Flexibly Freudian

The Collected Works of Jeffrey H. Golland, PhD

FLEXIBLY FREUDIAN

THE COLLECTED WORKS OF
JEFFREY H. GOLLAND, PhD

Edited by David Hamilton Golland, PhD

IPBOOKS.net
International Psychoanalytic Boo

International Psychoanalytic Books (IPBooks)
New York • http://www.IPBooks.net

Flexibly Freudian: The Collected Works of Jeffrey H. Golland, PhD

Published by IPBooks, Queens, NY
Online at: www.IPBooks.net

ISBN: 978-1-956864-84-7

For Marcia

Contents

PANELS, POLITICS, HISTORY, PHILOSOPHY

CONCLUDING ESSAYS

Editor's Foreword

Being the son of a Freudian psychologist/psychoanalyst—even a self-declared *flexible* Freudian—is complicated, to say the least. Dad insisted that he never analyzed his children, but such an absolute statement was surely aspirational rather than actual. What has become the butt of jokes in the public imagination has nevertheless been a net positive for me, as I have benefited from my own analyses—a lengthy child analysis, a brief adolescent analysis, and a lengthy adult analysis in my 30s. Not only have these been helpful as I have navigated my own life, giving me the tools to better understand who I am and why I feel the way I feel and do the things that I do, but my experience as an analysand has also helped me as a historian—especially when I was working on my second book, a biography (D. Golland, 2019, 2024). I was able to apply a psychoanalytically-grounded understanding of myself to my historical analysis of the subject individual. Similarly, my analyses have helped me in the present volume, for in the examination and evaluation of my father the scholar, it has been instructive to think of my father the man.

Since I became a scholar myself, Dad and I have occasionally toyed with the idea of working together. While queuing in a failed attempt to see Sam Waterston embody Abraham Lincoln at the Cooper Union, while revising my dissertation into a first book (D. Golland, 2011) and contemplating potential second projects, we discussed the idea of co-authoring a biography of Erik Erikson which would have combined my skills as a historian and then-nascent biographer with Dad's understanding of the field. Later, when I was well underway with my second project, Dad started explaining his concept of *psychoanalysis as science*. Being a historian with one leg in the humanities and the other in the social sciences, I had a rigid understanding of the definition of science as limited to variants of biology, chemistry, physics, and (possibly) math. Of course, I thought, Dad was wrong: psychoanalysis, as a variant of psychology, was mere *social* science. But he laid out his argument and convinced me that science is not as hard a concept as I had

1

previously thought—and psychoanalysis not so soft. I encouraged him to write about it. Much later, after many more conversations, I agreed that the concept of *psychoanalysis as science* was but one of Dad's reconceptualized "three masters"— the other two being *psychoanalysis as healing art,* because it involves doctors and patients, and *psychoanalysis as philosophy,* because Freud, its founder and visionary, was accorded the final volume of the first edition of the Mortimer Adler and Robert Maynard Hutchins' *Great Ideas* series. Upon further discussion, we agreed that Dad's existing scholarly corpus—his published essays, books reviews, and paper presentations from more than five decades as a practicing psychologist/ psychoanalyst and more than three decades as a professor of education—were already nearly enough to constitute a book-length explication of his thesis. Those writings—with a few notable additions that pull it all together—comprise the present volume: both the collected works of a practicing Freudian and a critical reappraisal of Freud and Freudianism. Critical, yet warm. And timely.

Working closely with Dad on this project has been complicated. Occasionally I see earlier iterations of myself in his writing, evoking a variety of psychological responses as I relive some of the challenging moments of my past, a childhood fraught with disappointment for myself as much as those around me, seemingly with precious little of the promise of my present personal, social, and professional success. More often I see earlier iterations of Dad, and that has been enlightening in a more positive way.

Dad has supervised no doctoral theses and will receive no *festschrift*; as such, my work on this book serves as my celebration of his scholarship. I hope you can join me in that.

Author's Foreword

The title of the book sounds egocentric, a common term of Freudian derivation. I am hardly alone in being *flexibly* Freudian. Sigmund himself was a role model. Abraham Maslow, when asked, deemed Freud "self-actualized" because he could readily alter his ideas in the face of new experience. My development as a psychoanalyst began in an undergraduate course in child development. My psychological studies emphasized flexibility, as did my formal psychoanalytic training, completed in 1973. The caricature of the rigidly silent Freudian analyst—amply recorded in decades of *New Yorker* cartoons—is addressed in several papers in this book. Debunking that caricature is a major motive of this book.

I began thinking about writing a book over a decade ago, but watching my son work at his first two made the effort seem daunting. When I spoke to him later about a volume of collected papers, he was encouraging. When I began to review my work, I came to believe in the project. We initiated it in the fall of 2022. Editing 50-plus years of writing would occupy lots of time in a very busy new academic administrative position, especially since David is not a psychologist. I am very grateful to him.

Freud was both flexible and rigid; an explorer, a thinker, and a genius still often mentioned in the *New York Times* on a wide variety of issues. Patients with very strange symptoms puzzled him; the primitive neurology of his time was not helpful. There was no box to think outside of! His listening and thinking led to some remarkable discoveries, but it wasn't until the late 1890s that his first theories emerged and—almost by accident—a method: free association. Patients are to speak without censorship. In 1900, at not quite age 44, he published *The Interpretation of Dreams*, a tome reviewing the history of dreaming, beginning with the Biblical Joseph and ending with a theory of how minds work! He expanded and modified his theories for another 30 years, during which time World War I, the early death of his oldest daughter, and new puzzles uttered by his patients led to a nearly complete revision of his initial model of the mind. His final decade was a creative elaboration, with writing I consider "Freud's anthropology," the application of his model to the cultural products of human thought.

I call attention to Freud's many errors—all science evolves from thought to trial and error to more thought. I believe psychoanalysis is a science, using rational and empirical approaches to understand the irrationality of so much of human activity.

Alongside my always-part-time clinical practice, I spent 35 years as a teacher education professor at City University of New York. This book includes papers on teacher education that I hope will demonstrate that psychoanalysis has a lot to teach teachers.

Organization

The Introductory four papers provide an overview of my career and its evolution, emphasizing major themes I discerned during the writing process. Included are an example of the clinical range of the psychoanalytic paradigm and an argument that such a paradigm must be considered scientific.

The second section is comprised of early writing including the abstract of my doctoral dissertation, papers based on my work as an Army psychologist, and samples from my academic career as a teacher educator.

My writing skills were honed when I was invited to review psychoanalytic books. The third section includes my published reviews and some responses to published articles. The fourth section is comprised of teacher education papers.

The fifth section of the book collects my unpublished talks as a faculty member in the Division of Psychotherapy in the Department of Psychiatry at Mount Sinai School of Medicine. It is followed by a briefer collection of essays on organizational politics and argumentation supporting a scientific understanding of psychoanalysis.

The final section is an attempt to provide my most contemporary understanding of the field of psychoanalysis and a summary of my evolution within it.

Preamble: Three Masters

This preamble was originally written in December 2011, when I hoped to write my first book. That book wasn't written but this introduction, edited, seems an apt preamble for this one.

I am comfortable with short-form writing: reviews, commentary, journal-length papers, panel participation. My style, at least as I see it, prioritizes clarity and brevity. Book-writing, as I am learning—is different. When I showed my older son, now with a third book in print, an early draft of a chapter of my "Three Masters" book project, I was chastened by his direct reply: "You must be more discursive." I'm not sure I know how to do that; what follows seems to me as much memoir as treatise. An English professor friend tells me that although I think I know what I want to say, the writing itself will lead me in new and surprising directions.

The idea for "Three Masters" came to me during a morning jog. Not since I was fresh out of college had I had a book-length idea. That first one was "a theory of everything" based solidly on youthful ignorance. "Three Masters" continued to excite me, though my writing progress was slow. I was and continue to be busy, easily distracted by one small project or another, and now nine grandchildren and two great-grands.

"Three Masters" is taken from Sigmund Freud. In The Ego and the Id (1923), he used the phrase to describe the plight of the Ego, caught between demands of the Id, Superego and External Reality. I use the phrase to apply to psychoanalysis itself. Its three masters are The Healing Arts, Science, and the History of Ideas. Each of these domains has its own standards and limitations, and each imposes on psychoanalysis a set of demands that inhere in the respective domain in its ways of trying to understand and relate to the world. These disciplines have overlapping concerns but can also be in conflict.

Psychoanalysis began as Freud's brainchild. He nurtured and exercised control over it until his death. As he said in an interview recorded in London in 1939, he began as a physician trying to help his patients find relief from their neurotic symptoms. In the course of his labors, he was privileged to discover and develop a new model of the human mind and its products. Ambition was joined with genius to write a new chapter in the history of ideas—one that became the concluding volume of the series "Great Books of the Western World," published by the University of Chicago Press in the 1930s under the editorship of Mortimer Adler and Robert Maynard Hutchins.

Freud's first duty was as a healer; he later came to see this art as secondary to the creation of a science of mind. His science eventually became more speculative than empirical. Erich Fromm is quoted as saying that "Freud and Marx had this in common: both were the indispensable starting points for students in their respective subject matters, although practically everything they said was wrong" (Holt, 1973). Robert Holt counted Freudian thought as a vehicle of rhetoric rather than a scientific weighing of evidence. Rhetoric is not a pejorative term on Holt's part or mine: rhetoric, along with logic and grammar, comprised the "trivium," the essential curriculum of schools in ancient Rome. While the trivium was the etymological source of "trivia," it holds a respectable place within the History of Ideas.

I became enamored of Freud as a college sophomore at Brandeis University taking a child psychology course. Primary sources were routinely assigned then. Psychoanalysis was considered one of three psychological paradigms (along with behaviorism and humanism, the so-called "third force" whose most prominent advocate was the psychology department chair Abraham H. Maslow). We read Freud's Three Essays on the Theory of Sexuality (1905) and the then-recent first edition of Charles Brenner's Elementary Textbook of Psychoanalysis. The professor, Walter Toman, who would later write a psychoanalytically informed book on sibling position, provided what I still consider the best definition of "cathexis:" not about hypothetical quanta of energies but instead, simply, "learning to appreciate." I joked that most Jewish boys don't have epiphanies, but I did. I also remarked after reading the Three Essays that Freud must have known my mother!

I was in the tenth class to enter and graduate from Brandeis. Founding President Abram Sachar referred to us as pioneers. He was mistaken; this young school had already established its reputation as an elite institution by the time I applied for admission, just eight years after its opening. Among its early innovations—beyond attracting headline faculty like Leonard Bernstein, Eleanor Roosevelt and Max Lerner, and Nobel-winning biochemists Kaplan and Kamen—were the establishment of the first college counseling service and the first doctoral program entitled "History of Ideas." Herbert Marcuse was among its charter faculty. The works of three "godless Jews"—Marx, Freud and Einstein— were central to the focus of its interdisciplinary scholarship, and my education was strongly influenced by that culture.

My subsequent undergraduate education involved additional Freud readings, a smattering of social and existential psychology, psychosomatics, and rigorous courses in statistics and experimental psychology. Statistics was taught by a young professor, Ulric Neisser, who would come to coin the very term "cognitive psychology." That paradigm would become the new "third force" replacing Maslow's. The history of psychology course was taught by a young physiological psychologist, Richard Held. It was a tour de force of centuries of philosophy that led to the birth of a new discipline for a new century.

This late adolescent thought he had found a holy grail: Freudian psychology. Tempered by Abe Maslow, Dick Neisser et al, here was a master narrative of human thought and action that was at the same time a healing profession and a social movement. I had a theory, and I could become a clinician as well as a social activist. It almost made up for my nearly absent sex life.

I was then lucky enough to be admitted to a doctoral program that was psychoanalytic to its core. The Research Center for Mental Health at New York University was staffed with psychologists applying experimental methods to Freudian ideas. They were led by George S. Klein and Robert R. Holt, who even taught Freud's then recently (and posthumously) published "Model for a Scientific Psychology." Some of our teachers had also been trained as analysts when, in this country, that was uncommon for non-physicians. Our therapy supervisors were practicing analysts, most having had so-called "bootleg" training, or had trained at so-called "non-kosher" institutes like Theodore Reik's National Psychological Association for Psychoanalysis (NPAP) or the William Alanson White Society. My two therapy practicum supervisors had trained "legitimately" in the late twenties with Freud himself, while taking PhDs at the University of Vienna; no medical degree was required there. One of them, Esther Menaker, has a paper cited in Fenichel's encyclopedic 1945 volume, "The Psychoanalytic Theory of Neurosis."

NYU's clinical psychology program followed the "scientist practitioner" model, the predominant form then approved by the American Psychological Association. Research skills were honed; statistics was taught by a clinical psychologist, Jacob Cohen, using engaging clinical examples. Cohen would go on to measure the power of tests and to develop a statistic named for him. Dissertation research tested psychoanalytic hypotheses. Mine used subliminal activation of aggressive drive derivatives and measures of defensiveness; the results were significant. It was the first of over 100 dissertations using a method advanced by the late Lloyd Silverman, who would eventually reduce symptoms in schizophrenic patients with tachistoscope presentations of the subliminal stimulus "Mommy and I are one." This kind of research still goes on, for instance at the University of Michigan led for decades by the late psychoanalyst-researcher Howard Shevrin. We also had internships; mine was a three-year stint with the VA, exposing me to severely and chronically ill World War II and Korean War veterans, many of whom had been hospitalized since discharge. Psychoanalysis was then hegemonic in the mental health field, and it was taught as established knowledge—especially as to its treatment method.

You don't have to be Freudian to respect early influences. I became an Erik Erikson fan and learned to appreciate the post-oedipal, late adolescent and early adult phases as crucial to my own identity development. My pre-analytic education and training provided an imprint of science combined with practice as pillars of what would become my career calling, as well as a foundation in philosophy and the humanities that I refer to here as the History of Ideas.

I was a happy camper: I had a diverse set of skills and experiences to go along with my master theory. But the 1960s were coming to an end; what was known as "the psychoanalytic movement" was about to splinter. I had missed the first such major upheaval, the controversial discussions in England between the Anna Freudians and the Melanie Kleinians, when Papa Freud's death finally allowed analysts to engage in disputation (rather than the prior model of rebelling and being banished). My training—under the aegis of the American Ego Psychology articulated by Hartmann and clarified by Rapaport—deemed the Kleinians losers, and spoke of them with disparagement, if at all. Outstanding clinicians and theorists wrote nuanced papers with different points of view within that mainstream. My training, at an institute excluded from the American Psychoanalytic Association, emphasized those differences, many of which became part of the standard individualized basic theory of psychoanalytic technique. Psychoanalysis had a mainstream but was not monolithic. Even Edward Glover's survey of technical practices among British psychoanalysts (1955) showed striking variations of style.

The next decade witnessed the defection of a former establishment figure, Heinz Kohut, and the introduction of what became his alternate psychoanalytic paradigm, Self Psychology. Psychoanalysis evolved (or devolved) from a movement with a clear mainstream and a few tributaries—even, in Auden's 1939 eulogy of Freud, "a whole climate of opinion"—to what seemed and may still seem Babel-like, now referred to as "pluralistic psychoanalysis." Worse yet for this master narrative, Neisser's Cognitive Psychology had eclipsed both psychoanalysis and behaviorism to become the single dominant master theory in North American psychology. In the skilled hands of clinician-researchers Aaron Beck and the formerly very strange Albert Ellis, a short-term effective treatment modality, Cognitive Behavior Therapy (CBT), emerged. CBT became the first choice of third-party payers and the exemplar of "evidenced based treatments." Alongside this mostly talking cure, the psychopharmacology industry produced apparently effective drug treatments with less serious side effects than those of the early anti-psychotics, and whose distribution by general practice physicians would undermine the patient base for psychoanalysis and for much of psychiatry as well. Thus came about the reduction of the psychoanalytic movement to a seldom-recommended therapy whose evidence base was challenged by scientific psychologists and whose very rationale was denied by philosophers. Psychoanalysis is now studied more by literature majors than would-be clinicians. If it is to survive as more than a cult—and I believe it will—fundamental reassessment is required.

My clinical practice involved routine reassessment all along, and I was an avid follower of the burgeoning literature—which itself is a perennial exercise in professional reevaluation. As my supervisors and teachers had said, I would continue to learn a great deal from my patients—and at least as much from those with whom I did poorly as from apparent successes. I became more modest about my own skills and knowledge. The more I learned, the more awesome my ignorance. The mind was no longer readily explained by any master theory. Paradoxically, I became more confident in my work and more effective with my patients. In arithmetic terms, the numerator was increasing, but the denominator was increasing faster. I became a supervisor and teacher, trying to convey both how much psychoanalysis had to offer and how vast was what remained unknown about the human mind and brain.

My path through the three disciplines—ideas, science, and practice—was the opposite of the trail blazed by Freud. I have been bothered by contradictions among these masters for much of my career. That book was to be an attempt to have psychoanalysis come to better terms with—and perhaps better compromises in—these "masters."

The very aims and scope of Freud's ambition had contributed to the theoretical and clinical difficulties that have befallen his enterprise. Freud may have been overambitious on our behalf. We must try nonetheless to attain the possibilities of his ambition.

Freud's ambition led him far beyond his work as a physician. He reluctantly entered private practice because the antisemitism of his time and place would not allow an academic appointment as what we would now call a neuroscientist. Indeed, it was his medical practice that led to the development of the clinical method that became psychoanalysis. But Freud later feared that therapy might hinder the science, and he aspired to be a great scientist of the mind as early as 1895 when he wrote and discarded his Project for a Scientific Psychology. It was after both his clinical theory and his psychology were established that he came to address larger issues in Civilization and its Discontents, Totem and Taboo, Group Psychology, and Moses and Monotheism. These took him far beyond the evidence of the consulting room in attempting to understand the products of the mind: art, literature, sociology, religion, etc., topics indicative of his ambition to a prominent place in The History of Ideas, (despite being, in Alfred Tauber's term, only a "reluctant" philosopher [2012].) Ambition and genius combined in Freud to enable creation and discovery of a new enterprise that is also a part of the pre-existing epistemological domains Therapeutics, Science, and The History of Ideas.

Charles Brenner takes The Mind in Conflict as the title of one of his later books. Just as the mind may be in conflict, my "Three Masters" thesis is that psychoanalysis is itself in conflict, attempting to meet the demands of its three masters.

There may be a silver lining, if not a pot of gold. Adversity builds strength, and the travails summarized here have indeed brought about necessary reappraisal. There is within psychoanalysis recognition that some, perhaps many, of Freud's original contributions must be discarded. Many others, however, have led to further productive exploration. There is also a developing consensus around the validity of at least some of its major tenets, although academic psychologists call them by other names. Robert Bornstein (2005) and Jonathan Shedler (2010) are among those who point out that words such as "implicit" replace "unconscious" as a favorite adjective for psychological research that ignores Freud.

In his Freud lecture, Brenner (2007) listed what he considered five major Freudian contributions, any one of which, in his view, would have made Freud great. These are 1) free association ("a stroke of genius"); 2) that symptoms and dreams make sense; 3) psychic determinism; 4) that psychological conflicts are based in sexual wishes and fantasies of early childhood; and 5) that pathology and normality are linked in a continuum. For me, the last of these defines Freud's creation of an entire theory of personality—and may well be the most important part of his legacy.

Of course Freud, like the conquistadors among his role models, was guilty of overreach and error. But his willingness to discard ideas that proved unworkable has created an enterprise with unrealized potential. While the more speculative ideas of Freud's concerns are favored in humanities departments, they have little relevance in the consulting room.

This book comes after decades of often difficult clinical work. I noticed ways in which established theory was inadequate while also recognizing the amazing reach of theory as therapeutic activity. Alternate schools of psychoanalysis now seemed to have something to offer. Alternate methods of mental health treatment are practiced successfully by people I respect. Alternate applications of theories had enriching implications for the humanities, the arts, politics, even world peace. Leo Stone's 1954 idea of "widening scope" became wider still while continuing to arouse controversy. Debates over "the pure gold of psychoanalysis" and "the copper of suggestion" seem more fruitful. And the contradictions within psychoanalytic discourse make for a new round of explanation and new generative thinking. Old discussions about theory and practice, old arguments over the differentiation of psychoanalysis from psychotherapy, and old arguments about the very definition of psychoanalysis are now taking new shape.

The Freudian Unconscious itself is a mass of contradiction and conflict; opposites co-exist, psychic reality is timeless; anatomy is not destiny: in our innermost mind we are all bisexual and polymorphous perverse. These discoveries, hardly Freudian fantasies, apply to our approaches to practice, to science, and to epistemology itself. Psychoanalysis cannot be reduced to a simple set of ideas and practices: its subjects are too complex, its applications too many and varied.

Brenner's last book (2004) claims to be a new master narrative. His formulation that all psychological phenomena are to be understood as compromise formations, the bases of symptoms and character, is elegant. But the closure it offers is premature, even simplistic. His approach to treatment aims to induce better compromises, while life itself forces reassessment of heretofore stable ones.

Many might disagree with the very premise of the book that was never completed: that psychoanalysis has a place within each of the larger narratives of clinical art, science, and ideas. Within and without our field, there are doubts as to the effectiveness of psychoanalysis as clinical practice. Many—including some psychoanalysts—dispute its scientific status or aspiration. As to its status as an Idea (Platonic or Hegelian), Freud himself, in his references to philosophy, might not care. I believe we should!

Neither historian nor philosopher, while struggling unsuccessfully with "Three Masters," I came to see that Freud's ventures into what has been called "applied" psychoanalysis: art, literature, religion, came from his belief that these applications, like the methods of the consulting room, are derived from the overall psychoanalytic theory of mind and its products.

Psychoanalysis burst upon the world in the early years of the last century and immediately became part of the intellectual discourse. From early on, psychoanalysis was controversial, shocking the establishment and alienating some early adherents who posed ideas antithetical to Freud's. How psychoanalysis affects history and how history affects psychoanalysis are fascinating studies. Many consider Freud to have had an enormous impact on history, especially in advancing what became a revolution in human sexual mores. Historical events affected psychoanalysis directly and dramatically in the 1930s, essentially evicting it from MittelEurope and its native German language to the Anglophone world of England and the United States.

Psychoanalysis is my profession. My career choice was influenced by my childhood and youth. My family's assumption that I would be a doctor seemed unquestionable. By age 10 or 11, I was done with the supernatural. I entered college as an intellectual manqué. It took an act of rebellion during college to drop out of pre-med: my mother did not speak to me for a year. I soon found a field that satisfied my several motives but have only now come to fully face its complexities and richness.

The chapters that follow form a collection of my writing for over half a century, much of it unpublished presentations to peers in the Division of Psychotherapy at Mount Sinai School of Medicine. They speak to the scientific status of psychoanalysis and the issues differentiating clinical psychoanalysis from other therapies, as well as the range of activities that embrace a Freudian sensibility. I hope thereby to represent the "flexible Freudian" identity that defies the caricature best captured by decades of New Yorker cartoons and typifies so many of my colleagues.

I find my work invigorating. Psychoanalysis is a vibrant field with daily clinical challenges, and ongoing efforts to establish scientific principles within an exciting intellectual ferment. I don't expect to resolve the issues I address. It will be enough if I can articulate them with some degree of clarity.

OPENING ESSAYS

Family Therapy Without The Patient

Mount Sinai Therapy Conference—2/21/13

For my Thursday presentations, I usually address a clinical issue, and prefer to pose a problem with a current patient. This time my problem is my friend H—or rather his characterization of me. The clinical material is not current; the presenting problem was resolved in just six sessions over a four-month period, with e-mail follow-up four months later. The clinical issue might be called "applying clinical theory."

H is fond of the aphorism: "If all you own is a hammer, everything you see tends to look like a nail." Just recently that statement was seen twice in the popular press with attribution of the source: Abraham Maslow—with whom I studied as an undergraduate at Brandeis. Everyone in our group has a tool kit; M is fond of this metaphor. Our skills vary; we are more adept with some instruments than others. Tools that stay in the kit might get rusty. Patients stay with us who are more likely to be nails to our power hammers. H presented a case recently and F presented another more recently; each would challenge anyone's carpentry skills. Emergency and urgent situations, like the one M presented two weeks ago, also provide challenges. We dig more deeply into our toolkit and sometimes succeed. Sets of instructions for our tools may exist, but rarely match any individual situation.

H has painted me as an ideologue who sneers at anything other than a caricatured classical psychoanalytic treatment. Framed by his infectious humor, these remarks have over time convinced some here that my mind is, indeed, firmly stuck in the 19th century. Any fair hearing of my presentations and comments should by now have contradicted that view, but apparently not enough. Today's presentation is another attempt to describe what I call flexible Freudianism, a position committed both to flexibility and to the ever evolving 21st Century Freudian theoretical corpus.

According to Eric Kandel, psychiatry's sole Nobel laureate, "psychoanalysis represents the most coherent and intellectually satisfying view of the mind that we have." He says this for good reason, often lost in discussions around this table: psychoanalysis has a grand aim; it is not merely a form of psychotherapy, as great a contribution as that was. It is a bio-psycho-sociocultural-ecological approach whose founder was not only a genius but ambitious enough to attempt an overarching theory of mind and its products. Freud's drive theory (the "dynamic point of view") focuses on the biological; his "complemental series" idea addresses the relative weights of biology and the relevant environmental domains for each individual in each circumstance. In his recent paper, "The Stories," H referred to his approach with his hyper-anxious patient as biosocial; I replied: "that does not differentiate it from psychoanalysis." Wilhelm Reich—misguided though the evolution of his treatment technique and theory was to become—focused on developing a psychoanalytic biology, while Erik Erikson and others stressed social and anthropologic dimensions. H made no oedipal interpretations to his patient; that assertion also fails to separate his work from his bogeyman psychoanalysis.

Today's analysts rarely make frankly oedipal interpretations. When we see Oedipus taking the stage, it is enough for us to allude concretely and directly to the object-relational or transference situation without referring to the myth that for Jocasta, Laius and their son was directly enacted.

I don't like the term "psychodynamic psychotherapy" because it narrows the field to its dynamic point of view. That is, literally, the sexy part of the theory, but far from the whole story—or necessarily the most important part. For patients whose treatment I supervise at Mount Sinai, the structural point of view, often misnamed "ego psychology," is usually more relevant. For all prospective patients the structural point of view is central to evaluation during the consultation phase.

The genetic (or developmental) point of view is also centrally relevant. When S tells us he has little use for theory, I believe he sells himself short. We all think about what goes on with our patients when engaged directly with them, and between sessions as well. We try to understand what has gone on, what might go on: we think. Thinking is theorizing. There are ad hoc theories, and better and worse theories. We test our thinking in each encounter or intervention (including silences)—or in subsequent reflection on the encounter. S does this, H does this; so must we all—if we lay any claim to professionalism. [We might make an exception for followers of Bion's dictum: to work without memory or desire, but I doubt anyone achieves this state for more than moments at a time.]

Along with Kandel, I find psychoanalytic theory to provide the most extensive possibilities for thinking about patients—and about the human mind and its products; Hartmann called it a general psychology. Many of Freud's specific assertions have turned out to be limited or erroneous; psychoanalysis evolves. It is a broad and ambitious theory whose domain has several applications, some of which are therapies. I disagree with another H, who sees it as a Weltanschauung. I see instead a scientific enterprise subject to the tests of utility and generativity, though not to randomized, controlled experimentation.

The case I will discuss is not usual in my practice; nor have I read of a situation quite like this one—presented to me several years ago. An analyst colleague, a close friend of several decades, referred a family to me, friends of friends of his. I had not worked as a family therapist since being discharged from active duty in the U.S. Army 38 years earlier—and haven't done so since.

The Case Material

I will call this family the "Ables," for reasons which will become clear. I saw the parents and one of two adult children, each a graduate of a prestigious university. The younger—I'll call him Ishmael—was the identified patient; he had written three versions of a suicide letter, one to his best friend, the second to his girlfriend (with whom he was living), the third to his family. He was missing; I never met him. Also participating in the work were the best friend and the girlfriend. The notes were received a few days after Ishmael's disappearance. The mother called me. We set an appointment for the next afternoon; the letters were hand-delivered to my office earlier that morning. The family, girlfriend and best friend introduced themselves and the letters were read aloud, each person offering commentary. The sister had hacked Ishmael's computer and found the itinerary for a trip abroad, with departure the day he sent the letters. The family plan was to put someone in the next seat on an upcoming leg of the trip; the mother thought she should go. That evoked my veto. The best friend was Plan B, which I endorsed. The family had contacted the State Department and understood the limits of its authority.

I offered supportive words to all. The suicide plan was to travel until money ran out, then to walk into a jungle and starve to death. The threat seemed unrealistic; it was clearly not imminent. I concluded the first session—70 minutes—by supporting the group's "collective wisdom," and their wish to establish direct contact.

Thirteen days later the best friend came in. He had indeed secured a plane seat next to Ishmael and spent three days with him. Ishmael agreed to email and phone contact and did follow up. The friend, an impressive man, was prepared to return to "grab him up" if necessary.

The girlfriend had a session with me soon thereafter. This resembled a usual initial consultation with a prospective patient. The parents would support therapy for her, but this was our only meeting. She asked how to respond to Ishmael's emails. My only advice was that she try not to reassure him she was doing well— since, in fact, she was not.

Days later I saw the parents again. Remote contact was happening. I noted Ishmael's verbal abuse in the mails and their anger. They denied anger and I warned them about their denial. Otherwise, I made no interventions except to support the family's continued collective wisdom and reliance on the best friend as emissary.

Six weeks later a phone session with the parents described ongoing email and phone exchanges. The mother was getting impatient; I said they were doing all they could. Two months later a phone session with the family detailed an upcoming visit with Ishmael at his foreign location.

My remaining contacts with the mother were by e-mail. My comments were asked for and given. About a month later, Ishmael returned to New York—to be hospitalized for two weeks. While in hospital he took an overdose of a medication in a suicidal gesture, and then agreed to begin psychotherapy. The hospital made a referral as did I. On being asked, I agreed with the treatment recommendation and made an alternate referral. I have not heard from the family since December 2006. A few years later, the referring psychoanalyst told me he had recently heard that Ishmael had his life together, had a very good job position, and was soon to be married. No information was available on whether the original girlfriend was the bride-to-be.

Discussion

The skills I used in this work are easily described. They reflect what I view as a method for beginning any psychoanalytically informed treatment. I listened attentively to each speaker, asking an occasional question when I felt the need for clarification. I assessed the patient and the family from the structural point of view. I call the family Able for their high level of individual integration, their ability to listen to one another, and to add and amend each other's comments without offense. Since the presenting problem was a family crisis, I commented when asked on proposed plans and actions—nearly all of which seemed to demonstrate their competence. I spontaneously disagreed with the one idea they offered that I thought ill-advised (the mother's making the initial in-person contact). This reaction on my part came from classic clinical theory: that suicide expresses an unbridled, misdirected hostility to the mother who gave life.

Since this work was intermittent and limited, I saw neither sound basis nor useful opportunity for interpretation; should the treatment have continued with one or more of the members, my work would have been in a beginning phase, aimed at establishing a good working relationship. Transference, as understood today, is ubiquitous. My approach is the one suggested by Freud for the "unobjectionable positive" variety—it is not addressed or interpreted until it becomes a problem, a resistance. During the sessions a major intervention on my part was advising self-care for all those involved. Could I guess at individual or family dynamics; sure—but that would be speculation, hardly useful unless the family or an individual would enter a treatment that would go beyond crisis resolution. The relationship, which S and others claim as the change agent of good work, had little time to develop. What seemed to carry effectiveness was my demeanor; a responsiveness derived from my general experience and theoretical framework—enabling me to come across as confident in both listening and speaking, despite the unusual nature of the work.

Successful treatment might seem easy to define, but most definitional attempts fall short. H says religion has helped more people than all the mental health practitioners put together. That depends on the definition of "help." Religions surely have a mass appeal that can be helpful in dealing with loss, facing death or relieving guilt, sadness or anxiety. They can also provide a sense of community, and a set of ideals; for some, religion can generate euphoric or ecstatic states. These are legitimate aims that may overlap with what we offer as professional psychotherapists. Religions, like drugs, also have powerful side effects: war the most destructive. Most of us believe we are successful when patients are helped with their symptoms and other presenting problems, but we can't claim that an alternative approach would not have helped as much or more—or more cheaply.

Psychoanalysis sets a different standard: not just symptom removal or behavioral change, but self-knowledge and the development of long-lasting skills at regular self-reflection. Psychoanalytically-informed treatments—like the one described here—are less ambitious but assume what Schafer has called the "psychoanalytic attitude." Shedler's important paper (2010) on efficacy showed a greater long-term effect for psychodynamic treatments than for competing modalities. I have discussed the differences between psychoanalysis and psychoanalytic psychotherapy in earlier presentations. The goal of the work presented—a family consultation rather than a therapy—was to help this family rescue a member—this anomic young man—from his manifest suicidal intent.

Others may have achieved similar success from different frames of reference. It is my view that a broad and flexible psychoanalytic outlook is more likely to succeed with more (and more varied) patients and situations that present themselves. This is an empirical proposition still lacking adequate research methods for testing. Maybe one day a sound independent empiricism will catch up with good clinical work.

Musings of a Flexible Freudian

Presented at the American Institute for Psychoanalysis—3/15/13

I have had two parallel careers. I am a psychoanalyst, and for 35 years, I was a teacher education professor at CUNY. Teaching is very important to me; I take every opportunity offered. Lecturing is a respectable method; it has its place but is not always the most effective for learners. I don't know this group, so I hope we will collaborate, as we do with our patients, to make this a meaningful and mutual learning experience.

The title of this paper alludes to my past as a doctrinaire Freudian. I was lucky enough to be introduced to psychoanalysis as a sophomore in college. We read Freud's Three Essays (1905) and Charles Brenner's Elementary Textbook of Psychoanalysis (1955). At the tender age of 17, I became a Freudian. The NYU clinical psychology program, where I did doctoral studies, was psychoanalytic in orientation. My dissertation was conducted at the Research Center for Mental Health, run by George S. Klein and Robert R. Holt, each a distinguished psychologist-psychoanalyst scientist. My study was an experiment using a subliminal aggressive stimulus to see if Rorschach responses would increase or decrease in aggressive imagery depending on defensive style; I had good results. My analytic training and long-time affiliation were at what was originally called the New York Society of Freudian Psychologists, later the New York Freudian Society, and currently the Contemporary Freudian Society. I had read the "neo-Freudians" (Sullivan, Fromm and Horney) as well as Jung and Adler in an undergraduate course on personality. They were judged also-rans in prestige, and institutes following their teachings seemed to offer a too narrow perspective on psychoanalysis, one that—at least at the time—minimized the importance of infantile sexuality. The prestige hierarchy also considered my own institute "unkosher." I could dismiss that view because the medical institutes, with their "reporting analyses"—in which training analysts decided on their patients' academic progress—undermined the treatment value of training analysis; one could hardly speak freely to a judge. So I had it both ways: secure in being privy to what I then believed were essential truths, in a program that followed the IPA model long before qualifying as an official IPA institute.

The Abstracts of the Standard Edition were published in 1973, the year I completed analyst school. Robert Holt, a cherished teacher and mentor at NYU who at 97 remains an active scholar, wrote a 79-page introduction entitled On Reading Freud. Holt's essay began by recalling a remark by Eric Fromm: "Freud and Marx had this in common: Both were indispensable starting points for students in their respective subject areas, although practically everything they said was wrong." Holt then added, "In its dramatic hyperbole it was itself a very Freudian proposition… if one understood its vehicle as rhetoric rather than as scientific weighing of evidence" (p 3).

An honest survey of psychoanalytic literature would show that even orthodox Freudians like Phyllis Greenacre (1941) would compose papers in a particular format: calling Freud to task for an error or limitation, then putting forth their own ideas. I followed that format in the most clinical of my own published works, "Not an Endgame: Terminations in Psychoanalysis" (1997).

Charles Brenner, whose radical revisions of psychoanalytic theory included dropping the id-ego-superego model from his final formulation (2006), credited Freud with six major discoveries, any one of which would merit "genius" designation. For Brenner, these were: the free association method itself; the meaningfulness of symptoms; the interpretation of dreams; psychic determinism (derived from the study of slips and ordinary errors and leading to a general, not just an abnormal, psychology); the central role of infantile sexuality (still minimized or denied entirely, in Brenner's opinion, by alternate theories); and sublimation (first alluded to in Shakespeare and a precursor to understanding healthy compromise-formation). This is three times the number Freud (1919) used to define the essentials of psychoanalysis: transference and resistance. Brenner spent much of this 2007 Freud Anniversary lecture criticizing "deviants" from Jung and Adler to Horney and Kohut for evading the centrality of sex and aggression in human affairs. It is notable that Frank Summers, the current president of APA's Division of Psychoanalysis, declared drive theory dead, a position I challenged in the December 2011 issue of Psychoanalytic Psychology.

So far I still sound like a hide-bound inflexible Freudian. But Abraham Maslow's undergraduate course at Brandeis did plant seeds of flexibility. Maslow considered Freud to be "self-actualized" in that he frequently and dramatically modified his views in the face of clinical experience. In graduate school I learned that theories were always provisional and were to be judged by their heuristic value. Did they generate good ideas? Were they useful? At the Freudian Society, Leo Stone's "widening scope" (1954) was not considered radical, as it was at his own New York Psychoanalytic Institute. Furthermore, the practice of converting psychotherapy to psychoanalysis, then considered deviant by the medical institutes, was common practice among psychologists and was my own experience, since I could not afford four times weekly sessions while a graduate student and I wanted my training analysis with the same person.

My first course on psychoanalytic technique included sharply contrasting positions on practice as well as study of Edward Glover's technique survey within the British Psychoanalytic Society. The diversity of opinion on many so-called standard technical questions among a homogeneous membership numbering about sixty in the 1930s was illuminating. In that course we also read a still-neglected classic by Edward Bibring (1954). Bibring defined the difference between psychotherapy and psychoanalysis not as categorical but depending instead on the relative proportion of different types of interventions: specifically, those meant to allay anxiety and those that would increase discomfort by attempting to deepen the associative process. The instructor also addressed "analytic attitude," a phrase later adopted by Roy Schafer as a title for one of his most important books. That attitude was to follow psychoanalytic principles as much as possible, even in face-to-face treatments meeting once or twice weekly. I've written on the relationship between psychoanalysis and psychotherapy, making use of Leo Rangell's felicitous metaphor (1954) of day and night versus dawn and dusk; shades of gray, if you will. I became a Rangell fan early on—well before he named his approach "total composite theory."

Yet these seeds of a future flexibility did not keep me from being a rigid beginner. The most dramatic instance I recall was when a patient had forgotten her purse and had no money for bus fare on a very rainy day. She asked to borrow the twenty-cent fare (you can guess how long ago this was); I tried to analyze her request and I refused the loan. She sent payment for her outstanding bill, but never returned to my office. In my own analysis I became quite upset when my analyst broke a rule, waiving my fees for the week my father died—when I went to Florida for the funeral period.

In 1973, Irving Paul published *Letters to Simon*, a lovely little book about psychotherapy, presumably written to a nephew beginning graduate school in clinical psychology. One of Paul's technical suggestions was not charging for missed sessions, reversing a practice recommended by Freud himself (1913a). Newly minted as an analyst when I read Paul's book, I ignored this deviation from "standard" practice. 35 years later I took up the suggestion, reinforced by reading Herbert Schlesinger's (2004) book, *The Texture of Treatment*, and adopting it as a text for a course on psychoanalytic technique. I had been rule-bound even in my own analysis and with patients, and have become, well, flexible.

The year 1973 is notable not only for Holt's treatise, Paul's book, and my graduation as a credentialed analyst, but for what some might see as the start of the decline of psychoanalysis. Don't blame me; you probably know the many factors involved. When I began institute training, psychoanalysis was the dominant theory in clinical psychology and psychiatry and was the treatment of choice, not only for the neuroses but for the entire range of psychological and psychiatric problems, especially following Stone's "widening scope of indications" paper (1954). Anna Freud had advised, in rebuttal to Stone, that analysts focus on neurosis. The decline was steep; within 20 years psychoanalysis moved from a first-choice treatment to one of last resort, disparaged by the establishment in both psychology and psychiatry. Over its first century it had gone from a small practice hatched in the dirty mind of a Viennese Jew to a fashionable indulgence for the worried well, albeit a respected profession. It then devolved into what seems a disorganized theory and practice, with academic attention paid mostly in departments of comparative literature! What happened to Auden's eulogy (1940) in which he wrote that Freud was "no more a person but a whole climate of opinion?"

So let me shift voices, since I am a Freudian, and it is the climate of opinion that I view as Freud's most important legacy. For me psychoanalysis is not limited to its therapeutic applications. Freud began as a clinician trying to relieve the suffering of his neurotic patients. His ambition and genius led to the discovery/ creation of a new psychology: an overarching theory of the mind and all its products. Freud called psychoanalysis a scientific psychotherapy (1905). As he developed this therapy, the theory became a major contribution to the history of ideas, comprising the 54th and concluding volume of the University of Chicago's Great Books of the Western World.

Freud began as a doctor; my start was as a student at Brandeis University where the first department named "History of Ideas" was established. Herbert Marcuse, a Marxist and a Freudian, was a founding faculty member. The social and political branch of psychoanalysis continued with the work of Erik Erikson, inventor of psychohistory, psychobiography and life-span developmental psychology. It flourishes to this day in psychoanalytic approaches to schools, government, even international relations. Drew Westen has recently written a political version of psychoanalysis, trying to make the Democratic Party more effective electorally and legislatively. Sklarew, Twemlow and Wilkinson, in their edited volume *Analysts in the Trenches* (2004), describe several programs of pro-social activity by psychoanalysts from assisting police in New Haven with promoting anti-bullying education in schools to negotiating peace between Greek and Turkish Cypriots and Protestant and Catholic Irish. Twemlow is a current Sigourney Award winner, the psychoanalytic version of the Nobel Prize. The aesthetic branch of psychoanalytic theory started with Freud's paper on Leonardo and with his brief quasi-therapeutic encounters with the poet Rainer Maria Rilke and the composer Gustav Mahler. Freud's reliance on Shakespeare's psychological insight is also well known. This branch of applied psychoanalysis was extended by Ernst Kris, Gilbert Rose, Martin Nass and, more recently, by Julie Jaffe Nagel (Nass and Jaffe focusing on music, a subject Freud found alien).

Despite the critiques of narrow-definition hard scientists in psychology and psychiatry and the dismissal by relational psychoanalysts like Irwin Z. Hoffman, psychoanalysis also has a long and worthy tradition of empirical research. Recent panels led by Leon Hoffman at the New York Psychoanalytic Society and recent publications by Jonathan Shedler (2010), Paul Wachtel (2010), Wilma Bucci and the late Norbert Freedman, among many others, address not only the efficacy of the treatment, but the process and concepts deemed Freudian. Earlier narrow-minded analysts (including Freud himself) used to declare that the only valid evidence for psychoanalysis came from the couch; more of us now recognize the contributions of cognate disciplines and the convergent validity supported by varieties of evidence. A new field, neuro-psychoanalysis, is both empirical and philosophical. It attempts to solve the age-old mind-body problem. The South African psychoanalyst Mark Solms is a leader in this development.

I believe the term "applied psychoanalysis" has been used mistakenly to refer to the relevance of psychoanalytic ideas outside the treatment situation. I consider psychoanalytic therapies the most pragmatic application of this complex theory of the human mind and its products. I call myself a "flexible Freudian" precisely because much if not most of my clinical work for nearly 50 years has been psychoanalytically informed treatment, rather than 4-5 times per week couch-based psychoanalysis. Surveys in both the American Psychoanalytic Association and APA's Division of Psychoanalysis (39) strongly suggest that my practice is hardly unusual, even among medical analysts.

Furthermore, I view the contribution of psychoanalysis to the history of ideas as a radical challenge. Freud demolished a common-sense psychology of consciousness. He compared his revolution to Copernicus' heliocentric theory and Darwin's Evolution. Our planet is not the center of the universe; humans are animals; and we have limited awareness, let alone control, of our own minds. As a revolutionary idea, psychoanalysis is true to its own nature when it is not in fashion or fashionable. It provides a better treatment when it works with so-called "difficult" patients. Freud learned from his patients: we do not practice a formulaic methodology, we struggle to help our patients and to advance knowledge of the workings of the human mind.

Toward this end, innovators should not be exiled, a major error for Freud and the subsequent generation of establishment analysts. Neither technique nor theory should be written in stone. Freud overthrew many of his own central formulations when he faced new challenges in his consulting room. His mature theory was far more useful clinically than was his initial theory and technical model—and it remains a model to be corrected, improved and eventually replaced. A flexible mind set is necessary for a psychoanalyst, just as increased mental flexibility is a major treatment goal.

Freud endorsed both Anna Freud's creation of child analysis and August Aichhorn's application of psychoanalytic ideas to work with adolescents. Melanie Klein competed with Anna Freud as to whose child analytic approach was more Freudian. Jacob Moreno, Samuel Slavson, Wilfred Bion and others applied Freudian thinking to groups. Nathan Ackerman and others developed family therapy and couple therapy, with continuing work in that area by Fred Sander. Others—against both Freud's and his daughter's advice—applied psychoanalytic thinking to patients whose disturbances were more severe than neuroses or perversions. Freud's theory of mind was extended differently in the United States than in England and in France—reflecting cultural differences and generating new theory. At times the international psychoanalytic literature seems like Babel, but new ideas and new applications emerge. This must be very confusing to beginners and surely makes learning more difficult—but it is an indication of the vibrancy of our theoretical environment. I find good ideas in every issue of the psychoanalytic journals, and I try to listen openly and think flexibly in every treatment session.

Our theoretical diversity is not just problematic for students. To the extent that treatment is the major occupation of those who use the theory, therapeutic effectiveness is, necessarily, an issue—as is the economics of practice. What works?

What are appropriate criteria for clinical success? So-called "evidenced based" psychotherapy excludes psychoanalysis from its list, and—despite Shedler's (2010) meta-analysis—denies the efficacy of psychodynamic psychotherapy.

But absence of evidence is not evidence of absence, and even the American Psychological Association considers clinical evidence to have validity. Psychoanalysis is empirical but cannot be experimental. As Wachtel (2010) made clear, randomized controlled design is not a methodology applicable to psychoanalysis. Nancy McWilliams promotes a scientific view but opposes narrow scientistic critique. Yet there is a problem. There is no generally accepted criterion for clinical success. While any therapy must deal with symptoms and presenting problems, the very approach of psychoanalysis and its derived therapies see symptoms and presenting problems as coming from whole persons with complex psychological makeup, and its methods address the problems by aiming to understand both their psychological and social context.

In fact, Freud warned against "therapeutic ambition," expressed the fear that therapy could hurt the science, and—in his later years—wrote papers less about clinical matters than social and philosophical ones. A paper on termination (1937) that was promised 24 years earlier turned out to be essentially philosophical, not technical at all.

Sander Abend (2000), a leading contemporary Freudian, believes that a psychoanalytic therapy should reduce or eliminate symptoms; after all, that's why most patients consult most doctors. But Abend's approach is Freudian, therefore more ambitious: to understand the mind. Analytic methodology valorizes latent content and hidden meaning. Symptom removal is expected but, since 1897, is not the primary focus of psychoanalytic treatment. The implicit questions for psychoanalysis are "why" questions: Why this symptom? Why this association? Why now? Analysts adopt an "expectant attitude:" helping the patient to associate more freely will promote understanding; that understanding makes for a better life. Among Jonathan Shedler's (2010) most important findings was that patients in psychoanalytic therapy had long-lasting effects of this kind.

How we measure success is a much more complex topic than acknowledged by insurance companies. What makes people better is as much a philosophical as psychological issue. Religion surely helps many people to deal with mortality, loss and grief; it can provide a sense of community and sets of ideals, and sometimes even euphoric or ecstatic experiences. These are legitimate goals that have some overlap with ours. Religion, like drugs, also has side effects—war the most destructive.

In the century since Freud created this field, we have come to know a great deal; we also know how much more there is to know, not only about each patient, but about the human mind. Theorists argue; many seem to make valid points, however they might contradict one another. Do we have a unified total composite theory as Rangell was aiming for in his 2007 book *The Road to Unity*? Or do we have instead a pluralism in which several divergent psychoanalytic theories compete? Contemporary physics and cosmology have the same problem: alternate conceptions of the universe with no Grand Unifying Theory, so they continue to do their work.

The Sigourney awards began in 1990 and rotate among the three large geographic areas of the IPA. This year's winners represent sharply differing views of psychoanalysis: Stuart Twemlow, who calls himself a community psychoanalyst, and Salman Akhtar, also concerned with societal applications, contrast with the two other North American winners, Thomas Ogden and Laurence Freedman. Ogden originated the concept of the "analytic third," a co-created structure in the treatment room beyond the two individuals present; Freedman, author of *The Anatomy of Psychotherapy* (1998), has focused his incisive intelligence on many aspects of the traditional clinical situation. Twemlow and Freedman had a testy exchange in the 2005 issue of the *International Journal* on whether or not psychoanalysis has anything meaningful to say about terrorism. Later that year, Stephen Sonnenberg suggested in the same journal that in different ways they were both right. The issue is one that has been important to psychoanalysis since Freud shifted his focus from seduction to fantasy: that is, the relative roles of external and internal realities. Marion Oliner's new book, *Psychic Reality in Context* (2012), takes up this very problem with reference to her having been a child survivor of the Holocaust. My version of analysis deals with conflict and contradiction within a Freudian paradigm that makes no final truth claims.

Theory and practice continue to evolve. Freud did not care for philosophy, but we have philosophical—epistemological—problems. My favorite supervisor, the late Donald Kaplan, offered a challenging metaphor: "When in the course of unraveling a glove is it no longer a glove but just a handful of wool?" In his final paper, Kaplan also wrote that we have no idea what psychoanalysis will look like in the future. Our best writers continue to make cases for hard principles in defining the field. For Freud these essentials were limited to unconscious motivation, psychic causality, infantile sexuality as basic psychology, and transference and resistance as basic technical concerns. I am a Freudian and I agree with these as essentials. An open mind is not an empty head. But my evolution as a flexible

Freudian comes from facing the challenges of theory and the concerns of each patient in each clinical session. We must, then, assume as part of analytic attitude an essential modesty along with an adequate degree of confidence and conviction in what we do.

Psychoanalysis is Scientific!

Division/Review Forum, Division 39, APA, 7/20/16

This is a philosophy of science paper. I will summarize the emergence of psychology, psychiatry and psychoanalysis from the Western philosophical tradition, and use Bacon's definition of science (1620/1993) and the contemporary philosophy of "Critical Realism" to argue that excluding psychoanalysis from science rests on an erroneous valorization of subjectivity or a constricted definition of science.

My axiomatic assumptions: 1) I am real and I have some degree of will power; 2) You are real and, similarly, have will power. To believe otherwise would suggest "depersonalization," "derealization," and "abulia," impairments of mental functioning. Subjectivity is real and worthy of scientific study, but is not the sole reality for a scientific psychology. Descartes's "I think, therefore I am" is, despite post-Cartesian argument, correct; Berkeley's "to be is to be perceived" is not.

Exploring the world starts at birth, perhaps some few weeks earlier. Neonates have immediate sensations that slowly become organized, forming a core subjectivity that will be present throughout life. Toddlers begin to develop a theory of mind, an accurate belief that others also have a subjective core. Such recognition gradually leads (under supportive conditions) to "I am not the center of the universe; reality exists beyond my perception and will." Reality-testing—the differentiation of internal and external—is a basic, though imperfect ego function. This is a cursory ego-psychoanalytic description of early development.

That psychoanalysis is scientific has been disputed for decades; the debate remains heated. Recent issues of *Psychoanalytic Psychology* (2015) and the *International Journal of Psychoanalysis* (2015) were largely devoted to psychoanalytic research, and an extensive discussion played out on Division 39's listserv. Science advances from argumentation as well as data.

Healing, Science and Philosophy

I've proposed (pp 5–12 above) that the discipline of psychoanalysis, like Freud's ego (1923), serves three masters: healing, science, and the history of ideas. These domains have different standards and methods. Many conceptual problems in psychoanalysis stem from attempts to meet the conflicting standards. Epistemology is the philosophical context for psychoanalysis as science, with Ethics, the philosophy of values, also relevant. Science, philosophy, and history are intellectual domains. Clinicians must respect ideas while attending to the pragmatics of helping patients; in a treatment situation, therapeutic intent should have priority over scientific aims (Stone, 1954).

History

Psychology emerged by addressing three central philosophical issues: the problem of knowledge (cognitive psychology), the problem of action (behavioral psychology), and the problem of evil (clinical psychology). Psychiatry advanced from demonology through humane caregiving to become part of scientific medicine that itself emerged just a bit more than a century ago. Psychoanalytic treatment addressed the clinical phenomena of neurotic suffering. Freud advanced propositions and a method for exploring the dark side of human nature, a dynamic unconscious. "Social" sciences emerged: sociology, anthropology, economics and politics, each developing validity criteria and methods fitting its subject matter.

Philosopher Francis Bacon (1561-1626), called the father of empiricism, defined science as "an attitude toward the universe in which observations are made using the best methods available; logic is employed; and contradictions or magical, supernatural, and ad hoc solutions are rejected." Charles Brenner noted that all sciences are inferential and influenced by the observer's psychology, but facts rule (2006). Experimentation may be employed but is not required (e.g., Galileo's astronomy); quantification is a tool of science, not its essence. Two principles to add to Bacon and Brenner: scientific conclusions are tentative, and although "psychological reality" is rife with contradiction and paradox, its methods are rational and empirical.

Science was first called natural philosophy. Epistemology asks how we know. Plato's answer: look inward, using "the mind's eye" rather than easily-deceived senses. Aristotle declared otherwise: observation is primary. Descartes followed Plato: we know only what our minds can grasp; we think, we doubt.

The British empiricists, especially George Berkeley, extended Aristotle's program: perception defined reality. Perception enhanced by technology (the telescope, microscope, fMRIs) remains subjective. Science requires replication and consensus to validate perception; psychoanalysis attends to counter-transference. Renik's "irreducible subjectivity" (1993), suggests that subjectivity is altogether irreducible, rather than not reducible to zero. That we are imperfect instruments rules out neither scientific activity nor reality-testing. Physicians rely on subjectivity, asking patients to rate their pain; self-report and lab tests together validate treatment.

The Age of Reason led to the Age of Enlightenment, with observation and reason superseding revelation for comprehending the world. John Dewey's pragmatism (knowledge is what works), and Sartre's choice (of what to believe) are 20th Century contributions to scientific epistemology. Contemporary science rejects supernaturalism, and is uncomfortable with a radical relativism of choice. Post-modernism treats subjectivity as a spur to scientific inquiry, with certainty always beyond reach. Scientific disputes focus on methodology. Science is better served by "both/and" rather than "either/or" approaches to method. Aristotle promoted empiricism without rejecting Plato's rationality.

Critical Realism

Philosopher-psychoanalyst Charles Hanly, a former IPA president, described the central tenets of this epistemology (2014): A real world exists, independent of our senses. Appropriate scientific methods of observation can help us know reality to a degree, as can unaided observation that allows commonsense knowledge of other persons and other things. Following Freud (1927), Hanly goes on: Evolution has enabled the human mind to "develop precisely in the attempt to explore the external world (p 55)." Children learn to assess reality with degrees of accuracy. Freud asserts that the human mind is part of nature, knowable just as any natural object only in a mediated way, and that mind is determined not only by its own structure, but by the objects (i.e., people) that affect it—an early relational idea.

Freud's arguments support my critique of the distinction between "social" and natural sciences that implies lesser status. For Descartes and the empiricist philosophers, subjectivity was the basis for knowing, while naysayers see mind as unable to judge reality, leaving it only with constructions. Critical Realism sees subjectivity as a limiting factor, requiring continuous scrutiny of the reliability of observation, rather than dismissal or mushy relativism. Hanly states: "there is no end to observing and correcting our clinical observations (p 904)." [Ongoing debate about "truth" and the nature of evidence in psychoanalysis is addressed by Levine (2016) and others in a recent special issue of the Psychoanalytic Quarterly.] Psychoanalysis has abandoned the idea of a godlike analyst with immaculate perception. Busch's (2015) IPA Congress plenary address underscored tentativeness in clinical psychoanalysis as a major change from the approach of earlier generations.

There is hard science—and harder (not lesser) science that must contend with the problem of subjectivity. Rogers (2014), reviewing Stanislas Dehaene's "Consciousness and the Brain" (2014), supports this position. Dehaene acknowledges that subjective reports can mislead, but states that the subjective report of the viewer in the lab is exactly what is meant by conscious awareness. "Subjective reports are the key phenomena that a cognitive neuroscience of consciousness purports to study. They are primary data (p. 42)... along with... psychophysiological observations," and the self is "a statistical deduction from observation...." He added that "every self is different from all other selves, and differs from itself over time" (p. 113).

Reality-testing, an ego-psychoanalytic concept and emergent property of mind, is essential despite imperfect perception. For Plato, Descartes, the empiricists, and we healers who inquire about thoughts and feelings, subjective consciousness is a natural phenomenon subject to scientific exploration. Freud deepened the understanding of human subjectivity by focusing on meaningful unconscious mental processes (psychological reality), also natural phenomena.

Reductive Causality vs. Emergence

Reductive causality declares mind to be brain, brain to be chemistry, chemistry to be physics and physical particles and sub-particles to have their character determined ultimately by the Big Bang. A consistent reductionism would claim that our universe is not only determined, but predetermined; if we can state necessary and sufficient antecedents, everything follows. That seems as predetermined as the notion of an all-powerful god whose omniscience must include immutable knowledge, even of the future. Contra this radical determinism, scientific domains develop methods of study of phenomena not adequately understood by their contingent precursors. There is no dispute about proximal causality or causal chains; free association relies on such chains. Despite the claims of Churchland (2013), emergent phenomena cannot be radically reduced.

"Emergence" is a conceptual alternative to reductionist determinism. Particles come together to form atoms and molecules with properties different from the particles; these come together over a vast time span in which life emerges with reproductive abilities not present in earlier material forms. Evolution generates new forms by variation and mutation. Life evolves toward complex nervous systems and the human brain. The brain's properties include consciousness, self-consciousness, language, a procedural unconscious that allows walking and riding bikes thoughtlessly, and a dynamic, meaningful unconscious. At each level, the properties are natural phenomena—not epiphenomena—around which scientific disciplines develop. Each discipline focuses on phenomena within its domain, developing methods specific to their study. Humans continue to evolve to create groups, economies, polities and cultures. Each emergent form can be studied scientifically. Social, political and economic realities exist; science must be funded to survive. Borderline disciplines address transitions. The brain is the hardware of mind. Lesions and other hardware differences (variations, mutations) have effects studied by brain science. When neural hardware seems intact, psychology, psychiatry and psychoanalysis become relevant; philosophy's Problem of Evil will not be solved by biology alone.

Evolution is progressive because a few hardware changes, variety in a genetic pool, increase adaption and survival. Inbreeding produces fewer changes. Social evolution works in historical rather than geological or cosmic time. Evolution has accelerated since the 1890s: through technology (built on science), social equality (built on evolving value systems), and the population explosion (built on agricultural and medical advances). Science has become an industry with space-age applications that generate new questions and better answers.

In addition to the personal investment we have in our own offspring, every baby represents a potential Copernicus, Darwin, Freud or Einstein. The population explosion creates a new set of environmental conditions—not all beneficial, but every baby (including identical twins) is different from every other.

The complex phenomenology of humanity therefore extends itself indefinitely, as long as we do not destroy ourselves and the planet. Each baby is unpredictable. Individuals interact based on proximity, creating different cultures, political and economic systems, and now global connectivity. These phenomena are worthy of scientific study, not to be restricted (as was anatomy by religious bans on dissection), or—and this is important—demeaned by a scientific disciplinary hierarchy strangled by its narrowness.

The study of individuals addresses commonalities as well as uniqueness. No generalization fully describes an individual. Intensive individual study will be incomplete, but essential for understanding anyone. Individualized medicine assumes the same stance as clinical psychoanalysis.

Over-determination, "Multiple Function," Parsimony

Freud (1895) asserted that a "convergence of several factors" is required to generate a hysterical symptom; human behavior is not based on simple causality. Psychoanalysis replaces the search for causes with a search for motives operating together and sometimes in conflict; conscious intent is never the single or even dominant factor. A depth psychology is posited in which personal history, imperfectly remembered, contributes to thoughts, wishes, fears, symptoms and behavior. Waelder (1936) described "multiple function" as behavior serving several aims at once. Science eschews teleology in principle, but human minds conjure possible futures or fantasies that motivate behavior.

Over-determination and multiple function are concepts analogous to interactions in statistical analysis of variance and covariance, where outcomes result from single variables and interactions among them. Psychology is multifactorial and loosely assembled; rarely does simple causality help to understand people.

Parsimony is a scientific principle; it does not overrule actual complexity. Though I admire its elegance, I find Brenner's parsimony inadequate for my own clinical work.

Free Will

Philosophy of science discussions are often sidetracked by semantic issues. Free Will is an issue that appears to contradict science. The seeming paradox of the psychoanalytic "free association," which we know is not at all free, is resolved by semantic precision.

"Freedom" is a concept, applicable in several domains: statistical, political, and psychological among them. For traditional science everything is determined (unfree). Contemporary science recognizes emergence as a property of evolution. Statistics uses "degrees of freedom" to measure indeterminacy. Political science measures freedom by rating elections, independent judiciary and press freedom to compare nations. According to Natan Sharansky, he had more freedom in the gulag than did his guards: freedom of thought. Freedom in any domain is a relative matter; it is a Platonic Idea. Enhanced agency is a primary aim of psychoanalytic treatment, freeing people from inhibitions, symptoms and anxieties.

Modesty, Ambition and Progress in Science

Scientists focus on specific phenomena to fit their methods. Dissertations include a section on limitations of the study that may limit generalization (e.g., sample size and population). Research programs address limitations with further research. Scientists must be modest in their claims.

Scientists are also expected to be ambitious. Research aims for generalization and for applications. Freud was ambitious, attempting a complete understanding of the human mind. His range came to include humor, art, literature, and the psychopathology of everyday life. Darwin's propositions have become the overarching paradigm for life sciences.

Ambition leads to error. Freud made many. The subtitle to his Narcissism paper (1914a), "An Introduction," could apply to much of his writing. Freud is chided for having no summary. This omission may be his recognition that his system, like Darwin's, was incomplete. Freud's view of psychosis is questionable; his psychology of women is undermined by its phallocentric viewpoint. "Anatomy is destiny!" was publicly challenged in 1951 by Christine Jorgenson, recently by Caitlin Jenner, following a 40-year political movement by the transsexual demographic. Freud's "bedrock" (penis envy in women, castration anxiety in men) was a leap of faith. His rejection of other-than-clinical research promoted an isolation that still hampers scientific progress.

The atomic physics of the 1940's gave way to nuclear physics and to strange entities; even to "quantum weirdness." Nobel Laureate physicist David Gross sees ignorance—and new questions—as driving science. Scientists must be ambitious and modest. Ambition expands the frontiers of knowledge; modesty limits premature claims. Scientists devise more refined methods to make progress. Popper led a philosophical assault on the scientific standing of psychoanalysis over 50 years ago; Grunbaum continued the assault more recently. Responding to Grunbaum, Howard Shevrin conducted a series of increasingly refined studies. The philosopher cried "Uncle" acknowledging Shevrin's (2012) work as a valid demonstration of psychoanalytic hypotheses.

Best Evidence; Convergent validity

"Best evidence" is a complex concept," determined—always provisionally—by social, cultural, even political consensus. The FDA recently approved a new pill for enhancing female desire by a vote of 18-6—a cogent example, I think, of consensus rather than certainty as criterion.

Despite Meehl's (1954) finding statistical prediction superior to clinical judgment, the latter is standard for individual decisions in all health care practice; cases also remain the primary source of psychoanalytic data. Experimental findings don't readily translate to individuals; operational definitions and exclusion criteria limit generalizability, and patients may be statistical outliers. Statistical significance often falls short of practical significance, experimental conditions differ greatly from those of clinical practice, and contamination and fraud are not unheard of. Failure to replicate is common for all areas of scientific research. Randomized controlled trials (RCTs) are considered a "gold standard" for empirical research, but a close look at RCTs comparing drugs or psychotherapies frequently shows results to be tarnished (Wachtel, 2010), leading to "fool's gold" claims (Shedler, 2015). It is understandable that practitioners are critics of controlled research; Hoffman's rejection of quantitative studies (2009) drew a standing ovation at his invited APsaA address. I read summaries of research papers, often finding full articles dull reading and rarely directly relevant to my practice.

Yet I must admonish fellow clinicians that an art whose claims are more than aesthetic needs more than claims for affirming its value. A google search shows nearly 500,000 listings for psychoanalytic research; with significant support for treatment effectiveness, as well as clarification of therapy concepts and process. Many studies use quantitative methods to provide normative data; social policy research is scientifically respectable. "The Authoritarian Personality" (Adorno, et al, 1950) initiated political psychology. Clark, Chein and Cook (1952) were cited in the Supreme Court's 1954 decision outlawing school segregation.

Scientific method begins with systematic observation, and correlation; clinical evidence may be limited to these methods. Psychoanalysis is not unique in this regard (e.g., meteorology, astronomy), nor is it unusual for much of health care practice. Scientific judgments are based on current empirical evidence and best rational arguments. "Convergent Validity"—a preponderance of observation, correlation, relevant experimentation, and findings from related disciplines—is a proper standard for "best evidence." Life forms evolve; subjectivity seems to have infinite potential for variation. Lest we find ourselves in the hatchery of Aldous Huxley's dystopic "Brave New World," individuals must be treated as unique. Science corrects its findings with changing consensus over time. There can be no complete theory of everything (Critchley, 2015). Researchers and clinicians should stop fighting. "The farmers and the cowboys should be friends" (Hammerstein, 1943).

Epistemophilia and its Discontents

The urge to know motivates infants. Freud spoke of an epistemic drive. Panksepp's recent work (2012) supports this idea. Curiosity is basic to science and to the future evolution of our species. Knowing is resisted because knowledge can be painful. Weaning requires accommodation to a reality beyond personal need; toilet training inhibits urges; the Oedipus complex redirects and defers desire; mortality leads to adaptations, from depression and despair to the search for meaningful lives. The Western creation myth forbids tasting the fruit of the Tree of Knowledge; Biblical knowing is a synonym for sex. What Freud made explicit has been in plain sight since Eve met the serpent. Science aims to discover realities. Psychoanalysis focuses on subjectivity and approaches its task with the best methods available.

Daily headlines demonstrate the failure to solve the Problem of Evil. Science is not alone in its efforts; by evoking personal engagement, the humanities provide a second path. Freud was as inspired by Sophocles, Shakespeare and Goethe as he was by Brucke and Meynert. Psychoanalysis bridges C.P. Snow's (1959) "Two Cultures." The study of superego phenomena exemplifies a psychoanalytic approach. Religion may provide comfort to multitudes, but its "side effects"— intolerance, fanaticism, cultism and holy war (common expressions of a punitive superego)—undermine its claims. Freud's genius allowed him to create from his efforts to heal a new science that has become a permanent contribution to the history of ideas. This science, a disciplined curiosity based on a set of ideas, continues to address the challenges of the Problem of Evil.

EARLY ESSAYS

Effects of Experimental Drive Arousal on Response to Subliminal Stimulation

Reprinted from *Dissertation Abstracts* 26 No. 11 (1967)

This experiment was designed to test the hypothesis that effects of an aggressive subliminal stimulus vary as a function of aggressive schemas being active in the individual and as a function of the individual's typical pattern of coping with aggressive drive (i.e., defense mechanisms).

Aggressive schemas were activated by the technique of "priming," i.e., an aggressive passage was read to Ss as a memory task. The individual's typical pattern of coping with aggressive drive was assessed by means of four different measures: baseline aggressive responses to inkblots, Buss-Durkee-Sarason Combined Inventory, Rosenwald Story Completion Test and threshold for recognizing the aggressive subliminal stimulus.

The aggressive stimulus was a drawing of one man stabbing another man, the control stimulus was a drawing of the same man giving a birthday cake to the other man. They were subliminally presented by means of a tachistoscopic shutter projector to Ss in groups of from five to twenty. Ss were 160 female university students.

The dependent variables were: a. Change in Aggressive and in Aggressive-Subject responses to inkblots from a baseline of four cards to a critical series of six cards during which the stimuli were presented; b. Changes in response to six mood adjective items: "annoyed," "angry," "suspicious," "inhibited," "anxious," "nervous" from a baseline administration to an administration after stimulation.

Session I of the procedure involved: a. administering the adjective checklist and the baseline series of inkblots; b. "priming"; c. administering a second set of four inkblots and a second checklist as independent measures of the effects of "priming"; d. administering the critical inkblot series and adjective checklist

43

during which aggressive or control stimuli were presented. The experimenter was "blind" with regard to which stimulus was used for any group.

Session II involved threshold and discrimination checks on subliminality and administration of the Buss-Durkee-Sarason Combined Inventory and the Rosenwald Story Completion Test.

The design was a factorial analysis of variance for each dependent variable to assess the effects of "priming," aggressive subliminal stimulus and their interaction. Each measure of defense was correlated with each dependent variable for each experimental condition and correlational differences between conditions were tested by means of the Fisher z-transformation. The independent effects of "priming" were assessed by t-tests for each of the dependent variables (using change from baseline to second measure) between "primed" and non-"primed" groups. Each measure of defense was also correlated with these "prime"-check variables for "primed" and non-"primed" Ss.

It was hypothesized that non-defensive Ss would give a greater increase in aggressive inkblot responses and certain of the mood adjectives when "primed"' and aggressively subliminally stimulated than defensive Ss or Ss who were only "primed," only shown the aggressive stimulus, or were untreated.

The results were consistent with the part of the hypothesis that defense is a necessary consideration when drive is at issue. All but one positive effect were obtained with non-defensive Ss. "Priming" had an independent effect as drive arousal, but it was found that this was not a necessary condition of the aggressive subliminal effect although it might help to make the effect more observable. Effects of "priming"' were found in mood changes: particularly "angry" and "anxious."' The Aggressive inkblot variable was not sensitive to the aggressive subliminal effect; the Aggressive-Subject inkblot variable was.

It was concluded that effects of aggressive subliminal stimuli are, in part, a function of defense and of response modalities. The hypothesis that drive arousal is a necessary parameter was not supported, but could not be rejected either. It was concluded, further, that "priming" is a successful technique for activating aggressive drive schemas and that effects of the technique of "priming" also vary, in part, as a function of defense and of response modalities.

Measures of defense were not substantially correlated with one another although each was an important parameter of some obtained effect. It was suggested that measures of defense be validated against specific theoretical definitions of particular mechanisms of defense.

Summaries of Two Research Experiments

Should WISC Subjects Explain Picture Arrangement Stories?
Journal of Consulting and Clinical Psychology 33,
No.6, pp. 761–762 (1969)
with James M. Herrell

To determine whether requiring Wechsler Intelligence Scale for Children (WISC) subjects to explain their Picture Arrangement (PA) sequences affects PA scores, 78 subjects were given the WISC and asked to tell PA stories, and 57 subjects were given the WISC under standard instructions. Forty-two pairs of subjects were matched for age, Full Scale IQ, and reason for referral. The subjects who told PA stories had an average PA score of 2.12 scaled score points higher than subjects who did not tell stories (p < .01). Similar differences significant at or beyond the .02 level were found for subjects referred for behavioral-emotional problems, subjects with IQ below 100, and subjects nine years old or less. Trends (.05 < P < .10) were found for subjects referred for academic-intellectual problems and subjects with IQs greater than 100. No significant difference was found for subjects > 9 years. Clinicians were urged to be aware of the apparently facilitating effects of subjects explaining PA stories when interpreting the WISC.

Should WAIS Subjects Explain Picture Arrangement Stories?
Journal of Consulting and Clinical Psychology 35,
No. 2 (1970), pp. 157-158
with James M. Herrell and Michael Hahn

To determine whether requiring Wechsler Adult Intelligence Scale (WAIS) subjects to explain their PA sequences affects PA scores, 56 subjects were given the WAIS and asked to tell PA stories, and 102 subjects were given the WAIS under standard instructions. Thirty-seven pairs of subjects were matched for age, Full Scale IQ, and reason for referral. No significant differences were found between subjects who told PA stories and those who did not. These findings were contrasted with those of Golland and Herrell (1969), who found a 2-point scaled score increment on PA for Wechsler Intelligence Scale for Children subjects who explained their sequences.

Training Army Psychology Technicians for Intake and Evaluation

Hospital and Community Psychiatry, December 1971, pp. 373–374.

In 1968, the Army had used psychology technicians to administer and score psychological tests under professional supervision for more than a quarter of a century. Five such technicians were on duty at the psychiatric clinic at Brooke General Hospital in Fort Sam Houston, Texas, when I initiated a program to train them to handle patient intake and evaluation.

The clinic procedures at the time were typical of many such clinics, civilian as well as military. New patients were seen for an extensive interview by a psychiatrist; he would make a diagnosis, sometimes with the aid of psychological tests, and a disposition, which sometimes involved the social work service. Patients accepted for treatment were most often treated by a combination of pharmacotherapy, attempts at environmental manipulation, and regular but generally infrequent visits to a psychiatrist or social worker.

Although these procedures were followed for many years, they seemed inefficient because the psychiatrists were so heavily involved with evaluations that they could only do very minimal and infrequent psychotherapy. Meanwhile, psychology technicians and psychologists did not seem to be contributing as much as they might to the overall functioning of the clinic.

Use of the technicians in intake and evaluation involved several changes in clinic procedures. New patients would be interviewed by a technician, who would refer acute emergencies to one of the professional staff. The interviewer would discuss nonemergency cases with his professional supervisor, who would help him organize his interview data and prepare a tentative disposition. The technician would present the material to a weekly disposition conference of the chiefs of psychiatry, psychology, and social work, who would then briefly interview the patient. Psychiatrists, psychologists, and social workers would be primarily involved in offering treatment for which they had the requisite training, including intensive psychotherapy.

To effect the plan, the technicians had to be trained to interview patients, They had to learn the elements of mental- and social-status examinations and social histories, and to distinguish an emergency from a nonemergency. The learning had to take place while they continued testing duties.

A total of ten men received training in the program; only one was a career soldier. The first five men, aged 21 to 26, were trained as a group over a two-month period. Two had bachelor's degrees, two had completed a year of college, and the fifth had a high school diploma. All had received eight weeks of training in psychological testing at the U.S. Army Medical Field Service School.

Five other technicians, men aged 22 to 27, were trained one or two at a time, as they came on the job. Generally, their training period lasted four weeks. Two had master's degrees and three had bachelor's degrees; four of the five had majored in psychology or sociology. Only two had been trained as testers by the Army.

Slightly different training procedures were used for the first five technicians than for the later trainees. Common to both procedures was extensive observation. In the first, a technician sat in on all initial interviews conducted by the psychiatrists. In the second, a technician observed interviews conducted by me or his already trained peers. The three men who were not trained testers also observed other technicians administering tests.

Didactic presentations and discussions were also used in both procedures. The first group attended classes held by the chief of psychiatry or social work or by me, as chief of the psychology service. The subjects were the various theories of emotional disturbance, signs and symptoms of various psychiatric syndromes, elements of mental- and social-status examinations, elements of social histories, and principles of interviewing. The classes began simultaneously with the interview observations, and were held for an hour four times a week for four weeks. In subsequent training, I was able to cover the same material by myself in four to six individualized sessions, because of the higher educational level of the later trainees and their backgrounds in psychology or sociology.

Didactic sessions for the first group were followed by five hour-long role-playing sessions, in which each technician played interviewer to my portrayal of various patient types. Twenty minutes of roleplaying was followed by 40 minutes of discussion. We did not feel role-playing was needed in the more individualized training given later trainees.

When the first group completed the role-playing sessions, they began conducting actual interviews with me present; I would add to or terminate the interview as I felt necessary. Each interview was followed by a discussion with me. The second five trainees began the joint interviews and discussions after completing the didactic sessions and after at least five sessions in which they observed experienced interviewers. Each of the ten technicians participated in at least three joint interviews. Three of the ten needed a fourth such session before we felt they were prepared to interview by themselves. When training was completed and each technician began to interview patients on his own, he was assigned a professional staff member as supervisor. The supervisory staff saw any emergency patients encountered by the technician, and, in weekly meetings, each supervisor helped his technician improve his interviewing techniques. Supervisors were rotated every three months to allow the technicians to learn a diversity of professional approaches.

The supervisors believed that most of the problems encountered by the new interviewers were related to the interviewer's own anxiety in dealing with stressful interpersonal situations. To deal with that anxiety, I suggested that a sensitivity group be formed. The first five technicians readily agreed, and I became the leader of the group, which met for 90 minutes weekly. All new technicians voluntarily joined the group. Later, after all ten technicians had been trained, some of them expressed a need for more feedback about each other's technique and style. By then, four had been transferred to other assignments, and the remaining six began to sit in periodically on each other's interviews.

The technicians' assumption of the intake role allowed professional staff more time for intensive psychotherapy, and also made it possible to incorporate a greater variety of therapeutic modalities. The changes led to increased cohesiveness and morale for the entire staff. Some technicians worked overtime voluntarily, something that had not occurred before and is rare among noncareer soldiers. They often spoke about feeling more involved and useful in their jobs, and several expressed increased interest in professional training.

Although the ten technicians achieved varying levels of skill and proficiency, only one was considered at any time to be performing below minimal standards. Interestingly enough, he was among the better-educated, with a bachelor's degree, but was hampered by personality problems. His workload was cut down, and with closer supervision he was able to meet the standards set by the chiefs of services.

On the other hand, the level of skill of some was considered so high that their intake role was expanded. Four technicians were trained to do brief phone screenings and were considered for training as supportive counselors or therapists under professional staff supervision.

Such plans were scuttled when a major turnover in professional personnel took place. The plans for counselor training were abandoned, but the technicians and their replacements maintained the intake and evaluation roles for which they had been trained. At least three went on to professional schools after military discharge.

Clearly the small number of personnel involved and the lack of control procedures limit generalizing this approach to in-service training of paraprofessionals in other mental health facilities. However, the approach was highly successful in the setting in which it was used, and that the experience might serve as a beginning for standardizing such training, or as a baseline for further approaches.

A "Hello" and "Goodbye" Group

International Journal of Group Psychotherapy. 22,
No. 2 (February 1971), pp, 258–261

This paper reports a group experience in which "hello" and "goodbye" became the almost exclusive issues of interaction. The implications of this experience for group therapy in general are discussed.

The group was formed among the staff at an Army Community psychiatric clinic as an "interaction group" or "personality laboratory" designed to help each member better understand himself and the way he related to others, so as to better interact with patients being seen in intake interviews or for psychological testing. It began with the author and the four paraprofessionals (Army Psychology Technicians) then on duty. All newly assigned paraprofessionals and the newly assigned psychologist voluntarily joined the group as they began their duties. The group varied from four to seven male paraprofessionals, age 20 to 26, and one or two clinical psychologists as leaders.

It was the military setting which gave the group its issues. In this situation. men were haphazardly assigned to the clinic, ordered to other assignments, or completed their military service so that, after two months (and aside for an occasional few weeks within the 14 months that the author led the group), there was at all times either a new group member or a soon-departing one. These comings and goings, it seemed, would either destroy all continuity in the group or, as it turned out, become the major issue of the group.

The first two new members joined the group at the same time and were known to the others as they had previously been assigned to another section within the same hospital. An ingroup and an outgroup formed immediately, with the original four members resenting the intrusion of the newcomers into what had become a comfortable and enjoyable group situation. The newcomers resented being treated as intruders. The leader's focus on the inter-clique conflict led the members to express their feelings and modify them as their knowledge of one another increased. This development of familiarity was characterized by the group as a welcome, or a "hello."

Vietnam intruded. When the group came together again—in about a month—two members, one from each of the two previous cliques, had received their orders. The group's initial reactions included denial ("It must be a mistake") and avoidance ("No need to talk about leaving; we'll be writing to each other, keeping up the friendship"). The leader confirmed the reality and pointed out the avoidance until the group was able to begin its "goodbyes." These involved considerable expression of feeling by each man for each other man, and a great feeling of closeness in the group as a whole. In response to one member's avoidance ("Why bother? People come and go all the time"), the leader was able to recall his own regrets, wishing he had said some things to someone who had gone from his life. The group recognized this experience and took the opportunity for saying like things before separation.

A new leader (coleader) joined the group then and was surprised that the members began relating to him ("hello") in his initial session. When his welcome had been accomplished by his fourth session, and he was accepted as coleader, he told the group about his previous experience in a similar setting during his internship. No one had focused on him at first and he assumed a detached observational role, never getting to feel like a participant in the group. The feeling he experienced—that groups were of little or no experiential value- was quickly changed.

Two more paraprofessionals were then assigned to the clinic and joined the group. Again, there was a "hello," but it deepened the concept of "hello" for the group. One of the two, a Black man, recalled to the others a previous Black member who had left for Vietnam; the other was cast in the role of the other man who had left the group, whose job he was filling. The newcomers resisted being considered replacements, and this led the group to see them as distinct individuals and to regard "hello" as much more than a perfunctory, assembly-line interpersonal technique.

The next man to join did so before the previous newcomers had accomplished becoming part of the group, and an older member received transfer orders on this man's first day in group. This led to some insight into the problems of getting to know people at different stages of relationship and of problems of simultaneous "hello" and "goodbye." These problems were focused upon. "Goodbye" was seen to have priority because of its finality, and "hello" occurred in the course of this "goodbye." The group came together again.

Next came a "goodbye" to a member who was being discharged and who was surely the most disliked group member. Feelings of antagonism had been expressed to him previously, but his very rigid defensive structure kept him from understanding them. Envy of his discharge added to his unpopularity, but the group had learned the power of "hello" and "goodbye" and was hopeful that the last weeks with this man would be another worthwhile experience ending with good feeling.

The learning experience occurred, but without warmth and good cheer. The group expressed its negative feelings and tried to eke out positive ones. The leave-taker was unresponsive. In his last session the other members looked to the leader to save the day. They wanted to see whether he would try to smooth things over with pleasantness or be honest and express his continued annoyance and frustration at not getting through the leave-taker's defensiveness. "I'm really sorry I couldn't get to like you; I hope you become more likable" was the "goodbye." "Byes" can't always be made "Good."

One other "goodbye," a good one, preceded the author's, also a good one; and each had become a less final goodbye. The then-current group members, today all dispersed, have maintained their friendships via mail and visits.

While the group was not a therapy group, the intensified learning about "hello" and "goodbye" proved readily generalizable to therapy groups run concurrently and subsequent to this group. "Hello" and "goodbye," as issues, incorporate many experiences and emotions common to most patients and most people. They recapitulate earliest experiences with new siblings and with individuation and independence-seeking; they reproduce current adult situations in a way that can be enlightening because of therapeutic scrutiny; they lead to increased and accurate feelings of self-worth as the individual is welcomed or wished farewell, and they prepare us for the ultimate "hellos" and "goodbyes"—births and deaths.

"Hello" and "goodbye" tend not to be easy. Individuals and groups avoid doing either well and fully. The group therapist's awareness of these issues and his focusing on their avoidance when it occurs form part of the foundation of a therapeutic group experience.

Mainstreaming and Teacher Preparation

Golubchick, L. H. and Persky, B. (Eds.), *Innovations in Education* (Kendall/Hunt, 1975)

Myron Brenton's (1974) article, "Mainstreaming the Handicapped," pointed to current trends suggesting that physically handicapped children will, in increasing numbers, attend school in regular classrooms. He cited statistics estimating 2.7 percent of the population under 17 as having some limitation of activity. The implications of "mainstreaming" such a large group are, he said, staggering (p. 20).

But, what is "mainstreaming"? It is not simply the placing of children in regular classrooms (the mainstream). It is, instead, an attempt to treat all children as "normally" as possible, while making the necessary adjustments, and *only* the necessary adjustments, for their exceptionalities.

In the case of physically disabled children, all too often they have been placed in special settings going far beyond their needs for special attention. These placements have stigmatized them and have added social isolation and rejection to the handicap imposed by the physical disability. In a sense, mainstreaming is a reaction to excessively special placement. More to the point, however, mainstreaming is an attempt to find the *correct* educational placement for the exceptional child, a placement that is increasingly likely to be closer to a regular placement.

Mainstreaming, as Brenton (1974, p. 20) correctly points out, essentially involves the placement of physically handicapped children, many of whose disabilities require no special educational approach. A ramp or an elevator might be all that is required for a wheelchair-bound pupil to attend a regular class. Learning problems do not follow from the orthopedic disability. Likewise, children with cardiac problems might need only a limitation of vigorous activity, if that, and children with seizure disorders might require medication to enable them to learn in a regular classroom.

Children with seeing or hearing impairments will require special educational measures such as braille reading or speech reading, but, aided by such measures and the availability of a special resource room, even a blind or a deaf child might be placed in a regular classroom for much of his learning!

Some authors extend the concept of mainstreaming to mean the elimination of all special classes and schools. Heffernan (1974) argues that current diagnostic labels are indefensible and special placement following from such labels as "emotionally disturbed," "brain damaged," "mentally retarded" and "learning disabled" are equally indefensible and should be eliminated. He calls for the dissolution of special-education classrooms and the individualizing of regular classrooms.

While there are problems in defining emotional disturbance, brain damage, mental retardation and learning disabilities, such labels are not indefensible. Each of these terms has objective referents, though at times diagnosis may be difficult. Often enough, however, children can be correctly diagnosed and, while the philosophy of treating all children as "normally" as possible still applies, in many cases the possibilities will exclude a full-time regular placement. While we must applaud Heffernan's call (1974), among many others, for individualization, we must recognize that we are sometimes unable to meet the needs of the special child without detracting excessively from the attention required by the rest of the class. It would be a shame to lose the benefits of many fine special placements because we overextend the concept of mainstreaming.

The mainstreaming approach is, however, applicable to groups other than the physically disabled, provided we do not throw out the baby (special education) with the bath water (excessively special settings). Many emotionally disturbed children can be well-placed in special classes within regular schools instead of in psychiatric hospital-schools; many brain-damaged children can be in special classes or even in regular classes on a part- or full-time basis as well. Some mentally retarded children can participate in monitorial activities, assemblies, and physical activities with the other children in a regular school rather than a special one. One retarded young man in a special class became the pride of that class when he was chosen for and succeeded in being a crossing guard! Most learning disabled children could spend most of their school time in regular classroom settings, with part-time special teaching enabling them to move fully into the regular classroom.

The mainstreaming approach will require additional training of regular classroom teachers. Few states require such training, Brenton (1974) noted, and funding cuts have reduced existing programs already (p. 25). Teachers must, nonetheless, become familiar with the characteristics of "exceptional children."

The term "exceptional children" refers to all children different enough from the statistical or medical norm of a specific trait to make a practical educational difference. Generally included as specific traits, in addition to physical capabilities, are cognitive skills, social behavior and cultural differences. While acknowledging the difficulty of estimating the prevalence of exceptional children in the schools, Dunn (1973, pp. 13-14) cites a figure of *12 percent* as the traditionally accepted estimate, and this figure excludes the large group of those who are culturally different from the white middle class.

Exceptional children will be found in regular classrooms for reasons other than mainstreaming, such as failure to identify the exception, and inadequacy or unavailability of appropriate special placements. In addition, certain exceptional children, most notably those with specific learning disabilities, are often not recognizable before school age.

It is clear that *every* teacher comes into direct classroom contact with exceptional children and, therefore, that regular classroom teachers, especially those in early childhood and elementary classes, should be prepared to identify an exceptional child, to refer that child appropriately for further evaluation, and to work with the child in the regular classroom part- or full-time should that be the placement of choice. Such preparation has generally been limited to special education programs.

When an early childhood and elementary education program was introduced at Bernard M. Baruch College five years ago, it was designed to include training in special education for the regular classroom teacher. In the upper junior semester, teacher-candidates take two corequisite courses: "The Exceptional Child in the Regular Classroom" and "Field Work with Exceptional Children." The field work involves 30 hours in a school or agency working with a group of special children. The settings have included classes for children of retarded mental development ("educable" and "trainable"), classes for brain-injured children, schools for children with emotional disturbances and specific learning disabilities, schools for the deaf and for the blind, classes for children with speech and hearing handicaps, "health classes," and classes for intellectually gifted children. For the most part, settings have been public ones, but private agencies have been included as well. In some settings, those for the deaf and for the blind in particular, children were frequently multiply-handicapped. In a weekly seminar hour, students share their experiences with one another under the guidance of a professor.

One may ask why students are placed in special classes rather than assigned as a single exceptional child in the regular classroom. The answer is twofold. First, we want our students to appreciate the full extent of defined exceptionality, i.e., how different is the exceptional child and how different are the special programs geared to that child. It is probable that such differences would be less clear-cut in a regular placement. Second, we want our students to learn that even the most exceptional children in special educational placements are *less* different from other children than common stereotypes would have it. This second lesson is almost always understood after the first field visit. Even when working with blind, multiply-handicapped children, our students have been impressed with the fact that people have more in common than they have differences or, as Harry Stack Sullivan put it, "We are all much more human than anything else."

The classroom course is aimed at developing the required skills by reviewing the characteristics, problems and educational approaches for children with a wide variety of exceptionalities. Students are presented with definitions of such terms as "normal" and "exceptional" and, with examples from their own fieldwork experience, come to see that, on the one hand, it is in specific traits that children may be either exceptional or within the normal range, and, on the other hand, that every child is unique. Disability, handicap and stigmatization are viewed from both the individual and the social perspective, and it is seen that all pupils need to be treated as exceptionally as their uniqueness requires, but as similarly to others as their uniqueness allows and their common humanity requires. Compassion must be coupled with respect in working with special (as well as with nonexceptional) children. These knowledge and attitudinal components of the course have recently been supplemented by evaluation of skills, wherein students are tested on their ability to identify different types of exceptional children seen on videotape recordings.

The results have been promising. We have "lost" several students to graduate programs in special education. Those who have gone on to practice teaching in the regular classroom have reported a greater sensitivity to the uniqueness of each child.

The goal of having "every teacher a special teacher" is amply justified, not only by the trend toward mainstreaming, but by the need of exceptional children for early recognition and referral. This goal can be met, as it has at Bernard M. Baruch College, with generalizability to the education of normal children an additional benefit.

The Status of Mainstreaming in the United States

**Golubchick, L. H. and Persky, B. (Eds.), *Innovations in Education*
(Kendall/Hunt, 1975)**

It has been reported (Brenton, 1974) that current trends suggest physically handicapped children will, in increasing numbers, attend school in regular classrooms. This shift of the physically handicapped has been referred to as "mainstreaming." As I have pointed out elsewhere (pp. 57–60 above), mainstreaming is neither limited to the physically handicapped nor mandates full-time attendance in a regular classroom (the educational "mainstream"). "It is, instead, an attempt to treat all children as 'normally' as possible, while making the necessary adjustments, and *only* the necessary adjustments, for their exceptionalities." It involves, for each child's educational placement, finding the least restrictive educational alternative. Leaders in the field of special education have been strong in endorsing mainstreaming, so defined. .

This article reports on the extent to which mainstreaming is being implemented throughout the United States. It is based upon a survey of State Education Departments (conducted by the author) which asked for each state's definition of mainstreaming, the formal policy of the state and the procedures for implementing that policy including funding, training and evaluation programs. One half of the State Education Departments responded to the survey.

As will be seen, no state has implemented, funded, trained for, and evaluated mainstreaming programs as fully as adherents would wish or as fully as several of the states themselves would want. I will report on significant aspects of the findings in order to clarify the issues involved and to focus on some of the problems encountered in attempting to implement mainstreaming.

Definitions

Most states have defined mainstreaming as I have done above, using a variation of the "Least Restrictive Alternative" wording. Others used wording which was different, but was near in meaning to the "Least Restrictive Alternative" and stressed the meeting of individual needs, increasing contact between handicapped and nonhandicapped, and the use of the regular classroom as much as possible. They have not limited the notion to the physically handicapped, but referred instead to all children; nor have they mandated full-time regular classroom attendance.

Policy

Most states have a formal mainstreaming policy: a few have public laws defining the policy, most have rules and regulations which are in force throughout their jurisdiction. These policies, by and large, are promulgation of the definition of mainstreaming, dissemination of information, and, in a few cases, provision for supportive services, funding and training.

Implementation

The major implementation procedure for mainstreaming is "encouragement and dissemination of policy." Several states have not proceeded beyond that in attempts at implementation. Some states, however, have specific pilot projects on mainstreaming; others had workshops and conferences and give "technical assistance" to districts. One state monitors districts to insure policy implementation; another reports developing teacher certification for resource room specialists. Two states place implementation of mainstreaming within the overall special education program. Three states report implementation in quantitative terms (25, 600, over 400 districts) which were not adequately defined. One state asserts that the majority of *physically* handicapped children are enrolled in regular education programs.

Funding

A few states have special funding policies for mainstreaming as distinct from the general category of Special Education funding. These fall into the following categories: (1) use of federal funds (Title VI, Education of the Handicapped Act), mostly for training; (2) additional state funding for itinerant teachers and resource rooms; (3) special funding formulae within Special Education funding for mainstreamed pupils, providing financial incentives to districts; (4) development of diagnostic-prescriptive centers, and coordination of agencies. Clearly, limited resources are being used in very limited ways in the quest for mainstreaming; but the last-mentioned item, development of diagnostic-prescriptive centers, provides a promising example of specific spending to implement mainstreaming.

Training

Some states have federally-supported in-service training for mainstreaming, mostly in the workshop format. Others have state implementation of in-service training. A few report such training being carried on by some localities. Four states have instituted pre-service training for mainstreaming at one or more universities within the state; three states report universities planning such training. The few in-service programs that have been established can hardly be expected to prepare large numbers of regular classroom teachers for at least the part-time inclusion of exceptional children. The few pre-service programs established or planned, while likely having a greater long-range impact, can prepare even fewer teachers for mainstreaming in the near future.

Evaluation

Very few states report evaluations of mainstreaming; a few more are planning or in the process of carrying out evaluations. Two states cite "favorable site visits" as evaluatory evidence; a third indicates the reduction of stigmatization and increased social and academic progress for handicapped children with individualized programs, but does not include the research evidence.

One state has published several evaluation reports conducted with EHA Title VI support. One report was a survey of literature from 1932 to 1967 comparing special and regular placement of educable mentally retarded pupils on academic and nonacademic measures and showing several studies favoring each type of placement. Two reports were anecdotal, supporting the success of mainstreaming. One report was a description of a rating scale for individual progress on mainstreamed pupils.

Two reports, however, were apparently well-designed and well-implemented empirical studies comparing experimental (mainstreamed) educable retarded pupils with control (self-contained classroom) educable retarded pupils. The first of these showed academic progress to be significantly higher for experimental pupils and had not analyzed the data regarding behavioral and psychological variables. The second, comparing mainstreamed and self-contained classroom retarded pupils in three different school settings, found mainstreamed pupils to have made more progress in reading, spelling, and math as well as having increased in self-esteem and parental favor. Differential results were found for different school settings and results on some variables were not conclusive. These reports are an effective demonstration that evaluation can be made a part of educationally innovative practices, and make the lack of more widespread evaluation procedures all the more deplorable.

Problems

The problem most frequently reported in the implementation of mainstreaming has to do with teacher resistance. It has taken various forms including: (1) regular teacher reluctance due to lack of training and understanding of the handicapped; (2) regular teacher fear that mainstreaming will serve as an excuse for "dumping" the handicapped into regular classes, enabling the elimination of special education and supportive services; (3) communication problems and conflict between special education teachers and counselors, on the one side, and regular teachers, on the other. These issues underscore the critical importance of pre-service and in-service training.

Lack of funding and supportive services are, of course, major problems as well. So too is the sense of lack of clear definitions in mainstreaming and in special education, generally. The lack of clear-cut criteria for placement of handicapped children is another critical problem.

We may conclude by bemoaning the limited extent of implementation of the widespread mainstreaming policies, criticizing legislatures for the limited funding that has been provided for such implementation, getting angry at the lack of in-service and pre-service training that makes untrained teacher-related problems, and joining so many others in lamenting the dearth of good research on educational issues.

We may choose, instead, to note the consistency of definitions of main-streaming, to laud the extent and consistency of formal policy development across the country, to support the attempts at innovative program implementation by supposedly bureaucratic departments, and to acknowledge the recognition of the need for funding, training, and evaluation on the part of these institutions.

It would be most correct, however, to recognize both the problems and the progress in the move toward mainstreaming in special education. With that recognition we may work toward overcoming the problems without being overwhelmed by them. That work may lead to a broad enough implementation of mainstreaming to allow for its thorough evaluation. If that evaluation is consistent with the few research findings we now have, many handicapped children will be in a much better educational environment.

Developmental Psychology and Psychoanalysis

American Psychologist (1980)

The October 1979 special issue of *American Psychologist* on psychology and children was a welcome and timely one for the international year of the child. For one segment of its readers, however, a major omission Is striking: psychoanalytic research and practice are given short shrift. While Scarr notes the "healthy diversity of psychological approaches to children's issues" (1979, p. 809) and White notes the "cosmic theorizing" aspect of developmental psychology (1979, p. 813), neither acknowledges the work of Sigmund Freud, nor of current psychoanalytic developmental psychologists.

Closer study of the special issue confirms this omission. Of 45 contributors writing 42 papers, not one is a psychoanalytic developmental psychologist, nor is one article devoted to the current psychoanalytic developmental literature; whereas there is a full paper on behavior therapy (1979, pp. 981-987), one on family theory and therapy (1979, pp. 988-992), and several articles from a cognitive point of view.

Intensive and systematic study of children has been a major influence on psychoanalytic theory and practice for the forty years since the death of Freud. Works such as Brody and Axelrod (1978) and the annual *Psychoanalytic Study of the Child* have been given regular and favorable reviews In *Contemporary Psychology* (1979, pp. 868-869; 1978, pp. 869-870), attesting to the fact that there exists a thriving psychoanalytic developmental psychology. Most developmental psychology texts (e.g. Biehler, 1976) affirm this view in the coverage given to Freudian theory and to the work of Erikson.

One may argue that the failure to include psychoanalytic authors in the special issue does not prove the absence of psychoanalytic influence. To test this proposition, I reviewed every citation in the Issue (n = 871), counting the appearance of any psychoanalytic developmental psychologist in the bibliographies. For this review I define as a psychoanalytic developmental psychologist Sigmund Freud and anyone who has published In Psychoanalytic Study of the Child (through 1978). There are 433 such persons. Of the 42 papers in the special issue, eight cite psychoanalytic authors, with 20 citations (2.3%) of 14 authors. Six of these citations appear in but one article (Ainsworth, pp. 932–937), two of the eight articles citing (Ainsworth; Hetherington, pp. 851–858) have psychoanalytic citations from the past decade. Three articles directly cite Psychoanalytic Study of the Child (Ainsworth, 3 times; Hoffman, pp. 859–865 and Lipsett, pp. 973–980). Three of the psychoanalytic authors (Bowlby, Spitz, J. Wallerstein) account for eleven of the 20 citations.

This quantitative view may not do justice to a special issue in which many papers should not be expected to be influenced by psychoanalytic views. A content analysis reveals, however, 22 papers where psychoanalysts have contributed to the topic of concern. These papers have 607 citations and include the eight which do cite, and the 20 citations (3.3%). It seems clear, then, that the psychoanalytic point of view has been, by and large, ignored.

In that the special issue purports to be representative of American developmental psychology research and practice, the absence of a psychoanalytic perspective is a serious limitation on that claim. In 1979, the year that APA established a Division of Psychoanalysis, it is ironic that such an omission should occur.

REVIEWS AND
COMMENTARIES

Introduction

I have long considered these papers to exemplify both my learning to write for publication and to include some of my best writing. The Richard Chessick review, for instance, began a ten-year relationship with *Psychoanalytic Books*, a private journal, successor to *Review of Psychoanalytic Books,* each founded and edited by the late Joseph Reppen, PhD. I appreciated the opportunity and found that reading and writing about the work of others deepened my connection with the intellectual ferment of psychoanalysis. Joe's wife, the late Francesca, was the managing editor and entire staff. She would copy-edit my submissions and improve them. Over time I became one of the most frequent contributors with fewer and fewer edits needed. Sometime during that decade Fran told me I had "a voice," a recognizable style. I had not thought that concept applied to me! Naively, I believed I was a neutral referee. I began to appreciate my writing beyond having learned from a book—and it took on a greater purpose for me. I frequently mention Fran Reppen as the person who taught me to write well.

Joe Reppen closed his private journal in 1998, a year after becoming the third editor of *Psychoanalytic Psychology*, the official Division 39 journal. I'm glad I was a division board member at that time because Joe's appointment required a political process. Despite Joe's qualifications, clearly superior to those of the other applicants, important organizational positions require political support. Joe repaid my efforts, inviting and publishing my comments thereafter.

Some years later I led the fundraising for the inclusion of *Psychoanalytic Books* in PEP-Web, the electronic repository of world-wide psychoanalytic writing. This was not simply selfless; more of my own writing is now in that permanent archive.

Joseph LeBoit and Attilio Capponi (Eds.)
Advances in Psychotherapy of the Borderline Patient
NY: Jason Aronson, 1979
viii + 526 pp.
Psychoanalytic Review 68, No. 3, 452–453 (1981)

According to its preface, this book aims to go beyond the substantial literature on borderline (and narcissistic) conditions by presenting recent advances in psychoanalytic thinking by prominent analysts from the United States and abroad. Some of the papers had been presented at a conference under the auspices of the Advanced Institute for Analytic Psychotherapy, with which both editors are affiliated. In addition to the editors, who each wrote an introductory chapter, the contributors were Adler and Buie (on aloneness), Giovacchini (on helplessness), Grotstein (on the borderline concept), Kernberg (on technical considerations), Rey (on schizoid phenomena), Rosenfeld (on treatment difficulties and on transference psychosis), Searles (on countertransference and on jealousy of an internal object), Spotnitz (on technique) and Volkan (on the "glass bubble"). The papers are organized into three sections: the concept, the technique of treatment, and the therapeutic situation.

The book misses its aim. This is less a function of the individual papers than of the absence of an editorial point of view. The contributors' earlier and present works are summarized by LeBoit in the first chapter, but without highlighting agreements or disputes, nor clearly presenting the specific advance of the current contribution. Capponi's chapter is a historical review of the borderline concept which is scholarly and has good summaries (especially of the works of Klein, Bion and Kernberg) but achieves only a weak integration. Several of the papers go over much of the same territory as does Capponi, and would have benefited from editing. It also becomes clear that the contributors are frequently discussing patently different patient populations, making their findings lack the comparability implied in the singular "borderline patient" of the book's title.

Some of the book's failure is a function of the general state of understanding of borderline and narcissistic conditions. Many phenomena discussed are acknowledged by the various authors to apply to psychotics and neurotics as well. In addition, disagreement exists in theory, particularly between explicit Kleinians (whose views are extensively and cogently represented here) and analysts of other persuasions. Here again, however, the absence of editing is notable: the two latter subdivisions of the book seem arbitrary, and the papers in each could have been switched to the other without making a difference.

The strengths of this book are in some of its individual papers. The clinical descriptions convey the experience of the authors, and the technical suggestions often seem well worth trying. The narrowly-focused papers such as Adler and Buie's, Giovacchini's, and Volkan's do make clear and specific modest contributions to clinical knowledge. Searles' paper, "Jealousy Involving an Internal Object," is an excellent contribution with many clear examples, and his paper on countertransference is the only one in the collection which explicitly debates with another point of view (Kernberg's). Spotnitz's paper, however, with a ten-step outline of once-a-week treatment, falsely conveys the impression that the field has attained a high degree of mastery of psychotherapy of borderline conditions.

In addition to the major editorial failures, there are disturbing production errors (e.g., a chapter is differently titled in the contents and on its initial page). Books based primarily on conference proceedings rarely succeed. This is no exception. The better papers would be better disseminated through journal publication.

Richard D. Chessick
The Technique and Practice of Listening in Intensive Psychotherapy
Northvale, NJ: Jason Aronson, 1989
xxii + 274 pp.
Psa. Books 2, No. 3 (1991) pp. 401–404

Richard Chessick has been writing about psychoanalytic psychotherapy for more than 20 years. His books are easy to read, informative about current theory, and full of clinical examples. This book is no exception.

This volume focuses on psychoanalytic listening as an interpersonal art and a technique that can be learned. Chessick presents five listening "channels" derived from (1) Freud's drive/conflict/defense orientation (the classic approach); (2) the object-relations orientation of Melanie Klein and Bion; (3) the "sociocultural" or phenomenological approach of Hegel, Fromm, Lacan, and others; (4) Kohut's self psychology; and (5) the interactive approach of Thomä and Kächele (among others).

The book's thesis is that there are different and irreconcilable positions within psychoanalysis and that each is needed for our clinical work. The thesis is valid because each position contributes meaningful understanding and because, like physics, psychoanalysis has, as yet, no Grand Unifying Theory. Chessick attempts to demonstrate his thesis by presenting the varying contributions of each theory and listening channel (or stance) to cases exemplifying broad diagnostic categories: psychosis, borderline, neurosis, narcissism, and the "difficult" patient.

In his two introductory chapters, Chessick articulates this thesis. He declares at the outset that Freud's model is "the primary [one] in approaching any patient material" (p. 16), and he states that "any departure from this channel should be tentative..." (p. 16) and should alert us to the possibility of defensive collusion. He then aligns himself with Schwaber's recent perspectives and conclusions (in her work from 1981-1987), placing the therapist's clinical stance at the heart of psychoanalytic listening. He asserts that the therapist's empathic attunement defines a new position, seeing things from the patient's perspective. Assigning Schwaber to the self psychology "stance," he states that he considers her outlook indispensable to psychoanalytic technique (p. 21), though more extreme than Kohut's.

This matter of giving categorical primacy to a model, aligning himself with another persuasive one, then relegating that one to but another of five models needs to be addressed at this point. Chessick persuasively argues for the validity of each model. This argument is consistent with, and provides the articulation for, his thesis, and yet he seems routinely to be hedging his bets (mostly between Freud and Schwaber). This is a different way of approaching the lack of a Grand Unifying Theory than those chosen, for example, by Pine (1990) in his work on the four psychologies of psychoanalysis and by Silverman (1986) in her multi-model approach. While those authors see different models as complementary, Chessick seems (at least temporarily) to lose other channels when he tunes in to any one. This seems less a rhetorical device than an actual discontinuity for him and may be either the major strength or a fatal flaw in the Chessick thesis.

The demonstration of the thesis, that is, its clinical application, occupies the largest part of the book, its middle five chapters. Four cases of psychosis are described: one from Binswanger, one each from Kraepelin and Kahlbaum, and one from Lacan. Each case is a dramatic treatment failure and demonstrates, in Chessick's view, the danger of a single-channel approach. I could easily see the clinical failure of the Binswanger and Lacan approaches, as well as of the two pre-analytic therapies, and could, with Chessick, see how the other models might approach the material more productively. No evidence is provided, however, that the use of all the channels together or in some sequence would, indeed, provide a sound clinical demonstration.

Three cases are presented in the chapter on borderline patients: one from Basch, one from Chessick's own practice, and one from Tolpin. Again, treatment failures are presented, but they seem to be failures of the therapist, or of the suitability of the patient, or of the match, rather than demonstrations that channel shifting would work better.

The case of the Rat Man is offered as a neurotic example, along with its well-known critiques and follow-ups. Kohut's Mr. Z. is the example of treatment of narcissism. Arlow's case of a "difficult" patient (as reported by Schwaber, 1985) provides the last example. For each of these cases Chessick notes shortcomings in the listening approach, which he contends could be overcome by shifting channels.

These clinical chapters are offered to illustrate Chessick's thesis and, as such, are the weakest part of the book. While scholarly, astute in the demonstration of error and of the complexity that must characterize psychoanalytic understanding, and descriptively excellent, they fail to do more than reassert the thesis without providing evidence for it.

In his summary chapter, Chessick focuses on learning psychoanalytic listening. The need for empathy (though not necessarily its sufficiency) is emphasized.

Wide reading is urged. Non-psychoanalytic contributions to therapeutic skill are acknowledged. Social, humane, and personal considerations are noted. Chessick is wise to remind us of these matters, which are not often fully attended to in the literature on technique.

Chessick also provides, in this book as in his others, an international perspective and a philosophical one, both of which are sound and useful and are usually absent from our technical literature.

In the absence of affirmative clinical examples, the use of the five models becomes an academic exercise. We may, however, thereby see what he may fail to see: that these five are not coequal stances, nor is each incompatible with all the others. Implicit in classical theory was object relations theory, and these are, despite their imperfect fit, commonly used together. The phenomenological approach has offered a perspective, but not a coequal stance, for most psychoanalysts. Empathy is accepted as necessary in mainstream psychoanalysis, but the claim for its primacy in therapeutic action has increasingly isolated the Kohutians from that mainstream. The interactive channel remains, in Chessick's own words, "the most controversial and most poorly delineated" (p. 48). Chessick's thesis, then, is at best premature as a basis for comprehensive technical recommendations.

In conclusion, this book has value because of the clarity of its writing, its scholarship (particularly the unusual international and philosophical perspectives), and its raising the issues related to irreconcilable positions that beg for a unified technical theory in psychoanalysis. Its limitations, however, render it a disappointment in its real aim: to be a landmark, state-of-the-art treatise on psychoanalytic listening.

Jennifer Stuart, Elliot Adler, and James Hansell
Listening to Discover Unconscious Processes
APA Division of Psychoanalysis (39)
April 5, 1992

The three papers we have heard presented reflect the richness and diversity of our intellectual tradition as psychologists. Coming from, respectively, an empirical experimental point of view, a scholarly clinical point of view, and from the point of view of rational conceptualization, they study our main behavior as psychoanalysts, listening, in such a way as to provide concrete recommendations for our therapeutic endeavor. I will discuss each in turn, in the hope that the points that most interest me, and some challenges I will put forth, might provide for a lively exchange among us panelists and with you, our audience. Such exchanges are what we come to these meetings for, and our analyses benefit from the excitement and intellectual nutriment we bring home to them.

Jennifer Stuart's interesting paper presents a perspective specifically representative of psychologist-psychoanalysts: that of subjecting operationally defined aspects of theory and/or practice to experimental methodology. The strength of the approach is that it helps us to focus on specifics and to test them in a way as to assess their validity. This aspect of psychoanalytic work aims for refinement in our theory of listening such that our technique may be more precisely taught and practiced.

Unfortunately, it is the very precision that quantitative studies seek that subjects them to important methodological critique and limits the useful generalizations that might be made. Stuart's paper avoids this weakness, in part by refocusing on her qualitative results with heuristic value, and expanding on her ideas with a qualitative review of the quantitative data. Additionally, her definition of metaphor as requiring interpretation and mutuality, and as always simultaneously revealing and concealing is cogent.

Stuart's particular perspective follows that of a distinguished line of thinkers concerned with figurative language, our working medium. Beginning with Freud's Psychopathology of Everyday Life and his "joke book," this line includes Ella Freeman Sharpe, Jacob Arlow, Roy Schafer, Victor Rosen, and even Jacques Lacan.

Among the general methodological problems are:

1. Limited therapist experience (5 beginners or near-beginners), with too few in each of three experience categories for meaningful comparison. The training of even the two experienced therapists is not specified.
2. The related countertransference or inexperience factors (blind spots and dumb spots) that make some clinical examples less than useful representations of psychoanalytic work.
3. The failure to distinguish psychoanalysis as a clinical method from psychoanalytically informed psychotherapies.

More specifically, the quantitative results don't pan out. They are neither convincing nor illuminating from a listening perspective. The *a priori* operational distinction, most important in dissertation research, between "frozen" and "novel" in particular, doesn't pan out because we know that it is the value placed in the language by the individual (conscious and unconscious)—not an external judgment about a metaphor—that is crucial for its understanding. While more unusual ones might be hypothesized as more likely to be personally invested, even cliches can become cathected.

This criticism is recognized by Stuart in her own conclusion. We might add that socially reinforced metaphors, cliches, may become useful for development of character style (e.g., "hot water" in a patient of mine had great strength in understanding many aspects of his character and symptoms while being quite clear in its social meaning).

Another specific critique, again of operational definitions central to dissertation research, is the matter of criteria for "process-enhancing" vs. "process-blocking." We occasionally, but not routinely, find responses to our interventions in the moments immediately following them.

In reading a paper with technical implications as its intent, we are concerned with interventions based on listening, and the *a priori* approach can lead us astray regarding affect as a basis for intervention and a measure of it. That is a too-conscious, manifest content approach. We need to remind ourselves of Bertram Lewin's sleep-wakefulness model of the hour, as Adler does. When a patient is too sleepful (in a primary process mode), our interventions awaken; when too wakeful (defensive), our interventions promote regression to primary process functioning. Intense affect is not a simple dependent variable: "too" regressive or "too" affectless are matters of clinical judgment.

Yet another problem is that the experimental microanalysis of minutes doesn't recognize process issues of larger timeframes within and beyond the single session.

Stuart's finding—that the novel is more associated with defense—is discussed well in her qualitative section, which goes on to provide the proper corrective for much that is weak in the experiment. For us, this forms the meat of the paper: we should focus less on words and more on their revelatory or concealing function.

The clinical examples largely reflect therapist inexperience and countertransference. Stuart provides useful discussions of these errors. My view of the presented data is that blocking is more related to therapist error than to aspects of language. A pitfall of quantitative research is often, though not here, to miss that kind of finding. Even therapist C's talking for two minutes blocks the patient, despite a good intervention.

Correct listening is more important than language itself. We all speak in metaphor. When analysts speak accurately, in timing, focus, and meaning, we enhance the process; when we are off in one way or another, we block it. The transference focus remains central to good work as Stuart's examples demonstrate. We intervene when either drive or defense is excessive. Analysts' metaphors are important, but not nearly as important as other matters.

The Ice King example is good therapy. Analysis is not enhanced, though, by the essence of the metaphor but by its use in the transference—as Stuart shows. The novelty of the figures is not so important. Other issues are more so.

As to Stuart's recommendation for more microanalysis, I doubt its relative clinical utility. Her recommendation that we drop the frozen/novel distinction is better. In my view, Stuart's general conclusions have more validity than the original focus of the study, the attempt to specify in advance language which promotes or blocks analytic discovery.

As Stuart takes metaphor as her listening focus, Elliot Adler offers Freud's dream psychology as a framework for understanding a patient's expressive language. His perspective is that of a working clinical analyst and his model brings us back to basics in several important and useful ways.

Adler reminds us that the first psychological psychoanalytic model of mind was dream psychology and recalls for us Lewin's transposition of this model to the general understanding of analytic sessions. We don't hear often enough these days of the psychoanalytic cognitive psychology of primary and secondary processes and how these interact to produce manifest mental contents.

Adler critiques Freud's listening metaphor of the receiver as vague, correctly substituting Arlow's focused listening technique while pointing out Loewald's corrective of Arlow: that unconscious derivatives may be vitalizing and creative as well as distorting and pathogenic. (While Loewald is right in principle here, Arlow's focus is usually right in clinical practice.)

My first psychoanalytic reading, some 33 years ago, was Brenner's elementary textbook. Brenner describes analysis's first principle as radical casualty, and Adler calls us back to that still essential position. He goes on effectively to refute a current listening mode, the so-called empathic one of Kohut and Schwaber. Manifest content and affective states are not *all* that analysis is about; in fact, analysis was born when what was latent and required interpretation called itself to Freud's attention.

In clear clinical examples, some including important "I said—She said" dialogue, Adler gives us six concrete listening principles that mark him as a most effective supervisor. Useful gems are found even in his footnotes!

If this seems to be a glowing review, it is meant to be. I wish I had written this paper. My criticism, which at first I felt obligatory, was to note that Freud's dream book was never meant to be applied to psychoanalytic technique, and that Adler was forcing things. My second reading, however, resulted in my coming to understand *how* Adler means what he says, i.e., this paper is not a technique paper in the sense of what the analyst does, but instead in how the analyst listens. As such, there is no better place to begin than with Freud's self-described masterpiece.

Adler reviews basic principles in such a clear, concrete and effective way that a review becomes a new and important contribution to the literature on psychoanalytic technique.

James Hansell takes a third approach to the study of the listening process: a conceptual one. He is concerned with refining the idea of neutrality in analytic therapy. His thesis is that neutrality should be defined by its aim, not its techniques; and its aim is to create conditions for expanding access to the patient's inner life.

Hansell is not satisfied with the state of the definition of neutrality, which he feels has become too broad. He reviews some aspects of the psychoanalytic stance which define for him four categories of neutrality: value neutrality, abstinence, non-gratification, and opacity. He specifies their definitions and delineates the theory of technique which supports the place of each in good psychoanalytic work.

Hansell's metaphor of the surgeon and the operating room is engaging. It is a good way to comprehend what are the non-specific but necessary factors in our theory of therapeutic action and what, by contrast, are specific agents of the action. Many writers use figure-ground analogies and I am fond of using it in the way that Hansell uses surgery.

It is not ironic, but intrinsic to the development of technique for a century, that our methods are usually defined by what we don't do, but this fact cannot be overstated.

Where I find fault with Hansell is not in what he has to say about practical matters; it is instead with his conceptual thesis, the purpose of this paper. I disagree that we have had no clear definition of neutrality; Anna Freud's definition, what Hansell calls "value" neutrality, has been widely accepted since it was promulgated. Abstinence, frustration, and analytic anonymity are related but different concepts, with related but different purposes, as Hansell clearly shows.

It seems to me that Hansell is defining neutrality to include several aspects of what may better be called "analytic stance" and my reading of his paper is such that at times he seems to be broadening the concept of neutrality to be congruent with our entire technique.

In my view, our technique as a whole has the aims ascribed by Hansell to neutrality, while neutrality has more specific purposes. The aim of our technical procedures is what Hansell here claims for neutrality. In doing so, he can then call anything neutral that fosters the treatment, nullifying its utility as a concept and a part of our stance.

In the case described, Jacobs, not Hansell, is right. Jacobs had deviated from neutrality and from the classic model. Perhaps this was necessary; I'll take Jacobs' word, though others might be successful in traditional ways. His stance did resolve the impasse and might, following Eissler, be thought of as a parameter which would, when possible, be analyzed.

Reassurance may include an implicit interpretation, as may other interventions. As such, it is better thought of as an interpretation with a parameter or a non-specific agent added, rather than, as Hansell says, an "extremely neutral" intervention. Such usage makes neutrality synonymous with the pragmatics of therapy and renders it conceptually useless.

I agree with Hansell that the concept of neutrality is central to the psychoanalytic process; I disagree with his redefinition of it.

These three papers, representing three intellectual perspectives, vary in their success. Stuart's paper demonstrates many of the flaws of the experimental model in its attempt to be useful to the psychoanalytic enterprise. Her paper succeeds in the more rational reflective assessment of its own findings. Hansell's work is in our important tradition of rational refinement of analytic conceptualization, and he boldly attempts to come to grips with important aspects of our analytic stance.

Some of our concepts surely need broadening or dismissal; neutrality needs to be narrowly understood. Adler brings us back, in a most engaging and useful way, to our basic and classic literature. I thank our three panelists for their papers and I thank the program committee for inviting me to be the discussant.

Althea J. Horner
The Primacy of Structure: Psychotherapy of Underlying Character Pathology
Northvale, NJ: Jason Aronson, 1990
xxi + 306 pp
Psa. Books 4, No. 1 (1993), pp. 29–33

Horner, Clinical Professor of Psychology at UCLA, uses the concept of structure to unite a series of her papers aimed at creating an integrated psychoanalytic approach to the treatment of character pathology. She uses the structural concept to refer to structure of character, rather than in its more familiar form referring to Freud's second tripartite model of mind. Her particular blend of object relations, drive-, ego- and self-psychology is applied to several diagnostic entities while it directs treatment approaches toward underlying character formation.

Horner begins by placing herself in the psychoanalytic landscape. She values object relations over drive theory, focuses more on dyadic than on triadic relations, considers empathy and reparation more significant therapeutic agents than she does insight, and sees herself a humanist concerned with the use of the real relationship in treatment. A therapist is a model and therapy creates a new attachment; establishing trust and preserving the patient's self take priority over protecting autonomy and promoting initiative.

Dividing her papers into categories of Development of Character, Character Pathology, and Treatment, Horner explicates her general position with essays on development and associated pathologies, the roots of anxiety, and processes of identification. She then focuses on depression, bulimia, self pathologies, and obsessive disorders. Her section on treatment deals with group psychotherapy, short-term treatment, and the concepts of alliance, resistance, will, and neutrality.

Throughout these papers, emphasizing a cautious approach to diagnosis and treatment, Horner notes therapy's potential for harm and the pitfalls of countertransference gratifications. She underscores the fact that development is a complex matter and that truly microscopic understanding is necessary for valid structural/developmental diagnosis and treatment.

In comparing and trying to integrate the viewpoints of four major analytic dimensions (object, drive, ego, and self), Horner shows familiarity with the relevant literature (from psychology as well as psychoanalysis), sensitivity to the meaning of interactionism in developmental psychology, and obvious experience as a therapist and supervisor.

It is in the area of diagnostic understanding that Horner makes her most cogent contributions. Her four chapters on gender identity elaborate on boys' dilemmas regarding mother as caretaker versus sexual object. Her paper on depression eschews the trend toward a biological view, and her chapter on bulimia details the complexity of compromise-formation in this condition.

It is in the area of treatment recommendations that Horner left me dissatisfied. Despite her call for precision in treatment based on a detailed developmental and structural understanding, the chapters discussing treatment speak of contraindications for group therapy, cautions about short-term treatment, and suggestions for creativity, but provide neither differentiations among treatment modalities nor indications for one or another approach. Horner's integrative stance falls victim here to an eclecticism she wishes to avoid.

Nowhere in this book does one find a theory of technical modalities that suggests systematic differences between psychoanalysis and various psychotherapies, nor does one find an organized matching of diagnosis with therapy that the early chapters lead us to expect. Instead, we find an approach that challenges some traditional views, but does so, in my opinion, ineffectively.

The first ineffective challenge trivializes the negative therapeutic reaction by suggesting (in chapter 3 and again in chapter 16) that such a reaction may be due to therapist error. This position does not acknowledge the very definition of the negative therapeutic reaction, a worsening clinical picture following an accurate interpretation, and it slights the centrality of the discovery of this phenomenon to Freud's reformulation of his model of mind.

In other instances, Horner makes her arguments by setting up what can only be called straw men: classical theory is pathologizing (pp. 68, 217), reductionistic (p. 71), and rigid (p. 151); it analyzes away positive developments (p. 79).

False dichotomies such as gratification seeking versus object seeking are emphasized to the disparagement of classical theory, and understandings derived from early ego pathologies are applied across the range of diagnoses. Neutrality is criticized (chapter 19) because it is imperfect, and, in its stead, the real relationship is vaunted but without specific technical recommendations. In attacking rigid application of analytic theories, Horner disparages several theoretical positions as essentially countertransferentially resistant (p. 151) and offers an undefined flexible creativity as an alternative.

Horner's discussions of transference resistance and acting out (chapter 20) define these phenomena as specific to character pathology and do not take into consideration the extensive and detailed literature on these ubiquitous clinical happenings.

Horner suggests that the developmental task of gender identity for boys is more difficult than for girls (p. 116), just as sexist a position as Freud's opposite view. She calls the concept of penis envy "anathema" and "ego-alien" (p. 248), whereas most analysts recognize it as a recognizable clinical phenomenon, though much less central to a general theory of female development than Freud had posited.

Horner is at her weakest in her most specific technical recommendations (see especially chapter 17), denigrating technique (p. 199) and promoting what seem at times to be behaviorist and suggestive approaches. She describes "active promotion of emotional connectedness" (p. 196) and suggests that a patient write to her during a separation. She "held and rocked" a patient (p.100) and gave another a transitional object (p. 101). Recognizing these obvious departures from standard analytic technique, she neither deals with their implications nor discusses the basic sources on variations of technique (Bibring, 1954; Eissler, 1953).

Horner's essays on short-term treatment (chapters 21 and 22) seem entirely too pragmatic, referring to pressure from third-party payers and ignoring both the fact that our field has no established system for matching treatment type with diagnosis and her own diagnostic caveats.

Going beyond my substantive critique of Horner's text, I need to state my misgivings about this work as a book. Thirteen of 22 chapters are articles that were published as many as 17 years ago. There are some jarring redundancies that call for editorial revision. Two of the new chapters together total only five pages. I doubt they would be published in a journal. One seventh of the book consists of blank pages. The tripartite division of the chapters is arbitrary, and many chapters could have been placed in any of the sections. Clinical case material includes too little data for the systematic exposition the book seems to attempt.

While there are useful insights to be gleaned from this work, and while readers may find some congruencies with their own experiences and viewpoints, I cannot recommend this book as a meaningful contribution to our literature.

Roy M. Mendelsohn
How Can Talking Help? An Introduction to the Technique of Analytic Therapy
Northvale, NJ: Jason Aronson, 1992
xiv + 314 pp.
Psa. Books 4, No. 4 (1993), pp. 503-506

The nature of the action of psychoanalytic therapy has been a significant question for the entire century of the existence of the enterprise. Freud's early answers included abreaction of affects. Classical formulations evolved to the position that conveying insight was the essential ingredient of the treatment effect. The nature of the action was not seen, however, as relying exclusively on this central element.

Freud spoke of the unobjectionable positive transference and of tact as being necessary ingredients of the treatment. Strachey emphasized the effect of the analyst as a benign superego substitute. Winnicott introduced the idea of a "holding environment." Loewald underscored the position of the analyst as a new object and of integration of therapeutic gain by way of the interaction between analyst and patient. Kohut postulated the curative role of empathy. Classical (structural) theory has come to accept that several ingredients may operate to make treatment effective but that insight is primary and others are secondary or incidental. Background conditions are assumed in psychoanalytic therapy, but the focus, for structuralists, remains insight.

Roy M. Mendelsohn, former Director of the Washington University Child Guidance Clinic in St. Louis and a Chicago-trained psychoanalyst, offers this book as a study of the positive forces at work in therapeutic relationships. A "widening scope" theorist, he uses psychoanalytic theory to develop a comprehensive approach to the treatment of seriously disturbed and neurotic patients. In a well-constructed presentation, he draws respectfully on classic drive conflict theory, object relations theory, self psychology, and ego defect theory. He organizes his thinking around four ingredients: the central role of insight, constructive positive identifications with the therapist, the place of regression, and new actual experiences in therapy. Mendelsohn focuses on what have been assumed by structuralists to be implicit background factors and finds them to be essential therapeutic agents, especially for more disturbed patients. The relative prominence of one or another ingredient, in addition to insight, depends, for him, on the nature and extent of the patient's psychopathology.

Mendelsohn's basic thesis is that, since more difficult patients make less effective use of word symbols, those patients require analyst behavior beyond interpretation in order to be helped. This argument is not new and has been the subject of debate now for at least 35 years. What is useful about this book is its nonpolemical, integrative viewpoint in the face of the current controversial new pluralism in psychoanalysis. The book has a logical and coherent organization, makes extensive use of detailed clinical material, and thoughtfully anticipates the reader's questions and concerns. Furthermore, it delineates the risks of failure to distinguish between empathy and countertransference on the part of the analyst and reenactment and acting out on the part of the patient.

Mendelsohn takes care to emphasize and exemplify the primacy of interpretation under conditions of abstinence and neutrality as providing not just insight but identification and support. He speaks of the therapist's attitude and personality, rather than technical modifications, as providing a basis for identification. He differentiates positive from destructive regression. He then calls for flexibility in applying psychoanalytic principles to the treatment of the most primitively organized patients.

Reading Mendelsohn's book is like spending several hours with a senior supervisor who has drawn for himself a coherent picture of psychoanalytic psychotherapy and who enjoys its articulation. He compares theory to a spiral, and the simile applies, as well, to his style in organizing this book. He introduces his basic ideas early and then deepens each one, returning to elaborate on earlier ideas with the depth achieved as he goes along. His organization is also unusual, at least in the first four (of eight) chapters. He provides a brief exposition of an idea, detailed summary footnotes describing significant contributions to the idea, and extended case material illustrating its use. At first this format was distracting, as was his frequent use of the concept of projective identification as a ubiquitous defense underlying all transference phenomena. As I became accustomed to it, however, I came to see the format as integral to the presentation and as conveying an important aspect of Mendelsohn's implicit style: deferring to and utilizing the creativity of the others who are his forebears or his patients.

The book's title is misleading in its simplicity. This work is neither simple nor introductory. It is a sophisticated discourse looking at many issues relevant to technique in the widening scope of psychoanalytic therapy. Understanding Mendelsohn requires a familiarity with both theory and practice, at least at the journeyman's level. A novice might be misled into adopting a posture of promoting identifications and new experiences in treatment in ways that Mendelsohn, himself clearly conservative, would likely find "wild" or unanalytic.

Mendelsohn does not address the technical differences between psychoanalysis and psychoanalytic psychotherapy. He speaks generically of the latter. His case examples include several children and adolescents as well as adult patients, and he does not speak to issues of differentiation of treatment by age group. Touching only briefly on the use of frequency and recumbency in technique, he considers them as options dependent on the patient's structure and feelings. He does not deal with issues of analyzability; instead he considers his version of psychoanalytic treatment as making use of proportions of ingredients appropriate to the patient. He recognizes that this approach requires precise and accurate assessment but gives too little space to how to make such an assessment.

Mendelsohn is aware that there are theoretical incompatibilities among the sources he cites and that the field has yet to achieve an integration some think it used to have. He honors the uniqueness of each patient, therapist, and treatment, and he gives examples of the ongoing process of learning from errors.

In this book, Mendelsohn demonstrates how talking helps some of his patients. Spending a few hours with it is likely to be helpful for our patients as well.

Jean Sanville
The Playground of Psychoanalytic Therapy
Hillsdale, NJ: The Analytic Press, 1991
xx + 288 pp., $36.00
Psa. Books 5, No. 2 (1994), pp. 211–214

This is an ambitious book in which the author hopes to cast our understanding of psychoanalytic treatment in terms of play. To accomplish her goal, she uses a metaphoric style in which the book is a play with a prelude and several acts. Play is its theme and its lens; the psychoanalytic situation is a playground; dreams are private playthings. Psychoanalytic concepts are to be played with; the goal of treatment is to render a person better equipped to live life as play.

Jean Sanville, a training and supervising analyst at the Los Angeles Institute for Psychoanalytic Studies, takes off from Freud's metaphor of "transference as a playground" and Winnicott's elucidation of that notion. She develops her thesis with an extensive review of infant observational research (especially that of Stern and of Emde) and reference to Erikson's ideas. Her sources range well beyond the psychoanalytic to include poets, linguists, anthropologists, philosophers, biologists, and general as well as child psychologists.

Sanville's integration leads her to view infants as stimulus seekers rather than as hiding behind a stimulus barrier. That view pertains through the life cycle and results in a humanistic emphasis on agency as a critical dimension of psychoanalytic psychology. Following Winnicott and Spitz, she places the concept of mutuality next to agency. Psychopathology, for Sanville, frequently involves the derailing of dialogue, and therapy aims at its rerailing.

Beginning with examples from child treatment, first of a child who cannot play, then of one who can, Sanville extends her ideas to adult treatment and acknowledges the work that must often precede play. Looking at space and time from philosophical and literary perspectives, she gives details about her playground/workspace. Trauma and reparation, myth as cultural play, and terminations as beginnings are issues similarly studied and played with.

As the book proceeds, Sanville presents a coherent model of psychoanalytic therapy that is easily understood and that makes use of a few well-delineated clinical examples. These show Sanville to be a seasoned, flexible, empathic analyst at play. The model emphasizes hermeneutic narrative, early development, reorganizing meaning rather than seeking hidden meanings, and reparation through the therapeutic relationship. It is anti-doctrinaire, respects the uniqueness of each patient and each treatment, stays close to the analytic surface, and offers hope as a major therapeutic ingredient. The British independent group, especially Balint, and Kohut's self psychology are important sources of Sanville's integrated model.

Had Sanville been content to look at the role of play in treatment and to view treatment issues from the perspective of play, it would be easy to judge her book a success and to recommend it. But Sanville's ambition, both between the lines and on them, is to postulate her view as the new integrated model of psychoanalysis. Such an ambition is premature at best, and, as her readership is likely to include those new to practice, it is potentially harmful because it hides the current intellectual ferment in the field.

An example of Sanville's claims is the following: "We have moved from [a paradigm] based on Freud's instinct and defense, to Erikson's identity and the life cycle, and currently to one based on death and the continuity of life (Lifton, 1989)" (p. 165). Few psychoanalysts would, I believe, consider Lifton to be the author of the new paradigm in our field.

In my own view of the current state of affairs, several paradigms are in competition. Some theoreticians attempt to establish the primacy of their theoretical position; others try to work with multiple approaches while we await a new unity; still others, notably Rangell, see psychoanalytic theory as a developing composite that integrates new theory and modifies itself as new experience and new thoughtfulness dictate. My sympathies lie with Rangell (1990), who decries those in our field who create so-called new paradigms out of partial aspects of psychoanalytic knowledge while they ignore or shunt aside hard-won knowledge of other pieces of the composite.

Sanville disparages the classical tradition when she states that "*even Brenner*" (italics mine) sees interpretation as collaborative (p. 211). Interpretation has long been seen as nonauthoritarian and collaborative in the several current analytic paradigms; her view is hardly new in this regard.

Sanville eschews definitions (p. 92), questions the "very word 'technique'" (p. 87), and feels that the "old distinction between therapy and analysis ... has broken down" (p. 221) and that "whether the child is transferring or is making a working alliance is not of practical concern" (p. 223). While her views on these matters are disputable, I would challenge the sense conveyed that her views are both the new wave and the new established theory—that, in effect, her playground model has replaced what she calls an old "battleground model" (p. 218).

In her claimed overturning of the old model, Sanville sets up straw men, that is, authoritarianism, symbolic dream interpretation, drive psychology. She supports an extreme of the idiographic approach in which any theory development would be highly problematic. She makes note of, but does not deal with, epistemological issues, leaving her conclusions at least as suspect as those with which she finds fault. (How do we know, for example, that Stern's findings will not come to be reevaluated, as have Mahler's?)

In presenting her actual technique, Sanville argues for elimination of the free association rule, against recommending to patients frequency of contact or recumbency, and for answering direct questions and sharing her own musings. In contrast, she speaks in favor of the classical maintenance of anonymity. Rather than discussing her rationale for these recommendations and the fact that they are not necessarily commonly accepted, she treats them as established new technique.

I find an unfortunate seductiveness in the approach of authors like Sanville, who describe human psychology and psychoanalysis primarily in their playful, loving, reparative, relational, and growth-oriented facets and who seem to avoid conflict, resistance, and unpleasant affects. It is only an apparent paradox that these writers, like Milner, whom Sanville cites with admiration, have worked with very difficult patients. It may be that a very playful and loving therapy is most effective with some of these patients. Good theory, however, cannot be constructed solely on the basis of data from those whose primary need is therapeutic safety and support.

Sanville does a fine job in elucidating the role of play in psychoanalytic treatment. She overreaches when she makes play a new paradigm, undermining what could have been a very meaningful contribution.

Horowitz, Kernberg, and Weinshel (Eds.)
Psychic Structure and Psychic Change: Essays in Honor of
Robert S. Wallerstein, M.D.
Madison, CT: International Universities Press, 1993
xiii + 373, $40.00
Psa. Books 6, No. 1 (1995), pp. 108–112

Having published over 200 works and served as president of both the American Psychoanalytic Association and the International Psychoanalytical Association, Robert Wallerstein is among the best-known psychoanalytic practitioners and theorists. This book is a Festschrift edited by three well-known colleagues and presented to Wallerstein at the conclusion of his service on the IPA Executive Council. It addresses psychic structure and psychic change, which have been ongoing concerns of Wallerstein.

In his book *Forty-Two Lives in Treatment* (1986), Wallerstein reported findings from the Menninger Psychotherapy Research Project, a major longitudinal study he headed for many years. His IPA presidential addresses, "One Psychoanalysis or Many?" (1988) and 'Psychoanalysis: The Common Ground" (1990) focused the profession on their title themes. Several papers in this Festschrift begin with issues raised in these seminal works, and the volume may be viewed as an extension of the presidential themes. Its contributors, 16 prominent analysts from Europe, the United States, and South America, represent major positions in the field and have made detailed clinical material (the presumed common ground) a substantial part of each paper.

While some of the papers are modifications of work for which the writers are already known, the majority are original works. Each work is of the highest quality both in the way in which it is written and in the ideas presented. Particular themes of note come from key Menninger Project findings—that psychotherapy may result in structural change, and that supportive interventions are an effective part of emotional experiences—are revisited with new implications for the theory of technique. Convergences among competing psychoanalytic paradigms are also explored.

Hoping to develop a new integration of theory with practice, the editors have asked the contributors to address the questions of how and why structural change occurs. Several contributors support this integrative effort. Others, reflecting on the diversity of the field, demonstrate in their papers that true integration remains something to be hoped for rather than already realized.

The volume begins with Mardi Horowitz's attempt to translate psychoanalytic vocabulary into that of academic psychology, particularly the schema theories of Bartlett and Piaget. Horowitz presents schematic diagrams to emphasize the complexity of the process. Next, the essential concepts of American ego psychology are reviewed by Edward Weinshel, who demonstrates the extent to which the self-observation of the analyst characterizes its technique. Change, not cure, is the aim of the process, and understanding always remains incomplete.

In an integrative essay of striking clarity, Joseph and Anne-Marie Sandler define structural change and the elements that contribute to it. Interpretation and the analytic relationship are explored for their relative impacts. A dynamic neutrality is posited in which countertransference floats and is then focused upon. The hardly "schematic" (p. 73) theoretical presentation of the Sandlers is exemplified with a clear case of resistance analysis.

Harold Blum analyzes the structures of superego and ego-ideal and more concretely, values in formation and conflict. Paul Dewald offers a demonstration of technique as he focuses on interpersonal aspects of the treatment situation.

In the first of the papers to take up a finding from *Forty-Two Lives in Treatment*, Anton Kris deals with support as a part of, rather than in opposition to, interpretive technique. Following his own earlier work on divergent conflicts, Kris redefines support as a sense of endorsement coming from effective, early interpretation of punitive self-criticism. Kris demonstrates how such interpretation is functionally neutral and results in a mourning process. That Kris's paper is one of only two of the volume's contributions to generate a response from another contributor reveals the all-too-common failure in volumes like this one to engage the contributors in conversation.

Like Kris, Owen Renik takes his cue from the findings of *Forty-Two Lives in Treatment* and elaborates on the role of countertransference enactments. Renik gives a cogent demonstration of the ubiquity and utility of these countertransference phenomena, which he appropriately parallels with transference enactments. In his discussion of questions of indulgence as well as corrective emotional experiences, Renik posits safeguards against the former and more analytically useful definition of the latter, provided that manipulative techniques are avoided.

Leo Rangell's essay summarizes the contributions by representatives of the branch of psychoanalysis usually referred to as "classical." Like other classicists, Rangell demonstrates a range and flexibility of concepts and practice that belie the frequent caricatures devised by the antagonists of classicism (within and without psychoanalysis). Rangell's composite psychoanalytic theory is antagonistic to Wallerstein's pluralistic position. In this volume, Rangell reviews the history of the theory of change, describes agents of change including relational ones, and details the results of change. He looks for and finds common ground with Wallerstein, the Kleinians, and self-psychologists. Rangell relates change to his own theory of action, which involves psychoanalytic ideas of will, courage, and integrity.

The Dutch analyst Nikolaas Treurniet provides a significant integrative paper (in the spirit of Rangell), which details the action of psychoanalysis in both its noninterpretive and interpretive aspects. Treurniet, who followed up on the papers of Kris and Renik, is the only author to attempt a correlation with the ideas presented in this book. Treurniet's paper shows how each aspect of treatment is both supportive of and aimed at promoting the analytic process. Treurniet attempts to resolve various conflicting positions (e.g., drive-conflict vs. developmental failure) by making use of ideas derived from Winnicott, Balint, Loewald, and Bollas, among others.

Following Treurniet's discussion, two papers, one by Janine Chasseguet-Smirgel and Angela Goyena, the other by Horacio Etchegoyen, do not have a correlative intention. The French Chasseguet-Smirgel and Goyena take issue with the very concept of structure and the Argentine Etchegoyen essentially ignores structure. Finding psychoanalytic structural psychology too abstract, Chasseguet-Smirgel and Goyena represent a non-Lacanian French school of psychoanalysis, which emphasizes interpretation of core fantasies, particularly of the libidinal roots of these fantasies. Etchegoyen focuses on change occurring within the session. A representative of modern Kleinian practice, Etchegoyen offers examples of interpretations and responses which, he asserts, are comprehensible and testable.

Max Hernandez, a Peruvian trained in the British middle-school orientation, believes that paradox and "not knowing" are factors necessary to create a new understanding and change in the structure of symptoms. Betty Joseph, a British Kleinian, introduces the concept of "non-resonance" in an attempt to better understand a small group of patients who did not change. Joseph, who stays away from theoretical formulation in this paper, provides vivid descriptions of a meaningful clinical picture.

In the volume's concluding chapter, Otto Kernberg summarizes distinctions between psychoanalysis and psychotherapy and outlines goals of analysis. Despite differences between the schools, Kernberg specifies convergences between ego-psychological and object-relational approaches, to which he has been a major contributor. Itemizing agents of change relevant to both patients and analysts, Kernberg promotes a totalistic view of countertransference, working through and considering deviations from technical neutrality when necessary to preserve the integrity of patients and their treatments.

This Festschrift is more than a testimonial to Wallerstein. It is also a testimonial to the richness and diversity of psychoanalysis under the aegis of its international organization. For a reader trained in the North American "classical" tradition, the vitality of Wallerstein's approach is well-documented. For such a reader, some of the divergent contributions may be jarring. Even these divergences, however, defy the caricatures such classical training may once have fostered, and may be appreciated for generating useful ideas, in good measure because Wallerstein's leadership has fostered a new openness.

The format of this book and the choice of contributors might compel even adherents of Rangell's composite theory to acknowledge that our field may not be an integrated discipline. As the second century of psychoanalysis dawns, if quality essays like those in this volume have resulted from such a divergence, it can hardly be considered a dismal state of affairs.

Richard Chessick
A Dictionary for Psychotherapists: Dynamic Concepts in Psychotherapy
Northvale, NJ: Jason Aronson, 1993
xvii + 405 pp., $50.00
Psa. Books 6 No. 3 (1995), pp. 463–466

The venerable Samuel Johnson has been a model for many dictionary writers and Richard Chessick explicitly takes Dr. Johnson as his ideal in this enterprise. While acknowledging his debt to several pioneer dictionary writers in the field of mental health, Chessick makes reference to Johnson more than any other author except Freud, Melanie Klein, Kohut, and himself. Composing in a discursive, narrative style, Chessick succeeds in putting a very personal stamp on what is usually a more formalistic reference work.

Writing for the practicing psychoanalytic psychotherapist, Chessick aims to give practical advice on clinical matters and to avoid metapsychological controversies. The audience he seeks includes both experienced clinicians and those in training. The latter group would use it as a reference; the former, he hopes, might read it from cover to cover.

For more scholarly definitions, Chessick recommends Campbell (1989) and Moore and Fine (1990); his is a clinical approach.

Chessick's ambitious goals require a double focus of the reviewer. Surely the book must be read cover to cover and its several aims evaluated as to their relative success. The book must also be judged as the reference work its title and format imply. As a book, rather than a dictionary, this work is a series of essays of various lengths on the many topics of interest to the author. As is true of much of Chessick's prior work, there is a heavy emphasis on philosophical roots of dynamic psychotherapy, and there are multiple citations of authors like Comte, Heidegger, Kierkegaard, Sartre, Marx, Dilthey, and Jaspers. Entries such as "Mind-Body Problem" typify this philosophical bent. There are, in the Johnson mold, frequent literary references too, with Shakespeare and Dostoyevsky having prominent places.

Chessick takes a biographical approach as well, and uses several such entries (e.g., Ferenczi, M. Klein) to describe the clinical and theoretical contributions of their subjects. In some cases (e.g., Lacan), biography is entirely subsumed by professional contribution.

A historical perspective characterizes many entries. With such entries as "cathexis," that perspective becomes appropriately lexicographic. There is also a socio-political orientation and sensitivity, exemplified by discussion of the application to women of "castration complex," and of "homosexuality." The presence of these many perspectives demonstrates Chessick's erudition, and his strong qualifications for the task of reference-writing.

Within the psychoanalytic frame of reference, Chessick is clearly indebted to the Freudian corpus, taking it as the starting point for all dynamic psychotherapies, but he is not reverential. He provides sympathetic renderings of theoretical modifications and deviations, especially those of Bion, Melanie Klein, Lacan, Laing, and Kohut. As in his book on psychoanalytic listening (1989), he asserts his belief that multiple theoretical foci are necessary to the therapeutic enterprise. Despite this theoretical catholicism, Chessick's frequent technical recommendations are, by and large, on the side of conservative Freudian caution, and are presented in an avuncular and authoritative, though rarely doctrinaire, manner.

Several entries provide summary comparisons among different psychoanalytic perspectives, hardly avoiding metapsychological controversies, but usefully clarifying them. Other entries (e.g., "ego consciousness, ego experience, ego feeling") provide an edifying blend of philosophical and clinical considerations. Chessick clearly recognizes the differences between philosophy and therapeutic practice, and the limitations of the application of metapsychology, even developmental theory, to clinical work. He notes the absence of sound empirical research regarding many of the practical issues he addresses.

The cover to cover reading offers both an overall sense of the Chessick view of dynamic psychotherapy, as well as several essays that could easily stand on their own for clarity and brevity of exposition as well as importance. Among these are "beyond interpretation (Gedo)," "borderline," "female sexuality," "empathy," and "metapsychology, mental apparatus." In the essay on "borderline," Chessick provides various descriptions of the clinical picture, a critique of the term, and recommendations for a flexible approach to treatment, all in a mere five pages.

In contrast to such entries, however, are many that seem to me to go beyond the esoteric, and to take away from the continuous reading of the book. Some of these references are philosophical (e.g., "gelassenheit [serenity, composure]," "ge-stell [en-framing]"). Others (e.g., "allon, the [Straus]," "aphanasis," "dialogue, dialogism [Bakhtin]," "fusion of horizons") are historical or from literary analysis. Their utility for the practitioner is not demonstrated; nor would they be likely to come up for the user of a dictionary for psychotherapists. Some entries are rather archaic (e.g., "direct analysis") yet seem to be written not merely for historical interest.

The length of entries varies considerably. In some instances, they seem much too long (e.g., "allon," "leisure"); in others (e.g., "archaic transferences and ego states") they are too short to do the topic justice. There are also entries which require so much more than a dictionary can provide (e.g., "depression," "dreams"), and whose length seems arbitrary.

Labeling items as esoterica and questioning the length of entries are personal judgments about a dictionary with an explicitly personal stamp. To me, the extent of the personalization, however, comes close to being idiosyncratic, and takes away from the book's claim as a reference.

In the breadth of coverage attempted, Chessick succumbs to inconsistencies. "If the phrase 'adhesiveness of the libido' is not obsolete, it should be" (p. 9); yet it is "of great significance in understanding the etiology of neurosis" (p. 52). The term "cathexis" "is technically difficult to defend" (p. 48), yet it is used to explain "corruption." The DSM-III-R approach to definitions is often contrasted to psychoanalytic approaches which Chessick clearly favors, yet he recommends being "thoroughly conversant with the standard disorders as they are delineated by" that work (p. 224). "We should never forget that in psychoanalytic work we transmit to our patients and our students the status of our value system" (p.60); yet the analyst should "refrain from value judgments" (p. 257). A totalistic definition of countertransference is approached with a thorough literature survey, yet the technical recommendation includes the statement that countertransference "always interfere[s] with correct understanding of and interpretations to the patient" (p. 68).

It may be that a dictionary format can successfully become a personal treatise in very few hands other than those of a Samuel Johnson. The alphabet is not the best organizing principle for essays on dynamic concepts in psychotherapy. Chessick has done better book writing elsewhere. Nor would a student be well-served by this volume as a reference work. Would a student therapist look up "idols" in such a volume?

Despite the many useful essays, this book, due to its dictionary format, is not likely to sustain the interest of most readers; nor, because of its almost idiosyncratic selection of entries, is it likely to become a standard reference work.

A.K. Richards and A.D. Richards (Eds.)
The Spectrum of Psychoanalysis: Essays in Honor of Martin S. Bergmann
Madison, CT: International Universities Press, 1994
xxix + 409 pp., $55.00
Psa. Books 6, No. 4 (1995), pp. 649–654

As a candidate in psychoanalytic training over 25 years ago, I began a course taught by Martin Bergmann. I was surprised to find the class attended by many more than the usual limit of ten, and that the students included members and people unaffiliated with the institute as well as fellow candidates. It was clear even in the first session that Mr. Bergmann's following was well deserved. Further along in my training I was privileged to take a regular-sized class and two individual tutorials with him. That he was someone quite special was underscored by his being, at the time, a faculty member of the institute without being a member of the sponsoring psychoanalytic society.

I then became informed that Mr. Bergmann was known primarily as a teacher of private seminars. He was also known as an analyst and supervisor of remarkable skills; one senior analyst spoke of his therapeutic effect as "magical." His coedited book on the history of psychoanalytic technique (1976) immediately became a standard text, with his own introductory chapter becoming required reading in any technique seminar. His professional presentations regularly drew capacity audiences and were characterized by an enviable erudition, and by an awesome telling rather than reading his paper.

His work on psychoanalytic Holocaust studies (1982) was recognized by his being honored (with his wife, also a distinguished psychoanalyst) by the United Jewish Appeal. His book on love (1987) may have brought him to the attention of Woody Allen, in whose movie, *Crimes and Misdemeanors*, Bergmann plays a Primo Levi-like character. His latest book, on religion and mythology (1992), resulted in a lively exchange in the *New York Times Book Review*. He was the first nonmember nonmedical psychoanalyst to deliver the plenary address at a meeting of the American Psychoanalytic Association.

So, Martin Bergmann has been and is a well-known, highly productive, respected and creative psychoanalyst. Yet, as in my first encounter with him, there has been for me a sense of surprise each time I heard something new about him. And, until I came to read the book under review, I did not pay much attention to that sense of surprise.

The loving preface by Carol Munter and Judith Pekowsky, the family pictures, the 80th-birthday poem by Eugene Mahon, and the papers about Bergmann, one by Arlene Richards (discussing his life and his ideas) and the other by Irene Chiarandini (on his special qualities as a teacher), helped me to understand my surprise. For all of his Olympian stature and intellectual breadth, Martin Bergmann conveys to each of his students, and undoubtedly to his analysands, a modesty and a personal presence that create an individual relationship that is shared with no one else. This creation supports an illusion that he is there solely as one's own private teacher, analyst, even parent, and renders surprising, though not upsetting, the reality of his place in the outside world.

In collecting the essays of this festschrift, Arlene and Arnold Richards have produced a worthy gift for Martin, a valuable book. The prefatory and introductory chapters already cited convey the feeling and spell out the substantial contributions of the man. The organization of the balance of the book is in four parts: clinical theory, psychoanalysis and love, psychoanalysis and political systems, and the creative process, corresponding to the areas of Bergmann's own contributions. The authors are some of our most accomplished colleagues and represent diverse geographical locations. In each paper either a direct reference to Martin or a commonality of interest is plainly evident.

The book's contribution to psychoanalysis rests on the uniform excellence of the individual papers and on the collective depiction of the spectrum of psychoanalytic thinking that Bergmann's own work encompasses. Psychoanalysis can be likened to a range of colors, blending yet distinct. Bergmann is among the rare few who works on its several wavelengths. For most of us with narrower range, it is good to be reminded so effectively that psychoanalysis is not only a clinical science but that its ideas illuminate the social sciences, the arts and the humanities as well. Yet even many of the papers in the nonclinical sections speak from or to clinical data, honoring Martin's routine question, "So what does this tell us to say to the patient?"

The seven contributors to psychoanalytic clinical theory fit Bergmann's definition of theory extenders, and some go on to be modifiers in the work presented here. Elsa and Harold Blum combine biological sophistication with psychoanalytic understanding to extend our comprehension of the psychosomatic issue of premenstrual phenomena. Peter Neubauer informs us about absence of a sense of time as he came to understand it developmentally in each of two analysands. With solid observation and keen use of theory, he clarifies the clinical issues as well as relating them to mythology, group formation and the idea of eternity, each special interests of Bergmann's. Norbert Freedman writes on clinical transformations occurring through enactment in psychoanalytic space. He modifies our psychoanalytic theory of action by proposing and exemplifying acts as initiators of reflective process.

John Gedo deals with the matter of form in psychoanalytic interventions, contrasting our usual objective language with the tropes of shared language, especially with their emphasis on the paraverbal. Using clear examples, he shows us how form can be a tool of treatment, not merely its ineffable artistic aspect. In a paper rich with a sense of history, Alma Bond rescues the often ignored or disparaged economic point of view and applies it to a theoretical study of fusion and de-fusion. She demonstrates the vitality of each concept, the value of healthy de-fusion, and the continuing utility of Freudian metapsychology.

Arnold Richards takes up Bergmann's classification of psychoanalytic innovators as extenders, modifiers or heretics. Aiming beyond extension, Richards ventures with humor and respect into modification of Bergmann's thesis. He applies his evolving understanding to the work of Kohut and the relational theorists, suggesting that these works may be heresies. Graciela Abelin-Sas writes poetically about a clinical type, the headless woman: a woman like Scheherazade, who is manifestly a prisoner of masculine power, but in fact is a victim of her own identifications. With a keen psychoanalytic understanding of gender, Abelin-Sas redefines appropriate phallic power as a merging of masculine and feminine identifications.

Two papers comprise the section on psychoanalysis and love. Peter Gay presents a lovely piece of applied psychoanalysis in describing, biographically and with reference to his writings, the love life of Goethe. Paulina Kernberg and Arlene Richards present the results of their review of preadolescent children's letters on love, written to Kernberg for her column in an elementary school magazine. Detailed descriptions of the ideas of youngsters are placed in the context of the vicissitudes of the Oedipus complex, providing us with a normative, descriptive, applied, yet essentially psychoanalytic, study.

Mortimer Ostow begins the section on psychoanalysis and political systems with a paper on apocalyptic and fundamentalist thinking in mental illness and social disorder. He develops a typology of such thinking which he sees as regulating affect swings in individuals, and, on the societal plane, as leading to the Holocaust. Janine Chasseguet-Smirgel reflects on the disappearance of symbolic capacity in

Nazi racial theory. She presents examples of the subversion of symbolism, which in the ultimate case leads to murder or suicide. Ruth Lax, in an astute historical and sociological review, presents a study of superego pathology focusing on the universal, yet commonly violated, biblical injunction, "Thou shalt not kill." She makes clear the defense mechanisms involved in the hypocrisy concerning violence in both individuals and society.

Otto Kernberg extends psychoanalysis to a new level of integration with group (mass) psychology. He reviews the contributions of Freud and Bion, relates these to his own work in which the role of aggression is central, and proposes new ways for understanding leadership. Kernberg urges psychoanalytic study of mass psychology to meet the threat posed by group regression and violence in contemporary society.

Jacob Arlow offers observations on the blood libel accusation against Jews in an essay on aggression and prejudice. Gathering historical, literary, and mythological evidence, he constructs a case for sibling rivalry as a central dynamic in prejudice.

Five papers on the creative process begin with Jerome Oremland's distinguishing between talent and creativity. He uses case examples to show how talent can serve as a defense against creativity, and that analysis may threaten defensive talent, but enhances true creativity,

Joel Whitebook takes up the concept of sublimation, aiming toward its revitalization. With philosophical, literary, and artistic examples, he shows the necessity of the concept, defining it as a transitional idea on the frontier between internal fantasies and their external realization. Gilbert Rose looks at dreams as a means of understanding creative vision in an attempt to extend and modify affect theory. He relates dreaming, poetry, music, art, and scientific discovery to biological rhythms in a heuristically appealing essay.

Maria Bergmann presents three cases of creative individuals with work inhibitions and shows how an object relations understanding may be combined with modified technique to undo the inhibition and release the creativity. Joyce McDougall's concluding essay relates creativity to sexuality. She creatively presents clinical examples to demonstrate that creativity is as intricate, mysterious, and complex as love and that the two may be similarly inhibited or expressed.

The spectrum of psychoanalysis represented by these papers testifies to the range of influence exerted by Freud's discoveries beginning a century ago. Psychoanalytic ideas, reflected and refracted, have altered the fields of philosophy, literature, music, art, sociology, and politics, among others. Martin Bergmann is a psychoanalyst whose interests and contributions span this spectrum in a way matched by few. Some readers may, therefore, find some of the papers less interesting or informative than others. The book may surely be read selectively. Any such selection will not, however, disappoint. This festschrift is a banquet of excellent choices.

Josephine Klein
Doubts and Certainties in the Practice of Psychotherapy
London: Karnac Books, 1995, x + 290 pp., £21.95.
Psa. Books 7, No. 4 (1996), pp. 499–502

"Modesty and Assurance in Heterodox Psychotherapy" might be a more apt title for this collection of essays by Josephine Klein, an experienced and thoughtful British therapist, not well known to most American readers. The book is of the genre of offerings by senior teacher/supervisors who, one can easily imagine, have been urged by students to bring their ideas to a larger audience. This is Klein's second such effort. It is composed of 10 chapters, one of which is a reprinted paper; seven are versions of recent lectures. The pieces are woven together with clarity and style to form a singular perspective with minimal redundancy. It is an easy read, but its themes and theses challenge concepts (particularly, transference, countertransference, fantasy, and construction) widely held in most psychoanalytic communities. It is also a book that seems to ignore the tripartite definition of psychoanalysis as theory of mind, method of inquiry, and treatment modality, considering only the last, and its application to difficult patients, to be important.

Klein begins with two chapters on values. She holds an egalitarian worldview and cautions as to difficulties of empathy across class, gender, and ethnic lines. She identifies with the disadvantaged, including her own roster of patients who tend to present concretely and superficially, and who are often unreachable with interpretation. She emphasizes the need for caring, openness, and imagination, against which she contrasts establishmentarian orthodoxies she associates with professionalism. Klein concludes this section with exhortations for courage, honesty, and intelligence. For me, her values provide a useful reminder of the revolutionary spirit that attracted many of us to psychoanalysis. They are also consistent with the pluralism of ideas that compose the current *zeitgeist*, and they define Klein's heterodox motto: "free thought" is better than institutional thinking.

Theories and techniques are the subjects of the middle six chapters. Klein's recommendations focus on treatment of "difficult" patients. She takes a common-sense, down-to-earth approach to both goals and methods of treatment. Her major intellectual forebears are Bowlby, Winnicott, M. Balint and Searles. Jo Klein is explicitly not a Melanie Kleinian. She emphasizes listening, accepting, and clarifying over intervening. In her chapter on holding, the best in the book, she articulates the nontechnical ways we hold patients. She cautions against special activities and recommends a balance between integrative interventions and a holding that might foster interminability. So far so good.

Klein's special thesis, her unique contribution, is contained in two chapters that speak about patients unready for interpretation and about the inappropriateness of transference interpretation in particular. She argues clinically, and from epistemological and moral positions, that interpretation can be harmful, that no standard of knowledge is sound, and that interpretation is a form of brainwashing. She asserts that deeper is not better and that her therapeutic aim is simply to help patients feel better and enjoy life. Transference analysis is, at best, a rarefied technique, not useful in most therapies. She concludes this discussion with avowals that she is a therapist, not an analyst, and that psychoanalysis is for itself, rather than for its patients.

In what amounts to an antipsychoanalytic, antitheoretical, anti-intellectual diatribe, Klein decries the concept of transference neurosis as iatrogenic, finds countertransference analysis "not my brief" (p. 153), and rejects a focus on internal fantasy and developmental construction. Despite her more balanced statements, Klein seems to dismiss some of the most central psychoanalytic ideas.

In her later clinical chapters, Klein resumes a more modest and cautious posture, providing a set of recommendations about analyzability and a theory of the development of well-being. Klein's concluding theoretical chapters take up the evolution of the idea of fathering and the contrasting histories of psychoanalysis in the United States and the United Kingdom. For her, there is no a priori gender orientation, nor oedipal primacy in theory-building. She encourages openness to cultural variants on fathering and is critical of the work of Chasseguet-Smirgel.

Klein sees theories to be historical accidents rather than rational developments. In the enisled United Kingdom, with no place to go, controversy led to useful ideas, which led beyond the clinical situation to the field of education. The frontier mentality of America led to splits, dispersion, and a great flowering of ideas.

It is here that she articulates what, for me, is the major flaw in her technical argument: "What psychoanalysts actually did, in the privacy of their consulting rooms, was left relatively unaffected by these benign explosions, with the results that, until recently, psychoanalytic practice in the United States seemed like a fly in amber to British analysts, so closely did it adhere to what had been orthodox in the 1920s" (p. 234).

In a review that closely follows Roazen (1975), Klein describes American psychoanalysis's four strands as the dissenters: neo-Freudians, Erikson,

Horney, Fromm, and Kardiner; the Chestnut Lodge group: Sullivan, Fromm-Reichmann, and Searles; Hartmann, followed by Kohut and Kernberg; and the empirical developmentalists: Spitz, Mahler, Ainsworth, and Stern. Her view of psychoanalytic technique as fossilized follows, it seems to me, from a lack of recognition of the contributions of Stone, Jacobson, Arlow, Brenner, Rangell, Gill, Wallerstein, and others in what is commonly considered the American psychoanalytic mainstream.

Klein is so catholic in praise of pluralism that she sees "well outside psychoanalytic boundaries though originating within... another outburst of creative therapeutic ideas: Encounter, Gestalt, Bio-energetics, and Transactional Analysis, and other such" (p. 259), but she has hardly a kind word for what is the Anglo-American drive-conflict-defense model.

In fact, there are a few kind words for Fenichel and for Greenson, a frequent utilization of Sterba's ideas (without attribution), and only a passing reference to Schafer. But this is the work of a champion of heterodoxy. Her antiestablishment position, justified, at least in part, by a now-crumbling medical orthodoxy, has resulted in a distorted perception of American psychoanalysis. It also might explain the rejection of central psychoanalytic ideas that forms the core of her clinical thesis.

Josephine Klein shares a too common error of many new paradigmatists: the claim to be psychoanalytic while, in effect, declaring psychoanalysis obsolete or dead. Her book is even more problematic, though, because it seems to be directed at an audience of novices and is couched in jargon-free, straightforward language. It uses diagrams, drawings, poems, and other literary references to enhance effective teaching. The danger of miseducation cannot be minimized.

This volume turns out, then, to be a disappointment to one who was looking forward to learning from a seasoned and talented psychotherapist from across the ocean.

Irving Steingart
A Thing Apart: Love and Reality in the Therapeutic Relationship
Northvale, NJ: Jason Aronson, Inc., 1995
xxvi + 291 pp.
Psychoanalytic Review 84, No. 1 (1997), pp. 156–158

Irving Steingart's *A Thing Apart: Love and Reality in the Therapeutic Relationship* is an important and wide-ranging book. It concerns the philosophical undergirding of psychoanalysis, the special nature of the psychoanalytic relationship, and the evolution and (mis)use of language as action on the part of certain analysands. It presents a clear and cogent argument for an ontology of realism in the face of hermeneutic alternatives. It parses the several components of the analytic relationship to show that therapeutic action is provided through committed interpretive intervention. It explicates a theory of language development and a theory of action, offering the idea of "enacted symbols" as vehicles for the analytic process. In this postmodern age of multiple psychoanalytic approaches, with their frequent claims for new paradigm status, this book provides an enriched renewal of the "ordinary," or "normative" Freudian paradigm, as well as a demonstration of its complexity and relevance.

Steingart's approach is challenging, written for experienced analytic therapists with theoretical sophistication, well-versed as to contemporary controversies. Steingart respects readers and expects them to work with him on the issues he discusses. He does not shy away from the intricacies of thought, providing extensive endnotes for each chapter. The book is not an easy read, and the author does not oversimplify; he respects and loves his subject, and he does it justice. Readers must be prepared for serious study to do justice to this work.

This is a well-structured book, akin to a modern symphony in classic style. It is textured, polychromatic, and multi-thematic. Its themes are supported with instrumentalities from related disciplines (psychology, anthropology, linguistics). Its chapters are of strikingly varied length, in consonance with the topics rather than to a preset form. Its tone is often conversational, its metaphors evocative. Earlier themes are reintroduced as they may heighten understanding of subsequent ones. Its concluding chapter is an integrative coda that, nonetheless, treats additional issues such as homosexuality and creativity in the context of riffs on developed material.

A Thing Apart is not merely strung together. Its topics are woven into a coherent, yet complex thesis that requires book-length exposition, rather than a series of papers. This is a major work by a major thinker.

Steingart's exposition of Freudian psychoanalysis gives the lie to common stereotypes. He shows Freudian practice to be an intensely involving, moral activity based on the axiom that self-awareness is therapeutic. This approach is essentially nonauthoritarian, with valid interpretations always offered in a collegial spirit of conjecture. Its results are based on deeply felt, connected experience. Its method constructs the development of psychic reality from material and historical truth, frequently imperfectly understood. Countertransference experience (but not action) is ubiquitous, recognized, and accepted as a crucial, not detrimental, part of the analytic relationship. Freudian analysts are not blank screens. Nonetheless, a basic percept of technique is to avoid confusing real and unreal. No participation beyond interpretation is required of the analyst; no pressure for change is placed on the analysand. Countertransference feelings are not revealed; the analysand's life is the subject of treatment discourse.

Steingart supports his exposition with a noncombative detailed debate of his concept of "comparative therapeutics," with the germane clinical positions of Gill, Hoffman, Schafer, Levenson, and Schwaber. Steingart differentiates analysis from the management techniques of Gedo and of Modell. He specifies the problems of Ferenczi's active techniques. He compares his own ideas on borderline and narcissistic analysands with those of Kernberg and of Kohut, and his concept of enacted symbols with Jacobs's ideas on enactment. Steingart's positions demonstrate a deep clinical wisdom, as well as a respect for the useful, clearly articulated contributions of those with whom he disagrees.

The core of Steingart's position comes not from debate, however, but from his treatment of the ideas of reality and of love as central and therapeutic within a normative Freudian paradigm. He analyzes the components of the analytic relationship, that is, transference, countertransference, empathy, work style, and mature love, and holds them up against his realistic ontology. He next traces the ontogeny of the sense of reality, with special focus on language development and its relation to action. He then returns to the clinical situation, focusing on enacted symbols, wherein play replaces fantasy as a special form of acting out seen with "widening scope" analysands. Finally, he shows how interpretations may be "tilted" in form and style to provide these analysands with insights made meaningful, meshing with their anal/rapprochement developmental conflicts.

In addition to Freud (whom he reads in a nondogmatic manner), Steingart acknowledges particular debts to Mahler, Stone, and Loewald, major innovators within the Freudian mainstream. He is also beholden to an empirical analytic research tradition, which, he believes, will continue to strengthen the realist ontology of psychoanalysis.

Nonetheless, the book is clearly original, built on a lifetime of practice with children, adolescents, and adults; on a career as teacher and supervisor; on collaboration in research on language behavior, kinetics, and other topics. As such, it cannot truly be summarized; gems are to be found on diagnosis, on psychotherapy as distinct from psychoanalysis, on memory, on masochism, on pretense, etc. I also found the book to be immediately helpful to my current practice, indeed a morale-booster (as Steingart himself finds the clinical enterprise).

With this book, Irving Steingart emerges as a major theorist to be reckoned with. This book should be widely read and discussed by analysts of all persuasions.

Elizabeth Young-Bruehl
The Anatomy of Prejudices
Cambridge, MA: Harvard University Press, 1996
632 pp., $35.00
Psa. Books 8, No. 2 (1997), pp. 231–236

Elisabeth Young-Bruehl has written a bold and important book of comprehensive scope, and she has done so with historical and psychoanalytic sophistication. She addresses a topic of utmost concern to citizens of good will, and she treats this topic with full respect for its complexity.

For over 40 years Gordon Allport's classic (1954) work has been the definitive social psychological statement on prejudice. Mainstream social science has operated essentially within its outlines. Allport's main thesis, that prejudice is a singular social psychological structure with multiple roots and varied targets, is subjected to successful challenge by Young-Bruehl. Allport's prime examples, antisemitism and white racism, have both been subjects of extensive research and analysis, complementing, extending, and filling in the Allportian thesis. Until recently, in the case of racism however, African and African American perspectives were excluded. Such views now begin to provide a different outline (e.g., Gaines & Reed, 1995). Young-Bruehl reworks our understanding of antisemitism and racism but casts a wider net to cover sexism and homophobia (neither of which had even been defined at the time of the Allport opus).

Known to psychoanalytic readers for her definitive biography of Anna Freud, Young-Bruehl comes to this topic in the same progressive spirit as had Allport, Adorno and the Frankfurt school, and the social psychologists who followed them, viewing social science as having a meliorative mission imbued with democratic values and aiming for progressive outcomes. It is clear to Young-Bruehl, as it must also be clear to us, that studies of prejudice have thus far failed to meliorate much. Black church burnings and incidents of gay bashing compete for headlines with rape and synagogue desecrations. The postwar American pragmatic resolve to erase prejudice has been reduced to rubble in the wake of the racially bifurcated reactions to the O. J. Simpson verdict and the confusing "don't ask, don't tell" policy of the United States Armed Forces regarding homosexual orientation. [Addendum: *Since publication of this review, we have seen the election of a Black US president, legalization of same-sex marriage, and the seating of four women on the US Supreme Court, suggesting progress is being made*].

106

A professional scholar, Young-Bruehl begins by faulting scholarship for its failure. She deconstructs the literature on prejudices to show that 1) Allport's singularity thesis is wrong—prejudices exist instead in the plural; and 2) the rejection of a psychoanalytic perspective in favor of cognitivism by those who followed Allport have so vitiated their work as to render it impotent.

Psychoanalysts are not let off the hook. In the author's view, we have avoided issues of prejudice by shaping our discipline around an increasingly narrow individual clinical focus. With the notable exception of psychoanalytic Holocaust studies, usually clinically based and arguably related to self-interest, this seems an apt criticism. In addition, unlike Freud himself—and Young-Bruehl cites his more progressive views—psychoanalysts have been resistant to viewing the homosexualities from other than a medical perspective and were too complacent for too long with respect to their overly simplistic psychology of women.

Young-Bruehl's deconstruction is a critique of overgeneralization in the contexts of politics and political change and of history and the history of ideas. Concluding that prejudices are indeed different, she nonetheless pays close attention to their similarities and overlaps. Her reconstruction is based on theory rather than "data," and she uses theory from several disciplines, as did Allport. Her central thesis is built around a psychoanalytic typology of what she calls "ideologies of desire" to understand the four focal prejudices. These ideologies of desire are contrasted with ethnocentrism, the common prejudice of the social psychology cognitive model. She derives her typology from Freud's paper on libidinal types (1931). Racism is associated with the erotic (hysterical) type, anti-Semitism with the anal (obsessional), and sexism and heterosexism (offered as perhaps a better term than homophobia) with the narcissistic personality.

This summary of her typology cannot do justice to her clear and consistent recognition of complex admixtures as well as "pure" types, nor to the detailed use of Anna Freud's notion of developmental lines. Each prejudice is followed ontologically through childhood and adolescence, with useful emphasis on the importance of the latter phase in the consolidation of prejudices. There is also the salutary psychoanalytic distinction consistently made between manifest prejudicial behavior and latent dynamic meanings.

Young-Bruehl then places her typology in the context of differing societal styles that produce different versions of each prejudice. Individual and social variables are respected as interacting, with neither set being privileged over the other.

Along the way, Young-Bruehl provides penetrating and wide-ranging reviews and critiques of the literature about each of the four prejudices. These might stand on their own were they not so well woven together in comparison and contrast. Hannah Arendt, also a Young-Bruehl biographee, and Richard Hofstadter are important sources for understanding antisemitism; C. Vann Woodward for Jim Crow racism; Gerda Lerner for patriarchal sexism. But Young-Bruehl always goes well beyond even her favored sources, applying her own insights to their advances in understanding. The newer literature on complex prejudices like sexism-racism and sexism-classism are also well explored. Anthropological and cross-cultural studies are not neglected.

The concluding portion of the book looks at each of the prejudices from the points of view of the victims. Young-Bruehl's purpose here is to provide diagnostic understanding of oppressors and therapeutic understanding for victims. Here again, wide-ranging review and critique provide considerable insight as the author extends the analyses of Primo Levi, Sartre, Wright, Baldwin, Myrdal, DuBois, Malcolm X, and Fanon regarding anti-Semitism and racism; and Millet, Genet, and others on the narcissistic ideologies of sexism and heterosexism. Young-Bruehl is respectful of the contributions of those who precede her but does not shy from criticism of their limitations as she builds on their work.

The epilogue to this book is more of a political tract than the text it follows. That may be the only possibility at this stage of our understanding. Young-Bruehl is candid about the loose ends and incompleteness of her contribution (although it is nonetheless a new classic and clearly state-of-the-art), and she calls for more study and research as she makes her political proposals. She would hardly claim her work to be dispassionate scholarship.

Well aware of the limitations of such methods, Young-Bruehl calls for political coalition building and education as partial solutions, while also attending to economic and social reforms. She differentiates approaches following her typology and based on the history and refined understanding of each prejudice. Programs to combat sexism seem to her to be most difficult to conceive. Ultimately, she calls for a new enlightenment and the development of a new intelligentsia. Implicitly, the entire work seems to be in the psychoanalytic tradition that takes as its axiom that insight is curative.

There are occasions when the political tract goes too far and detracts from the scholarly work. There are ad hominem attacks on researchers' anality causing their neglect of anal dynamics; there is the labeling of William Buckley as "an exemplary obsessional intellectualizer" (p. 445); there is the idea that welfare reform and opposition to affirmative action can be understood only as symptoms of prejudice; there is an assessment of the relative dangers of Ross Perot, Pat Robertson, and Louis Farrakhan. While we might agree that the political is personal and the personal is political, pathologizing those with whom one disagrees is unlikely to be effective, either psychologically or politically.

If we are to consider bigots of the various types as diagnosable and in need of treatment, we must also recognize that modern psychoanalytic technique goes beyond confrontation and the provision of insight. A therapeutic object relationship provides the necessary framework within which resistances may be analyzed. But, alas, bigotry is not usually a self-defined symptom promoting the seeking of treatment.

Young-Bruehl, in her literature reviews, uses the idea of stages to understand certain lines of development. There seems an optimistic evolutionism implicit in this structure. While I share this optimism, I am skeptical about its being more than wishful. Humans seem to have a still uncanny propensity for evil that has bedeviled every historical attempt at understanding.

Young-Bruehl's thesis, her typology, is well presented and well supported and should provide, in its myriad details, many avenues for further work. The very complexity of her typology, though, at one time obviates and vitiates its utility in understanding individuals and may, like diagnostic statements in general, be of limited value.

My misgivings regarding Young-Bruehl's political methods and her optimism notwithstanding, this book is a most welcome contribution and will likely stand as the basic text on its subject for some time to come. It will also be a morale booster for psychoanalysts who will see demonstrated the continuing relevance of psychoanalytic ideas to social issues about which most of us care a great deal. Our frustration at the lack of concrete suggestions will be mitigated by our seeing in this work on prejudices much in common with our work with individual persons.

Rose Marie Pérez Foster, Michael Moskowitz,
and Rafael Art. Javier (Eds.)
Reaching Across Boundaries of Culture and Class: Widening the Scope of Psychotherapy
Northvale, NJ: Jason Aronson, 1996
xvii + 275 pp., $35.00
Psa. Books 8, No. 4 (1997), pp. 499–503

This volume takes Stone's (1954) "widening scope" beyond diagnostic indications into the domains of class and ethnicity. In doing so, it carries forth Freud's (1919) program of applying psychoanalytic insights on a large scale. The "psychotherapy" of the subtitle is used to mean psychoanalytically-informed treatment. As no special attention is paid to any distinction between therapy and analysis, the Freudian (1919) metaphor of a copper-gold alloy seems implied. What alloys lose in purity they may gain in strength.

The editors—Rose Marie Pérez Foster, Michael Moskowitz, and Rafael Art. Javier—are ambitious. They aim to renew the development of a psychoanalytic cultural anthropology, and they venture boldly into the philosophical realm of values and the impact of those values on theory and practice. Their impetus is, however, most pragmatic: psychoanalysis is endangered, in part because of the economic and cultural narrowness of its patient base. Continued failure to address the issues raised could be fatal.

Collectively, the authors offer a deconstruction of psychoanalysis from an ethnopsychology perspective. The 19th-century Middle-European roots of Freudian theory and the 20th century American roots of Hartmann's modifications are outlined to provide an initial approach to the complex task of developing a contextual psychoanalysis. The papers selected attempt to show hidden ethnopsychological assumptions of psychoanalysis, to demonstrate clinical variations in intercultural therapeutic dyads and to propose modifications in technique. The book speaks directly to working with resistant, silent, undeserved and prematurely terminating non-European American patients, and of the effects of the trauma of cultural oppression.

Individual authors take differing stances regarding the editors' proposal that paradigm modification is needed. Following Bergmann (1993), some might be considered extenders, while others might be thought of as radical revisionists or even heretics.

The first four chapters comprise a section on "fundamental issues." Rose Marie Pérez Foster, in the keynote paper, asks "What is a multi-cultural perspective for psychoanalysis?" She answers: a two-person psychology with each person beginning with a distinct metapsychology, and with the work concerning the bridging of differences; a drive psychology is not helpful; relational revisions are more useful. Michael Moskowitz then addresses the social conscience of the psychoanalytic profession. He provides a clear and cogent critique of the bifurcation between our politically progressive self-image and the growing social irrelevance of our practice. He suggests an integrationist perspective for dealing with this split. Mario Rendon examines psychoanalysis from historical and economic perspectives to show that poor people do not get good psychotherapy services. His suggestion is for radical theoretical and technical revision. Alan Roland questions the universality of Western psychoanalytic conceptions of self, criticizing major theorists from Freud through Kohut, based on his own experience with Asian patients. Roland claims a paradigm shift to have already occurred.

The four chapters in the second part deal with diversity of 500 therapeutic dyads. Rafael Art. Javier questions the assumption that the urban poor are ridden with deficits and sees the provision of concrete services as depriving the poor of psychodynamic opportunities. He gives examples of varying techniques using psychoanalytic principles with those of Hispanic culture. Cheryl Thompson takes up the psychodynamic treatment of African Americans. She discusses similar and dissimilar dyads, the issue of trust, race as a defense, and gender issues. Michael Gorkin describes treatment of Israeli Arabs by Israeli Jews. He offers a good beginning typology of cross-cultural countertransferences and of their effective management. These three essays provide extensive clinical data in what Bergmann (1993) would likely call extensions of technique. George Whitson deals with working class patients, citing many of our usual technical recommendations as unwise totems. He tries to provide balance to his iconoclastic polemic, but his attacks on straw men seem radically overdrawn.

The final grouping of papers presents a useful miscellany dealing with language differences, skin color, the transference-countertransference matrix, and analyzability. Moskowitz introduces the latter topic with the intriguing title, "The End of Analyzability." He concludes, less categorically, that cultural sensitivity makes us ask, "Who is analyzable by me?" Addette Williams provides a detailed catalog of a special problem within the African American community: reactions to skin color differences. Javier and Pérez Foster separately treat aspects of bilingualism, with Pérez Foster providing another good catalog, in this instance for use by a monolingual therapist. These papers are successful in offering specifics of cultural sensitization and, as such, extend the range of theory and practice. Neil Altman proposes a reconstitution of psychoanalysis into a two- or three-person psychology to take culture into account, joining Rendon, Roland, and Whitson in what I consider the revisionist group.

In using Bergmann's (1993) categorization, I reveal my reservations with aspects of this book. While the editors were explicitly aware of disagreements among authors, the titular aim of the book, to encourage and empower therapists to reach across boundaries of culture and class, is at risk of being diluted in the turmoil of postmodern paradigm battles. Those I deem revisionist seem more intent on grinding axes of two- or three-person psychology, or of relational or constructivist theory, or of a too-political agenda, than in promoting the book's main purpose. The less polemical authors present information readily put into practice, without either ducking social issues or distancing themselves from critique.

I am also concerned with the risk of a recrudescent cultural relativism in a new guise: contextualism. Might honoring cultural or class values mean sequestering them from analytic scrutiny? To use one of Javier's examples, machismo may contribute to Hispanic males' unwillingness to use psychoanalytic treatment. Is that not considered a resistance, albeit a cultural one, subject to analytic inquiry? Character traits, especially those with obvious gender-identity relevance, provide compelling analytic material. Since character is ego-syntonic by definition, we must approach any patient's traits with care, and without condescension. Several authors are properly concerned that persons of different class and culture are offered second-rate therapy. I am concerned that revisionist ideology risks alloys of psychoanalysis so weakened as to do no better.

The proposed contextualism raises a perhaps more basic question about the psychoanalytic enterprise: Is our work in the service of finding universals in human psychology? This question has presented a paradox from the outset. Freud was interested in discovering universal laws of mental functioning, and scientific psychoanalysts share that quest. He invented an idiographic methodology par excellence, in both its therapeutic and its research approaches. Contextualism is central, therefore, to analytic work since each patient must be understood in a unique bio-psycho-sociocultural context. This book usefully highlights class and cultural dimensions, too often neglected in our literature, if not in our best practice. It has value as a significant extension of an inherently contextual methodology, neither revisionist nor necessarily inimical to its scientific aim.

As is true of many edited books, contributions vary in both level of discourse and of scholarship. Those papers that deal with matters of philosophy, history, economics, and anthropology might have benefited from coauthors from those disciplines. The editors are, nonetheless, to be commended for their integrative focus and for their new beginning to what indeed may be a matter of analytic survival. Despite my reservations, their effort must be considered a success.

Frederic J. Levine and Arlene Kramer Richards
Countertransference and Enactment in Psychoanalytic Process
APA Annual Meeting, March 11, 1996, Toronto, Ontario

This symposium began with Frederic Levine's literary account of the forces and feelings that come into prominence in a very private relationship between two people, A. and P., who turn out to be characters from John Le Carré's espionage thriller *A Perfect Spy*, but who sound remarkably like analyst and patient in the intimacy and mutuality of their encounter. Dr. Levine went on to review the history of ideas regarding the analytic relationship. He demonstrated that a countertransference/enactment model is not a new psychoanalytic paradigm but is rooted in Freud's technical papers and has evolved and been elaborated upon within a psychoanalytic mainstream that includes works by Reich, Fenichel, Fliess, Zetzel, Greenson, Beres and Arlow, Heiman, and Bird.

Dr. Levine then focused on Boesky's idea that psychoanalysis always involves mutual enactments, cautioning us that the jury is still out, and that much of the time these enactments might be at a small-scale signal level. He concluded by suggesting that frequent sessions per week provide better for the self-monitoring required, that study groups and supervision remain invaluable at all stages of an analytic career, and that we to need be wary of an "objectionable positive countertransference" and over-attention to the analyst's feelings at the expense of understanding those of the analysand.

Arlene Kramer Richards presented an intriguing clinical example of a patient who tested her clinical skills by canceling many sessions, evoking in the analyst feelings of withdrawal, fraudulence, impotence, diffidence, and anxiety; contemplation of premature termination; and lapses of communication. Dr. Richards' enactment involved using the patient's empty hours to read books he had recommended and to use the reading material as a form of bibliotherapy. The patient discontinued treatment after a year, leaving Dr. Richards with the question of whether she had done too little of the suggested reading, insights from which might have provided for more effective interpretations.

In a most literary style, Dr. Richards developed an understanding of her patient as a "Little Prince" (following Saint-Exupéry), and of her countertransference and role in the enactment as helpful tools for empathy. Dr. Richards concluded that analysts might consider reading what their patients read and seeing the movies they see in order to better understand and help them.

114

The sensitive topic of the analyst's participation in the process is Dr. Levine's keynote. He gives us a selective and pointed history to demonstrate that a countertransference-enactment model does not now comprise a new psychoanalytic paradigm. Instead, it is an elaboration and evolution of ideas that are rooted in Freud's technical papers. Freud's ideas have often been cited out of the complex context of his developing theory and practice so as to support one-sided views of the psychoanalytic enterprise for either promotion or debunking.

While Freud's dictum that countertransference is to be overcome can be seen as dominant in mainstream theory until the 1970s, the second view of an "ambiguously presented oracular idea," that countertransference is to be used, was taken up by Reich, Fenichel, Fliess, Kohut, Beres and Arlow, Paula Heimann, and Bird. I would add to the list Stone's classic monograph of 1961 (*The Psychoanalytic Situation*) and offer another reminder that the myth of the perfectly analyzed analyst was first debunked in 1928 (!) by Edward Glover. While my own training from 1968 to 1973 included study of Eissler and the so-called basic model, it also gave prominence and weight to this second view. I always understood the mainstream to include important eddies and cross-currents (like those of Robert Fliess).

Today, there seems to be a neglect of the complexity of our history in the apparent glorification of countertransference and enactment as new action techniques. Rooted in Ferenczi's experiments, anti-Eissler and, to my mind, anti-Freudian, they do not acknowledge that Ferenczi, himself, rejected active technique after his experiments. Nor do they recognize that Alexander's corrective emotional experience model became, after 1954, a psychotherapy alternative from which psychoanalysis could be meaningfully distinguished.

An appropriately more elaborate view of countertransference and enactment exemplified by Reed's survey of training analysts, and by Boesky and by Owen Renik, each editors of a most mainstream journal, *The Quarterly*, demonstrates the evolution so well described by Levine. He then poses the right question: Is our more elaborate understanding of action in technique part of our "margin of error" or an epistemic necessity for psychoanalytic knowing?

Sound psychoanalytic theorizing raises questions and poses judicious suggestions, and I like Levine's. We should pay special heed to his warnings about the risks of manifest prescriptions and about the risks of focusing more on the analyst than the analysand in the necessary oscillation of our attention.

What I would like Levine to tell us more about is his felicitous idea of the objectionable positive countertransference, that potentially delusional *"folie a* deux," and if I may, in this bilingual country, "*folie a deux personne psychologie*" in which we are fully, mutually and gratifyingly, participants—rather than, as recommended by Sullivan, participant-observers.

Unanalyzed countertransferences and unwitting enactments are surely opposed to what psychoanalysis has been and needs to be about, and can lead, in the extreme, to the boundary-breaking to which Jung, Ferenczi, and also Freud succumbed. As frontiersmen, they did not know better; Levine helps us know better.

Dr. Richards presents an intriguing clinical example of a patient who tests our technical skills and raises concrete versions of Levine's epistemic quandary. In a literate and most literary style, Richards vividly describes her patient's life and his dynamic conflicts, as well as the countertransference pressures he exerted. These resulted in a sense of fraudulence over taking money for work not performed; lapses in communication; feelings of withdrawal and of impotence; anxiety over an implicit suicidal threat and at listening to a man's genital anxieties, and diffidence in becoming her patient's flower. Such reports are most important, both for Richards' courage in expressing them, and for us, so that we may recognize the commonality of such feelings in analytic work.

The enactment on which Richards focuses is the use of her patient's empty hours for reading what he read, and the use of the reading for discussion as a kind of bibliotherapy. Are these acts what Levine might call our margin of error? Or, as Richards seems to suggest while nonetheless questioning their legitimacy, are they part of the necessary way we come to know these patients, and may they be suggestive of new and beneficial active techniques? Was the possible error in not doing more and better bibliotherapy?

Richard's conclusion is intriguing and goes to the heart of the matter. It encourages analysts to know as much as possible about their patients by attempting to experience as much as possible of what their patients experience. This seems both desirable and impossible, and highlights what has always been a quantitative dilemma: how much do we have to share of the patient's subjectivity to be effective?

In this short, interrupted treatment, we can only speculate on what might have been. I see this patient as exploitive as much as exploited; and especially as exploiting the vulnerabilities of his analyst, finally enacted in not paying her fee. I believe he was a little prince not only on the model of Saint-Exupéry, but of Machiavelli. I believe his associations would ultimately yield material about these identifications and others, without requiring Richards to be slavish in educating herself further in one or the other. Such reading, in my view, would amount to her being dominated by him, and risk her being drawn into his web: a morass of manifest content. Being his flower might mean having her petals torn off but that would remain for Mr. T. to discover, as he learned about love, intimacy and genital fears, and his defenses in the face of each. The possibility of this treatment blossoming into a full psychoanalysis might have been enhanced by a more traditional neutral posture. But who can really know?

It is nonetheless clear that countertransference and enactment are no longer viewed as destructive phenomena which must be reduced to zero effect. They must be studied, understood, and utilized. The questions, of course, are in which ways, and with what activities on the part of the analyst? In a recent paper, three Canadian psychoanalytic scholars (Bouchard, Normandin, and Seguin, *Quarterly*, 1995), offer a comprehensive and descriptive framework for understanding countertransference. They distinguish and describe in detail three types of mental activity on the part of the analyst: an objective-rational non-defensive observation mode; a reactive defensive mode; and a reflective mode (of immersion in one's induced affective states). Clinical illustrations are provided to exemplify each of the three modes.

Passionate personal participation of the analyst has, since Freud, characterized psychoanalytic method. Freud's (1900) Chapter 7 model shows thought and action diagrammed as polar and mutually exclusive. That early position may well have inhibited the development of an adequate psychoanalytic theory of action, but such inhibition no longer obtains in our rich and complex mainstream. The presentations by Drs. Levine and Richards continue that mainstream evolution, and they further the quintessential psychoanalytic goal of understanding human passions.

Chaya H. Roth and Steven D. Kulb
The Multiple Facets of Therapeutic Transactions
Madison, CT: International Universities Press, 1997
xvii + 308 pp., $45.00
Psa. Books 9, No.4 (1998), pp. 455–459

Chaya H. Roth and Steven D. Kulb have produced an ambitious work written with modesty, innovative yet steeped in respect for traditions. It is also a clinical work with annotated transcripts, yet most of its pages are devoted to explication and elaboration of theory. Roth and Kulb have attempted a major integration of competing psychodynamic models (and models outside psychoanalysis) and have developed a research tool for testing their integration. Readers will differ in evaluating the success of the integration; I believe all will agree that Roth and Kulb are seasoned, responsible, and effective clinicians with a great deal of wisdom to convey.

This book is based on nearly two decades of observation, treatment, and teaching at the Parent-Infant Development Service founded by Roth at the Department of Psychiatry, University of Chicago. It is sustained by a core axiom: that the infant-parent unit is the model for psychological functioning and its form is universal in design. For the authors, treatment principles are also universal, although the specifics of both development and treatment are always unique. Patients are studied individually as well as in dyads and triads for their uniqueness, and, simultaneously, from the perspective of Roth and Kulb's universal infant-parent model.

The authors aim to provide a replicable system of diagnosis and treatment across ages and pathologies. The system would encompass differing therapeutic modalities, including short-term work of limited focus. Although their core axiom places them squarely within the relational orientation, their approach is nonargumentative, detailed, and rigorous. They are highly respectful of the complexity and multidimensionality of human relations and of the contributions to understanding presented by the several psychoanalytic schools and by non-analysts.

The "multiple facets" of the title are four in number: interpersonal, developmental, characterological, and intrapsychic. These are described and related to one another in several chapters following a philosophical and conceptual overview. Roth and Kulb's philosophical stance emphasizes three ideals: 1) patients need to understand diagnosis and treatment for accountability; 2) shared ignorance makes for equality of privilege; and 3) information is routinely exchanged between therapist and patient.

The authors' conceptual overview begins by comparing Buber's "I-It" experience with his "I-Thou" relationship as the essential sources of self-definition. They spell out several assumptions: human behavior is motivated, goal directed, and meaningful; all aspects of human functioning are operative in elemental forms from birth; the unexpectable and unknowable must be calculated in a causal interactionism; and inventive capacity is a central human trait. Many aspects of Roth and Kulb's discussion of these matters are both welcome and unusual in a psychotherapy technique text.

In their chapters describing the four facets, the authors outline the domains, principles, aims, and "conservative tendencies" (coping strategies, defenses) of each facet. They refer to the contributions of seminal authorities, such that within each facet there is an excellent review of basic theory. Roth and Kulb are consistent in noting relationships among theoretical elements and in comparing theorists. Knowledgeable readers will experience a sense of familiarity; novices will come to appreciate the complexity of psychoanalytic ideas, while being helped by a series of charts and appendices to organize their own understanding.

In advance of delineating their treatment approach, Roth and Kulb address the problematic area of diagnosis. They relate ideas of deficit, delay, arrest, and conflict to models of psychoanalytic evaluation and to the behavioral DSM of psychiatry. They use clinical material to argue that DSM may provide a good beginning to multifaceted analytic thinking and that deficit, delay, arrest, and conflict provide complementary rather than competing orientations.

Also, before presenting their treatment approach, the authors render their understanding of the evolution of the psychoanalytic theory of technique. Again they review familiar work, and they posit a developmental line leading to their own specific integration. Loewald's theoretical contributions are central to theirs. Piaget, Gedo, structuralism, and systems theory are also influential for them. They liken their work to the multifocused approaches of Pine and Chessick. They pose the all-important question for multiple model approaches: how and when does one shift from one model to another? This question would then be answered from their therapeutic principles: explore, learn, understand, and practice (work through), in the context of their basic therapeutic aim: to restore balance among the four facets of psychological functioning, the interpersonal, developmental, characterological, and intrapsychic.

Roth and Kulb's unit of interaction (for therapists and patients alike) is the "bid," or communication component. This unit is the essential basis of their research contribution. Specific bids include silences, smiles, bodily and facial gestures, and a wide range of verbal communications from mirroring and probing to coaxing and other noninterpretive statements, and including interpretation, classically defined. Aiming to provide a lexicon, the authors describe simple and complex bids. They then offer six categories of bids: Humane, Supportive, Insight orienting, Containing, Internally orienting, and Negative. (Some negative or antitherapeutic bids are overriding, underinvolvement, sleepiness.)

Roth and Kulb are judicious in warning readers against mechanistic application of rules in following the schematic aids provided. Timing and transference-countertransference considerations are crucial. The authors' specific innovation, however, is the coding of all (save negative) bids by category, for each participant in the therapeutic interaction. This coding is meant as a classification and description for the purposes of training and research.

Finally, Roth and Kulb present coded transcripts of sessions from several treatments, exemplifying both individual and parent-infant/child treatment. The interactional treatment approaches are inspired by the work of Fraiberg and that of Mahler and Furer. These transcripts and the beautiful discussions of them serve a dual purpose. They demonstrate the Roth and Kulb coding scheme, and they show some exquisitely sensitive, psychoanalytically-based treatment.

The authors' concluding remarks emphasize the beginning nature of their work and the hope that others will replicate it. This modesty is appropriate yet also suggestive of the limits of the presentation: despite its ample virtues, this book disappoints.

Two paradoxes stimulate the disappointment. First, despite modesty, the authors seem to see their effort as a completed integration or one that is at hand. Yet the integration often blurs rather than solves active theoretical controversies. Loewald, Bion, and Kohut are treated as similar in approach; differences between Kernberg and Kohut are glossed over. While some controversies lend themselves readily to their integrative resolution (e.g., two-person versus one-person models), major attempts to resolve theoretical pluralism (e.g., Wallerstein, Rangell) are entirely ignored, while other attempts at paradigm making (Arlow and Brenner, Greenberg and Mitchell, Stolorow, Gill and Hoffman) are given affirmative nods but short shrift. Roth and Kulb's answer to the key question of the multi-model approaches they admire (Pine, Chessick), that is, how and when to shift gears, is never clearly articulated. The authors' modesty regarding their integration is more justified than their ambition.

The second paradox is the presentation of a yet untested coding tool as a research framework. The authors claim interrater reliability, and the coding is, indeed, consistent with one or another of the theoretical facets they explore. But the major portion of text devoted to explaining and demonstrating the coding system provides neither empirical data nor testable hypotheses. Roth and Kulb's second contribution is only a small beginning to the research program they wish to promote.

Another source of disappointment comes from the authors' style. Their prose is repetitive, sometimes turgid, and frequently makes use of new terms that are unlikely to catch on. This makes for patches of difficult reading without the novelty to justify the effort.

There is, nonetheless, much to admire in this book. Its theoretical chapters are respectful of the major streams of psychoanalytic thinking and that of related disciplines. Its clinical examples demonstrate responsible therapeutic work artfully described. Its empirical research aim is praiseworthy. The Parent-Infant Development Service at Chicago will, deservedly, be better known and perhaps emulated as a result.

"If It's All the Same to You…:" The Politics of Leveling
Psychoanalytic Psychology 16, No. 1 (1999), pp. 103–109

This commentary rebuts James L. Fosshage's (1997) conclusion that there is no meaningful distinction in the process between psychoanalysis and psychoanalytic psychotherapy. Fosshage's position is seen as part of a politics of leveling, an unfortunate alternative to the politics of pluralism in our discipline.

For psychoanalytic psychology in the United States, the decades of the 1950s and 1960s were especially fruitful. The development of psychoanalytic research programs led by psychologists such as George S. Klein and Robert R. Holt (in the tradition of David Rappaport) provided strong impetus for a psychoanalysis grounded in psychology rather than in medicine.

Subsequent decades saw a major increase in the numbers of psychologists (and other professionals) interested in psychoanalysis while psychiatry was becoming non-psychoanalytic and medicalized. With the advantage of hindsight, it seems natural that psychoanalytic training is now offered by psychology faculties at universities (e.g., New York University, Adelphi University), that nonmedical institutes flourish, and that (albeit spurred by a lawsuit) even traditional medically-oriented institutes welcome nonmedical applicants.

The diversity of professional backgrounds and the variety of training sites have enriched the ideological debate in psychoanalysis and contributed to what is now an acknowledged theoretical pluralism in the United States as well as in the international community.

The professional practice of psychoanalysis has also changed significantly since midcentury, and not for the better. It is challenged on two fronts: the popularity of safer medical treatments for emotional problems and the industrialization of practice under managed care. Unfortunately, a third enemy for psychoanalytic practice, one that operates ostensibly from within the profession, has evolved from a particular politicization of theoretical pluralism.

A. D. Richards (1999) has written informatively on the sorry effects on theory of the "politics of exclusion" practiced by organized American medical psychoanalysts over many decades. Happily, dialogue among theoretical schools is now common in a "politics of pluralism." There is another trend, however, in which premature declarations of victory create what I call a *politics of leveling*. Fosshage's article (1997), concluding that there is no meaningful distinction in the process between psychoanalysis and psychoanalytic psychotherapy, is one egregious example.

Fosshage argues that theoretical pluralism erodes traditional criteria for psychoanalysis; that theory, research, and practice undermine both extrinsic and intrinsic criteria for psychoanalysis, and that what he considers fundamental features of psychoanalytic process can include all current approaches. I argue that although there is room for debate on issues he raises, his conclusion is premature at best. I argue further that his approach does damage to psychoanalysis and is part of a politics of leveling that is as misguided as the former politics of exclusion.

Fosshage's Arguments Rebutted

Fosshage's (1997) review of the theory of distinctiveness of psychoanalytic technique properly relies on the works of Gill (1951, 1954, 1984), Rangell (1954, 1981), and Stone (1954, 1982) while improperly drawing unfounded conclusions from them. Fosshage cites striking changes in the Gill (1954) position, emphasizing here-and-now transference interpretations (Gill, 1984) while maintaining the earlier stance eschewing exclusive use of extrinsic criteria. It is Gill's evolution that serves, exclusively it seems, as rationale for Fosshage. While noting Rangell's (1981) more balanced view in his critical response to Gill, and Rangell's citation of Bibring's (1954) seminal article describing the several types of technical intervention whose proportions define the distinctiveness of psychoanalysis, Fosshage considers the Gill shift to summarize the history and to provide definitive evidence for an absence of distinctiveness.

Fosshage's review of research findings also limits itself to a single work, Wallerstein (1986), and within that work, to a single finding: that structural change could not be linked to interpretation alone. Fosshage notes several challenges to traditional beliefs raised by the Wallerstein opus and states that these support Rangell's view (of Bibring's position). Notwithstanding the contradiction between Bibring's and his own views, Fosshage concludes that these empirical findings (along with supervisory experience) "make it clear that our theory of technique... has been far too narrow" (p. 413).

As important as the Wallerstein (1986) research may be, psychologist-psychoanalysts would hardly consider a single study to provide such clarity nor to be conclusive. Such a finding should lead, instead, to refinement of thinking about the nature of change and as a spur to further research. Mainstream psychoanalytic literature is imbued with such thinking, although unhappily with too little empirical research. Traditional technical theory has, at least since Bibring (1954) and Loewald (1960), held a more complex view of the process than that characterized by Fosshage (1997). Citing Rangell as supportive of his reductionism is a disingenuous distortion of Rangell's well-known balanced, comprehensive theory.

Fosshage's understanding of current practice is as tendentious as his reading of the theoretical and research literatures. He speaks of a paradigmatic shift from positivism to relativistic science in which interpretation can be equated with suggestion and words with actions. This viewpoint is, indeed, a position taken by some new schools of psychoanalysis. I would assert, however, that these schools compete in a pluralistic field and have not achieved paradigm status. I would further argue that a sophisticated ontological realism (Steingart, 1995) remains vital within our debate and that similarities and differences between interpretive and suggestive interventions, and between words and actions, must be understood and accounted for (Golland, 1995). For mainstream schools of psychoanalysis, neither hermeneutics nor blurring of differences are generally accepted approaches. In current mainstream psychoanalysis, relational effects (Loewald, 1960) are not dismissed but are considered instead as necessary—but not necessarily sufficient—aspects of a complex psychoanalytic process.

Fosshage's major effort is to reassess traditional extrinsic and intrinsic criteria in distinguishing psychoanalysis and psychoanalytic therapy. Here he uses obvious exceptions to the rule to leap from the flexible understandings of our essentially idiographic enterprise to the astounding conclusion that the criteria have no validity whatsoever! That some treatments may develop an analytic process at a frequency less than four times weekly does not prove, as Fosshage would have it, that frequency is irrelevant to process (A. K. Richards, 1997). That some patients may prefer to work face-to-face is a diagnostic indicator rather than support for Fosshage's belief in the obsolescence of the couch (Moraitis, 1995). That psychoanalysis has a widening scope of indications (Stone, 1954) and that psychoanalytically informed treatment may be helpful to persons who may not respond to a more strictly defined procedure have long been known and hardly support Fosshage's denial of a distinction between psychoanalysis and psychotherapy. Being certified as fully trained does not guarantee success, and talented supervisees may do excellent work, but neither fact indicates that completed training is a meaningless distinction. Yet Fosshage makes each of these assertions about Gill's (1954) extrinsic criteria.

Fosshage treats Gill's intrinsic criteria similarly. He uses our increasingly complex understanding of transference and the transference neurosis for simplification (and obfuscation). He claims that interpretation is always—rather than at times—a form of suggestion. He denies that quantitative differences between transference and transference neurosis might become qualitative ones. (He ignores Rangell's [1954] compelling metaphor that the phenomena of dawn and dusk do not obviate day and night.) He uses Wallerstein's (1986) findings as a "demonstration" (p. 417) that various interventions are similarly effective, and he denies the use of Bibring's (1954) distinctions among various types of intervention with the rhetorical artifice "as we have seen" (p. 417).

To his own satisfaction, Fosshage presents technical neutrality as a concept "riddled with problems" (p. 418) yet offers a relational understanding of this concept that would support discarding it as a differentiating criterion. This is not the place to elaborate on neutrality as a matter of technique nor to provide a fuller description of a traditional treatment model. Suffice it to say that the issues raised are debatable in respectful dialogue but instead get short shrift in Fosshage's polemic.

Fosshage concludes by offering a two-pathway understanding of therapeutic action from self-psychological and intersubjective perspectives. The two pathways are empathic and other-centered listening. These provide him with a clinical example in which a "non-analytic" (p. 419) extra-transference inquiry was notably successful. His fear of criticism for being nonanalytic, in the example, is misplaced and might only come from the later Gill he admires. The intervention is readily supportable within a traditional perspective, at least since Stone (1954) and Loewald (1960). Fosshage's polemic, however, seems to require that he create a traditional straw man based on a narrow understanding of Gill's (1954) definition. Fosshage endorses certification of training (contradicting his earlier facile argument) to claim, with Gill, that analysts almost always practice analysis, but then joins more traditional analysts in questioning Gill's extremism with regard to transference interpretation. Fosshage routinely picks and chooses among Gill's statements rather than evaluating various positions elaborated by Gill over a long and distinguished career.

The two-factor theory offered by Fosshage is an attempt to simplify psychoanalytic listening. It stands in contrast to approaches developed over a century of study and practice (exemplified by Rangell's total comprehensive model) that require more complex guidelines to do justice to human psychology. Freud (1914b), at one point, also offered a two-factor formulation: "Any line of investigation which recognizes these two facts (transference and resistance)... has a right to call itself psychoanalysis" (p. 16). This turned out to be an over-simplification.

Leveling and Sharpening: The Politics of Leveling

Among the lines of research developed in the 1950s and 1960s was that of *cognitive styles* (Gardner, Holzman, Klein, Linton, & Spence, 1959). Two predominant styles, *leveling* and *sharpening*, were most clearly defined. The former, in which individuals minimize meaningful distinctions, may be likened to a hysterical approach to cognition. The latter, in which trivial distinctions are exaggerated, is related to an obsessional approach. The "new look" in perception research was essentially informed by a psychoanalytic sensibility. Fosshage's thesis exemplifies the leveling style. Rangell (1954) and Bibring (1954) make unmistakable briefs for a meaningful distinction between psychoanalysis and psychoanalytic psychotherapy, briefs that Fosshage fails to rebut. These distinctions continued to be useful for practice, supervision, and teaching. Why the need to level rather than engage in respectful debate?

Fosshage espouses a position that psychoanalytic practice cannot be defined by traditional criteria such as frequency and the use of the couch. Because his attempt to sustain that denial is supported by neither cogent and coherent theory, nor research, nor predominant practice, its purpose is best understood as political. Such argumentation does nothing to further professional discourse. Instead, it exemplifies a politics of leveling, a basically anti-intellectual enterprise, having much in common with the Freud bashing so stylish of late.

The leveling cognitive style exemplified by the Fosshage thesis asserts, "It's all the same," and, in doing so, proposes to raze (level, demolish) the (admittedly imperfect) theoretical and clinical edifice painstakingly constructed over the past century. Those who applaud the "no difference" approach forgo the opportunity to learn and practice psychoanalysis. It may be understandable that some clinicians victimized by the politics of exclusion and who could not benefit from a rigorous training may be receptive to the notion that what they practice is all the same as traditional psychoanalysis. Such a political position, however, does not make it so.

Readers of this journal should not be misled by Fosshage that psychoanalysis is other than a special enterprise worthy of respect and thorough study. Psychoanalysis as a discipline will continue to develop; it would be unfortunate if psychologists interested in psychoanalysis excluded themselves from that development by accepting the illusion that a politics of leveling had replaced the politics of pluralism.

R.D. Hinshelwood
Therapy or Coercion? Does Psychoanalysis Differ from Brainwashing?
London: Karnac Books, 1997
xii + 249 pp., £19.95

Stephen Frosh
For and Against Psychoanalysis
London: Routledge, 1997
x + 271 pp., $20.99
Psa. Books 10, No. 2 (1999), pp. 162–167

These two provocatively titled volumes are worthy British contributions dealing with psychoanalysis and philosophical issues. The first describes a personal and clinical struggle with the ethics of practice. The second confronts the most difficult questions facing psychoanalysis as a discipline. R. D. Hinshelwood, a well-known Kleinian analyst, presents a defense and redefinition of the moral position of psychoanalytic treatment in the face of existential questions about the ethics of influence. Stephen Frosh, a scholar/therapist, offers a more wide-ranging evaluation of psychoanalysis as science, as treatment, and as critical social discourse.

Hinshelwood begins with an account of his conflict over the coercive nature of the psychiatric practice of his training days, and his attraction to the alternatives of the therapeutic community, antipsychiatry, and psychoanalysis. He reflects upon his development of a treatment philosophy grounded in Kleinian ideas. Frosh, in a well-documented and tightly argued exposition, evaluates with remarkable objectivity the extensive criticisms to which psychoanalysis has been subjected in the past quarter century. Pulling no punches, yet avoiding the rancor of the Freud bashers, Frosh is successful in preserving much that he finds good and useful. His conclusion supports his title. He is, and we are persuaded to be, both for and against psychoanalysis.

Hinshelwood reviews moral positions in psychoanalytic theory and practice since Freud, for whom the discovery of truth was both the aim and its own moral justification. With Freud's redefinition of his structural theory, psychoanalysis came to be centered on unconscious guilt, and practice moved away from a medical model to a treatment of persons as moral beings. While Freud himself shied away from philosophy per se, Hinshelwood calls us to an ethical focus. He describes that focus from ego-psychological, Kleinian, and British middle group perspectives, opting ultimately for Klein's language and theory. He then organizes his exposition around four philosophical themes: the unity of the person, problems of autonomy, the ethics of influencing, and the study of persons in relationship to society.

As to the issue of the unity of the person, Hinshelwood takes us on a historical tour from the Enlightenment through the several principles underlying professional ethics in general (informed consent, paternalism, rationality, cooperation), to a discussion of the Freudian discovery of resistance. He then examines primitive mental phenomena (splitting, projection, introjection) in clinical practice and in everyday life. He concludes that psychoanalysis has discovered a mind essentially divided, and that this fact undermines any simple ethical view of human autonomy.

Regarding his now complex view of autonomy, Hinshelwood delves further into the division of the mind (via repression and splitting) and its implications for consent. He presents and rebuts several arguments for paternalism, finding them each flawed, especially in light of the recent emphasis on the analyst's subjectivity. He concludes this segment of his exposition by positing his central thesis: integration, the Kleinian mechanism of therapeutic action (involving undoing of splitting and projective identification), results in a person's regaining lost parts of the self and developing an enhanced capacity for self-reflection. Integration thereby provides us with an ethical principle more useful than alternate attempts.

In the light of the principle of integration, Hinshelwood reexamines the ethics of influencing to conclude that psychoanalysis is a moral practice, perhaps *the* moral practice, because its aim is to make a person more autonomous and rational. He argues that, by the very nature of the process, such a result cannot be coerced. In a thoughtful chapter on the nature of professions and their power, Hinshelwood evaluates the ways in which professions can, indeed, be coercive. He provides, through the concept of an integrative aim, an ethical alternative.

In his final section, addressing the social context of individual development, Hinshelwood attempts a psychoanalytic social psychology and derives from it a prospect for a healthy society. He deals with the ethics of political systems, the case of consumerism, and the matter of cultural relativity.

To me, Hinshelwood provides one useful model for the kind of philosophical thinking that psychoanalysts should demand of themselves. Ultimately, though, his effort disappoints. While he faces important issues and offers some solace to those less familiar with the ethics of influence, he admits that his philosophical analysis is amateurish. While he writes from a Kleinian frame of reference in a style that is clear to a non-Kleinian and not heavily laden with unfamiliar or off-putting jargon, his conclusion seems more in the service of his theory than convincing on its own. His technical stance is abstinent and his clinical experience and sensibility are always evident, but the task he sets himself requires more.

Hinshelwood knows that his philosophical position is easily challenged but he claims that the empirical findings of psychoanalysis (namely, splitting, projective identification, and integration) make philosophical objections irrelevant. His argument that his version of psychoanalysis is not parapsychology (actual thought transfer from one individual to another) will only convince those already converted. Much of his argumentation involves the setting up and demolishing of straw men. Finally, Hinshelwood's application of his ethics to social and political issues is less well developed than his applications to the treatment situation and is therefore even less cogent as an effective resolution of issues.

Where Hinshelwood faces challenges seemingly to test and reaffirm his faith, Frosh takes on greater challenges and follows them to often disconcerting, but more thoroughly grounded, conclusions. Placing his work within the context of the history of ideas and its postmodern turn, Frosh's tripartite aim is to review critiques of psychoanalytic epistemology, of psychoanalysis as a therapy, and of psychoanalysis as applied to the social issues of racism, sexism, and homophobia. In each case he finds the critiques to have significant, perhaps crippling validity, but he also finds hope for our discipline.

While not a trained analyst, Frosh is fully conversant with the Freudian, Kleinian, and Lacanian systems and their relationships with each other and with their critics. He is also well informed regarding American relational models and feminist critiques. In many ways he writes like a good analyst would practice. He confronts us with matters we might prefer to avoid, yet he does so with sympathy and respect, and in an alliance aimed at furthering understanding. The issues are: the weakness of the ontological and epistemological bases of our discipline; our failure to demonstrate either the effectiveness or the ethicality of our treatment procedures; and our more recent difficulties with diversity of gender identification and with race. Frosh asks: How may psychoanalysis deepen knowledge about philosophy, treatment, and diversity? Is the theory consistent, coherent, evocative—or sterile?

Frosh also deals respectfully with our critics, but does not join any hostile attempt to declare psychoanalysis bankrupt. He is intrigued by the discovery of a dynamic unconscious and cannot imagine modern intellectual history without it. He encourages us to be more self-critical in light of this most significant discovery.

For Frosh, psychoanalysis has lost its way by shifting from a revolutionary stance to a reactionary one. The shift was evident even in Freud's own movement from outsider to recognized great man. It was furthered by Hartmann's program of extending psychoanalysis as a general (adaptational, normative, implicitly conformist) psychology. It reached a mature establishmentarianism with its mid-century domination of American psychiatry.

Frosh's discussions of Science, Therapy, and Society are so well presented that a summary would not do them justice. His thorough analysis of the Science versus Hermeneutics debate finds that the dynamic unconscious by its very nature disrupts evidence that might meet scientific standards. Frosh then offers the important idea that the psychoanalytic process of argument around these issues, "however slippery" (p. 45), is itself a genuine knowledge endeavor, requiring the rigorous pursuit of criteria broader than either positivism or hermeneutics.

As to clinical practice, Frosh poses the baldest critical challenge: that talking makes things worse. He then analyzes the complexity of evaluating outcome in the intersubjective domain. Thoroughly knowledgeable about matters of technique and arguments over them, Frosh avoids polarities and introduces clear, generative and integrative ideas from authors with whom I was unfamiliar. He is also thoroughly conversant with the essentially unfavorable research literature but finds its methodologies inadequate to the task. Yet he wonders, properly, why psychoanalysis has not, after a full century, developed its own appropriate research methodology. His provisional conclusion about treatment is that, despite the inadequacy of evidence (from which we must not hide), the richness of the psychoanalytic discovery process cannot be dismissed.

Frosh's concluding section studies aspects of what he sees as the awkward relationship between clinical and so-called applied psychoanalysis in what he calls the politics of identity. Social theory asks explanations from psychoanalysis for the irrational (subjective), for example, war as always a war of fantasies. The Kleinian view of fantasy as what the mind does is contrasted with the Freudian view of fantasy as an alternative to reality. Again, modernist rationality is compared with postmodern critiques with a thoroughness and thoughtfulness consistent with Frosh's involved yet dispassionate truth-seeking.

When he focuses on the areas of gender, homosexuality, and race, Frosh is equally thorough and dispassionate. Here, his conclusions are that, for the most part, psychoanalysis has been guilty of promoting norms rather than understanding fantasies. Freud's views on women have been both acknowledged as passé, and superseded by a productive feminist psychoanalytic scholarship. Freud's views on homosexuality were more enlightened than those of the succeeding psychoanalytic establishment and, here too, advances in theory may lead to some reconciliation and renunciation of homophobia. Racism, Frosh finds, has been shamefully neglected, and psychoanalysis has been exclusionary. His view is that psychoanalysis should be an eccentric discipline, but has not freed itself, nor can it, from its social surround. Here again, he introduces newer psychoanalytic thinking that may promise reconciliation. Psychoanalysis would then have its own critical and self-critical theory, which might result in mixed and complex, yet more satisfactory, answers.

In each of the three areas of concern, Frosh comes out both against and for psychoanalysis. He is against its complacency and conservatism regarding its own epistemology and social relevance, and against its taking its therapeutic practice for granted. He is for its therapeutic caring, patience, subtlety, and intersubjective focus; for its dealing with both the pragmatic and the poetic; for its opportunity to exert progressive force. Frosh is aware that his own position can be deconstructed, and that one may argue for psychoanalysis as both eccentric and normative. He occasionally trivializes clinical conflicts like that around frequency of therapeutic contact. He does not cite a recent landmark work on sexism, racism, and homophobia (Young-Bruehl, 1996). But these are mere cavils in evaluating a major work.

Hinshelwood's treatise can be read with benefit by analysts hoping to engage with the axiology of their practice; Frosh's book should be required reading both for psychoanalysts and their critics. The renewal of the international exchange of ideas exemplified by the distribution of these volumes in the United States can only be of benefit to the psychoanalytic movement.

Irene Fast
Selving: A Relational Theory of Self Organization
Hillsdale, NJ: Analytic Press, 1998
xii + 183 pp. $34.50
Psychoanalytic Psychology 17, No. 1 (2000), pp. 186–189

William James's insight into the dual nature of self (as both object and subject, "me" and "I") provides the starting point for Irene Fast's theory of self organization. The theory centers around Fast's conception of the "I-self," an identity structured from interaction schemes (following Piaget's usage). The essence of I-self is "selving": The dynamic self is what it does. By comparing selving with related streams of psychoanalytic thought, Fast aims to contribute to the proliferation of theories and part-theories in the development of a relational framework for psychoanalysis.

In three introductory chapters, Fast describes inadequacies in earlier psychoanalytic conceptions of self, develops her own, and defines its basic structures and its ways of making meaning. She then deals with the development of the I-self in the first 2 years of life, when I-schemes are global and unaccompanied by a subjective sense of I-ness. She goes on to treat the post-2-year-old's construction, respectively, of an inner world and an external world. Ending each chapter with a summary and a connection to the next, Fast concludes with an overview of the range of characteristics of the dynamic I-self.

The dynamic I-self includes what traditional theory would consider the several ego functions, which develop, Fast says, through relational interactions. The functions (or actions) of the self are the self. The I-self comprises the dynamic processes of the mind. The id and the ego of traditional theory are each aspects of I-self, with agency (purposiveness) its intrinsic characteristic, and a subjective sense of self its developmental achievement.

Fast makes extensive use of the ideas of Piaget, as well as those of Winnicott and of Stern, to explicate the early structuring of the I-self from I-schemes, through processes of integration and differentiation. Interactions, rather than sensory perceptions, form the units that constitute such schemes. Me-self representations form from I-self interaction schemes. Although schemes do not form in response to any objective (positivistic) world, they develop increasing accuracy through pragmatic testing. Following Schafer, Loewald, Bowlby, Spence and others, Fast outlines an agentic theory of meaning making, involving metaphor and narrative.

Failures in meaning making (dissociations) result in reliance on action modalities (in lieu of thought) modalities. In adults, these failures lead to enactments.

Fast considers undifferentiated I-schemes to be more explanatory than concepts such as id, paranoid-schizoid positions, primary process, part-object relations, or rapprochement difficulties. Undifferentiated self states involve attributions and misattributions of agency and affect and may evoke annihilation anxiety. I-schemes are, Fast believes, more useful concepts than splitting, affect dominance, or poor reality testing.

Building on the work of Fonagy, Fast explores the complexities of selving, and her theory of internalization follows closely the Piagetian processes of assimilation and accommodation. Maturity is defined as the complex integration of multiple cognitive and affective schemes. Fast's dynamic I-self is, then, active, agentic, experiencing, constructed, bodily, intersubjective, and both individual and relational.

Fast's explication of her concept is well argued, accompanied by vivid clinical and developmental descriptions, and closely compared and contrasted with select traditional and object relations approaches. The present work grows out of her own earlier theorizing and research. It also makes useful reference to related developmental research.

Having offered a contribution to psychoanalytic psychology focusing on an important conceptual issue that has dogged theorists for over a century, Fast might well be commended for achieving her explicitly modest aim. She describes this work as schematic and suggestive, promising implicitly to explore in the future its application to major issues such as gender organization and psychoanalytic technique.

Also implicit in this book are two basic and questionable assumptions that permeate the work. They are far from modest. First, Fast takes it as axiomatic that all psychologically relevant experience (what traditional psychoanalysis would call psychic reality) is self experience. She offers her I-self concept to include all dynamic processes of the mind. In doing so, she presents, in my view, an overarching replacement theory rather than a schematic approach to a specific conceptual problem within psychoanalytic thought.

Fast is in good company, going back to the defections of Jung and Adler and including the contributions of Wilhelm Reich, Melanie Klein, Jacques Lacan, and Hans Kohut (who, surprisingly, is not cited for comparison in what is a new psychology of the self). Like these theorists, Fast finds serious fault with an aspect of traditional psychoanalysis. For her, it is the impersonal energic nature of the systems "Das Ich" and "Das Es." She believes Freud to have understood the personal nature of self but to have become caught up in the mechanistic scientific discourse of his time. His errors were then compounded, first by Abraham's reliance on drives and drive distortion of positivistically conceived reality, then at midcentury by Hartmann's ego psychology, which achieved conceptual dominance (and concluded the evolution of traditional theory).

Subsequent theorists like Winnicott, Loewald, Schafer, Spence, Eagle, Ogden, Kernberg, Stern and Fonagy are, in Fast's reading, not party to an advancing, evolving, self-correcting dialogue within what Rangell calls total composite theory. Instead, these theorists are partly in error and partly implicit supporters of the new relational paradigm. In common with the battling theorists of the 1930s (Bergmann, 1976), Fast seems to consider her work and that of her close allies (like Davies) as true heir to the original Freud.

What I see as Fast's replacement theory is accompanied by new language in which, for example, *dynamic* seems to mean *motivated* or *agentic* and *self* seems to mean *mind*. New terms (e.g., I-self or I-scheme) predominate in the discourse. Although recognizing that language may confound understanding, Fast explicitly excludes from her new language the familiar terms of Freud's second tripartite model, as well as references to sex, aggression, unconscious processes, fantasy, conflict, compromise-formation, and biological influences on psychological development. Fast cites Schafer's (1976) proposed action language, which also made central the issue of agency. In my view, he provided that necessary corrective to ego psychology. Schafer, however, felt able to retain the more familiar traditional concepts and the evolving theory, whereas Fast substitutes a new psychology of the I-self for virtually all of traditional psychoanalytic theory. In doing so, she calls to my mind Kaplan's (1995) question regarding theoretical revision: When, in the course of unraveling, does a sock become a tangle of thread?

In fact, Fast is quite explicit in her exclusion of unconscious processes, making her work seem closer to a psychology of consciousness than to psychoanalysis. Her second major assumption is that id and unconscious processes are not easily accommodated in relational perspectives and are increasingly outdated and "of no more than historical interest" (p. 94). If Fast is correct, her relational perspectives are part of a different discourse than what I find abundantly available in contemporary pluralistic psychoanalytic literature. I see her assertion repeating a common error of substituting a single idea, in this case the agentic I-self, for the complexity and richness of interrelated ideas that constitute evolving psychoanalytic theory. Such errors risk balkanization rather than the dialogue necessary to advance theory and practice.

One may quarrel, and I do, with others of Fast's assumptions and assertions. She disputes philosophical realism yet substitutes *actualities* for *reality* and speaks of *misattributions* for *distortions*, as if renaming resolves epistemological problems. Her concept "selving" serves as a totalistic substitute for "psychology," reminiscent of Skinner's similar use of "behavior." She views enactments as reflecting an absence of I-experiencing, neglecting their now recognized ubiquity. Fast concludes, by assertion, that her theory encompasses individualism and aloneness, body and mind, and a development of a cohesive self-concept, but her text does not provide ample support for this reclamation of a desirable richness.

Readers may find much of value in this book related to Fast's explicit modest aim, which I would paraphrase as a Piagetian understanding of the development of a conscious sense of self. In my view, that value is undermined by the implicit but pervasive offer of an overarching theory that is unidimensional and by the explicit rejection of so much of what has heretofore been considered the domain of the psychoanalytic enterprise.

Alan Sugarman, Robert Nemiroff, and Daniel Greenson, Eds.
The Technique and Practice of Psychoanalysis, Vol. II
Madison, CT: International Universities Press, 1992
Psychologist Psychoanalyst 21, No. 3 (2001), pp. 64–65

When I began psychoanalytic training, Ralph Greenson's technique text was new. Greenson was himself already very well known for his scholarly contributions as well as for being analyst to Hollywood stars and the putative model for "Captain Newman, M.D.," a World War II psychiatrist portrayed on the silver screen by Gregory Peck.

Volume One of The Technique and Practice of Psychoanalysis (1967) was a most welcome contribution. Prior to its issue only two works could claim the status of texts in the field of psychoanalytic technique. Glover's volume (1955) was an updating of lecture notes compiled originally in 1928 before the maturing of the structural theory. Fenichel, Greenson's own analyst, had written a brilliant monograph on technique in 1941. Each work provided a compendium of technical wisdom in the absence of a text by Freud.

Greenson set himself the task of creating a state-of-the-art text arranged in a highly organized and teachable format with numbered sections and subsections. He went to press with the first volume (covering the central issues of resistance, transference, the working alliance, and the psychoanalytic situation) when his ambition to cover treatment issues sequentially (beginnings, interpretation, etc...) would have resulted in too long a delay in publication. His second volume was outlined, with some chapters begun or completed, when illness intervened. We waited a quarter century for its posthumous publication.

Greenson's Volume One did not disappoint. It evoked contradictory feelings, however, in this beginning candidate. On the one hand, the clarity of exposition and the unprecedented (and still rare) open discussion of clinical details in a thoroughly engaging personal style led to the distinct (albeit naïve) feeling that this humane and exquisitely individualized technique could, in fact, be learned by following a text. On the other hand, the definitive and confident nature of Greenson's formulations was awesome, suggesting, perhaps, that only someone of his unique talents could master psychoanalytic technique.

Personal development as a psychoanalyst as well as professional change in the field over the decades since Volume One have made it plain that psychoanalytic technique cannot be learned from a text. Supervision, clinical experience, and peer group study provide an individual analyst with skills that may continue to develop toward a personal but very incomplete sense of mastery as each analysand disappointed textbook seekers, at least in North America.

Then, in 1992, there appeared Volume Two!

Lovingly and painstakingly put together by Greenson's son Daniel with Alan Sugarman and Robert Nemiroff, under the auspices of the San Diego Psychoanalytic Society and Institute, an organization whose birth was assisted by the elder Greenson, Volume Two appears from the same publisher and with the same title, cover, and typeface as its predecessor. The editors invited nineteen contributors, most of them well known from prior writing, to address the topics in Ralph Greenson's original outline. A section on goals was added as were some additional topics of interest to the invitees. Also included are Greenson's introduction and the four chapters he had written. Except for a chapter by the Shanes (from a self-psychological perspective) and one by Brandchaft (a critique of the working alliance concept from the intersubjective point of view), each a former student of Greenson, the book takes as its orientation modern conflict theory. Its authors, mostly psychiatrists, were trained at and/or belong to institutes of the American Psychoanalytic Association.

In his introduction and chapters on beginnings, acting out, countertransference, and termination, Ralph Greenson treats the reader, as in the first volume, to beautifully expressed, experience-rich and thoughtful ideas, anecdotes, and examples (but without the subsection numeration). It was a pleasure to be again in his company across decades. In his familiar authoritative tone, Greenson reminds us, nonetheless, that every case is different, and specific technical recommendations are always unpredictable in their effect.

Each of Greenson's chapters is followed by at least one contemporary paper on the same topic. This is felicitous editing, involving both update and critique. Daniel Greenson writes on assessment of analyzability and provides useful caveats against poor assessment. Haig Koshkarian makes good suggestions on managing acting out and he deals well with related countertransference issues. Morton and Estelle Shane render a cogent critique of Greenson's assumptions about the reality perspective from which transference and countertransference are understood. Sanford Izner postulates a useful differentiation between countertransference and counter-defense. Jack Novick offers compelling, transcript-like material from the terminal phase of treatment of an "interminable" analysis, demonstrating the importance of the phase and its issues.

Analytic goals are discussed by Robert Wallerstein, then jointly by Edward Weinshel and Owen Renik. Each essay, rich and informative in its own way, shows that agreement on the aims of psychoanalysis, if it ever existed, is largely absent today, even from within a common theoretical orientation. As chapters 3 and 4, these papers also serve notice that Volume Two is not a coherent single-voiced text. Although mostly organized as Greenson had outlined, topics such as interpretation (S. Levy and L. Inderbitzen, A. Skolnikoff), abstinence (P. Dewald), reconstruction (R. Tyson), dreams, (A. Grinstein), and working through (S. Wilson, S. Izner) are presented in papers that would be readily published individually by our best journals. Intellectual (and sometimes emotional) connection to Ralph Greenson seems the thread holding them together. Such is even more the case with the closing papers by Rudolph Eckstein and by Vann Spruiell. These are significant contributions to technique with widening scope patients and include, as was always the case with Greenson, detailed clinical material and innovative ideas.

Comprised, then, of excellent papers better described as a festschrift then as a text, Volume Two may disappoint readers who still wait and hope for a textbook. Such a wish, eschewed by Freud, was likely always a vain one, psychoanalysis being in its essence an idiographic domain. The current phase of theoretical pluralism makes a definitive text even less likely. Volume Two will not disappoint serious readers from any psychoanalytic persuasion, however. The quality of the papers and their continued relevance three decades after publication, the detailed clinical material, and the special opportunity to experience previously unpublished writing from Ralph Greenson give this book lasting value.

Festschrifts rarely serve as vehicles for influential contributions to the literature. Most authors prefer to submit their best work to the guaranteed readership of major journals. This book may be a happy exception, in that eight years after publication it was reissued in paperback. While its physical resemblance to Volume One and its title may be something of a marketing ploy, that seems a small indiscretion in the service of our continuing education.

Richard Tuch
The Single Woman-Married Man Syndrome
Northvale, NJ: Jason Aronson, 2000, xxiii + 310 pp., $30.00.
Journal of the American Psychoanalytic Association 49, No. 4 (2001),
pp. 1457–1459

Identification of a syndrome in either the medical or the behavioral realm is a matter of great import, with both practical and theoretical consequences. An interpersonal syndrome identified by a traditionally trained psychoanalyst would be a major contribution. This book's title not only promises a syndrome, but the particular area of study has social significance and would likely draw a wide audience. If the work succeeds, both the public and the profession of psychoanalysis would gain. There is a risk, however. If science and scholarship do not support the assertion of discovery, the work may amount to little more than sensationalism.

This book by Richard Tuch, a Los Angeles training and supervising analyst, has as its general topic extramarital affairs, and its ambition in part is to provide a window into related male-female issues and the nature of love. Richard Tuch's thesis is that the single woman–married man syndrome is specific and includes particular patterns of behavior, feelings, and attitudes not previously described in the literature. The syndrome has an incidence, a typology, and particular dynamic constellations. It is unlike most psychoanalytic syndromes in being essentially interpersonal; only *folie à deux* and sadomasochism are similar, in that they involve two persons with complementary intersubjective states. The key dynamic issue for both parties is interpersonal power and control.

Tuch provides a clear descriptive overview, and full-length chapters presenting his data from each of three different perspectives: the single woman's, the married man's, and the wife's. He then focuses on the issues of marital discord and extramarital affairs as significant social-psychological phenomena within which this syndrome resides. Tuch's concluding chapters are on gender, treatment implications, and the nature of man-woman love.

The author makes clear that any observations on the topics he addresses are culture-bound, and that monogamy is not the human norm. He is also assiduous in his several disclaimers regarding his evidence and the generalizations he draws. He takes an analytic attitude toward his subject matter, one that avoids blame, dismissive stereotyping, and voyeurism. He seeks to specify the unconscious nature of the motivation of the parties to the syndrome.

Tuch finds single woman–married man relationships to be longstanding and without psychological-mindedness in the participants. They do not lead to marriage but instead often turn ugly. He finds the single woman to be seeking a dangerous, clandestine relationship, usually motivated by unrequited oedipal love. The married man is looking for good sex. The wife is often masochistic. These admittedly simplistic descriptions are elaborated with more complex typologies and with an appreciation of individual differences.

Tuch begins each chapter with a pointed quotation from Shakespeare. The book is replete with examples that read more like short stories than stodgy science or scholarship, and literary sources are amply cited. This is a style that puts Tuch in the good company of the founder of psychoanalysis. The book concludes with a relevant poem on aspects of mature love by writer/ psychoanalyst Judith Viorst.

This book seems aimed at both professional and popular audiences. Its second chapter, from the single woman's perspective, is entirely about Monica Lewinsky and Bill Clinton and is based solely on the public record developed by Kenneth Starr and Lewinsky biographer Kenneth Morton. The rehash of what was for too long fodder for the media adds nothing for a professional reader, except that Tuch claims that the story supports his thesis. For the lay reader, the accounting is tendentious and, by now, tedious. That Tuch leads with this narrative as his first major piece of evidence is telling.

Most of the remainder of Tuch's exemplary stories are from non-psychoanalytic sources and do not go beyond phenomenological description. Included are lay treatises, social psychology studies (and even a physiological study) of dubious merit, and speculative works whose limitations are acknowledged. Few are from any clinical setting, and fewer still are from his own practice. Clinical examples are given very few pages, while nonclinical ones are extensively described. From an evidentiary perspective, the book makes large claims, despite its disclaimers. Tuch in fact retreats from his thesis in the face of his own evidence, finally calling the "syndrome" merely a tentative hypothesis. Thus he dashes the hope engendered by his title and initial assertions.

Along the way, Tuch provides occasional interesting psychodynamic speculation, as well as some trenchant observations on the more general topics of gender and love. For the psychoanalytic reader there is a thoughtful delineation and critique of Kernberg's views on mature love. On the matter of treatment implications, Tuch articulates his reluctance to present anything specific and, but only as a concession, briefly summarizes the basic elements of the psychoanalytic attitude. A substantial syndrome would likely have treatment implications beyond analytic attitude. In his concluding essay, which though not about his thesis turns out to be the best chapter of the book, Tuch questions his own presumptuousness in discussing the nature of love.

The author asks himself why this work is a book rather than a journal article. His answer is not satisfactory. A refereed journal article posing a hypothetical syndrome and offering some psychodynamic speculation, subject to further study, would likely have served scholarly purposes better. Tuch's interesting views on related larger topics might be more appealing had they been subjected to peer review. Further, it would have been useful to read the author's theoretical ideas on the interpersonal (as against the intrapsychic) dimensions of the hypothesized syndrome, a promise unfulfilled in the text.

Stephen K. Firestein
Termination in Psychoanalysis and Psychotherapy (Revised Edition)
Madison, CT: International Universities Press, 2001
Psychologist Psychoanalyst 22, No. 4 (2002), pp. 36–37

Beginnings and endings have fascinated people well before the advent of psychoanalysis. Anthropologists have studied creation myths for a century, while dramatists have focused on life's endings for millennia. Psychoanalysis began with questions about origins, causality; outcome, goals, aims, teleology, were thought better left to philosophy. Freud (1914b) offered recommendations on the technique for beginning a treatment and promised a discussion on its ending. When he came at last to write on termination (1937), his ideas were more in the domain of philosophy than of technique.

My scholarly interest in beginnings and endings (1972) predates completion of my analytic training. Twenty-five years later, from a psychoanalytic perspective and experience, I again wrote on the subject (1997). Early in this time span, Stephen K. Firestein's first edition (1978) appeared; it was the first book-length treatise on the topic. American psychoanalysis had passed its hegemonic period. Analyses were becoming longer, alternate and briefer treatments were competing, and the mainstream ego-psychological perspective of American psychoanalysis was experiencing its first challenge from within (Kohut, 1971). Firestein's text was a research report based on his study of eight analyses conducted by candidates at the treatment center of the New York Psychoanalytic Institute. The research was stimulated in part by the completion of his "own didactic analysis a year or so before" (p 1).

My analysis, while meeting training requirements, continued beyond graduation and was never considered by me "didactic." Its difficult termination phase stimulated quick purchase and reading of Firestein's book. I was left disappointed and angry. Not one of the eight cases presented seemed to have had a termination resembling my own, nor did any match my own clinical or theoretical understanding of the phase. Each was, in my view, a too-short treatment in which termination was usually analyst-led, and for reasons that seemed arbitrary at best. Decisions to terminate often seemed confounded by issues associated with the eight student analysts' completion of their own training. I dismissed the book as uninformative and I awaited further developments in the literature and in my own clinical practice.

Over time, Firestein (1978) became a routine citation in the burgeoning literature on termination, with my reaction apparently not shared by others, at least explicitly. Such routine citation seemed, in fact, to have given the book near-classic status. In my own teaching, I felt obliged to include it in the bibliography but passed it over with brief negative comment on its database.

When, 28 years later, the current revision appeared, I was again eager to read Firestein's work. No longer a new analyst, his contributions to the profession and to the literature, including additional work on this topic, were most respectable. Since he and I seemed, from my reading of his other work, to share a common contemporary Freudian frame of reference, I expected the revision would deal well both with psychotherapy terminations (promised by the new title) and with a review of the many good papers published on the subject in the intervening years.

As is my habit, I read the table of contents in advance of beginning the text. I was shocked. Pages 1-215, including the original introduction, each of the eight clinical examples, and the "substantive conclusions" chapter are identical to those pages in the original, and they even appear to be from the same galleys! What is new is a brief introduction to the new edition, an expanded reference list, and a 25-page concluding chapter (replacing the last two chapters of the original). Again I found myself disappointed and angry at what now seemed like a publisher's scam.

The book turned out to be better than I expected or recalled. The clinical descriptions that form the essential content of the book are extensive and rich. They make it clear that, even with training cases selected by narrower criteria of analyzability common to the early '70s, psychoanalytic treatment is always unpredictable and complex. A range of reactions to termination of treatment and ensuing difficulties are presented. The clinical chapters are not scholarly, nor meant to be. Citations are all but reserved for the concluding chapters. I found this a plus, allowing for engagement in the clinical matters and the theoretical matters separately. Diverse perspectives on both clinical and theoretical issues are, nonetheless, presented. Such diversity is not an innovation of the current era of theoretical pluralism. It has long been a feature of sound psychoanalytic training, and it results in highlighting the individuality of each treatment. For me this is a hallmark of the anti-normative psychoanalytic technical approach. A focus on the subjectivity of the analyst, with an emphasis on counter-transference as potential interference, is another unrecalled strength of the presentation. Some of the substantive conclusions, identical in the two editions, an admittedly modest attempt, seem consistent with current thinking, at least my own. Among these are: that there is a termination phase focusing on ending and extending beyond the cessation of formal sessions; that this phase is marked by affective intensification and, not uncommonly, acting-out; that the treatment alliance is tested and strengthened; that shorter treatment breaks are not predictive; and that there is an emotional impact on the analyst. These multiple assets combined to dissipate the disappointment and anger with which I had begun my reading.

The book, though, is hardly definitive as to the "state of the art" on its titular topic, and still wound up leaving me disappointed, if less angry than at the outset. First impressions of long ago were not completely off the mark. The eight cases presented were training cases of candidate analysts. The topic of termination was raised after from 3 ½ to 7 years, often by the analyst, and the analyst seemed to lead the process most of the time. The length of the "phase" was as often measured in weeks as months. One of the eight terminations was forced by the analyst's relocation; two seemed clear treatment failures. All were close in time to the analyst's own termination, noted (in the first edition) as a high-risk factor for countertransference interference. While this latter situation is unavoidable at one time for every analyst, a researcher should not consider it exemplary. In other words, the database for termination research was seriously compromised.

Despite the limitations of the data, the non-clinical chapters in both the first and the current editions are surprisingly valuable. In fact, the two excised chapters, one on methodology and one a literature review, might well have been profitably included, with some extension. As to methodology, psychologist-psychoanalysts would likely raise different questions than did Firestein. Given the pioneering nature of this project, his questions and answers are, nonetheless, useful. The literature review (itself adapted from a 1974 article) dealt with criteria, technique, special occurrences and post-termination developments in a way not as well covered in Firestein's new concluding chapter.

External factors impacting termination, while acknowledged, are given short shrift. Unpredictable factors influence the course of every analysis and its termination. Providing for optimal termination in their face seems to me a critical dilemma to be addressed.

Firestein's actual revision, the new concluding chapter bearing the book's new title, aims to extend his early study from psychoanalytic to psychotherapeutic terminations, psychotherapy as defined by Wolberg (1954) and by Fromm-Reichmann (1950). Firestein finds many considerations in common and he highlights some differences. Matters of technique and risks from countertransference reactions are emphasized. This chapter, for me, was sketchy and something of a teaser; much more could have been said about each of the important topics raised.

This book is closer to a re-issue than a revision. Its strength lies less in the treatment of its stated topic than in the presentation of rich clinical psychoanalytic material, and in the broaching of multiple considerations related to the topic. I had hoped, perhaps as naively as I did when I bought the original, for a definitive text. There may never be a definitive text on any psychoanalytic topic. Perhaps the best we can do is to continue to discuss the several facets of important issues, gaining incremental insight as we go. This formulation may parallel one for psychoanalytic treatment itself. I was especially disappointed, though, that Firestein chose to make his concluding statements on the arbitrariness of termination. While I would not disagree with them in substance, such an ending leaves a false impression. Termination work in any individual treatment can be much better than arbitrary. Study of the now fulsome literature when combined with a sensitive accounting for everyone's unique circumstances can result in successful terminations in both psychoanalysis and psychotherapy. In the end, what does this book contribute? A useful increment, a set of considerations, a wish to know more. I prefer the original, with its now excised chapters, to the revision, while hoping for more papers on the subject from the author.

David Shapiro
Dynamics of Character: Self-regulation in Psychopathology
Basic Books, 2000
Psychologist Psychoanalyst 23, No. 2 (2003), pp. 46–47

A potent mix of ideas attracted many of us to psychoanalytic psychology in the 1950s and 1960s. Psychology had evolved as an attempt to "scientize" the philosophical problems of action, knowledge, and evil; volition, thought, and feeling were its subject matter. Mainstream American psychology had, ironically, come to be dominated by a radical focus on action (behaviorism) that negated volition while dismissing unobservable thoughts and feelings. Its clinical psychology branch, however, addressed the problem of evil, with psychoanalytic ideas comprising the primary paradigm.

Psychoanalytic practice was then a virtual medical monopoly in the United States, but its ideas were not to be contained by a medical model. Important scholars in psychology like Jerome Bruner had come under the influence of psychoanalytic thought; psychoanalytic psychologist David Rapaport and his students were organizing ego psychological propositions so as to subject them to empirical study. Psychiatry, led by psychoanalysts, was attempting to meld psychodynamic thinking with its more traditional psychiatric nosology and treatments. For those of us inclined to pursue it, there was a developing and vital psychoanalytic psychology, allied neither with a sterile behaviorism nor with medical psychiatry.

One young contributor to this psychoanalytic psychology was David Shapiro. In his classic 1965 treatise, *Neurotic Styles,* he impressed us with gripping clinical descriptions and penetrating thought. He made it clear that understanding "styles" need not result in diagnosis-driven treatment. He emphasized the uniqueness of each therapy patient as central in any clinical situation. Commonalities and differences among and between styles could be discerned though, with the insights gained providing helpful things to say to our patients. Although not associated with any particular school of psychoanalysis, Shapiro's first book was must reading for any serious would-be clinician at the time, and to my mind still is.

For nearly four decades, Shapiro has continued to work the soil he first furrowed. Still an individualistic thinker (with an academic position on one coast or another), he has remained true to his initial interests. In his current offering, he presents the boldest extension of his thinking to date. He compares neuroses

147

and psychoses in what becomes an impressive challenge to the current trend to see the latter as solely a set of biological conditions; and he does so by maintaining his long-time focus on volition, or (in his preferred terms) decision-making, self-regulation, responsibility, and agency.

For Shapiro, "defensive self-estrangement" marks all forms of psychopathology. Self-deception and lack of planning are its important elements. Symptoms are not specifically related to trauma or to biology; instead they manifest a whole character. Self-estrangement is exhibited in the different forms of passive-reactive, rigid, and driven character types, each with varieties. Anxiety-laden situations do not provoke defense; instead, defense results as character exaggerates trivial situations. Shapiro presents a theory of character development in which affects trigger action only for the infant. As development ensues, conscious intention and will power evolve while more mature and complex motives provide context for responding to immediate situations. Defenses are part of character rather than mechanisms employed by it. Actions emerge from choice and responsibility, as well as from conflict and anxiety. Adults do not passively act out biological programs or family dynamics; nor do they regress. Instead they act adaptively or defensively, sometimes using pre-volitional modes. In more severe disturbances, defenses are extended and exaggerated, rather than broken down. Loss of reality sense, blurring of self-object differentiation, degradation of affective experience, and limitation of volitional direction are all characteristic of neurotic as well as psychotic conditions.

In what amounts to a major reformulation of several tenets of current theory, Shapiro presents a holistic, humanistic perspective on character pathology and the workings of the mind. He does not merely assert alternate positions. His views are supported by numerous examples from descriptive psychiatry and clinical wisdom, by reference to ideas derived from both psychoanalytic and psychological thought and empirical study, and by refined argumentation. He neither minimizes nor avoids the complexity of the ideas he discusses, and he acknowledges the incompleteness of both his formulations and the current understanding of psychopathology, especially psychosis.

Shapiro's reformulation is specifically directed at (and within) modern conflict theory. He does not address relational theories, object relations approaches, self-psychology, or other models extant in today's psychoanalytic pluralism. Nor does he address matters of technique except by asserting the principle that an incorrect message is given when models not based on "agency" guide our thinking. Shapiro does not deal with current "hot topics" in psychoanalytic psychology: two-person psychology, self-disclosure, gender issues, social issues, therapeutic outcome, or empirical validation. His work evokes (for me) the fundamental and still exciting issues of the 1950s and 1960s.

Shapiro's work is unusual also for its emphasis on two matters commonly overlooked by psychoanalytic theory: action and consciousness. Behaviorism devoted itself to the study of action only. Psychoanalysis emphasizes internal psychological events prior to action. Shapiro notes his dissatisfactions with Schafer's earlier attempt (1976) at developing an "action language" to emphasize agency but finds the even earlier psychoanalytic views of Hellmuth Kaiser (1955) on responsibility to be consistent with his own. Cognitivism, American psychology's current paradigm, devotes itself to conscious (usually rational) experience. For many psychoanalysts, "the unconscious" is the core of psychoanalysis, despite more modern and now long-standing structural theory. Action and consciousness are then seen as preoccupations of an anti-psychoanalytic American psychology. Shapiro attempts to reorient psychoanalytic psychology by giving equal respect to the three problems central to the original evolution of psychology from philosophy.

Shapiro's bibliography may seem timeworn or unfamiliar to contemporary readers, while warming the hearts of those of us still taken with the ideas of mid-century psychoanalytic psychology. 75 of his 89 citations predate 1990. They include early psychoanalysts like Abraham, H. Deutsch, Erikson, Fenichel, the Freuds, Guntrip, Nunberg, Rapaport, and Waelder. Inspiration from psychiatry comes from Andras Angyal, Arieti, Bleuler, Freeman, Sechehaye, and Sullivan. Lewin, Piaget, Werner, and Kurt Goldstein are psychologists cited. A more contemporary source is Louis Sass, whose notion of "double bookkeeping," a clinical description of pathological thought, provides Shapiro with a helpful means of understanding schizophrenia. An unfortunate anachronism is Shapiro's use of the male pronoun for all patients but hysterics, whom he refers to as female.

Some will find this an old-fashioned book; I find it a worthy new look at old problems yet unresolved. Some will find it narrow, focusing on complex issues through the single lens of agency; I find its ideas to be wide-ranging and evocative of Hartmann's ambition that psychoanalysis be a general psychology. It is a small book (160 pages of text) but it is not a quick or easy read. It is all meat and sometimes tough going. Shapiro's clinical descriptions amply justify the price of admission; his theoretical contributions will reward the effort required to study them.

Joseph Newirth
Between Emotion and Cognition: The Generative Unconscious
NY: Other Press, 2003
pp xviii + 255
Psychologist Psychoanalyst 24, No. 2 (2004), pp. 37–38

Pluralism is the watchword of the day in psychoanalysis. The final issue of the 2003 volume of *the Journal of the American Psychoanalytic Association,* a supplement addressing psychoanalytic politics, honors outgoing editor Arnold Richards. His own target paper on psychoanalytic discourse is subtitled "a plea for a measure of humility." The issue includes authors whose work would not likely have appeared in *JAPA* before Dr. Richards's decade-long editorial tenure. Despite Richards's plea, partisanship trumps humility in several of the compiled papers. Even the postscript essay on the history of Argentine psychoanalysis ascribes a political rationale to rejection of the North American ego psychological model. These essays provided a backdrop for this review.

Between Cognition and Emotion is a contribution to the comparative theory of technique. Joseph Newirth, director of the postdoctoral programs in psychoanalysis and psychotherapy at Adelphi University, has been in practice for over a quarter century. He offers here a new integration of what he sees as evolving psychoanalytic theory. He calls his integration neo-Kleinian. It attempts to transcend what he perceives as shortcomings of traditional ego psychology, and to go beyond the insights of self-psychology and the relational turn. Beside those of Klein, the writings of Winnicott, Bion, Lacan and Matte Blanco most inspire his new perspective, one that postulates a "generative unconscious" to help in understanding poetry, art, love, and friendship as well as clinical work, and to turn on its head Freud's own pre-structural goal of making the unconscious conscious.

Newirth's model focuses on subjectivity and the subject, as distinct from ego or self, and on meaning instead of conflict. He favors a post-modern, two-person approach to the treatment of apparently functional individuals whose problems center on feelings of being deadened or disconnected. The culture of narcissism (Lasch, 1978) suggests to Newirth that this "hollow man" typifies the psychopathology of our time, replacing "guilty man" and "tragic man," Freud's and Kohut's respective patient populations.

In a scholarly, thoughtful, and astute presentation, and with clinical examples from his practice and supervision, Newirth demonstrates the refinement and utility of his approach. He speaks to the development of symbolism and its failures. He incorporates Lacanian views on language and its contribution to meaning. He sees pathology as a paranoid expression of a shameful reality experience, and as an externalization of hatred. He postulates development from omnipotence to subjectivity and resulting in the ability to sustain illusion. Technical recommendations include welcoming paradox and dialectic, addressing power issues to approach complementary relations, and the use of the transitional states of reverie, play, and enactment as treatment modalities.

Newirth is especially clear in his articulation of Winnicott's contributions to technique, and in the description and use of the ideas of Matte Blanco. This book is an excellent example of a seasoned clinician describing his own mature thinking about the clinical psychoanalytic enterprise, and making suggestions regarding newer, helpful ways for others to think about their patients, particularly the deadened and disconnected.

Why, then, would I begin this review with reference to psychoanalytic politics and humility of discourse? I found Newirth's comparisons to be unfairly directed at an outdated caricature of my own traditional training and work. He seemed gentler with the interpersonalists (among which he includes self-psychologists, intersubjective analysts, and those of the relational school), whose approaches he generally supports and tries to extend. Perhaps reviewers from these camps would also find him unfair. My formal training, completed over thirty years ago, was suffused with the humanizing influences of Stone and Loewald. Winnicott's contributions and those of Guntrip and Balint were well appreciated. Kohut's new theory was respectfully read, and his insights taken seriously. Freudian analysts have long viewed Freud's own technical recommendations to be more concerned with taboos than with affirmative methodology, and have modified accordingly the rigid techniques of the first generations of analysts. We approach analysands with respect; we aim to enhance their personal agency, and to foster their creativity and individualism. From the earliest days, Freudians have eschewed authority as suggestion, and have used our own inner experiences (the analyzing instrument) to achieve understanding, not merely to avoid counter-transference interference. Our work has been enhanced further by more recent theoretical challenges calling for closer scrutiny of authority issues and countertransference, and by feminist critiques.

Newirth conveys the not uncommon triumphalist attitude that I find to be a weakness of several new theorists: giving an impression that their ideas had already supplanted prior theory instead of, more humbly, attempting to build on it. It is as if he were to say, "The traditional approach, whether called ego psychology or modern conflict theory, has been replaced by several post-modern, two-person theories, and my proposed revision improves upon and replaces these." Freud saw himself as a conquistador; would-be successors adopt this posture, however implicitly, at their own risk.

One troubling technical recommendation is Newirth's proposal for analytic spontaneity in response to difficult clinical situations. I wonder how spontaneity can be taught. All analysts rely on integrated unconscious resonance with the affects and actions of analysands. The "not-neo" Kleinians considered these resonances all to be projective identifications. What is the test? In one detailed clinical example, Newirth describes what became the ritual acceptance of a gift of a piece of doughnut from a patient. Winnicott is said to have taken tea regularly with his patients. Like Winnicott, neither Newirth nor his patient brought this event into verbal discourse, but it was used by Newirth to help explain treatment gain. *Post hoc* explanations can be offered by any of us; they no longer provide effective argumentation. No analyst analyses everything. I might have failed either by biting or refusing the doughnut, but to offer non-discussion of a treatment event as exemplary is neither consistent with a talking cure nor with an accountable two-person psychology. Newirth might reject my view as mere traditional rationalism. I will stand with Fenichel (1941) in defining psychoanalysis as a necessarily rational study of human irrationality.

Along with many other post-modern, two-person theorists, Newirth calls for optimistic, affirmative language not focusing on patient deficits. His reliance on Klein's paranoid-schizoid and depressive terminology as central to his own formulation is both inconsistent with that goal, and unlikely to succeed in influencing a standard discourse. (For an important effort to introduce a neo-Kleinian perspective to American psychoanalysis, see Schafer, 1995).

Readers of this publication may be especially prone to buy into what I see as triumphalism. Relational theorists hold sway in Division 39. Newirth, by accepting many of their basic premises, takes pains not to offend them. Psychoanalytic discourse is, however, much more diverse than Division 39's seems to be. It is only in the past decade that the American Psychoanalytic Association has come to see its politics of exclusion as harmful to both theory and practice, and to embrace the pluralism of American and international psychoanalysis. It would be a mistake of equal proportion for Division 39 to repeat the insular pre-lawsuit history of "the American."

This book is recommended. Many of Newirth's critiques and syntheses are both detailed and helpful. I have emphasized what I see as shortcomings because I do not think we are close to a new paradigm in psychoanalysis. Instead, with Rangell (1988), I believe we have a total composite theory: unsettled, with many rough edges and lots of problems, nowhere near final. Newirth's integrative attempt is a welcome addition to the discourse. I join Richards in hoping we can debate psychoanalytic ideas with greater humility on all sides.

Laura Heims Tessman
The Analyst's Analyst Within
Hillsdale, NJ: The Analytic Press, 2003
viii + 363
Journal of the American Psychoanalytic Association 52,
No.4 (2004), pp. 1269–1273

This book offers even more than its engaging title promises. It addresses a central feature of what is therapeutic about psychoanalysis, and how the process may work. Questions about therapeutic action have generated considerable discourse, yet consensus remains elusive. Insight theory is challenged by reference to the power of the analytic object relationship. Interpretation competes as explanation with interactional experience. In a recent contribution, Gabbard and Westen (2003) propose a systematic view that postulates *actions* rather than a singular action.

Laura Heims Tessman, in a work both ambitious and modest, addresses several questions related to therapeutic action. Her ambition is demonstrated by a research model appropriate both to the complexity of psychoanalytic process and to its essential subjectivity. Her modesty is shown by explicit acknowledgement of the limitations of subjectivity, especially of the particular subjects of this study, as well as by her goal of raising illuminating questions rather than trying, prematurely, to test hypotheses.

Tessman studied a specific facet of psychoanalytic action: the internalized effect of analyst on analysand following termination of treatment. Her subject "participants" were themselves analysts, who had of course been analysands. An open-ended interview format focused on participants' structured and free reflections. Tessman's aim, as her title suggests, was to understand how the analyst's own analyst continues to function *within* the mind of that analyst.

The author's basic assumption is that conscious and unconscious memories of the analyst have important effects in the post-termination life of any former analysand, that is, that the internalized therapeutic object relationship is of central importance in analytic action. The 34 volunteer analysts recruited as participants (30 of them members of the Boston Psychoanalytic Society, 11 of them now also training analysts) had 64 analyses among them. Tessman met individually with participants for from two to eight hours, recording responses to questions submitted in advance, as well as spontaneous narrative.

Much of the text is devoted to selected transcripts of these responses. These transcripts are highly engaging for an analyst reader. Memories of one's own analysis are immediately and continually aroused in response to the recollections and reflections of the participant colleagues. These memories interact with the text to produce strong affective reactions. I found myself cheering apparently good and condemning apparently bad work, and alternately elated and rueful about my own internal analyst. This book is unusually powerful in the emotions it evokes.

The transcript data are initially organized according to the participants' judgments of whether an analysis was "deeply satisfying," "moderately satisfying," or "highly dissatisfying." Analyses are then categorized by the gender-pairings of analyst and analysand and by the decade during which the treatment took place. Gender and decade breakdowns are presented in a table for statistical perusal. Transcript excerpts are presented for their relevance to the issues (raised by the pre-submitted questions) of termination, mourning, leave-taking, self-analysis, and post-termination contact (commonplace for this subject population). Finally, Tessman offers refined additional questions showing appreciation for the complexity of the analytic process.

Dissatisfying analyses were easiest to describe. Tessman places them into four categories: a hostile atmosphere in which the analysand felt blamed; an intrusive agenda on the part of the analyst; a detached analyst; and specific analyst vulnerabilities. The key to the nature of satisfaction seems to lie in the perceived communication of the analyst, such perception evolving over the course of treatment. The most striking findings were related to prominent dissatisfaction during the 1965-1975 decade, the time during which the Boston Institute was itself splitting, and to male-male pairings, especially in that decade. Tessman relates these findings to the authoritarian attitudes of the era, and to the stereotyped male roles and homophobia seemingly promoted by some male analysts. Training analyses that were "reporting" were uniformly dissatisfying (this procedure only being dropped officially by the Boston Institute in 1990), as were terminations that were either analyst-led or influenced by Institute guidelines.

The more satisfying analyses involved cross-gender matches and they tended to occur during more recent decades. The analysts described in these treatments seemed of two varieties: assertive or resonant-receptive. Tessman attributes greater satisfaction to a general shift in theory from one-person to two-person psychology, and to a more egalitarian attitude. Theories of attachment, infant study, and comparative psychology contribute to Tessman's explanation of her findings, as does current research on interactive aspects of psychoanalytic treatment.

Tessman believes that an analyst's theory of action itself affects outcome. Her two-person emphasis is evident throughout and is woven into her concluding reflections. Her debt to Loewald is clearly articulated. Her theoretical leanings are not, however, polemical; her discussion fits as easily with Rangell's total composite theory as with the relational approach she seems to favor.

The author is diligent in noting limitations of generalizability and is explicit about outcomes being most attributable to the particularities of each analytic couple. The highly individualized nature of psychoanalytic treatment is underscored by scrutiny of six instances of a common analyst for two participants and, more often, of different analysts for the same participants. Tessman's only serious lapse of data description is that, despite stating proper cautions, she presents a simple statistic (percent) when the numbers of subjects per cell is never more than seven. Describing six of seven treatments as 86% can be misleading.

The transcripts also make clear that, satisfaction notwithstanding, an abstract ideal complete analysis is nowhere to be found. That all issues would be analyzed, irrespective of the analyst's gender, is refuted. No woman participant and few men recall erotic transferences with female analysts; nor were paternal transferences with female analysts remembered. Non-specific factors (listening and empathy), and non-neutral modeling are credited by participants as therapeutic more often than is interpretation of content.

Tessman's work raises important issues in addition to that of analytic action. Evaluation of psychoanalytic results may be even more problematic than attempts to understand action. In this study, while conscious self-report and recollection, years and decades later, may be sound measures of satisfaction, recall may be less telling as explanation, or than ideas that might address unconscious processes. My own analysis, a deeply satisfying and transformational experience, involved a male-male gender pair and took place largely during the decade Tessman found to be least productive of satisfaction, and my own responses to her questions include several in which I am at odds with the approach of my analyst. Global conscious satisfaction may or may not be more valid than specific memories brought to mind, and neither conscious satisfaction nor memories would, themselves, satisfy validity criteria.

It should not surprise us that analysands, even in training analyses, desire relational gratification, and respond to it or to its absence. What may be surprising, and it is not apparent until near the end of the book, is that the participants all sound like reasonably well-analyzed people, independent of their level of satisfaction and of the treatment limitations described (including some analyses of rather short duration). Although transcripts cannot convey all dimensions of analytic success, they provide some evidence. One way analyses are judged by those outside the analytic pair is by whether an individual "sounds like" an open, flexible, reflective person. Participants in this study all sound "analyzed." Tessman discusses resilience in analysands. It may be that where an analysand begins treatment is as important to its outcome as the recalled characteristics of the analyst.

If accurate, my impression of the uniformly successful outcomes may have implications for yet another important issue raised by this work, the place of the personal analysis in our training model. While Tessman might have us pay more attention to the training analysis, it is equally plausible to recommend greater attention to supervision and curriculum, since training analyses are most difficult to influence. Assessment of "analyzability" (yet another knotty problem) might also compete for designation as the most important factor in analytic outcome.

Tessman's approach, her findings and her discussion, each of interest on their face, support her relational orientation. In addition, they raise important questions about basic aspects of the psychoanalytic enterprise at this point in its history. Tessman's work also provides one of too few sound research paradigms for clinical psychoanalysis. This book is highly recommended.

Neville Symington
Psychoanalysis as Science *and* Religion!
The Blind Man Sees: Freud's Awakening and Other Essays
London: Karnac, 2004
x + 226 pp, $35.99 paperback
PsycCRITIQUES 50, No.4 (2005)

American psychology offered to its mid-twentieth century neophytes a great opportunity to bring a scientific perspective to philosophy's big questions: Mind-Body, Free Will-Determinism, Good-Evil. Operational definitions, quantification, and empirical testing by often ingenious methodologies promised progress akin to that in the physical sciences. A sterile Skinnerianism soon brought disappointment to those committed to a humanist perspective and its related social issues, and to others who were intrigued by psychoanalytic ideas. Isidor Chein (1972) provided a cogent attempt to integrate scientific and humanistic psychology. Psychoanalysis, defending against attacks on its own scientific standing, adopted, in the United States, a medical professional model.

For millennia, religious thinking had taken the big questions under its umbrella. Conflict between religion and science had, itself, become a critical schism in the quest for knowledge. Skinner eschewed religious thinking as adamantly as did Freud. Separate yet interacting developments in religion, psychology and psychoanalysis have led to an even more complex state of affairs today. Religious practice attracts new adherents while conflict alternates with dialogue among denominations. Psychology, with its multiplication of specialized divisions, asks itself if there remains a common set of principles. Psychoanalysis sees the flourishing of diverse schools of thought, competing over both theory and practice. Are any unifying visions on the horizon?

Neville Symington is a prominent and prolific Australian psychoanalyst, trained in England and, for over 30 years, a leader in the "British Independent" tradition. He came to psychoanalysis after being educated in philosophy and theology. His writing has dealt with the big questions. *The Blind Man Sees: Freud's Awakening and other Essays,* includes papers from 1975 until the present. With his specific thesis that psychoanalysis is both a science and a religion, he offers a comprehensive vision. Psychoanalysts, scientists and religious people alike, however, may well be put off by his arguments.

In the absence of data, quantification and hypothesis testing, these papers may not seem like psychology to Americans. While British Independent thinking has become familiar to them, psychoanalysts have long taken umbrage at being classified with religion, and they may find Symington's philosophical and theological approach alienating. Along with his redefinition of spirituality in exclusively rational and emotional terms, Symington treats "revealed" religion as psychopathological, a position sure to offend believers.

Symington's definitions are unusual. Science is systematic and orderly thinking about a determinate subject matter (p. x, in keeping with Collingwood, 1969). Religion is an interpersonal and spiritual rationale for loving others (p. ix; Chap. 13). Psychoanalysis has at its center Freud's dynamic unconscious, but its major concerns relate to good and evil as inner states (p. 136). From these premises, several essays elaborate different but convergent lines of thinking.

Freud's awakening examines stages of development in religious leaders (e.g., Buddha, Saint Paul) and the development of their religious institutions. Later chapters criticize inconsistencies in Freud's thinking, providing as corrective a more prominent role to the mental agency of conscience. The amorality of the Freudian unconscious is challenged. For Symington, the only reason for repression is to destroy knowledge that highlights immorality. Sounding quite post-modern, Symington considers Freudian "reality" (psychic reality) to be a value judgment. Understanding is a creative act, assisted by the removal of repression. Psychoanalysis should concern itself with how people live, behave correctly, do right, and find fulfillment, purpose and meaning.

Although Symington describes the psychoanalytic treatment process, this is not a book about technique. His interesting clinical vignettes are used in support of ideas, not as specific recommendations for practice. Symington, like Freud, extends his ideas to the social realm. His concluding essays are ones of cultural analysis and criticism; he considers their topics as examples of religious failure. These essays deal with freedom, curiosity and imagination. The last one treats antisemitism as an example of social narcissism. Symington is also critical of American psychoanalytic ego psychology and does not address matters of central concern to newer American psychoanalytic schools such as self psychology (see Kohut, 1977) and relationalism (see Aron, 1996).

The very nature of the Freudian unconscious is actively and dynamically to resist awareness. Symington has no expectation that his views will be readily acceptable. An admired model for him is the philosopher Giambattista Vico, whose ideas achieved only posthumous appreciation (see Berlin, 1980). However, these essays, despite (or perhaps because of) their unusual assertions, have much to offer to an open-minded reader.

Traditional religionists will find understanding and appreciation of Western and non-Western religious contributions to human welfare. Symington does not reject religious teachings, only the institutional requirement that they be taken on authority rather than through personal, existential reflection. Psychologists will find Symington's ideas consistent with the recent emphasis on positive psychology, dealing with topics like love, imagination, curiosity and resilience. He takes Freud to task for defining the homeostatic pleasure-unpleasure principle as the foundation of human motivation.

The pluralism evident in psychoanalytic thinking today has gone far beyond the "third ear" suggested by Reik (1948). Newer psychoanalytic schools have given clinicians additional dimensions to their listening stances to help them understand those who seek assistance. Whether Symington's is an eighth or a twelfth ear, it should be a welcome one. His career-long study of the problem of evil is a theoretical challenge. It can also be a useful clinical tool, providing language to which some patients will respond.

In his shortest chapter (14), Symington offers a concise statement of the aim and process of psychoanalytic treatment (pp. 162-163). Few analysts would disagree; non-analysts may gain in comprehension of this alternate psychology. Although this is a compilation of essays written over decades and lacking explicit editorial integration, Symington's conversational writing style and his non-temporal organization of chapters lead to a book with structural integrity. The effort to overcome his unfamiliar approach and potentially alienating ideas will reward those still interested in the big questions of philosophy and those whose own thinking continues to allow for the openness to ideas that should always characterize psychology and psychoanalysis.

Dismissing the Past: Not Unique to Gen-X
Psychoanalytic Psychology 22, No.3 (2005), pp. 445–446

"Nobrow," Carlo Strenger's (2004) paper examining cultural discontinuity and identity formation in Gen-Xers, is a strongly written essay with a vivid clinical example. It makes the case that connection to the past has less psychic reality for this sociological cohort than for its forbears. Since connecting with one's personal history has been considered central to psychoanalysis, a new dilemma is presented for clinicians. Strenger suggests a therapeutic technique more sensitive to current social and cultural upheaval.

While Strenger's sociological scholarship is interesting and his clinical narrative engaging and almost compelling, reservations are in order. Strenger recognizes that his work with gifted Gen-Xers is "not statistically relevant" (p. 514), but takes it anyway to corroborate his thesis. His case example—Ben, a twenty-seven-year-old "star," unschooled but nearing millionaire status in start-up ventures whose product his analyst does not understand—is hardly typical of his generation. The media hype lionizing such individuals is at least as likely a blip as a historical trend (as was the dot-com economic bubble).

For psychoanalytic psychologists, it is even more important to question the utility of Strenger's clinical method. A face-to-face therapy, in which the analyst's more successful interventions are described as "asides . . . , little pieces of wisdom of Life 101" (p. 507), and include joining in a decision for geographic relocation (thereby ending treatment after a year and a half), seems more like an example of supportive therapy than a treatment promoting an exploratory psychoanalytic process.

The central intervention described by Strenger, in which, at long last, he expresses his frustration about his patient's dismissive and rude behavior and thereby alters the nature of the work, seems to be offered as innovative technique. In fact, Strenger's extended passivity in the face of his patient's resistance is a caricature of psychoanalytic posture. The use of evoked feelings, whether called countertransference or not, has been central to clinical technique for several decades, and not limited to the British Kleinian tradition. Confrontation itself is a basic technical intervention. When mainstream analysts joined Ferenczi (1950) in rejecting some specific approaches of his active technique, the standard model developed an expectant stance, not to be misunderstood as a passive one.

I do not mean to question Strenger's clinical work with his patient. It may have been the best possible therapy under circumstances more fully known to the treating analyst than to his readers. The work as presented, however, is neither innovative nor exemplary, and it seems a stretch to use it to promote a reorientation of clinical theory.

What seems most cogent to Strenger about his patient is Ben's disconnection with his personal history. Rather than being specific to Gen-X, such dissociation is a common phenomenon in psychoanalytic treatment, generally understandable as transference. Likewise, a sense of fraudulence (Ben's presenting and continuing symptom) and exceptionality are topics each with a rich heritage in the psychoanalytic literature. To dismiss our own intellectual and professional history in favor of an ephemeral social present is a sad and inadequate response to patients who dismiss their own and our common history.

Toward a Balanced Consideration of Telephone Analysis
The Round Robin 20, No. 3 (2005), p. 9

Batya Monder (*Round Robin* 20, 2005) errs when, in her recent editorial, she requires those who would write about telephone analysis in these pages to have experience with that modification of the setting. Theory development does not ask that we engage in Ferenczi's mutual analysis to comment on it, nor does it call for us to practice relational self-disclosure to critique its technical utility. Arlene Kramer Richards (*Round Robin* 20, 2005) is unnecessarily polemical in decrying those who might differ with her views as bureaucrats relying solely on tradition.

Good analysts are always concerned for the well-being of their patients. In my view, sound practice is evident in each of the clinical examples presented by the four telephone treatment advocates. Stanley J. Coen (*Round Robin* 20, 2005) judiciously considers indications for telephone sessions, and Stanley Moldawsky (*Round Robin* 20, 2005) uses his study group to assist him to evaluate both process and countertransference.

There is no ideal psychoanalysis, but there are better and lesser conditions for its success. Practice routinely varies to meet special circumstances of both analysand and analyst. Most would agree that telephone analysis is better than no treatment, and may also be better than available alternatives. Coen and Moldawsky acknowledge, though, that it may not be better than in-person analysis.

Richards recommends telephone analysis for those with "major mental illness." Her examples extend beyond that category to include telephone analysis as a regular option, including training analyses. One of the problems in our field is that exceptional approaches creatively applied by experienced analysts tend, in discourse, to become overly generalized. Promotion of a more traditional psychoanalytic process may thereby be discouraged or even disparaged. Interpretation of transference resistances, critically important for many analysts, may be given short shrift.

Variations of technique must be open to balanced discussion. Telephone treatment is no longer a taboo topic. Training institutes may, however, legitimately expect candidates to conduct their few supervised treatments in a near-standard manner without being considered unfriendly to their trainees.

A skeptical view of innovation should not be dismissed as stodginess. It is an essential component of a scientific attitude. Space permitted to letters is hardly adequate to fairly evaluate the Round Robin telephone analysis issue.

Rangell, L.
My Life in Theory
(NY: Other Press, 2004).
Psychologist Psychoanalyst 25, No. 2 (2005), pp. 42–43

Leo Rangell should need no introduction to a psychoanalytic readership. But because this book—a professional memoir—acknowledges that the "mainstream" is no longer main, and because many readers of this newsletter may not even be in his stream, perhaps he does. Rangell is only the fourth person to be named Honorary President of the 95-year old International Psychoanalytical Association (IPA), following Ernest Jones, Heinz Hartmann and Anna Freud. He and the late Merton Gill (separately at the same watershed symposium) provided overlapping statements of the psychoanalytic method of treatment (1954). For over half a century, their formulations have defined "standard technique." Rangell's contributions include 450 papers and 7 books. He was twice president of the American Psychoanalytic Association (1961-62, 1966-67) and served two consecutive terms as IPA president (1969-73). He coined the phrase "total composite theory," and is the leading advocate for that paradigm. Among other things, this book is an argument against eclecticism and pluralism, and in favor of a "unitary psychoanalysis."

Total composite theory rests on the premise that recurrent theoretical divergences result from misguided attempts at creating replacement systems overemphasizing an important element while neglecting or dismissing others. Such *pars pro toto* thinking, abetted by group psychopathology in response to charismatic leadership, has generated several new psychoanalytic theories. Earlier in the psychoanalytic century, schism (e.g., Jung, Adler) and exclusion (e.g., Reich, Horney) were common. More recently, eclecticism and pluralism keep divergent groups under a common administrative umbrella. Rangell sees this internal incoherence of theory and practice playing a major role in the diminished standing of psychoanalysis as an intellectual discipline, with public confusion and low confidence as sad results.

Alternatively, total composite theory is open to inquiry, inclusion and change, but newer discoveries neither displace valid older ones nor do they make for exaggerated corrections. Over time, innovations achieve standing in the composite, with challenged concepts becoming fine-tuned or dismissed. Applying Freud's notion of "complementary series" to several of the dichotomies that led to splits (e.g., drive–object relations, oedipal–preoedipal, transference–reconstruction, historical truth–narrative truth, authority–egalitarianism), Rangell proposes "both–and" as an antidote to "either–or." He provides numerous examples to illustrate his "both–and" solution.

Full disclosure is in order. I have been an adherent of Rangell's outlook from my training days (1968-73), and my own thinking, teaching and writing have been strongly influenced by his. When I met him for the first time in the 1990s, I told him he was "my favorite analyst I hadn't met." When I volunteered for this review, I had little doubt I would enjoy the book and favor its approach. While I have some reservations and will not simply applaud, my anticipation was accurate, or perhaps self-fulfilling.

Rangell aims in this memoir to supplement his scientific record. His choice of title, My Life in Theory, is especially welcome now, when Darwinism is attacked as "merely a theory" and when therapists may claim to be good clinicians while denigrating or even dismissing theory. While warmth, intuition, and tact are necessary components of good therapy, they are not sufficient. Rangell shows how theory, a set of conceptualizations providing coherence to discreet phenomena (as Freud's did with symptoms, dreams and slips, and with the normal and the pathological in psychic life), is essential both to psychoanalytic treatment and to a scientific worldview. And, for Rangell, psychoanalysis must be scientific.

Another of Rangell's themes is that science is not simply an objective enterprise. He describes the interaction of the personal (affective) and the theoretical (cognitive), using as prime examples his own biography and his relationships with other leading analysts of the past fifty years. This affective-cognitive dichotomy is shown also to be a complementary series, although he sees theoretical progress evolving by separating the poles and minimizing the personal and political. Rangell's review of even early divergences finds a cognitive/rational perspective to be opposed by an emphasis on the affective/inspirational/identificatory dimension. Following Fenichel (1945), he views ideas and affects as equally important subjects for study, but with rationality, not affect, guiding theory and method.

Divergences leading to the current pluralism are ascribed to the seminal breaks of Melanie Klein in London, George Klein in Topeka, and Heinz Kohut in Chicago. Personal interactions with Ralph Greenson, Anna Freud and Kohut are offered as examples of subjective influences on psychoanalytic politics and on theory. Much of Rangell's text is devoted to a chronology delineating agreements and differences with Joseph Sandler, Robert Wallerstein, Roy Schafer, Charles Brenner, Peter Fonagy and Gill, among others. In each instance, he aims to demonstrate that his is the inclusive theoretical frame, and that alternate views, when not incorrect, can easily be subsumed. George Klein (1973), with his separation of clinical theory from metapsychology, and Wallerstein (1988), with his sanctioning of multiple theories, are seen as the major adversaries of total composite theory. Rangell's argumentation reprises much of his earlier work and I find it effective.

One particular issue where I judge Rangell's discussion to be weak is in regard to the controversy over "lay analysis" in the United States. He considers the exclusion of non-medical analysts by the American Psychoanalytic Association (APsaA) as having been an error, but he believes that this issue is improperly confounded with opposition to the ego-psychological stance, resulting in hostility both to the politics and the theory by those who were excluded. I have made the same point regarding the confounding of politics and theory (Golland, 1991). But Rangell minimizes the "lay" issue when he asserts, however correctly, that physicians and non-physicians alike have held to both good theory and bad. He neglects his own thesis regarding the interaction of personal/political factors with theory by not recognizing that the large-scale, systematic exclusion from the political center of psychoanalysis in America had large-scale effects on alternate theory development. And Rangell, unlike his paradigm rival Wallerstein, was neither leader nor participant in the political change. The wounds resulting from the exclusion of non-physicians are not fully healed. Despite Freud's coinage, most of us feel "lay analysis" to be an inappropriate and disparaging term. A unified psychoanalysis must include analysts, independent of their academic background.

There are also elements of style that may create some dissonance. Editorial discipline cannot be easy in memoir writing. Rangell devotes many pages to the politics of psychoanalysis in his home city, Los Angeles. Details of his rivalry with Greenson are as fascinating for a reader as good gossip can be, but as an admirer of Greenson's monumental text on technique (1967), I felt like a child listening to his parents fight. A similar feeling was evoked from descriptions of the machinations involving Miss Freud around Rangell's rivalry with Kohut for the IPA presidency. Rangell uses published letters to support his views, but these necessarily one-sided, sometimes angry and negativistic accounts may muddy rather than enhance understanding of the theoretical issues at stake.

Rangell does not neglect more current theoretical controversies. He discusses relational psychoanalysis, two-person psychology, and the technique of self-disclosure. He reviews Schafer's attempt to unify Kleinian and Freudian approaches. He challenges Brenner's recent rejection of the tripartite structural model. He welcomes indications that some alternate theorists, like Jay Greenberg, have moved to more inclusive positions, but he remains uncompromising about what he takes to be errors of thinking.

Now in his nineties, Rangell continues to develop theory. He extends his own original contributions regarding unconscious active decision-making as an ego function, and his treatment of the moral dimension (first proposed in his 1980 book on the Watergate scandal). He sees his election as Honorary President, after two decades of absence from the IPA executive council, as indication that his views may again be ascendant. He hopes that psychoanalysis will move forward by addressing topics in moral psychopathology and by approaching new frontiers with the study of freedom, sincerity and courage. Despite the inevitable discovery of a hero's limitations, I remain in awe of both his intellect and his feistiness.

But are we really near a unified theory? Brenner's conflicted patients suffer from maladaptive compromises, and Kohut's from the tragedy of narcissistic wounds. Schafer has come to find his patients plagued by projective identifications. Wallerstein finds common ground in actual clinical practice but is challenged in this view by Paniagua (1995). Rangell sees common ground in a unified conceptualization, but theoretical differences are still pronounced. I join Rangell in hoping for a unified theory, but such a goal remains elusive.

Those who are unfamiliar with Leo Rangell will find this memoir to make important contributions to their understanding of psychoanalytic theory and practice. Those who know Rangell's work will appreciate many aspects of this book, and especially that the work goes on.

Bruce Sklarew, Stuart W. Twemlow and Sallye M. Wilkinson
Analysts in The Trenches: Streets, Schools, War Zones
The Analytic Press, 2004
xi + 331 pp, $39.95.
Psychologist Psychoanalyst 25, No. 3 (2005), pp. 65–66

The title is true to its word. This book is about psychoanalysts working in mean streets from New Haven to New Orleans, plying their trade in violence-ridden public schools and responding to casualties of war in Angola, Bosnia and the former Soviet Republic of Georgia. Other workplaces include municipal halls, police stations, earthquake-damaged areas, and "ground zero" in Lower Manhattan. Racism, child abuse and homelessness are among the traumatic situations leading to the announcement of a new identity within our profession: the community analyst.

Twenty-three contributors describe their work in twelve essays, most with gripping clinical details. Some have practiced community work for decades. The editors, Bruce Sklarew, Stuart W. Twemlow and Sallye M. Wilkinson, contribute two chapters and an introduction that together provide a theoretical frame and general methodological considerations for community practice. The final essay, on mental health intervention and preventive approaches, addresses issues of research and policy. Those whose work has been limited to clinic and consulting room will be enlightened, impressed, maybe even a bit envious. These authors report impact in the larger world, while most of us treat fewer and fewer psychoanalytic patients.

What's going on out there in the trenches? Isn't psychoanalysis about intrapsychic and interpersonal psychology? Isn't it our job to help people understand transference and resistance? Don't we promote insight leading to personal agency and resolution of maladaptive compromises? Isn't work in the trenches for the less well-trained psychologists, psychiatrists, social workers, nurses and paraprofessionals?

The term "applied psychoanalysis" has generally referred to non-clinical applications of our theory in the arts and humanities. Psychoanalytically-informed applied psychotherapies have been considered distinct from the intensive, couch-centered treatment that Freud (1919) described as "pure gold" (p 168). Along with the contributors to this book, I would use the word "applied" to cover *all* applications of psychoanalytic understanding, including the "pure" treatment method.

Freud's abandonment of the seduction theory of hysteria is thought by many to have exchanged an external locus of motivation to an internal one. It is more accurate to say that a focus on fantasy life became central to his subsequent theoretical advances. Freud never rejected the importance of external influences on psychological functioning, and Hartmann's adaptive point of view restored their status to the organized theory. This book has as its theme the effects of trauma and their management, both with individuals and with populations, and it provides several examples of the utility of a comprehensive psychoanalytic theory.

The editors' introduction demonstrates how community analysts rely on understanding unconscious motivation to create methods that are active and group-based, and which aim to change (rather than interpret) transference and dynamics. A neutral posture is recommended for consulting on social conflict, but personal relationships and collaboration are core principles of the work. A flexible, helpful approach is advocated, eschewing both credentials and a posture of expertise. The history of this new specialty is traced to Anna Freud, August Aichhorn, John Bowlby, Erik Erikson, and Karl Menninger, among others. The American Psychoanalytic Association (APsaA) endorsed community work in the 1970's, but until the past decade, APsaA seemed to have dropped it from the agenda. Two of the co-editors, Sklarew and Twemlow, have led APsaA to a more activist stance, and support of this book's publication is one result.

It is at this juncture that a review of an edited compilation would typically provide brief summaries of the chapters. An earlier draft had laudatory but inadequate words that failed to convey the richness of detail and clarity of presentation in what I consider to be exciting, even heroic efforts on the part of the contributors. But these are not easily summarized. Like all compilations, chapter styles vary, but unlike most, there is an overall coherence that is conveyed only by reading the entire book. The different voices comprise a consonant choir, not needing an editors' summary.

I would be remiss, however, if I did not acknowledge Vamik Volkan, the pioneer (and perhaps still lone) practitioner of international psychoanalytic intervention, who describes his work over three years on a once-in-five-months visiting schedule with an émigré family displaced by war to Tbilisi in the Caucasus. I must also cite the exemplary William Granatir, who presents a memoir of his decade of volunteer work as a retired psychoanalyst in inner city schools, beginning at age 76.

I identify myself as a "classical Freudian" and my own institute teaching emphasizes the "standard" technique applied to intensive individual treatment using the couch. How can I heap praise on and express envy of the dramatically different methodologies of this book?

I see psychoanalysis as a psychological theory, akin to the Theory of Evolution in biology, the Theory of Relativity in physics, and the Big Bang Theory in cosmology. Although the discovery and creation of psychoanalysis took place in his consulting room with its data drawn from intensive couch-based psychotherapy, Freud was ambitious and saw its applications going beyond a mere method of treatment for neuroses. "Standard" clinical practice is, for me, our laboratory, the site where discoveries continue to be made to modify, extend and correct the theory. Its methodology is central to its advances, and it is unique in being simultaneously a research tool and a clinical application. A theory must also be useful beyond its laboratory or it will be elitist at best, or altogether irrelevant. Methods adapted for clinical situations different from the "standard" have led to the vast enterprise of psychoanalytically-informed psychotherapies.

This book is a landmark in defining newer methods for situations that cry out for psychoanalytic understanding. It does not read like typical analytic literature, and many names in its bibliography were unfamiliar to me. I reviewed it while also reading a series of papers in the *Psychoanalytic Quarterly*, a somewhat disjunctive experience. The *Quarterly* papers address intrapsychic conflict, delineating the ideas of outstanding theorists from several diverse psychoanalytic points of view. The abstractions and the clinical inferences were of a different order than those in *Trenches*. Psychoanalytic thought advances, though, from both metapsychology and phenomenology. *Trenches* provides the latter. Analysts may be committed to refining theory and the intensive individual analytic practice from which it evolves, while at the same time supporting social applications.

How can psychoanalysts engage in community psychoanalysis? Economics make it difficult. Fee-for-service models were the mainstay of practice, at least until insurance companies came to dominate health care. Like many of the contributors, community analysts often hold university faculty appointments, or they work for agencies. Grant support is needed to underwrite projects, and is not easy to come by. The larger society's priorities do not emphasize mental health activities we psychoanalysts value.

I believe we can and must attend both to our practices *and* to the ills of the world. We can improve our methods in the laboratory in which psychoanalysis was discovered, and work to apply our knowledge beyond the consulting room. I have spent the last 35 years as a teacher educator. Only in the last decade of that tenure did I begin more explicitly to connect my analytic thinking with my work in public schools, and I have tried to develop communicable methodology for this application (Golland, 2002). *Trenches* has advanced my thinking. I can now more fully embrace the role of community analyst while I continue to practice intensive individual treatment.

Stephen Frosh
Hate and the 'Jewish Science:' Anti-Semitism, Nazism and Psychoanalysis
Palgrave MacMillan, 2005
Psychologist Psychoanalyst 26, No. 4 (2006), pp. 66–67, 71

Hatred rules! As I begin this review, hundreds of missiles rain down daily on Israelis and Lebanese while frustrated diplomats scurry about for a ceasefire formula. A secular Jew living thousands of miles from the Middle East tinderbox may reflect and write, while action-oriented individuals rally to Israel's cause, with "Never again!" on their lips. World opinion seems ever ready to condemn my tiny tribe with its small patch of sovereign soil, even for defending itself against those who would destroy it utterly.

How has such a small group become more than a blip on the historical screen? How has this sect managed to defy statistical prediction in its impact on civilization? Why does it attract such enmity? Psychoanalysts since Freud have addressed these questions, trying to provide rational answers for understanding irrational hate. Yet rationality is not an abstract entity; observers bring their own history and culture to every act of reflection and understanding. Stephen Frosh, a prolific British psychoanalytic psychologist and scholar, brings his subjectivity to the study of hate, and his rationality to the persistent and virulent version of hatred known as antisemitism.

In this slender volume, Frosh investigates his topics as they play out in the history of psychoanalysis, especially during and following that most heinous and hateful period of Nazi ascendancy and crime. Three "case studies" comprise his format: Freud as a Jew; the response of organized psychoanalysis to Nazism, and an examination of theories of anti-Semitism. His aim is polemical: to assist in curing this social pathology. His approach melds psychological formulations with social, economic, and historical considerations.

Freud's conflicted feelings about his Judaism have been well documented. While he objected to his discovery/creation being thought of as a "Jewish science," Frosh finds this characterization to have been useful for initial group identity, though costly for Jews and for psychoanalysis. Frosh develops the argument that psychoanalysis does, in fact, have its roots in Jewish identity and culture, and he describes the continuing effect on the development and content of our discipline. He notes that several scholars have depicted "psychological man" (p. 11) as the epitome of modernism: rational, critical, interpretive, subversive—and Jewish. Outsider status promotes such a perspective and also a cultural cohesion. A major negative result was antisemitic activity directed against psychoanalysis. Freud's own thesis on Judaism (1939) claims superiority for his culture, and itself provides ammunition for antisemites. Another negative consequence was Freud's siege mentality and his excessive concern with loyalty, personal and theoretical, an attitude that continues to hamper scientific progress.

Frosh's second case study recounts the fate of organized psychoanalysis during the Nazi era, a story whose details did not emerge for a quarter century, and whose issues remain inadequately understood. That the IPA will hold its second German post-war congress in 2007, this time in Berlin, underscores the current relevance of this history. Those who have become familiar with the events Frosh recounts will appreciate the details provided. They will also appreciate his demonstration of avoidance and denial prevalent even at the IPA 1985 Congress where clinical rather than moral issues dominated the program, and where the welcoming remarks of Hamburg's mayor were more poignant than those of the psychoanalysts present.

Nazism forced gentile psychoanalysts to choose: collaborate or die. Mixed responses of cowardice and courage are difficult to unravel. Some cases are more easily judged than others; each challenges us to walk in the shoes of those facing a horrible choice. Frosh parses the words and actions of Jones, Jung and Goring, and offers no easy answers. Freud, himself, and Anna were hardly heroic figures in this battle, but Frosh believes that faulting them would be an unfair blaming of victims, and antisemitic to boot. Two myths are compared: 1) that psychoanalysis as such was erased during Hitler's Reich; and 2) that, instead, psychoanalysis resisted the nightmare. Each holds a kernel of truth; neither convinces. Frosh describes collective defenses and the return of the repressed. He suggests that a form of psychoanalysis is compatible with social conformity despite the idealistic wish that psychoanalysis be inimical to coercion.

Frosh's third case study begins with the question: why does psychoanalysis not yet have good enough insight about antisemitism? He reviews the literature of the "Christian disease" (p. 151), finding formulations to be based on too thin data sets. Kleinian splitting and other theoretical propositions are also found inadequate, although Frosh believes that each of the proposed dynamic understandings has a ring of truth. He concludes his critique in a brief chapter in which he offers a social psychology for psychoanalysis, one based on the developmental task of coping with "otherness."

Otherness is described as a primary source of human subjectivity. For Frosh, subjectivity is formed by identifications and repudiations, by contrasting self and other on various axes, including the categories of class, race, sex, and gender. The experience of otherness is uncanny and complex, id-like. The "other" inside us is dreadful, requiring extrusion. Joy and shame are associated affects. Frosh sees his theory as relevant for black color racism and, now, anti-radical Islam. But 2000 years of history have made Jews the "universal stranger" (p. 198) of Western society. That Jews are targets of projection is fundamental for social and psychological organization; they are not merely convenient scapegoats. "All otherness in the West is Jewish, including that inner otherness that is unconscious desire" (p. 215).

Frosh concludes that antisemitism is an extreme phenomenon calling for a strong formulation. He makes two such statements: Psychoanalysis is Jewish in important ways, as is the Unconscious. Antisemitism is not just an example of irrational group hatred like misogyny or colonialism, it is central to all aspects of relating to others.

The final statement seems to go beyond his evidence and his argumentation. In his earlier book, *For and Against Psychoanalysis* (1997), Frosh was meticulous in respecting the complexity of issues, and was rigorously fair in presenting alternative perspectives. In my view, his judgments of some gentile analysts are overly balanced and generous. But I believe he gives uncalled-for priority and centrality to antisemitism over other social pathologies. In what is the least developed but most original section of this book, Frosh acknowledges racism and sexism, but does not demonstrate that these or other "isms" are less important than antisemitism as axes of otherness. Nor does he, for all his sound scholarship, cite the classic Allport (1954) or the more recent Young-Bruehl (1996) contributions, which are works that provide more balanced understanding of the multiform varieties of prejudice.

For me, the great strength of this volume is not to be found in the subject matter of its title and subtitle. In discussing Freud's Jewishness or the Nazi era, little new ground is broken, but those unfamiliar with these topics will learn a great deal. In discussing identity-formation based on identifications and repudiations, Frosh provides instances of well known "me-not me" developmental theory, consistent with our understanding of reality-testing and self-object differentiation. The excellence of this book lies in its extending Frosh's more ambitious long-term project: that of studying psychoanalysis not merely as a clinical treatment or a psychological paradigm, but as a major chapter in the history of ideas.

In contrasting Freud's "Jewish science" with the Aryan version of psychotherapy that smothered it during Hitler's 12-year abomination, Frosh addresses a major philosophical issue. Freudian psychoanalysis adopts a critical and self-critical, even ironic, worldview—one that depends, he argues successfully, upon its outsider status. The Aryan approach is a conformist psychology in which the human spirit is to be harnessed in service to society, e.g., the Nazi State.

The implications of this contrast are manifold and contemporary. Thomas Szasz saw mental illness as a sane response to an oppressive environment; Soviet psychiatry defined political dissent as mental aberration. Schools of psychoanalysis may find themselves closer to one pole or the other. A medical orientation leans toward the conformist end when compared with approaches emphasizing autonomy and agency. American ego psychology is criticized (especially by European and South American analysts) for its emphasis on adaptation. Brenner's model of therapeutic gain—more adaptive compromise-formations—is subject to this same critique, as well as begging the question of who defines "adaptive." Two-person approaches may similarly end in an accommodating, socializing approach to treatment, while one-person models may be scored for suggestion and potential abuse of authority.

Like Freud, who believed psychoanalytic ideas are applicable far beyond the consulting room, Frosh asks that we consider social, economic, political, and historical factors in a comprehensive psychoanalytic theory. He challenges us also to avoid complacency about our clinical methods and their implicit values. His value is clearly on the side of a less conformist psychoanalytic praxis.

Has Frosh provided a solution to the problem of antisemitism? The history of ideas, like psychoanalysis, seeks rather to extend knowledge. The implicit belief in both fields is that knowing is beneficial, but it "works" at a very slow pace.

As I conclude this review, missiles have stopped falling; there is a shaky truce in the Middle East. Each side claims victory, but death and destruction are the undisputed winners. And, as this month-long conflict pauses, war still rages in Iraq where death claims even larger numbers. As you read my words, perhaps collective wisdom will have advanced a bit and we will see more peace and less hatred and violence in our world. It is my belief that psychoanalysis contributes toward this goal. Stephen Frosh's scholarship makes a contribution as well. This book is highly recommended.

Matthew von Unwerth
Freud's Requiem: Mourning, Memory, and the Invisible History of a Summer Walk
NY: Riverhead Books, 2005
x + 244 pp. $23.95 (cloth), $15 (paper)
Psychologist Psychoanalyst 27, No. 2 (2007), pp. 40–41

Ferenczi's "confusion of tongues" (1980/1933) spoke to differences between adults and children. The metaphor could easily be applied to a much broader range of issues in today's psychoanalysis. Ample grounds for confusion were provided by Freud. As we know, he used the very term psychoanalysis to describe at least three different enterprises: a theory of mind, a theory of psychopathology, and a treatment method. Many of our seemingly basic terms are similarly used in so many ways even in one language, let alone the many into which Freud's work has been translated. The ways in which we speak with one another include cultural, linguistic, and substantive differences often difficult to untangle. A considerable literature has addressed definitional matters, but the present state of affairs has gone, it seems, beyond mere confusion to Babel.

It is easy to decry this situation, and those concerned with psychoanalysis as a science (as was Freud), may be among those most troubled by it. As an alternative perspective, the very subject matter staked out by the founder is so complex in its nature—encompassing the multiple dimensions of human nature—that this century of definitional confusion has been both necessary and heuristic. The human mind/brain is comprised of trillions of synapses, with a factorial algorithm of possible meanings approaching infinity. Psychoanalytic psychology created a new approach to its exploration and discovery. Our "Babel" is a necessary stage for dealing with such complexity.

Toward this end, clinical psychoanalysts and research psychoanalysts should welcome what has been called "applied psychoanalysis," if only to extend the reach of phenomena subject to analytic scrutiny. *Freud's Requiem* is a most worthy contribution.

Cited in a recent *Newsday* article and favorably reviewed in the *New York Times*, this is a book whose popularity is good for psychoanalysis. That Freud's name should be associated with a Catholic mass for resting souls may seem incongruous, as he was, famously, a Godless Jew. But Matthew von Unwerth demonstrates throughout this almost poetic work Freud's preoccupation with mortality and his attempts to come to grips with it, not only personally but scientifically. This book is simultaneously about psychoanalysis, the first psychoanalyst, science and art, poetic inspiration, psychoanalytic methodologies, and the dilemma of human existence.

Trained in literature, von Unwerth has been a librarian at the New York Psychoanalytic Society and Institute for a decade. More recently, he has undertaken clinical psychoanalytic training. His literary background melds with his attraction to psychoanalytic theory to inform and inspire this book.

Stimulated by Freud's 1915 essay "On Transience" (provided as an appendix to the current volume), von Unwerth deals with the essay's theme, and with Freud's concurrent thinking that would be revealed in "Mourning and Melancholia" (1917a). Using episodes from the lives of Freud, Rainer Maria Rilke and Lou Andreas-Salome (these latter two reasonably presumed to be the characters referred to in Freud's essay), von Unwerth weaves psychoanalytic theory, poetry and biography to grapple with the domains of art and science, epistemology, and mortality.

Freud has often been cast as a pessimist. In contrast to the poet in the essay who experiences the transience of beauty as depressing, Freud argues that its very transience provides a scarcity value that is inspiring. Freud is here an optimist; those who cannot mourn are depressed. Andreas-Salome introduced Rilke to Freud, and also recommended analysis for the then-blocked poet. She soon retracted her advice, fearing that treatment would stifle his creativity—a sad but not uncommon view, even today.

Freud's psychoanalysis promoted rationality over inspiration (the oceanic feeling). Freud respected poetic intuition and loved poetry, but could not connect emotionally to it, or to Rilke. Freud's art appreciation was intellectual; he did not consider himself creative. For Freud, art is irrational and related to psychosis; he cared not at all for music.

Andreas-Salome is considered the most important female German writer of her time. She was a biographer and lover of Nietsche, Jung, and Rilke, and she became a psychoanalyst and a member of Freud's Wednesday group. Rilke's writing block was undone without analysis and the literary achievements that followed were major. Andreas-Salome was able to mourn Rilke's early death, in part by writing about him.

Much of this book describes Freud's neurotic object-relations and their relationship to his ideas and to the history of the psychoanalytic movement. An adolescent crush leads to a rejection of emotionality; Freud commits himself to science, but his work redraws boundaries between art and life. Self-analysis poses an obvious scientific problem (objectivity); yet Freud writes often about artists and writers. Freud identifies with Ulysses, and Goethe is also a major hero for him. Establishment science rejects Freud while art embraces him; Freud would disagree with both judgments.

Von Unwerth deals with Freud's smoking and his cancer, his collection of antiquities, his love for his dogs, his Lamarckianism, and his being a political reactionary, yet engages neither in Freud-bashing nor hagiography. He moves fluidly from each topic back to his two central themes: death as Freud's preoccupation and mourning as the alternative to depression.

This book attempts to unite art and science. Like Freud and others before him, von Unwerth's success is limited. Unlike Freud, he does not engage in theory-construction, although his grasp of psychoanalytic theory is impressive. With artistic flair, he engages our interest in the details of his presentation and in his themes.

Like Hartmann (1964/1944), I view psychoanalysis as an overarching general psychology. I count the "standard" psychoanalytic treatment situation also to be one application of the general theory. I believe that psychoanalytic knowledge may be derived from the couch, from standard research paradigms, and from biography, literature and other sources of human endeavor. The state of our knowledge, although extensive after a century of exploration, remains limited, and our pluralism can seem like confusion. Von Unwerth's is an important new voice—and this book is a good read as well.

Kenneth Eisold
"Psychotherapy and Psychoanalysis: a Long and Troubled
Relationship"
International Journal of Psychoanalysis
2006

In an impressive essay, Kenneth Eisold views the issue of psychotherapy vs. psychoanalysis from several angles not usually considered: historical, political, economic, scientific and international, to name the obvious ones. Unlike Fosshage (1997), who concluded that there is no difference in the process, a position I took pains to rebut (1999), Eisold does not address clinical process. That is where I find the analysis-therapy distinction to be most useful.

My view is inspired by Rangell's (1954) metaphor about day and night, dawn and dusk, and (with more specificity) Bibring's (1954) distinction between therapeutic and technical interventions. The latter paper is a pillar of my teaching about technique. Abreaction, suggestion, manipulation, clarification and interpretation are defined, with their proportions (and whether the intent is anxiety-reduction or stimulation to further association) indicating a more analytic or more therapeutic process. On a moment-to-moment basis, clinical judgment will always decide the issue. For treatment-as-a-whole, the preponderance of the technical or the therapeutic, and of the five intervention types, will make clear the distinction.

Many dimensions are relevant to clinical process, among them Gill's (1954) external criteria of frequency and use of the couch. We may also include preference for transference or extra-transference work and the degree of attention paid to the analyst's emotional responses, however defined. My own psychotherapy practice (as it has become for many, the larger part of my work) typically includes an attempt to move toward analysis, because I believe it is a deeper and more beneficial experience. I recommend the couch and frequent sessions, and I favor technical interventions.

Wallerstein's Menninger study (1986) showed disappointing results for my side, and we tended to ignore it for nearly two decades. We were elated to see Blatt and Shahar's (2004) study, reviewing Wallerstein's data to find that analysis works better with some people and therapy with others. Like most process and outcome research, now thankfully plentiful, additional study is needed. Objective research is no quicker at finding "truth" than is clinical psychoanalysis, and seekers must be open to alternative pathways.

Eisold speaks to the "macro" level and includes the multiple contextual issues needed for sound discussion of similarities and differences between psychoanalysis and psychotherapy. It is the "micro" level of clinical work that continues to reinforce my conviction that the distinction remains critically important.

Brenner and Rangel, Revisited

Charles Brenner
Psychoanalysis or Mind and Meaning
NY: The Psychoanalytic Quarterly, 2006
vi + 140 pp., $25.00 (paper)
PsycCRITIQUES 52, No. 33 (2007)

For over half a century Charles Brenner has been the foremost theoretician of what was once the mainstream of American psychoanalysis. His "modern conflict theory" is one of several parallel or divergent streams in a clinical discipline now characterized by pluralism. In this perhaps valedictory volume, published at age 93, Brenner argues against both the pluralistic *zeitgeist* and the alternate "total composite theory" of his peer Leo Rangell, the honorary president of the International Psychoanalytical Association (IPA).

I first read Brenner's *Elementary Textbook of Psychoanalysis* (1955) in an era when psychology professors often assigned to undergraduates original work by Freud and other psychoanalytic authors. Brenner's clarity of exposition (and of course the subject matter) strongly influenced my own career path. Few can compete with his writing style. The current work, like his *Elementary Textbook*, is jargon-free and easily understood, even by a "lay" readership.

The word "lay" should rankle. Brenner was among the leaders of psychoanalysis in the United States who for decades supported a medical monopoly on its practice. He is considered an archconservative in this regard, and those unfamiliar with his writing mistakenly view him as a pillar of Freudian orthodoxy. Along with his closest collaborator, the late Jacob Arlow (1964), he has been a radical revisionist of the most basic of Freudian tenets. I have referred to him in conversation as "the William of Occam of psychoanalysis." Brenner's razor has shaved away so many constructs (lately even the id/ego/superego schematic) that many Freudians find too little left in his spare formulation. This book presents the current state of his pared-down theory in a mere 96 pages (plus appendices).

Brenner organizes this "purely personal statement" (p iii) according to: a) conclusions about mental development and functioning, b) treatment principles, and c) observational data supporting these conclusions and principles. His five untitled chapters cover: 1) psychoanalysis as science, 2) the basic theory, 3) evidence, 4) technique, and 5) applications beyond therapy. He challenges those who differ to present their conclusions and evidence. He believes such argumentation will winnow away alternate or composite theorizing.

For Brenner, psychoanalysis is a natural science following Francis Bacon's (1620/1993) definition: an attitude toward the universe in which observations are made using the best methods available; logic is employed; and contradictions or magical, supernatural, and *ad hoc* solutions are rejected. All sciences are inferential and influenced by the observer's psychology, but ultimately facts rule. Experiment may be employed, but is not a requirement (e.g., Galileo's astronomy); quantification is a tool of science, not its essence. The brain is the organ of the mind.

Psychoanalysis is a theory of meaning. Mental events are never random. Psychoanalysis translates the apparently random into cause and effect statements. The pleasure principle reigns, with unconscious pleasure explaining apparent anomalies. Pleasure and unpleasure (reactions to the miseries of life) necessarily collide; mental compromises are then created to maximize the former, minimize the latter. Crucial conflicts are over sexual and aggressive impulses of early childhood, especially the ones ascendant at ages 3-6. Brain development and language must precede mentalization of conflict and compromise-formation. Affects are sensations associated with ideas, memories and fantasies. They are classified by intensity, content and origin. Anxiety anticipates danger, while depressive affect is a belief that a calamity (parental abandonment or hate, castration) has already occurred. Any mental content may be used to defend against unpleasure.

The main data supporting conflict theory originate with Sigmund Freud's (1901/1953) description of the psychopathology of everyday life. Additional data accrue from the clinical situation but, Brenner acknowledges, these data strain attempts at generalization. Ordinary psychological phenomena (e.g., generosity, career choice, optimism) provide clear though less reliable evidence. Fiction, fairytales, myths and religions add to Brenner's dataset, as do humor and the preoccupation with sex and violence in newspapers and best-sellers. The ubiquity of these phenomena makes them too normal to be considered pathology; compromise-formation is how the mind works. Psychopathology is quantitative, a matter of too much or too little.

Psychoanalytic technique is too individualized for written summary. Brenner defines the aim of therapy: alteration of compromises to yield greater gratification, along with reduction of anxiety, depressive affect, inhibition, self-injury and self-punishment. Concluding a treatment is always based on clinical judgment, not specific criteria. Curiosity (rather than approval, disapproval, encouragement or discouragement) is the essential analytic attitude; the method is to convey understanding. Interpretations are always conjectures, but analysts derive authority from their knowledge of the workings of the mind. Various aspects of the psychoanalytic setting are described as aiding the process, not basic to it. (Brenner is often cast as dogmatic about technique; he is not.) All interpretations are inexact; listening involves a general set of expectations based on theory. Treatment progress is measured by the patient's greater understanding and toleration of mental contents.

Brenner's writing has heretofore been about the application of theory to practice. In his closing chapter, he gives a general description of the life cycle, and he discusses morality, creativity, daydreams, religion and politics. Each domain is illuminated by his theory of conflict and compromise-formation. His appendices expand on issues raised in the chapters, providing elaboration and both clinical and applied examples.

Brenner's theory melds the program of one of his teachers, Heinz Hartmann (1947/1964), who defined psychoanalysis as a general psychology, with the specific focus of another teacher, Ernst Kris (1947/1975), who defined psychoanalysis as "human behavior viewed as conflict" (p 6).

For a few years following the lawsuit that ended medical exclusivity of internationally-recognized psychoanalytic training in this country, I participated in a weekly supervision group led by Jacob Arlow. It was among the first non-medical groups he had agreed to teach. I had long considered Arlow and Brenner to represent the gold standard in theory and practice, but was uneasy with that idealization. Beyond my resentment of their long resistance to non-medical practice was a sense of exclusivity, inconsistent with my social values. Membership in the New York Psychoanalytic Society, their home organization, remains open only to graduates of their institute (now including psychologists and doctoral-level social workers), while other historically-medical societies welcome Freudians like me who are members of the IPA.

My unease was not just political; it was also theoretical and clinical. Could I work with the implied and sometimes explicitly-stated purity of their psychoanalysis? Not quite. This book enabled me at last to articulate my concerns.

Brenner's psychoanalysis as method takes a narrow-scope perspective. I find Stone's (1954) "widening scope" more useful. Patients may not meet narrow criteria for analyzability, nor are many these days willing to undergo the rigorous schedule and abstinent procedure that lends greater probability to establishment of the process described by Brenner. Yet psychoanalysis may have the best chance of helping people, especially those for whom other treatment approaches have failed.

Brenner's psychoanalysis is based on a level of brain development capable of storing verbal memories, not attainable before age 3. No one doubts that experience in the first three years of life affects human development. Just as embryology is a science different from psychoanalysis, Brenner considers the "pre-oedipal" period not to be open to psychoanalysis. Along with many others, I believe the first three years are worthy of an analytic perspective, despite the difficulties of understanding early experiences.

Brenner ignores theorizing from other psychoanalytic schools, risking a conceptual narrowing of scope. Attachment theory is rejected as concerned with too-early development. That therapy involves two persons in close emotional interaction is not addressed by him. Transference and countertransference, central to clinical theory for many other authors, is subsumed under object-relations and given short shrift.

Brenner's evidence is problematic. The data of clinical psychoanalysis are not limited to what might be transcribed; unspoken thoughts and feelings of the participants are crucial. Yet Brenner presents much of his clinical data already filtered by his theory; it is not close enough to raw. Likewise, he takes non-clinical data to be clear and convincing, when alternate interpretations are readily generated. As a Freudian in clinical practice, I am persuaded by his data; as a psychologist, I find them plausible. I doubt, though, that outsiders would be convinced. When Brenner writes about applied topics, a departure for him, his theory fits, but is far from conclusive.

There also may be a logical fallacy in Brenner's overarching concept of compromise-formation. If all mental products are compromise-formations, can their components (wishes, affects, defenses) also be considered compromises? Brenner may be postulating an infinite regress.

Despite my reservations about the theory, this work is invaluable. Brenner is unsurpassed at providing clear definitions for the concepts he addresses. His discussion of psychological defense, rejecting A. Freud's (1936/1966) classic catalogue, is consistent with current, widely-accepted clinical understanding. His flexible technical attitude is a breath of fresh air amid sharp controversy over current diverse practices.

Still, I find Brenner's pared-down theory premature. Psychoanalytic data are far too messy at this time for the law of parsimony to be invoked. This book is, nonetheless, a work to be learned from and reckoned with; it is essential reading. Psychoanalysts of every persuasion will be challenged to refine their thinking. Psychologists and laypersons alike will find it a clear treatise on the current state of a major stream of psychoanalytic thought.

Leo Rangell
The Road to Unity in Psychoanalytic Theory
NY: Jason Aronson, 2007
pp ix +133, $34.95
Psychologist-Psychoanalyst 27, No. 3 (2007), pp. 67–69

The massacre at Virginia Tech last April recalled for me what sparked my initial interest in psychoanalytic psychology. The "problem of evil," once the province of religion and demonology, later of philosophy, was passed to psychology. Psychoanalysis is the most serious attempt to deal with its complexities. Freud offered a method that was both a therapy and a means of understanding. Rejecting medicalization of his findings, he saw and stressed the continuities of normal and abnormal in a broad theory that aspired to be inclusive of individual and mass psychology, as well as of the creative products of the human imagination. Heinz Hartmann and David Rapaport elaborated Freud's vision, developing psychoanalysis as a "general psychology."

This grand plan reached an apex about thirty-five years ago and has fallen on hard times since. We no longer seem to have a comprehensive theory, but instead a host of competing formulations. Some ideas are offered as new paradigms while others are eclectic. Some seek integration or common ground, say, in the clinical situation.

Leo Rangell believes that theoretical pluralism has fragmented our field, accounting in good measure for its decline both as a therapy and as a respected social and intellectual force. A major extender of the Hartmann/Rapaport project for over half a century, Rangell has promoted his "total composite psychoanalytic theory" for at least a decade. This book is his latest attempt at restoring theoretical unity.

Readers of this newsletter, the house organ of perhaps the very hotbed of pluralism, might need a reminder of Rangell's credentials. In 1954, he presented what was to become one of two overlapping standard definitions of the treatment method of mainstream psychoanalysis. Merton Gill's was the other. Rangell was twice president of the American Psychoanalytic Association (APsaA) and twice president of the International Psychoanalytical Association (IPA). His publication list is vast in number and scope. A nonagenarian, he is honorary president of IPA, a distinction held by just three others before him: Ernest Jones, Hartmann and Anna Freud.

Rangell published a professional autobiography (2004) that I reviewed in 2005. The current volume reprises psychoanalytic history and his own place in it; it goes beyond, though, to answer critics like me and to advance a program for promoting reunification.

Unlike the autobiography, this is a short book (for the statistically-minded: 17 brief chapters across 133 pages). I will not repeat my discussion of the rich detail provided in 2004. Rangell's central and repeated points are but two:

- False dichotomies characterize most psychoanalytic controversies. Rangell offers a "both/and" approach in place of "either/or" splitting. He emphasizes the centrality of Freud's (1917b, p 347) "complemental series" concept and Waelder's (1962) use of that idea regarding levels of abstract and clinical theory.
- Formulations other than his total composite theory have erred with *pars pro toto* thinking: they exaggerate a new issue while ignoring or discarding older discoveries that should be retained.

In, Out, Pending

Rangell is clear with regard to what is included in total composite theory, what is excluded, and where the jury is out. "In" are: objective rationality, transference from the past, uncovering unconscious conflicts, interpretation and reconstruction, and the Oedipus complex. "Out" are idiosyncratic concepts that have not found general acceptance: e.g., "self-object," concrete early fantasies, "without memory or desire," and symmetrical two-person psychology. Decisions pending are, e.g., projective identification, depressive and paranoid positions, "analytic third," "analytic space." He explains how many ideas can be subsumed within existing theory: e.g., mind and body; attachment and mentalization; asymmetric two-person psychology; narcissism (not as a diagnosis, but as a central psychological issue on a par with anxiety).

Who decides? The general theory evolves by consensus; individual analysts work with preferred ideas that may or may not survive. When innovation arouses group excitement (e.g., Owen Renik's challenges to received technique), modifications are widely attempted in what is intrinsically a flexible method. The faddish falls away, leaving enduring contributions. Theoretical conflicts are routine in any evolving science; contradictions are not allowed.

Rangell summarizes his own additions to the overall theory: 1) similarities and differences between psychoanalytic and psychotherapeutic treatments; 2) a theory of choice and action; 3) the concept "compromise of integrity" on a par with neurosis in human affairs; 4) the concept "human core," with sexuality remaining a central issue; 5) unification of theory; and 6) advances in large-scale group psychology.

Polemic

This book is a polemic. Its aim is to return us to a time when theoretical argument was captivating, and psychoanalysis was an inspiring social movement. Rangell sees the irrational, our subject matter, as having invaded the method—inevitable in large group process where democracy rules over science, where each analyst is an uncalibrated instrument defining personal practice, and where every child can overthrow parents. Pluralists, like groups in general, are seen as dominated by irrationality.

These are meant to be fighting words, and while I am sympathetic with their aim, I question the likelihood of their efficacy. Rangell cites Martin Bergmann (from an historical perspective) and Arnold Richards (from a political one) also as sympathetic, each offering skepticism similar to my own. Bergmann emphasizes the ferocity of dissidence. Rangell believes history is moving his way, citing as

187

evidence recent work by Renik, Green, Chusid, Greenberg, and Schafer, and noting that Wallerstein, Kernberg, Fonagy and others are writing about theoretical convergence. Rangell praises Reed and Baudry's (1997) questions designed to promote rational discussion—as against affective decision-making.

Interestingly, Rangell does not directly challenge fellow nonagenarian Charles Brenner, as he had done in the earlier work (Rangell, 2004). In his sole citation of Brenner (p. 76), he finds agreement that psychoanalysis is a natural science. In his concept of unconscious choice, Rangell directly opposes Brenner's central formulation (that all psychological products are compromises) but he does not address Brenner's more recent elaborations. Nor does he note that Brenner's theorizing entails a radical paring of concepts, in striking contrast to his own additive approach (Golland, 2007).

Lay Analysis

In my earlier review, I faulted Rangell for his discussion of "lay analysis." Although he now devotes four chapters to the topic, two of every seven pages of text, I remain disappointed. Rangell separates the politics of theoretical pluralism from the issue of political exclusion, a position I had taken much earlier (Golland, 1991), and he provides many examples of medical and non-medical analysts in different theoretical camps. But his list of theoreticians does not reflect the demographics of exclusion. When I began my analytic training in 1968, programs admitting psychologists were nowhere to be found in the United States outside of New York City. Many of my teachers were products of "bootleg" training. As we know, it took a lawsuit to end exclusion by APsaA, the settlement of which Rangell claims here was "universally applauded" (p 47). The lawsuit was initiated in the face of intractable conflict; its resolution was not easy. The defendants' applause was mostly for APsaA's avoiding bankruptcy; there was hardly a warm welcome for the plaintiffs or their group.

Rangell considers his discussion of "lay analysis" a digression (p 77), one taken, perhaps, in response to my criticism. He seems not yet to recognize its centrality to his earlier thesis (Rangell, 2004), the interaction of personal factors with theory, nor that righteous indignation is a legitimate part of the political psychology in which he is a pioneer (Rangell, 1980). The very phrase "lay analysis" still rankles. Rangell credits my home base, the predominantly non-medical New York Freudian Society, with hosting his theory in 1996. Many in Division 39 consider those like myself who have joined APsaA to be sleeping with the enemy. That this controversy remains effectively unresolved for so many represents an essential psychoanalytic truth: traumas of the past manifest themselves in the present.

Is a Psychoanalytic Social Psychology Possible?

Psychoanalytic controversy has often centered on the issue of inner vs. outer reality. Freud's complemental series concept, consistent with the Hartmann/Rapaport model and with Rangell's position, should resolve this conflict. But a psychoanalytic social psychology remains elusive. Pluralism and exclusion are each highly charged issues. Group emotions are more difficult to comprehend than individual ones, especially since there is no evading the participant/observer dilemma.

Rangell's theory encompasses person and society (p. 76). Yet, unfortunately in my opinion, neither "compromise of integrity," nor his more recent discussion of public opinion (2005) has gained consensus—even as being proper psychoanalytic topics. Freud's own essays in social psychology have experienced a similar fate. Alfred Adler, the neo-Freudians, and even Erik Erikson go unrecognized within much of current theory, apparently for their external emphases.

Rangell notes pressures for social applications of our theory, as well as the demand for results, but he recognizes that pragmatism is often at odds with an open search for coherent understanding, our primary refined tool. Group applications (e.g., Sklarew et al, 2004) are often disparaged as diluting theory for pragmatism. Untangling subjectivities is a major focus of psychoanalysis as practiced today. How much more difficult is it to separate oneself in trying to analyze group or political issues in which one is a participant? Rangell's own application of psychoanalysis to the larger political arena is often viewed with suspicion, as are psychoanalytic commentaries on politicians from Barry Goldwater to George W. Bush.

In the clinical setting, confrontation is a technical intervention used sparingly; exhortation is not consistent with an analytic attitude. Can polemic be more effective (and analytic) in achieving consensus in our own professional group—or in any group?

Rangell presents a sophisticated discussion of "applied" psychoanalysis, but states that confirmation comes from "free associations of living beings" (p. 75).

Clinical technique remains a matter of much controversy; surely, we are further from consensus about any methodology beyond the consulting room.

Rangell is a keen observer of the interaction of personal factors with theoretical development; but can he separate them any better than analysts can separate affect and intellect in our offices?

Is Theoretical Unity Possible?

I am a scion of the Hartmann/Rapaport era, and I identify myself with Rangell's phrase "developed Freudian" (p. 8). Rangell's work supports Freud's (1927) sentiment: "The voice of intellect is a soft one, but it does not rest until it has gained a hearing" (p 53). His strong voice and emotions are entwined with his life in theory. I have highlighted here issues that might limit his success. It is far from clear that psychoanalysis will reunify, but Rangell's efforts are admirable and his words merit a respectful hearing.

Herbert J. Schlesinger
Promises, Oaths, and Vows: On the Psychology of Promising
NY: The Analytic Press, 2008
pp xiii + 216
Psychologist Psychoanalyst 28, No.4 (2008), pp. 50–51

In a year of presidential politics, promises abound. Is a candidate who goes back on a promise adaptive and pragmatic—or a flip flopper? Is one who holds to a promise despite changing circumstances idealistic and principled—or rigid? Simple answers are the stuff of promotional sound bites. This book is about psychology, not politics, but its study of promises and their variations reaches conclusions about morality and integrity, traits that should be central to the politics of a free society.

After earning his Ph.D. at the University of Kansas 55 years ago, Herbert J. Schlesinger completed clinical training at the Topeka Psychoanalytic Institute. He was among the first very small cohort of psychologists to be accepted for full training under the aegis of the American Psychoanalytic Association. He became a supervising and training analyst in 1960. After heading the Menninger Foundation's psychology staff, he moved to academic, administrative and clinical positions at the University of Colorado Medical Center, and then to the training directorship of the clinical psychology program at New York City's New School. He was appointed to a professorship at Columbia University's Psychiatry Department in 2001, and at its affiliated Weill Cornell Medical College. He is also a supervising and training analyst at the Columbia Center for Psychoanalytic Training and Research.

Schlesinger's first published paper was co-authored with George S. Klein in 1951. Topics he has addressed alone and with colleagues include projective testing; memory, cognitive styles and defenses; gender, ethnicity and age effects; managed care and insurance, and specific training and clinical issues. More recently he authored two widely acclaimed books: *The Texture of Treatment: On the Matter of Psychoanalytic Technique* (2003), and its sequel, *Ending and Beginning: On the Technique of Terminating Psychotherapy and Psychoanalysis* (2005). These books condense his half-century of clinical wisdom in a jargon-free and practical style. I adopted the earlier book as the text for my psychoanalytic technique course, and I modified my own clinical work and my teaching to incorporate some of what I learned from reading his books.

Schlesinger's clinical practice provided impetus for the current volume: his curiosity was aroused by a patient's broken (though uncalled-for) promises. The psychological and psychoanalytic literatures were limited on the topic of promises (and their stricter forms, oaths and vows), so he set himself the task of filling the near void.

In doing so, he came to a conclusion reached by neither social nor developmental psychologists: that making and keeping a promise "could be a, if not the defining act of moral maturity" (p xii).

The book's organization reflects Schlesinger's career as scholar, clinician and thoughtful theorist. Its first chapters comprise a critical conceptual review: various definitions and the reasons behind the act of promising are offered; the relationship of promising to mental development, especially from the standpoint of ego psychology, is explored; and empirical studies of promising and moral development—the larger psychological category it implies—are surveyed (e.g., Piaget, Kohlberg, Lewin, Zeigarnik).

The next set of chapters is clinical: the implicit promises of analytic treatment; the disparate pathologies of promise-breaking and their compulsive keeping; mature and regressive determinants of promising; a character typology of promising, and specific clinical recommendations. While Schlesinger's theoretical commitments are explicit, his examples are concrete and pragmatic, as in his earlier books on technique.

The final set of chapters enters the realm of what is usually called "applied psychoanalysis." Schlesinger provides a *tour de force* study of Greek drama and of Shakespeare through the lens of promises, oaths and vows, and he then deals with various forms of promising in religion.

The organization of this work brings to mind Freud's own progression from a masterpiece scholarly study of dreams, to clinical papers rich with recommendations, then to extending psychoanalytic ideas to the domains of literature, society and culture. In his conceptual review, Schlesinger's basic training as a psychologist shines through. In his delineation of ego functions (memory and perception, self and object differentiation, senses of time and inner and outer experience, and language and action), his mastery of the Hartmann/Rapaport ego psychology in which he was trained is abundantly evident. In his clinical discussion, his debt to Freud's theory of psychosexual phases is clear. In his foray into literature and religion, Schlesinger joins the late Charles Brenner (2007) in relating clinical findings to cultural products, as well as understanding these products as sources of convergent evidence for psychoanalytic ideas.

On every page, Schlesinger's commitment to a naturalistic worldview is most apparent. In his chapter on religion, he acknowledges that holders of faith-based epistemologies "may object to the very premise of my investigation" (p 176). This book also resembles an outstanding doctoral dissertation, albeit one written after a lengthy post-doctoral career. From this perspective, recommendations for a follow-up study would ask for greater detail contrasting pathological outcomes of promising (reneging or too rigid adherence) and its pathological sources (magical thinking, *hubris*) with the achievement of a moral maturational ideal.

Herbert Schlesinger has been a prolific contributor to psychoanalytic psychology. With his third book of our new psychoanalytic century, he demonstrates the continuing vitality of traditional psychoanalytic ideas and his own ongoing generativity.

Dale Boesky
Psychoanalytic Disagreements in Context
NY: Jason Aronson, 2008
xx + 229 pp., $85 (cloth), 44.95 (paper).
Psychologist Psychoanalyst 29, No. 3 (2009), pp. 51–52

"Congenial inclusiveness (is) not... enough" (p 75) concludes Dale Boesky in his chapter on comparative psychoanalysis, evoking association to Bettelheim's (1950) famous title. This book is Boesky's attempt to develop a method for contextualization of clinical material from which we might develop useful comparisons within and between our differing theoretical models. It can be considered another effort on the theme "pluralism and its discontents," begun by Wallerstein (1988) and more recently addressed by Pine (2006) and Rangell (2007). Boesky's aim is to provide a philosophy of science grounding to extend recent successes in achieving professional congeniality, and to help adherents of different models to stop talking past one another.

Boesky considers his aim narrow and modest, focusing solely on the mind of the analyst as interventions are formulated and prioritized, rather than on specifics of technique or the truth claims of different models. Along the way it becomes clear that his task is highly ambitious, even "daunting" (p 117).

Clinical examples are discussed in four chapters. The first addresses the well-known Casement (1982) paper about token physical contact with a patient, and its many published discussions extending over two decades and exhibiting "two dozen analysts divided into two opposing camps, each of which [omit] important data... "(p 34). Boesky offers eight contextual criteria—defined as bridging tools, "dynamic themes that link theory, context, and technique" (p 34)—and suggests rules of evidence that he believes could usefully guide a psychoanalyst's thinking. His next example takes up several works of the Boston Change Process Study Group (BCPSG), and concludes that their promotion of "sloppiness and indeterminacy" (p.71) is a "category error," an "unrecognized misunderstanding of the nature of the things being discussed" (p 9).

A third clinical example, from Boesky's own practice, attempts to show that one- and two-person psychologies are compatible rather than contradictory. A final example offers contextual criteria to clarify a dispute between Brenner (2003) and himself over a presentation by Kogan (2003), a disagreement between adherents of the same theoretical model. In this example, Boesky argues that "equifinality"—the assumption that most analysts get good results (all roads lead to Rome)—is based on faith, not evidence, and is fallacious.

In three concluding chapters, Boesky focuses on what are his basic concepts: associations, contextualization and hermeneutics. Psychic determinism is axiomatic for him, and a patient's associations are privileged in the search for hidden meanings. Boesky believes our several models agree on seeking hidden meanings, but notes that not all consider determinism and association to be essential. He explicates and subscribes to the "critical realism" of philosopher-psychoanalysts Charles and Margaret Ann Fitzpatrick Hanly (2001) and Marcia Cavell (2002) in contrast to perspectivist claims. He posits hermeneutics as a heuristic strategy consistent with science, rather than a competing epistemology. He emphasizes throughout the need for clinical evidence, clear definitions, and sound research, and laments their inadequacy in every one of our models.

This book is well worth the effort to work through its closely reasoned arguments, laden with extensive footnotes and several heavily philosophical sections. Recognizing that most analysts are not experts in such discourse, Boesky provides a glossary and an extensive list of supplemental readings, but several chapters seem to have been presented as stand-alone papers and are not smoothly integrated, with redundancies that add to the difficulty of comprehension.

A greater difficulty might be Boesky's evaluation of points of view differing from his own modern structural theory, perhaps straining congeniality. While he lauds pluralism and considers theoretical eclecticism necessary, and he claims (despite acknowledged bias) to "not have a horse in this race" (p 8), a string of judgmental words: "error," "fallacy," "flawed," "misleading," "contradiction," "conflate," would result in many—perhaps all—of the other horses being "scratched." Those betting on other entries will not likely be persuaded. In his recent review, Arnold Goldberg (2008), a self-psychologist, while praising the scholarship and clear-headedness of the book, is virtually dismissive of Boesky's central attempt at finding common ground.

This problem is not new. The theme of the recent IPA Congress in Chicago was "Convergences and Divergences." The search for common ground within pluralism was also begun by Wallerstein (1990). Yet when leaders of various schools are asked to present arguments, mutual dismissal is routine. Recently, Henry Smith (2007), the editor of *The Psychoanalytic Quarterly,* commenting on papers invited for a special supplement issue on therapeutic action, sharply criticizes several contributions on logical and philosophical grounds similar to Boesky's. Does this problem represent the long-standing conflict between "thinkers" and "feelers?"

Most of us might join Boesky in endorsing Arlow's observation that an "analyst must have both a soft heart and a tough mind" (p 163), but we fall easily into caricature in judging models different from our own. Attempts at congeniality and inclusiveness may be necessary to promote discourse, but the details of the discourse carry the risk of re-alienation.

I prefer a version of Boesky's model, but I am troubled by his central assertions about equifinality and clinical error. Lack of evidence and slippery slope are his two objections to equifinality; each argument could be applied to many of our theoretical assertions. Lacking consensus on a definition of treatment success, it seems premature to dismiss claims of models other than our own. I have been surprised recently to discover groups of therapists practicing gestalt therapy and even orgone therapy, among other nominally psychodynamic approaches. I had thought that these offshoots had been found obsolete decades ago. It will take much more time—if we can achieve it at all—to create a definitive clinical psychoanalysis, since we all properly lionize both individuality and the uniqueness of each patient-therapist pair.

As to the possibility of error in clinical interventions, Boesky admits that the "list of possible meanings (of associations) is inexhaustible" (p. 160). He claims, nonetheless, that if some details are not considered, we are in a situation he analogizes to risking erroneous medical diagnosis. Contextual considerations are proposed as remedy, but different models disagree on contextual priorities. Boesky's assertion is reminiscent of Glover's (1955) views on inexact interpretation. Errors in clinical work, and better and worse interventions, surely exist. Unfortunately, we lack agreement on how to judge them. Boesky's quarrel with Brenner is most telling in this regard, and reminds me of my own study groups in which disagreement on specific clinical interventions is routine, welcome, and experienced as useful—but rarely leads to conclusions. I find Fred Busch's (1993) "in the neighborhood" notion to be a more useful guide than a Glover-like perfectionism I read into Boesky's warning about misdiagnosis.

My own resonance with much of the substance of this book leads me to hope it will find a readership and stimulate useful discussion, instead of falling victim to dismissal. Boesky concludes that we must keep trying to come together, so "we will be better able to follow Beckett's famous advice: 'Fail again, fail better'" (p 204). Boesky has not failed, but our recent congeniality and inclusiveness has not been nearly enough to render psychoanalysis a consensually understood, coherent therapy among its diverse practitioners.

Daniel Burston
Erik Erikson and the American Psyche: Ego, Ethics and Evolution
NY: Jason Aronson, 2007
xiv + 219 pp. $37.95 (paper)
Psychologist Psychoanalyst 30, No. 2 (2010), pp. 33–34

I have been a fan of *Childhood and Society* for more than a half century and have used Erikson's (1950) epigenetic schema of the life cycle as a central theme in teaching human development, both to prospective teachers and to psychoanalytic candidates. This one book initiated the field of lifespan developmental psychology while also situating basic psychoanalytic theory within a socio-cultural context. As I followed Erikson's subsequent writing, I admired his creation of psychohistory and psychobiography, and was proud that a practicing clinician and major extender of Freudian thinking was also a public intellectual. Over time I became puzzled that both the professional literature and institute curricula seemed to give his contributions short shrift. A 2007 citation count showed Erikson to be widely quoted in journals in other disciplines and in the popular press, but not in psychoanalysis.

Upon Erikson's death I organized a symposium, presented at the Division 39 1995 meeting and subsequently published in a special issue of *Psychoanalytic Review* (1997). The neglect of Erikson's ideas seemed especially incongruous in light of Wallerstein's obituary (1995) proclaiming him "a true genius." Daniel Burston has solved my puzzlement! In the closing chapter of this book, "Erikson's Erasure," he provides a complex and convincing set of reasons implicating *Childhood and Society* (professional and cultural), and respecting the core Freudian idea of overdetermination.

This wide-ranging and closely reasoned yet accessible book is more than an excellent psychobiography and a sound description of much of psychoanalytic history in the United States. It is also a comparative psychoanalysis including commentary on Freud, Jung, Adler, Rank, Federn, Anna Freud, Melanie Klein, Reich, Fenichel, Hartmann, Rapaport, Waelder, Eissler, Fromm, Winnicott, and Lacan; and a comparative philosophy discussing Kant, Nietsche, Darwin, Marx, Freud again, and the Frankfurt School. A scholarly *tour de force*, on many pages reading like a novel, it provides even more: Insights into Luther, Gandhi and the psychology of religion, and the development of conscience through intergenerational identification; dream psychology, and social commentary. The book is also a testimony to the multiple domains to which psychoanalysis belongs: a theory of mind, a theory of psychopathology, a healing art, a science, and a major addition to the history of ideas.

Burston, professor and chair of the psychology department at Duquesne University, is not a clinical practitioner. The author of numerous books and articles on the history and theory of psychoanalysis, and the many points of convergence between psychology, philosophy, religion and culture, he is neither a basher nor idolizer of Freud or Erikson. He offers incisive critiques of them and the several thinkers he discusses, admiring strengths and noting weaknesses as he sees them. Until the 1970s, he tells us, psychoanalytic history was "a meager field dominated by the Freudian faithful or those with some sectarian axe to grind" (p. 170). Since then seasoned historians, philosophers and independent scholars have taken up the task.

As a clinician, I find Burston's intellectual range awe-inspiring and his argumentation fair. I will take note of three focal topics: Erikson on superego development, Erikson on dreams (two areas in which I feel well-informed and in agreement with Erikson's modifications of the Freudian canon), and Burston's ethological critique of Freud (where I find the ideas to be less convincing).

Burston's Thesis

This book is more than biography or historical treatise, however informative readers will find those sections. Burston has a thesis from which he draws his own conclusions about the contemporary "American Psyche" of his title. His thesis is that Erikson is not an ego psychologist, but instead a creative theorist impossible to pigeonhole, and a "crypto-revisionist" (p. 90). Burston shows Erikson's exaggerated loyalty to Freud to conceal a creative revisionism under the guise of orthodoxy. This professed loyalty did not protect him from rejection by the psychoanalytic establishment (most notably his own analyst, Anna Freud); nor did their rejection protect what was once "a movement" from the energy-sapping schisms that have weakened it.

For Burston, Erikson's single most important idea is "intergenerational identification," a cultural and historical concept that "clinicians, with their narrow focus on treatment issues, generally overlook" (p.3). It is about the relationship of adults—engaged in their middle age generativity conflict—and their adolescent children who need good role models in their quest for identity. "Intergenerational identification" extends the psychology of superego development forward from the Oedipus complex and is as well, in contemporary terms, relational. Failures of intergenerational identification can result in cynicism, indifference, or rigidity. Successful identifications result in judicious ethics and flexible minds. Erikson's insistence on ethical concerns was a reproach to the more rigid stance of many of his psychoanalytic contemporaries. Burston's conclusion is a rebuke to the current technological culture in which anonymous internet relationships replace authentic intergenerational ones.

The Specimen Dream

Erikson's best known clinical contribution, "On the Dream Specimen of Psychoanalysis" (1954), appeared in the second volume of the *Journal of the American Psychoanalytic Association.* Here Erikson reanalyzes Freud's Irma dream and offers a prospective approach to the meaning of dreams, consistent with his own ideas about identity-formation; this in addition to Freud's archeological and decoding method. Burston, with the benefit of subsequent commentaries and later emergent biographical material, provides an even more complex understanding of this basic clinical text. From his exegesis, we learn more about Freud, Erikson, and the art and challenges of clinical dream interpretation.

Instincts and Civilization

"Freud's contention that instincts and their derivatives lack realism and restraint and hamper the organism's adaptation to reality" (p.85) is seen by Burston as inconsistent with ethological observations that instincts are naturally selected "to enhance adaptation, not to obstruct it" (p.85). It is a "civilized conceit" Burston argues, "that aggression is unchecked in nature ... or that restraints... are all a product of 'civilization,' as Freud contended" (p.86). For Erikson, "aggressive tendencies...ascribed to the 'death instinct'...are rather a product of... socialization" (p.86): *Instinctive* means adaptive; *instinctual* means excessively libidinal or aggressive, and "divorced from instinctive patterning" (p.86). Burston sees Erikson's views as avoiding the "closet metaphysics" (p.85) of the Hartmann/Rapaport model, opening psychoanalysis to data from outside the consulting room, and supporting a social psychoanalysis. Although I question this very specific application of the ethological point of view to psychoanalytic drive theory, Burston's conclusion that Erikson's views conflicted with the standard psychoanalytic theory of his contemporaries is on the mark.

A Critique

Burston's view of Erikson as a "crypto-revisionist" is a significant but only partial truth. Like Freud, Erikson's intellectual ambitions were not limited to clinical practice. "Totem and Taboo" (1913b) and "Moses and Monotheism" (1939) are two examples of Freud's attempt to create a complete theory of the human condition. Erikson might better be considered an "extender" (Bergmann, 1993) of this line of the Freudian agenda. His was an attempt to account for the interaction among the biological, psychological, social and cultural contributions to human development. At a time when psychoanalysts dominated mental health practice and were protective of the purity of that practice, Erikson's theoretical forays and his popularization were seen as "not psychoanalysis," speculative, and indicating dilettantism in a man who did not spend his time in one place and could not, therefore, be a clinician dedicated to an increasingly long-term treatment model.

As a psychologist who was also excluded then from the psychoanalytic establishment, I found Erikson's work to be broad and unifying, and his influence on people like Dr. Benjamin Spock and Mr. Fred Rogers to be salutary. I find his work to be consistent with the "developed Freudian" of Rangell's (2007) total composite theory. The contents of recent newsletters of the American Psychoanalytic Association and the International Psychoanalytical Association suggest that the "establishment" may itself have become more Eriksonian now that it can no longer impose a narrow-scope, pure and exclusive psychoanalytic model of theory or practice.

Clinicians might find some of Burston's points inadequately appreciative of clinical realities, and there are occasional misspellings and injudicious comments (e.g., p.142, "Hartmann's work just sounds silly nowadays"). We should, however, be grateful for this important volume, and should hurry to invite Burston to speak at Division 39 conferences.

This book appears under the imprimatur of *Psychological Issues*, an excellent monograph series founded by George S. Klein in the 1950s and currently edited by Morris Eagle, a former president of the division. Kudos to Morris.

"Wild Analysis" Revisited: A Comment on Summers (2011) and Zamanian (2011)
Psychoanalytic Psychology 28, No. 4 (2011), pp. 581–583

Papers by Frank Summers (2011) and Kavah Zamanian (2011) each take inspiration from Freud's 1910 paper, "'Wild' Psychoanalysis" (1910). They are worthy in their own right, but they also demonstrate the ongoing generativity of Freud's ideas and the creative use to which they can be put. These authors are not the first to find this paper evocative.

Roy Schafer (1985) introduced the idea of "tame" analyses in a paper that is a model for comparative theorizing. He postulated criteria by which an analysis might be considered wild, depending on one's theoretical perspective. He compared Freud's original concept—wildness as interpretation that ignores resistance and precedes the development of a benign transference—with Freud's actual practice, wildly associative in theoretical trail-blazing, yet contextual in clinical work. Schafer compared Freud's understanding of "wild" with the then-current approaches of Gill, Kohut and Klein, and he inferred their responses to his comparison. He saw that accusations of wildness could effectively be hurled in all directions, as could the alternative of being tame in the face of the complexity and intensity of psychoanalytic work.

Summers' novel idea is to consider "wild" any psychoanalytic treatment conducted from an essentialist position, i.e., with preconceived ideas about what is likely to be discovered. He contrasts this wildness with what he believes should be an open-ended process in which results cannot be foreseen. Claiming that drive models have been overthrown in contemporary psychoanalysis, he evokes a parallel with the shift in the humanities from neo-classicism to a romantic viewpoint. He sees current practice as defined by its method of inquiry rather than theory, with the aim of self-realization via an expansion of personal subjectivity. Praising Freud's method of evenly-hovering attention, Summers asserts as invalid Freud's insistence on the centrality of sex and the Oedipus Complex. To the extent that any of our theories impose norms, Summers counts them as wild; only the patient's experience deserves analytic focus; anything different is oppressive.

An astute theorist and experienced clinician, Summers answers several theoretical challenges to his ideas along the way, and his clinical examples effectively demonstrate his approach. But Zamanian (2011), in the paper immediately following, presents a strikingly different position, regarding both "wild" analysis and drive theory. The placement of the two papers is an editorial coup—attesting to the vitality and excitement of contemporary psychoanalytic theorizing.

Zamanian emphasizes a traditional reading of Freud's distinction between sex and psychosexuality, always controversial and often ignored (as Freud indeed pointed out in the original 1910 paper). Freud's position has been increasingly defended, at first by his own "romantic" followers (Ferenczi, Balint), currently by the desexualized approach of attachment theory and, shockingly to both Zamanian and me, even by nominally psychoanalytic clinicians who, instead of offering analysis, refer patients with sexual issues to sex therapists.

Zamanian asserts that Freud recognized attachment as obvious and instinctual, but chose to focus on psychosexuality as drive (and related fantasies) in his own project. By distinguishing between drive and instinct, a new psychology— psychoanalysis—is created, based in bodily experience yet responsive to the external world. Infantile sexuality assumes bisexuality, polymorphous perversity and zonal dimensions, along with primary and secondary identification, as determining an individual's psychological makeup.

Zamanian resurrects Freud's (1920) concept of *Thanatos* as critical to this model, as a biological fact, and as a matter of human character. He sees it evidenced by repetition-compulsion, and incorrectly dismissed by too many contemporary analysts. Aggression and sex are issues too wild for those who cling instead to romantic notions of love and intimate attachment while ignoring the ubiquity of war and sex in the cultural surround as striking evidence of repression and acting out. He argues as well for metapsychology as necessary for understanding issues like masochism and gender identity.

I take no issue with Summers' encouragement to listen to our patients and to appreciate individual variations of the human condition; this has always been basic to Freud's talking cure. I also expect to be surprised and often to be wrong in my interpretive conjectures. But Zamanian (not to mention Brenner [2006], and many European and South American analysts) shows that Summers' claim that drive models have been overthrown is premature at best, and his romantic view extreme. Summers states that Bion's (2001) admonition to be without desire or memory is fanciful, yet he promotes its spirit and stance: his thesis being that all theory-based work is wild analysis. Schafer was already a hermeneutic, two-person psychologist in 1983 when presenting his paper at a plenary session of the American Psychoanalytic Association and when he said of Freud, "He made his discoveries by knowing what to look for, and his discoveries helped him look for more and to find it, to our lasting benefit" (1985, p. 279). How can we as psychoanalysts not have our own ideas, however much we may be open to the unknown and accepting of our patients' thoughts and experiences? (Or, what's a two-person psychology for?) Summers seems to create an unnecessary dichotomy between his romantic approach and the neo-classicism he asserts is superseded.

For Zamanian, it is the romantic view that is reactionary. Although he recognizes attachment theory as important, and attachment itself an instinct (rather than a psychological drive), he treats the matter as obvious and almost unworthy of psychoanalytic interest, claiming that Freud thought similarly. His very title asserts that attachment is used defensively, to the detriment of psychoanalysis. Like any other psychological event, attachment may be used in the service of defense, but it seems, nonetheless, a valid area for research, and it has potential clinical relevance as well.

When I first read *Beyond the Pleasure Principle*, I was thoroughly taken with the beauty of Freud's (1920) metaphor of the struggle between Eros and Thanatos. Nearly a half-century later I still appreciate its poetry and I consider aggression and sexuality basic drives central to psychoanalytic theory and practice, but I do not find persuasive Zamanian's attempt to revive Thanatos as a clinically relevant concept.

I very much appreciate Summers and Zamanian for placing their psychoanalytic thinking in the context of the history of ideas (neo-classicism, romanticism). For me, clinical psychology and its most complex and useful theory—psychoanalysis—are rooted in philosophy, specifically The Problem of Evil. That sexuality is intricately implicated in a psychology of Evil (as a function of superego development) is a major Freudian contribution; that aggression is centrally related to Evil seems too obvious to belabor. These two thoughtful and scholarly papers, especially as they are paired, attest to the ongoing and open-ended excitement of psychoanalytic ideas.

Daniel Benveniste
The Interwoven Lives of Sigmund, Anna and W. Ernest Freud: Three Generations of Psychoanalysis
International Psychoanalytic Books, 2015
pp xvii+668
International Psychoanalyst, 2015

Daniel Benveniste has produced a massive and complex work. At its core is a biography of one man, Ernst (1914-2008), the eldest of Sigmund Freud's eight grandchildren, the only one who became a psychoanalyst. It is also a partial biography of Sigmund himself, dating from the birth of this grandchild, and of Anna, a foster mother to Ernst, also his child analyst, and eventually his professional mentor. The book is about their respective psychoanalytic careers and the times in which they lived; it evolves into a psychobiography of Ernst.

Benveniste is an accidental biographer, having first sought a meeting with the elderly Ernst to discuss the *Fort Da* game. Ernst was the toddler observed in Freud's first report of *Fort Da* (1919 footnote to Freud, 1900, p. 461), an observation that became a part of a major revision of drive theory (1920). Benveniste was pursuing his own interest in the psychology of games. Ernst, like his famous forbears, was reluctant to cooperate in an authorized biography, but a mutual cathexis occurred nearly immediately in their second meeting, when Ernst drafted Daniel for what became a fourteen-year labor of apparently mutual love.

This triple biography offers an even greater number of voices than subjects. Benveniste cites many sources in a 23-page bibliography; countless letters among the principals, their friends and acquaintances; and extensive interviews with Ernst, his friends and colleagues, even his ex-wife and ex-brother-in-law. These are provided as direct quotes and transcriptions in a gray matte background to contrast them with the author's narrative and to provide a greater sense of authenticity. The unusual gray pages provide multiple witnesses to the colorful lives of the three Freuds. Benveniste adds yet another voice, that of Ernst's mother, Sophie Freud Halberstadt, who died of Spanish flu when he was not yet six years old. Sophie kept a baby diary, a fine example of child observation before this became a psychoanalytic practice. Appendices provide the diary translated into English, and in the original German. Benveniste's singular voice sounds clearly in the last forty pages of this tome, arguing that a 1936 case report by Anna, later elaborated as "Frank O." (Sandler et al, 1980), was a disguised version of Ernst's child analysis—

from which Benveniste provides conclusions about Ernst. Benveniste's original interest is discussed in a 27-page appendix: "The reel [sic] meaning of *Fort Da.*" A series of photographs, most from Ernst's collection, separates the book's several sections.

Benveniste asks if W. Ernst Freud merits a biography in his own right, and answers, "Absolutely not" (p 2). This book is primarily a contribution to the history of psychoanalysis. Its first and longest section focuses on Sigmund Freud's final quarter century of life, years in which he developed his mature theories, and extended them. World history (The Great War, Nazism) is also a major character. The escape and exile of the Freud family reads like a thriller novel, despite general knowledge of these events. Ernst, age 25 at Freud's death, was a victim of fate: his father's wartime absence, his young mother's death while pregnant with a second brother, his favored younger brother's death, his becoming a foster child cared for by relatives. He did poorly at school and seemed without direction. It was almost accidental that he was included on the short list to be ransomed from Nazi horror: he was unemployed and living with the Freuds and Burlinghams at *Bergasse 19*. In England, Ernst served as his grandfather's chauffeur, driving him to medical appointments.

These 250 pages are thoroughly engaging. They provide an important section on the Hietzing School, founded by Anna Freud and Dorothy Burlingham for the Burlingham children and the children of friends. Teachers included Erik Erikson, Peter Blos, Sr., and Esther Menaker, one of my first supervisors, then a candidate at the Vienna Institute. This small school and its communal life provide a stunning rebuke to promoting psychoanalysis as prophylactic, and may surprise those unfamiliar with the absence in the pioneering days of therapeutic boundaries now taken for granted. Suicides, neuroses, and interpersonal conflicts are reported within the extended Freud family, and among their analytically-oriented friends and acquaintances. Every Hietzing student was in analysis with Anna, including her nephew, who had been her first patient earlier in his life. In a series of cameo appearances, many of Ernst's classmates are profiled—several were also interviewed. This method (cameos and interviews) continues throughout the book with scores of Ernst's contacts having their accomplishments noted, while lending their voices to describe "that Halberstadt boy" and each other. Erikson and Blos get mixed reviews as young teachers.

Benveniste's account of the *Anschluss* and the eventual escape of the Freud family are painfully detailed. Freud's long-standing naïveté regarding Nazism, and his stubborn wish to die at home delayed his decision to flee. Benveniste believes

Freud's succumbing to "the narcissism of minor differences" in his concern about Anna's being unwelcome among English Kleinians was a "bizarre, blind denial" (p 230) of the larger Nazi menace. In physical distress from cancer and multiple surgeries, Freud after age 70 is quoted as feeling he lived too long, though his productive work continued unabated. Defensive? Post-Hartmann psychoanalysis would count this a most admirable adaptation.

Anna Freud is the dominating presence of the second and next longest section (160 pages), though Ernst's adulthood is described in exhaustive detail. Interned enemy-alien, marriage and fatherhood, college, adopting the Freud name, starting psychoanalytic training; even his institute curriculum is recorded in full. Slowly emerging from an aimless youth, Ernst made few friends. Among these was Leopold Bellak, a boyhood chum who was making his impressive way in the United States. This relationship, like others, remained at a distance; Ernst's letters to Bellak are admiring and envious. Though identified with his aunt in the Klein-Freud split, he felt disrespected by the Anna Freudians, and his psychoanalytic practice did not thrive. His work was mainly at Hampstead, under Anna's aegis. Even in old age, he blamed the jealousy of others for his not living up to his famous (adopted) surname and legacy. Ernst did not find an independent career focus until his late fifties; his sense of identity seemed mature only in his seventies, following his aunt's death. He kept his distance as her health was failing, and—conspicuously—did not attend her funeral.

Ernst lived on for nearly 26 years, 20 of them productive. For these 20, Benveniste dubs him "The Lone Wolf," playing on his given name, Ernst Wolfgang, the W mysteriously placed first when he became an Englishman. Those close to him called and spoke of him as Ernst. Major personal markers of this period were divorce, relocation to Germany to take up with a lover, and the accidental death in 1987 of his only child, Colin, from whom he had become nearly estranged. Ernst wrote and lectured internationally about the infant observation research he had begun at Hampstead. He was disappointed in his wish to relocate to the United States when his resume proved insufficient for landing a funded position, despite support from several prominent American analysts. Benveniste remarks on his scholarly productivity: in the two decades following Anna's death, Ernst more than doubled his published output compared with the years at Hampstead. In 2002, shortly after extensive conversations with his biographer, Ernst moved into an assisted living facility where he deteriorated physically and mentally for six years, dying at age 94.

In his concluding chapter, Benveniste focuses on Oedipal issues (a father at war, a doting mother), loss (the deaths of mother, brother, aunt and son), and sibling rivalry as major themes reflected in Ernst's character. In their conversations, subject and biographer came to see the death of the unborn brother as of deepest significance, reflected ultimately in Ernst's involvement with research on pre- and perinatal development. These formulations fit well with the plentiful material provided. Sibling rivalry is also posited as a thread connecting the three generations: Sigmund/Julius, Anna/Sophie, and Ernst/Heinerle. Finally, and primarily with literary references, Benveniste argues for *Fort Da* as the central theme of Ernst's life and elaborates in an appendix on *Fort Da* as an important psychological phenomenon.

While reading this book, I often thought of "personology," Henry Murray's personality theory, grounded in psychoanalysis but also a precursor to contemporary "positive psychology." Ernst's life could be judged as one of pathological compromises, a personality disordered in reaction to multiple traumata. That verdict would not adequately reflect the record of evidence provided by this thorough study of his life. Slowed but not overwhelmed by early losses and family instability, Ernst made friends, found love, and achieved meaningful professional success. A patient's memoir speaks of the selfless and sound help he provided as her analyst. His admission to obstetric and neonatal intensive care hospital units though lacking medical or academic doctoral credentials confirmed recognition of his research efforts. Benveniste correctly calls it unfair to compare a child with a brilliant aunt or a genius grandfather. Ernst was a "normal neurotic;" a contemporary phrase for reasonable adaptation to life's vicissitudes and the human condition.

Implicit in the book's title is an attempt to shed light on mechanisms of intergenerational influence through "the study of lives," this phrase being the title of a *festschrift* for Henry Murray (White, 1963) that includes essays by Erikson and Bellak. Benveniste provides more than ample evidence that Ernst's psychoanalyst namesakes had enormous influence over him. Benveniste's conclusions and his discourse on *Fort Da* are worthy contributions. Specific mechanisms of identification remain an area for further psychoanalytic investigation.

Daniel Benveniste has made a major contribution to Freud scholarship. Those interested in the intensive study of individuals will appreciate this report on these lives. The book has recently earned Benveniste well-deserved honorary membership in the American Psychoanalytic Association.

**Steven D. Axelrod, Ronald C. Naso, and
Larry M. Rosenberg, (Eds.)**
Progress in Psychoanalysis: Envisioning the Future of the Profession
NY: Routledge, 2018
xxii + 305 pp, $44.95 Paperback, $160 Hardback
Psychoanalytic Psychology 38, No. 2 (2021), pp. 157–159

It is with some trepidation that I began to read this book. I've avoided edited volumes, usually finding the several contributions inconsistent in the writing, and often redundant. I try to keep up instead by reading journal reviews of such books. This one is a striking exception. Each chapter is a gem that could stand on its own, though several relate explicitly to the others. Easy to read but disquieting, the difficult truths and "sclerotic culture" (p.7) described throughout the volume are matters of critical concern. The editors' summary brings them together to create coherence, but psychoanalysis *is* in crisis, and while these superb essays attempt to intervene, resolution remains elusive: this book is aspirational, perhaps even utopian. Complex and nuanced recommendations reflect the history of conflict in our field, despite decades of compulsive repetition.

The book is divided into three sections: Perspectives, Research and Training, and Relevance beyond the Consulting Room. It was published in 2018, so I must first address recent events that provide a more current context for evaluation.

Trumpism, Covid-19, and the Murder of George Floyd

About 75 million US citizens voted to re-elect Donald J. Trump, the largest number for a presidential candidate in US history but one, Joseph R. Biden, Jr., whose popular vote total was several million more. Mr. Trump left office contesting the result as fraudulent, even inciting an insurrection that attempted to overturn it. His unreality remains supported by many of his voters. Confidence in the electoral system itself is threatened by "alternate facts" and "fake news," claims that gainsay any evidence-based truth-seeking. This attack on epistemology itself may be a perverse sequel to the post-modern replacement of logical positivism, with frightening implications for respectful collaboration, the very foundation for progress promoted by the writers and editors of this book. Can we (the people) get along?

For psychoanalytic clinicians world-wide, the Covid-19 pandemic shifted practice in a matter of days to remote technologies that had been controversial within the profession. Early research on remote treatments (Bekas et al, 2020) found the shift far less traumatic than anticipated. In less than a year, psychoanalytic practice is adjusting to the pandemic, but there remains controversy as to how changes will affect practice over time: Will it remain recognizably psychoanalytic?[1]

The police murder of George Floyd returned American racism to a top priority issue in US politics and underscored the perennial failure of our profession to "look like America." Psychoanalysts remain overwhelmingly economically-secure white people, despite the greater focus on diversity and inclusion in journals and the meeting programs of local and national organizations.[2] Can't we do better than talk among ourselves?

It is no accident that of the 17 contributors to this volume, only two are physicians. Ending the monopolistic medical orthodoxy described by Eissler (1965) required, 20 years later, a restraint-of-trade lawsuit against the American Psychoanalytic Association (APsaA) and its affiliates. APsaA policy requiring training analysts to report on the analyses of candidates also met its well-deserved end. Such analyses were almost necessarily superficial. A psychiatrist friend wondered during training how he could be open with his analyst when his career hung in the balance. While some of those trained under this policy may have had valid treatments, others did not. A fully-credentialed medical psychoanalyst spoke of learning a lot from his training analysis though his career evolved toward anti-analytic bias. Others—meeting with rigidly silent, rule-bound analysts—became vocal opponents. The lawsuit saved APsaA; when psychiatrists stopped seeking its training, its membership ranks were filled mostly by psychologists.

Contents and Some Discontents

Despite editorial coherence, the five "Perspectives" chapters are at some odds with one another; differences among them reflect contemporary pluralism. Elliot Jurist

---

1 Two papers published by European colleagues (*IJPsa* 2020, 101:3) might be summarized, only half facetiously: "If you can't smell the patient, it's not psychoanalysis." One suggested discontinuing the work until in-person sessions could resume.

2 The Metropolitan Institute for Training in Psychoanalytic Psychotherapy in New York City is a notable exception; its holiday parties are striking in the visible range of ethnic diversity of party-goers.

calls for coexistence between science and hermeneutics, offering "mentalization research" as a unifying method to lead toward a "strong pluralism." Paul Wachtel reiterates his longstanding advocacy of clinical integration as the proper response to competing orthodoxies that include CBT. Ronald Naso introduces a novel term, "fictionalism," to support coherent narrative and fantasy as pillars of good theory and practice. For Naso, psychoanalysis is a metaphorical enterprise in which fantasy has causal power. David Lichtenstein sees the divided self—and especially the unconscious—as *demanding* multiple theories and *unintegrated* practice. He claims that mastery is illusory; consensus and coherence can only be partial. Lichtenstein makes the case for welcoming multiple points of view as representing the illogic of the dynamic unconscious. Morris Eagle finds fault with that position, urging a responsible integration toward a theory of mind, while respecting a therapist's primary responsibility to the patient. Eagle sees no real progress in the controversy so far (p 112), joining consensus with barely hidden skepticism.

In the spirit of inquiry, I raise some questions: To Jurist: Does "mentalization" owe a debt to "object constancy," a concept advanced by Margaret Mahler? I'd ask Naso whether "fictionalism" is not too easily parodied. I'd ask Wachtel whether the overt antagonisms often referred to as the "Therapy Wars" (Burkeman, 2016) can be overcome by pleas for goodwill collaboration with those who attack therapeutic analyses as malpractice. Lichtenstein's understanding of Freud's *Ucs* seems reflected in the unresolved issues of our profession, but is there no chance for the soft voice of intellect to be effective? This section is rich in detail and exciting to read.

The four chapters comprising part 2, "Research and Training," are not in conflict; they are mutually supportive, and easy to endorse—if our history of conflict is ignored. In the first research chapter, Elizabeth Graf and Diana Diamond discuss three evidence-based psychoanalytic treatments known best by their leaders' names: Kernberg, Milrod and Fonagy, respectively. Clinicians support research in principle and are pleased that successful outcomes are reported, but the standing ovation given to Irwin Hoffman's (2009) APsaA plenary address shows that resistance is strong. Practitioners find research studies, typically focusing on specific diagnoses, inapplicable for work with either clinic or private practice populations.

In the second research chapter, Sherwood Waldron and colleagues update his 35-year program studying 27 cases recorded by seven psychoanalysts, with new statistical tools enabling a focus on treatment process (what works and doesn't work). The acknowledged small and dated sample, with adequate funding absent and replication unlikely, might well account for this project's marginality, except that psychoanalytic research remains, unfortunately, largely marginal and ignored by clinicians.

Erika Schmidt, in the first chapter on training, urges institutes to go beyond preparation for practice to address the social function of psychoanalytic ideas, as do many recent open professional meetings. She emphasizes the critical problems of teaching both norms and individualization, and of promoting curiosity while offering comforting structure for neophytes.

Norka Malberg's chapter focuses on development, Freud's genetic metapsychological point of view. In my opinion, this is the most influential societal contribution of our field, and is fundamental to developmental psychology and education, though mostly unacknowledged.[1] John Dewey's progressivism was consistent with psychoanalytic values; Benjamin Spock's *Baby and Child Care* (1946) was Freudian-based, and once the all-time best-seller after the Bible, and TV's Mister Rogers was perhaps its most effective champion.

The concluding section, "Relevance beyond the Consulting Room," offers three approaches aimed at recovering social relevance for psychoanalysis. Kerry Sulkowicz's chapter on leadership is especially notable as its author is incoming president of APsaA, a position typically held by a clinician. Sulkowicz, a certified psychoanalyst, has made a career as a consultant to industry, finding his clinical training transferable to the dynamics of business leadership. He emphasizes leaders' ability to inspire, a non-rational proposition (p. 112).[2]

Kimberlyn Leary addresses public policy as a domain calling out for a psychoanalytic sensibility. She outlines modifications of approach needed to promote psychoanalytic values in healthcare reform, most especially with heretofore underserved populations.

Larry Rosenberg's chapter directs analysts to take consultative, teaching, and supervisory roles in a mental health workforce whose direct providers far outnumber psychoanalysts. He also takes up the problem of burnout, asserting that psychoanalysts are best able to help to reduce it among therapists.

---

1 Jonathan Cohen's (2018) efforts in the area of social-emotional learning in schools is an important exception.

2 By not citing occasional phrases and allusions, I've followed Sulkowicz's admonition that we take Freud off his pedestal, expecting readers of this journal to get them by immersion in Auden's (1940) "whole climate of opinion."

This domain of this third section of the book was named "community psychoanalysis" by its pioneer, Stuart Twemlow. He and his colleagues described multiple non-clinical roles in their edited work, *Analysts in the Trenches* (Sklarew et al, 2004). Among the unusual roles: riding with police on emergency calls and participating in city council meetings. Such opportunities are scarce, and usually short-lived: the next election ended the analyst's city council role. 17 years on, institute curricula remain largely unaffected. These careers are unlikely to provide remunerative employment, and the work itself may not be easily recognizable as psychoanalytic. There is also a risk of giving short shrift to unconscious motivation when dealing directly with politics, business management, crime and racism; external realities are likely to override internal ones.

The editors' summary is not simply a list of the ways forward; each recommendation is nuanced and recognizes many limitations. One general conclusion is that psychoanalysis (in theory and practice) aims for "radical honesty." In the face of Freud's most basic discovery—the universality and depth of self-deception—this aim is resisted constantly. Consensus regarding treatment follows Shedler's (2010) six-point model for psychodynamic psychotherapy, and Pine's theoretical agnosticism, de-idealizing purity for a system of thought with philosophical, clinical, theoretical and pragmatic perspectives. Social psychoanalysis looks for species and cultural manifestations of resistance, while individual treatments utilize resistance to understand character, the etched-in aspects of personality.

The editors support "mentalization," i.e., *learning to appreciate* alternate points of view, and to engage in reflective functioning. I first heard this phrase, "learning to appreciate," over 60 years ago as an undergraduate; it was the instructor's very definition of *cathexis*, serving me far better than attempts to quantify or concretize psychoanalytic ideas. My training, a half-century ago at the Freudian Society, followed a flexible model centered on the misnamed Ego Psychology. Most instructors were psychologists, with backgrounds in philosophy of science and research; they judged theories on utility and avoided reification. Kurt Lewin's "there's nothing more useful than a good theory" was foundational, balanced with J-M Charcot's "theory is all right, but it doesn't prevent something from existing" (Google translation). Models are tentative, as befits a scientific attitude. Their very inadequacies promote inquiry and discovery. A central attraction of Freudian theory was its ambition: a theory of the human mind and its products. Helping people was not enough; most professions or trades could make that claim.

It should not be surprising to psychoanalysts that stable consensus is an idealized fantasy, as was the idea of "psychoanalytic cure." Lichtenstein notes that this state of affairs seems to mimic the operations of the unconscious, where opposites co-exist, paradox is more common than clarity or consistency, and ambivalence and frustration are universal conditions of mind. In Freud's *Ucs*, the fabled rabbi is right: incompatible propositions co-exist! But we must still hope that Eagle's critical thinking, the soft voice of intellect, might find a place.

The consensual respect for research is well-supported by this journal and repeated frequently in this book. Yet there is still only minimal effect of research on training curricula,[1] and collaboration between researchers and clinicians remains uncommon.

Associations Interminable

Mid-20th Century psychoanalytic literature spoke with declarative confidence; since then, authors aim to be evocative rather than definitive. This change parallels the evolution of technique from expert analysts providing interpretations to collaboration in a therapeutic partnership. This book's chapters demonstrate a similar shift, with truth-seeking replacing truth-telling. They are stimulating, and not the dystopia forecast by Bornstein (2005). The crisis is not over; it may be interminable. Pluralism has led—in principle—to open criticism and new ideas.

My preferred psychoanalytic model—Leo Rangell's (2007) "total composite theory"—was also aspirational; this book has converted me to Jurist's "strong pluralism." As a young reader, I found the battle between Eros and Thanatos the most striking of Freud's poetic images, sealing my commitment to psychoanalytic theory. Conquistadorial fantasy must be tamed along with therapeutic zeal. This book, especially in its contradictions, encourages us all to appreciate our profession and to struggle with its full complexity. I urge you to read it.

---

1 An exception: A research course is required for New York State's license in psychoanalysis (LP).

An Elaboration of my Published Review of Axelrod, et al

November 19, 2021

I was truly surprised that writing a book review could alter my position in the theoretical spectrum of psychoanalysis. I patted myself on the back about my identity as a flexible Freudian. I am also someone who prefers order and stability, but I've come to understand that such an orientation is grossly inadequate for understanding the mind, or for that matter much of the world. I also enjoy reading lengthy obituaries, especially of people I've never heard of who have made important contributions to knowledge. In July I read about the life of Richard Lewontin, an outstanding geneticist. He took what has become an old saw: "the more you know the more you know you don't know" to an extreme. He said in 2009, "I think most of the interesting questions about human individual and social behavior will never be answered. The human species will be extinct before they are." I believe this to be true of our field, and to require a modesty of assertion regarding any contemporary claim to large T truth.

In late September, a patient who'd been away on his traditional September vacation called to tell me he was, despite being fully vaccinated, in the hospital with Covid, and would call me when he was up to making a next appointment. I called the following week a few times, only to leave a message. This patient was 82 years old and with cardiac and other health problems. I became concerned for his life. I called his home number and spoke with his wife, who told me he was now on a ventilator and couldn't speak. I was relieved that he was alive, but no less concerned for his life. Some days later I called again, and he answered. Off the ventilator but still hospitalized and awaiting readiness for transfer to a rehab facility, he expressed appreciation for my call. I told him I appreciated hearing his voice.

The necessarily brief call called to my mind the apocryphal story I heard in my first technique course at the Freudian Society: A.A. Brill passed a patient on the street and did not acknowledge the patient's greeting—so as not to violate confidentiality or compromise the transference. My teacher pointed out the absurdity of the first rationale and the cruelty of the second. The psychologist-psychoanalyst Fred Busch wrote a paper entitled "Not your grandfather's psychoanalysis." Indeed! The rigidity of mid-century psychoanalytic technique, enacting a "silent treatment," turned off many, including some in my group. The decline in popular acceptance of psychoanalysis has many reasons. The future of psychoanalysis hinges upon conveying the humanistic essence of the Freudian paradigm that brought its initial success.

Postscript: September 2022

My conversion to a flexible (strong) pluralism was premature. Attending a meeting celebrating the latest Morris Eagle book brought me back to hope for the possibility of a comprehensive theory, one which Eagle's book shows can be based on elaboration of the ego psychological model in which I was trained. My flipflop underscores the Lewontin position discussed above.

Post-Postscript: January 2024

At a recent Zoom conference, at which Morris Eagle was the discussant, I believe I heard him say something to the effect that we are unlikely to resolve our pluralism. Another flipflop supporting Lewontin.

EDUCATION

Humanizing Education

Presented to the Public Education Committee
of West Orange, NJ, 4/8/76

How interpersonally sensitive should or could teachers and administrators be with children and families? And how much focus should or could there be on emotional education?

As a practicing psychoanalyst, "Humanizing Education" is indeed exciting to me. It is also central in my work as a professor and chairman of a university education department. It is even more important to me, as it is to you, in that we are parents of young children. My psychoanalytic background would suggest, correctly, that I bring an emotional focus (and bias) to my role in training teachers and administrators. As department chairman, however, I have come to understand and respect differing focuses and biases.

Tonight, I want to share with you some of the several issues involved in this topic. I want as well to give you some specific approaches to emotional education from both the curriculum and the human relations points of view. (I believe these are complementary rather than contrasting). I hope to stimulate ideas and questions, rather than present definitive answers. Education is much more art than science. Settled answers are few, differences plentiful.

The first is whether or not to "humanize" and, if so, how much. We can cite contrasting positions on the mission of the schools: Shall our emphasis be on cognitive development or emotional development? On product or process? On facts or on values? On passing on the culture or on stimulating ideas and criticisms of it?

These alternatives have been posed from Plato's time to John Dewey's, and continue to ours. To say a little of both—or a balance between them—begs the question in that the school day is time-limited, and funds are scarce. Should we hire a reading resource specialist or a sex educator (when we can't afford both)?

Should we focus on mathematics or on developing patriotism? Writing skills or intergroup relations?

Last year's annual Gallup poll of adult attitudes toward education—a survey of adults and high school seniors—gives us little guidance on this problem. There is a great concern with lack of discipline, problems of integration/segregation, the use of drugs, and inadequate funding, but the solutions all involve more money, and focus on a "more diversified curriculum" and suggestions like the return of prayer to public schools. There are other indications that large numbers of Americans would prefer school to keep out of areas like sex, political controversy and other value--laden issues, leaving emotional and moral development to the home. Your committee's concern for what we're calling "humanizing" education may not be widespread!

Indeed, there have been strong arguments for concentrating on basic skills and cognitive development. The three Rs are certainly a central part of the mission of the schools—teachers are trained to teach them and not effectively trained in emotional or values education, and can get into serious trouble with the community, even if trained. Methods for teaching skills have been better researched than methods for emotional or value development. Results of teaching basics are more easily determined. Why would any teacher venture into the deeper, more turbulent, less well-charted seas of emotions and values. Surely, the argument goes, these are areas for parents, psychologists, and the clergy.

Additionally, there is some evidence that success in life is not much influenced by non-academic aspects of the school experience. Just plain luck, family background, and formal academic achievement (in that decreasing order) seem to have much greater influence. Think of what has influenced your own life.

Despite these arguments, however, let us go with our gut feelings that we want our children to be happier in school, and that success should be judged in emotional terms as well as by objective criteria. Let's look at what humanizing education might mean.

First, let me point up examples of the specific interpersonal problems that occur in the schools: Teachers and parents often have conflicts not only over what to teach, but how. A teacher may see Mary as lazy, not working hard enough; the parents may be encouraging a relaxed approach to school. A teacher may see Johnny as taking a normally long time in learning to read; the parents may be pressing for faster results. The child's welfare may be paramount to both, yet each sees the situation differently.

Conflicts between teacher and child often take the form of discipline battles: chewing gum, talking out of turn. The teacher needs to deal with an entire class—a disruptive child's needs might be felt to interfere with the needs of others. Some teachers have told me, by contrast, that they have conflicts over wanting to be closer with the children and focus more on individual needs, but this is seen by supervisors, parents, and spouses as too emotionally taxing, when compared with a cooler, "professional'" approach.

Administrators and parents are in conflict over the nature of the curriculum, the methodology and the choice of teachers. The professional feels better trained to make such decisions, the parents feel they have a right to a part in the decision-making process as it affects their own children. This, by the way, is a central battle in what is referred to as "the Politics of Education."

Administrators often are placed in conflict with children by virtue of their role as the school disciplinarian. The burdens of paperwork often keep them from being the all-too-rare principal who knows every child by name.

Administrators and teachers are in conflict in what may be considered the typical management-labor model. Although education has been trying to operate in a professional rather than industrial model, the needs for hiring, evaluating, supervising, making salary recommendations, and firing, have made potential adversaries out of professional colleagues. Unions and the tenure system are also at issue here. Additionally, administrators and teachers may disagree as to how much individual curricular and methodological innovation is acceptable. These are just some of the conflicts over principle, that are human interaction conflicts in significant part.

How to deal with these conflicts and solve these problems is the task before us. I would like to focus on the non-emotional aspects of the solution first as my own work and that of my colleagues has convinced me they play a significant role.

1. We must deal with children in terms of what we know regarding stages of development. While there are no sharp age borderlines, most children between ages of three and seven are not prepared for heavy dosages of factual learning in written form. This is a time for Early Childhood Education, which emphasizes freedom of activity, much variety of subject matter, lots of leaving the child to his or her own devices, and lots of learning through play. None of these principles requires throwing out structure or elimination of achievement goals.

2.   Let me skip to the developmental stage of pubescence, ages approximately 11 to 14, when a child's "juices are flowing" in the process of biological change toward reproductive potential. We make a dreadful mistake here by demanding a departmental level, high-school-like academic performance. No wonder Junior High Schools are considered the most difficult level by teachers. We demand cognitive focus from students in biological turmoil! In contrast, we often require little of kids from seven to eleven, a period where biological growth latency and cognitive readiness could allow for tremendous academic achievement! You must be aware of the energy level and concentration involved in stamp-collecting and model-building. It's a shame schools have inappropriate age-stage expectations. We must use tested new curriculum when it's available. A quality curriculum results in a quality lesson, resulting in an excited teacher, a stimulated and happy child, and good feelings in administrators and parents. Some examples:

   a.   Using cutouts for concrete teaching in mathematics: Remember quadratic equations?
   b.   MACOS: Man, A Course Of Study—Exciting descriptions of how humans survive in different ways
   c.   Curricular guides to interpersonal sensitivity

3.   We must individualize the placement of all children. Different children need different styles of teaching and degrees of structure. Some kids do great work in open classrooms, others excel in Montessori settings, yet others thrive in traditional settings. It is often possible to make a learning diagnosis which is followed by a teaching prescription. Trained personnel are, of course, needed, and carrying out of these recommendations are costly.

Now we can look at the non-academic approaches to the solution of the conflicts we've outlined. Let me group these under the heading of "fostering human understanding and self-reflection."

There is a particular problem when discussing human understanding, that is, what are the criteria of good-understanding, or, what are the criteria of good human relations, or of good mental health!

There are two schools of thought here. The dominant one in the United States is the behavioristic school. It answers these questions in terms of overt, objective evaluations. Good human relations (for school children) might be defined in terms of the absence of overt conflict, the participation in peer group activities, the successful completion of academic work.

For behaviorists, only overt behavior is an acceptable criterion for any psychological statements. The advantage here is obvious. Overt behavior can be objectively and scientifically judged.

Unfortunately for objectivity and science, many of us in psychology, human relations, and education know that important things occur within and between people which are not overt: these are thoughts, wishes, fears, whims—the whole area of subjective experience. We non-behaviorists choose to include the subjective experiences of people in our study, at the risk of being less scientific, because psychology, without focusing on internal experience, would be—for us—a hollow shell, a computer model, a distinctly non-human endeavor.

Studying internal experience is difficult mainly because we can never be certain that we are not subjectively biased in what we observe, based on our own thoughts, wishes, fears and whims. We are not suggesting that studying experience should replace observing behavior, but that the two must be combined. Obviously, a person who is doing well may or may not be feeling well; likewise, someone who feels well may or may not be doing well. The method of understanding internal feelings is called "accurate empathy"—knowing what is felt. How do we know what is felt? Because as adults we should have experienced the full range of feelings, not necessarily to the same degree. These feelings we have experienced can be triggered in us if we are in tune with another in such a way that we know how they feel, though not necessarily how deeply. This can be called "grooving," "being on the same wave length"—but it's not magical, it's based on common experiences. Spouses frequently think the same thing at the same time. The better we know someone, the more alike we are, the more accurate our empathy can be. The more different, culturally or generationally, the more likely we'll make errors. No teacher is likely to be accurately empathic on the first day of school.

How to improve the accuracy of empathy? Two ways: by familiarity with the other person, and by greater knowledge of our own feelings and what arouses them. This is where training comes in; training in many forms: meditation, self-reflection, psychotherapy, T-groups (the first group training method aimed at developing accurate empathy); classes (human relations courses are required for all New York City teachers between their bachelor's and master's degrees). Participation in these group activities is aimed at understanding our own emotions through emotional learning. There's been notable success at this in many settings.

The development of more accurate empathy should allow us, whether teachers, administrators or parents, to relate to others so as to understand both their needs and our own, so we may reach the best compromises and resolutions of conflict. We can become aware of the anxieties of teachers (regarding job security, economic and educational status in relation to us) so we can more honestly, and less threateningly, relate to them. Many in our generation are more educated than teachers. This doesn't mean we know more about teaching. With accurate empathy and self-awareness, we can be more open and stop playing power games, and come to respect one another, as we are all more human than otherwise. Should we be able to do this, we may then be able to accept and even help the young, inexperienced teacher, we may be accepted by the older, perhaps rigid principal— we may be able to replace frozen conflict with open communication having a chance for conflict resolution. After all, teachers, parents, administrators, and children are not natural enemies--though their pressures and anxieties may make them act that way.

So, let me conclude with a direct answer to the two questions originally posed:

1. Teachers and administrators can and should be interpersonally sensitive with children and families; but only if they have adequate curriculum, methodology, placement of students, smaller class size and interpersonal sensitivity toward them from parents as well.

2. Emotional education can be adequately pursued in the context of modern curriculum developments, with trained empathic teachers, administrators and parents—without formal lessons on values, but by identification of adult role models who are open, flexible and empathic.

I have left one issue for last, not as an afterthought, but for emphasis. That issue is research. As I said at the outset, the field of education is more art than science. The science of education can and must be more adequately developed so as to end that part of educational controversy which is clearly testable. Funding for educational research has been a very low priority and the quality of educational research reflects that. The area of "humanizing education" has even less meaningful research activity than other areas because applying scientific methodology in human research is harder. We can more effectively humanize our schools if we could more adequately demonstrate scientifically some of the points I've made with this paper.

Empathy as Teachable

American Psychologist (1981)

Kenneth Clark's (February 1980) emphasis on the neutral substrate of empathy is unfortunate in that it weakens his very important argument for its teachability. To consider bigots (or those with only "chauvinistic empathy") to be morally inferior on a constitutional basis seems more a retaliation against the false accusation of black intellectual inferiority than an assertion based on evidence.

As a social scientist whose early research contributed to a national policy of school desegregation and as one who continues to exert positive influence on education as a member of the New York State Board of Regents, Clark takes an unduly pessimistic position regarding social change through social action and education. This position may, however, be consistent with his earlier call (Clark, 1971) for a biochemical approach to the control of national and international leaders as well as criminals.

Clark's biological emphasis detracts unnecessarily from the critically important topics of his article—the teachability of empathy and the need to control human destructiveness by education in empathy. In pointing out the neglect of these issues by a behaviorist research establishment in American psychology, he performs a service that should be supported by those of us who value the realm of the subjective, a realm to which empathy is a major access route.

Why Reading? Why Math?

Reading Improvement 32, No. 1 (1995), pp. 63–64

In responding to serious problems like school violence, school finance, and school quality, educators must not lose sight of issues of pedagogy. This paper focuses on teacher enthusiasm for subject matter as a central pedagogical matter that may too easily be neglected.

The field of education is beleaguered with problems unanticipated when I began my teaching career over thirty years ago. School violence tops the list of concerns of teachers and communities. Inequities of school funding attacked in court decisions in several states, and funding inadequacies compounded by defeat of school budgets in many localities, plague teachers and school administrators. Uncertainty regarding the quality of their preparation for the vagaries of the American economy has students frightened for their futures.

These serious problems are being addressed in many forums and by political leaders as well as educators. Recent reform reports have, at times, aroused in me a nostalgia for more narrowly defined pedagogical problems that might be more easily solved.

As a teacher educator, I instruct students on the complex set of social and economic issues that form the context for education in the nineties, and on issues and methods of classroom management. I also deal with aspects of pedagogic performance that can contribute to a positive classroom atmosphere and improved learning. In that regard, and in a nostalgic mood, I thought back to some of my earliest experiences supervising student teachers in secondary schools.

Trained as a psychologist with prior teaching experience at college, graduate, and secondary levels (the latter in Chemistry and General Science), I looked forward to my first supervisory assignment with a mixture of interest and anxiety, as I was to be supervising in English and mathematics classes. I had been told that such out-of-specialty assignments are common in small teacher training programs, and I accepted my responsibility with what grace I could muster.

My first observation, two weeks into the semester, relieved my anxiety considerably. I found, as I had been assured by my department chair, that my skills as an educational psychologist, bolstered by my own secondary teaching experience, enabled me constructively to critique the lesson observed. It was the major criticism of that English lesson, and those I went on to observe in a mathematics class, that suggested the questions that form the title of this communication,

The student teacher was reviewing a short story dealing with the theme of hypocrisy. The class was well prepared and already seemed comfortable with their young instructor. The pupils responded well to his questions and seemed to have gotten the point of the story. They were able to cite examples from their own lives to demonstrate a fine understanding of the concept. Assignments were given and the class ended. My question to my student was: "What makes this an English lesson?"

The student teacher did not understand the question, He assumed that going over the content of a short story was indeed a complete English lesson.

I asked why the class could not discuss the concept of hypocrisy without having read the story. If this was an English lesson, was not a significant issue how a piece of literature contributes to our understanding? Should not the artistry of the writer be brought into focus? Might there not be an opportunity to discuss the derivation of certain words in which the class showed interest?

The student teacher thought that such a focus might be irrelevant and boring to his pupils. If that is true, I countered, playing devil's advocate, why read short stories at all? Can't youngsters learn about hypocrisy and other human foibles through other media—television, radio, discussions—all without reading? Might reading not be obsolete?

The student teacher was taken aback. "No," he asserted. "I love to read. Reading a good writer results in something besides information, and the good writer gives vitality to the content he deals with."

"They need what you take for granted—appreciation," I told him. "Part of your responsibility is to communicate your appreciation to them." I had placed a new issue into focus for him. He said he'd never thought about it before!

A month later, another student teacher, also facing a well-prepared and friendly class, was teaching the measurement of an angle formed by a secant and a tangent. She was relaxed, elicited a wide range of pupil response, and was able to respond well in turn. The pupils seem to have understood the measurement and its proof. Something was missing, however. The lesson was not as exciting as I thought it could be.

I raised this point with my student and she was puzzled. "It's just a matter of understanding the steps and memorizing them. It's not really supposed to be exciting," she said. "If it's not exiting," I countered, "why should they care?" Again, playing devil's advocate, I suggested that, perhaps, math was boring and, with the availability of inexpensive calculators, maybe it was becoming obsolete.

This second student, like the first, was taken aback, but she rose to the challenge as had her classmate. "As far as I'm concerned, math is fun and exciting." "Fine," I answered. "Let's see why, and let's see if you can convey it."

We looked over the lesson and found the points that, if highlighted, would convey excitement: 1) In math, the derivation of formulas is not just an exercise, it is challenging and aesthetic, and the resulting formulas make problem solving easier (rather than the enigma many feel it to be); 2) neither are the proofs mere exercises without import; they give mathematics one of its essential ingredients, generalizability. In the case of the lesson observed, an angle formed by any particular set of a secant and a tangent is measurable by the very same formula; a universal law is discovered.

My student happily began to prepare her next lesson, seeking to highlight aspects that would convey her appreciation of her subject to her pupils.

These two vignettes suggested the focus of my efforts in many supervisory sessions. Overcoming my students' self-imposed limitations, and their inability to convey appreciation and enthusiasm, became one of my chief goals. Such conveyance leads regularly to what we call "pupil motivation."

Teachers need to remind themselves of the appreciation, excitement and value they place upon their self-chosen discipline so that they may convey that appreciation and excitement, and articulate the value to their pupils. My student teachers had not known this, either from their pedagogical study or from their subject area courses.

It seems to me that unless teacher educators pose such questions and help students to find answers to these significant challenges, would-be teachers are in great danger of boring their pupils and themselves by losing the interest and excitement that originally motivated their choice of profession.

Teacher enthusiasm is, of course, hardly the only factor leading to pupil motivation. Selection of materials, cooperative learning, and appropriate pre-evaluation are among the methodologies new teachers need to learn and master.

Issues of school violence, school funding, and school quality are, appropriately, high on the educational agenda. Many teachers would, as well, appreciate having the well-prepared and responsive classes described in my two vignettes, and they work toward making that a priority. Old-fashioned pedagogical issues, including the promotion of teacher enthusiasm, cannot be left aside, however, if education is to be successful.

Good College Teaching

College Student Journal 29, No. 3 (1995), pp. 308–311

College teachers have rarely been trained to teach. Facing less well-prepared students in recent decades, they have tended to let them sink or swim, or have lowered standards. This paper posits several elements of good college teaching that help avoid either of these mistaken tendencies. Starting from the premises that learning is a process, that learners have different ways and rates of learning, and that teachers are facilitators who convey love for a discipline as much as its substance, I discuss elements of structure, field experience, self-teaching, the use of consultants, self-analysis, experiential workshops, varied time frames, lectures and silences.

In recent decades, open-admissions policies brought many underprepared students through formerly closed doors. For some teachers this presented no problem: the students would sink or swim in the old-fashioned way. Other teachers adjusted their teaching to the needs of their learners, and some did so inappropriately. Reduction of standards, grade inflation, watering-down of courses, and creation of content-weak courses were among the outcomes. This was, of course, as insensitive as the sink-or-swim approach. If the new students would not fail, they would hardly achieve meaningful success. The value of their college education would be held in disrepute.

Good college teaching exists, and involves neither the social Darwinian approach nor the dispensing of shoddy goods. It starts from a different set of premises, intuitive or trained. These premises are: a) that learning is a process; b) that learners learn in different ways and at different rates, and c) that teachers are learning facilitators, not information-dispensing machines. A teacher has a love for a discipline and wishes to convey that love so that a student will appreciate that discipline's beauty as well as its content.

Even before open enrollment, students were short-changed by bad teaching. Those who succeeded often developed a sterile mastery of facts and a relief at getting past a subject, rather than appreciation of all subjects, which is the hallmark of educational success.

This essay describes several methodologies, some of which may be adapted to any discipline. The general purpose of the varied methods is to escape from total reliance on the lecture format. More specific purposes include promoting active learning, promoting interaction, developing self-confidence in learners, and teaching in the affective domain. I have found that their use enhances student motivation and approaches the goal of teaching appreciation as well as content. The use of these methods in various forms also serves to keep the teacher alert and interested in the teaching process and concerned with the individual success of students.

I believe that the use of multiple methodologies is critical to good teaching regardless of its locale or level, and regardless of the preparation level of students; hence, the general title of this essay.

Structure. The first class meeting must introduce the course in each of its aspects. The requirements should be clear as should be the grading standards. Distributed written materials should describe the course content and structure. The fact that different formats will be used should be made explicit. I tell students that some of the course consists of "interrupted" lecture and that it will be their responsibility to interrupt: with questions, comments, or even confusion. I let them know that professors are prone to lecture indefinitely and that they must work to keep this from happening. I let them know, also, that I reserve the right to raise or lower the final grade up to one letter depending on factors such as participation, attendance, punctuality and change in performance over time.

Examinations and other evaluations are described. Their dates are known at the first meeting. I have found that quizzes given more frequently than the traditional midterm and final are most useful. They reduce the pressure (each being worth less than 50%), spread out studying time, provide for more frequent feedback and for greater opportunity to improve one's standing. I go over each quiz, having graded them by the next class meeting. I require those with grades of D or F to see me individually, and I invite others to do so at their own initiative.

Research papers are required and a descriptive instruction sheet is distributed. Topics for the papers are left to student choice within the constraints of course content. If students are in doubt as to whether or not their chosen topic is acceptable, I tell them; but I never choose the specific topic. I require that the papers be brief, and I return them for resubmission if standards of written English or of source citation are inadequate.

There are, frequently, field work assignments related to my courses. Regular reporting, also meeting appropriate writing standards, is required. I have found that every student's writing improves significantly when written assignments are frequent and when they are returned for resubmission as needed.

The structure can be described in the first class session but it will bear repeating from time to time as questions arise and as graded assignments or quizzes are returned. Students get a clear idea that they will work hard to master a significant body of knowledge and that they will enhance their basic learning skills as well.

Fieldwork. In education courses, students are frequently placed in field sites for a specific number of hours over the semester. When this is not formally the case, I try to provide some "real world" assignment. In one course, I require students to attend meetings of school boards and to report on them. I describe, in a handout, the necessary contents of their observation report, often directing students to specific matters such as "describe the nature of the community that this school board represents." Structuring their reports gets them to focus on the content-related purpose of the field assignment. In some courses, oral reports are presented by the students and they become discussion leaders, after I have modeled discussion-leading for them.

Students Their Own Teachers. This last point introduces another methodological approach: getting students to the front of the classroom. I have assigned students to prepare topics in small groups to present before the class. The assignments are made early in the term with presentation dates toward the end. Groups meet me before presenting to assess their mastery of content and the form of their presentations. Sometimes presentations are a series of mini-lectures, but I discourage that. Instead I suggest debate, role-playing, skits or other types of performance.

As most of my students are preparing to teach, this activity matches their goals. It is equally important for other students. Declamatory skills are cultivated and content is more thoroughly learned when it has to be presented to others.

Bringing Outsiders In. Rarely is any one of us the best possible teacher for all content aspects of our courses. I have made it a practice to invite guest experts to share their expertise with my students. In a classroom management course, a senior school teacher visits so as to inform students of the most current problems and practices. In a course on disabling conditions, I have invited disabled friends to describe their educational experiences. Whenever possible, I have these visitors videotaped. Two particularly timeless recordings I show routinely. Others in my department who teach the same course have also used these videos. One, of a woman crippled by polio, is so emotionally gripping that, if students miss that class session, I require them to view it on their own.

Self-Analysis. Video technology has demonstrated its usefulness in many skill areas. My students have lessons recorded at their placements, or record mini-lesson simulations with their peers, and then use the videos for detailed study. Some aspects of the teaching are so specific and focused that only this technology allows for adequate evaluation. Precision in self-analysis leads to a self-awareness required in teachers. For just that reason, college faculty also record their work so as to foster growth in professional skills.

Experiential Workshops. Some learning tasks require active structured experiences. The field of group dynamics is best understood by group experience followed by analysis of the experience. Toward that end, workshops in which I have divided the class into discussion groups deal with a (controversial) topic I have selected. Such topics as "being accused by parents of racism" always provoke involvement and interaction which, when interrupted, shed light on group process.

Empathy is difficult to teach. Putting oneself in another's place is an experience that can be structured for its teaching. In my special education classes, I run workshops in which students take on handicaps like a blindfold, a hand splint, or a wheelchair. Tasks are presented which cannot easily be performed and feelings are elicited and spoken. Few students are immune to such empathy induction.

I have had students teach one another in small groups with one role-playing a disruptive child. The teaching student attempts to control the disruption and resume the lesson. At the end of the exercise the group provides feedback.

In some of these situations I am the active leader-director; in others, I am absent from the room. These latter situations, mostly in graduate courses, provide opportunity for a different, authority-free, exchange. Such exchanges give students a good taste of the professional peer evaluations we hope they will engage in throughout their careers. There are many instances where there is no best (or professor's) answer, so we do well to foster helpful brainstorming.

Time Frames. None of the workshops just described fits a usual class period. We all know that knowledge does not come in neat blocks of 50, 75 or 100 minutes and that these time frames are but a necessary logistical constraint in an institutional setting. With ordinary course content I let the class end at the bell, with the frequent loose ends needing to be picked up next time. With workshops like those described, I schedule differently. I have found no objection on the part of students to having one 200-minute class in a course, or one all-day session provided, of course, that it is scheduled at the start, and that an equivalent number of regular class hours is eliminated (usually at the end of the semester).

Students tend to report both that the content of the workshop is meaningful and that the variation in the schedule winds up being advantageous, e.g., in giving them more time at the end to study for final exams in other courses.

Lecturing. Nothing I have said thus far should lead to the conclusion that I do not lecture, even, sometimes, without interruption. When I do lecture, however, I don't find it useful to have students trying to write my every word, or even audiotaping the class. I prefer students to listen actively so that they may think and question. Toward that end, I often prepare and distribute lecture notes in an outline form. I tell students that, while it is not a transcript, what I have given them is the essence of what facts they should learn and that, in exchange, they may not take notes except at appropriate pause points.

My lectures are designed to be lively, evocative, and provocative. I want students to be engaged by the material. I try to engage them with my own enthusiasm. I move around, gesticulate, change my tone, and sometimes even shout. If students are sleeping, they won't get much of the lecture. In my classes, however tired they may be, it is hard for them not to stay awake.

Silences. However lively the performance, I am still reluctant to convey the impression that full-period lecture is a common occurrence. It shouldn't be. At least it's not sound pedagogy for it to be.

When I am responsible in a class for most of the talking, I know I must insert pauses. Research in teaching has shown that a pause of less than three seconds following a question isn't effective, but counting three seconds after every question does elicit responses. Pauses are not just for allowing responses to questions. I give pauses for putting notes on my outlines. I give pauses for questions and reflections. I give pauses just for rest, after a difficult bit of work. These latter pauses must be palpable and must, therefore, take, perhaps, at least ten seconds. Ten-second silences will seem strained at first, to the teacher and to students not prepared for them. They will, however, pay dividends in participation and in effective learning.

Bad college teaching abounds. Good college teaching exists. It takes a commitment to what is now known about the nature of learning and the nature of learners. It involves structure, participation, variety in methodology, and awareness that we are all teaching more than our discipline's content. It involves breaking stereotypes and rules.

College teaching can be as good as good teaching at any level. That it involves hard work is not a surprise. What may be a surprise is that every class session can be a joy and can renew our commitment to keep improving our craft.

A Lesson Plan Model for the Supervision of Student Teaching

Education 118, No. 3 (Spring 1998)

Abstract: A model for the supervision of student teaching is presented. The model uses the elements of lesson planning for its structure. A conceptual review of the planning elements is followed by a description of a flexible supervisory procedure in which the elements are integrated to meet the learning needs of the student teacher. The aim of the model is to enhance the effectiveness of supervisory teaching across grades and across curricula.

Supervision of student teaching is the typical capstone instructional modality in preservice teacher training. Its goal is to advance the student's integration of skills and to determine if an independent teaching assignment may be taken on in short order.

The supervisory experience is often paired with an integrative seminar in which a group of student teachers learn from the diversity of its members' experiences. This paper, however, focuses on individual supervision. It describes a model for supervision which can be applied across grades and across the curriculum. The flexibility of the individual experience is emphasized.

The Lesson Plan as an Outline for Supervision

The lesson plan has been an essential tool for teachers since its formulation in the nineteenth century. Those aware of the history of the teaching profession are familiar with Herbart's important innovation as it evolved to a "gospel" in the premature formalization of normal school methodology. Variations on lesson planning now abound, and they are more in keeping with Herbart's creative spirit. The elements of the lesson plan are still recognizably Herbartian, but the words have changed, and the understanding of the elements has become complex, sophisticated, and flexible as the disciplines of psychology and pedagogy have developed. I will describe the elements as I use them for supervisory teaching. I will then integrate these elements as a model for supervision.

Elements of Lesson Planning

1. Objective

All lessons must have an aim, purpose or objective. The teacher must be clear about the objective to get a successful learning outcome for any block of time. In order to choose an appropriate lesson aim, the teacher must work "backwards" in each curriculum area. For example, what are the general purposes of science education by the end of high school? I suggest that they include enhancement of curiosity about the natural universe, development of a modern scientific attitude including skepticism and familiarity with criteria of proof, and knowledge of basic findings and their applications in the several sciences. I urge student teachers to articulate this level of general purposes as a first step in lesson planning.

The next steps in backwards planning are a) defining the annual objectives in the curriculum area (usually provided by state education guidelines), b) specifying unit objectives, and c) choosing a series of lesson objectives consistent with annual and unit objectives.

While the choice of a lesson's primary aim is important, it must be kept in mind that lessons almost always have secondary aims. These include the development of listening and speaking skills, and vocabulary; the development of writing skills; the development of social skills like politeness and teamwork, and the development of quantitative thinking. Lessons will vary in the amount of attention paid to such secondary aims, but they are rarely to be ignored.

2. Pre-assessment

This component of the lesson plan determines the appropriateness of a specific primary objective. It involves evaluation of the level of skill and knowledge called for and determination of the difficulty of the lesson: too easy, too hard, or just right. We may not be able to make that determination accurately until we are in the midst of the lesson. For this reason, unit planning necessarily precedes lesson planning. The teacher must be able to move on quickly (or in greater depth) if the lesson is too easy (or slow down, of course, if it is too hard).

Pre-assessment is not just of the group we call a class, but of subgroups and of individuals. Teachers must develop a sound way of knowing where each pupil is in each curricular area, as well as how to construct small learning groups. Pre-assessment is best understood as individualization in the context of group learning.

Pre-assessment includes the allotment of time. A class period is an administrative unit which may not provide an appropriate teaching unit. The nature of the subject and the learning readiness of the pupils provide the best gauges for timing. For early childhood teaching a five- to fifteen-minute span is most often right; for high schoolers double-periods may be useful for many lessons.

Pre-assessment may not be visible in the execution of every lesson, but it must always be an explicit part of the planning process.

3. Motivation

I have found that many student teachers misunderstand the concept of motivation. They often assume it to be the "focusing event" which calls pupils to attention. Motivation is, instead, a psychological state within each pupil of wanting to learn what the teacher wants to teach. As such, motivation should not be a mere gimmick at the lesson's start; it must be an attitude sustained throughout the lesson. Too often lapses in motivation are what capture teachers' attention. Lapses take such forms as daydreaming or problems in classroom management.

When lapses occur, the lesson cannot continue according to plan. Unmotivated pupils are not likely to be learning what we intend. The formal plan must be suspended until motivation can be reestablished.

Sound motivation comes from a hierarchy of motivators. First, the subject matter is to be intrinsically motivating. If student teachers do not understand the intrinsic value of a lesson, they must be helped to do so. Elementary-level student teachers who find decimal fractions dull should find out why this mathematical idea generates excitement in their math major peers or a math teacher. Relevance or pragmatic utility may be a part of intrinsic motivation. If teachers do not understand the intrinsic value of a curricular area, it will be impossible to engage pupils effectively.

The second motivator is teacher enthusiasm. It flows from an understanding of intrinsic motivation and adds to it. Authenticity is important; pupils can tell when teachers are feigning. Good acting ability, however, may help.

Thirdly, we come to focusing events. These may be of use in particular lessons. Usually the first two motivators will suffice. A focusing event must not only gain the attention of the pupils, but it must be a natural lead-in to the lesson, and relevant. It may be the first activity of the lesson rather than a special event, since active learning is itself engaging.

Dull lessons not only fail to achieve their objectives, they tend to dull children to the process of school learning. Motivational thinking remains central to the avoidance of this more general dulling.

4. Techniques and Sequencing

Beginners' lessons typically focus on sequence and specific techniques. Activities, demonstrations, questions, reinforcements, and medial and closing summaries are addressed here. The use of materials, audiovisual aids, grouping, etc., are also covered. These items comprise much of traditional lesson planning, and justifiably so. The wide range and variability of techniques appropriate to differing curricula is generally well-covered by special methods courses.

5. Application, Evaluation, Follow-up

These concluding parts of the lesson plan speak to the matters of utility, effectiveness, and the place of the lesson in the learning sequence. Aristotle emphasized utility in his thinking on education; educators who ignore utility risk irrelevance. Modern ideas about applications are not, however, limited to the concrete, economic or practical; we understand utility to include the development of thoughtfulness, aesthetic sensibility, and democratic attitudes, among other aims. The teacher must, in planning, know the place of each lesson with regard to one or another application.

Evaluation of a lesson provides information as to its effectiveness, the degree to which it has achieved its primary and additional learning aims with each pupil. The teacher cannot successfully continue with the lesson if pupils do not achieve the performance objectives. There are many assessment devices, formal and informal, individual and group. Each device has advantages and limitations. Some are more useful in particular curriculum areas. Whatever the device, the lesson plan must always address the issue of evaluation.

The idea of follow-up emerges from the very fact of a lesson's embeddedness in a unit and in a curriculum. Lesson time blocks are arbitrary in regard to the curriculum: learning is not neatly packaged in forty-minute parcels. Pupils must learn also that each lesson is meaningfully connected to the next in its subject (and, where possible, to other subjects). The planning process must provide for those connections.

6. Interpersonal Skills; Classroom Management

Although not formally part of a lesson plan, these elements of the teaching process are important and need to be addressed in planning and in the supervisory situation. They can be thought of as potential emerging errors by the teacher and by the pupils, respectively (although there are often mutual influences). When a lesson is going well, we may not notice these elements; when a lesson goes badly, we should quickly look at them.

Interpersonal skills in teaching come in many forms and styles but they emerge from calm, kindly, caring, respectful attitudes. When teachers feel a good deal of stress, interpersonal skills fall short and sometimes mar a lesson's execution. At a calmer moment, the bruised feelings of pupils can be easily resolved by the usually-caring teacher. If apologies become a too-regular occurrence, counseling may be needed.

The effective handling of classroom management problems results from training and experience, and is often based on specific knowledge of the stresses on the individual "culprit". Consideration of the cultural and linguistic diversity of students may also serve to aid understanding and prevention of disruptions. It is also common that management problems erupt, particularly with novices, from an inadequately engaging, poorly structured lesson.

Use of the Lesson Plan in Supervision

Each student brings to the student teaching experience a set of aptitudes and attitudes along with skills and knowledge. The model of supervision I propose recognizes the uniqueness of the set of tools and the personal history that has formed it. From such recognition an individualized experience may be constructed.

A few weeks into the semester, when a comfort level with the class has been reached, I ask my student to prepare for a first observation "cold." I want to see a demonstration of a beginner's skills with minimal focus on what I might be looking for. I try to assure the usually anxious student that I am not expecting a perfect lesson; the ideal doesn't exist even for experienced hands. I want the first observation to set a baseline from which I might address individual needs and strengths.

At the lesson's start, I am given a written lesson plan. I study both the plan and its execution. As I observe, I keep my model plan elements in mind. I note the clarity of aim(s), the appropriateness of content, the motivation level, and the sequence and methods employed. I also make note of interpersonal skills and their variation, and of classroom management issues and their handling. As the lesson draws to its close, I note the application, assessment and follow-up, if these elements are present. At the end, I ask the student teacher to prepare a written self-assessment of the lesson's shortcomings and strengths, and we arrange an appointment, preferably for the next day, to discuss our respective evaluations.

We begin the post-observation conference by reading each other's reports. I then respond to the student's self-evaluation. I frequently find student teachers to be overly self-critical and limited in perceiving their own strengths. After commenting on the student's report, I ask for responses to mine. My reports typically are in three parts: I describe the lesson, I enumerate the strengths observed, I then focus on the student's errors of omission and commission. I try to engage the student in a conceptual discussion of those elements most relevant to the lesson observed, and I will also offer concrete suggestions. We write up and exchange reports of our discussion.

Subsequent supervision follows a similar format except that the student is expected to utilize insights from prior lessons in planning later ones, and I am available in advance to help with such planning.

In subsequent reports, I comment on the student's progress with the elements dealt with earlier, and I focus on additional issues as they emerge in the new lesson. No report is a checklist; each is a narrative which addresses the specifics of the lesson. While the proposed model guides supervision, my reports and conferences are not boilerplate. They are designed to hone the unique set of tools brought by each student.

Evaluation and Self-Evaluation: Toward Professionalism

I expect student teachers to be at a minimal competency level. This is usually assured by prerequisite courses and field experiences as well as grade-point averages. My grading is essentially based on the student's growth as a result of supervision, as demonstrated in conference discussions. I look for enhanced conceptual understanding of the planning elements; for teachers to become professionals they must be able to explain what they do and why they do it. Performance skills will emerge in increments and only with practice.

It is my aim to provide student teachers with a model of evaluation which might also be useful for ongoing self-evaluation. The conceptual scheme for lesson planning described here provides me a context for evaluation and can provide the student with guidance for self-evaluation. Professionals are never done with evaluation; accountability requires it. The model offered is flexible and modifiable as the teacher gains experience and in-service mentoring. It might also prove useful for peer supervision and consultation.

Conclusion

I have presented a model of student teaching supervision which uses the elements of lesson planning for its structure. I hope to have demonstrated how such a model may be effective in developing a conceptual understanding for novice teachers, while being flexible and modifiable for different individual needs and teaching situations.

Reprinted courtesy Project Innovation Austin LLC,
https://projectinnovationaustin.com/

What are Schools For? Everything!

June 13, 2002

Every society has set goals for schooling as some combination of the intellectual (to sharpen the mind and the senses), the economic (to prepare youth to contribute to the commonwealth), and the cultural (to pass on the values of the adult generation). The United Nations Convention on Rights of the Child calls for education to include the development of the child's personality and talents, as well as developing respect for parents, human rights, the natural environment, the child's cultural and national values and the values of others. These general statements provide a large framework for addressing the question. They fall short of answering it.

For Plato, schools were to teach music and gymnasium. By "music" he meant the subject matter of the Muses: poetry, painting, theater, dance, philosophy, and so forth. We call these subjects the humanities. The goal of Athenian education went beyond developing citizens of sound mind and body; it was to have them live like the Olympians, Homer's hedonistic community of immortals.

Roman curriculum consisted of seven subjects known as the trivium (grammar, logic, and rhetoric) and the quadrivium (arithmetic, geometry, astronomy, and Plato's music). The quadrivium extends the Greek ideal but gives more weight to the practical subjects of mathematics and science. What of the trivium? Why were these language arts given top priority? The aim of Roman education was to empower its elite citizenry to conquer and rule the known world; to create and sustain an empire. Mathematics and science enabled construction of aqueducts and viaducts. Emperors, without benefit of phone, fax or e-mail, needed to be unambiguous in sending orders to their generals in the provinces. Verbal errors could mean life or death. For effective rule, the Roman elite had to communicate in clear, exquisitely refined classical Latin.

Current systems may need greater historical perspective before similar concise characterization. An international perspective may help. Canada's public schools are organized by its two main churches, Catholic and Protestant. Schools of the former Soviet Union and of the People's Republic of China aimed to develop socialist citizens. Israeli Kibbutz schooling also promoted a socialist vision.

American history may be a better guide. In earlier times in this country, there seemed some general agreement as to the purposes of public schooling. Literacy promotion would support religious and political freedom, job skill training would provide for economic self-sufficiency, and the principle of local control would foster community values and individual liberty.

Three American educational principles, articulated by Horace Mann in the 1840s, had developed over the preceding two centuries: 1) universal public education to literacy, 2) which shall be secular, and 3) locally controlled. Religious freedom was a major motive of the first European colonists. To promote universal literacy through a system of public education would free individuals from the wiles of the "Old Deluder Satan" by providing direct access to the wisdom of the Bible. To establish a continental-scale democratic republic, in which leaders are civil servants subject to electoral evaluation, would require a citizenry literate enough to follow press accounts of political performance. Mann's secularism was derived from the compromises made in the drafting of the United States Constitution; neither Maryland's Catholics nor Pennsylvania's Quakers nor Carolina's Baptists would wield the authority of government as had England's state church. Mann's principle of local control would empower parents in their own communities to determine the value-content of school curriculum, rather than leaving such matters to a distant central government.

These principles were never without complexities or controversy. Universal literacy was initially based on very limited conceptions of both universality and literacy. The struggle to include girls, children of diverse racial, ethnic, and economic backgrounds, and those with disabilities may be considered the defining issue in the history of American education—and its most important contribution. But taxpayers have been routinely vexed with the question of how much literacy should be provided at public expense. Jefferson may have thought a fourth-grade level to be adequate for political literacy; despite a recent New York appellate decision suggesting that a ninth-grade level might meet the State's burden, most of us have higher expectations.

Secular education, more easily accepted in Mann's day, when an eclectic Protestantism could pass itself off as secular, still generates controversy. How can this nation provide for both religious expression and freedom from religious coercion? A recent federal court ruling found the words "under God" in the Pledge of Allegiance to be unconstitutionally coercive. Local control was also a matter of contention when it came into conflict with the other two principles, and Federal courts were called upon to outlaw State-sponsored racial segregation and school prayers.

The knowledge explosion of the 20th century put strains on attempts to define literacy; the technology revolution made obsolete most programs of skills training, and the increasingly notable diversity of the American population (coupled with powerful assertions of racial and gender equality) made attempts at defining community values problematic.

The public continues to have goals for schooling despite absence of consensus on what these should be. There is no shortage of complaint regarding school system failure to ensure literacy, and a "back to basics" movement is sometimes a popular approach. There are school districts that now require in the primary grades that each school day's morning hours be devoted to literacy studies. Periodic testing in mathematics and reading (annually, according to a recent Federal mandate) has become a major focus for many schools and a major matter of contention as well.

Nor is there a shortage of advocates for different curricular emphases. Those who would promote the Athenian ideal of "sound body" remind us that obesity is a major American health problem, and they promote strengthening school nutrition programs. Athletic facilities are underutilized even when available. For example, New York City school swimming pools go unused while a shortage of trained lifeguards limits access to public beaches.

Safety is high on the agenda of parental concerns and courses in driver education are considered important. Such specific curricula have taken a back seat, however, to the physical protection of students following a series of school shootings, especially the killings at Columbine High School in Colorado. School violence prevention programs have been established in many states, though they have yet to demonstrate effectiveness. The US homicide rate remains dramatically higher than that of Western Europe countries.

The tragic attacks on this country on September 11, 2001 have added to pressures on schools. Student scores on "pop" culture exceed those on American history. How can a nation be at war while its young citizens are unaware of the tenets of patriotism and the requirements of citizenship?

Several months after the 9/11 attacks a study claimed 15% of New York City's third through eighth graders showed signs of the psychiatric condition Post-Traumatic Stress Disorder. As with violence prevention, programs of social-emotional education are recommended. Where are they to be placed on the crowded school agenda?

Social-emotional education goes to the heart of value-oriented teaching, and yet values conflicts abound. Do we agree that children should be taught honesty? Why then did a Kansas school district fire a teacher and a principal for disciplining students guilty of plagiarism? Are educators trained to avoid being punitive with their charges? What of new immigrants, like many from Asian countries, who see the schools as overly permissive and who see rewards for good behavior as bribery? Laws are inconsistent from State to State: Texas supports corporal punishment; New York bans it. And what of those who, like Alfie Kohn, eschew a reward and punishment system altogether? How do we counter bullying when we promote self-assertion? Will the teaching of patriotic values spill over into chauvinistic propaganda? Is gender equality a communal value in all areas of this country? Debates over values-based teaching are not new but remain highly contentious.

Vocational education is itself a subject of controversy, beyond the problem of obsolescence. Parents often shy away from enrolling their children in technical programs in favor of a focus on college preparation. Indeed, higher education has flourished in this country in the last half-century, making it the envy of the world as well as the assumed baseline level for upward mobility and economic security. But what of those who do not aspire to college? How much should a public compulsory education system do to prepare them for embarking on a career?

The economics of education do not stop at the door of curriculum controversy. Schools have become major employers. Privatizing such functions as transportation, food services and security (as a management tool) has threatened the employment of drivers, cooks, and guards, often the only community residents to be employed in some school districts.

Issues involved in defining the aims of education in this country are myriad, and the list could go on. Wishing for simpler times and clearer goals leads to oversimplification and problem-avoidance, not resolution. What are schools, then, to do in the face of so many legitimate demands? How are time and money to be spent to pack in everything and to satisfy everyone?

When asked why he robbed banks, the infamous Willie Sutton responded, "That's where the money is!" Schools were the major arena for civil rights struggles of the last century, and they remain so for many American controversies because that's where the children are. Public education serves some 90% of America's children. Schooling is a government function, a collective responsibility. Defining the goals of the educational enterprise cannot be avoided, no matter the difficulties.

Horace Mann's principles may still provide a framework for guidance, even as we recognize their complexity. Universal literacy's current task is elimination of the continued disparity between "haves" and "have-nots." Racial and ethnic minorities remain heavily over-represented among "have-nots." The assertion of the principle of equality among citizens, and its acceptance as public policy, were 20th century revolutions. Full actualization of the principle is the task of the 21st century. Resource differentials between well-off and poor school districts must be abolished, as several State courts have ruled, and weaker school districts must be assisted by States and by the Federal government to achieve more success.

Expansion of the definition of literacy is a second continuing task of the principle of universality. Leaders must promote newer areas and levels of literacy as normative. Educational attainment through high school and into college has become commonplace for most Americans. Few doubt that this rise in the level of education is unrelated to the historically unprecedented creation of economic wealth. Educators must press the point that expanding educational opportunity will continue to promote both democratic values and the wealth needed to support the expansion of such opportunity.

Yes, then, to everything: basic literacy skills; health and physical education; safety education and violence prevention; civics and social-emotional learning; the arts, and preparation for vocational possibilities. The strongest arguments against curriculum expansion involve limitations of time and money; both can be made more available for schools. Schools also provide jobs. School employment contributes to community development at the local level as well as to the larger economic wellbeing of the citizenry. When it comes to learning, children could have it all, and the public schooling enterprise can provide it.

Horace Mann's second principle, secular education, offers some specific guidance as to *how* to have it all. Secular education may be understood in our era as fostering pluralism and diversity. This redefinition suggests secularism as an alternate to sectarian parochial views rather than to spirituality.

Secularism is not a platform for Godless public schools. It teaches children that diverse views are consistent with the religious freedom sought by the original colonists. It teaches the many ways human beings have lived and learned in different times and places. Throughout our nation's history, communities have imposed narrow values on their schools' curricula. This is true of recent immigrant communities just as it had been for older ones. Pluralistic education would consider such local values to be parochial and, instead, would propose exposure to the varieties of human experience. A secular American education would promote tolerance of differences, in part because our society is itself variegated, and in part because we can see the dangers of intolerant monolithic values turning schooling into indoctrination, here or elsewhere in the world.

Secularism expands the curriculum within the context of the overall knowledge explosion of the last century. Exposing children to differences does not add subject matter to burden students and teachers. Curricular expansions such as a growing music repertory or literature or DNA-based biology are not incorporated in curriculum by providing more facts for student digestion, but by teaching skills of knowledge acquisition. As such they lead to methodological innovation for teachers and continuing stimulation to personal inquiry and intellectual growth on the part of students.

What then of Mann's third principle, local control? It remains the valid means for assuring individual parental rights within a democratic context. American schools will not be clones of any one model or national program. By engaging parental support and cooperation known to be a crucial component of student success, schools will reflect the unique styles and character of their communities. As in the past, parochialism resulting from the principle of local control will be subjected to balancing with the principles of universality and secularism as provided by the institutions of American government. Legislators and jurists remain the arbiters of our national and local democratic systems.

Some schools will provide more resources for arts education while others emphasize athletics. Rural schools may promote agricultural studies. It is not necessary to see different emphases as competing with one another but instead as providing varied contents for the development of learning skills. Long term educational achievement of its students will also affect a school's approach; if students are less successful in achieving their own goals, the school must change its approach for the next cohort.

Value controversies must be engaged at a local level. Debate is a means for involving parents in defining the mission of schools while at the same time providing parents with continuing education. Parental participation at schools and at school district deliberations offer, after voting and jury duty, the most common opportunities for democratic participation. Democracy entails an evolving set of ideas. Participation of individuals and communities is central to its evolution.

No simple answer is provided for this paper's titular question. Instead, I offer an historical perspective on the development of universal public education in the United States as a framework for continuing discourse on what may be unanswerable in any simple way. The world is complex, and the planet consists of interdependent nations. Horace Mann understood the principles he espoused in much simpler terms than we do. His limitations cannot be ours. The principles frame ongoing discussion and debate, and their scope expands. There may be no better arena in which to understand and attempt solutions to social problems than that of the public school. Schools can be for everything!

What Do Teachers Want (From Psychoanalysis)?

Journal of Applied Psychoanalytic Studies 4, No.3 (2002), pp. 275–281
Updated 1/2/23, 3/6/23

A central theme of my presentations over the past 18 years here has been that psychoanalysis is not limited to traditional clinical practice. Beyond the several psychoanalytically informed therapies are its "applications," a term typically used to refer to the use of its theory beyond treatment. But my focus has been on psychoanalysis the paradigm, a comprehensive attempt initiated by Sigmund Freud to understand the human mind and its products. Toward that end, I've spoken about an edited collection, "Analysts in the Trenches," published in 2002, describing the application of psychoanalytic ideas in violence-ridden public schools, municipal halls, police stations, earthquake damaged areas, "ground zero" in Lower Manhattan, and in response to casualties of war in Angola, Bosnia and the former Soviet Republic of Georgia. I've also discussed my 35-year career as a teacher education professor at the City University of New York.

In his *New Introductory Lectures,* Freud (1933) stated unequivocally that education was the most important of the possible applications of psychoanalysis (p.146). Why this should be so seemed obvious. Psychoanalysis had discovered the roots of adult psychology in childhood, and the roots of psychopathology in the immature ego of the young child. To approach the teaching of children with psychoanalytic knowledge could only promote sound development. Anna Freud had already adapted psychoanalytic technique for therapeutic work with children, and August Aichhorn had applied psychoanalytic principles to work with delinquents (1925).

Freud warned (1933) against prophylactic use of psychoanalytic treatment for children, anticipating public outrage. Psychoanalysts have heeded this warning. He viewed education as a critical social institution whose primary aim must be a taming of instincts, even with the inevitable risk of neurosis. The primacy of this aim has never won wide acceptance, nor had it even been seriously considered by most educators. Freud challenged educators to steer between the shoals of frustration of, and non-interference with, children's drives, a quaint-sounding formulation today, yet one that resonates with the ongoing educational conflict between more traditional and more progressive teaching philosophies. Freud emphasized total respect for the individual differences of children, and most teachers would agree.

His most specific recommendation was that teachers undergo psychoanalytic training, especially including a personal analysis (noting that often the most effective help for children was personal analysis of their parents). He had earlier suggested (1925) that such training would, in fact, qualify teachers for clinical practice. This recommendation was, of course, ignored. Sharing society's apprehension of psychology and resistance to psychoanalysts, teachers would reject the notion that they all need to be analyzed. Freud also warned against a psychoanalytic stance that would run counter to a school's conformist social mission. Only those few teachers adhering to a social reconstructionist educational philosophy would consider it.

Freud's recommendations and warnings and their limited acceptance, even briefly noted, call to mind his description of psychoanalysis and education as two "impossible professions" (1925). Their interaction may be doubly impossible. When we consider that 90% of schooling in the United States takes place under the auspices of government (Freud's third impossible profession), it might seem that only the most foolhardy would consider engaging in the application of psychoanalysis to education.

I am grateful that many individuals, hardly foolish ones, have tried. In fact, in the quarter-century-long postwar heyday of psychoanalysis in the United States, departments of teacher education (rather than of English or philosophy, as in the current milieu) provided academic homes to many psychoanalytic psychologists, myself among them. Traditional psychology departments were much less welcoming as they shifted from behaviorism to cognitive psychology in their scientific (and often anti-psychoanalytic) orientation.

I came to teacher education in 1970 while engaged in clinical psychoanalytic training. Richard Jones had been my undergraduate teacher of educational psychology, and he taught the subject from a distinctly psychoanalytic perspective (his 1968 book was called *Fantasy and Feeling in Education*). Initially, I understood my task as bringing that same perspective to students preparing to teach in early childhood, elementary and special education, as well as in secondary school academic subjects. I would do so via required courses in developmental psychology, classroom management, and the teaching of exceptional learners. While eventually I expanded my range to include pedagogic methodology, educational sociology, individual supervision of student teachers, and a leadership course for prospective educational administrators, my influence as a professor would remain limited to the intellectual and personal.

Beyond the influence of effective teaching by individuals with a psychoanalytic orientation, psychoanalysis applied to education came essentially to mean some form of clinical consultation for troubled youngsters while they were, necessarily, also in school. Psychoanalysts working with children and adolescents were usually aware of the need also to relate to school personnel (teachers, guidance counselors, school psychologists and social workers), although all too frequently such relationships were of minimal impact.

I'll now address the three programs, each discussed in papers published with the original version of this essay.

Farley and Manning

The Houston program described by Farley and Manning is a well-conceived and well-implemented intervention designed to go beyond individual efforts of psychoanalysts working with school personnel. Its systematic three-tiered approach originated in structuring consultations on a regular and consistent basis with a large number of schools and daycare centers. The idea was to treat the children through the teacher, as Freud had treated Little Hans (1909) through his father. The second tier, a therapeutic preschool for more difficult youngsters, evolved from this consultation program. Psychoanalytic treatment of parents of these youngsters became a significant adjunct to the work of the preschool, following Furman's (1969) model. For children in the preschool suitable for and needing psychoanalysis, a third tier was developed, the provision of parent helpers as an adjunct to child treatment. The most essential elements of the clear effectiveness of this approach is the use of volunteer time and the commitment to regular and long-term work. What school would refuse such a program?

Psychoanalytic consultation to schools can be effective when offered freely and with commitment, and when misbehavior (psychopathology) of the child is the focus. Such an approach challenges neither the educational goals of the school nor the individual sensibilities of the staff. Influence is exerted, over time, by interpersonal transmission of a psychoanalytic ideology. That such a program is systemic provides social support, enabling individual teacher acceptance. Resulting reduction of misbehavior in the children (and their exclusion when misbehavior disrupts class functioning) clinches the deal. Free, long-term consultation and support for occasional exclusion is certainly what most teachers[1] want of applied psychoanalysis. The trick is to develop willingness on the part of psychoanalytic organizations and their members to sponsor such a program at no cost. The payoff seems obvious, but the start-up inertia may be formidable. The Houston-Galveston Institute is to be congratulated for their work on this.

Sklarew

Congratulations are also due to the District of Columbia's School-based Mourning Project described by the late Bruce Sklarew. Groups of inner-city elementary school youngsters, experiencing grievous loss simply as a result of the violent nature of the inner city, were recruited to discuss their feelings with psychoanalytically-oriented group facilitators. Recruitment of subjects was difficult, and creative means were utilized. Anecdotal examples of the benefits of such groups were supported by more formal research methodologies demonstrating their utility. The essence of its application to education *per se* was that subjects were children and sites were schools.

Again, teachers would welcome and be impressed by this heroic project, whose ambitious social aim is disruption of the cycle of inner-city violence. Unlike other programs with that aim, Sklarew's addresses the inner lives of individual youngsters. The welcome would result, as in the Houston program, from the focus on the child and the lending of psychoanalytic expertise. Sklarew hoped the success of the project would motivate counselors, teachers, and principals to be trained in the psychoanalytic understanding of inner-city violence. That hope might be as ambitious as his social aim. While many individual educators are sympathetic to psychoanalytic ideology, the profession as a whole is much less so.

---

1 Exclusion has become a major controversy in education. Most teachers of regular classes favor it, special education teachers are divided, and policymakers are increasingly in favor of its alternative, inclusion, but adequate funding and support of inclusion by school districts remains unusual.

Kusche and Greenberg

While the Houston and District of Columbia projects clearly follow the lines of development pioneered by Anna Freud and August Aichhorn respectively, and each represents an excellent example of what has become the usual application of psychoanalysis to schools, the PATHS (Promoting Alternative Thinking Strategies) curriculum is much closer to what Freud had in mind when he spoke of applied psychoanalysis. Not merely a treatment or consultation approach with people who happen to be schoolchildren, it draws upon psychoanalytic theory to develop an educational curriculum. While ostensibly cognitive in title and in several of its aims, it is essentially an approach to affective education. Its focus is not on the psychopathology of misbehaving youngsters but, instead, on the ordinary emotional lives of the general population of elementary schools. And it is clearly psychoanalytic in its outlook.

An ambitious and thoroughgoing curriculum, PATHS trains teachers to deliver lessons planned for the full range of the elementary grades. While its aims include prevention of psychopathology, and reduction of both emotional distress and risk for later problems, they emphasize emotional literacy, social competence, general development, and improved classroom atmosphere. Psychoanalytically-oriented consultants are the trainers, and teachers are the "primary attachment objects" and implementors of the curriculum. An educational, rather than clinical, approach is expected of the trained teachers, although training would promote teachers' empathic attunement and emotional relatedness. An additional important focus is the training of parents as partners with teachers in this curriculum, supporting the ideal educational model of such partnership development for the standard academic subjects.

Like the Houston and District of Columbia programs, long-term commitment of consultants is an essential feature, as is a research paradigm. Success is reported with different populations, in different states, and in Great Britain as well.

Among the features attractive to teachers would be 1) the respect shown for teaching skills, with the use of the teacher as implementer; 2) options to infuse social-emotional learning in the standard curriculum; 3) improved classroom atmosphere and academic achievement; and 4) prevention of misbehavior. It may be ironic, then, that although the latter features are exactly what most teachers want, the first two features might pose obstacles to wider implementation.

The Demands on Teachers

Teachers are challenged by the PATHS program to develop additional curricular expertise at a time when they stand accused of inadequacy with regard to traditional curriculum transmission, and, in many school districts and states they are pressed to improve their skills to meet higher standards for job retention.

To psychoanalysts a social-emotional curriculum like PATHS would likely seem a high priority in a nation made more aware of social-emotional problems by the epidemic of school violence. I know that many individual teachers would agree with that priority. I also know, however, from being in schools while supervising student teachers, that most have other concerns. In one school district I visited, no subject other than language arts may be taught in the morning! Seasoned and creative teachers may, of course, meet this restriction nominally while providing a rich experience for their pupils. Many teachers find it easier and wiser to comply with such a directive in the service of raising test scores. In other school districts, in-service training is comprised of routine conformity with pet projects of the administration or school board. In yet others, especially districts with limited resources and inadequate salaries, many teachers are unlikely to agree to additional professional development without immediate and concrete incentives.

PATHS has been more successful than most in selling itself. Another social-emotional curriculum, one aimed at older children, *Facing History and Ourselves* (*FHAO*) has also been successful. Not based in any psychological theory, *FHAO* uses the subjects of the Holocaust, genocide, slavery, sexism and homophobia to achieve democratic attitudes and feelings in pupils. A charitable foundation has been established to expand its impact from the Boston area to several other locations across the nation. Centered on teacher training like PATHS, it still requires sales expertise to gain acceptance by school districts. And we are well aware of political opposition to such a curriculum in more conservative states, e.g., Florida's "don't say gay" law.

Teachers feel overburdened by external demands in their impossible profession, and are likely to greet additional training requirements and curricular innovation with caution.

The Matter of Values

Kusche and Greenberg recognize another source of potential resistance to their program.

They omit sexuality and oedipal themes from their curriculum, consistent with their own understanding of the needs of latency-age children. They also hope to skirt parental and teacher rejection. For this latter reason, they similarly avoid important feelings about death and grieving. Freud thought (1933) that those who would apply psychoanalysis might be considered trespassers in the fields of application. Talking about sex or death would risk wearing out the welcome of psychoanalysts in schools. There is little doubt that Kusche and Greenberg are wise to avoid such risk. Sex education has been a major curricular battleground, even without a psychoanalytic cast. A combination of the puritan strain in American culture and psychoanalytically-understood resistance provides a formidable challenge even at the end of what some have called the Freudian century.

The *FHAO* curriculum meets resistance that PATHS tries to avoid. Even with older children some teachers and parents object to strong emotionality. Kusche and Greenberg recognize that, for many, any emotional expression is tabu, and any such curriculum may be disparaged as "touchy-feely." Additionally, *FHAO* has a clear ideology that defines antisemitism, racism, sexism, and homophobia as social pathologies. These definitions run headlong into value-diversity. Psychoanalysis also rests on values, and on an ideology with which not all would agree. Analysts may be uneasy with the compromises PATHS adopts to foster acceptability, while recognizing their necessity.

Teachers, like most people, are not receptive to challenges to their values. As psychoanalysts know from the clinical situation, confrontations can be useful only after a relationship of safety and a working alliance have been established.

What Do Teachers Not Want?

The principle of universal education was put into practice only over the course of the past century. During its first fifty years, the teaching field established itself as a profession. In the latter fifty years, high school graduation became a general expectation, and college attendance became commonplace in industrialized nations. Teachers are no longer more educated than members of their communities and, following traditions going back to the colonial area, ordinary citizens feel free to tell teachers what and how to teach. Recently, we've seen an upsurge of conservative efforts to exclude books from libraries and schools. Teachers accept many such directives and school boards support them, since schools are, in fact, owned and supported by their communities.

Teaching is, nonetheless, a profession with developed knowledge and skills. Teachers do not want to be told (particularly by experts from other professions) what their aims should be or how they should go about achieving them. Neither do they want to be told that their own personalities and values need to be adjusted. Instead, most would want assistance with problems that they define themselves.

Conclusion

The three programs under discussion provide fine examples of psychoanalysis as applied to the field of education. The Houston program provides consultation for teachers in dealing with children with behavior problems, as well as opportunity for out-placement and treatment of these children. The District of Columbia program provides a specific intervention aimed at preventing violence for inner-city youngsters. The PATHS program provides a curriculum and a training program for interested teachers and school districts. To the extent that these programs are made available by psychoanalysts, rather than imposed on teachers, they will be welcome.

Freud's (1919) metaphor of the pure gold of psychoanalysis alloying with the copper of suggestion to achieve mass effect implied an elitist view toward applications and, too often, their derogation. Fortunately, those who hope to influence the development of children by the application of psychoanalysis have created some focused approaches that are successful. Eschewing grand results on a mass scale once foreseen by Freud, they reflect an appropriately modest stance consistent with current clinical psychoanalytic method. Teachers and psychoanalysts have good reason for guarded optimism in their *not* impossible collaboration.

Psychoanalysis in Public Schools:
A Contextual Approach

Presented as part of an Introductory Talk at Mount Sinai School of Medicine, 12/7/04

August Aichorn was the first to apply psychoanalysis to education with *Wayward Youth* (1925). Anna Freud supported this work and, along with (and in opposition to) Melanie Klein, went on to create child psychoanalysis. The theorist best known to teachers is Erik Erikson, inappropriately maligned by psychoanalysts for being a popularizer. Would there were more such creative popularizers! A beautifully titled book by Eckstein and Motto, *From Learning for Love to Love of Learning* (1969), was for me of special importance. Another book, by my teacher Richard Jones, *Fantasy and Feeling in Education* (1968) was also inspirational.

Psychoanalytic work in schools has typically taken the form of clinical consultation and referral. Among the projects psychoanalysts have initiated is one at the Houston-Galveston Institute (led by Farley and Manning) in which children are treated through work with their teachers (as Freud treated Little Hans through his father). The Institute also provides a therapeutic preschool for more difficult youngsters, as well as treatment for parents. In Washington, DC, a school-based project focused on mourning (led by Bruce Sklarew) provides psychoanalyst group facilitators for the many elementary school youngsters who have experienced grievous loss because of the violent nature of their inner-city life. My own Institute, the New York Freudian Society, supports a candidate doing such work in a New York City private school, and the other IPA historically non-medical group, IPTAR, has members and candidates working in public schools in this neighborhood. Crisis intervention is a related approach. Following the Columbine High School massacre, the Denver Psychoanalytic Society provided *pro bono* debriefing as well as regular consultation for school mental health professionals.

Following the attacks of 9/11, psychoanalysts were among those who went into schools to work with children and teachers.

Another approach, closer to what Freud had in mind by applied psychoanalysis, is curriculum development in what is called social-emotional (or affective) education, with training programs provided for teachers. The focus is on the emotional lives of the general population of elementary school, rather than the psychopathology of misbehaving youngsters. Emotional literacy (i.e., naming and understanding feelings), social competence, and improved classroom atmosphere are its aims. It works by helping teachers to become more empathically attuned and emotionally related. Parents are also enlisted to be partners in the educational enterprise. Good work has been done to reduce bullying, the scourge of middle school youngsters.

My education practice has, for the past decade, been primarily in public schools. I work with student teachers, new teachers, and principals. I do not identify myself as a psychoanalyst, but I have come more clearly to see the work I do as essentially psychoanalytic. My work with principals occurred accidentally. When I enter a school building, courtesy requires me to touch base with the boss. For the past few years, when principals see me, they break away from what they are doing for five, ten or twenty minutes for what I have come to see as a monthly therapeutic consultation. They speak with me as someone not in their hierarchy. Essentially, I listen. What I say would rarely be called interpretation, but it often seems to be what the principal needs to hear. Once I "ordered" a principal, in the face of her felt pressures, to absent herself during Christmas recess, when no one else would be in the building and when she was in fact sick with flu-like symptoms. She followed my advice and was able to return to work refreshed.

One example of psychopathology stands out. A 9-year-old boy walked threateningly around the classroom, grunting and, at times, striking his classmates or throwing objects. Attempts at exclusion and special education placement failed on procedural grounds, with the mother standing as obstacle. The boy's father had committed suicide two years earlier and his mother was sleeping with her son for her own comfort. In my monthly visits and frequent e-mails with the talented first year teacher, this boy was a major focus of discussion. Despite the principal's assistance, procedures moved at a glacial pace. With my help, the teacher was able to deal with her own feelings and those of the other children. She was able to work with this seemingly feral child so that his behavior, while still grossly inappropriate, became less and less disruptive in the classroom. By the end of the school year, any of us, or any teacher, would still see this boy as seriously disturbed, but the incremental changes induced in him were important for the wellbeing of both the teacher herself and her other pupils. The boy was left back again. Although we are not good at prediction, without help I see him becoming a rapist by early adolescence. In my opinion, this boy requires major psychiatric and family intervention. This example suggests that psychoanalytic involvement in schools may achieve some success, but to do so it must address contextual issues, in this case a dysfunctional system for getting help for disturbed youngsters in disturbed family situations. The issues involve understanding the bureaucracy and the law—and being able to work under conditions vastly different from those of the consulting room.

My own work in schools has nothing to do with abstinence or anonymity. It has much more to do with being a contributing partner on an educational team, offering my skills to other members of the team and, on occasion, to the children. I am reminded of the time during my psychology internship when I worked on a violent ward of a veterans' hospital. I was told I needed to sit in the day room for a few weeks before I would be accepted by patients as a piece of furniture, and before any individual meetings could be useful.

The New York City school system is enormously complex. None of its chancellors has achieved more than limited success, nor has anyone ever figured out how to run a 1.1 million-child system for the benefit of every child. To be effective in any situation, an analyst must become familiar with its workings, just as we become intimately familiar with the workings of individual minds. While it may seem obvious, this is what I mean by the subtitle of this talk, "a contextual approach." I know the bureaucracy and can provide empathy for beleaguered principals and information and guidance for novice or even experienced teachers.

Over a 34-year period, I have worked in different settings. The Greenwich Village School, PS 41, where one of my own children was a pupil, is in a community with medical, law and doctoral degrees about two to a family, and with parents ever-present and tending to intimidate teachers. Attorney Joel Steinberg was so intimidating that he had to kill his 6-year-old illegally adopted daughter, Lisa, before laws were changed to require reporting of suspicion of abuse, and child neglect and abuse were to become a focus for educators. In the south Bronx, where I now do my educational practice, parents are hardly to be found—even when teachers are willing to make home visits. Children may be able to learn reading and writing without parental support, but successes will be far fewer, and principals will be fired more frequently for school failure measured by inappropriate high-stakes test scores.

At the national level, we have the "No Child Left Behind" act, with its great title and great goal. Its neglect by under-funding and its abuse for the sake of political sound bites are notorious in education circles.

As aware citizens you have some familiarity with the problems of education. Education and government are Freud's two other "impossible professions." The question I ask myself, and the one for which I seek your help, is how we may develop and extend successful methods for using professional psychoanalytic knowledge in this arena. To the extent that the school experience of children contributes to personality development, for psychiatrists such work should be considered early prevention. For psychoanalysts, it is another important domain in which to apply our worldview.

A few weeks ago, we heard a scholarly and informative talk about psychiatric practice with Orthodox Jews in Monsey, New York. Giving medication to adolescents to reduce libidinal feelings seems at best to be an instance of searching under the lamppost, rather than in the dark where we have lost our coin. The social pathologies of cultism, sexism, and sexual denial call out for psychiatric and psychoanalytic attention, but, alas, we have no sound tested methodologies. It seems to me that the challenge facing us is to bring our understanding out of the consulting room where we have plenty of light, to the darker corners of social arenas, schools prominent among them, where our skills and knowledge are sorely needed.

For me psychoanalysis provides a frame of reference for this adventure.

Reading, Writing, and Therapy: Psychoanalysts in Schools

with Bruce Sklarew, *The American Psychoanalyst* 39, No. 4 (2005), p. 40

A new psychoanalytic subspecialty has recently been defined: the community psychoanalyst. Schools are one prominent setting for this practice. Analytic work with children began with Freud's consultation about Little Hans; it advanced through the creation of child psychoanalysis by Anna Freud and Melanie Klein; and it expanded its horizons with August Aichhorn's work with delinquent adolescents.

Analysts who work with children have typically been involved with aberrant behavior and, in schools, with special education. Gilbert Kliman's Cornerstone Project, reported in TAP in 1997, is an outstanding example and resulted in the prevention of multiple foster home placements. Many programs are geared to early intervention with preschool children. A fine example is Donald Rosenblitt's work at the award-winning Lucy Daniels Center for Early Childhood ("Lucy Daniels Center").

Redl and Wineman were the first to extend psychoanalytic ideas to the general classroom and school building in 1957. More recently, systematic approaches have been developed for the kindergarten through high school years. Bruce Sklarew's clinical/research collaboration with the Wendt Center for Loss and Healing—the School-based Mourning Project in Washington, D.C.—is one important example. Innovative group techniques developed by Dottie Ward-Wimmer provide inner-city children opportunities to deal with their common experience of grievous loss associated with the multiple traumas of lives of poverty. The Stuart Twemlow team's innovative work on bullying is another admirable enterprise ("Schoolyard Bully"). Identifying the role of "bystander" and developing teaching strategies for undermining peer tolerance for bullying have led to improving both the social and the intellectual climate in elementary schools. Robert Pynoos works in schools for traumatized children. In locations such as Columbine High School, Los Angeles, Armenia, and Bosnia-Herzegovina, his interventions have enhanced the recovery of students and staff, improved overall functioning, and contributed to a healthy school atmosphere.

Analysts have also been involved in curriculum development. Carol Kusché and Mark Greenberg have created an approach to the "regular" classroom, Promoting Alternate Thinking Strategies (PATHS). Elementary school teachers are trained to teach emotional literacy as a regular "subject" along with reading, math, and the rest of the standard curriculum. Henri Parens made the teaching of parenting skills the core of his approach to providing curriculum for 5- to 18-year-olds in regular school classrooms.

Others have developed collaborative efforts to provide clinical consultation for pupils, faculty, and administration. Art Farley and Diane Manning provide a multi-tiered approach to supporting children's emotional development, including consultation with teachers, a therapeutic school for 3- to 8-year-olds, and parent assistance for children in psychoanalysis. William Granatir, following his retirement from clinical practice at age 76, has been a volunteer school psychoanalyst for the past 13 years. He organized a demonstration clinic in a D.C. inner-city elementary school and acted as liaison between the highest levels of the mental health and education systems.

Beyond the participation of well-trained analysts, what makes these programs analytic? Each takes as basic the importance of unconscious mental life, emotional development, and the interrelatedness of social, emotional, and cognitive growth. Each, whether working with pupils, their parents, or school staff and leaders, focuses on the meaning of behavior. They differ from clinical psychoanalysis in that the analyst is a team member with other respected professionals, rather than an authority imposing expertise with esoteric methodology. Where clinical psychoanalysis analyzes transference and resistance, school psychoanalysts use their understanding to modify more directly these phenomena for the benefit of the children and the school community.

"Applied psychoanalysis" has been disparaged by clinical psychoanalysts for far too long. Despite his expressed wish that psychoanalytic technique be modified for its more widespread utility, Freud's own "alloy" metaphor may have promoted this attitude. But alloys are created because they are stronger than pure elements. While research is yet to establish the strength of school psychoanalysis, Freud thought education to be the most important of applications.

The projects reported here should help to end the false conflict between clinical psychoanalysis and community work and will surely upgrade the public image of our science and discipline.

Parenting Teens: Helicopter or Jet?

Presented to the Dobbs Ferry, NY, Parent-Teacher-Student Organization, 3/21/07

A New York Times front page headline on March 17, 2001 claimed: "For Teachers, Middle School is a Test of Wills." One key issue raised was "the topography of the adolescent mind." I've spent much of my career as a teacher educator in public school buildings: mostly in Greenwich Village, an affluent, professional community where my kids still found trouble in middle school; and more recently in the south Bronx, where dedicated teachers made home visits, frustrated in their attempts to locate most parents.

One could attribute many problems to economics, but one son's elementary school was where Lisa Steinberg was a first grader. Lisa was brutally murdered by her lawyer father, initiating requirements for reporting child abuse in New York State. He was a helicopter parent of the nightmarish kind, whose spinning blades were lethal. To call parents of the south Bronx "jets" would be stretching a metaphor. Mostly solo custodians with urgent needs to put food on the table, they spend their days and nights cleaning homes and working in sweatshops.

There are no formulas for raising children or dealing with teenagers. Sara Delano Roosevelt was a helicopter parent well into her son's mature years; her daughter-in-law couldn't stand her. Ben Franklin's parents sent their son from Boston to apprentice in Philadelphia as a young teenager, without suggesting that he "go fly a kite." My psychoanalytic understanding is based on generalizations that won't apply to individuals, and on lots of individual situations that might offer some helpful perspective.

Generalizations I

The message of the 2006 movie Babel was, I think, "keep a close watch on your kids; the world is a dangerous place." It is. Current news reports remind us that binge drinking has become basic to the college experience, as have explicit sex journals and videos. Younger teens are hardly much different, though more secretive in their behavior. Middle school and high school cultures seem to assume the availability of drugs of both the legal and illegal sorts. Chances are good that your child participates or has close friends who participate in activities that would frighten you.

The good news is that most kids grow up navigating dangerous conditions (as well as parental errors) to become adults facing the ordinary triumphs and tragedies of life. We can't make things perfect for our kids; nor will most of us ruin them. The bad news is that whatever we do as caring parents, life will be risky, and we will be unable to protect our kids from inevitable pain and accidental tragedy.

Adolescence is a time of turmoil, a second individuation—the first one being toddlerhood, when kids start saying "No." Teens will rebel in overt and covert ways. For most adults, there is an emotional amnesia about the pain of adolescence. We may recall events, but our minds protect us from intense emotional memory.

Men can't imagine the pain of childbirth; my cousin told me the day after her first delivery she would never do it again. Two more kids and forty-odd years later, she doesn't remember the pain. Recently I became a victim of low back pain, I hurt today; it's not easy to recall that today's pain is much less intense than last month's, and to know that I am in fact recovering. I know by remembering that I whimpered in the morning, and I don't now.

Just as we can't remember, we are also caught up in the universal generation gap. The next generation is always "going down the tubes." They're rude; their music is horrible. But the gap goes two ways: our middle-school kids think we're inept at best, and that our ideas on just about everything are obsolete. Most often, we are not their role models, as we were when they were just a few years younger.

Individual Situations I

A "terrible two" who remained difficult until age 25 threw a punch at his father at age 17; the second time the police were called to scare him, and parents inquired of an attorney about a PINS petition, only to be laughed off. A tough love eviction followed on his 18th birthday.

A teen was arrested for jumping a turnstile. His parents were distraught despite his release without charges.

15-year-old D's boyfriend escaped from a first-floor window upon her mother's early return from work.

A "good boy" arrested at 15, soon thereafter comes home drunk. A bed-wetter until age 16, when he ran away from home.

My 15-year-old grandson disses his "stupid" parents; his 13-year-old sister soon discovers their alleged stupidity.

A patient, daredevil at 16, stood on moving motorcycles, is now a clinical psychologist.

Another patient, age 46, a very good boy as a teen, but has been mildly depressed since then. He dislikes his psychologist father who didn't show him interest, and still seems uninterested in his concerns. He now notices he doesn't pay enough attention to his own daughter, 11, and son, 10.

Generalizations II

Recent neurological studies have shown a brain area, the nucleus accumbens, as the site of long-term goal-directed behavior. It is not fully developed in teenagers. This finding was part of the evidence influencing a Supreme Court decision limiting capital punishment for teens.

The late Erik Erikson, a most important psychologist of adolescence, spoke of this as the stage where the life task is to develop a solid sense of identity. In part, this means differentiating oneself from parents, lest we produce clones. It is a time for testing new roles and new ideas to see what fits. It is a time of rapid changes as styles, friends, interests, and beliefs are tried on and discarded. It is a time of anxiety about the future, and of moodiness.

Individual Situations II

The situations I described earlier each had positive outcomes; that's not always the case. Boys tend to get into trouble over violence; one youngster I know brutally beat another guy at the instigation of his girlfriend. Girls often get in trouble over sex and are more prone than boys to develop eating disorders (anorexia, bulimia). We are sadly familiar with school shootings like Columbine. The onset of schizophrenia is usually in late adolescence; early signs are often ignored. What about body-piercing, tattoos? I think of them as self-mutilation. Are they merely a style—or suggestive of a serious problem?

Conclusions

It's hard to be a teen or a parent of a teen. Parents have legal responsibilities, of course, and must also stand up for their personal values. They must provide structure and discipline, not as an exercise of power but as part of loving care. If parents don't stand up, kids will test their rebellion outside the home, with greater risk. No quick labels like helicopter or jet will apply to most situations. Individual differences are far more important than generalizations.

Good parenting can't start during adolescence; a sound basis for influence is based on a loving relationship starting in infancy. If adolescence becomes mostly a power struggle, parents can't win; kids will outlast them and become emancipated. For parents, adolescence is about giving up control; sound relationships with adult children depend on it.

Life can be understood as a series of separations, disillusionments, losses, and mourning. Loving families can provide crucial balance to these sad realities. Poets and playwrights provide important insights; so can psychologists. I hope I've provided a few.

Education in the USA: Why Are Teachers Disrespected?

4/23/13

After my earlier presentations on American Education, a colleague asked why schoolteachers are held in low esteem. Sadly, the low esteem for teachers is an old story. Socrates' wife Xanthippe is said to have complained: "If you're so smart you'd earn real money instead of the few coins tossed at you by those rich young men." Centuries later, when I was chair of a teacher education department, I ran into my own sixth grade teacher on the street. We hadn't seen one another for nearly 25 years. I introduced myself and we spoke for several minutes. He turned to his wife and said with pride: "See, what I do matters!" as if there had been a running argument—just like that between Socrates and his shrewish spouse.

I knew about this disrespect long before I became a teacher education professor. Upon my discharge from the army, my mother met me at the original Barney's on Seventh Avenue (when it was not yet a high-end clothier). I needed two civilian suits for my new job. We met an acquaintance of hers who asked what I did. When I told her I was a teacher my mother's face dropped. "Where do you teach?" she asked. My mother's smile returned when I replied: "NYU Medical School."

Teaching is a "wannabe" profession, hoping for and working toward a status now accorded to the more established ones. The oldest of these (if we skip prostitution) are the clergy, the military, medicine, and law. Church and army achieved status and established their hierarchies by the claimed power of a god or the force of arms. Medicine was presumed to be based on the power of reason, but until the changes wrought by the Flexner Report (1910), it was really more like an alternate clergy, staffed by barbers and "sawbones" who could tolerate blood and death. Law was a scholastic enterprise, at first a specialty of the clergy for codifying and interpreting its rules and regulations. Shakespeare's famous line, "Let's first kill all the lawyers" was an assessment. In *Emile*, Rousseau's treatise on education, the clergy were derided as "indolent." It takes time and a valid demonstration of worth to achieve lasting social esteem. And, as we see with clergy scandals and lawyer jokes, in our post-modern and highly educated era, social esteem cannot be taken for granted.

As for teaching: following the first colonial education law in the 1640s, when communities had reached a certain size, their leaders hired a teacher for a one-room schoolhouse. This person—nearly always a man—was to be in charge of the school. He would teach all subjects up to preparation for college. He would also wield the mop and keep the building in good repair. The pupils were boys whose families could afford to spare them from labor. The teacher served at the pleasure of the town council, the hiring criteria being whatever pleased these community leaders. A similar model continued until the late 19th Century, with college graduates of the new colleges forming a pool of candidates, but high school graduates eligible for the post.

During westward expansion, job notices were telegraphed by growing towns to be posted at Harvard, William and Mary and the few other east coast colleges. Candidates would apply and those hired received a one-way railroad ticket. When a town's population expanded, a second teacher would be hired, then a third; the most senior would be designated "principal teacher," allotted some time for administration and supervision. Under the impetus of state legislatures whose constitutions provided regulatory authority, standard-setting for teachers and pupils began. The 1862 Morrill Act enabled states to build land grant colleges, so they needn't rely on the east coast to generate teacher candidates. By the end of the 19th Century, teacher training schools—so-called "normal schools" (for teaching norms or expectations)—were created to produce cadres of teachers to meet the demand of an exploding population. The early 20th Century saw the development of high schools, then junior high schools, and a fuller realization of Horace Mann's first principle: universal public education to literacy, including availability of higher education. Normal schools, like the medical and law schools of the era, were alternatives rather than add-ons to liberal arts colleges. Doctoring, lawyering, and teaching were taught to high school graduates—when there were still relatively few. In New York and most other states, teachers' colleges evolved to become the dispersed campuses of current state university systems. The bachelor's degree became a requirement for a teaching job. It remains the entry-level degree, though in most jurisdictions a master's degree is required by the end of a few years of service. It is important to remember though, that unlike medical residents, who presumably work under close supervision, even the newest and least-experienced teachers are alone in their classrooms nearly all the time, every day.

Perhaps the most significant historical change in the teaching profession was the gender shift. A profession of schoolmasters became, in the early 20th Century, a low-paid job for women. Men remained the subject-matter teachers in high school and junior high school, or at least the science and math teachers, while women became dominant in elementary schools, and nearly the whole workforce in the early childhood specialty. After World War II, college education became a new standard for the middle class, and the most able women entered professions that welcomed them: first nursing, then social work and teaching.

The principle of gender equality is a major historical movement in our lifetime—in this nation and in the industrialized world. It is a work-in-progress, with 20 women now seated in the US Senate, a similar percentage in the House of Representatives and three of nine Justices of the US Supreme Court. A majority of law students are now women, and medical students are at near parity. When most of us were in training, women were a distinct minority in both psychiatry and psychology. No more. An unintended consequence of women entering the more prestigious and more lucrative professions was the decline in the overall academic standing of those going into teaching. My career in teacher education, 1970-2005, tracked that decline. My experience with students and student teachers was that most were not the most talented ones like my own wife, who became teachers in an earlier generation.

Another parallel shift was taking place across generations. Immigrant parents and grandparents respected teachers who were usually far more educated then they were. I was the beneficiary of teachers, both men and women, who—during the Depression—were eager to take secure teaching jobs. At my high school, Stuyvesant, many had PhDs. They enjoyed teaching smart kids, and chose to make a career of it.

Teaching had become, nominally, a learned profession with the National Education Association (NEA) its standard-bearer. By the end of the 1950s with an expanding post-war economy, the meager salaries of teachers became an issue, and teacher unionization began. The NEA resisted identification with labor, and promoted, for at least twenty years, a learned society organizational model. In 1961 and 1962, the New York City's teachers union affiliated with the national American Federation of Teachers, held one-day strikes, and established themselves amid much controversy as the legal bargaining agent for their members. By the late 1960s, lengthier strikes took place, led by Albert Shanker—whose name provided a joke in Woody Allen's movie, *Sleeper*. Although Shanker had marched with Dr. King, the issue in the strike focused on race: community control vs. employment rights. These strikes resulted in a major schism in the Civil Rights Movement alliance between Blacks and Jews, one never fully repaired. The NEA soon gave up its organizational model and became the labor union for rural and suburban America, with the AFT smaller nationally but dominant in large cities. This evolution led to a diminution in professional respect for teachers who came to be seen as just another labor union—just at the time when organized labor was experiencing a major loss of political power.

As a teacher, I now offer a medial summary: Teaching is disrespected because it requires less schooling than more respected professions; because teaching is women's work, and no longer the brightest women at that; and because it's part of the labor movement, evoking stereotypes of featherbedding and corruption, as well as disruptive and illegal strikes. Unlike "real" professionals, teachers are public employees working within a bureaucracy with little say as to policies and procedures. Worse still, teachers do not have continuing education requirements once they have completed masters' degrees and earned statutory tenure, and—it is said—their unions care more about job protection for mediocre and poor performers than for the welfare and achievement of children.

In fact, teachers are, by and large, public employees—putting them in an adversarial position with their employers, the taxpayers. In all but the largest cities, school budgets are voted on by these taxpayers, and salaries are negotiated by unions sitting opposite school district officers trying to construct budgets that will be approved. Teachers and taxpayers are financial adversaries. Private and religious school teachers are not in this adversarial position but they usually work for considerably less remuneration in exchange for avoiding the diverse student bodies generally found in public schools. And all teachers are smeared with the accusation of laziness: their official working hours from 9-3, their many holidays, and their long summer vacations.

To complete this picture, our nation's overall education level has gone up considerably in our lifetime; middle class people may have as much or more schooling as teachers, and nearly everyone has direct experience with kindergarten through grade twelve education and, having spent those years with teachers of varying ability, can claim a self-defined expertise about good teaching based on that personal experience—no matter how biased and idiosyncratic that claim might be. Parents who are more educated can be condescending, even intimidating. Attorney Joel Steinberg bullied teachers into silence while abusing his wife and finally killing his six-year-old daughter—leading to adoption of child abuse reporting laws. Many highly educated or high-earning parents have abandoned the public school system entirely. A recent *New York Times* article in the real estate section found middle-class families to routinely budget for private schooling. As the middle class abandons public schools, teachers in those schools are seen as "the inadequate monitoring the unwashed." "Those who can, do; those who can't, teach" has become a motto of what is now an anti-teacher movement.

Is it any wonder that teachers and their unions have become the *bêtes noirs* for a so-called school reform movement that focuses on their inadequacy and blames them for educational decline?

Beyond the history, sociology and economics of teacher disparagement, there is also a psychoanalytic consideration: teachers are major objects of identification in the important stage of middle childhood, and—as authority figures—are also objects of ambivalent transferences. Even our best teachers have been our judges and disciplinarians. During adolescence, teachers can be objects of scorn and mockery, even teasing and harassment, as teens test their new physical and mental skillsets. No one—neither teacher nor ordinary citizen—is without bad memories of a teacher.

The current "school reform" movement has been defined by the 12-year Bloomberg mayoralty, not just in New York City, but nationally. Its major thrust has been one of measurement of teacher effectiveness and student outcomes. There is now a track record, noted primarily in newspapers and newsmagazines.

I completed 12 credits of statistics and I support appropriate assessment. I was also on the CUNY-wide council of education deans from 2000-2001, the year the New York City Teaching Fellows program was initiated as a pilot project of the Board of Education and three campuses of the City University of New York. In September 2001 I attended the meeting where the Chancellors of the School System and of CUNY jointly announced, with no data yet recorded, that the program was a resounding success and would be expanded to all eight CUNY senior colleges. I participated in the development of "rubrics," presumably objective measures of teaching effectiveness. I was skeptical at the onset but now align myself with Diane Ravitch, the educational researcher who was once a leading proponent of this kind of reform and is now a leading critic. The New York City model was duplicated just a few years later by Michelle Rhee, then superintendent of the Washington, DC, school system—and similarly in Atlanta, where the former superintendent, originally a New York school administrator, is now the chief defendant, indicted in a major scandal over falsifying results. Ms.

Rhee is herself now facing a hearing in DC on allegations of cheating during her tenure as chancellor.

The pilot Teaching Fellows program was based on rubrics which attempted to enumerate all the skills teachers should possess. Every possible teaching skill was added to the list. I called it the "kitchen sink" approach to measurement. Later, my son became a teaching fellow in Washington, DC, and is now an elementary school teacher there. An outstanding and enthusiastic teacher, when a few of the laundry list of items were not observed during a supervisory evaluation, there was a markdown in his total score.

Poor teaching is identified as the prime culprit in educational failures in the United States. Getting rid of bad teachers protected by statutory tenure and by their unions has become a major aim of so-called reformers. I have no problem with that aim; nor has Randi Weingarten, president of the American Federation of Teachers. She has worked diligently to streamline the process of teacher dismissal while protecting the rights of accused teachers from those who, for reasons of their seniority-based salaries or personal antagonisms with supervisors, might be inappropriate targets. Recent studies show few teachers to have been dismissed based on these dozen years of presumably "better" evaluation. A much bigger problem is the fact that schools cannot *keep* teachers in whom they have invested training resources. Many teachers leave the profession within five years, including the vast majority of participants in teaching fellows programs and the much vaunted *Teach for America* program. Despite his rating in the top tier each year and being recognized at Kennedy Center ceremonies, I am concerned that my son, now in his second decade in D.C., will leave the work he loves because of the pressure of these inappropriate evaluation measures and the linking of pupil achievement scores with job security and pay. In 2002, at the start of his mayoralty, Michael Bloomberg asked to be assessed on his record with the public schools. Now completing his extended tenure, he has had to defend re-evaluation of initial scoring reports that show little overall positive effect.

Of course teachers are important to learning. Of course there are better and worse teachers as there are better and worse lawyers, doctors, and psychoanalysts; the normal curve applies to most group measures. Teaching fellows programs and *Teach for America* are predicated on the notion that attracting Ivy League graduates to school careers would make a big difference. I taught and supervised the first cadres of New York City teaching fellows and indeed they were more academically able then their less selectively chosen peers. Some were good novice teachers, some were terrible and quit within months of working in a classroom.

Few stayed on beyond their commitment, able to use their teaching experience as a resume enhancement to seek more remunerative work. A *Times* article in early January called *Teach for America* as valuable a credential as working for McKinsey Associates, the financial consulting giant. W.E.B. DuBois spoke of the "talented tenth." Even if the teaching profession could attract and draw more of these people—the aim of fellows programs and *TFA*—there would not be nearly enough to fill classrooms in a nation promising education for all.

Blaming teachers and imposing high-stakes testing on children has not improved our schools. Our best schools exist in communities that support them and—frankly—in those that are comprised of children from wealthier families. Forcing teachers to teach to the test and to make every lesson focus on reading and math will not succeed. A top-down business-model, closing schools and re-opening them with new personnel, hiring principals in their 20s with no experience as teachers, promoting competition (as in "Race to the Top"), and multiplying independent charter schools are approaches that are already proving—despite spotty successes—to be mostly disappointing reforms.

Freud was right: government, psychoanalysis and education are three impossible professions. Every citizen claims to know how to govern, most people believe psychology is common sense, and every former student—i.e., everyone—is an expert on teaching. In his articulate *New York Times* op-ed of ten days ago, Jal Mehta, of Harvard's Graduate School of Education, calls for a true profession of teaching, for which there are successful models in countries that now outperform ours—and in several of our most successful school districts.

Two older writers need to be re-read: John Dewey, especially his *Democracy and Education* (1916) and Jonathon Kozol, especially his *Savage Inequalities* (1991).

As much as I have enjoyed attending graduations and theater and orchestra performances at the suburban schools attended by my three older grandchildren, I cannot help but compare the quality of the programs and their love for many of their teachers with the circumstances at the South Bronx elementary schools at which I supervised student teachers and teaching fellows—and recognized these savage inequalities. The economic disparities that were highlighted in the recent presidential election are most striking when Westchester or Suffolk districts are compared with those of the South Bronx or Central Brooklyn. I've called my grandkids "overprivileged." Their parents are correct to object. A good education should be a right, not a privilege.

When we disrespect and disparage teachers we engage in scapegoating—we project our inadequacies as a society. Teachers provide a target to let us evade collective responsibility for the education of all children.

Ethics Education for Civic Virtue: A Knotty Issue

Introduction to a Panel, October 12, 2017

Three aims characterize all educational systems: the Intellectual, the Practical (economic), and the Cultural (passing on values). There is conflict within and between these aims: Liberal educators fight over critical thinking or a core curriculum; Vocational education presses for greater emphasis. For our topic, Virtue, we must ask whose values are taught in a multicultural society.

What is virtue? Jefferson was a slaveholder; some would argue the economics of slavery overrode its immorality, at least for a time. Fossil fuels drove 20th Century economic progress. Do Republican economics override caring for the least among us, or those struggling in the middle, or the survival of our planet?

The question of indoctrination, or propaganda: The first amendment limits government in contradictory ways (establishment; free exercise), with private and religious schools free to indoctrinate. Athenians jailed and executed Socrates; Spartans taught war. Soviet schools banned religion; Chinese teach that the Dalai Lama is a war criminal. Saudi and Palestinian madrassas teach hatred of Jews. States control curriculum in the United States. De jure segregation was outlawed in 1954 but not legislatively banned until 1964, while de facto segregation continues, even in New York City. Southern and Midwestern states are gun cultures, coastal states mostly not. Does patriotism mean "my country right or wrong," or "toward a more perfect union?"

Even in authoritarian and parochial schools, adolescent rebellion exists, so does adult resistance. Children may or may not learn attendance, punctuality or fairness in kindergarten. How do we influence or shape values in children, adolescents or adults? Psychoanalysis has ideas; in practice, even in individual therapy, changing minds is difficult and unpredictable.

The development of individuals is determined by genes and learning. Biologists now hope to change genes (CRISPR) and the epigenome. It's no less complicated, probably more so, to induce learning; uniformity of results could lead to the Brave New World of Huxley's automatons, or the marching army of Kim Jong-Un.

Each generation claims a decline in manners or virtue in the next. Are we right—or just old? Many young people have values akin to ours, and we differ. History will judge, and the future, if there is one, will judge what is to come.

De gustibus non est disputandum. But calling it a matter of taste trivializes deeply felt values. This is not an organized panel; none of us know what the others will say. I'm eager to listen.

Maslow and Me—A Memoir

February 21, 2019

I thank Hillel Swiller for suggesting I talk in the Mount Sinai group about Abe Maslow.

Abraham H. Maslow was recruited from Brooklyn College in 1950 by President Abram L. Sachar and came in 1951 to found and chair a department of psychology at Brandeis University. Dr. Sachar began departments at the fledgling school, founded in 1948, by selling people like Leonard Bernstein, a native Bostonian, and Benny Freedman, the first Jewish All-American football star—yes, Brandeis was to have a football team, but only for its first decade—on the idea that they had an obligation to make this new university instantly elite; it was the first—and still sole—non-sectarian institution of higher education founded by the American Jewish community. It was founded in response to Jewish-exclusionary quotas at the many prestigious private institutions founded by Christian denominations (think Columbia, Yale, Harvard).

Maslow did well, as did the other department chairs, including two Nobel Laureates in Biochemistry, matched in 2017 by two in Biology. He recruited a group of young men, none yet with great academic accomplishment. They were each superb teachers and went on to become leaders in American psychology. He also recruited one older European woman, Eugenia Hanffman, not as a teaching professor, but to create the first college mental health center. It became the model for such offices now nearly universal at American and European colleges.

I became a freshman at Brandeis in the fall of 1957. I was pre-med, as were most of the boys in my corridor of a dormitory built to resemble a medieval castle, inherited from the defunct Middlesex Medical School. Only two walls remain today of the Castle, rehabilitation being far more costly than building a new contemporary dorm with a clear view of Boston, completed last year. My first elective was to be in the spring, but Abe taught the introductory psychology auditorium lecture only in the fall. My intro teacher was the guy who taught in spring, Ricardo Morant, and a terrific teacher he was. It wasn't until fall of 1959 that I met Professor Maslow in his small seminar on motivation and personality, the title of his 1954 book.

I was a shy young man. Others complied with Abe's insistence that he be called Abe; I couldn't do that with this distinguished man 33 years my senior, sporting a bushy moustache. Though I've grown a few beards and moustaches in my time, I could never produce a bushy one like that. A psychology major, after declining early acceptance to Johns Hopkins's then-new quick Bachelors-Medical degree program, I learned a lot in Maslow's informal seminar. When asked by my first grad school psychotherapy supervisor at our first meeting, he an American graduate of the Vienna Institute, for my most important influences, I cited Freud, of course, Wilhelm Reich for his Character Analysis, and Abraham Maslow, for the humanistic context required, in my opinion, for all psychological work.

I returned to Brandeis for my fifth anniversary reunion, having just earned my PhD, and I spotted Dr. Maslow walking on campus. I eagerly engaged him, telling him of my accomplishment. His response was chilling. He seemed clinically depressed and said he regretted everything he'd written, especially the popular abnormal psychology text with Bela Mittelmann (1951), and he was unhappy with the field in general. He had just been elected president-elect of the American Psychological Association. He left Brandeis three years later for a position in Southern California and died of a heart attack in 1970 at age 62. My 1966 encounter with him colored conversations I had about him for decades. I would summarize Abe as an outstanding faculty recruiter, whose teaching was limited to anecdotal schmoozing, hardly organized or scholarly. It is only in the past decade that I've come to appreciate again how much he taught me.

The most prominent memories that come to mind: "What do you call a nudnik with a PhD? A Phudnik!"

"Peak experiences are exceptions. If you're single, you have to go home; if you're married, you have to go to sleep."

"Was Freud self-actualized? Yes, as amply evidenced by his ability to change his mind frequently on very important matters in the face of new evidence."

And: "No one who really wants to be president is psychologically qualified for the job. The only nominee I could ever support, therefore, was Adlai Stevenson." Abe died before the election of Barack Obama.

Though he came home every night, my dad Jerry was largely absent in my day-to-day life, working six days a week as a retail shoe clerk, with side jobs most

Sundays. I've joked that he worked 25/8 to barely support my mother, my younger sister and me. Errors of judgment led to three business failures that put him in debt to brothers-in-law. Bankruptcy was not an option; family debts had to be repaid. He was rarely visibly upset; the exceptions being when my mother would berate him. At the age of 54, while I was in college, he started a small business—a specialty shoe store (ladies sizes 9-13) where he was pleased to serve tall women and transvestite men. He achieved a small success, enabling a modest Florida retirement at 65.

Abe, two years younger than my father, seemed completely at ease as a teacher, and a successful man in his prime. He may have lectured in his introductory auditorium class, but in our seminar, he sat behind a desk, schmoozing with us. We had readings of course, but I don't recall lectures; he was anecdotal. Without much awareness on my part—and not much interaction—Abe became a role model. That his younger daughter was my Brandeis classmate surely supported this identification.

My father rarely conversed. My mother was the voluble one, and her friends and their husbands were his friends. I recall only five conversations with him, when a few years ago I began to search for specific memories.

1.   At about age 13, I asked: "You work and can't go to synagogue; do you believe in God?" "If there's a God," he replied, "he knows I'm a good person."
2.   At age 16, about to leave for college, when urged by my mother, he asked: "You know about girls?" "Yes." "Good."
3.   At about age 20: "Did you ever have a mistress?" "Who could afford one?"
4.   On returning from military service I displayed a framed picture of my Texan girlfriend who would become my first wife. He asked—invoking the name of his own father who died in my infancy—"Has she agreed to name your first son David?" "Yes."
5.   On announcing my engagement some months later: My mother: "How could you get engaged without asking us?" My father, interrupting: "A man doesn't ask his parents' permission to get married."

Each of these memories was pregnant with meaning and had deep influence in my development.

I always felt my father's love and pride in me, and I credit a very long psychoanalysis for my learning to appreciate him fully, and for my ability to express my love to him in his last years. "Learning to appreciate" is a phrase I learned from

Brandeis psychology professor Walter Toman, a native German who provided that experiential phrase—"to appreciate"—as the best definition for Strachey's neologism, "cathexis." Cathecting my father is the example I still cite as the most important outcome of my personal analysis, a result no other treatment approach would be likely to claim.

Even during the years following our encounter at my Brandeis reunion, when I was not appreciating Maslow, I would speak of him as a talent scout of genius. The psychology faculty at Brandeis during my era was—pound for pound, as we would say of boxers—the best department in the nation. Having taken every course offered, I missed out on teachers in other disciplines like Max Lerner, Eleanor Roosevelt and Herbert Marcuse. My class produced an unusually high number of mental health professionals, and we all knew at the time that we were in the presence of great young men. I followed their careers. One of them, the late Ulric Neisser, coined the term "cognitive psychology," and headed the APA task force that provided rebuttal to "The Bell Curve," the 1994 book by Herrnstein and Murray that claimed the intellectual inferiority of Black people. I spoke with Neisser a few years ago, when he was preparing his essay for a volume of the annual series, "The History of Psychology in Autobiography." When he joined the Brandeis faculty, he told me, there were three main paradigms in psychology: Freud's psychoanalysis, Skinner's behaviorism, and Maslow's humanism, referred to then as "the third force." Little did Neisser suspect, he said, that his brainchild, cognitive psychology, would replace Abe's as the third—now most prominent—force in American psychology.

None of Abe's recruits' names have become as well-known as his. Morant, my psych 101 teacher, became long-term chairman of the department following Abe's departure. Toman returned to Germany and published on sibling relationships. Richard Held moved to MIT, where he became a leading vision scientist, Dick Jones went to Oregon and wrote about education, James Klee went to the University of South Georgia, where he became the most popular professor on campus. David Ricks had a career at several colleges, including Columbia.

Abe's reputation continues to flourish posthumously. A 2002 survey had him as the tenth most cited psychologist of the 20th Century. Two particular phrases of his have become cultural staples: Maslow's hierarchy of needs, and "Maslow's hammer." Hillel enjoys using the latter to criticize psychoanalysts—"if all you have is a hammer, everything looks like a nail"—but without citation (The Psychology of Science, 1966). I only learned from Wikipedia while preparing this article that this phrase is Maslow's.

Much of what follows is likewise gleaned from Wikipedia, which I had believed to be an unreliable source. While not a scholarly encyclopedia, its reputation has improved. The more prestigious Encarta is now seen by scholars as far less satisfactory.

Some biography: born and raised in Brooklyn, Maslow was the oldest of seven children. His parents were Jewish immigrants from Kiev, then part of the Russian Empire, who fled from Czarist persecution in the early 20th century. They came to New York City to a multiethnic, working-class neighborhood. His parents were poor and not intellectually focused, but they valued education. He had various encounters with anti-Semitic gangs who would chase and throw rocks at him. Maslow and many other young people struggled to overcome such acts of prejudice in the attempt to establish an idealistic world based on education and economic justice. The tension outside his home was also felt within it, as he rarely got along with his mother, and eventually developed a strong revulsion towards her. He is quoted as saying

What I had reacted to was not only her physical appearance, but also her values and world view, her stinginess, her total selfishness, her lack of love for anyone else in the world—even her own husband and children— her narcissism, her Negro prejudice, her exploitation of everyone, her assumption that anyone was wrong who disagreed with her, her lack of friends, her sloppiness and dirtiness.

He also grew up with few friends other than his cousin Will, and as a result he grew up in libraries. It was here that he developed his love for reading and learning. He went to Boys High School, then one of the top schools in Brooklyn, where he served as the officer of many academic clubs and became editor of the Latin Magazine and the school's physics journal.

As a young boy, Maslow believed physical strength to be the single most defining characteristic of a true male; he exercised and took up weightlifting in hopes of being transformed into a more muscular guy. His actual appearance and studiousness made him a failure at that goal. Maslow attended the City College of New York after high school. In 1926 he began taking legal studies classes at night in addition to his undergraduate course load. He hated law and almost immediately dropped out. In 1927 he transferred to Cornell but left after one semester due to poor grades and high costs. He later graduated from City College and went to the University of Wisconsin to study psychology. In 1928, he married his first cousin Bertha, still then in high school. Maslow's psychology training at Wisconsin was decidedly experimental-behaviorist. He pursued a line of research which included investigating primate dominance behavior and sexuality under the guidance of Harry Harlow (of monkey mothering fame). Maslow's early experience with behaviorism would leave him with a strong positivist mindset. He wrote his master's thesis on "learning, retention, and reproduction of verbal material." He regarded the research as embarrassingly trivial, but completed his thesis in the summer of 1931 and was awarded a master's degree. He was so ashamed of the thesis that he removed it from the psychology library and tore out its catalog listing, a reaction strikingly similar to his expressed wish 35 years later to destroy his books. Yet his professor admired the research and urged him to publish it. In 1934 it came out as two articles.

He continued his research at Columbia University, finding another mentor in Alfred Adler. From 1937 to 1951, Maslow taught at Brooklyn College. During the years following World War II, he began to question the way psychologists had come to their conclusions, and although he did not completely disagree, he had his own ideas on how to understand the human mind. He called his new discipline humanistic psychology. Maslow was already a 33-year-old father of two when the United States entered World War II. He was thus excused from the draft, but the horrors of war inspired in him a vision of peace leading to his groundbreaking studies of self-actualization. The studies began under the supervision of two mentors, anthropologist Ruth Benedict and Gestalt psychologist Max Wertheimer. These two, such "wonderful human beings" in Maslow's eyes, inspired him to take notes about them and their behavior. This would be the basis of his lifelong research and thinking about mental health and human potential. He extended the subject, borrowing ideas from other psychologists, and added new ones: hierarchy of needs, meta-needs, meta-motivation, self-actualization, and peak experiences. He built a framework that allowed others to conduct more comprehensive studies. Maslow believed that leadership should be non-intervening. Consistent with this belief, he rejected a nomination in 1963 to be president of the Association for Humanistic Psychology because he felt that this particular organization should develop an intellectual movement without a leader. In 1967 he was named Humanist of the Year by the American Humanist Association.

Abe's last years at Brandeis were not happy ones. Always a political progressive, he became upset with what he saw as the radicalism of late-60's student movements: civil rights, anti-war, gender equality and sexual diversity. He supported the causes but was offended by the methods. He had become a consultant to businesses and rejected as utopian the views of his Brandeis colleague Herbert Marcuse, and the public intellectual, psychoanalyst Erich Fromm. To be sure, Abe was no feminist. Brandeis students came to see him as an old-fashioned liberal and withdrew their affection. Students occupied a major classroom building there in 1968. Unlike the uprising at Columbia, where police were brought in, a negotiated outcome ended the Brandeis occupation and led to creation of an African and African-American Studies Department. The year 2018 saw the 50th Anniversary of the founding of this Department, with Angela Davis, Brandeis Class of '65, one of the symposium speakers.

Abe and Bertha had two daughters, Ann, and my classmate Ellen. Ann graduated from Bennington in 1958, first worked in social agencies, and then became a small business owner, living in Indiana and Ohio. She married and had a daughter. I found a 2015 profile; the word "obituary" was left blank.

Ellen was one of those radical women dismissed by her father. She deferred Brandeis graduation to work in the civil rights movement in Mississippi, and to participate in other "movement" projects. She returned to Brandeis to graduate in 1967, and she earned a PhD in clinical psychology, practicing for decades as a psychotherapist in Boulder, Colorado. She married and had three sons and died in 2009. She never came to class reunions.

Reaching its peak in the 1960s, the main point of Maslow's humanistic movement was to emphasize the positive potential of human beings. Maslow claimed his work was a vital complement to that of Freud: Freud supplied us the sick half of psychology and we must now fill it out with the healthy half. Maslow focused his studies on mentally healthy individuals, self-actualizing people, claimed as a coherent personality syndrome representing optimal psychological functioning, and a life in harmony with oneself and one's surroundings, and with frequent peak experiences.

Maslow's hierarchy is applicable to topics such as finance, economics, history and criminology. A letter to the *New York Times* on October 30, 2018, about the possible Sears bankruptcy stated:

When I began teaching management to M.B.A. students in 1971, a major company goal was customer satisfaction through outstanding employee performance. Great emphasis was placed on employee motivation, performance and loyalty to the company to maximize customer satisfaction. Frederick Herzberg's theory of "job enrichment" and Abraham Maslow's "self-actualization" were introduced to students as methods to add meaning and challenge to jobs and to stress employment achievement.

Then in the mid-1980s the emphasis shifted to shareholder value, and many employers began to view employees as commodities to be bought and sold. The profits and stock prices in quarterly and annual reports became the holy grail of organizational effectiveness. Pensions disappeared, employee loyalty declined, and the result has been an unfortunate decline of the American employee (Goodale, 2018).

Doctors similarly became "service providers."

Humanistic psychology has become better known as "positive psychology," promoted most prominently by the University of Pennsylvania's Martin Seligman, himself a past president of APA.

In addition to those who thought his politics establishmentarian, Maslow had professional critics. Biographical analysis as a method is based on the inevitably biased subjectivity of the researcher. Humanistic psychology suits people who emphasize the positive side of humanity and free will. It is criticized for its lack of empirical validation. It is also not applicable for treating specific problems or mental disorders.

Maslow's 1968 book, *Toward a Psychology of Being*, stressed the importance of what he then called transpersonal psychology, writing: "without the transpersonal, we get sick, violent, and nihilistic, or else hopeless and apathetic." Human beings, he believed, need something bigger than themselves that they are connected to in a naturalistic... but not a religious sense: Maslow was an atheist and found it difficult to accept religious experience as valid. Transpersonal psychology became popular within psychology, and the *Journal of Transpersonal Psychology* was founded in 1969. In the United States, transpersonal psychology promoted recognition for non-western psychologies, philosophies, and religions, and understanding of "higher states of consciousness," for instance through intense meditation.

The oldest of Abe's hires, James Klee (1916-1996), in his young forties then, was the only department member who teased Maslow. Abe used the word "instinctoid" to mean "sort of" instinctual: Klee said you might as well use "ecoloid," "sort of" environmental. Maslow posited self-actualization as the antithesis of psychopathology; this binary is far from the nuanced interactionist model that is widely accepted in the human sciences. Abe called his research "studies," and was not an experimentalist.

In setting up a positive or transpersonal psychology, Maslow seems to have ignored the work of older contemporaries, notably Heinz Hartmann (1894-1970) and Erik Erikson (1902-1994). Hartmann's project was psychoanalysis as a general psychology, Erikson's a lifelong development model. The second edition of his *Childhood and Society* (1962) includes a discussion of human strengths and virtues, the latter encompassing hope, will, purpose, competence, fidelity, love, care and wisdom to complement his eight developmental stages along with their life tasks. Abe's narrowness in this regard is evident today in what I see as the "silos" of professional groups in our field. Psychoanalytic society meetings I attend have minimal overlapping attendance, despite great theoretical commonality. We all await an inclusive paradigm in the human sciences—a grand unifying theory—but we don't work closely enough with each other. Freud referred to this phenomenon as "the narcissism of small differences."

What remains of Maslow's contribution to general psychology? Like gestalt psychology, it has properly infused the profession without becoming a major specialty. While Fritz Perl's students maintain a gestalt training institute that eschews his more controversial approaches, that institute is small, and I cannot discern its unique contribution. Though there are undergraduate courses in positive psychology, transpersonal psychology, and humanistic psychology, these are rarely used as professional identifiers.

I'll close with another memory: While serving at Brooke Army Medical Center as a clinical psychologist during the Vietnam era, I engaged with the civilian professional community. Two prominent local psychiatrists began a group therapy training program, and I joined as a student. At the initial meeting, one of them asked, "What's the first thing you notice when you meet a patient?" The brash young Freudian that I was responded quickly: "Transference and resistance." "No," he admonished. "It is the patient's humanity!" Believing that such a sentiment should be in one's bones, rather than conscious thought, I snottily replied: "If you have to think about it, you're in the wrong field!" He did not throw me out, so that riposte may in fact have been unspoken, but is now recalled as part of my personal myth (Kris, 1956). I learned a lot in that program that was directly relevant to the several therapy groups and the process group I led as an Army psychologist.

As the rabbi says, both positions are correct. Human beings are exceedingly complex creatures, and both collective and individual complexity become more evident as we learn more. Any paradigm that would be useful must attend both to individual differences and to common humanity. Maslow's may have been an overreaction to the pathologizing of patients, but he had good reason for it, and is properly esteemed for his contributions. Though I've treated sick patients, the vast majority has not been "mentally ill," and I'd be happy to have some as friends if they weren't my patients. The DSM expansion of diagnoses is the creation of a monster. Maslovian thinking would have that expansion dramatically reversed.

Like each of our mentors, and all great contributors, Abe Maslow was a limited human being. But I am grateful for having known him.

MOUNT SINAI
PRESENTATIONS

I was appointed to the voluntary psychiatry faculty at Mount Sinai School of Medicine in 2005, following a year as a faculty conference guest. I am most grateful to the long-term director of the Division of Psychotherapy, the late Hillel I. Swiller, MD, for his invitation and for his friendship. Hillel trained as a psychoanalyst when that was expected of psychiatrists, but he defined himself as a physician and took pride and pleasure criticizing my Freudianism.

Many papers in this collection were responses to Dr. Swiller's humorous putdowns as we became foils for one another during conferences. I interacted with the group, often by direct reference to their presentations or commentary. I cite others without full references and have anonymized most colleagues' names. Redundancies occurred as I tried to correct misapprehensions about Freudian practice and to elaborate on core principles of Flexible Freudianism. These interactions helped me appreciate the thinking of those whose views differ from mine as I articulated and modified my own. Note also that several papers here are discussion of books I reviewed (see the earlier section).

Consensus and Controversy in Dynamic Psychotherapy

4/14/05

This talk was stimulated by several of the talks that preceded it in our Thursday sessions. I hope you are tempted to interrupt. I ask you, though, to wait until I have concluded, and my overall theme is clear. There will be ample time for rebuttal.

Introduction: Have We Moved Toward a Scientific Psychotherapy?

It is about 45 years since my first undergraduate course on personality theory. The essential message of that course was that every theory reflected the personality of the theorist. Recognizing the validity of that thesis, I was even then troubled by it. Surely there must be some general truths about human psychology out there. My quest for those truths attracted me to psychoanalysis and, despite the arguments of post-modernism and their legitimate criticisms of positivism, I continue to find total composite psychoanalytic theory to contain much more than a hint of truth. Following Leo Rangell, I believe there is one complex theory of the human mind and interaction, and that the many "alternate" theories are instead partial ones that can be subsumed and integrated in an approach of "both-and" rather than "either-or."

Psychoanalysis has no final answer to the questions of ontology and epistemology, nor is integration the current and widely accepted approach. We must surely welcome and respect legitimate differences of opinion to refine both theory and practice. But what are *legitimate* differences, and can we approach a scientific psychotherapy?

This introduction was stimulated by a brief conversation with a colleague following an excellent presentation here on attachment theory. In that

291

conversation, we found accidental events to have turned this colleague away from a psychoanalytic practice—and me away from group psychotherapy. The paper generated other thoughts germane to this presentation. The process by which Margaret Mahler developed her psychoanalytic developmental theories, and the same process by which they are critiqued by attachment theorists, is the unified process of scientific advancement. The personalities of Mahler and John Bowlby, as well as those who choose to work within their respective models, however, can hardly be discounted in what remain inconclusive findings. The model claimed by the paper for attachment theory is one in which a goal is to distinguish "normal" and "at risk" populations as early as possible. I acknowledge the category "at risk of serious psychopathology," but find Freud's ideas pointing to similarities and continuities between normal and pathological to be more compelling, and I worry about the lack of reliability of very early childhood assessment in the domain of human psychology.

Soon after I began attending these sessions I was struck by the sharp differences of opinion in the room. When our chair accused a presenter of malpractice for what I considered exquisitely skillful transference work with a woman the chair had referred to the presenter, I was shocked by the intensity of the exchange and impressed that such an exchange could occur in the context of obvious mutual affection. As I listened closely, at our several conferences, I continued to be struck by differences of opinion in the room (including differences I had with one or another speaker or discussant)—and with the continued maintenance of collegiality. I hope that will apply when I have finished reading today.

Eventually, another observation forced itself upon me. Sometimes differences seemed to be papered over by the friendly atmosphere or simply dropped, rather than fully explored. This is understandable. As a division of an academic department that defends talk therapy, once the mainstream in psychiatry and now unfortunately marginalized, we should not fight among ourselves in the face of external challenges from predominantly chemical approaches or by managed care. It is also a matter of available conference time and of the rabbi dilemma: "They can't both be right? You're right too." Perhaps just exposing ourselves to within-group different ideas is good enough. Acceptance of alternate points of view is useful in clinical study groups where even practitioners of similar theoretical persuasion will have different "takes" on clinical material and will suggest new angles of observation from which a presenter may learn.

But, 100 years after Freud published his brief essay "On psychotherapy" (1905), our profession seems far from agreement on even the basic components of a scientific psychotherapy. I decided, therefore, to make note of differences expressed here in the hope that we might approach some consensus on what could be considered validated ideas and practices and, alternatively, that we might define more clearly the controversies. We might then decide to become more ambitious and sort controversial ideas into categories of good, promising, and debunked. If not, we might at least have fun trying to be more scholarly and scientific.

A Paper on Dreams

I'll begin with the December 9th presentation by M, "The Dream in Psychotherapy." To my listening, the dream presented from a neighbor demonstrated M's intuitive grasp. I mean intuitive in Aquinas's sense: the immediate grasp of a truth, not requiring sequential steps of cogitation. I am not so talented in this regard and must work more ploddingly. M had some confirmation of his understanding of the meaning of the dream, and yet, around the conference table, alternate views abounded, each with its own rationale. If dream interpretation is so disparate in a room of experienced therapists, well trained in one or another psychodynamic tradition, can it have *any* validity?

And what of the "Dream Breakthrough" model presented by D in November as *predicting* adolescent psychosis? D expressed his strong preference for avoiding false negatives to catch and prevent potential psychotic breaks, over the risk of false positives. I would be concerned about iatrogenic effects of false positives in his approach—just as I am with attempts at early detection in toddlers of "at risk" behaviors.

F on the Management of Medication Corollary to Psychotherapy

Just a week after M's presentation on dreams, F presented a treatment with inadequate communication between a psychopharmacologist and herself in which each doctor seemed to assume primary responsibility for the patient's care. The psychotherapy was put into jeopardy. We know about split transferences. Do we know how to be effective in limiting their potential for blocking treatment? And what of another colleague's comment that the patient described was altogether unreachable? And an opinion that the apparently insensitive pharmacologist may have been closer to the right approach? How may we adjudicate these matters for the benefit of a patient—and of the scientific psychotherapy we claim to practice? I am raising questions of *knowing* who or what may be more correct, rather than just trying to figure out what seems to make most sense in a specific clinical example.

In this regard, I was also reminded of M's earlier presentation in which he disappointed me deeply when he said, almost as a matter of course, that he prescribed medication for the patient—for fear of her having an anniversary reaction leading to decompensation while he was away on vacation. And I had thought, despite our chair's objections, that the talk therapy by itself was on track. Who is right? How can we know? If we are to pretend to a scientific approach, we must ask these questions.

Papers on Sex Therapy and Group Therapy

What about our different modalities? L recommended sex therapy on a few occasions, including in December with A's patient. Others—in a different clinical presentation—asserted the value of group therapy. Do we favor what we enjoy practicing? Adherents of each of our modalities develop lists of indications and contraindications to claim theirs is not merely personal predilection. For individual patients there can be no adequate controlled study. Does the patient go to the most forceful personality, or does she go to the seemingly most empathic?

In an exquisitely detailed presentation in early March, we heard some effects of the entry of a new and unsuitable patient into a group engaging in mourning the death of a long-time member. Our colleague sought interventions and ideas alternative to the ones she used. To my thinking, our group provided little more than bromides; surely none of us knew with any confidence how to work better than the therapist with what she had described.

More Examples

In December, D presented a control patient in thrice-weekly psychoanalysis. He welcomed the several differing opinions, which included alternative diagnostic and treatment recommendations. I felt we were blind people feeling different parts of the elephant—or characters in *Rashomon.*

Z's December presentation seemed to equate external stimulation with trauma, to my mind an erroneous parsimony like calling countertransference anything and everything a therapist feels or thinks about a patient.

I include myself among many who value Wilhelm Reich's work on character but judge his orgone energy theory as either simply wrong or part of his own pathological thinking. A colleague, a serious and creative thinker, supports orgone theory and yet another spoke recently about "medical orgone therapy." Most professionals believe that approach to have long been debunked. When can an approach be rejected?

A Defense of Psychological Theory in the Face of Brain Science

In late January we heard a most scholarly paper by P. He took us from the Golden Age of Greece through a history of Western philosophy and medicine and provided strong support for our commitment to psychological treatment. It was only in his vignette regarding the successful alleviation of depression in a politically well-connected mogul that I found myself disappointed. The guy felt better after talking—and that's enough to count the treatment as psychotherapy? I look at symptomatic improvement as important for the development of a treatment alliance that may lead to an understanding of the patient's problems embedded in character. Abreaction or catharsis may be a good first step. Effective psychotherapy requires more extensive work.

Feeling Better

Our chair has suggested that getting a dog is therapeutic for some people. He has described some aspects of his practice (having lots of pictures of grandchildren in his office) as making *him* feel better. In a presentation that I truly respect as the beginning of a subspecialty, F described her work with a family as "anything that might help." I encouraged her development of theoretical formulations to have her work evolve to subspecialty status. I cannot believe, however much feeling good is a necessary aim for our patients and ourselves, and however much effort we put in to achieve that aim, that it is sufficient to define sound psychotherapy. Lots of things contribute to feeling good, and many things may be helpful in general. D's excellent presentation last week on placebos demonstrated sometimes dramatic effects of any intervention, for good or ill. As scientific practitioners, we must attempt to tease out nonspecific effects from interventions that have more precise and predictable therapeutic potency. What is our professional, scientific contribution—the part that justifies our fees? And what interventions enable us to go beyond suggestion and promoting good feelings? To take a preemptive shot at one theme suggested, to what extent are we different than the cleric or prostitute?

Theory as fantasy?

It's been stated here that whatever our theory, we find data for its justification. There is some truth in that claim. I believe, nonetheless, that theory is absolutely necessary for developing and understanding method, and that there are not several theories, but one that, like Darwin's and Einstein's, provides a good roadmap. Rangell calls it "total composite psychoanalytic theory." Like the theory of evolution is to biology, its aim is to comprise all psychological phenomena. Like Darwin's theory, its specifics are tested and refined. It is at one time a theory of everything and also an incomplete theory. We minimize its importance to the detriment of our science.

Tentative Conclusion

I must admit that I often feel that the rabbinical approach is best: they're all right. And on some matters (listen to the patient; be warm, thoughtful, and tactful; listen for alternate possibilities) the rabbi is surely right. When we are with like-minded colleagues with whom we are comfortable, we find benefit in alternate hypotheses that may help our patients. There are surely highly empathic and intuitive individuals who seem to understand people more quickly than most. I must work hard at the necessary but insufficient nonspecific factors of warmth, intuition, and tact. These are not my talents.

But we must recognize that the divergences of opinion sampled here cannot *all* be right. How can we look at the claims made in these conferences—going beyond respectful listening and challenging to refinement of our thinking and our practice?

I will conclude by recalling Henry Murray's renaming personality theory "personology." This was his attempt to define our work as an *idiographic science*.

I agree with Murray, and I find the uniqueness of each patient or analysand to make our work unfailingly interesting, day after day, hour by hour. Surely, it is my anal character that pushes me to seek order amid the chaos of individuality. I learned 45 years ago that character influences viewpoint, but if that is a universal psychological law there must be others. If we make any claim that our work is based in science, we need to seek more such laws. Please, let's talk about it.

Analysis in Foxholes

September 22, 2005

This talk was stimulated by the 2004 book *Analysts in the Trenches: Streets, Schools, War Zones,* co-edited by Drs. Bruce Sklarew, Stuart W. Twemlow and Sallye M. Wilkinson. My change in title from "trenches" to "foxholes" was an attempt at some originality—and to evoke, of course, the aphorism "there are no atheists in foxholes." The settings described, and others I will discuss, are better thought of in terms of collaboration.

My central thesis is one I have stated here before. Psychoanalysis is far more than a specific form of psychotherapy. Instead, for me, it is a worldview, a comprehensive psychology, incomplete, but with great explanatory power not at all restricted to the consulting room site of its original and continuing discoveries. Like evolution in biology, relativity in physics, and the "big bang" in cosmology, it is a master theory. It was made so by the imagination and genius of its founder whose interests ranged widely among the humanities and the sciences—including those sometimes referred to as "hard."

Leo Rangell's term is "total composite theory," one that adds to its own range, is self-correcting, and has virtually unlimited potential application in the spectrum of human affairs.

Traditionally, the adjective "applied" has been used to refer to non-clinical domains. Freud wrote both clinical and applied treatises, but he also saw therapeutic utility beyond the practice of intensive, individual, transference, resistance, interpretive treatment. He wrote famously in 1919 of alloying the pure gold of psychoanalysis with the copper of suggestion to create therapies that would be more widely useful. "Alloy" has become an unfortunate metaphor, in that for many it suggests a watering down. Taken literally, the metaphor should not be pejorative. Iron takes strength from the elements with which it is blended to form steel. Pure gold may be ever so beautiful, but it almost never appears in its 24-carat

298

pure form. I doubt that psychoanalysis as traditionally practiced is ever more than 18-carats, and my own wedding ring is a mere 14, but is nonetheless a cherished piece of jewelry. Ideals serve as conceptual beacons, but even Kurt Eissler, who gave parameters their psychoanalytic definition (1953), acknowledged that no analysis was ever conducted by interpretative interventions alone, or without asking a question.

Psychoanalytically informed psychotherapies are, themselves, applications, alloys, and they have proven to have enormous range, utility, and strength. Purists and blenders should cease the antagonism that has contributed to casting psychoanalysis and its related therapies into current disrepute.

The book on which this talk is based is true to its title. It describes work by psychoanalysts in mean streets from New Haven to New Orleans, in violence-ridden public schools, and in response to the casualties of war in Angola, Bosnia and the former Soviet Republic of Georgia. Other workplaces include municipal halls, police cars and precinct houses, earthquake-damaged areas, and "ground zero" in Lower Manhattan. Racism, child abuse and homelessness are among the traumatic situations leading to the announcement by the book's editors of a new identity within the psychoanalytic profession, that of *community analyst*.

The editors provide a theoretical frame and general methodological considerations for community practice, and they and others address issues of research and policy. Freud's abandonment of the seduction theory of hysteria is thought by many to have exchanged an external locus of motivation for an internal one. It is more accurate to say that a focus on fantasy life became central to his subsequent theoretical and clinical advances. Just as he never discounted biological factors when he laid aside his *Project for a Scientific Psychology* while awaiting advances in his original field of neurology, Freud also did not reject the importance of the myriad of external influences on psychological functioning. Hartmann's adaptive point of view in his consideration of psychoanalysis as a general psychology served to restore the status of life experience to the organized theory, and Greenson's (1967) classic text on technique made explicit use of noting adaptive reasons for analysand behavior.

Analysts working in either trenches or foxholes deal with the effects of trauma and their management, with individuals and with populations. I will discuss several examples from the book, and some others. I will then attempt to describe what makes these approaches "psychoanalytic," and how they differ from, for example, community psychiatry as practiced by many in our group. I will conclude with some ideas as to how the classical psychoanalytic treatment model, unique in being simultaneously a research tool and a clinical application, might serve, as it always has, as a laboratory for new ideas and new theory. I especially hope our discussion will help me toward that end.

Schools as Foxholes: Long history, New Efforts

I have spoken before on psychoanalytic work in schools, and of my own career as a teacher educator. As I report in an article (co-authored with Bruce Sklarew) to be published in December's issue of *TAP,* much of school-based work is related to aberrant behavior and "special education." Typical reports are of clinical cases with most programs geared to early intervention with the now-misnamed preschool age cohort. Fritz Redl and David Wineman (1957) were the first to extend psychoanalytic ideas to general classroom and school atmosphere. More recently, Bruce Sklarew (2002) and his colleagues in Washington, DC, have created the School-based Mourning Project. Inspired by Freud's classic paper *Mourning and Melancholia* (1917a) and Sklarew's prior 30 years of work, weekly therapeutic groups are provided at an inner-city school for children who have the too common experience of grievous loss. Many are orphans. They have suffered abandonment and have lost family members to street violence. The subject matter of group discussion is, inevitably, their reactions to the multiple traumata of lives of poverty.

Stuart Twemlow's research on bullying, the scourge of middle schools, has identified the central role of "bystander" and developed educational projects to reduce bullying by addressing most kids, who are neither victims nor perpetrators.

Systematic programs for clinical consultation in schools were developed in Houston by Arthur Farley and Diane Manning to include consultation with teachers and parents, and the creation of an affiliated therapeutic school. William Granatir deserves special mention. He retired from practice at age 76, and has for the past 13 years served as an individual volunteer, then a project leader, in the Washington, D.C., public school system. He schmoozes, takes referrals, gets involved with a few individuals, and starts groups. He has also provided liaison between the upper administrative levels of the education and mental health systems there. Like Granatir, Harold Wylie works in schools in nearby Montgomery County, Maryland, in regular collaboration with administrators, teachers and other professionals.

Others have approached school psychoanalysis by developing curriculum and training teachers in its implementation. Carol Kusche and Marc Greenberg's

Promoting Alternate Thinking Strategies (PATHS) is one such curriculum for grades 1-6, and Henri Parens has made the teaching of parenting skills to kids age 5-18 central to his curricular approach to school-based psychoanalysis. Jonathan Cohen has founded the Center for Social-Emotional Education, jointly affiliated with Columbia's Teachers College and the City University of New York. His group has consulted in this country and in Europe in an attempt to take advantage of the fact that every teacher from preschool through 12th grade can be of major influence on individual emotional development.

Mean Streets: Ready Theory; Newer Applications

In his paper *Life Without Walls* (2004), Alan Felix of Columbia University describes his work with New York City homeless people, a population victimized by severe trauma and neglect in childhood and abused in adulthood by the many correlates of homelessness. Based on theoretical principles drawn from Erikson, Winnicott, Bion, Mahler and Gill, an outreach program for caseworkers and their clients has been developed. Practical problems are rife, but the demand is great, and the principles are available and teachable.

At Yale, supported by my late friend Donald Cohen, Steven Marans developed the Child Development-Community Policing Program, based on the insight that police officers are first responders to many severe family crisis situations. This program has been extended with federal grants to other cities and to the formation of a National Center for Children Exposed to Violence. Its analyst participants are on-call to join the police, for example, at scenes where a child has witnessed the murder-suicide of his parents. In New Orleans, Howard and Joy Osofsky have worked with the police in their LSU-based violence intervention program, as well as with the teachers and social workers whose caseload makes them ready candidates for "burnout."

Natural and Man-made Disasters; War Zones: More Drama

Robert Pynoos, affiliated with both UCLA and Duke University, describes responses to sexual abuse at a day care center in Norway, to a school hostage situation, to the aftermath of the Taiwan earthquake of 1999, and to the traumata following the war in Bosnia-Herzegovina. These interventions aimed at providing a sophisticated approach to current circumstances, as well as creating long-term mental health care for traumatized populations.

Martha Bragin, also of Columbia University, reports on developing culturally competent services for healing the psychological wounds of war in Angola, as well as on her more-local work combating recidivism in New York City's Juvenile Justice system.

In what reads like a clinical case report, the University of Virginia's Vamik Volkan, probably the leading "international interventionist" psychoanalyst, describes his work over a three-year period, on a once in five months visiting basis, with a family of émigrés who were forced to relocate following civil war in the former Soviet Republic of Georgia. His work with them enabled their resumption of community leadership, now in a new location.

There have been multiple reports of mental health interventions at "Ground Zero" during and following the destruction of the World Trade Center. While more services were offered than immediately desired by many first responders (police, firefighters and EMS), a literature on the several issues of what we may call "emergency" psychoanalysis is evolving. Jeffrey Taxman, a former New Yorker, flew in from Milwaukee to be at the scene, and his paper describes what he learned about massive community trauma. The New York City Disaster Counseling Coalition, a group formed on 9/12 of 2001, provided free services for first responders. After Hurricane Katrina, this group consulted in the formation of similar programs in other cities.

Once the fabled home of psychoanalytic mecca The Menninger Clinic, by the year 2000 Topeka, Kansas, was a city in chronic crisis. Stuart W. Twemlow and Sallye M. Wilkinson responded with the launch of the Healthy Community Initiative. Could an entire city be put on the couch? Using volunteer facilitators from "stabilizing groups" (law enforcement, clergy, educators, social service workers), and involving successive mayors, an integrated methodology attempted to engage the entire city population.

Ricardo Ainslie, a private practitioner and professor in Austin, Texas, is a psychoanalyst who has worked in a foxhole, not a trench. Following the dragging murder of James Byrd by white supremacists in the East Texas town of Jasper, he spent three years interviewing residents of this notorious small town. In doing so, he developed his own methodology of empathic interrogation while at the same time providing a therapeutic experience for his many interviewees and for the town.

Overall, these projects should easily give the lie to the accusation that psychoanalysis is an elitist enterprise treating only the "worried well," or that it is the "purchase of friendship," an insulting phrase coined by the behaviorist O. Hobart Mowrer in the '60s. In fact, though it may no longer be well known, psychoanalysis has historically included community and political activists, among whom were major theoreticians like Otto Fenichel, Wilhelm Reich and Annie Reich.

But you may ask, "What's new about creative individuals working in new settings?" or "Why can't all of this easily be considered community psychiatry?" I will now present a contrast between psychoanalysis and psychiatry. It derives from an essay by Marvin Hyman, presented ten years ago at the annual meeting of the American Psychological Association. It was the "con" side of a debate I moderated there, entitled, *Is psychoanalysis health care?* Marvin's paper was called *Why psychoanalysis is not a health care profession.*

Psychoanalysis was indeed created as a medical specialty in the attempt by Freud to cure his neurotic patients, and its bedrock discoveries were made in that physicianly attempt. Over time, psychopathology (as in "The Psychopathology of Everyday Life") evolved into "psychodynamics," with "pathology" as metaphor. Neurosis was no longer seen a disease, but instead as the human condition—perhaps at its best. Ultimately, in "The Problem of Lay Analysis," Freud defended Theodore Reik against criminal charges of quackery, and declared his own brainchild *not* to be part of medicine, psychiatry, or even medical psychology, but instead to be a branch of psychology itself.

The medical model treats symptoms by studying pathology and etiology. Treatment generally follows meticulous diagnostic procedures. In psychoanalysis, one might well describe the entire procedure as diagnostic, since we do not fully understand the issues until the treatment is successfully concluded.

In the medical model, the doctor is an expert whose treatment recommendations are to be followed to rid the patient of unwanted symptoms over which there is no self-control. In psychoanalysis, there is a collaboration in which active engagement with the analysand as partner is required for there to be a reasonable chance of success. Symptoms are understood as adaptive responses to internal conflict and unconscious compromises and, at least in part, as desired by the analysand, for they include a wish. Coming to take responsibility for one's wishes is central to the favorable resolution of symptoms.

In medicine, understanding is a first step preceding therapeutic intervention; in psychoanalysis understanding defines the entire process. In medicine, the outcome is evaluated; in psychoanalysis it is the process that is judged. Outcome is much too complex to be defined simply as success or failure.

Finally, beyond the participation of well-trained analysts, these programs are psychoanalytic because each takes as basic the central importance of unconscious mental life, of emotional development, and of the interrelatedness of social, emotional, and cognitive growth. Each program, independent of the population served or the setting, focuses on the *meaning* of behavior.

All applications of psychoanalysis aim to understand aspects of the human condition. Just as in clinical applications, where collaboration is central to the process, in community psychoanalysis, analysts are explicitly members of a team rather than its leader. They work with other adult professionals (teachers, police, social workers, politicians, diplomats) and respect their perspectives and expertise. The analyst's unique contribution remains the conveying of understandings about psychological aspects of the overall situation, by making use of theories of transference and resistance, of development, and of the several additional dimensions of psychoanalytic psychology. As in the classical clinical situation, the analyst is necessarily and simultaneously a transference object, an ally, and a real person, and must understand and work within each role. Unlike the classical couch-based situation, no esoteric methodology is employed.

Psychoanalysts acknowledge both biological and environmental influences on behavior. To the extent that the latter predominate, the expertise of others will be more important than an internal psychological focus. It will be likely, however, that a psychoanalytic perspective will be useful even in situations of biological compromise or severe trauma. To whatever extent psychology is relevant, the most complete perspective must include the understanding of unconscious mental operations that has evolved from over a century of psychoanalytic work in and beyond the consulting room.

It is not enough to declare these programs worthwhile, or to talk about a new community psychoanalysis. While the programs have face validity, various kinds of research and documentation are necessary, both to determine their precise value, and to define the elements central to their replication. These tasks require financing. Most who are engaged in this work have academic positions and/or grant support. A fee-for-service model is neither appropriate nor feasible. Nor is managed care a suitable model. Getting the word out may engender some public support, but mental health work is not yet a societal priority.

It is also true that the case for specifically psychoanalytic pieces of these projects is not yet adequately made. Theoretical connections remain broad, and the general understanding of transference and resistance, despite Freud's oft-quoted comment, is only the beginning of psychoanalytic understanding.

How much copper? How much gold? What alloy for which circumstances? Of course, pharmacology is in no less need of similar work. The action of most drugs is poorly understood, and their individual dosing remains as much art as science.

It is my belief that psychoanalysts can and must attend *both* to our 18-carat practices and to the ills of the world. The consulting room is the laboratory in which psychoanalysis was discovered, and it will likely continue to be the best source of new and useful theory about unconscious mental life. We should also leap at opportunities to apply findings to other settings, but we must work to demonstrate both the utility of our applications and their reliance on a specifically psychoanalytic world view.

The examples I have described demonstrate wide-ranging possibilities. The second century of psychoanalysis may have started off inauspiciously. There is, however, good reason to be hopeful.

Psychoanalysis: Therapy and Worldview

February 28, 2006

Introduction

I have been asked to define what I mean by "psychoanalysis." Readers may have many different orientations to psychotherapy. Although some may be identified with psychoanalysis, with an approach most often congenial with my own thinking, many may consider themselves dynamic psychiatrists. Some trained as analysts no longer identify as such. One colleague told me that being a physician was his initial goal and being a man of medicine—a healer—remains his primary professional identity. From his perspective, psychiatry is a medical specialty, and the various psychotherapies are sub-specializations.

My professional identity is that of a psychoanalyst. My initial training as a psychologist is sometimes relevant to my thinking and my work, but often at odds with it. If psychoanalysis were not a healing profession, I would not have found it attractive. I am comfortable with Leo Stone's (1961) description of a "physicianly" attitude as fitting that aspect of my work, and I would not be content pursuing theory or scholarship alone. I view psychoanalysis as not only a healing art, and surely not a branch of medicine or, as Freud famously put it (1938), even of "medical psychology." It is a global psychological theory, to my mind the most complex available. I admire its complexity as a match for its complex subject matter. My problem with Charles Brenner's brilliant theorizing is that he keeps eliminating concepts; he is our William of Occam. I can't do with so few concepts as Brenner would leave us.

I also believe psychoanalysis to be a *basic* science, and a worldview.

The need for definition responds to an unfortunate legacy: Freud used the word "psychoanalysis" for three related but distinct enterprises. Psychoanalysis is first a theory of mind, as Hartmann called it: a general psychology. Second,

306

it is a theory of psychopathology or neurosis, as Fenichel (1945) described its findings. Third, it is a specific method that serves as its main treatment modality. These distinct but related enterprises emerged in reverse order, and Freud's own development from neurologist to psychiatrist to psychoanalyst gives the language of psychoanalysis a medical vocabulary inconsistent with its creator's ultimate view. The problem that vexes many is that the very same word, psychoanalysis, is used for the global psychological theory, for the clinical theory, and for the treatment modality itself. In fact, matters are confounded further by Freud's also considering the treatment technique as a research method. If an astute and well-educated dynamic psychiatrist might be confused, imagine the chaos of understanding in the public at large.

Therapy and Meta-therapy

My first feeble attempt at dealing with this linguistic problem came over 40 years ago as a psychology intern, untrained but already committed to psychoanalytic thinking. In "bull sessions" with peers and supervisors, many of whom challenged psychoanalysis as an esoteric therapy useless for what we now call "widening scope" patients (Leo Stone, 1954), I called psychoanalytic treatment a "meta-therapy." I had neither the conceptual tools nor the clinical experience to go further at that time, but I already understood that classical psychoanalytic practice had broken away from its medical roots, that "analysands" were not "patients," in the usual sense of having diagnosable pathology, and that this esoteric and refined treatment had ambitions that were more in keeping with promoting a self-reflective and emotionally rewarding life than with any notion of "curing" a disease.

Bibring's seminal paper (1954) pointed the way for clinical theory to understand and subsume any psychological treatment approach, including Cognitive Behavioral Therapy (CBT), and he showed, for example, how "catharsis" could explain the success of some "alternate" therapies, or how "clarification," (what might today be called "cognitive restructuring") could explain other successes. Aaron Beck countered that CBT includes psychoanalysis. Although we were looking through opposite ends of a telescope, we were asserting the same premise. We each hold that our preferred theory is an overarching conceptual paradigm, in Thomas Kuhn's sense (1962), with the ambition to explain all psychotherapeutic approaches and, in principle, all psychological phenomena.

Psychoanalysis's self-inflicted semantic wounds are unlikely to heal. In these quarters, though, we may see them for what they are, and specify which "psychoanalysis" we are addressing.

As regards the treatment modality, following Bibring (1954) I see the general theory as having multiple applications. I use the word "applications" not in the usual sense of psychoanalysis and the arts, but for all pragmatic work guided by the general theory of mind. All therapies are to be understood as psychoanalytic, in the same way Beck would understand all therapies to be based on learning theory. An applied psychoanalysis respects the significance of the dynamic unconscious and listens for the latent meaning in human communications. Treatments might approach more or less the "standard" five times weekly, couch-based practice, and here our theory of technique would come into play—and get us well beyond today's topic.

All treatments may be thought of, then, as "applied psychoanalysis," and I have said elsewhere (2005) that Freud's (1919) metaphor of alloying the pure gold of psychoanalysis was an unfortunate one, in that it mistakenly implied dilution and weakening. Alloys, in fact, are created for their utility and strength, as steel is an alloy of iron. The various therapeutic uses of psychoanalytic theory have not been adequately tested for relative strength, and controversy reigns in the argument over psychoanalysis vs. psychotherapy, an argument now, sadly, over fifty years old.

My own clinical preference is for "pure gold" whenever possible, and with Arnold Rothstein, I believe standard technique to be more applicable for many than do most practitioners. But I surely respect other applications, including the combination with medication or with CBT. I would claim, though, that such alterations or alloys of "pure gold" are consistent with a more general psychoanalytic understanding, following Bibring (1954). For example, medication can serve to modulate intense anxiety or depressive affect or may reduce disinhibitory mechanisms by directly affecting brain chemistry (in ways, however, that remain far from adequately specific and known), while cognitive methods can be understood as using that most extraordinary evolutionary achievement, reflective consciousness, an ego function. I also favor "standard technique" where applicable, as providing the best research method for further psychological discoveries about the workings of the human mind.

When I supervise psychology interns on their psychotherapy at Mount Sinai School of Medicine, I appreciate that their patients are often severely impaired, and that for most of them medication is the primary treatment, psychotherapy an adjunct or, sadly, an afterthought. The psychotherapy I teach, however, is conducted as an attempt to understand structure and psychodynamics, with interventions directed to the day-to-day needs of the patients.

Beyond Therapy

There are non-clinical applications of psychoanalysis, with several examples provided in Sklarew and Twemlow's 2004 book *Analysts in the trenches: Streets, Schools and War Zones*. Freud (1926) thought treatment to be just one application of his discovery, and perhaps not even the most important one. Much of my own work has been with teachers and principals in the public schools of New York City. Colleagues on the American Psychoanalytic Association's Committee on Psychoanalysis in Schools do similar work. Twemlow calls himself a community psychoanalyst, applying his skills with mayors, police chiefs, judges, clergy and other civic leaders. Laurence Friedman challenged Twemlow as to community analysis being real psychoanalysis. Steven Sonnenberg, citing Freud's paper "On War," sees Friedman's position as closer to Freud's, but agrees with Twemlow (and me) that social applications are an important and appropriate frontier. Following Leo Rangell, I believe we should seek a "both/and" resolution of this conflict, rather than "either/or."

Although I have no expertise in the areas commonly known as "applied psychoanalysis," literature, linguistics and the several arts, I am respectful of the psychoanalytic thinking that illuminates those areas of human endeavor—and I play close attention when we have papers on film or great music. In American universities, psychoanalysis is rarely taught in departments of psychology, where I first encountered Freud as an undergraduate. Instead, Freud is read in departments across the humanities curriculum. It is regrettable that there is a major disconnect between those faculties and clinical faculties, such that there is great "confusion of tongues" on those rare occasions when they speak with one another. The linguistic theories of Jacques Lacan, not held in high repute in American clinical circles, are quite influential with humanities faculties, and we are grateful for having learned here about Lacan and French psychoanalysis.

Clinical Theory Today

Some of the clinical psychodynamic thinking seems based on largely outdated theory that some would now consider wild analysis. Clinical practice for both the "standard" method and for the related psychotherapies has become refined in the past thirty years in reaction to theoretical challenges from within. Kohut's self-psychology, then British Object Relations thinking, was followed by the newer relational and inter-subjective approaches and even a resurgence of Kleinian thinking catalyzed by Roy Schafer. These have challenged Modern Conflict Theory's once dominant position, resulting in greater definitional clarity and understanding of clinical practice, and an ongoing search for common ground.

Psychoanalysis and Science

Respectful external challenges from newer neurology have brought psychoanalysis back into the realm of science from the isolated *sui generis* position defensively favored by Freud. Respectful psychologists have, now for several decades, produced a body of empirical research on process and outcome, and on qualitative aspects of the psychoanalytic situation. These research programs led by individuals such as Howard Shevrin at Michigan, Sidney Blatt at Yale, Lester Luborsky at Penn, Robert Wallerstein and Weiss and Sampson in San Francisco, Norbert Friedman's group at the Institute for Psychoanalytic Training and Research (IPTAR), Peter Fonagy's group in London, Sherwood Waldron's group at Mount Sinai, and research psychoanalysts like Drew Weston at Emory and Jonathan Shedler at Colorado have served also to bring psychoanalysis back into alliance with empirical science. A *New York Times* op ed by Adam Philips reminds us, though, that science is not only a quantitative discipline, and that psychoanalysis requires methods consistent with the emotions and interactions that are its central phenomena.

Less respectful attacks on psychoanalysis have implied that the behavior of its practitioners, including Freud's analyzing his own daughter and numerous boundary violations and inadequate therapies revealed by letters and historical research, has undermined its claims for validity. A presentation of the history of psychoanalysis in France led me to ask how the ideas could possibly survive the people who proposed them. I take heart that only a psychoanalytic perspective provides ideas that can unravel and understand the utter messiness of human behavior and the universality of feet of clay.

Psychoanalysis is a peculiar science and has not yet developed research methods fully adequate to satisfy simultaneously its own data set and a more standard science. That the classical treatment method is its own adequate research instrument is an idea held by Andre Green but challenged by many besides Robert Wallerstein. Freud, in his concern that the treatment could destroy the science (1926), was contradicting his own apparent welcome of treatment alloys (1919).

Psychoanalysis as World View

I am touching on some of the newer trends in a vibrant discipline, one that is thriving intellectually while its public reputation remains greatly undervalued. These various enterprises involving psychoanalytic thought come together for me as a world view.

Psychoanalysis is not just its classical therapy, its related treatments, its applications in the artistic and social spheres, and in the world of ideas, it is itself a *Weltanschauung,* at least for me. I filter virtually all my life experience through my psychoanalytic lens. To risk the accusation of grandiosity, I sometimes find it akin to Superman's X-ray vision. It enables me to understand my world, and to give me both relief and pleasure through understanding. I remember being in a clinical supervision group with Jacob Arlow, one of the first he provided for non-medical practitioners. One of us would present process notes for discussion. Often Arlow would utter a few words about it and it was as if klieg lights had been lit. The increased depth and clarity of understanding was frequently immediate and consensual—and we were, even at that time, not an inexperienced group.

Melanie Klein might diagnose me as suffering from epistemophilia. Anna Freud might call it intellectualization. Klein is closer to the mark, since my defenses involve little by way of isolation of affect, and lots of "philia," the love and enthusiasm for making sense of the world. I believe that psychoanalysis (necessarily corrected and modified by experience) provides core insights that continue to offer unparalleled means of understanding people. I remain a modernist, as I was educated, not a post-modernist. A worldview that provides this extent and complexity of understanding may be deconstructed but cannot be easily dismissed.

311

Philosophers have enshrined Freud in the pantheon of the history of ideas. His basic discoveries remain both vital and generative. It is my hope to have contributed something to their definitional clarification.

Notes on the 150ᵀᴴ Anniversary of Sigmund Freud

5/4/06

Many events were scheduled in New York and elsewhere to commemorate the sesquicentennial of Freud's birth. Freud's work remains important—and well beyond his creation of a psychotherapy method. The paradigm for a worldview is even evident in a panel held at the New York Public Library, under the auspices of its *Dorot* Jewish Division, celebrating the 150th anniversary of Freud's *bris*. Entitled "Freud's Foreskin," it includes a historian, an anthropologist, a religious studies professor, and a cultural studies specialist, discussing scholarship about circumcision, a procedure now being recommended to curtail the spread of AIDS.

Freudian analysts like me are no longer able to wrestle a god, as did Jacob. But the Jewish tradition encourages intellectual and emotional struggle, so we continue to wrestle with Freud—and with each other.

There has been an explosion of psychoanalytic knowledge in the past 30 years, some from empirical research, some the assertion of new paradigms like Self Psychology and Relational Psychoanalysis (much of these being refinements of what I would call the "basic treatment model" and "mainstream" theory), some of it from interaction with cognate disciplines like neuroscience. Those who are not regular readers of psychoanalytic journals are likely to have their understanding fixated at early formulations of the state of psychoanalysis, what I would now consider caricatures of current practice and theory.

Bob Lewis's talk presented at a recent conference on Attachment Theory is worthy of serious discussion. The New York Psychoanalytic Institute of his training era, from both his perspective and my own, presented a curriculum reflecting a narrow-scope approach to psychoanalysis, one consistent with the views of Anna Freud, but not with those of their own Leo Stone.

What follows are some disparate thoughts stimulated by Lewis's work in the context of the Freud anniversary.

1. Margaret Mahler comes across as a *bete noire* while the ongoing work of her collaborators, Fred Pine and Anni Bergmann, continues to demonstrate the flexibility of her theory. Mahler developed a major *piece* of theory, not a paradigm. Her paradigm, really a sub-paradigm, was ego psychoanalytic developmental psychology, and she did not exclude developmental issues beyond those addressed by her research, essentially on toddlers. As an aside, the foibles of theorists should not be taken as arguments against their ideas, lest all ideas join our feet in the clay. Ideas stand or fall independently from the *mishagas* of their creators.

2. Today's psychoanalysis is no longer stated in the all-knowing tones of Fenichel's encyclopedic masterpiece (1945). Today's understanding is both more extensive and more modest, as theory is challenged, and new knowledge accrues.

3. Analysts must not disparage consciousness. It is, after all, a terrific evolutionary achievement, and it informed Freud's first formula of the action of psychoanalysis: to make the Unconscious Conscious. Treatment depends on it and a complete psychology must include it.

4. Freud was worried that psychoanalytic treatment might kill the science, and did not consider treatment to be the most important application of psychoanalysis. Others worry that science, or rather a rigid scientism, will kill both the treatment and the real science that is psychoanalysis. Freud's worry had to do with the need to modify our methods because they might be too difficult to employ. Of course we must modify them when they are limited or wrong, but the risk of focusing on symptom relief, a la Dr. Feelgood, remains an omnipresent danger.

5. When I teach "toddlerhood," I start by debunking "negativism" as did Selma Fraiberg. I then review "anality," "autonomy," "separation-individuation," "attachment" and the move toward "object constancy" as important dimensions of a complex developmental phase. I think of these concepts as Netter drew them in his magnificent anatomy charts, overlays that add to understanding but do not substitute for one another.

6. Peter Hofer's paper "Reflections on Cathexis" (2005) related the term to Winnicott's "holding" and Bowlby's "attachment." I would suggest that these are interesting and important *findings*, but not a new "paradigm," certainly

not in Kuhn's (1962) sense, now the common use of the term across the sciences.

7. The hope for early prediction seems doomed to failure, as was Freud's theory of psychosexual fixation. Early experience contributes to what will be a complex organization navigating the vicissitudes of each developmental phase. Specific early predictors are notorious for their unreliability.

8. Lewis' work is consistent with the move toward "positive" psychology, as compared with a psychology derived from pathological findings, the accusation leveled at Freud, psychiatry, *and* clinical psychology. It is a useful addition, not a replacement paradigm. Andras Angyal, a humanist psychoanalyst, wrote in the fifties of the concept "homonymy," a counterpart to "autonomy" as a goal for mental health. My teacher Abraham Maslow, Carl Rogers, and others in the humanist camp were precursors of positive psychology, yet their "movement" generated little in the way of broad theory, and certainly no new paradigm.

9. My friend, the late Ester Buchholz, wrote about the positive effects of "solitude" in infants and adults as a balance to her view that the Beatrice Beebe research program was too one-sided in its observations.

I hope readers can see my appreciation and enjoyment of the ideas stimulated by Bob Lewis's work.

Whatever Happened to Erik Erikson?

1/29/08

Though I never met the man, I've been a fan of Erik H. Erikson's since my undergraduate days. I taught developmental psychology to prospective teachers for 35 years and Erikson's work was central to my syllabus well after I felt I had to minimize references to Freud, Spitz, and Mahler, even Selma Fraiberg. Over time I developed my own version of Erikson's stages, essentially removing the "vs." from his well known tasks, "trust vs. mistrust," etc . . . , replacing them with "ands." Each stage results in a proportion of the two sides of the task contributing to individual character. To be all trusting would be gullible, and to be totally mistrusting would be an extreme of paranoia rarely seen even by psychiatrists.

Erik H. Erikson died in 1994 at the age of 92. An obituary (1995) by Robert Wallerstein, published in the *International Journal of Psychoanalysis*, proclaimed him a true genius. At the 1995 Spring Meeting of the Division of Psychoanalysis (39) of the American Psychological Association, I chaired a memorial symposium focusing on Erikson's contributions to clinical practice. The papers were published with my introduction and summary in *The Psychoanalytic Review* in 1997.

Among the topics discussed was Erikson's marginalization among his own colleagues. Hope was expressed that our papers might help to return to prominence in the field the contributions of one of its most creative theorists. This has not occurred.

A study group to which Bill Greenstadt and I belong recently discussed Erikson's "Eight Stages of Man" chapter (1950), his best-known contribution to developmental psychology. We followed that discussion by studying the papers that comprise the published symposium. We were impressed with the continuing clinical relevance of Erikson's early ideas, especially his chapter on "zones, modes and modalities." We speculated as to why Erikson seems to be off the map of current psychoanalytic scholarship.

The group suggested three reasons, the first of which was discussed at the symposium by Margaret Brenman-Gibson (1997), Erikson's role as a popularizer. Such scholars are often disparaged within their disciplines. For psychoanalysis to have done so is especially unfortunate. It reflects a narrowness and elitism, each of which has contributed to its diminished contemporary standing.

The second reason was that Erikson substituted a developed bio-psycho-social model for psychoanalysis, a decidedly non-medical model put forth when the locus of psychoanalytic power had shifted to the United States where the field had been officially co-opted (against Freud's wishes) as a medical specialty within psychiatry. Official psychoanalysis, i.e., the American Psychoanalytic Association (APsaA), had to be sued for restraint of trade to acknowledge that psychologists, social workers and other non-psychiatrists might be appropriate candidates for full clinical training.

The third reason, perhaps an extension of the second, was Erikson's attempt to develop a social psychoanalysis. In the attempt to maintain a distinction in mid-century between psychoanalysis and what was then seen as a "watered down" dynamic psychiatry, psychoanalysts insisted on a *solely* intra-psychic focus to define their discipline. Interpersonal theorists like Sullivan and the "neo-Freudians" were considered beyond the pale; others, like Franz Alexander, were deemed apostates.

I will briefly review the highlights of the 1995/1997 symposium. Brenman-Gibson's contribution (1997) was a highly personal memoir about a mentor who became a cherished friend. The first non-physician to be allowed official training within APsaA, she recounted Anna Freud's disparaging remarks about Erikson, Ms. Freud's own analysand. Morris Eagle (1997) addressed Erikson's two major theoretical contributions to psychoanalysis: 1) the influence of society and culture on ego and identity development, and 2) the positing of developmental phases to extend through the life cycle. Irving Steingart (1997) discussed, with clinical examples, Erikson's being "prescient" (p 352) regarding the importance of object relations and enactment in clinical work.

To the ideas of my invited panelists, I added that Erikson is the acknowledged founder of psychobiography and psychohistory, and widely recognized for bringing a psychoanalytic sensibility to the fields of education, anthropology, and art.

Erikson's work may well be viewed within the spirit of the then-contemporary Hartmann/Rapaport program, psychoanalysis as a general psychology, as well as what I see as that program's current version, the total composite theory posited by Leo Rangell (e.g., most recently, 2004). His work can also be readily identified as a forbear of the current "positive psychology" movement—so popular now in undergraduate psychology education—in his delineation of strengths and virtues specific to each of the eight developmental stages.

Erikson is a subject of scholarly interest, though not in his own discipline, as I will show. A recent biographer (Burston, 2007) noted that his popularity peaked between 1965 and 1975, but even then Erikson considered himself misunderstood by his own colleagues. Despite his being eclipsed within psychoanalysis by luminaries such as Kohut, Loewald, and Kernberg, to name a few, and in academe by Lacan and postmodern perspectives, Burston finds Erikson's ideas compelling and relevant to a host of contemporary issues, including the very decline of psychoanalysis.

Today I note Erikson's critical contributions to clinical psychoanalytic listening. For example, the three adult stage tasks (intimacy v. isolation, generativity v. stagnation, and ego-integrity v. despair) can help clinicians gauge whether initial complaints are age-appropriate, suggesting a more favorable outcome—or more regressed. Erikson's strengths and virtues help us listen to, respect, and address the whole person, not just psychopathology. Our study group looked closely at "zones, modes and modalities" as providing yet another useful listening dimension.

Erikson is honored by the well-known Austen Riggs Center at Stockbridge, MA, which has named its education and research institute in his memory, and which holds annual conferences. But his continued exclusion from psychoanalytic theory and training can be documented quantitatively with bibliographic searches of databases.

A search of Erikson's citations since his death is revealing. His ideas continue to exert influence in the fields he founded: psychobiography, psychohistory, life-span developmental psychology. In addition, his work is cited in such diverse publications as *Substance Use and Misuse, Social Behavior and Personality, American Behavioral Scientist, Journal of Vocational Behavior, Human Resources Management, British Journal of Educational Psychology, Arts in Psychotherapy,* and *American Psychologist,* to list just a few.

A perusal of my own Institute reading lists shows Erikson to be minimally represented—an exception being his "specimen dream" paper (1954)—while each of the others to whom I have compared him is prominent in bibliographies.

That Erikson remains marginalized within his own discipline seems evident. That his ideas are widely appreciated in other disciplines is equally apparent. He is, we might say, quite alive and very well.

There is perhaps another reason for Erikson's eclipse within psychoanalysis: So many of his ideas have become part of our culture, at least its college-educated segment. Erikson may be the only psychoanalyst commonly studied in undergraduate psychology and education courses. Many of Erikson's contributions, like "identity crisis," have become cultural assumptions. While this is hardly a horrible fate, I prefer recognition to anonymity. Although I am now in Erikson's eighth stage—on Medicare and contemplating mortality—when I was a beginning teacher decades ago, I required students to know the names of contributing scholars, not just their conclusions.

Our planet's population explosion and its knowledge explosion coincide with the birth of psychoanalysis just over a century ago. These explosions combine to make for an industrialization of science and the creation of knowledge. With very few exceptions like Crick and Watson or Freud, individuals are less likely to achieve a general fame than they were in prior centuries. Knowledge is an industry both highly specialized and often esoteric, and even great discoveries may become common knowledge, with the author forgotten. Erikson is no Freud, but giants are still too few to deserve neglect within their own fields. A theorist who has brought psychoanalytic ideas to so many should be lionized, not eaten by wolves.

An Alternative to the DSM:
The Psychodynamic Diagnostic Manual (PDM)

September 23, 2008

The Diagnostic and Statistical Manual, now in its fifth version (sixth if we count IVa), has been a standard in psychiatry for several decades. It is a major project of its publisher, the American Psychiatric Association, in the understandable quest for uniformity of evaluation in the field of mental illness, and it is considered the official manual for psychiatric diagnosis. Its most recent versions, designed to be independent of any theory, have (at best) disappointed those of us with a psychoanalytic or even a psychodynamic orientation. In our own conferences here at Mount Sinai, non-analyst speakers on topics as varied as learning disabilities and neuropsychiatry have also disparaged DSM, both conceptually and practically. A recent speaker claimed that it distorts far more than it clarifies.

That diagnostic accuracy is considered a *sine qua non* in every medical specialty may be too obvious to belabor. But even before the advent of DSM, this axiom faced challenges in psychiatry from iconoclasts like Thomas Szasz and R.D. Laing. Harry Stack Sullivan, a more mainstream figure with a wider following, offered his interpersonal theory, redefining psychiatry as about problems of living rather than disease entities. Our own Dr. P, as mainstream as we get, often reminds us that psychiatric illnesses have neither genetic markers nor adequately objective sets of signs and symptoms.

My problem with psychiatric diagnosis began prior to the phenomenological approach of the DSMs. As an intern in psychology, I spent most of my scheduled work time doing "diagnostics," i.e., administering test batteries that included the Wechsler, the Rorschach, the TAT, the Bender-Gestalt, the House-Tree-Person drawings and others, and composing detailed reports of my evaluations. Each report was required to end with a sentence, "The diagnostic impression is of . . . ," and in the pre-Vietnam era Veterans Administration, that sentence would usually conclude, "... schizophrenic reaction, chronic undifferentiated type." With these veterans of World War II and Korea, by then long-term patients, we rarely saw acute problems or even the then-extant subcategories catatonic, hebephrenic or paranoid; the first two of these are now obsolete terms.

What really bugged me was that the referring psychiatrist seemed more interested in this concluding sentence than in the details of the report, endowing the label with a meaning it did not have. The details were mostly about various ego functions and included some dynamic hypotheses. This detailed text, however, was what we were trained to care about and focus on—and to have some confidence in. Virtually the same reductive attitude was encountered with nearly meaningless full-scale IQ scores, since the best available test, the Wechsler, could only provide 95% confidence in a 16-point IQ range. Variations among the several IQ subtests, as well as specific unusual responses hinting at structural or dynamic issues, were of much more interest to us and were much more useful clinically than the full-scale IQ scores.

I am getting to the topic of this presentation, an alternative to the DSM, while trying to provide a context, not just a psychoanalyst's disdain for labels that cannot be reliably supported and whose validity is far from demonstrated.

Motivation for replacing the DSM with the PDM came from several sources, all concerned that the descriptive official manual did injustice to patients and their troubles while offering little or no direction for useful treatment. The PDM is a collaborative effort of five organizations: the American Psychoanalytic Association, the International Psychoanalytical Association, the Division of Psychoanalysis (39) of the American Psychological Association, the American Academy of Psychoanalysis and Dynamic Psychiatry, and the National Membership Committee on Psychoanalysis in Clinical Social Work, united as the Alliance of Psychoanalytic Organizations. Forty distinguished researchers and practitioners are listed as task force members and consultants. The chair was Stanley I. Greenspan, MD, of George Washington University; associate chairs were Nancy McWilliams, PhD, of Rutgers (a past president of Division 39), and Robert Wallerstein, MD, of the University of California, San Francisco (a past president of both APsaA and IPA).

The manual they produced is over 800 pages in length, weighs 3 ½ pounds, and has three parts: a classification of adult mental health disorders, a similar classification for child and adolescent disorders, and a series of articles dealing with the historical and conceptual foundations and the research foundations of the earlier parts. Part three is greater in length than the first two combined. In tribute to the DSM, the editors have indicated parallels wherever possible.

It is not hard to understand why psychoanalysts might like the PDM, and why I do. The three dimensions, P, M and S, speak to our traditional concerns: P=diagnosis as a character typology; M=diagnosis as an evaluation of ego-functions, and S=diagnosis as an empathic appreciation of subjective experience. These are the very dimensions that guided the lengthy reports I was trained to write, and they remain central to my less formal diagnostic—or rather evaluative—thinking as I listen to both analysands and patients.

These three dimensions speak also to a modesty that was uncharacteristic of mid-20th Century psychoanalysis—at least as represented by Fenichel's (1945) encyclopedic tome *The Psychoanalytic Theory of Neurosis.* At that time, psychoanalytic writers, drunk on its revolutionary discoveries and its domination of psychiatry and clinical psychology, claimed to know much more than would later be validated. Today, we are more impressed by our vast ignorance of the mental processes that are presented to us. A multi-dimensional evaluation does more justice to both what we know and do not know than does a very premature and reductionist Kraepelinian approach to diagnosis.

There are critics who see any attempt to label, categorize, generalize, and diagnose as wrong-headed, the Chicago-based relational analyst Irwin Z. Hoffman prominent among them. He criticizes the PDM as just another dehumanizing scheme. He is even more critical of one of the instruments described in a Part 3 paper, the Shedler-Westen Assessment Procedure (SWAP), a 200-statement inventory from which a subset of statements is derived to describe patient psychology. That SWAP has achieved very high inter-rater reliability is, to Hoffman, only an indication that therapists are willing to reduce their patients to a series of statements rather than appreciate their full complexity. "Who would want such a therapist for themselves or family members?" he chides. Yet another critic, Arnold "Ted" Rothstein of the New York Psychoanalytic Institute, believes that diagnostic labeling is a countertransference phenomenon designed to make us feel superior to our patients, and should be treated as such.

Many psychoanalysts believe that a diagnosis can only to be determined at the conclusion of treatment, a turning upside-down of the medical model, but an assertive statement that meaningful concise generalizations about individuals can be made only following a thorough understanding of that person's complex psychological functioning.

So we return to an initial conundrum: to assess in some concise way—or not. The lack of conciseness of PDM is its compromise and, I believe, one of its strengths. It acknowledges complexity and provides lots to read and to ponder—

and its authors view it as a work-in-progress. Its compromise also includes limited ambition—to complement rather than replace the DSM, when, in fact, its approach is strikingly different. So I pose the conundrum differently: Is diagnosis a short statement or, instead, an ongoing evaluative process in psychotherapy?

I wrote to Nancy McWilliams, asking if PDM diagnoses would be accepted by insurance companies and, perhaps more important, Medicare. Not only did she express doubt—insurance companies prefer the reductionism of the DSM, Medicare approval would require extensive lobbying—but she noted that the hope and aim for PDM is that people will read it and think about the issues raised. It was published by the five cooperating organizations to keep its price affordable for students, with, therefore, limited advertising and distribution. She was happy to hear about this talk because she feared that only she and Jonathan Shedler, co-author of SWAP, were peddling the product.

After eleven decades of the psychoanalytic enterprise, we know a great deal about both evaluation and treatment; we also are much more aware of how little we know. Learning from PDM, this alternative approach to diagnosis, is one important way to extend our understanding of psychology and psychopathology.

Do I believe there are mental illnesses? Of course. Our patients may suffer from their unconscious fantasies but do not suffer from a myth. We remain at an early stage in attempts to adequately define and describe these conditions. The mind/brain is the most complicated subject of both scientific and philosophical inquiry. I applaud neuroscientists, pharmacologists, philosophers, and others who are seriously committed to understanding the mind/brain. I don't know what a new synthesis will look like any more than anyone else. Furthermore, any mental illness resides in a person and interacts both with that individual's total personality and with the interpersonal, social, cultural, and ecological surround. Justice cannot be done with a label; nor do we have specific treatments that are demonstrably effective for specific diagnostic entities, as in other medical specialties. Psychiatry must interact with its basic science of psychology; and, according to psychiatry's sole Nobel laureate, Eric Kandel, "Psychoanalysis still represents the most coherent and intellectually satisfying view of the mind that we have."

Psychoanalytic Principles in Psychotherapy Practice

A Clinical Presentaton, April 30, 2009

How does a Freudian psychoanalyst work when conducting psychotherapy rather than a more intensive psychoanalytic procedure? This presentation attempts to provide some answers. It also aims to make transparent the work of *this* psychoanalyst. Such transparency has become common in the psychoanalytic literature in the past few decades, though it was rare earlier—in the literature, in supervision, and in seminars—when non-transparency was part of what alienated many here.

There were and remain good reasons for lack of transparency. The novice clinician wants desperately to know from the master "how to do the work; what to say;" and the scientist expects public data to support theoretical propositions. But privacy concerns for the patient are essential to both intensive on-the-couch analysis and psychoanalytic psychotherapy, and issues around confidentiality have a complexity of their own. (Clinical presentations may compromise confidentiality.) Perhaps equally important: therapeutic interactions are in principle never formulaic; they are not to be imitated. There are many apt things to say (as well as apt silences) in every treatment hour, and it is only in the crucible of the consulting room, where nonverbal cues and the therapist's immediate internal reactions are available that the most useful interventions (including silence) can be determined—or attempted as trial and error. Psychotherapy does not follow procedures that fit the training paradigm: "see one, do one, teach one," so central to medical education.

Of course, there are analysts who want to protect their own privacy, some—as Irwin Hirsch told us—to cover over their use of the therapy situation for personal satisfactions. And the spontaneity of the clinical interaction frequently results in off-target interventions and even errors that we may be reluctant to expose. The shame that had to be mastered during the supervisory experience of every analyst and therapist may also serve to deter ongoing exposure. But less than optimal interventions are not necessarily harmful in an ongoing treatment; they may be learning experiences for both parties. Yet we should not underestimate shame-avoidance as a motive for concealment.

The processes of analysis and therapy are loosely coupled; rarely does an intervention lead directly to a therapeutic result. Interventions are hypotheses, to be tested over time. "The Sopranos" and "In Therapy" show these processes as drama; actual treatment is painstaking and would surely bore a television audience. Much of what an analysand or a patient says is "manifest content" whose full meaning is far from clear in the moment; much of what goes on in the analyst is internal, therefore invisible. (Some transcripts attempt to capture the analyst's thinking in parentheses, but even these attempts do not reproduce the situation.)

Some of the best writers have made major contributions to clinical theory while presenting little or no clinical data; Hans Loewald is prominent among these. Yet "he said/I said" clinical material has become more commonplace. The late Hartwig Dahl used a transcript of a complete analysis as data for a major long-term research study.

Diversity of opinion was most impressive during a 2009 presentation by Jack Herschkowitz in which his patient was interviewed live, to ascertain our diagnostic impressions and therapeutic recommendations. With over 30 therapists in the room, with the collective experience of centuries and an average IQ at least two standard deviations above the mean, disagreement was extreme and telling, although there was some overlap of impressions. [*A clinical vignette was presented and discussed.*]

Psychic Reality: Phenomenon or Epiphenomenon?

November 17, 2009

Dr. William Greenstadt is my inspiration for this paper. Bill and I have been colleagues and collaborators for over four decades, and members of four study groups, two of them lasted for over 19 years. Bill had encouraged me to affiliate with Mount Sinai for at least 10 years until, in the spring of 2004, anticipating my retirement from City University, I made application.

Bill and I worked most closely when he was president of the New York Freudian Society, and I was Director of its Training Institute. Readers should be familiar with his rigorous and creative psychoanalytic thinking. I get to benefit from it an additional twice monthly at study group meetings—and more recently for a third time at monthly process group leaders meetings. I continue to learn from his mastery of Freudian theory and its application to the clinical work presented in our groups. There has been one—just one—serious point of disagreement between us. Bill is a proud, nearly knee-jerk exponent of scientific reductionism; I have found reductionism to be problematic from the time I first engaged in undergraduate debates on the topic.

This paper is an elaboration of my respectful disagreement with Bill. Although unlikely to resolve the issue, I will touch on a number of philosophical issues to which others have spoken here with far more erudition. I will also mention other sciences than ours, and the arts. (Even the arts are subject to scientific study as natural phenomena. The bigger APA, the American Psychological Association, has a Division of the Arts dedicated to the scientific study of aesthetics). Interspersed, and concluding, will be references to the clinical situation. Bill and I had some recent in-person exchanges, followed by e-mails. Part of our disagreement may be semantic; he will likely rebut me on the rest. I hope there will be other rebuttals and I will not be preaching to a choir.

My first negative reaction to reductionism inspires the subtitle of this presentation: phenomenon or epiphenomenon. As a college freshman taking introductory zoology, I heard the teacher say that biology going forward would only need to study the vicissitudes of DNA; the lives of individual organisms being merely distracting "epiphenomena." Perhaps I was too naïve to know she was joking, but I soon changed my major from pre-med/bio to psychology.

"Epiphenomenon" seems always to have been an epithet, dismissing as unworthy matters in which the speaker has little interest. The psychology department at the then 9-year-old Brandeis University, led by a great talent scout if not so great theorist Abraham Maslow, was especially open to ideas ignored by the establishment—and its teachers represented many points of view. We studied Piaget before his work was well known on this continent; we studied existential psychology; we had experiential courses, process groups in fact though not yet so named; we even had a course entitled "Choice, Will and the Ego." We did not memorize then-current behavioral research. I was anxious that this preparation would impact my GRE score in psychology; I need not have feared. The diversity and excitement of our curriculum—in which we also carried out experiments, but no professor put down the work of others as epiphenomenal—was successful. Several of the then young faculty members went on to distinguished careers in their respective branches of academic psychology, and an extraordinarily high proportion of undergraduates went on to careers in psychology and psychiatry.

Mid-twentieth century American psychology aspired to be a traditional science. Modeled on physics, its aim was prediction and control. Even then, clinicians were skeptical of that orientation. Paul Meehl (1954), a psychologist sympathetic to clinical—even psychoanalytic—concerns, began an important series of studies comparing actuarial (i.e., statistical) and clinical prediction. The findings disappointed clinicians and have yet to be accepted by us as conclusive. Skinner's behaviorism was the dominant paradigm of academic psychology, but clinical psychology's guiding theory was psychoanalysis and its ego-psychological elaborations. Individualization was—and remains today for any psychodynamic approach—essential for evaluation and treatment. The late Louis Linn would say we are all Darwinians, and I agree. His negative take on Freud is similar to we contemporary Freudians. We note our differences with Freud, (my most cited paper, on termination, is called "Not an Endgame"), but we are all Freudians.

Can psychoanalysis argue for its status as a scientific discipline while it eschews a normative approach in clinical practice? Psychoanalysis is both nomothetic and idiographic in its methods (Bornstein, 2007); each of these research approaches

327

aims for valid and useful generalizations. Freud drew conclusions from intensive work with individuals, conclusions he believed were universally applicable. Many of his ideas have been discarded, others remain convincing, while several have evolved and been modified. Piaget's science was likewise idiographic, generalizing about cognitive development from intensive non-standardized work (and play) with individual children. The Nobel laureate physicist, Murray Gel-Mann, speaking about Freud, praised his idiographic method, including the study of his own dreams, with the statement that if something is true of any one of us, it must be a piece of universal truth.

Psychoanalysts in clinical practice use current normative understandings while valorizing the uniqueness of each patient; this makes good sense. Alternating focus between norms and variation is central to all critical thinking (and even to good statistics). When we discuss phenomena of any kind, we compare and contrast them with other phenomena. Comparison notes similarities; contrast focuses on differences. Psychological science is *both* normative and differential. Variations from norms are not "errors of measurement," as some statisticians suggest, but of interest in their own right—and centrally important to clinical work. "Error of measurement" and "error variance" are terms referring to what is unaccounted for by statistical algorithms; use of the word "error" suggests that the unknown is a bothersome epiphenomenon. Clinicians are interested in individuals, even those who defy normative evaluation, outliers like the "dog whisperer" described in a recent *New York Times* article. That man's abilities seem uncanny, but as clinical scientists we must consider them natural phenomena worthy of curiosity and understanding—although successful understanding of such outliers may defy the best of our current methods, even psychoanalysis.

Biological science has found the human genome to have over 95% commonality with those of other primates. Much research in comparative biology is based upon that great commonality. Are differences between humans and apes not also important? In psychotherapy, every patient is subject to DNA-based determinism. Important generalizations about causal factors also come from domains studied by psychology, sociology, and anthropology, even economics and politics. Among the most significant generalizations are interaction effects measured by sophisticated statistics like ANOVA and ANOCOVA to show how and to what extent environmental factors interact with genetic dispositions to yield specifiable degrees of probabilistic prediction.

I take the word "analysis" to mean separation of a complex entity into its components. This applies in mathematics, chemistry, political science or psychoanalysis; in my view "analysis" differs meaningfully from "reduction." In mathematics, a reductive analysis by factoring is perfect. Eight *is* two times two times two; and quadratic equations can be perfectly solved $[(a+1)(a+2) = a^2 + 2a + 2]$. In chemistry, politics, or psychoanalysis the parts do not completely explain the whole. A water molecule consists of two parts hydrogen and one oxygen, yet water is very different than either; the two gases cannot simply be mixed to form the compound. A compound necessary for human life—salt— is comprised of two highly toxic elements. A dream has multiple determinants: manifest and latent contents the understanding of which can make dream analysis of clinical value; a dream is not an epiphenomenon. As with the old Jewish joke about *hamentaschen,* the gestalt principle applies: the whole is more than the sum of the parts. Humpty Dumpty is more than broken eggshells. Ernst Mayr's concept of emergence regularly applies.

Each patient is—and must be addressed as—unique, unlike *any* other person. While it is often a useful clinical intervention to let patients know their experience is like that of others—to universalize—respect for and understanding of individuality is at least as important. Commonalities and uniqueness *together* comprise the text for psychoanalytic study; the traditional method aims for as thorough an understanding of each patient as might be practically achieved.

The actuarial/clinical distinction applies as well in everyday life. We calculate the odds of choices exactly, approximately, or implicitly. Context, specific issues, and the trait of risk-aversion influence every decision. Often enough some of us go against the odds, acting on hunches. Hunches sometimes prove correct, more often for some than for others. Are successful hunch-takers merely lucky? Luck is neither an entity nor a phenomenon; it is a portmanteau word for the combination of incalculable or unknown factors that influence any outcome beyond individual control. In that sense, we are all lucky every day. Those with lots of good luck may be more perceptive while having no clear explanation of their skill. We infer that they are better at quickly and accurately sorting and judging more (and even more subtle) information than others.

Sensitivity and intuition are skills that vary among clinicians. These differences in clinical talent provide one argument against comparing mean success scores of various therapies whose subject pool includes more and less skilled therapists. Some narrowly defined "evidence based" research attempts to control for therapist variability with scripted protocols, avoiding variation, the very individualization that is the *sine qua non* of psychodynamic therapies. (I am aware of the work of the Columbia research group led by Fredric Busch that is attempting to script psychoanalytic therapy, but I do not believe they can study the individuality that is central to psychodynamic treatment).

Psychotherapy involves more than one person, and each is affected by multiple and varying factors. Some therapist-patient pairs may be more likely to achieve success; others may be a better fit for unhappy or happy stalemates, the latter a form of *folie a deux*. Our profession is far from ready to forsake either actuarial or clinical prediction, nomothetic or idiographic approaches. After about 110 years, we continue to discover greater complexity in every human mind and in every interaction; reductionism—a central tenet of traditional science—is at best premature in ours, and, I believe, wrong-headed.

Beside norms vs. individuals, another false dichotomy is surface vs. deep description—in psychoanalysis it is represented by manifest vs. latent meaning, consciousness vs "the Unconscious." This dichotomy tracks the conflicting epistemologies of phenomenology (e.g., those of Aristotle or John Dewey), in which observation and experience are decisive, and idealism (e.g., Plato, Hegel) in which ideas are central. Good science requires both. What is the truth about color? Is it a matter of perception or of wavelengths of visible light? Neither science nor philosophy has yet bridged this divide. Is one epistemology more real? Psychology and physics are surely related, but not identical. Both perception *and* the color spectrum demand study. The problem of consciousness (perception) has interested philosophers for millennia but continues to defy reductive solution. Consciousness is as relevant to our clinical work—and was Freud's original aim for treatment outcome—as are unconscious processes. These battles represent antinomies: contradictory principles, each true, while apparently, only apparently, mutually exclusive.

All science begins with phenomenology—raw observation. Modern science has developed tools and methods for more precise observation. The closer physicists look the more they see, beyond the atom to subatomic particles. Cosmology has been dominated for a generation by string theory, a set of mathematical propositions with not one shred of empirical support. Yet it remains a viable, even dominant paradigm.

When we apply the manifest-latent distinction to our profession, matters are no more decided. Freud's self-proclaimed masterpiece, *The Interpretation of Dreams* (1900), made the initial distinction regarding dream contents, and it turned out to be a heuristic hypothesis with demonstrable clinical utility. The method of association remains central to psychoanalysis, though Freud discovered other psychological phenomena important in treating his patients (e.g., transference, countertransference, narcissism, superego, etc...). We continue in our evolving clinical science to modify both our theory and our practice.

Renik (1993a) uses the concept "irreducible subjectivity" to challenge epistemological claims for psychoanalytic objectivity. Certainly, all perception is subjective, but his radical position would undermine all science that necessarily rests on observation. This is a *reductio ad absurdum* since science seeks truth. How can we reconcile subjectivity of observation with any truth claim? Some postmodernist contextualists even see mathematics as a product of social conditions rather than yielding transcendent truth. Plato spoke of consistency of ideas, Aristotle correspondence, Dewey consensus and pragmatics. When a work of art or literature moves masses emotionally or intellectually, something about collective subjectivity may be deemed objective—and that something—a real phenomenon—would be a common psychological resonance. Anne Perry's recent World War I novels, for example, evoke the smells, sounds and sights of war in the trenches and aboard ships, and these perceptions evoke emotions and a sense of understanding that suggests a common reality. The reader has only personal subjectivity; this best-selling author—and any true artist—evokes a generalized human understanding.

Let me take another example from the so-called arts or humanities. In his *New York Times* article of September 27th, "A Fine Instrument, a Classic Instinct," Anthony Tommasini, a classical music critic, interviewed Barbra Streisand about vocal technique, the mechanics of what's happening with air in her body. Streisand works intuitively, and insecurely asks, "Did you like (my rendition of) "Smoke Gets in Your Eyes'?" Tomassini's reply: "Did I like it? Are you kidding?" Streisand produces vocal art without scientific understanding. We can look for understanding at both the physical and experiential levels. Each level is legitimate and—I claim—irreducible, like the wavelength of a color and its experiential *qualia*. These alternate ways of understanding are antimonies, different but not mutually exclusive; each focus is required to approach complete understanding.

Not only did I reject my zoology professor's biology for my own career, I found what to some biologists may be another epiphenomenon, the mind, to capture my interest and passion. Do quantum physicists reject mechanics? Do physicists consider chemistry epiphenomenal? Do chemists put down biology? Science has as its domain the *entire* natural universe, extending to the very fact of subjectivity and beyond, and to social sciences including economics and politics. Each of these "epiphenomenal" domains entails a greater complexity of variables and much less precision in prediction and control than aimed for by "harder" sciences. Their commonality rests on the scientific attitude that aims for deeper understanding of the phenomena being studied, continuously asking not only "what," but "how" and "why."

For Freud, unconscious processes—convincingly inferred explanations for otherwise mysterious observations—provided a basis for the development of a new science. Psychic reality is comprised of both consciousness and unconscious processes. IPA Honorary President Leo Rangell, writing in the *Huffington Post*, notes that "There is psychic reality as well as material reality. A thing is not only what you can touch; it is also what you feel. A mood is a thing, an entity. It comes from somewhere and can lead to something. Depression can lead to death; anxiety to almost anything." Rangell would not deny a neuro-chemical substrate of depression or anxiety; but the psychic reality is worthy of attention; it is not epiphenomenal.

Charles Brenner agreed with Rangell and me about the importance of psychic reality. On another level he was the psychoanalytic William of Occam, reducing the number of theoretical concepts and the range of psychological phenomena appropriate to psychoanalytic study. He held firmly to belief in the narrow scope of indications for both psychoanalytic treatment and study. His position was that so-called pre-oedipal events were not amenable to psychoanalysis because the method requires language development and verbal memory and a more myelinated brain than is to be found in children before age three. I disagree. While I find Brenner's theory the most elegant and parsimonious of competing psychoanalytic approaches, it does not provide adequate scaffolding for my thinking and responding as I sit with a patient.

On the other hand, Freud developed new theory to account for his discoveries of new psychological phenomena like transference, resistance, countertransference, narcissism. These are real, *not* epiphenomena. They led Freud to an expansion of theory, especially including the principles of over-determination and multiple function, and the several metapsychological points of view. Committed to the law of parsimony, Freud was nonetheless forced by the complexity of psychic reality to an expansion—in fact several *explosions*—of theoretical creativity.

I am committed to drive theory and to Brenner's focus on conflict and compromise in trying to understand and help my patients. Sex and aggression are central to my clinical thinking and interventions, but I do not believe these drives comprise a complete explanation of human motivation. Sex drive diminishes as a function of aging, and aggression is similarly reduced. Even violent imprisoned felons become less aggressive and dangerous as they age. Classic psychoanalytic theory offers sublimation as an explanation, but that term is merely descriptive; it is phenomenological in the pejorative sense, not explanatory. Hartmann's delineation of libidinal economics such as cathexes and anti-cathexes, expanded by Rapaport and his students, is hardly referred to today. It is speculation about unconscious processes that seems no longer to have heuristic value—though the problem of quantitative differences remains unsolved and of ongoing interest.

My initial and continuing commitment to psychoanalysis as a master theory of psychology came about because its tenets—even over a half century ago when I first read them—were sensitive to what I had already observed and what I continue to see in people, a perhaps infinite complexity. Freud became bothered in his later years that therapeutic concerns might threaten the scientific development of his discipline. I am more sympathetic to Leo Stone's position that we must privilege the therapy over the science when the two might conflict. Our science remains young and inexact. When confronted with the inconsistency of various propositions by our study group, Jacob Arlow shrugged his shoulders, indicating that this is the best we can do at this stage of our knowledge. I agree.

Furthermore, and perhaps most important, effective therapy requires an attitude that is explicitly anti-reductionistic. Patients need to be understood in their uniqueness, not by any generalization, let alone a formula. Our work of exploring a patient's mind aims to help increase comfort with internal complexity, contradiction, even and especially conflict. While still a candidate, I was elated when a patient commented that my words did not seem to come from a book; that they were specific to her.

To conclude: psychic reality is a natural phenomenon and a legitimate domain for scientific study, not an epiphenomenon. Our clinical work must be accompanied by the attitude that this reality, while partaking of human and primate commonalities, is also rich and unique. No patient is to be reduced, conceptually or otherwise.

Defining Transference

July 19, 2010

In her 1965 paper on Acting Out, Anna Freud spoke to the issue of evolving definitions in our field. It is clear that definitions change, for good or ill, and that psychoanalytic discourse can become confusing. Transference, as Erik Gann's letter to the *International Journal* (2010) indicates, is a basic concept that has become subject to a confusing evolution (devolution).

Our literature is replete with papers using and gradually redefining transference. I often find these semantic changes unfortunate. The "transference-countertransference" matrix has come to be equated with the entire clinical psychoanalytic situation, and has thereby—to my mind –become useless as theory.

Transference was one of Freud's most basic and important discoveries. For me it has two clear definitions, psychological and clinical. Psychologically it is the transfer of memories such that the present is perceived to varying degrees in terms of the past (a universal phenomenon). Clinically, it means references (manifest and latent) to the psychoanalyst, reflecting attitudes, thoughts, feelings and fantasies (conscious and unconscious) from earlier, usually primary, object relationships.

Psychoanalysis is exceedingly and increasingly complex, both as a theory of psychology and as a clinical practice. We need all the good ideas we can muster, but we also need to define and distinguish among concepts. Clinically, transference is a most important idea; so is counter-transference. Of course these phenomena interact in the two-person relationship of the clinical situation, as do other phenomena.

Our "confusion of tongues" might be eased if we were less inclined to change Freud's definitions (especially inadvertently) as we develop both theory and practice.

Psychotherapy, Terminable or Interminable: A Clinical Discussion

February 3, 2011

I've been interested in endings for more than forty years. In 1972 I published a paper in the *International Journal of Group Psychotherapy* entitled "A Hello and Goodbye Group." It focused on a process group I led for my staff of psychology technicians when I was an officer in the United States Army. From the start of the group—which continued following my discharge—the main topics were greeting new members and saying farewell to others, some of whom were departing to Vietnam and possible death.

In my own subsequent and lengthy psychoanalysis, the ending was especially difficult. Stephen Firestein's book on termination came out during that time and I hated it for conveying the impression that it was a relatively routine matter. All his patient reports were training cases at the NYPSI clinic, and nearly all his terminations were what we would now call "therapist initiated" or "forced," determined as they were by the candidate's graduation and the wish not to continue treatment of very low fee patients.

About 20 years ago, several long-term relatively successful analyses in my own practice came to termination. Those hours of intensive treatment were never fully restored with analytic patients; most of my practice since then has been psychotherapy.

In the mid-nineties I was coordinator and reporter for two panels on termination at Division 39 conferences, panels which led to now-frequently cited papers by Martin Bergmann, Donald Kaplan, Jack Novick and others. I spoke with Jack about my terminated treatments, and he became excited, exclaiming "You have lots of data, write it up!" My paper, "Not an endgame: terminations in psychoanalysis," was included along with the panel presentations in a special issue of *Psychoanalytic Psychology* in 1997 and appears in this book.

In 2002, I was invited to review the revised edition of Firestein's book. There was no new clinical material and the new introductory and concluding chapters were not as good as in the original book. Less angry, I found the book to present lots of interesting clinical process, but little to inform about termination itself.

In 2005 I was a pre-publication reviewer for "Termination in Psychotherapy," published by APA Press in 2007. Like many research-oriented books, this one attempted generalizations that would not likely help any of us with the unique presentation of any specific patient. I was thrilled, however, to see my paper not only cited several times but once even alongside the master himself: "Freud said... Golland said... " (I received more mentions, in fact, than Freud).

So I am sort of a recognized expert by dint of having contributed to and followed the growing literature on this topic. And here I am, again puzzled over the work with two of my psychotherapy patients who seem more than ready to complete successful work but are so far unwilling to begin termination.

This issue was addressed by Franz Alexander in the 1950s. Alexander developed and recommended a tapering technique for psychoanalysis in which dependency would be gradually reduced. Both the technique and Alexander himself were soon expelled from mainstream psychoanalysis. "Real" psychoanalysts were to analyze and resolve dependency, never attempt to manipulate it away.

My own view, for psychoanalysis as well as psychotherapy, was summarized in the four principles that concluded my 1997 paper: Follow the patient's lead; keep the treatment process consistent with the treatment that preceded the termination phase, do not value idealized scientific considerations over therapeutic ones; and devote time and thought to every termination.

As to following the patient's lead, I wrote that the analyst could surely infer allusions to termination and introduce the word, but that the ending process would be collaborative; analyst-directed or forced terminations were always to be avoided. Central to a psychoanalytic approach is the aim of expanding a sense of agency (see Abend, 2001). Furthermore, except for very disturbed patients who might be judged "lifers" and require supportive treatment indefinitely, interminable treatment avoids processes deemed essential to maturity and psychological health: the ability to mourn central among them. Analysts provide interminability only by denying their own mortality, or by creating an "until death do us part" context, suitable for marriage but not therapy. A termination phase strengthens what Melanie Klein called "the depressive position," essential to a sound treatment outcome.

Freud's 1937 paper, "Psychoanalysis Terminable or Interminable," was philosophical rather than technical. In important ways the issue may be essentially philosophical rather than clinical—although as clinicians we cannot avoid the clinical implications of our explicit or implicit philosophical stance.

My 1997 paper explicitly eschewed such a doctrinaire approach. Every treatment is unique, and we have recommendations, not rules, about experience-based best practice. But I think I may have fallen unwittingly into a doctrinaire position, forgetting that most therapy endings are the result of unplanned external circumstances.

The newest psychoanalytic theory of termination—Brenner's—has it that we can never do better than to help our patients achieve more gratifying, less symptomatic and less inhibited compromises; treatment is not concluded to meet any ideal, and actual termination is always arbitrary.

On Herbert Peyser, *Osheroff v. Chestnut Lodge*, and "Repetition, Recollection and What?"

Herbert Peyser was a Distinguished Life Fellow of the American Psychiatric Association who trained when psychoanalysis was the dominant theory. More allied with medical approaches, he was a scholarly authority on alcoholism and other psychiatric conditions while also engaging in organizational leadership. We were colleagues at Mount Sinai for a decade, enjoying friendly debates at conferences and over frequent lunches. I was flattered in 2013 when he asked me to discuss the two papers. Herb died in 2015 at age 90. My discussions follow with, I believe, clear enough exposition of his views to allow for expression of mine.

Osheroff v. Chestnut Lodge
February 12, 2013

Herbert Peyser is one of the most erudite members of the Mount Sinai discussion group, able to recite entire poems or aria lyrics precisely relevant to the subject at hand. We share an interest in ontology (particularly the mind-body problem) and epistemology, but Herb is an expert and I an amateur. Herb and I have another common interest: we have each been activists in our respective APAs and their affiliate professional groups. We know that the work we do is not related solely to personal skills; it is embedded in philosophical, historical, social, political, and economic contexts. The inexact nature of mental health practice makes it especially subject to outside forces that may be unrelated to clinical issues. As regards the case of *Osheroff v. Chestnut Lodge*, the judicial system itself—even in this case settled with no trial record—promoted a sea change in "best practice," virtually requiring that severely disturbed individuals be treated with psychoactive medication as well as suggesting psychoanalysts consider combined treatment rather than their traditional practice eschewing medication.

Herb and I enjoy our debates, often lengthy e-mail exchanges continuing discussions started in group. Debates are about differences; in fact, Herb and I agree on far more than what divides us. We usually conclude online by noting the overlap of our positions and the insolubility of our minor disagreements.

I have little quarrel with the substance of what Herb has written on *Osheroff*. I will address several of his points in ways that might make us seem more at odds than is the case.

First is the matter of ideology. Adherents of any theory risk becoming ideologues, but we don't necessarily fall victim to that risk. I call myself a flexible Freudian. I understand that theories are heuristics, not ideologies (or religions). They serve only as long as they generate ideas and prove useful. Some theories achieve more than heuristic value. Evolution is an accepted paradigm for biology, for instance. That is not the case with psychoanalysis, despite its founder's wishes and claims. Many of Freud's propositions were in error. He often corrected central ones himself as he learned more from his patients, and thought more deeply. Ironically, he had more faith in rationality—with his own ideas the standard—than has turned out to be warranted. So, point one in response to Herb's thrice-stated francophone assertion: We know that theories don't create facts!

Herb is masterful in informing us of the complex set of facts in the *Osheroff* case: the range of personal, financial and professional problems that any competent psychotherapist would consider—for *Osheroff* or for any depressed or anxious patient. But a malpractice suit promotes an adversarial approach. For us a clinical matter should not engender a binary: that Dr. Osheroff had either a neurobiological disease or a psychosocial problem. Proper diagnosis in medicine is supposed to direct treatment; our field has produced nearly nothing so specific. None of us has first-hand knowledge of Dr. Osheroff, but we know that diagnosis is not always clear-cut, and available labels are subject to heated controversy—as witnessed in the recent deliberations about the Diagnostic and Statistical Manual (DSM), which most of us find highly flawed at best.

Why not *both* psychotic depression and narcissistic personality disorder? And if both, would medications necessarily work? They did not succeed in Osheroff's earlier treatment. Did Silver Hill Hospital get lucky? Perhaps the patient was more willing to be drug-compliant, or—invoking a medical model—perhaps the disease was in a later phase when he arrived at Silver Hill. The Chestnut Lodge approach has been successful with many patients and produced an important literature on the treatment of schizophrenia. The late David Feinsilver, MD, my Brandeis classmate, spent his entire productive career there. Did the individual failure with Osheroff really show the Lodge's approach to be generally bad practice?

What is evidenced-based treatment? Inadequate evidence is hardly evidence of inadequacy. Paul Wachtel, in a brilliantly argued 2010 paper, shows "evidence-based" psychotherapy to rely on limited methodology and to be prematurely dismissive of treatments not amenable to randomized controlled study. Would any of us welcome a malpractice suit based on inadequate evidence of our own efficacy? The current state of "evidence" for many psychotherapeutic approaches would make nearly all of us vulnerable to claims our insurance carriers would urge us to settle!

Informed Consent and Patient Autonomy are Peyser's most important points. These are not simple matters. What do we mean by informed consent? Must we spend initial consultations reviewing several possible recommendations, emphasizing evidence and its absence to assure that a potential patient is adequately informed and enabled to exercise autonomy? I may be routinely in violation of my APA's ethics code on this matter; I use consultations to listen and learn as much as possible about both the problem and the person. When I make a recommendation, it is simply that—it is not coercive. While I usually provide a rationale, the person will accept my recommendation based on an intuitive sense that I have been helpful and will continue to be so—or not. When the going gets tough, as will always happen if we give any credence to the notion of resistance, we will try to work through the difficulty. Some patients leave, and sometimes that will be a sound decision. More often, in my experience, regressive phases and heightened resistances lead to a deepening of the treatment. In fact, it was the "negative therapeutic reaction" phenomenon that led Freud to a total revision, first of his model of mind, then of his theory of anxiety—leading to the more mature theory he bequeathed to us.

I am glad *Osheroff* did not go to trial. Whatever disputes we have in our literature, the public clash of mental health experts in a legal setting has, in my opinion, more often hurt than helped our collective reputation. Yet the case—despite not being tried—has had a larger effect than warranted, contributing to the demise of psychoanalytic hospitals, the Austen Riggs Center the major survivor. From a research perspective alone, a single case with its complexity ignored, in the limited public record, should not have had such power. I am surely not alone in having treated some psychotic individuals successfully without pills, and a recovery model is not the only possibility remaining for our difficult patients.

Stories and Medicine
June 17, 2013

Herb Peyser's erudition is always impressive; it can be dazzling: Aristotle, Hippocrates and Thales of Miletus; Shakespeare, Rimbaud, Camus, Faulkner and Miller; Helmholz, Charcot and Hughlings Jackson, and even more. The dazzle might distract us from the substance of the argumentation. I've had the privilege and luxury of reading this paper in advance—several times. I will use that advantage to acknowledge much with which I agree, but also to attempt what our chairman often suggests: to improve the presenter's understanding. This group will then adjudicate—and correct us both.

Dr. Peyser's paper shows deep respect for the History of Ideas: for history itself, and for philosophy, literature and mythology—despite his disparagement of what he sometimes calls "just stories." He makes good use of these humanistic domains, though, for surely they offer him and us windows on truth. He is adept at integrating and applying his vast knowledge of stories and myths—which he also calls "interesting ideas"—to clinical work.

Dr. Peyser's knowledge of Freud's psychoanalytic writing is nearly as impressive as his erudition. His summary of Freud's 1914 paper, *Remembering, Repeating and Working Through*, is terse and sound. He points out that Freud early on gave up relying on *Deutung* (interpretation) alone, while noting that even inaccurate *Deutungen* might be of value. He also discusses the shifting of responsibility in treatment, and the need for taking ultimate responsibility. Here he touches on the philosophical problem of "free will." Freud's 1923 superego concept launched the psychological study of conscience and responsibility, more clinically relevant than any philosophical approach.

Freud's psychoanalytic corpus spans 46 years, 1893-1939. The next generation of analysts took it as essential knowledge to be followed, rather than the heuristic brilliance of a genius. Subsequent decades of post-Freudian scholarship, research and clinical experience have made for an evolving scientific psychology not fully reflected in Herb's discourse. Psychoanalysis, like other scientific endeavors, other disciplines, other treatments, is guilty of major errors. Herb seems to take pleasure in continuing to judge it by its errors: "schizophrenogenic mothers," "ice box parents," homosexuality as illness, penis envy as the bedrock of female psychology among the most egregious, have long been abandoned.

Herb follows Ricoeur in counting psychoanalysis as *Weltanschauung* (or mythology) rather than science, as Freud claimed. Ricoeur's "vicissitudes of desire in its eternal debate with reality" is but a restatement of two of Freud's titles: *Instincts and their Vicissitudes* and On Theory—is also personal. Ernst Kris's 1956 paper, *The Personal Myth*, describes individual unconscious fantasies with great motivating power. We can study myths in general then, or individually. We can do so with rigor and can learn a great deal both about the human condition and individual psychology. Freud would appreciate Herb's reference to Sisyphus; it is consistent with his own final conclusions about resistance in treatment and the interminability of psychoanalysis (1937). The word "myth" can convey, however, a certain disdain. As both cultural and individual phenomena, myths are worthy of respect and understanding. Herb seems to be of two minds here.

So what about "working through"? Freud introduced this term in 1914 with only a brief comment: resistances must be aroused and overcome; it was left for others to elaborate on the idea. Brenner (1987) reviewed 70 years of literature only to dismiss working through as a technical concept. The term is still around because there is an adhesiveness of concepts in our ambiguous field. I borrow Freud's (1937) metaphor, "adhesive libido," to highlight two major problems in our field, definitions and conceptualization. "Adhesive libido" was coined to explain treatment failure; "working through" to explain the slow process of treatment. Each is a descriptive phrase, not an adequate explanation. Brenner's dismissal of the term reflects his valorization of theoretical parsimony; I believe his parsimony to be premature, if not misguided—like the creation of the series of DSMs. We can readily understand a collective wish for coherence within the staggering complexity of mind/brain phenomena. As to "working through," the literature Brenner cites provides heuristic utility. As to mind/brain phenomena, there are 3 trillion synapses, axonal spines as microscopic loci, and Llinasian resonance in just one mind—and these minds interact with one another in small and large groups. Ongoing discussion can lead to better understanding and practice, but a unified theory remains elusive: a wish, perhaps a fantasy. I applaud attempts to achieve it in our domain but I doubt we'll see success any time soon. We are not alone; physics also lacks a unifying theory. Such is the nature of the scientific enterprise.

Scientific? Science begins with systematic observation: specificity, context, record-keeping. Correlations among phenomena may then be found. A branch of science might develop methods suggesting causal relationships. Botany and astronomy are mostly systematic observation, some correlation. Determinism and causality are positivistic ideals, with prediction and control goals of positivistic science. Today these ideals and goals have been supplanted by probabilities, even in the physical sciences. More complex phenomena result in lower probability values. Clinical sciences rely on the likely repeatability of observations and the reasonable predictability of correlation, with the expectation of error. Randomized controlled designs are premature in claiming causality, and too often cheat. Failure to report negative findings, and testing only against placebo, not older drugs, are frequent examples of such cheating. Economics is called "the dismal science," its methods observational and statistical; they yield low probability predictions that may be useful anyway—not for picking individual stocks but in understanding the movement of the forces under study. Social science is science!

What about practice? Herb's comparison of psychoanalysis with Alocholics Anonymous (AA) is seductive but not persuasive. To meaningfully relate two approaches, we need both to compare *and* to contrast. The psychoanalytic method eschews exhortation and any promotion of faith. We explicitly avoid attempts to "persuade." Suggestion was a major bugaboo for Freud; he frequently disclaimed it. We now know that suggestion can be reduced but not eliminated; psychoanalytic technique tries deliberately to minimize suggestion in treatment. And rather than faith, the goal of analysis is conviction based on rational understanding within probabilistic limits. There is some similarity between AA's group process and the concept of therapeutic alliance. Resistance is a major Freudian discovery; breaks in the alliance and defensive denial are predictable and central to psychoanalytic work; they led Freud to the elucidation of defenses and character structure. Herb's claim that Freud's hope to change an attitude can be considered "sort of a behavioral approach" is wide of the mark. Attitude is a mental concept differing sharply from a behavioral approach or intervention. What Herb might mean is that psychoanalysis includes cognitive work; making the unconscious conscious and enhancing ego functions must surely be counted as cognitive.

Herb does better by reminding us about existential issues. Faulkner's essay on Camus is more useful than psychopharmacology. Faulkner and Camus told stories; Camus's wisdom about the constant search in life is in the realm of ideas. Facing illness and repetition characterize both psychoanalysis and AA. Aristotle and Shakespeare are important guides to the human condition. Existential philosophy has impact for us. Our chairman told us once that he chose psychiatry as his medical specialty because reading novels counts as work. For many of our patients it is a story—the "narrative approach" of Roy Schafer—that provides relief if not cure.

Herb presents a paradox with his obvious commitment to ideas and his idealization of a disease model. Both are relevant, yet they are at times at odds. Neither alone is adequate to the tasks we therapists face or to the struggles our

343

patients present. Healers try to heal; psychoanalysts to open a patient's mind, with self-healing or existential acceptance often leading to something like cure, more often to a better ability to deal with ordinary miseries of life. Thales' approach and Freud's may seek different ends for patients; our still-young profession is caught in their contradictions. I welcome medical advances and respect their effects, notably for chronic, severe disturbances. I do not believe they will solve the problems of living faced by most of our patients.

Herb's concluding remarks are sound. We move slowly down related and different paths to develop realistic and useful theories and methods, as do cognate disciplines—from which we also learn. Freud failed when he tried to construct a biology of mind but continued to wish for one. His "bedrock" statements were also wishes. Herb's existential conclusions are similar to my own. Instead of a direct therapy we give up therapeutic ambition and smell the roses, or take up Zen. A version of happiness better called wisdom involves recognizing limits and going on with life as best we can. Why should psychiatry keep trying, in Herb's brilliant imagery, like the stepsister with the big foot, to force itself into the glass slipper called medicine? Maybe it needs a different footing. Maybe it should swim. Maybe it's a swan, not an ugly duckling.

On Theory

May 30, 2013

1. I define theory as "how we think about what we do." Thinking is a major activity of the mind (an "ego function" in my theory of choice). Much of living consists of action-theory-action-theory sequences. Theory preceding action is planning; theory following action is reflection. We theorize routinely; we may do so well, not so well, or badly. Our actions are not reflexes; they are influenced by thoughts—both conscious and outside awareness.

2. A theory is not about "capital T Truth." It is a heuristic that may or may not prove useful. Theory also serves to generate new theory. According to Charcot, "Theory is good, but it does not impeach existence" (my translation). We test theories against observations; we confirm, modify, or refute our thinking. Scientific work consists of thought and checking our thought: theory and testing; rationality and empiricism.

3. Eric Kandel finds that "Psychoanalysis still represents the most coherent and intellectually satisfying view of the mind that we have." Freud did not complete his theory and it remains incomplete more than 80 years after his death. It will remain incomplete as a matter of scientific principle. Where it fails to help us adequately, new theory is required. Martin Bergmann categorized new thoughts by psychoanalysts: extensions, modifications, and heresy. Some of the heresy has provided useful additions to what Leo Rangell called "total composite psychoanalytic theory."

4. I teach what I call "the educated spontaneous response." In human relationships of all kinds, action must at times be immediate. It should also be authentic, our best effort. Spontaneity is based on the interaction of the perceived situation, conscious and unconscious memory, and temperament. After acting (and choosing silence or inaction counts as an action), we

reflect on the action, the session (or the lesson). Effective reflection makes subsequent spontaneity—our next try—a more educated one.

5.   Surely thinking can go wrong. There is transference to theory, intellectualizing as defense (in Kleinian terms, epistemophilia), and theory as a security blanket or strait jacket for the analyst. There is also a literature, i.e., attempts at refining thinking, or improving inappropriate or ineffective use of theory.

6.   Sympathy, kindness, dedication, acceptance, support, focused attention and reliability are among the non-specific components of therapeutic action. Fred Pine points out that for some patients these factors are quite specific and may be central to the repair of developmental deficits. Which interventions work best is often a matter of trial and error, as well as a prod to systematic empirical study, using appropriate methods for gathering evidence.

7.   Adolf Grunbaum himself has recently acknowledged that Howard Shevrin's psychoanalytic research program at the University of Michigan meets the criterion of falsifiability. Constitutional factors in development were routinely acknowledged by Freud and are explicitly included in his "complemental series" concept: We are bio-psycho-sociocultural-ecological creatures. Psychoanalytic theory has always been a comprehensive interactionism, while its unique focus is the study of intra-psychic conflict.

8.   The scientific theory of psychoanalysis is not limited to its clinical applications, where the primary task is effective treatment. Instead, the theory valorizes what physics Nobel Laureate David Gross calls the most important product of science: ignorance. Science is a search, Gross tells us, not just for knowledge but for better questions. Scientists are more engaged by questions than by answers. Ignorance drives science: curiosity is its engine. A Higgs boson physicist said the team was nearly ecstatic when tests confirmed their theory and isolated the particle. He added that it would have been more scientifically interesting had they failed.

9.   Science and clinical work are not perfectly correlated; at times they are even in conflict (note Sinclair Lewis's Dr. Arrowsmith). They interact. Each affects the other intimately.

10.   Our work reflects—among other things—our theories. Connections to interventions are more or less direct. Clinical work is an art grounded in theory and science. P's work is easily recognized as psychoanalytic. It need not connect any specific idea to a specific action or outcome; psychoanalysis is a holistic theory.

346

Psychoanalyic Imperialism?

February 27, 2014

This essay is my reply to the accusation of imperialism. On behalf of psychoanalysis, I plead guilty—or as we say in traffic court, guilty with an explanation. Ample evidence of the expansionism of psychoanalysis is found in studies of nonverbal aspects of the treatment situation and their relevance for theory development, psychoanalytic treatment of psychotics, psychoanalysis in non-clinical settings, and Holocaust studies. Much of the ongoing study is of pre-oedipal phases and of trauma and aggression, ideas initiated but not elaborated on by Freud, whose major clinical efforts focused on oedipal fantasies and the vicissitudes of libido. It is also notable that the recipients of the 2012 Sigourney awards, the psychoanalytic Nobel prizes that go to North Americans every third year, represent both narrow and wide-scope psychoanalysis, an ongoing controversy between those who would stay with the "pure gold" of psychoanalysis and those who develop alloys for their greater strength and wider applicability.

First, some thoughts on the appropriateness of imperialism in any scientific endeavor: All science must be imperialistic, although not in the political sense. Aristotelian science has as its aim the discovery of the workings of the natural world. All of nature is subject to its scrutiny as it tries to remove the veil of ignorance through processes of discovering. Looking at the world makes use of the technical extensions of our senses and our rationality; Aristotle had neither microscope nor fMRI.

Today we develop sense extenders with refined methodologies suitable to the aspect of nature on which we focus our metaphorical lens. Refined rationality is theory-building, our thinking as we attempt to organize what we observe. Scientific work consists mostly of observation and trial and error, but it always aims to extend the domain of understanding. Scientific reports focus on narrow topics while always aiming for something greater—a generalization about the essential nature of the world or, for human sciences, the nature of the beast. The image of blind men describing an elephant by touching its different parts is apt. Such reports might describe accurately a respective part—and claim or at least aspire to describe the whole.

Medicine itself is highly subspecialized; each specialty aims to understand the beast and, by such understanding, to heal. Physicians know very well, however, that they are not dentists. My internist refused to inject my trigger thumb with cortisone; he sent me to a rheumatologist. Medicine aims for an organismic understanding; many drugs have systemic effects while targeting a specific bodily site.

Thus psychoanalysis: a theory of mind and all its products, with a wide variety of approaches and targets. Recall the "sector therapy" developed by Felix Deutsch several decades ago, among the first treatments to be called a psychodynamic psychotherapy.

Two Sigourney honorees, each most worthy, are Stuart W. Twemlow and Lawrence Friedman. They take strikingly different positions in their respective definitions of psychoanalytic work. Twemlow published a paper in the *International Journal* in 2005: "The relevance of psychoanalysis to an understanding of terrorism." Friedman wrote a rebuttal; Twemlow a rejoinder. Their positions represent the best of "imperialistic" psychoanalysis and of the "narrow scope" perspective. My own view—consistent with that of the Sigourney trustees—is that these are each important spokes of an umbrella psychoanalysis that, like physics, lacks and seeks a Grand Unifying Theory. Psychoanalysis has wider and narrower applications; both types make good sense while seeming incompatible to some. The proverbial rabbi is right: each party seems right yet they can't both be right— or so it seems. I recall Jacob Arlow who, when confronted about an inconsistency in his wise pronouncements, simply shrugged. At the time I thought he meant "that's the best I can do for now." Today I believe him to have meant "that's the best understanding we have so far."

It is only proper to credit Leo Stone's paper "On the widening scope of indications for psychoanalysis," published in the second volume of *JAPA* (1954) along with a mildly critical discussion by Anna Freud. Reflecting what was already common clinical experience, Stone pointed out that analyzability was not well correlated with psychiatric diagnosis. *Contra* Freud, some psychotic patients could be treated successfully with full-scale traditional psychoanalysis. A radical formulation at the time, experience with "widening scope" patients would provide impetus for modifications of technique; theoretical innovations focusing on pre-oedipal issues, aggressive drive, and trauma (as distinct from the oedipal- and fantasy-based method for treating neurosis), and a proliferation of approaches within psychoanalysis that is described currently as "theoretical pluralism."

Like so many ideas in this field, the roots of "widening scope" are to be found in the writings of Sigmund Freud. While frequently repeating that his treatment method should be limited to the so-called "transference neuroses," Freud was unable to restrain himself from discussing psychotic phenomena. Of only five major case reports, the *Schreber case* (1911) was an account of *dementia paranoides*. Freud's work on primary process thinking resonated throughout his theory, from dreams to artistic creation. Many of his clinical examples would now be judged non-neurotic. Freud the scientist became less interested in clinical success—about which he became increasingly disappointed—than in what he could learn from his patients to elaborate his theory of mind while hewing to his primary technique of free association and his maturing theory. Other analysts, more concerned with treatment outcome, created new methods and new theory; August Eichhorn, Anna Freud, Jacob Moreno and Samuel Slavson are prominent among these pioneers. The new modalities often came to exceed the boundaries of psychoanalytic theory. An imperialistic theory—a paradigm, if you will—must extend its utility beyond its own laboratory or it will become irrelevant. Methods adapted for clinical situations differing from the "standard" have led to the varieties of psychoanalytically informed psychotherapies, including group and family work, focused short-term treatments, and Twemlow's "community psychoanalysis."

Today most analysts shy away from offering analytic treatment to psychotic patients. Some do not succumb though to the hegemony of biological psychiatry. Thomas Ogden, another 2012 Sigourney honoree, has written on the psychoanalytic treatment of schizophrenia. The 2012 book "Experiencing psychosis: personal and professional perspectives," edited by Geekie, Randal, Lampshire and Read, and reviewed by Richard Waugaman in a recent issue of *Psychoanalytic Quarterly*, challenges a derogation of analytic therapy with psychotics and provides evidence of its utility in combination, at times, with medication. The exquisite individualization of psychoanalytic clinical work suggests that some analysts can be successful with some psychotic patients. I don't claim that special talent, but one of my clearly psychotic patients seemed to have been "cured" of his psychosis in the evaluation of an independent clinical observer some years later—who considered the patient a sociopath. The jury remains out on the larger question of the effective treatment of psychosis—no matter the approach.

Frank Baudry is an exemplar of psychoanalytic imperialism, discussing clinical topics, teaching us about theory development from different psychoanalytic cultures and applying psychoanalytic ideas to the arts. Applied psychoanalysis is a phrase traditionally used for non-clinical applications—another relevant example of psychoanalytic imperialism. There is no gap between Freud's work and the present in the study of non-neurotic phenomena. Helene Deutsch's "as if personality," Michael Balint's "basic fault," and Donald Winnicott's "false self" are among well-known clinical concepts expanding the Freudian corpus. The subtitle "an introduction" to Freud's essay "On Narcissism" (1914a) could be added to nearly every one of his major papers. Martin Bergmann refers to elaborations of psychoanalysis—most responding to clinical findings—as extensions and modifications of theory and practice. If this be imperialism, it is the very hallmark of scientific advance.

Twemlow partnered with Bruce Sklarew and Sallye Wilkinson to edit "Analysts in the Trenches," a 2004 book I reviewed for publication. The book describes analysts working in mean streets from New Haven to New Orleans, plying their trade in violence-ridden public schools, and responding to casualties of war in Angola, Bosnia and the former Soviet Republic of Georgia. Other workplaces include municipal halls, police stations, earthquake damaged areas, and "ground zero" in New York. Racism, child abuse and homelessness are among the traumatic situations leading to a new professional identity: the community analyst—a title embraced by Twemlow and elaborated in his plenary address to the American Psychoanalytic Association (2013). In the 2004 book, 23 contributors describe their work with gripping clinical detail. Those of us who work only in clinic and consulting room will be enlightened and maybe a bit envious. Analysts typically see few patients—and even fewer using their traditional treatment approach—while these authors have impact in the larger world. The book deals with problems that are properly considered extensions of clinical practice.

Community analysts rely on understanding unconscious motivation to create methods that are active and group-based, and which aim to change (rather than interpret) transference and dynamics. A neutral posture is recommended for consulting on social conflict, but personal relationships and collaboration are core principles of the work. A flexible, directly helpful approach is advocated, eschewing both credentials and a posture of expertise. The history of this specialty is traced to Anna Freud, Aichhorn, Bowlby, Erikson, and Karl Menninger, among others. Among the "Trenches" authors is Vamik Volkan, the pioneer and premier practitioner of international psychoanalytic intervention, who describes his work over a three year period on a once-in-five-months visiting schedule with an émigré family displaced by war to Tbilisi.

I believe we can and must attend both to our practices and to the ills of the world. We can improve our methods in the consulting room laboratory in which psychoanalysis was discovered, and work to apply our knowledge beyond it. In my 35 years teaching a psychoanalytic perspective to teachers and prospective teachers, I tried to develop communicable methodology for this application of psychoanalysis to teaching (Golland, 2002), while continuing to practice intensive individual treatment.

George Moraitis, in the April 2013 *JAPA*, presents a belated review of his father's book "Psychoanalysis and Its Application to Education," originally published in 1928. The elder Moraitis was a Greek mathematician who became fascinated with "The Interpretation of Dreams," embarked on a self-analysis, and launched a program of teacher training based on its discoveries. He did not train as an analyst, but eventually did counseling and became the main expositor of Freud in pre-World War II Greece.

Laurence Friedman is a superb theorist of the traditional clinical analytic situation, what goes on between analyst and analysand in the consulting room. The range of his writing is extensive; his focus is intensive. His 1988 book, "The Anatomy of Psychotherapy," has become a classic. *Contra* the Sigourney trustees, he does not count Twemlow's community work as psychoanalytic. Friedman looks at psychoanalysis as a treatment suitable for the few. I see him plying his trade in the original psychoanalytic laboratory, the one that provided Freud with his revolutionary insights into the nature of mind.

Otto Kernberg, a past president of IPA, has exercised imperialism by extending a psychoanalytic therapy to borderline and narcissistic conditions. He developed a method he calls "transference-based psychodynamic therapy" and a research program to validate its utility. Kernberg follows Freud's 1919 idea that the pure gold of psychoanalysis be alloyed with the copper of suggestion (or, in some translations, lead) for greater applicability—and I note here again that alloys are created for their strength and should not be demeaned on aesthetic grounds; treatments must aim for effectiveness rather than elegance.

Robert Bornstein's 2005 paper "Reconnecting Psychoanalysis to Mainstream Psychology" addresses the decline of psychoanalysis, describing how 19th Century philosophy gave birth to two distinct approaches to a new discipline of psychology in which Wundt's laboratory method of nomothetic research competed with the idiographic approach of Freud's clinical method. By mid-20th Century, Freud's was dominant; now it has lost its position. I agree with Bornstein that the fault lies with psychoanalysis. At least in the United States, the organized discipline was insular, avoiding contact with the intellectual challenges of the academy and the larger scientific community. It held to inaccurate ideas, relying on the authoritative statements of its pioneers rather than evidence, and was often insolent, claiming a unique window on truth that would not be subjected to outside evaluation and critique. The result was not only reduced influence but near banishment from both academic psychology and medical psychiatry. This change is truer of American psychoanalysis than its European and Latin American counterparts—and much of it might be laid at the feet of what Kurt Eissler (1965) called "medical orthodoxy." Eissler accurately predicted hard times unless such orthodoxy gave way. It took a restraint of trade lawsuit 20 years later, supported by Division 39, to end medical orthodoxy in psychoanalysis in this country, but much damage had been done.

Bornstein fears that hard times for psychoanalysis could lead to its demise as a special discipline, or perhaps to cult status. What might alter this outcome are the many important ideas generated in the first psychoanalytic century, ideas supported by empirical research not well known to the current psychology and psychiatry mainstream. Bornstein shows how psychoanalysis has itself been imperialized without acknowledgement such that it is often unknown beyond its own sanctuaries. He shows how psychology has co-opted psychoanalytic ideas in what are acts he calls "unconscious plagiarism." Just as historians still study the legacies of the Austro-Hungarian and Ottoman empires, psychology and psychiatry believe they have eclipsed psychoanalysis and relegated it to historical artifact even as they have unknowingly absorbed a lot of it. Clinical researchers like Bornstein publish within and beyond so that its best ideas will not be buried like ancient Troy.

It is common to differentiate between clinical and applied psychoanalysis. I find that distinction unhelpful. I include clinical psychoanalysis and related therapies among the applications of an evolving scientific paradigm called psychoanalysis. It is ironic that psychoanalysis in academic circles has focused on its contribution beyond the clinical situation, that is, its relevance to the humanities and to history. Theorists as different from one another as Erik Erikson and Jacques Lacan are well known in academia while they are denigrated within establishment American psychoanalysis.

What is psychoanalytic method? Despite the efforts of the research group at Columbia University, most analysts believe it cannot and should not be scripted. It is an exquisitely individualized method with interventions geared to the specific patient in the specific moment, based on the best understanding of the situation, the history of the patient, and the history of the treatment relationship. When I taught a technique course, it was called "theory of technique;" we studied and debated issues about technique precisely because there is no prescribed method. I never know what will happen in any session—or even in the next segment of a session; this is one of the joys of the work: every session is a new experience. Surprises occur, challenges are frequent. In a recent review of a book on child and adolescent analysis technique, Martin Silverman (2013) recalls none other than Arlow saying in a supervisory session: "There are no rules. Well actually there are two rules: don't hurt the patient and don't let the patient hurt you. Everything else is a set of guidelines, to be applied individually . . . ." This is the idiographic approach that should be very familiar to physicians, most of whom tell their patients to ignore the dire warnings included in drug inserts—since the medication is prescribed specifically for them. This is the sense of a 2011 book edited by the fourth of the 2012 Sigourney laureates, Salman Akhtar, entitled, "Unusual interventions: Alterations of the Frame, Method, and Relationship in Psychotherapy and Psychoanalysis." Like Freud, analysts still treat patients and analysands according to our best understanding of who they are as unique individuals—and we expand our theory and practice as we share our experiences at conferences and in the literature. I don't often practice group or family treatment, but I welcome learning from those who work with groups and families.

Not only is there no prescribed method—making each treatment situation unique—but there are also differences of style within the same institute and, as has been pointed out here, with the same analyst working with different patients. There are also various sub-theories (the "pluralism" that includes traditional, relational, neo-Kleinian, Bionian, Lacanian and other variations), and there are cultural differences: the Latin American, French, Israeli and others; earlier the Viennese, the Swiss and the British. These differences are subjects of scholarly dispute. Such disputes are important for psychoanalytic discourse; we debate and try to achieve tentative consensus, with any consensus subject to further debate and modification. This is how I understand Leo Rangell's "total composite theory." The disputes themselves are means of refining the thinking of the disputants and their readers. A current book review essay by Carmeli and Blass (2013) challenges the enterprise of neuro-psychoanalysis as described in a recent book by Norman Doidge. They see Doidge's work as not only in error, but harmful to psychoanalytic practice because of its "simplistic view of the treatment." Blass has also challenged clinical approaches differing from her own and responded to rebuttals by Lewis

Aron among others. Such debates typify the exchanges that lead to advancement in any scientific field.

Jonathan Shedler's 2010 paper not only reviews decades of research literature supporting the efficacy of psychoanalytic psychotherapy but provides an excellent concise summary of the defining characteristics of a psychoanalytic therapy. Psychoanalytic therapies also rely on the several meta-psychological positions as they have evolved, with the structural, genetic, and adaptive points of view equal to or perhaps more important than the original Freudian psychodynamics (see Novick and Novick, 2002).

When an esteemed colleague demonstrated his understanding and clinical utilization of the imperial theory of psychoanalysis, he asked me if he was therefore an analyst. I replied he was not. The paradigm is indeed available to anyone for study and use. A psychoanalyst, however, is trained as well in the traditional treatment modality of intensive couch-based work. Such training includes a personal analysis and close supervision of cases treated with that intensive couch-based approach. I welcome all who wish to be psychoanalytically informed mental health practitioners; but there is a distinct group to which the psychoanalyst title applies. One may have the credential but not engage in the practice nor keep up with its evolution.

There are main ideas I hope will be taken away from this essay: First is that discussion or debate in our field should follow the essay format I learned in high school: compare and contrast. A subject is best understood by looking at its similarities with and differences from a related subject. Examples are psychoanalysis vs. psychoanalytic psychotherapies or CBT vs. DBT, individual vs. group vs. family treatments, and so forth. Another of the main ideas is that validation cannot be limited—as Freud and many of his followers mistakenly thought—to the methods being validated, but also with the caveat that validation models must fit the subject matter. Psychoanalytic treatment must have external criteria of success to remain a scientific paradigm, lest it become a religion or a cult. A paradigm needs both a rational frame of reference and appropriate empirical approaches to test its propositions.

Too often the problem is one of definition. Psychoanalysis began as a psychiatric treatment for the neuroses but extended its range beyond treatment to become a psychological paradigm for the understanding of mind and its products. It came to include varieties of treatment approaches. I call the paradigm psychoanalysis. Paradigms are imperialistic; they try to encompass all the phenomena within their domain. The varieties of therapeutic approaches have commonalities and differences, one of which happens, unfortunately, to be called by the very name of the paradigm. I believe our chairman's accusation of imperialism is directed more at the traditional couch-based treatment model than at the paradigm. In that sense the pejorative use of imperialism may have some validity. The traditional treatment approach has made unjustified claims. A more modest, probabilistic approach is offered by Kligman (2010), e.g., the Oedipus Complex "might be a relevant way of thinking about *this* patient" (emphasis in the original).

Did Freud discover or create psychoanalysis? Both words are apt. He created the method of free association and its application to talk therapy. With his method he discovered facts about his patients' minds and about the human mind. His theoretical formulations are creative constructions based on clinical discoveries. Each of us helps each of our patients discover the inner workings of the individual mind. We do this best when we engage in creative collaboration with our patients and with those who work in cognate disciplines. In this way psychoanalysis may return to its proper place at the forefront of psychological science.

Freud saw himself as a *conquistador*. His ambition was a theory of everything about the mind and its products. This remains the legitimate ambition for the paradigm of contemporary psychoanalysis. Call it imperialism if you will. Imperial works for margarine and for Chrysler, not so much for politics. This is the Empire State; I grew up on Empire Boulevard in Brooklyn's Crown Heights. An imperial psychology—a comprehensive psychology—is what we should all hope for. In agreement with Eric Kandel, I believe psychoanalysis is the best and most benign empire around.

Panel Discussion of the Film "Argentina"

February 11, 2014

The film provided more questions than answers, a result appropriate to the state of our profession worldwide. I will provide here a few reactions.

Argentina, Insel, Israel

By coincidence we saw the "Argentina" film on the very morning National Institute of Mental Health Director Thomas Insel was profiled in the *Science Times,* and that very day an evening program with similar content was held at the Academy of Medicine under the auspices of the Association for Psychoanalytic Medicine and the Columbia University Institute for Israel and Jewish Studies.

Dr. Insel began his career when what he calls a "cabal" of psychoanalysts ran psychiatry. His own long-term leadership in psychiatric research and administration has emphasized an exclusively biological orientation. The film we saw focused, by contrast, on the traumatic, cultural and historical contributions to personality disorders and the psychoanalytic commitment of the enormous middle class of an entire nation. (Insel also challenged DSM and Big Pharma, noting that psychiatry has made no significant impact on the incidence or prevalence of its "diseases" in contrast with medical specialties with biomarkers.)

That evening, Eran Rolnik, a psychoanalyst and historian at Tel Aviv University and the Max Eitingon Institute for Psychoanalysis, presented a paper "History and Theory: The case of Psychoanalysis coming to Palestine (pre-state Israel)." The paper was discussed by Fordham English Professor Anne Golomb Hoffman. Its parallels to the film "Argentina" were striking.

Insel's use of "cabal" and the current dominance of biological psychiatry promote "either/or" thinking; Mark Solms' neuro-psychoanalysis takes a "both/

356

and" approach, far more appropriate to our state of knowledge—and to the facts. History, culture *and* biology—are central to any meaningful psychology. Contemporary psychoanalysis can provide meaningful commentary on history and culture.

The Case of Argentina: Scope of Indications and Methods

Psychoanalysis in Argentina is seen as more psychological than psychiatric—even in a cartoon. Hospitalized psychiatric patients are treated with an emotionally sensitive and humane community approach that would be applauded by Harry Stack Sullivan. Argentine culture seems also to reflect Freud's position that neurosis is normal—or as good as it gets, at least for the middle class.

Argentine psychoanalysis includes individual, couple, family, and group modalities, without the exclusionary and divisive battles that have damaged the reputation of psychoanalysis in this country.

Psychoanalytic Activists: Argentina; the USA; "Disappeared" and "Tortured"

Argentine analysts take active political positions, in contrast to the American reluctance for public advocacy. Communist affiliations of psychoanalytically conservative analysts have only recently been explored by Arnold Richards. Stewart Twemlow, a Sigourney honoree who was among the speakers Saturday at the New York Psychoanalytic Society, and others who represent a social activist psychoanalysis by emphasizing the role of the community analyst, are only recently being accepted by the American psychoanalytic establishment. It is notable that Division 39 (Psychoanalysis) led the battle in the larger APA to declare unethical a psychologist's assisting in torture sessions at Guantanamo. That issue returned to the forefront as the APA (considerably involved with Defense Department grants) has dismissed on technical grounds the ethics charge against a man who was the most flagrant violator at Guantanamo.

When Rogelio Sosnik, MD, migrated here from Argentina to practice psychoanalysis, he did not bother to qualify for a medical license. Instead, when legislation threatened his practice, he qualified under the new regulations as an LP (licensed psychoanalyst).

Concluding Remarks

My idea of a psychoanalytic paradigm that includes but is not defined by its traditional therapeutic approach seems apt. Even in graduate school, we spoke of psychoanalysis as both therapy and meta-therapy. Psychoanalysis—as stated in the film—is about freedom of thought; it is incompatible with authoritarianism. I remain mystified as to how analysts conducted practices under dictatorships like those of the Argentine Colonels, when patients and analysts were expected to report subversion, and "disappearance" became a frightening risk for any dissident. That psychoanalysis survived and thrived in troubled Argentina is a national case study worthy of our attention.

With each of these strictures we have an apparently insoluble conflict. Like most of Freud's "principles" they are not absolutes, though his writing style sometimes makes them seem so. The mirror, the receiving instrument and the surgeon are three of the technical metaphors in conflict with a meaningful bond between analyst and patient, an affective bond that is almost always necessary for therapeutic effect.

With each patient our stance oscillates between austerity and indulgence, anonymity and disclosure, judgment and neutrality. Our aim is to oscillate in resonance with our understanding of our patient from session to session and moment to moment. That resonance is far from perfect. To help any patient it must be good enough. There is and can be no formula.

Thinking About Thinking in Psychotherapy

February 27, 2014

My group talks about therapy a lot. Our Tuesday conferences are, in fact, entitled "Psychotherapy." They offer a wide variety of topics we consider relevant; not just diagnosis and treatment, but literature, art, history, law—nearly anything of intellectual or cultural value—and we properly consider all these topics to be related to our work as therapists. The Thursday conferences are called "Group and Family Therapy" but have not been limited to these topics. Thursday conferences usually focus on clinical matters though, and problematic cases are often presented. I enjoy both conferences, but I regularly ask myself whether our therapeutics has any common core and, if so, can it be stated. My answer: "Not simply." We work with very complex systems: individual human beings, couples, families, and small groups, each system in a social, cultural, financial, even ecological context. The many factors we must consider in our work preclude short answers. For every difficult problem there may be a simple answer—and it is nearly always wrong!

Two key psychoanalytic ideas that address this complexity are "over-determination" and "multiple function." The first says that meaningful behaviors are not "caused" in a linear way; they result from the confluence of several motives and compromises.

The second says that such behaviors have multiple effects; they aim to satisfy id, ego, superego and external realities. Complexity is why Freud, in his introduction to August Aichorn's *Wayward Youth* (1925), called psychoanalysis the third impossible profession, the first two being education and government. That is why I reject single-factor theories like Becker's *Denial of Death* or Frankl's "search for meaning," despite the importance of these ideas both clinically and existentially. That's why therapy cannot be described in a single statement like: "It's just what goes on in the interaction between therapist and patient."

I focus today on how we **think about** our complex work. I won't try to be comprehensive; nor will I provide explicit clinical material. Instead, I will discuss several ideas worthy of the consideration of any serious therapist. Thinking, considering, rethinking, and re-considering our observations and experiences as we work is how I described theorizing, in a presentation here last year. Today's paper is also about theory, a topic that turns some of us off. I want to be clear, though: I agree completely with Charcot that theory does not determine factuality. I was warned in graduate school of the dangers of reification: theories are neither true nor false; they are judged by their utility and heuristic value. The eminent social psychologist Kurt Lewin declared there was nothing as useful as a good theory. I contend it is impossible for any of us to work successfully without theory; to try to do so would define us as thoughtless, perhaps even impulsive. Our minds cannot help but to create theory about our observations, in the same way preschoolers ask "why" and teenagers "why not."

Epistemology is the branch of philosophy that evaluates theories. It asks the perennial question, "*how* do we know?" How does a mind come to know anything? Aristotle applied a critical corrective to the abstract idealistic theories of Plato, his teacher. He promoted observation—which must then be subjected to logic, reflection, and further observation and thinking if it will achieve any potentially valid understandings. Post-modern philosophers have undermined the notion of valid understanding or truth. They tell us all is subjective, all is perspective. Their excesses have provided a gift to anti-intellectuals who deny global warming and evolution. Owen Renik, a prominent psychoanalyst, speaks of "irreducible subjectivity." The study of human beings is, of course, irreducibly subjective, meaning bias cannot be reduced to zero. But it is absurd to believe we can have no grasp of external reality or of the reality of ourselves and other people. The study called "theory of mind" is devoted, in fact, to how we come to understand others. Children develop a theory of mind in normal development; without it there can be only egocentrism or psychopathy.

A teacher of Victor Frankl's said that "life is nothing more than a combustion process." Frankl disagreed. A college biology teacher of mine announced in the first class session, facetiously I now hope, that our lives are essentially epiphenomena of the survival process of genetic material. My anti-reductionist position became clear at that time, and I later found like minds, Frankl's among them. Existentialists have posited an unfeeling universe in which our existence hardly matters. It depends on what we mean by "hardly." Frankl defined the life task as a search for personal meaning in the face of our puniness and our miniscule lifespan, at least when measured in universal time.

Is our therapy designed to help our patients find meaning? Are we philosophers? Adolescence is a stage in which we must ask philosophical questions; our minds achieve the Piagetian stage of abstract thought, of being able to revel in pure ideas, of possibilities rather than mere concrete actualities. Quantitative types often proclaim that anything that exists must exist in some measurable quantity. Not necessarily measurable, I'd reply. Can we measure love?

Professional philosophers train their minds with thought experiments. Heraclitus said, "No man steps in the same river twice." We know the water molecules we dipped into yesterday are all gone today. But a river is only partially defined by its molecules; it is also defined in larger terms: a body of water arising here and flowing there. Thinking is more useful if we leave the study of molecules to chemists and physicists and address a holistic reality and even metaphorical ones, or ideas themselves. What of Zeno's paradox? If we must cover half the distance to get from any one point to another, we would never reach our destination. Sound thinking rejects that premise. Covering half the distance does not limit us to half-steps; we can leap.

Freud's basic assumption about tension-reduction, considered axiomatic by Morris Eagle in a recent book (2011), leads to theoretical extensions that make no sense to me: a motive to reduce tension to zero; a death drive as basic. Risk-taking, curiosity, novelty-seeking, and the wish to be challenged are behaviors that come readily to mind as not best served by treating tension-reduction as a foundational axiom, although it has its place as a sometime explanation. A recent review of the newly translated work of French analyst Jean Laplanche (Scarfone, 2013) has him also disagreeing with Eagle on this matter. In like manner, Charles Brenner's most elegant, parsimonious model of the mind leaves me too few concepts to work with. His wielding of Occam's Razor to shave one psychoanalytic idea after another from our theory seems premature at best. For philosophers, teleological thinking is erroneous; a non-existent future cannot affect what precedes it. But, as philosopher/psychoanalyst Jonathan Lear pointed out (2017), teleology is an essential part of thinking: we plan, we anticipate, we hope, and we wish. These thoughts do not predict the future, but they are essential psychological processes that influence personal futures. Subjectivity and unconscious motivation, what Freud called psychic reality, are real; they are natural phenomena subject to study on their own terms.

We discuss ideas in many meetings and, unlike philosophers—who constantly challenge faulty thinking—we are nice people, do-gooders who try to find value in any set of ideas; and we try to avoid hurt feelings in anyone brave enough to present them. That's not all bad. But take Mark Solms' recent championing of a "conscious id." Solms's own research, especially on dreaming, is impressive, and in one talk before the group he showed himself to be a most impressive human being, but in this assertion, he is making what logicians call a "category error." Freud's "Id" is a theoretical construct. It is—by definition—a concept at the artificial and indeterminate border of biology and psychology, a bridge concept between two artificially but usefully segregated disciplines. The Id is an inference with potential heuristic utility, demonstrated in Freud's tripartite structural model and an internal conflict-based approach to psychology. It is not a locus in the physical brain as Maggie Zellner suggests, although there will be brain correlates; nor is it just a biological concept. It cannot be conscious other than as a thought experiment.

Solms's idea may lead us to question Freud's theory, and that is surely fine—but one cannot postulate a "conscious id" without scrapping a host of other concepts willy-nilly, i.e. without convincing evidence or argumentation, and without proposing an alternate psychology. The square root of negative one is an "imaginary" number in mathematical parlance; it is a product of mathematical reasoning. It has several implications for physicists in quantum mechanics and elementary particle physics, one example being the Higgs boson. I was delighted to discover that mathematicians are quite comfortable with both imaginary and irrational numbers within their useful sets of ideas. Minds imagine; imagination has effects, internal and external. Recall Freud's citing Kekule's dream that led him to discover the benzene ring.

This tangent may seem far from useful for therapists. But I am talking about errors of thinking that can lead us astray, and creative imagination that requires further thought, time, and testing. We are reminded regularly that we have a practical task different from that of philosophers.

Subjectivity is not only a limitation on objectivity; it is a human phenomenon worthy of study. It is not reducible to zero for any observer in any science. All scientists use an epistemology of best evidence combined with consensual validation, and they must be modest in asserting findings as facts. Falsifiability and replication are hallmarks of the scientific enterprise. Psychology is scientific and psychoanalysis is an important paradigm within psychology.

Next month we'll hear a second paper on the concept of "psychotic core," I heard the following whispered criticisms in group: "scholastic," "untestable" "unhelpful therapeutically." These negative reactions reflect problems inherent in evaluating psychoanalytic ideas. How do we define psychoanalytic? Its core premise is that the full meaning of psychological phenomena is often out of awareness and often also unavailable to awareness through ordinary cognitive effort. Among these phenomena are thoughts, feelings, behavior, and more complex manifestations such as artistic, musical and literary productions, and large and small group processes, i.e., the products of the human mind in social context. Scholastic? I would use the non-pejorative "scholarly," a major strength of the best professional presentations. Untestable? In the same sense that 1) axioms are untestable (e.g., natural selection, survival of the fittest) but, instead, provide frames of reference that generate specific testable hypotheses; and 2) testing propositions requires methodology appropriate to subject matter. A double-blind, randomized controlled experiment is not a method suitable for effective comparison of psychotherapies. Unhelpful therapeutically? Indeed, evidence of helpfulness is required. Anecdotal evidence is a start, but to declare ideas unhelpful without testing is to believe that the absence of evidence is evidence of absence. And I too frequently must remind colleagues that there is a considerable body of research going back over sixty years to support the efficacy of psychoanalytic treatment (see Shedler, 2010).

Psychoanalysis is a psychological paradigm created by Freud and elaborated for more than a century. Its original discoveries were anecdotal observations, and its evolving theory or paradigm was created by his genius. Though both the observations and the theory were born in a medical consulting room, early on (by 1895) they were defined as psychology, not biology. They were eventually extended by Freud to the world of art and literature. Ultimately, psychoanalysis-as-paradigm is a set of ideas. Its core idea—dynamic unconscious mental processes—is a major contribution to the History of Ideas, recognized as such by the inclusion of Freud's work as the concluding volume of the Great Books of the Western World series.

An essential characteristic of this core idea is that motivation is not directly observable. Instead, it must be inferred from overt manifestations (Freud's latent and manifest content). In this regard it is no different from nuclear physics. The nature of the atom was at first a postulate that might account for many observations. Einstein's theories did not receive empirical validation until several years after they were published. Tests demonstrated the utility of atomic physics, and in 1945 the world entered the atomic age. Physicists continue to observe and to find anomalies, observations not adequately explained by existing theory. Higgs and his fellow 2013 Nobel laureate postulated a particle, the boson, which only recently found empirical validation—at the cost of great scientific effort.

Many ideas derived from psychoanalytic observation have found validation, even beyond the consulting room; others have been shown to be in error or of more limited use than was first claimed. The field of early mental development is especially vexing, mainly because very young children cannot speak their minds. Child observation and experimentation have yielded results, but these remain incomplete, and many remain inferential or speculative. Some authors use the "primitive mental states" of adults to develop inferences and possible models of the infantile mind. Like the empirical test for the Higgs boson, major investigative expense may be required to assess these models. That assessment is likely to take several forms: direct observation of fetuses and infants, neuro-physiological study, clinical work with the very young (like Anni Bergmann's mother-infant observation program), and treatment of adult problems ascribed to "primitive mental states."

That such reports may seem scholastic or may be otherwise hard to grasp is due to the very subtle nature of the phenomena, whether mother-infant interactions or the fleeting affective states in the psychotherapy situation. Projective identification is one such subtle concept, one whose proponents I respect, though I have yet to find the concept useful for thinking about my patients.

The therapeutic value of a psychoanalytically-informed method relies for its effectiveness on patience, relationship-building, and gaining a highly nuanced understanding of the patient—perhaps even more so with more disturbed individuals. It cannot promise quick results and may not achieve success despite the effort expended. None of our therapies can promise success, though some fail more quickly. Psychoanalytic treatment may properly be—as it was originally and is again—for those who have not been helped by other methods. In his 1905 paper, *On Psychotherapy*, Freud endorsed any treatment that could achieve success more quickly or easily, even hypnosis, which he had given up in his own work. No one is coerced into psychoanalytic treatments or made to stay. Many leave unsatisfied; full satisfaction is not to be believed, let alone expected. The literature is replete with attempts to understand failed treatments. Trial-and-error remains the basic method of both science and clinical work.

Respect Must Be Paid

Sigmund Freud admitted his lack of music appreciation. He was a highly cultured man, knowledgeable and appreciative of arts and literature, with an outstanding collection of artifacts adorning his consulting room. He wrote about what is called "applied" psychoanalysis, the extension of his theories to works of art and literature—but, notably, not to music. Although several of his papers are now deemed philosophical, he explicitly disavowed philosophy. He did not comment on his own avoidance of music.

Fundraising efforts for New York's classical music radio station emphasize the importance of the experience of music for its listeners. An avid listener, I am also a donor. In 1697, 200 years before the birth of psychoanalysis, William Congreve wrote "Music has charms to sooth a savage breast." One would think that Freud the healer would follow Congreve's lead, as Freud focused on savage elements of human motivation. Recent commentary suggests that Freud's rationality and the therapeutic principles related to it—promoting awareness and ego strength—could seem incompatible with the direct experiential effects of music. Freud recognized the "oceanic feeling," a sense of unity with the universe, psychological and not necessarily religious, but he did not elaborate on it. Intense pleasure or rapture is about the pleasure principle; for his therapeutics, Freud promoted the reality principle.

The belief has been expressed that music is best understood through its intervals and other formal characteristics. That would make it part of acoustics, a branch of physics. Surely appreciation of music also has biological correlates but is not reducible to its physics or biology. Formal characteristics do not address the sometimes ethereal experience that can result for the same individual from different forms: baroque, classic, romantic, opera, jazz, Broadway show tunes, folk, pop, rock or rap. A guided tour of the Metropolitan Opera House moved opera higher on my own rapture scale. In my own musical tastes, I am almost as promiscuous as our group leader in his theorizing about psychotherapy.

This is a talk about thinking, not feeling, but feeling is central to the complaints of our patients and the savagery of their minds. Recent literature on psychoanalysis and music is being extended by Julie Jaffe Nagel, a Juilliard graduate and psychologist-psychoanalyst whose 2014 article *Psychoanalysis and Musical Ambiguity: The Triton in "Gee, Officer Krupke"* led an issue of *JAPA* and thrilled me, and whose recent book *Melodies of the Mind* (2013) extends her work. She deals with notes and intervals, but also with the dynamic unconscious. Otto Fenichel considered psychoanalysis an attempt for a rational understanding of the irrational. I remain with him in that regard.

Psychologists approach the study of creativity by differentiating two types of thinking: convergent and divergent. Convergent thought is linear, causal, and seeks specific answers that can be judged as correct or not. Divergent thinking is open-ended, associative (free-associative, perhaps), evocative with no specific correct answer. Scientists, like artists, must be creative; let's add therapists to this list. Jacob Arlow's (1979) paper, *The Genesis of Interpretation*, defines two phases: an initial associative one and an organizing, rational and evaluative one. We must first open our minds to possibilities as we listen to our patients, then we need to test our ideas internally against what we know of this person and this treatment, and we must organize what we will say. During any session, we oscillate between divergent and convergent thinking. With "imaginary" numbers, mathematicians pay tribute to imagination, enabling their creativity as it enables the creativity of all children and adults.

To distill in a phrase the most valuable thinking skill provided by my education at Stuyvesant High School and Brandeis University, I offer "compare and contrast." Whether in history (World Wars I and II), music (Mozart and Haydn), literature (romantic and 'beat' poets), or science (Newton and Einstein), such an analysis, inevitably evaluated by a final exam question, was routinely expected. This skill could be used with matters from the most abstract to the most mundane (like dinner menu selections). In the various controversies we experience in our field and in individual sessions, this type of thinking—how is today's observation similar to and how is it different from what preceded it?—are the questions that should be routine in our thought processes. This patient is like others (Sullivan's 'more human than otherwise')—and necessarily unique, unlike any other. Like control groups in experiments, compare-and-contrast is required for both effective thought and effective therapy.

When I was new to the field I sought a coherent theory and I thought I had found it. Ongoing study and clinical practice showed me its limits. I reject a premature attempt at refinement like Brenner's and am more tolerant of my own ignorance and the ignorance of our profession. A Grand Unifying Theory seems far away; it is of comfort that the same holds true in physics.

Psychotherapy: Considerations for Theory and Practice

November 18, 2014

My patients rarely speak of musical interests, except for one opera scholar from 30 years ago who went almost daily during the Met season for standing room. He was well-known to the regular ushers who would often provide him a vacant seat, and he'd published two opera books. He was sure I was as taken with opera as he, because, he said, he found me such a good listener. In fact, I'm an opera-liker, not a lover; I rarely attend but I do listen to WQXR while driving.

A 2014 piece in the Sunday Times Magazine, "My Problem with Music," by Dan Brooks, made the author's musical taste clear: counterculture. I knew few of the genres mentioned but was intrigued that one group he slammed—Journey—was my older son's favorite; he's traveled long distances to their concerts and even operated a Journey tribute website. I wondered how I might relate to Mr. Brooks were he to come to my office.

Similarly, I don't understand why as many as 65% of American households have pets. One of my sons has two cats; a stepson two dogs. In my first marriage, we had a cat I ignored. While I can intellectualize people's attachment to pets, I have little empathy. I've never treated anyone with gender dysphoria, and frankly find it easier to contemplate transgender men than surgery effecting the reverse. I learn a lot and believe I could work with such people.

Many years ago, I had a patient who was a Rolex fan, going into debt to add to his expensive watch collection while paying me a reduced fee. His therapy was reasonably effective. I cannot easily empathize, though, with the motivations behind such a purchase.

What have these thoughts to do with psychotherapy principles and practices? To my mind, it's precisely what characterizes the psychoanalytic approach: people are different from one another; generalization is—necessarily—overgeneralization.

Sullivan was right about our commonalities when he said, "We are all much more nearly human than otherwise," but psychotherapy is more about our seemingly infinite diversity. The people who show up in our offices asking for help will be similar and different from us and each other; they might include people we would avoid in our personal lives, or perhaps even despise.

The psychoanalytic paradigm expresses itself in a range of therapeutic approaches. Each treatment is unique, and surely differs from—but also even has commonalities with—non-analytic approaches. The work differs from active, focused or directive therapies, although they help many people and, in 1905, Freud wrote that quicker, cheaper methods should be preferred if they can be effective.

The principles and practices of what I call "flexible Freudianism" are not idiosyncratic; my approach is very much the way many colleagues think and work. We begin with the premise that we know very little about another person; inner life is hidden even from intimates. The treatment situation is one in which we try to learn about the other person (I refer primarily to individual treatment, though group, family and couple treatments have similar elements), and to help that person learn about him- or herself. A second premise, stated by physics Nobel laureate Murray Gell-Mann, is that anything true of any person is at least a partial truth about the human condition. This premise is central to the scientific aspiration of psychoanalysis.

The notion that we all do good clinical work is seductive, but unsatisfying. We are kind, experienced people, who listen well and engage with our patients by dint of our personalities and talent. But psychotherapy should extend beyond WIT—W. I. T., Warmth, Intuition and Trust—to merit respect as a professional enterprise.

WIT, whether word or acronym, is a necessary but insufficient set of conditions for successful treatment. (I may be overgeneralizing here: Ivar Lovaas's work with autistic children seemed to lack warmth; harsh authority can promote behavior change—and for some patients that's a reasonable goal.) The notion that WIT is enough denies that different theory and technique might yield different results. Success is claimed by analysts of many theoretical persuasions and is also claimed by "evidence-based" treatments that explicitly reject psychoanalytic ideas.

Is everyone doing good work? I think not. This should be an empirical question, but we differ over what we count as good work and what we accept as evidence. Paul Wachtel (2010) addresses specious claims in the evidence-supported treatment movement. The American Psychological Association counts clinical evidence as legitimate. We sometimes hear asserted that no evidence exists to support psychoanalytic treatment, despite considerable actual evidence (e.g.

Seligman, 1998, in the Consumer Reports study; and Shedler, 2010). Peter Kramer, a well-known proponent of psychotropic medication, argued against eliminating "stories," clinical narratives, in a recent front-page essay in the New York Times Sunday Review.

There are also the gurus and hucksters. Some invent new treatments most of us would disdain. We've been encouraged to be up on the methods being taught to psychiatric residents, including programs on Imago Therapy, Mindfulness, and Interpersonal Psychotherapy, all considered arrows in an eclectic quiver. This gives me pause, especially when the presenter seems more salesman than serious therapist. And we must also be careful about our metaphors: arrows in a quiver may be useful for hunter-gatherers targeting food or predators, or biologists attacking viruses and bacteria, but that kind of thinking might create a subtle ambience that puts at risk a self-discovery technique. Although many patients expect or even prefer a doctor to suggest and to guide, Freud's "receiving instrument" and Winnicott's "holding environment" offer a contrasting therapeutic attitude. The basic claim in clinical practice is that something works, but that depends on how we define "works."

Science and Practice

A prior paper about psychoanalytic research concluded with a quotation from Oscar Hammerstein: "The farmers and the cowboys should be friends." Researchers and clinicians don't seem any friendlier since I wrote that paper. I'm a clinician who supports sound research, but there are reasons for the unfriendliness. I call the researchers "farmers," since farming has methods and yields; the therapists are "cowboys," famously hating fences.

Farmers must accept that their fences provide only occasionally useful boundaries for cowboys, and cowboys must understand that boundless individualism is too wild for a respectable profession. Good research can provide some guidance, but not rules. Farmers and cowboys can both contribute to science and practice to advance convergent validity which must include best evidence as well as clinical wisdom.

The empirical research base for psychoanalysis goes back over eight decades. Studies fall into three categories: effectiveness, process, and conceptualization. Recent compendia have been published. Despite the latest efforts of Westen, Shedler, Jones, Bucci, and Bornstein, among a new generation of American scholars, psychoanalytic research remains dismissed or ignored by current mainstream psychiatry and psychology, and by most clinicians. Irrational bias persists; Freud's work was rejected for emphasizing infantile sexuality.

Researchers like Jacques Barber have bought into "randomized controlled" designs as a "gold standard" for psychoanalytic research, despite the lack of fit between that design and the spontaneous process typical of psychoanalytic therapies. Experimentation is a major empirical method; my own dissertation was an experimental test of aggressive drive arousal. Experimental research isolates and controls variables to focus on the relationship between one or more independent variables and an outcome. Scripted therapies attempt to control for therapist variability.

A Mentalization Modification Therapy (MMT) paper presented at Mount Sinai also controlled for time, limiting treatment to 20 sessions, but the presenter acknowledged that her clinical use of MMT had no fixed number. A psychoanalytic orientation requires an open timeframe, with unique interaction central to its therapeutic effect. Much of psychotherapy research supports the centrality of the unique relationship to positive outcome. Standardizing therapists distorts what is essential. Differences between laboratory and consulting room account for frequent dismissal of research findings by clinicians; the more elegant the experiment, the less it will simulate conditions of practice.

Research can help us to articulate relevant variables but clinical application cannot use such findings as a template. Each patient in each moment is best served by in-depth knowledge of that patient's life and concerns. Considering or requiring Randomized Control Trials (RCTs) as a gold standard is therefore not valid for most psychotherapy research. RCTs are standard in drug research, but are properly criticized for economically-interested bias, failure to report negative findings, testing against placebo rather than existing treatments, and other limitations.

Creative approaches to research can be far better than experimental control. At a recent lecture, V. S. Ramachandran stated that his dramatic cures for phantom limb pain using his ingenious mirror technique were dismissed for lack of RCTs or large enough sample size. Rejecting his clearly effective work is not sound science.

Stanislas Lehaene developed a single-subject experimental method to study consciousness, with the important strength of replication, true also of Ramachandran. Hasan Asif has used EEGs for brain diagnosis and treatment, also using single cases. Asif said that psychotherapy changes the brain; I've often spoken of my clinical work as non-invasive neurosurgery.

With its single-minded pursuit of profits, Big Pharma valorizes RCTs, but not so coincidently, RCTs often go unreplicated. Among scientific principles, replication is as important a principle as control or parsimony. Charles Brenner's theory represents psychoanalytic parsimony at its most elegant; I find that parsimony premature. Convergent validity is better attained by several approaches rather than one. Meta-analysis (Shedler, 2010) shows psychoanalytic psychotherapy as effective short-term, and more effective long-term than its competitors.

This research is ignored and dismissed because it is neither precise nor elegant; it relies on convergent validity rather than an acid test. It is also probabilistic, something generally true of social science research, which is favorably reported nonetheless in the pages of my favorite newspaper.

Robert Bornstein compared nomothetic to idiographic research; both are useful. The Times feature The Upshot reports daily on social, political, and economic issues from a statistical point of view. There was also a well-written explanation of statistics, useful for understanding complex issues of social policy, such as the government's exaggeration of the cost of college. Among the thoughts clinicians should have while listening to patients is "how is what I am hearing similar to or different from what is typical?" Norms can sometimes help us with what to say to the other person in the room. Numbers will also tell us that the average American family has 2.2 children; I've never met a fifth of a child.

Clinicians often find research papers dull. I read summaries to assess relevance but am unlikely to read many papers through. Researchers find clinical papers speculative, if not fanciful. Clinicians tend to find case reports more relevant to their work.

I appreciate good science that uses methods appropriate to the subject matter, and I welcome good interdisciplinary science. If RCTs are to be the gold standard, astronomy is an art form and Darwin a philosopher. After a quarter century, there is no evidence for string theory, yet it remains important in physics.

Theory and Practice

We are quick to agree with Charcot's "Theory is good, but it doesn't alter facts," but too often that statement is an anti-intellectual depreciation of theory, like the way creationists refer to evolution. Charcot's first clause, "theory is good," deserves more weight. The relationship between theory and practice refers to how we think about patients. Thinking is good; intellect is not intellectualization. We do more than think; we listen and have affective responses; we let our minds wander and resonate with what we hear; we also speak. Thinking can be more or less sound. Humans are unavoidably philosophers; it's the Piagetian epigenetic stage (ages 10-15) during which our minds develop the ability to speculate, to move from concrete to metaphorical to fantastic, to ask not just "why?" but "why not?" In other words: to be creative. Thinking must be subject to critical scrutiny; patients and colleagues should be encouraged to challenge our expressed thoughts. We need to hone thinking skills and test our theories empirically to improve them. We must not rely on personal theories, but we must count thinking/theory as central to our work. Everything in a session, including silence, is affected by our theory. Intellect is good; theory is good; it does not rule, nor should it be ruled out.

Both "neuro-psychotherapy" and cultural psychiatry are relevant to our work. Individual patients will at different moments benefit from a focus on one or the other. We don't know what our next patient hour will present and must be available for any possibility; sometimes biology, sometimes culture, sometimes personal history will be the issue. The only broad generalization is that humans are bio-psycho-socio-cultural-ecological creatures. Any of these domains may be emphasized at different times with the same patient.

Clinical Practice: Reflections on Papers by Several Colleagues

February 2014's day-long Symposium at Mount Sinai, sponsored by the Conference of Psychoanalytic and Psychotherapeutic Publications and Organizations (C3PO), was entitled "What works?" I found it rewarding not despite—but because—speakers offered different answers. One of our colleagues, S, articulated his belief that therapeutic effect derives from the pre-verbal and non-verbal communication characteristic of infancy, and evident throughout life. His presentation was emotionally moving. S cried when reading about a man's guilty confession for not having provided water for another man suffering from thirst; some of us also became tearful. The discussion came to near consensus that speaking unspoken thoughts and feelings in the presence of a supportive other is the essence of psychotherapy. I find that a strikingly incomplete answer to "What works?" a necessary but rarely sufficient condition.

Acknowledging hidden feelings was the essence of the Breuer-Freud method: abreaction of strangulated affects. Revolutionary 120 years ago, though known to our ancestors ages ago, its results were limited. Many people need more, so Freud proceeded to develop a deeper method, discovering transference and resistance as he went along, then narcissism, guilt, negative therapeutic reactions, and so much more—as new clinical situations led to new thinking, new theory, and new technique.

S's emphasis on the pre- and non-verbal is supported by Edward Tronick's demonstration that motherly gaze dramatically affects infantile well-being. Tronick and his colleagues identify as psychoanalysts; they study what Freudians call the "pre-oedipal" phases of development. Arrietta Slade, another major attachment theorist, spoke Sunday at an all-day meeting honoring Fred Pine. She was explicit in her debt to Pine's mentorship, and her commitment to contemporary psychoanalysis. Our colleague B's work relies on Bowlby, later attachment theory, and the work of Tronick and his colleagues. Our colleague F's several recent presentations on "psychotic core" emphasized pre-linguistic memory inscription (distinct from representational memory) as relevant to clinical work. F builds on the work of Winnicott, Bion, Green, Bleger and the Barangers to elaborate a theory of early development with possible clinical utility for patients formerly deemed unsuitable for psychoanalytic treatment. I was surprised to be reminded recently that Loewald also wrote on "psychotic core," a controversial proposition. This widening of the scope of psychoanalytic research challenges traditional approaches, specifically Brenner's insistence on verbal memories, available only from myelinated brains of the oedipal years. My review of Brenner's last book chided his narrowness; it flies in the face of a consensus that the earliest years of life impact significantly on later development.

What is admirable in early life research—"baby watching"—is its addition to our knowledge base, and its proposals for newer therapeutic approaches. Less congenial is any exclusive or primary focus as a generalization: what Leo Rangell called pars pro toto theorizing. Worse are formulaic interventions, be they routine praise offered for the merest discernable progress, as in a recent presentation on mindfulness with impulse-ridden patients, another presenter's mantra "feel good about yourself" in his mindfulness talk, or B's routine use of praise in a case presented a few weeks ago. I'm not against praise, and B's seemed to help this specific patient; my argument is with routinized interventions. When I was a patient I would have found such praise condescending.

Another colleague discussed her work with families of autistic children, recalling a mother phoning late at night, frightened by an impulse to kill her child. The therapist self-disclosed a similar impulse when—years before—her own baby was not sleeping through the night; her caller was immediately relieved. S opined this wasn't therapy; it was a simple humane response. The presenter agreed, saying she might not say the same thing in a session. But humane responses are integral and necessary within any therapy and contribute to its action. S was correct that these humane responses—often referred to as non-specific factors—are not of themselves therapy. They are far from sufficient, although, as Fred Pine has written, non-specific factors may be quite specific for patients with traumatic or neglectful early experiences. These responses can also backfire. Some patients have told me they don't want even my very modest self-disclosures. Others, of course, seem happy for my utterances, and still others ignore them. Self-disclosure, like any intervention, must be individualized and of the moment, not routine.

F's recent presentation of clinical examples drew a question: "What do you say to such a patient?" F provided a generic answer. A psychoanalytic approach offers no specific intervention for someone else's patient. Each intervention should be patient-specific, moment specific, and in the idiom of the dyad. Individualization is achieved over time, and only with increased understanding of the particular patient; instant cures are merely happy accidents.

Dan Birger once said if we had a transcript of his sessions in the course of a day, we couldn't tell it was the same therapist. To this I add: not only is each clinical dyad unique, but each hour is also unpredictable. Joseph Sandler called my Birger Principle "role responsiveness." Therapists must seek as much understanding of—and with—the patient as possible. Each dyad creates its own interaction, one that changes over the course of the work. S might call the Birger Principle "what goes on between the two people in the room." I believe Birger's and Sandler's to be more articulate; but I also bet, if we had the transcripts, we'd find some consistency. As I said at the end of S's presentation, what works depends on the answer to several questions: For whom, by whom, under what circumstances, and how we define "work."

One definition of psychology I heard in graduate school I immediately rejected: the science of behavior aiming for prediction and control.

Concluding Remarks

Forty years ago, as a recent institute graduate, I was asked by my favorite supervisor, then the program chair of the Freudian Society, to discuss a paper at an upcoming public conference. I read the paper, written by a senior member, and thought it was terrible. It reflected obsolete theory in the dogmatic, Germanic style then typical of some immigrant analysts who believed they knew all the answers. I tried to beg off the task, but my most admired mentor urged me to proceed. I came up with an organizing theme: "psychoanalytic papers are valuable to the extent to which they raise questions rather than provide answers." My words were disingenuous, a cover for avoiding frank disagreement. But it worked; the author thanked me when I concluded.

I now believe those words and consider them central to a contemporary psychoanalytic attitude. They are also central to my belief that psychoanalysis is a natural science. I am reminded of the Higgs boson scientist who commented after the empirical confirmation of the particle: The discovery was truly exciting, he said, but it would have been more interesting had they failed. A scientific attitude is characterized by disciplined curiosity, with questions more important than answers. As a clinical enterprise, psychoanalysis must seek and provide answers, different ones for each patient. As a scientific enterprise confronting the vast unknown of mind/brain phenomena within developmental, social, cultural, and ecological contexts, psychoanalysts and psychotherapists must accept and embrace ignorance.

Abstinence, Anonymity, Neutrality: Form or Formula

A Clinical Presentation, April 30, 2015

I sign up for a Thursday presentation before knowing what I'll present, though it will always be clinical work. One year I had trouble finding a topic. Even after finding one, I thought it was too abstract—closer to a previous presentation. About five weeks before the scheduled talk, a dear colleague apologized for her anticipated absence; I said she wouldn't miss much since I couldn't seem to get my paper organized. We then said to each other, virtually simultaneously, "maybe that's a good thing for you/me." I always admire another colleague's presentations, despite his self-described disorganization. I decided to allow myself to not organize, but I cannot shed my character style easily or completely. I took some inspiration from a heated exchange on the APsaA members list in response to the death of Robert Langs, a controversial figure in the psychoanalytic world. Contradictory opinions were expressed by people who knew him and by others who only knew his prolific writing. The exchange was a disorganizing experience, as I agreed with several writers on each side of the debate.

My late mentor Donald Kaplan's article, "The Future of Classical Analysis," was published in Psychoanalytic Review and reprinted as the concluding essay in a book of papers assembled by his late wife. It concluded by describing orthodox, liberal and progressive opinions—and his own. I'll paraphrase, but with some quotes:

The orthodox analyst is "concerned with proprieties and improprieties... manners more than science, he is no analyst but a dandy.... Sometimes amusing... largely irrelevant." The liberal is adaptable but cannot tell "when in the course of unraveling a sock... " we are left with only "a tangle of wool." The progressive, a pragmatist, is "an arch-cynic" for whom any cosmology will do; whatever works is fine.

Kaplan admired his contemporaries for improving on the past, while defining psychoanalysis "as a distinct theoretical program and methodology, ... one of the better ones." He believed in its necessity, its purpose, and its survival. Writing half a century ago, he seemed, presciently, to address the current theoretical diversity/ disarray and simultaneous continuing professional vitality.

For Kaplan (and me), questions are more revealing than specific answers. A psychoanalyst is engaged in a lifelong study of the human mind and its products; the clinical situation is the primary but not sole source of understanding. We join with others in groups open to new ideas, yet building on the contributions of Sigmund Freud, neither idealizing nor dismissing his work. Short answers won't do.

When I offer a clinical presentation, I try to present an actual problem in an ongoing treatment, or to focus on underappreciated aspects of the psychoanalytic theory of therapy. One reason, I'll admit, is that, in general, case presentations *per se* rarely hold my interest. Unless they ask for input from colleagues or address an issue or issues beyond the case itself, they often seem to me like engaging stories that may entertain—or sometimes show off—but do little more. In much of our literature the case is offered to support the author's position but is without dispositive value. I hasten to add that I am not disparaging great writing like Dan Birger's and certainly not Sigmund Freud's (though his cases are not examples of good clinical work). Case presentations are standard components of our initial and continuing education; listening to them adds several ears to Theodore Reik's three, and to our packet of listening skills. 120 years of cases also provide a degree of empirical, not experimental—the distinction is important—support for some principles.

I will address three classical recommendations of clinical theory, ones often seen as straitjackets to sound psychotherapy practice, dismissed or disdained rather than respected. These recommendations are caricatured in the picture of the silent analyst and countless jokes. One of my earliest supervisees—herself a most talented clinician—told me that her analyst's consulting room was darkened to near invisibility. Freud's descriptions of his own practice, and the several published reports by his patients, show a therapist ignoring his very own strictures and recommendations. He fed a patient, went for walks and vacationed with them, even recommended which woman to marry (in his "treatment" of Ferenczi). Freud treated his daughter, and she treated her nephew and the children of friends. Freud's housekeeper routinely provided tea and cookies in the waiting room. Abstinence, anonymity, and neutrality were, in fact, first offered by Freud, e.g., with his surgeon and telephone receiver metaphors, to create a professional public image and to prevent what we now refer to as boundary crossings, another example of which—Jung's romance with his student Sabina Spielrein—is dramatically if erroneously portrayed in the film "A Dangerous Method."

There is a clear rationale for observing what is now thought of as an austere psychoanalytic stance; the "projective hypothesis." Based on the idea that all perception combines sensory characteristics of the object and the psychology of the perceiver, it follows that the more ambiguous a stimulus, the more the reported percept will reflect the perceiver's inner life. Hermann Rorschach's inkblots and Henry Murray's TAT are two venerable tests based on the projective hypothesis. In "standard" psychoanalysis, to the extent that the focus is on the patient's inner life, an analyst would aim to minimize active participation. This approach is referred to these days, usually disparagingly, as "one-person" psychology. Even for those who lean toward this technical stance, however, contemporary technique places great weight on countertransference. It is simultaneously a one- and two-person method.

Over 70 years ago, Sullivan's interpersonal theory rejected the austere model, as did others, collectively called neo-Freudians. Mitchell and Greenberg inaugurated relational psychoanalysis in 1983 as a paradigm to compete with the then-mainstream Ego Psychology of Anna Freud, Heinz Hartmann, David Rapaport, and Arlow and Brenner. In more recent decades, the idea of "two-person" has become ascendant in the United States—in what is now described as a pluralistic psychoanalytic world. Even within "old school," the "transference-countertransference matrix" is a central tenet of clinical work; our own Richard Gottlieb used that phrase to describe the dominant perspective of the last 20 years.

Leo Rangell's "total composite psychoanalytic theory," on which I base my own flexible Freudianism, is inclusive. Differences in practice remain for future research and theory to resolve. Psychoanalytic practice has evolved from a "one-person" psychology to one more consistent with Freud's own interactionism: Human development as a bio-psychosocial-cultural-ecological process with relative contributions from each domain in what Freud called a "complemental series." My own psychoanalytic training emphasized continuum, rather than either/or, in which constitution interacts with experiential domains. This principle applies to the therapy process just as it applies to all aspects of human behavior.

That said, I will make a case for relative abstinence, anonymity, and neutrality, providing what I hope are cogent clinical examples to support these technical recommendations. I doubt that my arguments will settle the matter—but I believe they speak to Kaplan's and my own flexible Freudianism.

Abstinence

The classic definition of psychoanalytic abstinence is that neither patient nor analyst gain direct gratification from the work, a most austere statement—one that is impossible to defend in the extreme. There is, however, an alternate extreme: Dr. Feelgood, whose direct aim is to make the patient feel good, and to become enriched in the process.

Austerity and indulgence are also seen as negative polarities in child-rearing. Life experience from birth to death includes both gratification and frustration. An infant's needs—physical and psychological—must be satisfied; yet, as Harlow's monkeys showed, without frustration there is no achievement of maturity. Like Justice Potter Stewart's formulation, we know pornography when we see it, and we know overindulgence when we see it.

That last statement is ironic: relative gratification is in the eye of the beholder; we are back to subjectivity, which is better than caricature. Degrees of abstinence and gratification are matters of clinical judgment and personal-history-based character.

Anonymity

The blank screen is its clearest metaphor, an impossible standard. Even before Google, our professional credentials and history could be known. Office décor reveals something of our taste, our character, or both. National or regional accents are discernable. Wardrobe communicates an aesthetic. Even in a darkened room, we are not totally anonymous. We reveal ourselves, as do patients, from the first phone contact, a matter Robert Langs discussed in an early book. Initial impressions have some validity; to the extent that our patient is realistic, much about us is discernable. Some will have more accurate impressions, others less. This may indicate something about their perceptiveness. The opposite extreme is the exhibitionistic therapist who, rationalized as being a role model, narcissistically acts as if the patient should be like him or her.

My response to a patient seeking personal information: acknowledge the wish and explain that the patient's task is to say whatever comes to mind, and to deal with the problems saying it. Mine is to say what I hope will be useful.

Neutrality

Anna Freud's is considered the classic definition: the analyst should be an abstraction, equidistant between id, ego and superego. Currently, technical neutrality refers to not taking sides in the patient's life decisions: who to marry, what job to take, etc. Non-judgmental relating is a central tenet for Rogerian client-centered therapy as well as for psychoanalysis. Like abstinence and anonymity, it is impossible to be fully neutral. Even if we don't respond overtly, patients might discern our view—or may project theirs onto us. The extreme alternative includes "doctor knows best" therapy. In psychoanalytic therapy, however—as distinct from traditionally-practiced psychoanalysis—expressing judgment may be important, even necessary. Here I speak to the assessment of patients who may need us to provide prosthetic ego or superego functions. But I also recall a situation in which a patient told me that she believed her behavior was "morally reprehensible" and asked how I could disagree. Didn't I have value commitments that would condemn her multiple adulteries? And if so, how could I not be judgmental? My response: "Yes, we share a common culture and will agree that certain activities are immoral. It is my job to do my best to see things from your perspective: you can't help but behave as you do, and also to feel guilty and engage in self-punishment. Our work may lead you to behave differently by virtue of your own judgment." This patient was satisfied with my response. Another might not be.

The tightrope we walk is fairly represented by a paper by Stefano Fajrajzen. Presenting it initially at the Rome Psychoanalytic Center in 1973, and reprinted with a contemporary discussion (2014, pp 997-993), Fajrajzen argued that analytic neutrality must conflict with the "compulsion to judge." If we are involved with our patient as we must be, we are bound to veer from neutrality; if we don't judge, we are not involved enough to be a felt presence.

With each of these strictures we have an apparently insoluble conflict. Like most of Freud's "principles" they are not absolutes, though his writing style sometimes makes them seem so. The mirror, the receiving instrument and the surgeon are three of the technical metaphors in conflict with a meaningful bond between analyst and patient, an affective bond that is almost always necessary for therapeutic effect.

With each patient our stance oscillates between austerity and indulgence, anonymity and disclosure, judgment and neutrality. Our aim is to oscillate in resonance with our understanding of our patient from session to session and moment to moment. That resonance is far from perfect. To help any patient it must be good enough. There is and can be no formula.

Comments on Arnold D. Richards:
The Danger of Ideology

March 5, 2015

First let's acknowledge Arnold Richards's Brill lecture on "the politics of exclusion," later published (JAPA, 1999), and his multiple decades leading a politics of inclusion that is slowly bearing fruit within his two home organizations. Let's also acknowledge Herbert Peyser's talks on Max Weber and large group dynamics.

My vision of psychoanalysis has it as a paradigm serving three masters: the healing arts, science, and the history of ideas; these epistemological domains have validity criteria both congruent and conflicting. Richards gets much of the science argumentation right. I also argue that psychoanalysis is science. My research training promoted theories as heuristics, to be judged only by their usefulness; never as ideologies; and that reification of theoretical constructs was always to be avoided. Brenner could discard Id, Ego and Superego; I cannot do without this model in my clinical thinking and teaching—but only as a useful metaphor, not as concrete entities.

Richards's focus on NYPSI and APsaA is understandable but limited. The most popular Freudian Society supervisor, the late Irving Steingart, argued successfully against affiliating with APsaA, citing its abysmal record of stewardship and attempted sole ownership of psychoanalysis in the US. It was in 2014 that I learned of my own eligibility for NYPSI membership; that bylaw change remains unpublicized.

Human organizations have power dynamics and are always at risk of oligarchy, ideology, and corruption. The current publicity over the American Psychological Association's highly questionable behavior regarding torture—with psychoanalysts and Division 39 the leading critics—is another sad example. European, South American and independent IPA institutes in the US have very different histories and cultures than APsaA and NYPSI; none is without these and other problems, though many are more inclusive.

Worldwide psychoanalysis is currently caught up in a generative maelstrom of competing ideas, even within APsaA and its institutes, with a creativity that may come to equal that of the pioneering generation. American versions of Bionian and Lacanian thought are prominent in psychoanalytic debate. Who knows where the discussion may lead?

The crisis of psychoanalysis, at least in the US, is very real. One commentator identified the "mental health industrial complex" as the true enemy, and he called on psychoanalytic therapists to declare war on Big Pharma, the insurance industry, and superficial "positive psychology," rather than fighting among ourselves. "Freud the father" provides shadow and light. I agree with Richards that the light is worth preserving and fighting for, and we should be grateful for his persistent leadership and for continuing to move this important discussion forward.

Discussion of Sy Gers' Paper:
On a Revised Standard Edition of Freud's Work

January 19, 2016

Sy Gers's paper is a *cri de coeur*, albeit a cry in the wilderness. Two new English translations of Freud are now underway: Adam Phillips is general editor of the New Penguin Classics translations of Freud's writings, while Mark Solms is lead editor of a Revised Standard Edition. Most of us recall two earlier, competing English versions of Freud, the first by A.A. Brill and the second—and winner of the popularity contest—by the Strachey team. There is no question that economics is a consideration—but in a positive sense; commercial success relies on adequate demand.

It was only recently that I learned why the Strachey volumes were called "Standard." Remy Amouroux, in a 2011 paper translated from the French (and funded—not coincidentally—by the CP Snow Memorial Fund) wrote of the failed attempt to republish the *Gessamelte Werke* for at least two decades following Hitler's book burning. Despite considerable effort, with no German-speaking customers, the project was not economically viable. A standard edition, the Standard Edition, had to be produced in English, the common language of Freud readers post-World War II.

I've come to appreciate Sy's perspective on clinical matters. As he puts it: what goes on in the here and now exchange between patient and therapist is the essential vehicle of therapeutic action. Where he and I differ is on the relevance of theory, metapsychology, philosophy, even neurology and other disciplines. From my perspective, our difference can be boiled down to what I take as his claim to primacy of the affective exchange, especially non-verbal communication, and his implicit (and sometimes explicit) disparagement of other dimensions of the treatment process . My difference with Sy also reflects a difference with many here whose focus is exclusively clinical, while my understanding of the psychoanalytic paradigm is also about a science of mind, and the history of ideas.

Do we need a new translation—or two? This question requires much more than a yes-or-no reply. Sy praises Freud's "thinking and ideas" but says his genius "does not depend on his words." But how else could we know about his thinking and ideas? No serious reader questions Freud's literary achievement, for which he won the Goethe prize. Though many of Freud's statements are wrong, his ideas—expressed in words—have generated ongoing discourse, not only in mental health disciplines, but in several fields of arts and letters, and they have earned translation in the world's major languages. Freud's language is more evocative than definitive—and continues to be useful for clinical work, for science and for the history of ideas.

Translation is always interpretation; the two words are often used synonymously. Diplomats employ interpreters who, in fact, translate. Every language conveys meaning within its linguistic culture; some meaning may be lost in translation, but new audiences are gained; these audiences then participate in, and contribute to, Freudian discourse. Sy's critique brings to mind Justice Antonin Scalia's reading the Constitution for "original intent," while cabinet meeting records from the Washington Administration show that the document's authors couldn't recall the precise meaning of the words crafted by the Constitutional Convention. Freud himself frequently added footnotes in German to clarify his intent, or to revise a passage when his own thoughts were modified by further thinking and observation. Heinz Hartmann claimed to understand his own ideas better after reading David Rapaport's translation.

I teach Freud papers to novice therapists who struggle, especially with theoretical papers, concerned as they are with finding immediate utility for their work with patients. The criticism that theory and practice are unrelated, repeated for decades, is simply a canard. I reread papers before each class and make different underscores as I find new emphases relevant to my current patients. But my students have a problem beyond the conceptual and practical; Strachey's language is old-fashioned. The 23 volumes were published from 1953 to 1964, the index and bibliography in 1974, and the Concordance in 1984; for new readers, the Strachey translation is stilted. There is an entire sub-literature of scholarly dispute over the wording of his translation. The word most challenged is "instinct" for the German word "trieb," even addressed by Strachey himself in the Editor's Introduction to Volume 1. Bruno Bettelheim wrote about the loss of Freud's Germanic sensibility in the Standard Edition, for Bettelheim the very soul of the work.

Several English versions of the Bible followed the King James Protestant English standard. There are several Torah translations in English, the Reconstructionist version produced 25 years ago by my Brandeis classmate, Rabbi Arthur Green. Homer, Sophocles and Virgil have been retranslated into English several times over and to acclaim, likewise other Athenian immortals. A recent psychoanalytic paper discussed cultural issues in the Chinese Freud translation. How many of us would get through Chaucer in Middle English? A Revised Standard Edition project underscores Freud's importance in the History of Ideas, and aims to bring those ideas to readers in today's idiom.

Why Mark Solms? This scientist-practitioner-scholar has a personal charisma that, in addition to his own research, has brought him to prominence far beyond his South African homeland. He has been named research chair of the International Psychoanalytical Association and is a founder/leader of the cognate discipline of neuro-psychoanalysis. Strachey was the leader of a team of British literati/psychoanalysts; Mark Solms also leads a team. I was concerned when I learned that Adam Phillips was general editor of the new Penguin translation. Phillips knows no German, and his writing seems more self-advertisement than about psychoanalysis, while Solms clearly respects Freud. Solms is a member of his country's landed gentry. His economic circumstances may allow him availability for this project. I trust Solms to bring his intelligence, honesty and dedication to this project. It should be no surprise, though, that two necessarily different translations are in the works.

Sy prefers Solms's new ideas to his retranslation project. Solm's new ideas, though arguable, are welcome. But Freud's words matter. His evolution—in words—is a model of scientific attitude, with new observations generating better attempts to understand his subject. Words have connotations as well as denotations; they are evocative, metaphorical and ambiguous, only occasionally—though importantly—are they definitive. We debate words with words to find their meaning. How can we separate words from thoughts? Sy emphasizes non-verbal communication; none of us denies its importance. But ours is a "talk therapy," and non-verbal communication is even less precise and definitive. Sy's pressing for the non-verbal attacks a straw man; we get it. Our therapies depend, nonetheless, on language. Non-verbal communication between mother and infant may not require translation; patients' gestures often must be translated into words. For Brenner, psychoanalysis is the study of "Mind and Meaning." Non-verbal behavior is meaningful; verbal behavior is meaningful. Words matter. Metaphors matter. Translations matter.

In 1942, Susanne Langer (pp 26-27) wrote:

The importance of symbol-using, once admitted, soon becomes paramount in the study of intelligence. It has lent a new orientation especially to genetic psychology, which traces the growth of the mind: for this growth is paralleled, in large measure, by the observable uses of language, from the first words in infancy to the complete self-expression of maturity. There is an increasing rapprochement between philology and psychology—between the science of language and the science of what we do with language.

I expect the Revised Standard Edition will be marketable and useful. I doubt there will be a new "concordance;" scholars will likely cross-reference their citations. I also believe future translations will be produced as we continue to plumb the mind of this genius for meaning about the minds of our patients, and for our continuing attempts to map the mind. A contemporary translation will serve as standard until it is again revised; a final definitive translation seems highly unlikely.

I thank Sy for providing an opportunity to discuss these issues.

Clinical Applications of Freud's Theory

April 6, 2017

Regular psychotherapy conferences at Mount Sinai provide stimulation for my own clinical work and teaching. A recent exchange initiated this paper. A colleague told me he wanted to discuss his work toward a fully biological theory of mind and to compare it with "the Freudian model." Which model did he mean? 1895? 1896, 1916, or 1926? 1940? His retort, properly: "Today's."

One of the strengths and simultaneous difficulties of Freud's thought is that it is not a singular model, but several: a theory of mind, a clinical theory and a developmental theory most prominent among others. One generative aspect of Freudian thought is its openness to revision. Today's model includes what Martin Bergmann (1993) called "extensions, modifications and heresies," and defies easy summary. Freud's posthumously published "Outline" (1938a) was not an organized summary, and the years since have seen deconstruction, reconstruction, and expansion of the paradigm. This history is not unfortunate; it is instead responsive to the challenges of new findings about the human mind/brain, its environmental context, excellent clinical papers and theoretical proposals, as well as data derived from systematic research. The expansion of the paradigm helps therapists to listen more creatively. Theodore Reik's metaphor "listening with the third ear" (1948) could be extended to perhaps 17 ears... and counting.

Conflicting demands of intimacy and deprivation in our clinical work are essential for understanding the practice, but problematic for teaching technique. One guide was Leo Stone (1954), considered a radical at his institute at the time. Stone's work was central in my training and to my own evolution. The technique course at the Freudian Society was correctly called "Theory of Technique." Psychoanalytic therapies have neither scripts nor sets of rules; they have theory.

I've spoken and written about differences between traditional psychoanalysis, the intensive couch-based approach, and psychoanalytically informed therapies, usual referred to as "psychodynamic." Freud's alloy metaphor (1919) was about offering treatment to the masses. It is misunderstood as a watering down: metal alloys are created for their strength; for us, alloys extend the range of our work by being cost-effective.

Freud's several theories comprise a psychological paradigm, not solely a clinical method. My recent papers have focused on psychoanalysis as science; it is more welcome these days as a theory of culture within the humanities and the history of ideas, so-called "applied psychoanalysis." I say "so called" because I consider treatment the most important application of the paradigm. Freud has become part of our educated Western culture. "Anal" is a common, accurately understood personality descriptor. Like Moliere's Bourgeois Gentleman, we're surprised to realize we're speaking prose—or thinking Freud.

Since my graduate school days over 50 years ago, I've heard the canard that there is little relationship between psychoanalytic theory and practice. That rap is also about the inapplicability of psychoanalytic treatment to contemporary clinical problems. Alas, this understanding of psychoanalytic treatment comes from the rigid model experienced decades ago at the New York Psychoanalytic Institute (NYPSI), among the then-exclusively medical institutes. It ignores the last half century evolution of clinical theory and practice, both outside those institutes, and even within them.

Psychoanalytic practice has been extended since August Aichhorn's "Wayward Youth" (1925), an application to education and therapy for teens, accompanied by Anna Freud's and Melanie Klein's extensions to treatment of children. Group and family therapies began as extensions of the psychoanalytic paradigm and continue to be influenced by it. Even explicitly non-psychoanalytic therapies make extensive use of renamed ideas, usually without acknowledgment (Bornstein, 1999). Daniel Kahneman's Nobel-winning work on irrationality with his late research partner Amos Twersky (1979) is a tacit elaboration of a Freudian idea. We all speak prose dialects!

I strongly support systematic empirical research on psychoanalytic treatments, and I've lectured about several such programs. The Columbia program, led by Barbara Milrod and Frederic Busch, uses RCTs (randomized controlled trials), and has softened my critique of them. Their RCTs are manualized but not scripted, using blind inter-rater reliability to assess procedural homogeneity.

I give mixed reviews to many clinical presentations. Understandably, discussion focuses on the case material, often with 20 or more different opinions, while avoiding the ideas behind the treatment. That's fine when a presenter asks for help. In supervising, I emphasize that even a novice knows much more about the patient than the supervisor—or anyone else. Speculative group free association aims at opening a therapist's mind to additional ways of listening, some of which might be relevant to the case, and is the rationale for small clinical study groups.

Publication of clinical work raises several complications, among them the matter of confidentiality versus the distortions of disguising the material. I deleted clinical material from this written report; what follows instead are the issues raised by the presented paper and the group discussion that followed, with my comments on some psychoanalytic practices and principles.

1. How much time is a session? 50 minutes, 45, double sessions, marathons, frequency variation, and Jacques Lacan's short sessions are among the answers. Answers are provided by common practice, rather than systematic research. IPA now accepts a thrice-weekly model, pioneered by the French; the recent acceptance of the White Institute now takes 3-5 sessions as a new APsaA standard; debate continues. Like other psychoanalytic issues, there is no universal formula, but practice changes: we don't hear much about marathons anymore, and Lacan's truncated sessions not only got him kicked out of IPA, these days no one reports following that method of his practice.

2. One colleague said some clinical interventions seemed like "propaganda:" The problem of suggestion and authority began with Freud's own discussion and continues unabated. The concept of "working alliance" is one proposed corrective. It is recognized that therapeutic neutrality cannot be absolute. I do my best to avoid advising about life choices, but often offer direction regarding in-session conduct: I ask patients to associate and remind them frequently. I suggest they pay attention to my comments when they prefer to ignore them. How much of this is based on professional authority (one basis for charging a fee), and how much might feel coercive, varies with each patient. We are asked to help people change their behavior, feelings, symptoms. People change in a variety of ways! Autonomy is one of our major goals.

3. A presenter in my group spoke of "lulling" and compared it with active confrontation. Both are part of the psychoanalytic repertory. We "Accept, don't settle," according to Laurence Friedman (1988). Winnicott and Bion offer the container model for a therapist. Psychoanalytic confrontation is neither violence nor aggression, but the presentation of external reality in the face of pathological denial. Psychoanalytic therapies have many moments, and an array of useful interventions. I'm reminded of Edward Glover's 1938

survey of technique in the British Psychoanalytic Society, to which 25 of the 29 members responded. I also recall the paper by Kurt Eissler (IRP, 1974) on payment of fees, and styles of technique, a lengthy discourse that speaks clearly to the range of legitimate psychoanalytic approaches. (Eissler, remembered for his supposed rigidity, spoke at a large meeting sponsored by the Freudian Society, saying he regretted his term "parameters," as stultifying what should be a more flexible technique.)

4. Is there still a psychoanalytic taboo on the use of questions? Stanley Olinick wrote two fine papers on potential pitfalls of questioning (1954, 1957); Eissler stated there has never been an analysis without them. For Sullivan, recently "made kosher" but always a guilty pleasure for Freudians, questioning is a basic and frequent intervention. Edward Bibring (1954) wrote about the varieties of technical intervention, the most important distinction being those aimed at raising anxiety and those hoping to reduce it. The former predominate in more traditional treatments, the latter are never absent but are used more in primarily supportive approaches. The "silent analyst" has always been a caricature, though silence itself is an important and useful part of technique.

5. Hans Loewald (1960) promoted the idea of the analyst as "new object." Roy Schafer focused alternatively on theories of internalization. Modeling and promoting imitation are not explicit psychoanalytic techniques, though patients often use them, with or without our awareness. Analysts are likely to raise questions when they notice.

6. One member of my group is consistent in avoiding any theory. I do not question his clinical work, but I ask: How do we know and explain what we're doing in what he calls simply "the back and forth" of the therapy relationship? Theory, thought about between sessions, can help provide answers for self-assessment, for teaching, and for what we might lend an ear in a subsequent session.

Freud's 1923 structural theory (Id, Ego, and Superego) can provide a strategy. Attention to Transference and Resistance was his briefest statement of criteria for psychoanalytic treatment. Among the Kleinians, Strachey's superego psychology focused on the centrality of transference interpretation for therapeutic effect. Contemporary Freudians rely more on Nathan Leites's 1977 paper "Transference Only?" to say we need more interventions. Psychoanalysis aims to promote self-knowledge as a means for therapeutic action.

Clinical Differences:
Comments on the Work of Others and My Own

April 26, 2018

I make a clinical presentation on a Thursday each spring. Most often I provide material from my own work that seems relevant to a larger clinical issue. Today I will discuss recent clinical presentations by others and speak more fully to the issues presented than I could at the time. Our meetings stimulate many of my own papers; recently I made several presentations on the philosophy of science. Today's will be something of a potpourri and will include case material from my current practice. My hope is to evoke discussion of the issues. Though some of my comments are critical, I respect each of those I cite.

The idea for this talk followed immediately on a case report of an 84-year-old man with obsessional jealousy, a case for which a colleague and I were asked to prepare separate comments based only on the write-up of his initial consultation.

Hillel Swiller had taken a good history of a man whose mental status was normal and physical health good. He had a diagnostic impression of OCD, recommended meds combined with CBT and dynamic psychotherapy. Meds were refused; therapy accepted.

My colleague's prepared comments suggested a treatment approach focused on the patient's thoughts. My commentary supported the recommendation for open-ended exploration and suggested the possibility of a quick remission. Others speculated on possible dynamics: one asked how the symptom serves the patient and suggested asking for masturbation fantasies; others suggested a homoerotic dynamic; still others wanted to know more about the patient's history, relationships, and his affect. Some focused on countertransference. My colleague added, as did most others, that she needed to know more. I was most surprised by one definitive diagnosis: Obsessive Disorder, and treatment of choice: exposure therapy.

After all comments were heard, Swiller reported that in the next session or one shortly thereafter, the patient addressed his current situation and his symptom disappeared—as I'd suggested it might. Having "cured" this man, Swiller's anxiety about the case also remitted. With his usual theoretical promiscuity, Swiller had been ready to learn exposure therapy, but then returned to a default position of "Don't talk; don't do," a reasonable takeaway from this case, though a caricature of psychodynamic psychotherapy.

My subsequent thinking was about the contrast between the definitive diagnosis and treatment plan (Obsessive Disorder and exposure therapy), with most of the other speculations that would lead to further exploration rather than any quick conclusion and focus. My additional thoughts were about the commonality of the wish for quick fixes. In the days of psychoanalytic hegemony, psychoanalysts might dismiss these patients; the current psychoanalytic approach assumes the quick fix wish to be defensive, while using active listening in a consultation phase to see if the person might become a patient.

I also thought about Swiller's half-joking expression of envy of this patient's wealthy lifestyle. If this man hangs out with billionaires, my countertransference reaction might be hostile. Unless accompanied by serious discomfort that could allow for reflection on character issues, I would doubt my ability to help. "Masters of the Universe" don't often show neurotic guilt; many are amoral. I'd have seen this patient for an extended consultation and be glad he was quickly done with me. His dramatic remission exemplified an early Freudian discovery, to wit, that a symptom could result from avoiding consciousness of guilt while conscious acknowledgment could lead to dramatic remission.

Let me return to the Obsessive Disorder diagnosis. Is an obsessive thought or even a compulsive act sufficient to make a diagnosis? Is exposure therapy to be quickly recommended when many motivated patients are unwilling to subject themselves to that rigorous regimen? Studies report exposure therapy dropout rates ranging as high as 40%. I know this doctor to be a most thoughtful clinician, taking careful histories, and with what I think of as a "therapeutic personality." People feel better talking with him because of his very manner. Why the quickest and most definitive response to this initial session?

I've seen a man in his mid-50's for four months. He's caught in a love triangle, suffering intense anxiety and guilt because his paramour is pressing him to choose her, or break it off. His wife (and mother of their children) has always ignored his frequent dalliances, so long as he kept them from her. His problem is "he loves the girl he's near." He cannot stick with a decision because he wants both, as in the

1953 Alec Guinness movie "The Captain's Paradise." My patient was on medication well before seeing me, and—at his request—is now monitored by a colleague of mine. He believes medication enables him to work effectively and hopes to wean himself from it. I'm actively listening, and he seems committed to the work we do twice weekly. I hope to learn today how CBT might help this man.

Another colleague made a clinical presentation recently that included verbatim notes from sessions. It was asked how such detailed notes can be taken while engaged in the presumed psychoanalytic stance of "evenly hovering attention." An excellent question. Taking notes surely distracts some from evenly hovering attention while being an invaluable tool for precision supervision—and the case was supervised. Psychoanalysts know that whatever we do in treatment is imperfect—and might even be problematic. In this case, the conflict is between an ideal listening stance and highly accurate process notes. Both cannot be fully satisfied at the same time. Analytic listening is compromised but not eliminated. Other aspects of the colleague's stance (patience/expectant technique, non-judgmental positive regard) allow for a good enough result, despite the shortcoming in one technical ideal. Leo Rangell, my favorite theorist after Freud, criticized others for *pars pro toto* thinking—creating theory that overemphasized one aspect of theory, e.g., Kohut's empathy, rather than accepting complexity and conflict among many relevant concepts and issues.

During the reported treatment, the patient's parents divorced but this matter was not addressed by the therapist, who thought the matter of lesser importance than more internal issues. Hillel Swiller strongly disagreed with not focusing on the marital schism. True to his commitment as a physician-healer, Swiller prefers active intervention, though that might sometimes move him further away from his own conclusion: "shut up and do nothing." Here again two ideals (active healing, respectful listening) might conflict, and are used in different proportions by different therapists. Emphasizing one or another might make little difference—or possibly all the difference in the world.

Related general questions arise: Among several issues brought up by any patient (directly or otherwise), how do we decide which to address, and when? A psychologist-psychoanalyst from Chicago posted a comment on a professional listserv. It was about a long-term case in which alcohol use seemed to qualify as somewhere along the spectrum of abuse, yet the topic had not been part of the therapeutic conversation. J thought about the implications of the therapist's addressing the issue. Not to mention it suggests a certain kind of neutrality and fidelity to the potential transference focus of therapy was preserved, but at the cost of ignoring the alcohol problem, perhaps colluding in keeping it out of the therapy. On the other hand, had the therapist made it part of the explicit therapeutic conversation, there would be a different transference dynamic than if the therapist continued to say nothing about the client's drinking. J opined that either approach had psychodynamic pluses and minuses. And of course, there is also countertransference either way. All therapists have a "personal therapeutic approach." This doctor would not overlook an obvious substance use problem, just as we should also address divorce. These are therapeutic choices with psychodynamic impacts. These considerations extend to any role the therapist takes; for example, within a psychodynamic frame assigning homework, doing relaxation training/guided imagery/biofeedback, referring the client to a couples therapist or a psychopharmacologist. As a profession, we have no effective way to adjudicate these matters; where research exists, it is of limited value. We discuss them—and this presentation is one attempt to have that kind of discussion.

First Principles

The issue of self-disclosure used to be a controversial topic. It was postulated as a striking alternative to abstinence, anonymity, and neutrality, central principles of psychoanalytic technique. Of many technical recommendations these three set an idealized and false standard of the psychoanalytic stance, contributing to the caricature of the too-silent analyst. This caricature may have been part of the training regimen of early generations of analysts, especially at the then-exclusively medical institutes, but was not the case during my own analytic training begun nearly 50 years ago.

The principle of abstinence meant that analysts were not to use patients for the gratification of their own needs. It was introduced in reaction to what are now considered boundary violations by early pioneers, Jung and Ferenczi prominent among them. It was never meant to suggest that analysts should not enjoy their work.

The purpose of the principle of anonymity in psychoanalytic treatments is to maximize the understanding of transference. All perception is determined by the stimulus and the psychology of the perceiver. As a matter of technique, to the extent the analyst is an ambiguous stimulus (like a Rorschach inkblot), the patient's response can reveal aspects of the psychology of the perceiver. Transference is ubiquitous; it is equated today with subjectivity. In ordinary situations it is simply "personality." The psychoanalytic situation and its variants study individual subjectivity/personality by urging the analyst to be an ambiguous stimulus.

This has been caricatured. During my training, the analytic relationship was considered to have three aspects: an ambiguous transference screen, a therapeutic alliance, and an interpersonal reality—all wrapped up in one person. Nathan Leites's 1977 article "Transference Analysis Only?" summarized the already standard psychoanalytic answer: "Of course not." But whatever we do or don't do, say or don't say, affects our patients. And we do want to affect their perception of us as real people, as people worth joining in a therapeutic alliance, and as a somewhat ambiguous figure on whom to project their fantasies.

The principle of neutrality, like much in psychoanalytic thought, has an extensive literature, also subject to caricature. Neutrality is a technical posture in psychoanalysis and its derivative therapies without being absolute. How could it be? We have opinions and values, convictions, and biases; we also have professional standards. Freud went so far as to say our patients should be "of good character" (1905), but that is surely a subjective standard. Leo Stone's "widening scope" approach (1954) is more common among psychoanalysts. Neutrality means we try not to take sides in the patient's life choices: who to marry, where to live, what job to take and the like. I told my love triangle patient that I would not weigh in on which woman he should leave, but that it was unlikely he could hold them both. After going back and forth one time too many, his paramour left him. We may have an opinion, of course, but a more important principle is promoting the patient's sense of agency and autonomy. Our opinions about the treatment situation are another matter. I will or won't suggest the use of the couch, and following whichever posture I suggest, I will try to elicit the patient's expression of thoughts and feelings about my suggestion.

We are always self-revealing. When I complained about not knowing some facts about my own analyst, he correctly pointed out that I knew a great deal about him: his way of relating, his character. Even in the world before Google, I knew many facts about him.

None of us is a blank screen. Much of what we reveal is done without a specific decision to disclose this or that fact. The real question about self-disclosure has to do with what is deliberately disclosed. Psychoanalytic technique leans toward trying to understand a patient's request for information rather than providing direct answers, and generally eschews offering ourselves as role models. Being reliably present and prompt, speaking respectfully, smiling and laughing, are among the personal habits that can serve as models for some patients without being specific techniques.

Brenner and Stone debated in mid-century whether one should answer where the analyst was going on vacation. Brenner, clear as always, said no. Stone suggested that with some patients, "upstate" or "the seashore" would be ambiguous enough. The psychoanalytic issue would remain; what is the meaning for the patient of the non-response or non-specific response. The therapeutic issue would rest on clinical judgment of the patient's needs in the moment.

In my view, this is neither intuitive nor planned. I call it the "educated spontaneous response." Spontaneous because we need to say something or nothing in the moment, and educated because we know something about how to do the work, and equally important we have a sense of the patient (or couple, or family, or group). Our replies depend mostly on our experience of doing the work and our experience with this person. And, of course, our responses are subject to error. With some patients the errors will matter a lot, with others very little if at all.

My own routine disclosures are about what goes on in the room: I explain my method, often responding to a patient's question about why I said something. I don't want the method to be experienced as mysterious; it is enough that it is felt to be different from non-psychoanalytic conversations.

I'm treating a young man who came in on advice of his lawyer, while facing criminal charges. Deliberate self-disclosure would describe much of what I say to him lately in this twice-weekly face-to-face psychoanalytic psychotherapy. Research findings are minimal; nor is there a clinical evidence base for this kind of case. The meager literature suggests success is unlikely. We've been working for 21 months, and, having resolved the criminal charges with a misdemeanor plea, his participation is no longer compulsory; he has become interested in our work. The self-disclosures I make, beyond explaining my interventions, are of experiences from various stages of my life, and specific points where he and I agree or disagree on a philosophical or political position. In this case I'm offering a caring and responsible father-figure, since this man's mother lost custody early on to a father for whom "negligent" would be a generous description. There is nothing in this that is heretical to psychoanalytic psychotherapy. I'd likely do less of it if we were in a more intense traditional psychoanalysis.

A recent presentation on "Non-Obvious Treatments of Depression" offered techniques none of which would be my first-line approach. Resistance and transference were Freud's reply when asked for a summary of psychoanalytic treatment focus. For psychoanalysts, all patients are resistant. Some may have intractable symptoms. We don't keep repeating interventions that fail; clinical judgment and creativity make for new interventions that might succeed. If we keep failing, the patient leaves. If not, we ask why the patient keeps returning.

After the presentation, I learned of a patient who came each week for a year with no improvement, then suddenly had a remission that lasted. The patient was voting with her feet while something was going on (in the therapy or in life) that made for a surprising cure. Analysts would want to know why, of course, but a patient is not required to satisfy our curiosity.

Freud's concept of the Unconscious requires us to accept ignorance. Our task is to engage in a mutual search. Should the patient ally with us in exploration, the ego will be strengthened by that very engagement. Any "standard technique" is for teaching or research; from a psychoanalytic perspective, no treatment will strictly follow any such "standardization." Boundaries may be crossed, but each of us decides our own boundaries, and what counts as a crossing. Analysts invite a search for meaning for whatever occurs in the engagement. Boundary crossings are not necessarily boundary violations!

I choose to think of interventions not as cognitive or behavioral, but as ego psychological interventions to encourage thoughtfulness and judgment—ego functions frequently in need of attention. The psychoanalytic paradigm applied to treatment emphasizes a search process. We do not claim success with everyone. A recent paper on obesity was encyclopedic and full of important information. Obesity remains, however, a condition that rarely yields sustained success by any known methodology. In a presentation on an obese couple, we did not hear whether obesity was even addressed.

As to treatment failure, we heard a paper about Marilyn Monroe, followed by a dramatic reading from a play about her, a special case even among special cases. I doubt that success was possible for treating this woman—or in preventing her suicide. No *post hoc* test for suicide prevention exists; nor is there a possibility of controlled experiments, let alone randomized trials. Suicide prevention is successful, though: hotlines, therapy, medications have all contributed to reducing the incidence in populations. There remains, however, no standard of prevention or individual treatment. Kris and Greenson each recognized that Marilyn was unsuitable for traditional psychoanalysis. Marianne Kris hospitalized her, a move undone by Joe DiMaggio. Ralph Greenson provided near-residential treatment, available at any hour, even at his home. The first analyst, Margaret Hohenberg, seemed to work more interpretively, at least in the methodology of that time. This was likely a serious error, but Marilyn did not die on Hohenberg's watch.

Many analysts no longer make the distinction between traditional psychoanalysis as a method and psychoanalytically informed psychotherapy. I still find the distinction important, though there are surely gray areas. Marilyn was treated by psychoanalysts, not by psychoanalysis. Countertransference has been the most significant topic of technical attention for nearly thirty years; except as a taboo, this was hardly the case during Marilyn's short lifetime. We learn about these difficult cases as we try to learn about any psychological issue. None of it makes us able to claim success for all.

The essential characteristic of psychoanalytic therapies is listening. The primary task is to help a patient to speak as freely as possible. Some people do so readily and continue with minimal prompting until they say, "I don't know what else to say." Before that, prompts include the engaged, expectant look, varieties of "mm hmm," and clarifying questions. I introduce Freud's basic rule at the conclusion of consultation sessions: "Try your best to say whatever comes to mind, regardless of whether or not it seems to make sense." Subsequently, when patients feel they've run dry, I remind them of the rule, while acknowledging the impossibility of full compliance.

Listening is multifaceted. Extending Theodore Reik's well-known title, I call it "Listening with 17 Ears;" that number is arbitrary. From the first contact, I engage in free-floating attention to the words, the non-verbal presentation (especially affect), and to my own internal responses. Zvi Lothane calls this mutual free association. The essential difference between mine and the patient's is that I am mostly quiet, at least for a while.

If the person sitting opposite me is in visible distress, I would be more active— but the aim is the same: to relieve distress to promote additional speech and freer association.

This approach is flexible, and I find it to be nearly always effective as well for consultation. My consultations usually take two to four sessions for me to know enough to offer a recommendation. I don't know a person well enough in 50 minutes—yes, I still provide a 50-minute hour—to tell them much, other than to keep talking, until I have confidence that I've learned something about them that might be helpful. While assessing as I listen, I do not find diagnostic labels valuable. The image I've used recently in teaching is that of a large jigsaw puzzle: some pieces start to fit together, border pieces may firm up, a first central focus may come into view. This puzzle will never be complete, but it might offer good ideas for next steps. The puzzle is also subject to being shaken up, with the pieces landing in very different, sometimes more useful places. If treatment goes well, the patient and I develop increasing confidence that ideas we refine together over time are meaningful and helpful.

The late Swiss psychoanalyst Danielle Quinodoz wrote a remarkable book on traditional psychoanalysis for people over 80. On the rare chance that such a patient would be willing, it could be a very positive experience for both patient and doctor.

In a process group, I stated the notion that individual psychotherapy is about two ignorant people talking together, trying to learn as much as possible about one of them. A resident replied animatedly: "Why didn't they tell us this at the beginning?" The group agreed. This statement came to me in response to the report of the 84-year-old man discussed above. I must emphasize my view that we hardly ever know enough from the first session to do more than hope more material will be forthcoming. I believe the quick diagnosis and treatment plan offered was misguided, despite the medical training model and the desire of many patients.

In an initial session, I'm unlikely to address a person's history. I would note to myself whether they've lived a life with successful love, work and play, with an ego reasonably intact—or not.

A great deal may be learned in a single session, yet confusion is understandable. Few people develop obsessions of the kind this patient did in old age; the scant literature would not be helpful. I would likely have asked what type of therapy this man was hoping for; I would not have suggested medication and would certainly respect his refusal. I would have offered an ongoing exploration of the type Swiller recommended. I was not surprised that the obsession quickly remitted. A transference cure can be a therapeutic success.

I do not believe this patient had a successful life despite his riches, but I do believe he was of sound mind from a psychiatric perspective, having led a long life free from debilitating psychopathology. Despite my disclaimer about prediction, my idea about a transference cure possibility (regarding the symptom) was borne out. Specific symptoms frequently disappear after initial sessions. "Expectant technique" remains the best way to learn about someone. This patient was happy with symptom-relief, and that's fine with me.

60-plus years of empirical studies and even recently RCTs for psychodynamic treatments haven't influenced those who don't want to believe that psychoanalytic treatments are very often effective. When they work it is by trial and error, clinical titration of gratification (comfort, alliance) and frustration, challenge, and the search for meaning. Human systems are loosely bound; many errors are tolerated by some people, none by others. The different approaches presented are a mix of art and science: What we call art is when trial and error succeeds; the science is important, but necessarily always tentative and rarely applicable to an individual.

Psychoanalytic psychotherapy is neither a tool kit nor eclecticism. It is a coherent and integrated set of principles, flexibly used in responsive clinical practice. Unlike traditional couch-based, intensive psychoanalysis, it allows for providing auxiliary ego or superego functions and support for reality-based, reasonable wish-fulfillment. The reality principle has always been in trouble, but we cannot work unless we believe we have some connection to reality.

"Therapy Wars:" A Biased Commentary

June 25, 2019

My group was sent an essay "Therapy Wars: The Revenge of Freud" in January 2019, ten weeks in advance of a scheduled talk by Jonathan Shedler. The essay had appeared three years earlier in the prestigious British publication *The Guardian*. Oliver Berkman, the author, in engaging journalistic style, quoted critics of psychoanalysis. Since they use words like "scam" and "confidence trick," and make claims that psychoanalysis has "no posterity," it seems apt to call them "bashers."

Berkman addressed the "triumph" of CBT, his condensation of several short-term, actively focused non-drug alternatives to psychodynamic treatments. He described CBT's main thesis, did a quick summary of its history from Ellis to Beck, and noted that these therapies could now be administered by computer. He cited a patient complaint that a computer doesn't feel, and he introduced Jonathan Shedler, a leading "warrior" on Freud's behalf. Shedler's literature review showed CBT to fail long-term, a review central to his Grand Rounds presentation earlier at Mount Sinai, which disconcerted some in the audience—and even provoked complaints to our department chairman for allowing the talk to take place at all.

Evidence of complex unconscious processes, Berkman wrote, comes from the respectable field of neuroscience. For Berkman, its central finding—that the brain works far faster than consciousness can capture—undermines the basis for any cognitive-dominant approach. Berkman also dismissed psychoanalysis as science because of the uniqueness of patients, and the uniqueness of all people. He suggested that ignorance is the striking state of the mental health professions, and recommended modesty for therapists of all persuasions. The apparent paradox of resistance to voluntary treatment is, of course, a Freudian discovery; understanding resistance is a major focus of psychoanalytic therapies. Thus Berkman's subtitle: "the Revenge of Freud."

This essay uses "Wars" in its title because psychoanalysis, an incomplete, evolving theory of mind, has been under attack from the beginning. American psychology and psychiatry have each been disdainful of psychoanalysis in recent decades, in large measure for economic reasons. This gave Freud-bashers a great edge and has moved psychoanalytic therapies from their mid-20th Century dominance to a last resort; surely evidence of a battle, even a nearly-concluded war. Shedler is a general of an army in apparent retreat. Washington was such a general, retreating all the way to Cornwallis's 1781 surrender at Yorktown. My belief that psychoanalytic treatments will survive is supported by an anomalous situation in our own department. A so-called "triage" psychiatrist is employed here to meet with residents seeking therapy. Despite the minimal presence of psychoanalysis in the residency curriculum, referrals always go to a trained psychoanalyst.

Beyond the specifics that distinguish psychoanalytic therapies from structured and directive approaches, professional "wars" should not surprise us. Scientific status is also controversial within psychoanalysis. The French in particular, and some relational analysts, Irwin Hoffman prominent among them, eschew standard science criteria altogether, while major research groups continue to produce respectable studies. Marianne Leuzinger-Bohleber leads such a research group in Frankfurt; it has just published 3-year results of an ongoing longitudinal study, and Fredric Busch is a leader of the research program at Columbia.

We live in a world of conflict, often resulting in wars, cold and hot. Freud and Einstein corresponded in the 1930s about war; Freud also spoke of the "narcissism of small differences" leading to conflict between individuals, especially in intimate relationships. Ernst Kris defined psychoanalysis as the study of "human behavior viewed as conflict" (1947). The analytic paradigm aims to understand the human mind and its products. It remains incomplete, and its propositions have always been controversial. Controversy, conflict and even war seem "in the nature of the beast." It is also in our nature to seek conflict resolution—and love. "Thanatos" and "Eros" remain at war! Controversy is part of what keeps this work exciting for me.

Contrasting Psychotherapeutics

January 6, 2022

This essay was stimulated by a 2021 presentation on "Gottman Method Couples Therapy" in my group at Mount Sinai. I am grateful for my colleague's sharing her case notes with me, so I might approach accuracy in my characterizations. In my commentary at her presentation I praised her clarity of exposition but I remarked that there was nothing in the Gottman method that I would consider for my own practice. She explained their method and presented the case of a very difficult 10-year marriage. She acknowledged her skepticism about the Gottman approach, but—as has been a regularity in her presentations—she is always seeking new tools for helping those who seek her help. Despite her hesitancy, she studied the method well enough to teach us, and to conform her work to it with this difficult couple.

I'd also commented that I'd never heard of the Gottmans, underscoring a frequent observation I've made for many years: our entire field of "mental healthcare" exists in silos, not only between different therapy approaches, but within approaches: the several psychoanalytic organizations in New York have minimal overlapping attendance at their conferences. Silos hamper progress, even in the face of persistent, cogent efforts by promoters of psychotherapy integration like Paul Wachtel and Stanley Messer. I've noticed that silos seem also to exist in the "hard" sciences as well.

I will argue that striking schisms between approaches cannot be written off as "the narcissism of small differences," although this Freudian aphorism plays a part. IPTAR and the Freudian Society have no discernable conceptual differences and considerable overlap in membership, but they've rejected uniting in the 60-plus years since their founders withdrew from NPAP on ideological grounds.

One strength of the Mount Sinai group is that we do not split over differences. I learn from such differences, and have come to appreciate many treatment varieties, and especially the friendships we've made despite them. This is a tribute to our leaders, and I gather it is also the tone set by conference founder Aaron Stein.

As I understood the talk, the Gottman method has five phases: 1) Manualized Intake, 2) Establishing Trust, 3) the Physicality of Flooding, 4) The Perpetual Problem and its associated Dreams, and 5) Repair to reduce conflict (i.e., Stop Action). I find scripted psychotherapy anathema, but I was shocked with the claim that trust could be established in a few beginning sessions. We all expect initial rapport based on people having initiated contact and showing up: they know we are credentialled, and they can anticipate at least a modicum of relief talking about the upsetting matters that brought them in. It's likely we've all had *someone* not return for a second appointment, but that's a rare event. If the Gottmans called this phase "calm" or "comfort," I would not have been shocked, but trust is a complex psychological state with infantile roots, necessarily imperfect unless one is naïve or gullible—traits that would themselves attract our attention. We also often hear secrets revealed later in the treatment; some were consciously withheld precisely because we cannot expect deep trust until we are tested. In a basic sense, people cannot, do not, and should not trust others or themselves fully; secrets emerge in their own time in a sound therapy, often seemingly unbidden.

According to my colleague,

> Trust and Physiological Calm are the basics I am striving for at the beginning of each treatment. Why should a couple trust me, or this treatment or themselves to make change happen ... especially, since trust was the first thing that often had been eroded after the long stretch of marital strife. Or, after the traumatic discovery of an affair. The partners have lost trust in the safety of their relationship, have often lost trust in *deserving* a loving relationship, and they are now confronted with a therapist who is not known to them. They are also new to couples therapy and the triad dynamic.

She called it—correctly—a "sea of vulnerability, helplessness and mistrust."

It seems simply wrong to believe we can establish trust in a few meetings. We aim rather for a careful willingness to tolerate exposing pain to a stranger, and—in couples work—in the presence of the one seen as causing the pain.

The next phase is "flooding." Psycho-educational interventions are not excluded from psychoanalytic therapy but explaining physiology and its negative effects near the start of treatment seems like a distraction, intellectualized at best. Flooding often emerges early within treatment without assistance and can provide immediate cathartic effect. Abreaction can often provide some sense of relief and an eagerness to return. Freud's earliest theory saw abreaction as central to therapeutic effect, learning as he went on that its results were quite limited.

Phase Four—the Perpetual Problem and the Dreams that relate to it and should provide a pathway to Repair—sounds roughly like what analysts call individual or relational dynamics. When dreams were mentioned, I thought I'd hear something familiar, but instead "dream" is the Gottman word for wish, or conscious fantasy. It is not surprising that wishes and fantasies can conflict with reality, or with a partner's differing wishes. This exploratory phase seems too quickly concluded in the Gottman approach, and too readily satisfied with conscious and concrete wishes. For a psychoanalyst, this entire program could comprise an initial phase of what might evolve into a treatment process.

For a psychodynamic therapist, "repair" (or the reduction of conflict) would be where a therapeutic effect occurs. Psychoanalysts call that "working through," the repetitive and varied manifestation of a conflict that leads to depth in understanding. Co-morbid conditions having the potential to slow down or impair progress in the Gottman method, psychoanalytically oriented therapists would not think of marital strife as the sole focus of a treatment. "Co-morbid conditions"—a concept appropriate to necessarily-focused medical procedures should—in sound therapy—be addressed as integral to human intimate interaction. Psychoanalysts learned in the 1930s that psychological symptoms are generally embedded in the more stable mental structures that comprise the total personality or character, and that one or more of these co-morbid conditions could be relevant, or even at the core of a presenting problem.

I am grateful for more than the opportunity to rebut the Gottmans; that was easy. Writing this essay has led me to wonder why psychoanalytic thinking has been dismissed or ignored by so many. A sophisticated college classmate of mine, a retired English professor and award-winning poet, recently remarked that while he was a supporter of psychotherapy in general, he saw the psychoanalytic "protocol" as more ritualistic than useful, and he wondered how anyone could subscribe to it as a generalized treatment approach. I was taken aback by the word "protocol;" I'd never thought of even the intensive, couch-based approach as formulaic, a word nearly synonymous with "protocol." How have we allowed our work to be seen this way by highly educated people? The self-reflection required by a psychoanalytic orientation makes clear that the profession bears a heavy load of responsibility. Freud made a fetish of his isolation, eschewing bringing psychoanalysis to universities (a stance adopted generally in the United States, the Columbia Institute among too few exceptions). Freud also exiled dissidents, with separate lines of development only more recently welcomed back to psychoanalytic circles. The hubris of mid-century American psychoanalysis was elitist, demeaning many variations of therapy that have, nonetheless, thrived in the hurly-burly of American competition. The model was also purist, attacking deviations as "not psychoanalysis," berating Winnicott when he spoke at NYPSI. I've often repeated my rejection of the medical model for psychoanalytic treatment, but it took a lawsuit in the late 1980s to end the exclusionary policy of the American Psychoanalytic Association and the IPA (although Kurt Eissler, himself a physician, had decried medical orthodoxy in 1965). The situation was different in Europe and South America, where psychoanalysis has remained a strong presence in mental healthcare, as it has now become in Asia. Recent newsletters of the American Psychoanalytic Association show new member lists to be about 80% non-medical, while death notices are even more heavily comprised of physicians. Though weakened in this country, American psychoanalysis was rescued by the ending of exclusionary practices, acceptance of theoretical pluralism, and—as Freud had himself directed—training of and participation in the field by non-physicians.

The damage done in this country by exclusionary medical orthodoxy, and its silent analyst model, has left more than scars; it's been nearly ruinous. A 2021 lecture by Carolyn Ellman looked at this history from the perspective of Freud's rejection of his once favorite student, Sandor Ferenczi. While the clinical mainstream evolved along lines originated by Ferenczi, it was Mitchell and Greenberg's Relational Model that adopted him and used his banishment to deny changes well underway in clinical theory and practice, notably the contributions by Loewald, Winnicott, Bion, Guntrip, and Jacobs. Ellman's paper showed how organizational politics and personal animosities have been all too active in psychoanalytic history; no surprise, we are subject to the sins and pathologies of all human groups, though pathology—like sin—should be dropped from our therapeutic vocabulary.

Other examples of psychoanalytic purism: before 1990, psychotropic medication ruled out daily couch-based psychoanalysis, while now many patients begin psychoanalytic treatment already on medication. Participation in other treatments was also thought of only as resistance, while symptom-reducing approaches (like EMDR) would not today preclude—and in fact might support—even traditional psychoanalysis.

Having acknowledged some of our own faults, I'll now try to be clear about what I believe is a more accurate way to understand psychoanalytic therapies than the caricature of the blank screen or the notion of "protocol."

Despite my own training at a non-medical institute far less rigid than the ones from which I was excluded, I began my practice in a rule-bound manner consistent with my personality. That's probably true and perhaps necessary for most neophytes. We studied Freud's 1910 paper, *Wild Psychoanalysis*, and never want to be accused of it. At that time—the late sixties—psychoanalytic training for non-physicians was available in this country only in New York.

With time I loosened up. During the '90s, after concluding several traditional analyses, I found no new referrals who would agree to more than twice weekly visits, and most would not accept more than one weekly session, the preferred frequency of the insurance companies who'd come to own most of the patient population. I'd worked twice weekly, often using the couch, but I had to learn to make weekly sessions effective. I was able to rely for help on psychoanalytic clinical theory. The literature was there when I trained a quarter-century earlier, and my own teaching focused on a course called "Theory of Technique," not technique itself. I became more flexible. In the early 2000s I published an article arguing against phone therapy; with the advent of the COVID-19 pandemic, thanks to the guidance of my eldest grandson (now a doctoral student in clinical psychology), I became—as we all did—a remote therapist via Zoom and telephone. I found remote work surprisingly satisfactory for my patients but, having returned one day a week to office practice, I find in-person work more comfortable, and I believe my comfort must in some way contribute to the therapeutic effect.

This essay is not about my personal journey; it is about the distinctive difference between psychoanalytic therapies and more focused and directive mental health approaches. I'll offer a case vignette.

In 2021 I made a brief statement on supportive therapy in my group, baldly claiming there was no such thing. But support is central to every psychoanalytic approach. I'd been seeing a man twice weekly for three years when he experienced three major simultaneous traumas. His 25-year marriage ended; a young adult child struggled with an eating disorder that required hospitalization, and his highly successful 30-year professional career is ending involuntarily for what we can only term political reasons. I've made countless supportive interventions, validating his highly resilient and effective handling of each situation despite considerable anxiety, even suicidal thinking. I still believe however, there is no general therapy that is simply supportive. Exploratory work continues, focusing on strikingly negligent parenting he experienced through childhood and youth, and his oedipal wishes.

In my teaching, I emphasize the stance of "exquisite individualism." We are novices with every new patient, and we learn from the patient how to be helpful. Each session is an opportunity to learn more together. The lack of predictability of the process is what keeps the work interesting, even exciting, in every session, in my 59th year as a therapist.

A second vignette is about a woman I'd seen for five years, once weekly, with breaks for childbearing and -rearing. A woman of accomplishment, she ran a business and dealt with a difficult marriage and two very young kids. She avoided awareness, suppressed anxiety, rage, and depression, while overvaluing episodes of comfort and dismissing most interventions with concreteness and demands for advice. She found it difficult to stay for my 50-minute sessions and absences were frequent, payments often late. I often considered referring her, but I dealt with that feeling with a combination of patience, acceptance, and repeated attempts to promote associations. My encouragement to try to stay on Zoom for the full time bore fruit. Soon, when she cancelled an appointment, it would be with notice and a request for rescheduling. Eventually she gained the ability to talk about painful matters. I let her know that my job was to help her tolerate rather than avoid difficult feelings and thoughts, and most of my interventions were simply to ask her to say what came to mind. My patience paid off. I should add here, that—until recently—I'd treat absences, lateness, and fees as transference-laden and requiring exploration. I believe that approach is valid, but a patient's readiness is essential. Perhaps as relevant, my own relationship with time and money is more comfortable than when I had children to support. It's only recently that I've come to understand more deeply the admonition to "look at the countertransference." Early on that meant that the analyst's neurotic issues were intruding. But the definition expanded, even by the time of my own training (Racker, 1968), to using countertransference feelings to understand the patient's communication, paving the way to a fuller two-person psychology. It now also relates to the therapist's ability to tolerate greater discomfort to get to more primitive feeling states in the patient. Countertransference tolerance allows for more flexible boundaries in doing the work. Countertransference resonance also enables an ability to be "in the zone," with greater access to memories about the patient, even when personal memory may be slipping.

Charles Brenner, seen by many as a model of traditional psychoanalysis, was in fact a radical revisionary. Jacob Arlow and he (in their 1964 book) were the progenitors of "modern conflict theory." It might surprise readers to learn that over 30 years later Brenner wrote that psychoanalysis is not about "frequency or furniture." It is instead about helping patients learn about themselves. Its main feature is "analytic attitude," exemplified by the two vignettes I've shared.

Central to this attitude is a general orientation to learn about a patient's mind. The major technical stance is called "expectant technique," or active listening. Listening well may require prompts. Failures push us to keep trying. Silences are communicative; we make efforts to understand them.

Freud's short 1905 paper *On Psychotherapy* includes one of the many well-known images that won him the Goethe Prize for literature. He contrasted art forms: painting adds oil to canvas to create beauty, sculpture chips at and rubs stone to find beauty beneath. Freud likened his therapy to sculpture. Its methods attempt to get at the innermost part of a person. Its overarching aims are to promote autonomy and agency; the analytic attitude avoids directing life choices external to the consulting room, especially the most important of them. The principles of practice are about how a psychoanalytic therapist listens, thinks, and acts in sessions. Over time, a theory of mind evolved and continues to evolve to inform practice. A wide range of styles and interventions can be incorporated. Two more recent advances, no longer new (except to those unfamiliar with contemporary psychoanalysis): 1) We no longer dismiss enactments as simply inappropriate countertransference requiring the therapist's self-analysis; they are inevitable features of treatment, understandable within the two-person model, and useful in retrospect when recognized; and 2) Rupture and repair are common features of treatment. I like repeating the title of a paper by Fred Busch: "This is not your grandfather's psychoanalysis" (1994).

One more clinical example of psychoanalytic psychotherapy, "chronic undifferentiated type," going back 50 years: Mr. X introduced himself to me in the Bellevue outpatient clinic by jumping on my desk and shouting: "I just escaped from a mental hospital!" This was true, and for about six months most of what he would say in session could be called "word salad." My interventions were essentially: "Huh?" and "What are you trying to say?" He became more articulate over time. When I left Bellevue about a year later, he joined my private practice and made effective use of a few additional years of treatment with me. With an accidental follow-up several years later, I was able to confirm that he was no longer psychotic.

The Gottman method cannot fit within the capacious psychoanalytic model, just as—in the 1960s—Ivar Lovaas's disciplinary therapeutics with children did not fit. Nor can straightforward reinforcement methods or a strictly positive psychology of validation of strengths fit. Supportive interventions are included in dynamic psychotherapies but will be specific to the patient and the moment. Recommendations to take each opportunity to validate strengths would also not fit.

Human beings are complex; people are not to be reduced to presenting symptoms. Symptoms, behavior patterns and personality develop from a complex interaction of conditions from the biological to the social, political, and even temporal—understanding the pandemic, for instance, is important to our treatments. Psychotherapy focuses on motivations in the plural (the principle of overdetermination) that serve multiple functions. To the aphorism that for every difficult question there is a simple answer, I add: that answer is almost always wrong. Contemporary technique follows Shedler's seven points, the first being the privileging of affect, with each of the seven meaningfully present in any psychodynamic treatment.

Edward Glover's 1955 book, *The Technique and Practice of Psychoanalysis*, updated a 1928 verbatim report of six lectures he delivered at the London Institute soon after Freud's major revisions of basic theory (1923-1926). The report was itself updated in 1940, with some rigidities modified based on a survey Glover conducted in 1938. That survey, published in full in the 1955 volume, was sent to the 29 members of the British Psychoanalytic Group, and was returned by 24. Acknowledging the small sample, he nonetheless found some agreement about basic principles. When I first read the results—mostly short answers, not quantitative measures—I was unsettled by the striking differences among the respondents on several issues. Even in 1938, while Freud still lived, there was a proto-pluralism! Today, despite having been a vocal opponent, I've embraced what Elliot Jurist calls "disciplined pluralism:" necessary to the creativity required for studying the human mind.

Jay Greenberg, co- founder of Relational Psychoanalysis with the late Steven Mitchell, claimed at a 2015 conference that there could be no consensual validation of the work we do. I was uncomfortable hearing him say that but am now more in agreement. Professional differences in our field, where the very subject matter is subjectivity, are unlikely to be resolved—any more than are political ones in this country or internationally. Each of us here works differently from the others. What we do "works," in quotation marks because our criteria are varied and variable. We are all successful in economic terms: we make a living. Freud in the 1905 paper said that anything that works for a patient quickly is fine, though his conviction was that most problems don't quickly resolve. Martin E. P. Seligman, a psychologist not at all psychoanalytically inclined, reported on a large-scale Consumer Reports study (1995) that found long-term, open-ended (essentially psychodynamic) therapies to be more satisfying to former patients, and, more importantly, that the effectiveness and emotional impact was recalled many years after the end of treatment.

I've become more impressed of late with our ignorance, in general—and as part of analytic attitude and effective therapeutic stance. I have taken notice recently of entire domains of important knowledge, about which I am barely informed. We are familiar with the Rashomon effect, different people viewing the same events differently. I like the image of blind people touching the elephant in different places, generating vastly different pictures of the beast. That image extends beyond the various psychoanalytic schools to all psychotherapy. We each know what we experience, and our subjective experience has its own validity but is far from the whole story; each of us misses a lot. This is not identical to Bion's listening "without memory or desire," but it incorporates that possibility. I believe those who ignore motivation without awareness—the dynamic unconscious— are missing an essential way to understand patients' Dark Side. The professions of clinical psychology and psychiatry originated and evolved to address more empirically the philosophical Problem of Evil.

In 2019 I spoke in a public venue of my disbelief in the Death Instinct concept, and I denied its clinical utility. We recently heard an excellent summary of the conflicted history of this idea. Trumpism and Covid-19—and the greater proximity to my own mortality—have changed my mind. I believe Freud's Death Instinct is useful, but as metaphor—and talk therapies are most effective using metaphor. Individual, couples, and groups can be helped to address the Dark Side. Psychoanalytic theory has provided some light, as well as a clinical approach addressing aggression as a basic motivator. I once concluded a presentation with my favorite of Freud's images: Eros and Thanatos in perpetual struggle.

I hope to keep finding meaning in Freud's genius, and to use it to benefit my patients. I have attempted here to outline essential differences between psychoanalytic therapies and treatments that are focused, short-term, directive and results-oriented.

Remote Psychotherapy: Two Years Later

March 3, 2022

Most of our professional organizations have had discussions and even set up task forces on "teletherapy." Journal articles appeared as early as spring 2020.

My thoughts began in 2005, when I published "Toward a Balanced Consideration of Telephone Analysis" (The Round Robin, Vol. 20, No. 3, 9) in which I was generally opposed to remote treatment except for temporary or emergency situations.

I saw patients in my office on Friday, March 13, 2020, but by that Monday I was on Zoom, assisted remotely by my grandson, a PhD candidate in clinical psychology. I was pleasantly surprised that the work seemed satisfactory. That June I told a class that it was so—but I said I wouldn't begin with someone remotely. That summer, I relented, accepting a referral from my psychotherapist sister, and it was okay.

By spring 2021 the pandemic seemed to wane. I asked my patients if they'd return to my office and was surprised by the positive replies. I'd thought the absence of a commute would be decisive; it was for some. I rented space on Fridays at my former office suite, with two patients hybrid, one session in person, the second online. Only one patient in my always part-time practice made regular complaints about remote work—but she dealt with it. Others have been at least okay, seeming to do the work with me as they had been, pre-Covid.

With the two hybrid patients, I feel the difference most clearly. Zoom glitches, though rare, still occur and the possibility bothers me (more than it seems to bother the patients), and I'm more relaxed in the office, not attending to the technology. One hybrid patient in particular (who has chosen to use the phone)—a man who has had a traumatic last two years and deals with his harsh reality admirably, seems far more relaxed in person, where he often smiles. On the phone he always sounds tense, and I can't judge pauses as pauses or glitches without asking. He's now agreed to use video.

We are privileged. Many have suffered during the pandemic, psychologically and economically. Most of us have probably been protected from economic harm though we've not escaped entirely unscathed. With a major reduction in overhead, my net income increased, but I still wanted the pandemic over.

An ad hoc group on remote analysis in training outlined areas that require further thought and emphasized the need for more member feedback to facilitate broad discussion about the differences/similarities between in-person and what may be called 'tele-analysis' during training. Areas requiring further attention include the presence of Procedural Code discrepancies in already approved variations on analysis during training (shuttle analysis and condensed analysis) and the need for research data about the extent to which psychoanalytic identity and competence can be arrived at through tele-analysis.

Update, July 2024: Without Zoom or similar technology, our work would have been limited to telephonic communication. As with the patient I spoke of above, I would have found that too different from in-person treatment and unsatisfactory. In the time since I wrote these brief remarks, I've read several papers on the issue; none struck me as a clear enough verdict. In conversations with colleagues, I've continued to describe my impression of Zoom-aided psychotherapy as "satisfactory but not nearly as good." Most agreed but were grateful that the work could continue, as were their patients. Yesterday I read Mitchell Wilson's paper, "Property, Materiality, Proximity: The Analytic Frame and In-Person Work" (JAPA 2024, 84–107). He articulated differences that made clear the important limitations of remote psychotherapy. Despite the slow waning of the Covid pandemic, in-person treatment is now generally available. Convenience has provided much support for too many therapy pairs to continue remotely. I believe now, with Mitchell, that it is less than the best we can offer.

Supportive Therapy: There's No Such Thing!

March 16, 2021

The proliferation of "special" method therapies such as Emotion-focused Therapy (EFT), Interpersonal Therapy, Transference-focused Therapy (TFP), and others, have usually been developed to address a diagnosis with a standard, often manualized, approach. I don't believe psychiatric diagnoses are useful for clinic or private practice patients. Judith Caligor acknowledged upfront in her excellent presentation that TFP is a research protocol for Bipolar Disorder. Favorable results correlate with severity; less severe cases show more improvement. A psychiatrist colleague from my Army days ordered a Rorschach. I told him he could order an evaluation. Psychological "tests" are not like blood tests.

Most psychotherapies are "supportive." Supportive interventions are those that aim to calm the patient, whether by addressing anxiety, depressive affect, or other intense feelings. If the patient is willing to be with you at all and to return, the patient must sense an adequate degree of support. Support is an important part of what keeps any patient in the room; rarely does it address the distress that brings the patient for psychotherapy.

Edward Bibring (1954) classified treatment interventions as "analytic" or "therapeutic." The former might increase upset by challenging the patient in some way; the latter aims to calm. The proportion of these measures, silence among them, would for Bibring define the treatment as psychoanalysis or therapy.

Reassurance is a primary direct offer of support. Its effects, if any, are temporary at best. I'd have been insulted in my own treatment by direct reassurance; that's what I expect from friends, not a mental health professional.

In over 52 years of private practice, I saw only one patient I expected to stay with me for life (hers or mine), a so-called "lifer." I was happy to be wrong; in about 10 years, we completed the once-weekly, face-to-face treatment with meaningful success. The neediest patients may indeed need lifetime care. Would that be supportive—or palliative? Unless they are demented or imminently terminally ill, I would still try to challenge them. Palliative care is appropriate for terminal illness. If a patient could engage with me, I would avoid treating the situation as if mental life was dying.

In the variety of psychoanalytic therapies, interventions depend on the context of the treatment and the moment; they are exquisitely individualized. They also depend on the relationship, itself a complex concept. Greenson (1967) described three aspects to it: reality, alliance, and transference. Mistakenly, he treated countertransference as an obstacle. We now see it as a *possible* obstacle, but also as potentially important for understanding reactions that this patient tends to evoke. The transference-countertransference matrix is a primary—but not sole—concern of all psychoanalytic (psychodynamic) treatments.

The very concept of "supportive therapy" as *a specific methodology* undermines effective treatment—because it replaces critical thinking with mush!

Morbidity, Mortality and Ubiquitous Denial

April 28, 2022

In 2019 my group held a panel discussion entitled *The Impaired or Deteriorating Therapist*. The topic was deemed important enough to schedule it at each of two separate conferences. Our chair gave the keynote. One paper was sent in advance, two others spoke, and I made concluding comments before open discussion. We had also had a group discussion on this very topic two years earlier. The collective denial of mortality is an old story. My own forgetting the prior meetings until preparing for this one underscores the ubiquity of denial. Anne Ziff's book, *Your End of Life Matters*, was published in 2018, having originated with a presentation here a few years earlier. Six months ago, we were urged to read Irvin Yalom's book, *A Matter of Life and Death*, initiating today's event, and Becker's *Denial of Death* (1973) is frequently touted.

I was privileged to study with Martin Bergmann. One course was titled *Varieties of Technical Intervention*. Among its many gems was the clinical differentiation of repression and denial. Interpretation is the standard psychoanalytic intervention for repression; denial calls for confrontation. Despite its aggressive connotation, for psychoanalysts that word means simply stating an external reality. When repression lifts, the reaction is "Aha!" With denial, it's "Oh my!" with a slap on one's forehead. For denial of mortality, intellectualization and isolation of affect kick in for us obsessional neurotics to diminish the felt experience of existential dread. I've circulated a template for professional wills here and elsewhere. Three years ago, I'd encouraged both neuropsychological testing and professional wills; those colleagues I've asked recently hadn't done either. This essay is meant to provoke a collective slap on our own foreheads. In the face of denial, we must be confronted with potential disability and inevitable mortality.

My affairs are in order; my analyst called me counterphobic. Of course that's defensive but, a la Hartmann, defenses can also be adaptive. My father prepaid my mother's and his funerals, saving us from practical tasks and enabling our grieving when he died a few months later. I said then that I'd do the same, but I deferred for 35 years before acting, reminded only by approaching my father's age at death. Estate plans are important; they require a trusted younger executor. We should also have what Anne Ziff calls "the talk" with partners, adult children, and stepchildren. I've done it.

Most members of my group are old. We should have our mental status and memory evaluated. My second neuropsychological exam three years after the first had the same good result, but we are all in decline. By age 85, fully half of us are expected to be dementing. I see two patients whose prior therapy was aborted because of the therapist's dementia. We must prepare for disability! Not everyone can work until days before their demise, as did Louis Linn and Martin Bergmann. At my age I'm reluctant to take new referrals, as my treatment approach is explicitly "open-ended." Erikson defined renunciation as the strength of his eighth stage of life. I stopped skiing three years ago and gave up night driving last year. My mother's car, on the other hand, had a "for sale" sign for a full year before she accepted an offer.

Decline is harder for me to contemplate than death. A colleague told us he didn't fear death but dreaded painful terminal illness. I was a daily runner for over 30 years. I slowed to a jog, then a hybrid jog-walk; now I speed-walk but it might not look speedy. I'm careful on stairs, gripping the rail. I am no longer agile. I note increasing instances of forgetting. On the plus side, I seem still to have excellent recall with patients, and I usually feel "in the zone" when working. Ours is a great profession, and I'd have a hard time if I had to stop altogether.

This essay addresses self-reflection, but the issues apply equally to assisting colleagues. All our organizations have defined principles regarding assisting impaired co-workers and their patients. None has established a realistic protocol; things are left to friendly colleagues. I've spoken before about two dementing colleagues: when I approached the topic with one, she broke off our long relationship and dropped out of our study group; the other tested positive for Alzheimer's Disease, immediately closed his practice and moved with his wife to an assisted-living facility. Perhaps even harder is facing spousal or partner decline, and an ensuing "Caregiver Syndrome."

Finding the Right Words

When asked what I teach at Mount Sinai School of Medicine, my answer is always: "listening." The job is, therefore, to help patients (or couples, families, groups) find their own words, to help them untie their mental knots. Teaching is more word-oriented, its aim primarily cognitive. Words help us theorize. Here's my favorite set: "I'm a love doctor; I practice metaphoric cardiology."

A teacher in analyst school once said: "I made *ze* interpretation and ze patient *vus* cured!" Even in 1969 I didn't believe her. Merton Gill (1954) set a technical standard: "By interpretation alone!" Earlier, Strachey (1934) asserted that helpful (i.e., "mutative") interpretations must be "in the transference." In clinical discussion, our chair frequently asks the question: "What did you *say* to the patient?"

"The Evolution of Psychoanalytic Technique" (1976), edited by Martin Bergmann and Frank Hartman, outlined changes in psychoanalytic technique through 1940. That evolution has continued. It remains a complex issue. I often cite Fred Busch's phrase, "Not your grandfather's psychoanalysis" (1993). We now speak of a transference-countertransference matrix; of rupture and repair, and many additional concepts of technique, far more specific than "the relationship."

I'm frequently surprised at what patients recall of what I've said, and that they do not recall—at least consciously—what I thought was memorable. I've taught: "If you mean well, the words rarely matter"—except for the too easily offended (an assessment issue). Our colleague Daniel Birger reminded us, though, that you can't say, "blah, blah, blah." He also told us: we are different with each patient. In the exquisite individualism of psychodynamic treatments, we develop the idiom of each therapy (with each patient, couple, family, or group).

PANELS, POLITICS,
HISTORY, PHILOSOPHY

Brief History of the Affiliation of the New York Freudian Society and the International Psychoanalytical Association

with William M. Greenstadt, Ph.D.
Psychologist Psychoanalyst (1990)

Beginnings

At the 1986 Mid-Winter Meeting of the American Psychoanalytic Association, until recently always held at the Waldorf-Astoria Hotel in New York, Moss Rawn, then past president of the New York Freudian Society (NYFS), and William Greenstadt, at that time president of the NYFS, approached Robert Wallerstein, then president of the International Psychoanalytical Association (IPA), and told him that we had heard that the IPA might soon be considering applications for affiliation from nonmedical psychoanalytic societies in the United States. His response was guarded but positive, and he suggested that we "await developments."

In his role as President of the NYFS, Bill kept in touch with Dr. Wallerstein and arranged a meeting with him and other members of the IPA Executive Council at the Montreal IPA Congress in the Summer of 1987. NYFS members who attended the Congress participated in this meeting. We were told that several members of the American Psychoanalytic Association (APsaA) were going to propose an amendment to the IPA constitution and by-laws that would revoke the infamous "Regional Rule" that had effectively barred the way for nonmedical practitioners in the U.S. from obtaining "official" training and from full status as analysts within their profession. We were told at that meeting that the APsaA was taking an active interest in what would follow since it had a vital interest in preserving high standards for all officially recognized analysts in the U.S.

At length we were told that an organizing group was being formed that would work with applicant societies to formulate methods and procedures for application and the meeting of IPA standards. Since for what was being done there existed no precedents within the IPA, it was constantly emphasized that we would all be "feeling our way." The two leaders of this group were Professor Charles Hanly of Toronto (chairman), and Dr. David Sachs of Philadelphia, who later was appointed chairman of our IPA Site Visit Committee.

First Stage: 1987–1988

In collaboration with Professor Hanly, we began to accumulate data that would give the IPA some idea of the background and character of our membership. Accordingly, data were collected from each member on the number of patients he had in analysis at present, i.e., the character of his practice—how "analytic" it was. We also determined the number of hours in private practice each member was now undertaking, indicative of whether the practice of psychoanalysis was a "primary" activity of the member. Finally, we assembled data on the training and supervising analysts of each member: whether or not they were IPA-trained, and the number of sessions per week and the length of their own personal analysis and those of their training cases.

An IPA Site Visit Committee, consisting of very distinguished analysts from the U.S. (David Sachs), Mexico (Luis Feder), the U.K. (Moses Laufer), and Canada (Eva Lester), was appointed. Dr. Sachs was the chairman of this group, and I began a telephone liaison with him to prepare for our first site visit. In the meantime, William Greenstadt appointed our own IPA Steering Committee of seven, selected from members of the NYFS Board of Directors (and one non-member), with himself as chair.

A general meeting of all members of the NYFS was organized, at which the issues and current developments were discussed. It was the sentiment of the members to go ahead with the application.

The first of two site visits was held from May 15-17, 1988. Jeffrey Golland, as a member of the Steering Committee, was responsible for most institute matters from early in the application process, when he was vice chair of the Training Committee of the Institute and continuing into his chairmanship.

The IPA Site Visit Committee received in advance all our literature: our public relations/recruiting brochures, our bulletin and our forms. They wanted details about our procedures from a prospective candidate's first inquiry through graduation: standards and special responses, the steps in the admissions process, including the establishment of a file, the interview methods and criteria, the section criteria, and the telephone and letter responses to applicants. They were interested in our progressive steps of formal periodic evaluation: readiness-for-control and case presentation. They focused questions on both usual cases and individual variations.

In addition to our literature, the Site Visit Committee wanted to get a "feel" for the process. We discussed it with them, but we also showed it to them by taking them through the actual files (with names of the candidates, references, analyst, teachers, and supervisors having been previously redacted by Golland). They were interested in our record-keeping in general, and several files were similarly prepared for their scrutiny, representing both more and less successful candidates at the various levels of training.

Of course, in addition to its form and format, our site visitors wanted to know the substance of our training program. They had course descriptions and were shown outlines and bibliographies. They then observed four classes and nine supervisions, which had been rescheduled for the weekend of their visit.

The site visitors reviewed with us write-ups of evaluations reflecting the standards used in individual cases for making judgments on admission, readiness-for-control, and case presentation. Some of these were reviewed in the context of an actual Training Committee meeting (once again, rescheduled for the site visit weekend). At this meeting, the discussion of these presentations was at first observed, then joined in by our visitors. They also observed, at that time, the handling of administrative matters that come routinely before the Training Committee, and they had the opportunity to raise questions with each committee member.

The quality of our faculty and of our supervisors was, as would be expected, subject to evaluation by the site visitors. The process of selecting instructors and the criteria for appointment to the faculty were discussed (and this process was also demonstrated), and the regular evaluation process and its utilization were discussed. Sample evaluations of instructors (by candidates) were studied.

A final meeting between the Site Visit and our Liaison Committee was held to discuss the preliminary impression we had made on the visitors. Dr. Sachs and his committee prepared a report that was to be presented to the IPA Executive Council in London during the summer of 1988.

Second Stage: The Second Site Visit, December 1988

Early in the Fall of 1988, we were informed by Dr. Sachs that the Executive Council of the IPA, which had met in July 1988, had been impressed with us in general, but that our application could not go forward until we had altered our procedure for selecting training and supervising analysts. This was a major stumbling block. As a matter of policy, the NYFS had many years before adopted the rule that a candidate could undertake a training analysis or analytic case supervision with anyone who had been a full member of the NYFS (in adult analysis) for more than five years. We now were told that our selection procedure was unacceptable since it lacked quality assessment—mere seniority being an insufficient standard. We had, in the main, been satisfied that our candidates were in good analyses and supervision; the politics sometimes associated with selection at other institutes has been avoided for thirty years. The visitors had apparently been surprised that we did not agree with them on this issue, move to change our system, and then move on to other matters. We were surprised to find out after the first site visit that the matter was not really debatable: we would have a selection procedure acceptable to the IPA or the application process would not go forward!

A procedure in keeping with established IPA guidelines would therefore have to be devised and put into effect as soon as possible if our application was to proceed. By the end of September 1988, the NYFS board enacted a new guidelines procedure including quality assessment, but until we were putatively approved for IPA status, all former training analysts under the old system were to be considered *de facto*. At the next site visit, scheduled that December (1988), small groups of our more senior analysts (those actively involved in the education and training of candidates and in the administration of the Institute) would be asked to discuss a clinical presentation made by one of their number. Groups of three and four senior members participated in these "clinical discussion groups" with members of the Site Visit Committee sitting in and taking notes. The total number in this initial group was 23, out of a larger group of over 70. If this initial group were approved as IPA members "on the training analyst level" at the Membership Business Meeting of the Rome Congress (Summer, 1989), they could then evaluate the remaining training analysts in the NYFS, now using the procedures of the newly-adopted guidelines. This group (beginning with the 23 evaluated by the IPA Site Visit Committee), would then constitute the Panel of Training and Supervising Analysts of the institute.

A second issue was our aim to get our entire membership into the IPA. Earlier, Dr. Wallerstein had offered the tentative suggestion that not all of our members might qualify for the IPA, and that we might wish to form a second, IPA-sanctioned Freudian Society. This group could then selectively take into membership those analysts from the "old" Freudian Society who qualified under IPA standards. The NYFS weighed this and similar plans but felt that they were far too divisive and destructive to be considered. It was finally established that every individual member who applied to the IPA would be evaluated by the IPA Site Visit Committee in accordance with a complete and detailed curriculum vitae. If any "deficiencies" in IPA standards were found, a system of "functional equivalents" would be applied (for example, a member whose personal analysis had been conducted on a three session per week basis by a non-IPA training analyst might subsequently have engaged in extensive teaching in the institute, participated in private seminars with IPA analysts, and published papers in major, refereed journals). One or more of these would be considered as compensatory "functional equivalents" for the training analysis "deficiency." Of over 100 members who applied, only 14 had their membership delayed, during which time they could engage in additional training activities (e.g., supervision) to prepare for their presentation for membership at the next Congress in Buenos Aires (1991).

The second site visit (December 15-18, 1988) involved additional class and supervisory observations, discussions of research activities, and a review and evaluation of the activity of our Psychoanalytic Consultation Service. Finally, the Site Visit Committee evaluated us through the eyes of our candidates. Ten to twelve candidates at various levels were selected to meet with the visitors over lunch, with no NYFS member present.

While the atmosphere during the first site visit was felt to be somewhat chilling, the second was far more friendly. We came away from it with the sense that we were going to make it! Although socializing had been discouraged during the site visits, and after having weathered a difficult and disappointing first site visit, a final dinner party capped this most successful enterprise.

The Rome Congress: August 1989

We now held our collective breaths until the Rome Congress, when the results would be made known. Officially, we had no prior knowledge of the results of the two site visits, which were contained in a report of over 100 typewritten pages

427

and were sent in advance to the IPA Executive Committee. Those of us who attended the Congress found ourselves in a state of restless suspense until the Business Meeting—the morning of August 2, 1989. At about eleven that morning, we gathered outside the doors of the large meeting room, cheerily bantering with one another to compensate for our state of anxious anticipation. Finally, Professor Hanly emerged, congratulated us on a unanimous vote in favor of our membership, handed us official voting cards, and we entered the room to a standing ovation by the assembled members. The three presidents of the societies newly approved by the IPA membership made brief appreciatory speeches, and we were welcomed by Dr. Wallerstein. The experience was more vivid than reality, and it took some of us hours to believe that a state of isolation that had lasted for more than 50 years was now over forever!

The NYFS (along with two other societies in the U.S.) was now a Provisional Society of the IPA. This status means that all functions of the NYFS were in a state of continuous review by a Liaison Committee of the IPA until attaining full Component Society status. The IPA estimated that it would take 2-6 years for the three new provisional societies to reach full component society status.

Aftermath and Problems

One problem that was solved for all practical purposes was the making ready of the fourteen members whose IPA status had been delayed for their submission until the Buenos Aires Congress in July 1991. Their curriculum vitae were approved, and when the "functional equivalent" activity they undertook was satisfactorily completed, they could consider themselves "putative" IPA members.

Within a few years, almost all members with training analyst status under the old rules had been evaluated under the new Guidelines procedure. Each member presented an analytic case to five members of the Training and Supervising Analyst Panel.

The process of revoking all training analysts' status under the old rules, and "re-credentialling" each of them under the Guidelines procedure, proved to have had the divisive effects that were feared in the case of qualifications for IPA membership in general. In January of 1990 a group of twelve members, feeling that their training analyst status had been unjustly revoked, sued the Board of Directors and Trustees of the NYFS under the New York State law pertaining to corporations. They refused to have themselves evaluated under the Guidelines procedure. After much anguish and conflict, the suit was settled and the NYFS was faced with having to bind the wounds suffered during this period. If any moral may be drawn from this experience, it is that any psychoanalytic society contemplating applying to the IPA for membership should thoroughly explore the possible impact upon its existing structure and the morale of its members. Thus, intensive prior discussion within the society's membership is vital.

The Politics of Psychoanalytic Training

Psychologist Psychoanalyst (1991)

From its standardization in Berlin in the 1920s the tripartite model of training seemed to be eminently reasonable: training analysis designed to remove neurotic obstacles to the emotionally-taxing work; supervision to give a sound mastery of technique; coursework to expose students to the broad and complex issues of theory and practice.

Soon these cornerstones showed flaws. There was to be no perfectly analyzed analyst, and the inevitable limitations included transferences of both idealizing and rebellious varieties. Political conformity and political schism resulted as did attention to the central matter of countertransference. Supervision brought similar problems, The curriculum in any discipline needs regular review.

Matters of standards in the selection of training and supervising analysts, as well as of faculty, became subject to political considerations, with those in power codifying criteria and perpetuating their power. The reporting role of training and supervising analysts, as enforcers of standards, emerged as both a political issue and, in the former case, a matter that undermined the confidentiality essential to sound treatment.

Standards and standardization, then, created problems for the training enterprise, limiting openness, innovation and freedom—values espoused by the discipline. A particular standard adopted by organized American psychoanalysis, medical training, has at last been exposed as an economic (and therefore political) sham. This exposure resulted from the lawsuit but began with Freud's defense of Reik.

Need we reject a model because it is flawed? Must we reject authority because it is abused? Have the International Psychoanalytical and the American Psychoanalytic Associations lost all legitimacy because some standards were political and wrong? Specifically, have the regional rule and medical monopoly forfeited their authority?

We have learned from Kuhn (1962) that paradigms are replaced only when better ones are adopted. We vary aspects of our model in the hope of reducing flaws; no replacement model is yet cogently offered.

Those of us excluded for fifty years from "official" American psychoanalysis were trained in several ways: A small group was afforded the "waiver" and their names are well-known to us (e.g. Pine, Schafer, Spence) both for their outstanding contributions to the field and for their acceptance of "official" psychoanalysis in its political forms. Others formed their own training centers where (in New York) there were adequate numbers. These centers chose for their initial faculties those who adopted a third option of independent (or "bootleg") training. Independents were trained, often secretly, by APsaA members who did not accept the rules. This group replaced formal coursework with private study following a similar curriculum. While elements of the training programs at the non-medical centers varied from "official" standards (e.g. non-reporting training analyses, Neo-Freudian theories, reduced frequency of therapeutic contact), the tripartite training model remained standard and the publications of official psychoanalysis remained high on reading lists.

The lawsuit had as two of its achieved goals admission of psychologists to training in institutes of APsaA and admission of non-APsaA institutes to IPA. Clearly, IPA and APsaA have not lost their positions of authority by virtue of their exclusionary standards. It is necessary neither to idealize authority nor to rebel against it. What legitimate authority remains with IPA and with APsaA is that accorded these bodies for what contributions they made and continue to make to the discipline. Errors of theory and clinical practice need to continue to be debated at meetings and in the literature; political errors, when they cannot be resolved organizationally, may result in lawsuits.

Has psychoanalysis been in a period of stagnation resulting from the medical dominance of its American practice, as Shapiro (1990) has suggested? The evidence is to the contrary. American psychoanalysis has grown and developed in this country in the past fifty years and continues to do so. Hartmann's ego psychology resulted in dramatic expansion of theory and refinement of practice. Mahler's important emphasis on pre-oedipal development helped widen the scope of indications for psychoanalytic treatment, and for methods to work in this wider scope. It is also important to note that Rappaport's students, including psychologists Holt, Klein and Schafer, have made major contributions to the theoretical debate, resulting in the generative controversy over hermeneutics. Mahler's collaborators, notably psychologists Pine and Bergman, continue important research. The American post-ego psychology model has integrated these developments. Self-psychology was born in this era in an institute of the APsaA, and Kernberg's development of object relations theory grew in a similar environment.

The various definitions of psychoanalysis are much more problematic and pose significant political issues now that psychologists and others have begun to organize as analysts.

As a member of IPA, I subscribe to a definition of psychoanalysis which requires that training and supervised analyses be conducted at a minimum frequency of four times weekly, and that the couch be used. The matter of frequency has been referred to by critics as a "numbers game." That is a trivialization. Psychoanalysis, as a treatment and method of study, requires an analytic "process" in which regressive associational material can emerge. While such a process can occur in many ways, it occurs most reliably when a recumbent position and a high frequency of contact are maintained. Since training always occurs with the first cases seen by neophytes, it should provide the optimum conditions for the development of the process. The personal analysis of trainees needs to be similarly conducted.

The distinction between psychoanalysis and analytically informed psychotherapies is important. We often find ourselves more comfortable in political union with those who formerly excluded us but share our conception of psychoanalysis, than with many of our non-medical colleagues whose practice we may not see as analytic.

IPA-oriented institutes outside of APsaA are faced with a psychological and political challenge: Do we identify with those who, until now, have excluded us or do we identify with our still excluded colleagues? Do we reject our orientation as psychologists, or our commitment to a particular definition of psychoanalysis? Are we traitors to our kind?

Freud considered psychoanalysis a part of psychology. Our psychology training led us to the discipline of psychoanalysis. Exclusion from "official" psychoanalysis has led many of us to feel that what we were doing was better. We developed our own modifications of theory and came to believe our divergence was a sign of creativity and openness. To those of us oriented toward IPA, this historical process led to eclecticism, not to be equated with openness.

IPA, the political grouping with which some have now affiliated, will benefit from our political orientation as well as our contributions to theory and practice.

While IPA itself has never held to a medical model, it has now disowned that model in this country. We are not medical-model psychoanalysts and we will work to eliminate what remains of that orientation. IPA-oriented psychoanalysis can become politically open without yielding to eclecticism and what it considers to be unsound in theory, practice, or training. Far from being traitors, we hope to be in the vanguard of a politically open psychoanalysis that is also a sound psychoanalysis.

In earlier decades there was a psychoanalytic movement. It is unlikely that there will be a revival. It is too late for IPA-oriented psychoanalysis to resume possession of the name, since it has been adopted by many dynamic schools of psychology. More than 50 institutes came together in May (under the auspices of Division 39) and met again in November to develop an American federation of institutes outside of APsaA. The consensus at these meetings was for a non-exclusive organization, and anyone who claims the name psychoanalysis would be welcome. The numbers will likely surpass those of APsaA. Good ideas will emanate from that organization and psychoanalysis may well reclaim high public awareness and greater recognition by cognate disciplines.

There will then be a beneficial effect on training at most institutes. Psychoanalytic thought will resume a strong presence in graduate psychology and social work programs, and potential candidates for training will be better prepared to make educated choices. In the face of better-prepared candidate cadres, institutes will be stimulated to improve faculties and curricula, and will refine their versions of psychoanalysis.

With the success of the lawsuit, the admission to the IPA of non-members of APsaA, and the beginnings of a non-APsaA federation, American psychoanalysis has "officially" become more diverse. Talented, prepared individuals will define their orientations knowledgeably and choose training accordingly. The word "psychoanalysis" will continue to be an expanding umbrella; specific practices will achieve refined identities under it. Well-trained practitioners will work with a sense of authenticity in one or another version of psychoanalysis.

This rosy view is not an "end of politics" statement. Politics (and even politics as usual) seems to be, like sex and aggression, in the nature of the beast.

In the Hartmann era, psychoanalysis was not only to be a general psychology, but a world view. Now we are more modest as to our place in the world. We recognize that psychoanalysis exists in social, economic and political realities and, while its theory contributes to the understanding of those realms, its institutions cannot escape their laws.

Why Termination Has Become
the Achilles Heel of Psychoanalysis

Psychologist Psychoanalyst (1993)

A standing-room crowd of over 500 heard Section I President Oliver J.B. Kerner introduce invited panelists Jack Novick, Martin S. Bergmann, and Donald M. Kaplan, who would address the topic of psychoanalytic termination.

Dr. Novick's paper, "Termination—Conceivable and Inconceivable," has as its thesis that termination is hard to conceive of, both for patients and analysts, and it detailed the analyst's resistances, in particular. Novick cited Freud's technique with the Wolf Man, Brenner (1976), and Firestein (1978), as well as reports of the personal analyses of Brunswick, Gardiner, Sachs, Sharpe, and Little, to demonstrate that "forced" terminations are the historical norm which he called a "genetic defect" showing effective termination to have been "inconceivable, a trauma denied and repeated with each succeeding generation."

Novick then turned to the lack of mourning in training analyses, the related issue of post-analytic contact, the lack of expression of feeling in reports of termination, and the lack of appreciation of termination as a phase in which fantasies get worked through to underscore his thesis. Forced, unilateral, premature, and overdue types of termination were noted as comprising a tentative taxonomy. Novick concluded his paper by suggesting ways of making termination "conceivable" through analysts dealing with their own resistances to allow for endings in which treatment gains are consolidated rather than destroyed.

Prof. Bergmann's paper, "Why Termination has Become the Achilles Heel of Psychoanalytic Technique," began with a review of the literature from Rank, Ferenczi, Freud, Fenichel, M. Klein, A. Freud, A. Reich, E. Buchsbaum, M. Balint, and Hartmann to the more contemporary views of Arlow and of Brenner. That we force terminations or let them die of exhaustion, that we may not change our minds about dates or analyze dormant conflict, that we may be optimistic or pessimistic, were among the issues critically discussed. Our goals, means of evaluation, theory and technique determine our endings, noted Bergmann, and the literature is inadequately helpful.

Bergmann then presented his views on the difficulty of upsetting the ego's new analysis-based equilibrium, so the good becomes enemy of the better. We give transference love without demand, which may not translate into love in real life. Our idealization of termination is an obstacle to ending, and we ask analysands to leave with neither their former defenses nor further (non-analytic) contact. We seek endings unlike those in life, so that we may be available again, as analysts, should we again be needed. Our literature, Bergmann concluded, offers no paradigm, so premature terminations and overlong analyses cannot be avoided for now.

Dr. Kaplan's discussion praised the two papers' avoidance of blame and quick fixes in the absence of a sound termination paradigm. He clarified the difference between idealized cultural discourse and real data, which are lacking. The two papers pick up the threads of the issue, with theory in place ready to be mobilized. Novick's taxonomy is a useful heuristic. Bergmann's paradoxes are valuable in helping us dig out the substance in the analytic relationship. Ours is not the only field in which ending is a problem, concluded Kaplan, with examples from music and art.

The audience raised issues of the pragmatics of ending, the matter of psychotherapy endings, and the question of pessimism. Dr. Kerner had to close the meeting, although the panel and audience could usefully have continued if time allowed.

Is Psychoanalysis Health Care? A Debate

Affirmative: Stanley Moldawsky, Ph.D.;
Negative: Marvin Hyman, Ph.D.
Moderator: Jeffrey H. Golland, Ph.D.
Psychologist Psychoanalyst (1994)

Approximately ninety APA members attended the Section I symposium, a debate over the very premise of the Division 39 theme, psychoanalysis as a health care profession.

Marvin Hyman began the debate with a scholarly review of the evolution of the relationship of medicine and psychoanalysis. He provided a cogent contrast between the two enterprises, one being characterized as concerned with symptoms, the other the whole of mental life; one pertaining to pathology, the other to psychodynamics; one seeking physical, objective, and historical fundamental causes and cures for illness, the other studying subjective experience; one assuming responsibility for the patient, the other taking responsibility only for the process; one seeking to reduce the human condition to the biological and chemical, the other content with the psychical; one viewing mental illness as fact, with diagnosis determining treatment, the other seeing mental illness as metaphor, with treatment being diagnosis and vice versa; one emphasizing outcome, the other, process; and one seeing the professional as the responsible authority, the other requiring shared responsibility. Such an extensive list of contrasts implies that psychoanalytic psychology's efforts to be part of any health care delivery system will be to the detriment of psychoanalysis and analysands and in conflict with the very process of psychoanalysis.

Stanley Moldawsky began his rebuttal by agreeing with Dr. Hyman's distinctions, but taking a contrasting view of psychoanalysis having always been alternate health care in the nonmedical tradition of treatments such as vitamin therapy, nutrition, homeopathy, apitherapy, chiropractic, and osteopathy. From that perspective, psychoanalysts have therapeutic responsibilities to help patients with reality testing, provide referral for psychopharmacological intervention, arrange for hospitalization if indicated, and provide validation of patient experiences.

Psychologists had to struggle to establish their autonomy as alternate health care practitioners in the past, argued Moldawsky, and will need to struggle again in the current reform (and managed care) climate. Political organization is necessary now, as it has been before, to achieve inclusion of mental health benefits, inclusion of psychologists, substantial outpatient benefits, regulation of managed care, willing provider regulations, and point-of-service options. Removing ourselves from the system will work neither for our patients nor ourselves. Psychoanalysis may be excluded from the system but psychologist-psychoanalysts must not be, concluded Moldawsky.

Dr. Golland's discussion highlighted the contrasting positions of Hyman and Moldawsky by raising questions concerning the value of linking psychoanalysis with alternate health care such as bee venom therapy; whether a focus on psychodynamics eliminates the concept of psychopathology; whether external or psychic reality has priority in our work, our responsibilities as analysts, and appropriate evaluation of the work. He encouraged continued debate by raising the issues of analyzability and the distinction between psychotherapy and psychoanalysis.

Hyman and Moldawsky responded to each other and to Golland. Questions and comments from the audience stimulated further rejoinder by the debaters, who easily could have continued to respond meaningfully, except that the allotted time period came to an end.

Whither or Wither?

President's Column, *The Round Robin* (1995)

In the last issue of Round Robin, I expressed the hope that, during my presidency, I might articulate the special place of our section, Psychologist-Psychoanalyst Practitioners, in the highly populated world of professional organizations. I did not realize that this hope would immediately become a primary agenda item of the Section Board. Nor did I realize that such articulation might involve some reactivation of old political battles within the section.

From our birth 13 years ago, we defined ourselves as a section of trained psychoanalytic practitioners within Division 39, which is itself open to any APA member with an interest in psychoanalysis. We set standards of training for admission to the section which include lengthy and intense experiences in the tripartite model that has characterized our field since the 1920s. Of course, we recognized that American psychologists had to find different paths to such training, given the history here of medical control of psychoanalysis.

Our section has grown and continues to attract membership. Lately, most applicants have institute-based training experiences, following the historic Division-supported lawsuit which ended exclusion of psychologists from medical institutes and encouraged development of our own training centers.

Some nine years ago a group of Division members applied to the Division board to become a section of clinicians which would not have what they saw as exclusionary standards. The Division, with our section in strong support, declined to create such an alternate practitioner section, and a compromise was reached creating Section V, Psychologist-Psychoanalyst Forum, to which any Division member might be admitted. An uneasy peace characterized the relationship between Section I and Section V, until last year when Section V, following its own procedures, adopted a change of name to that which its founders had initially intended, Psychologist-Psychoanalyst Clinicians. The name change was reported in Division publications.

The board of Section I was taken aback by the reported change and noted its concern in Section News in the Division newsletter, while seeking a meeting with Section V leaders and seeking to place the issue on the Division board agenda. Organizations move slowly and the meeting with Section V did not take place until January, just before the Section board meeting. The Division board, hoping for an amicable resolution, offered mediation and did not put the matter on its own agenda.

Marvin Hyman and I represented Section I board, while Spyros Orfanos and Frank Goldberg represented Section V. Our meeting was a friendly one, but sharply differing positions were stated. We felt that they had unilaterally abrogated the terms of their creation; they felt they had, at last, properly defined their section.

At the Section board meeting in January a unanimous position emerged: a) to press the Division board to require a rescission of the Section V name change; and b) to create a Committee on Mission and Affiliation.

Section I board asserts, as it did when Section V originally came into being, that a clinical practice section of a psychoanalytic interest group requires appropriate standards, e.g., of intensity and duration of training. All Division members eschew inappropriate standards such as a medical degree; self-definition is also an inappropriate standard for a responsible practitioner/clinician group.

The Section V action catalyzed for our board a growing sense that the relationship between Section I and the Division had evolved in the last several years and needed reexamination. Reduced participation by Section I members in the leadership and programs of the Division, and a reduced commonality of interest, were felt to characterize the evolution. "Examine thyself" had been good humanistic philosophy even before it became a psychoanalytic tenet.

Board member and past president of both our section and the Division Ernest Lawrence agreed to chair the new committee. Along with our president-elect, Frederic Levine, our immediate past president, Marvin Hyman and myself; Harriet Basseches, Nell Logan and Judith Welles also agreed to serve. The committee has begun to work and will be deliberate in meeting its charge.

As trained analysts we do not, by habit, act in haste. The committee expects to be at its task for a good while in preparing a report and recommendations for our Board. As responsible organization leaders, we are committed to maintaining an open dialogue with our membership in advance of taking any significant actions.

Words matter to analysts; names matter. Organizations also matter, and a vital organization must be clear in its mission so as to provide meaningful programs and affiliation for its members.

All of us recognize the external threat to psychoanalytic ideology and practice. Some of us believe that a more serious threat may be internal: the inability to define clearly who we are and what we do. I conclude this column by restating the hope that we may articulate the special place of our section among psychoanalytic organizations, and by extension, strengthen the effective practice of psychoanalysis.

Compare and Contrast

President's Column, *The Round Robin* (1995)

If I were to distill in a phrase the most valuable skill provided by my studies at Stuyvesant High School and Brandeis University, "compare and contrast" might just do it. Whether in history (World Wars I and II), music (Mozart and Haydn); literature (romantic and ''beat'' poets); or science (Newton and Einstein), such an analysis, inevitably evaluated by a final exam question, was routinely expected. The skill could be used with matters from the most abstract to the most mundane (selecting dinner from a menu, for example), it provided clear organization for my thinking.

In psychoanalytic psychology, the related approach for me used Erikson's dual definition of identity: an identity involves similarities with others and differences from them. While we are, indeed, in Sullivan's words, "much more nearly human than otherwise," we are also, each of us, unique. To know oneself, a goal of psychoanalysis, is to know one's common humanity (compare) and one's special nature (contrast). Neglecting either component always does an injustice to the person or issue to be understood.

In this column I want to take up a few examples of what I consider such neglect: the first is organizational and continues the discussion begun in my last column on the Section V name change. The second is theoretical and responds to Jay Greenberg's "The Analyst's Notebook" contribution, also in the last issue of *The Round Robin*.

The reactivation of political battles engendered by our claiming a uniqueness within Division 39 has, it seems, intensified. My debate in these pages with Section V president Arnold Schneider was continued at the Division Board meeting in Santa Monica. An hour of agenda time was given to discussion of the Section V name change, the role of sections in the Division, and the special place, if any, of Section I. The discussion was serious and respectful. The matter will be revisited in August, with the Division board accepting responsibility for deciding on the acceptability of the Section V name change at that time. [You may recall the key point in my argument: "Clinicians" and "Practitioners" are synonymous; another section should not be allowed to take our name.]

Following that discussion, a new proposal emerged. Division Board member Lewis Aron, a member of both Sections I and V, suggested the dissolution of both Sections, each having served its historical purpose. Psychoanalytic credentialing, he argued, should not come about through Section membership, but instead through the newly created and independent ABPsaP. My mini-debate with Aron, with the participation of Arnold Schneider, will have been seen by you in the latest issue of the Division newsletter.

My arguments with Schneider and Aron boil down to an assertion of Section I's identity as an organization of psychoanalysts within APA that meets and supports standards of training involving intensity and duration. It remains for the Division and for this Section to determine whether such an organizational identity is acceptable or desirable in its present form.

If the Division approves Section V's name change (or denies us our membership criteria) it would be saying, with Aron, that APA will not be implicated in defining the clinical practice of psychoanalysis. It would say, thereby, that Section I and Section V are two versions of a common entity. In my view, such a denial of our unique identity would be an implicit dissolution. There may be many Division colleagues who desire such an outcome, contending that all Division members are similarly psychoanalysts and that our standards (differences) are irrelevant.

In the face of these possible Division actions, we must continue to ask what we are as an organization. Our Committee on Mission and Affiliation is taking up that question, but it is a question, ultimately, for the entire membership. Do we wish to ignore differences and be at one with our Division colleagues or, instead, is there some importance to asserting our uniqueness while maintaining common cause where warranted? If we have no special mission, no difference from other organizations within APA, we should, ourselves, consider the Aron (dis)solution. We all belong to several professional organizations; Section I should provide something special if it is to be a meaningful affiliation for us.

Greenberg's "Words and Acts" quite explicitly attempts to undo the distinction between words and actions, claiming everything the analyst does to be an action. His latter claim is, clearly, correct, but that hardly makes words and acts identical. The straw man Freudian "loyalists" created by Greenberg would be fools to assert the possibility of speaking without acting. But Greenberg believes his rhetorical claims (words) are able to demolish (a dramatic action) the idea that interpretation from a position of technical neutrality has any privileged status in psychoanalysis. He characterizes (with words) his recommendations as models of risk-taking (acts) which demonstrate the superiority of his interactive psychoanalytic process over "orthodoxies of received technique." His selected clinical example, as is common in our debates, seems to support his notion of a radical interactive model, but his argument blurs instead of elucidating the issue.

"Acting in the transference" and its more current version, "enactment," have been major topics of study in mainstream Freudian psychoanalysis for decades. What differentiates the mainstream study is its insistence on a thorough understanding of the complexities of the issue; comparing and contrasting, rather than declaring all types of interventions the same because they have commonalities. Such an approach has allowed mainstream psychoanalysts to expand their technical repertoire and become more effective practitioners with a wider range of analysands, while avoiding revision for its own sake and the loss of essential and hard-won psychoanalytical insight. Greenberg, an important and influential theoretician, is surely able to note the differences between words and acts: differences central to our "talking cure" from its beginning, differences not erased by rhetorical radicalism. By discussing only similarities between words and acts, his "Notebook" piece does justice neither to the issue he addresses, nor to his reputation for scholarly thoughtfulness.

Erik Erikson's Clinical Contributions: A Symposium in Memorial Tribute Introduction and Discussion

Psychoanalytic Review (1997), 325–328, 363–365

Erik H. Erikson (1902-1994) was, after two people surnamed Freud, the psychoanalyst best known to the educated public. His masterpiece *Childhood and Society* (1950) inaugurated the life-span orientation in developmental psychology and placed psychoanalytic theory firmly into social and historical contexts. He should need little introduction to readers of this journal who would know that his contributions to psychoanalysis and to general knowledge are of the first rank.

An artist and teacher, Erikson's range of interests even after he became an analyst were such that he can be considered almost solely responsible for the extension of a psychoanalytic sensibility to the fields of education, biography, sociology, and history. He is the acknowledged founder of life-span developmental psychology, of psychobiography, and of psychohistory. For many of us, his biopsychosocial approach was the first assertively nonmedical psychoanalytic model of the human condition, expanding a reductionistic and pathologizing vocabulary with his concept of life tasks and their derived vulnerabilities, strengths and virtues, related, nonetheless, to psychosexual stages. Erikson's life work seems, indeed, to go well beyond Hartmann's attempt to make psychoanalysis a general psychology. It serves instead to explore the not at all average expectable environment and to provide a multidisciplinary integration which breaks down false barriers between disciplines.

And yet, there is a great paradox. While no less a figure than Robert Wallerstein, in an obituary (1995) published in the *International Journal of Psychoanalysis*, proclaims Erikson a true genius, something has gone awry between psychoanalysis and Erik Erikson. His work is hardly cited in our journals nor

444

assigned in our institutes. In expanding the bounds of psychoanalysis, he has, it seems, been evicted from its narrow environs.

On the clinical level that for many of us defines those narrower environs, I have always found the Erikson sensibility to inform and to influence my basically classical stance. My own feeling is that Erik Erikson has made a most meaningful contribution to the practice of psychoanalysis which has not been explicitly acknowledged. This symposium is one attempt at redress.

Margaret Brenman-Gibson gives us a beautiful and loving paper with Erikson's unfortunate marginalization as its central focus. Morris Eagle has looked at the broad clinical implications of two of Erikson's most sweeping contributions: the interaction of individual and society, and the relative autonomy of the several developmental phases. Irving Steingart has concentrated on Erikson's particular and subtle influence on clinical thinking, and on the relevance of his thinking to some of the most current psychoanalytic controversies.

Erikson's marginalization, Brenman-Gibson tells us, can be attributed in good measure to the disdain intellectuals too often have for so-called popularizers. She is right, and they are more than wrong; for in being wrong they have contributed to the marginalization of psychoanalysis as a profession and as a way of thinking. My own experience as a teacher educator is that psychoanalytic thinking can effectively be made accessible, and that Erikson's ideas are especially useful toward that end. In teacher training, in fact, Erikson's ideas provide the primary exposure to a psychoanalytic point of view.

To the extent that psychoanalysis, as a treatment, has adopted Leo Stone's widening scope, rather than Anna Freud's narrower one (and that is mainly the case), Eagle's emphasis on Erikson's social point of view is most welcome. Freud was concerned with guarding against a parochialism in psychoanalysis, selecting the gentile Jung as first IPA president to avoid having his discovery seen as a Jewish specialty. We need to maintain a similar guard against psychoanalysis becoming a treatment for well-to-do Americans. We gain as well from an in-the-bones sensitivity to the crises of adult development of which Eagle reminds us, lest we be seen by our patients as interested only in the past, and insensitive to their adult concerns and needs. I have, in addition, found Erikson's life tasks to be useful concepts in diagnostic appraisal, asking myself during a consultation how close are presenting problems to adult normative tasks.

My "in-the-bones" metaphor applies most to Steingart's paper. He speaks of subtle, unconscious influences exerted by Erikson. Psychodynamics go well beyond our earlier focus on psychopathology. Erikson's ideas about hope, will-power, purpose, competence (to cite his first four "virtues"), and devotion, affiliation, production, renunciation (to cite his last four "strengths"), have enabled us as clinicians to better conceptualize and experience the full humanity of any of our patients, and, thereby, to do better treatment.

In closing, I want to note the man, Erikson, as a model of generativity, an idea he extended beyond mere productivity to include a long-term caring for what one produces; and as a model of ego-integrity, refusing McCarthyite loyalty oaths and living a good and principled life to its fullest. Thus he demonstrated the highest of virtues, wisdom.

This symposium provides evidence that, to our good fortune, such wisdom can be passed on.

Meet the Editors: Invited Symposium

With Jay R. Greenberg, Ph.D., *Contemporary Psychoanalysis*;
Adrienne Harris, Ph.D., *Psychoanalytic Dialogues*; Owen Renik, M.D.,
Psychoanalytic Quarterly; Joseph Reppen, Ph.D., *Psychoanalytic Books*;
and Arnold D. Richards, M.D., Moderator, *Journal of the American
Psychoanalytic Review*
Psychoanalytic Psychology (1995)

An inquisitive audience heard from and participated in discussion with editors of five of our leading psychoanalytic journals. The editor-panelists began the session by responding in turn to the moderator concerning their roles as trustees of the intellectual heritage of psychoanalysis, and their particular responsibilities to a specific readership.

The presentations described for the audience some of the history and focus of the journals, which vary in age from 6 to 82 years, and include independents and organizational affiliates. They have varying editorial procedures. One (*Psychoanalytic Review*) has newsstand sales in addition to subscriptions. Instead of emphasizing their roles about heritage conservation, each editor spoke of seeking novel and creative contributions from new voices and good writing styles, and each articulated a commitment to presenting a widening scope of theoretical orientations to serve their readers better than they had when there was a more parochial focus. I questioned the commonality in these claims, inquiring as to differences in approach. A lively and friendly interchange among the editors ensued, and differences emerged, particularly in the editorial process.

Many of the questions from the audience were on the nuts-and-bolts of that process: blind review, publication lead time, choice of peer reviewers, e-mail, and newer technologies. They elicited specific responses from the panel as well as philosophical musings on the welcoming of an interactive readership, the future of print journals, and the general state of writing. Other questions related to exposing readers to international literature (a regular feature of two journals and planned by others), to nonclinical pieces (also regular in some), to papers with minimal bibliography (more likely to be reviewed skeptically, but welcome, nonetheless).

One member of the audience summarized the overall effect of the session: the editors and their processes were humanized and demystified; he felt more comfortable with the idea of submitting an article for publication.

Other Voices, Other Visions

President's Column, *The Round Robin* (1996)

This, my concluding president's column, appears when I have already been succeeded by the able Fred Levine. It is a tradition that this column summarizes and thanks. Those tasks are, for me, interrelated. Appreciation is due to every member of the Section board, for supporting with one voice a vision of psychoanalysis and of the Section's role among psychoanalytic organizations, a role consistent since its founding. Especially stalwart was my predecessor, Marv Hyman, now Division president-elect, and Ernie Lawrence, who stays on as chair of our Committee on Mission and Affiliations. My thanks go also to our members, who have been most supportive of our efforts this past year, even in the face of attempts by some Division leaders to separate membership from the board's position.

Unfortunately, that attempt to divide may continue. The martial metaphors I had hoped would be put aside were escalated in the last Division newsletter, with references to the Bosnian war, to the conflict between Israel and the Palestinians, and to the Division's being "held hostage to factional disputes." Fully one-quarter of the newsletter's pages were devoted to a presidential vision which differs significantly from that of this Section, and which includes a tendentious reading of an ill-conceived survey, along with charts and bar graphs to imply a scientific objectivity that is far from the truth.

It is better that the Division and the Section move on, as mature organizations, to deal reasonably with the issues that define and concern them. It is my hope that the current leadership of the Division will move that way; I know that this Section is pursuing such a process.

That we are a rigid monolith eschewing diversity is given the lie by every issue of *The Round Robin*, by each of our three annual professional programs, and by even the most casual scanning of our membership roster. Section I embraces differing theoretical commitments, a range of professional concerns, and a variety of political positions. Where we hold fast is in our bedrock belief that analytic training includes personal treatment and supervision which has measurable intensity and duration, and that only such training qualifies one as a practicing clinical psychoanalyst.

Our work this past year in reasserting this position has resulted in a revitalization of commitment. Older and newer activists have put forth ideas that have become part of our dialogue. Two important such ideas suggested the title of this column. The first emerges from the deliberations of the Lawrence committee: that the Section may be more identified with a psychoanalysis that is not the province of other professions (medicine, psychology) and may, instead, continue its revitalization by welcoming those who may not be qualified as psychologists. The idea that psychoanalysis is a profession sui generis is not new. That a section of an APA division might be less identified and involved with APA is likely to be controversial and is a direct challenge to the vision expressed in the Division's most recent presidential address. It is worthy of our attention.

The second idea, long championed by Marv Hyman, is taken up by Patrick Kavanaugh in the last Division newsletter: psychoanalysis outside health care. This, too, is controversial, as we saw when Marv debated Stan Moldawsky (our member and now Division 42 president-elect) at the APA meeting in Los Angeles under the Section's aegis.

There are yet other voices and other visions in our diverse and vital organization. We can provide an appropriate arena for debate precisely because we recognize differences and yet maintain a commonality of purpose.

I close with thanks to our editor, Ira Moses, for taking this outstanding newsletter to new heights, and, again, to our membership for providing me with the privilege of its presidency.

Third Party Payments in Psychoanalysis: Clinical Implications

Discussant, APA Division 39 Meeting, Denver, Colorado—March 1, 1997

We're all nuts about money! Attitudes about money and time are psychoanalytically well-known areas for the manifestations of character dynamics. Eissler's (1974) paper on the payment of fees (Int'l Rev Psa, 1:73-101) remains a tour de force on many issues relevant to fee-payment in analysis. Freud (1913a) also addressed money matters, often wisely. His admonition regarding low- or no-fee treatment reducing analysand motivation, however, turned out to be a partial truth, not a sound guideline.

I believe we need a range of responses appropriate to different third-party situations. I think it unwise to have a general policy either a) rejecting third party for all patients; b) accepting the intrusions as part of the life of practice; or c) taking their money while fighting their procedures. Any of these alternatives may be appropriate in a specific situation; each of them has important implications for the treatment.

Outright rejection of third-party payers limits our practice to the well-off, yet may be advisable for individuals who can pay if they are advised of the tradeoffs. For others the third-party conditions may be the only ones allowing them treatment. Yet others may be helped by our joining their individual battles.

How we deal with any external situation in a patient's life, other than by neutral, engaged interpretation, may or may not limit the achievable results of the analytic work. How we deal with external situations derives from our theory of technique and therapeutic action. I consider myself conservative on matters of technique and would prefer to move as little beyond interpretation as possible, given the structure and needs of the patient, and given my own boundaries as to how far I might go. I have written to an insurance company for one patient, suggesting that legal action might be successfully waged against its jeopardizing the mental health of their insured. It is my general preference in technique not to do that for the patient.

Whatever stance we take with an individual regarding third-party payers, it is critical that we try to understand its impact on transference, alliance, and real relationship—to the extent possible. Some patients will ignore our efforts in this regard, and they are likely to be those who are unavailable for transference work in other areas as well.

On this issue, I come down as I do in many matters of technique: there is a useful model (in this case, to protect treatment from intrusion and to analyze the effects of any intrusion), and variation or even deviation are sometimes necessary. This may limit results, but results are never unlimited. In this impossible profession, essentially idiographic, it almost always depends.

Not an Endgame: Termination in Psychoanalysis

Psychoanalytic Psychology (1997)

For much of the history of psychoanalysis, the matter of termination received little attention. Freud's famous chess metaphor, offered in the paper devoted to the technique of beginning the treatment (1913a), designated termination the endgame, which could be subject to "an exhaustive systematic presentation" (p. 123). Freud did not take up that presentation, either at that time or later in his more philosophical paper specific to the subject (Freud, 1937). Ferenczi (1955) paid some attention to termination, bequeathing the notion that analyses would die from exhaustion. Annie Reich was astonished that these were the only two papers on the topic until her own (1950/1973), although seven other papers appear concurrent with hers in the *International Journal*. Glover's 1955 revision of his text was the first to define a termination phase per se, and Firestein's 1978 book was the first presentation of a series of extensive clinical examples to elucidate the process. Since then, the literature on termination has become quite extensive.

From the time of the endgame metaphor until recently, the relative absence of study paradoxically may have led to a sense that termination might, indeed, follow the metaphor. A few definable principles and variations would be available, as was seemingly true of analytic beginnings. Terminations would evolve, naturally, from properly conducted analyses; the phase would proceed from a mutually agreed-upon date and would include regression, reactivation of symptom complexes and a mourning process; the technique would be a continuation of transference and resistance analysis, especially regarding reactions to the fact of impending termination, with the only essential difference being the analyst's agreement to the actual date of ending.

This simple view is not supported by Firestein's early literature review (1974), in which he demonstrates the variety of termination criteria and the lack of unanimity regarding technique. Termination, however, is not often taught at our institutes (Blum, 1989), in part because the length of analyses has resulted in candidates having limited exposure to appropriate case material during their training. Despite the growing literature, which includes many warnings against a simplified view of termination, an idealized and simplistic view is nonetheless seen by some to obtain in practice.

Novick (this issue) asserted that an omnipotent perfectionism has kept analysts from facing issues of termination squarely, and he delineated several other factors, keeping the matter from appropriate study. Prominent among these is analysts' avoiding their own feelings of loss. Bergmann (1997) found criteria for termination often to consist of idealized statements, and he suggested that external realities, rather than psychoanalytic criteria, are usually determinative.

Shane and Shane (1984), reviewing and extending the list of indicators for termination proposed by Firestein (1978), discussed overall health, symptomatic improvement, structural change, intuition, increased autonomy, resolution of the transference neurosis, dream themes, continuity of self, and developmental attainments. They presented examples that they hoped would guard against the risk of idealization of any of these criteria. They showed, in particular, evidence that transference neuroses are modified rather than eliminated, and, in general, that partial achievements of criteria may be legitimately considered successes.

Oremland, Blacker, and Norman (1975), noting Freud's contention (1937) that all analyses, even successful ones, are incomplete, provided a follow-up study of two incomplete cases whose terminations were based on "reality resistance(s)" (p. 838). They concluded with a definition of successful termination that emphasizes significant alleviation of psychopathology and a mutual confidence that a self-analytic process would ensue.

Several authors attempted to develop principles while giving due consideration to the variability of the process. An early issue of Psychoanalytic Inquiry (Bornstein, 1982) is devoted to articles in this vein. Novick (1982) defined different types of termination (mutual, forced, unilateral), and suggested that attempts at unilateral termination may, for some patients, be a precondition for mutuality (the desired type). Limentani (1982), focusing on "unexpected" (forced) terminations, suggested that our theories (or idealizations) should not bind our practice. Dewald (1982), noting that some terminations are due to the death or illness of the analyst and leaving patients essentially on their own, emphasized the unpredictability of outcomes.

In 1982, Firestein noted that conditions for termination seem as idiosyncratic as the specific symptoms, character problems, and life situation of any analysand,

454

and that analytic technique in termination is as variable as it was when Glover published his well-known survey (1955). Yet he found consistencies involving an emphasis on clinical evidence of symptomatic improvement, and on maintenance of treatment style during the terminal phase. Gillman (1982), using a Glover-like survey, provided data on 48 successful cases without external determination. He found consistencies: For example, patients usually initiate the topic; mourning is common as is an increase in symptoms. He found variation as well: for example, some termination dreams and some attempts at prolongation of the treatment.

Rangell (1982) presented a model of termination strikingly different than most. He considered that roughly the second half of treatment is a moving toward termination in what he actually diagramed as a notched semicircle of the overall course of treatment.

Viorst (1982) provided data on various emotional reactions of analysts to the conclusion of their treatments, though Novick (1997) considered emotional reactivity to be rarely expressed, and Firestein (1982) considered most such statements to be professional rather than emotional.

Firestein concluded the Psychoanalytic Inquiry issue in 1982 by noting that aphorisms and metapsychology seem to be preferred to facing the difficulty of applying principles, such difficulty being the result of the extreme variation in endings of treatment. This conclusion is in agreement with those of both Bergmann (1997) and Novick (1997).

This article is an attempt to further the thesis that psychoanalytic termination is not simple and that the endgame metaphor has been unfortunate. With several clinical examples of treatment endings that do not readily fit endgame rules, I try to show that termination phase issues and technique are as complex as issues and technique in the overall psychoanalytic enterprise, and that terminations always fall short of any ideal.

From this demonstration, I try to develop some general principles, which, as in all of psychoanalysis, constitute recommendations, not rules. The actual work of psychoanalysis involves principles and variations from these principles due to the individuality of every particular analysand. Following Rangell's felicitous metaphor of dusk between day and night (1954), there are both nuances within psychoanalysis and things that are much more clearly either psychoanalytic or non-psychoanalytic. Reich (1950) for example, considered partial successes to make for non-psychoanalytic endings; I assert that all successes are partial.

To combat the idealizations that have developed, I propose that imperfect variations of psychoanalytic terminations are the norm and should not be considered as failures. Close study of such variations should serve to sensitize analysts to the theoretical and technical issues involved.

Case 1, A Case of Giving (It) Up (Exhaustion): Ms. A

Ms. A was in psychoanalysis for 12 years, following a 2-year exploratory psychotherapy. A 25-year-old when she began treatment, living with her parents and working as a temporary secretary despite holding a master's degree, Ms. A came for relief of depression following the breakup of an engagement. Over the course of the work, she separated from the parental home and developed a successful career. Depressive symptoms were resolved early on, but she continued to have a general unhappiness at not finding a husband. Intense attachment to father and rivalry with mother were the major themes of the larger part of the analysis. A late-in-life only child of Holocaust survivors, Ms. A was doted upon by father and dominated by mother into adulthood.

Ms. A is a strikingly attractive woman who had no difficulty finding suitors. Her family romance fantasy required that they be millionaires. To a man, they were inappropriate choices, and each relationship reached its fated end in weeks or months, although she would return briefly to some. To her chagrin, she found that three of her lovers slept with loaded guns at hand, and on one occasion, she and her date barely missed being accidental victims of an assassination attempt.

During the treatment, Ms. A had three abortions. Several of her lovers were married men. When a suitor seemed on several accounts to be suitable, Ms. A would pull away from the relationship in fear of betraying her father. On one occasion quite late in treatment, despite frequent confrontation and interpretation, she insisted on taking an unaccompanied vacation to Europe with her father. She would neither leave him nor give him the grandchildren he desperately desired, in a dogged insistence that she, not her mother, was his favorite woman. Guilty and self-punitive reactions to her living out Oedipal wishes formed a vicious cycle in her life.

The termination phase lasted approximately 2 years, initiated by Ms. A. One date was disavowed; a second, despite great anxiety, was met. This long and arduous treatment had achieved many life goals and some treatment goals (Ticho, 1972). It did not achieve, it seemed, a resolution of an intractable Oedipus complex, despite considerable apparent insight. Toward the very end, Ms. A articulated what

I felt: We'd done what we could, and she might or might not achieve her goal of marriage on her own. (About 2 years later, I received a birth announcement, and a lengthy letter of gratitude informing me that Ms. A had married 8 months earlier.)

Some would consider this treatment an analytic failure, its having ended with its central analytic issue unresolved. Some would consider it an overly long treatment that should have been ended earlier by the analyst. Some would question the 2-year termination period in which the first date was disavowed.

That the psychoanalytic process is designed to continue with post-analytic self-analysis (Siegel, 1982) and that significant changes may then be expected is now generally accepted. Although there are some who indicate that the analyst should suggest or take the lead in termination (following Ferenczi & Rank, 1925), such end-setting, despite Freud's using it with the Wolf Man, is not normative. Our therapeutic responsibilities, even in an analysis, include continuing to work with analysands so long as they wish, provided that our professional judgment suggests possible progress rather than irreconcilable impasse. That "the lion only leaps once" (Freud, 1937) regarding ending dates, is not consistent with other experience (Shane & Shane, 1984).

Ultimately, our judgments in each analysis are intuitive (Novick, 1982), making use of the principles and uncertainties we have learned as best we can apply them to each analysand. These judgments are, of course, subject to countertransference pressures. We must be wary both of holding on to patients for too long, and of succumbing to current values aimed at shortening treatments to fit approved nosological schemes.

Case 2, A Case of External Determination: Mr. B

External events precipitate endings in psychoanalytic treatment with high frequency. Such endings may be conducted as and considered legitimate terminations, rather than being automatically judged as premature and, therefore, unsuccessful. In fact, it is often enough the case that external events trigger a termination, that we need to understand the coincidence as fitting the needs of the analysand, and we need to develop principles that may be useful for these circumstances.

Mr. B, age 25, began an analysis that was to last almost 7 years, following 5 months of exploratory psychotherapy. Pressured into treatment by his girlfriend, he described himself as irresponsible, an abuser of drugs and alcohol, a spoiled kid now grown up. He also reported two episodes of impersonal homosexual activity while under the influence of alcohol, and was troubled by their possible meaning.

A financial whiz, Mr. B was a great success as a stock trader. His high income supported his substance abuse. A major issue for him was that his father's similar success was followed by forced bankruptcy for fraud when Mr. B was 9 years old. Following two suicide attempts, Mr. B's father became a passive man, with mother assuming breadwinning and family leadership roles.

The treatment was characterized by Mr. B's acting on his wishes, in and out of the transference, seeking gratifications and facing unhappy consequences with regret. Drunken homosexual episodes, impulse purchases, chronic lateness, and absences were frequent in the first few years of analysis. As the work continued, Mr. B supplemented it on his own initiative, with the structure of a 12-step program. He got sober, and internal gains began to match external success. Marriage and fatherhood followed. Economies taken in his industry made for cutting back on his lifestyle, especially with new family responsibilities, and his being laid off was not so much of a surprise that he hadn't made reasonable preparation for it. Such preparation included a 3-month termination period for his psychoanalysis, at reduced session frequency.

Although this termination was, from my perspective then, as well as the common wisdom now, a too-short and inadequately planned termination, I would now argue that a pretermination phase was in progress, with effective analysis of the negative oedipal constellation well along. The termination was similar in content, I would now judge, to what it would have been with more time available. A mourning process began; review and recapitulation of analytic work occurred; and Mr. B. demonstrated his most important analytic gain: a deliberative, reflective attitude that had, to a very significant extent, supplanted his impulse-ridden orientation.

Case 3, An Apparently Interminable Treatment of 17 Years, with Several Years of What Turned Out to be a Termination Phase: Mr. C

Although we have gotten used to the lengthening of analyses and have not adopted Freud's end-setting technique with the Wolf Man, very lengthy analyses are surely subject to legitimate questions as to analyzability, countertransference interference, and inadequate technical skill. This example is presented to demonstrate that, these legitimate questions notwithstanding, some analyses may require heroic expenditures of time, and some terminations may require years.

Mr. C, a 24-year-old recently married graduate student, began psychotherapy for fear of self-assertion, difficulties with authority figures, a general sense of passivity, and concerns about his hastily entered marriage. The initial recommendation was for psychotherapy, because concerns about analyzability were prominent. Mr. C's communication was vague and sometimes confused; he was anxious and had a propensity to overeat, and he suffered memory lapses. Four years of psychotherapy resulted in marked improvement in mental status, internalization of symptoms, establishment of a professional career, and a strong desire for psychoanalysis, which emerged following the death of his grandfather.

In the first 5 years of the analysis, Mr. C divorced and remarried, mourned the death of his grandfather as well as of his own father, became a father himself, and was diagnosed with Buerger's disease as the analysis seemed to be entering a pretermination phase. An additional eight years of analysis was required, during which the manifest focus was on his inability to give up smoking so as to prevent the amputation of his limbs (a frequent outcome of protracted Buerger's disease).

During this period, Mr. C quit smoking several times with the help of formal programs and on his own. He would relapse well before he had the confidence to propose an ending date. When off cigarettes, he would binge on food or go on gambling sprees. Frequent absences characterized several periods. Amidst these difficulties, meaningful analysis of transference fantasies regarding castration as punishment for voyeuristic wishes ensued. Eventually, an end-setting became possible with 9 months left to work. Smoking was given up, and a mourning process culminated in genuine gratitude.

Case 4, A Case of Weaning: Dr. D

Most psychoanalysts have not adopted Alexander's suggestion (1954) that analytic termination be a weaning process, and there has been little controversy in the field over this issue. Dr. D. began a training analysis that went on well beyond graduation for a total of 9 years prior to the start of a termination phase. He took an additional 2 years to complete treatment at a twice weekly frequency. Dr. D had, in the first 9 years, achieved many life and analytic goals he had set for himself but, despite discussion of the issue on several occasions, he was unable to set a date.

Dr. D himself decided on a reduced frequency of treatment; his analyst acquiesced. Other aspects of the conduct of the treatment did not change. After a year, Dr. D became able to set a date and to conclude his analysis.

Although we make recommendations as to frequency for principled reasons, we respect the patient's autonomy in accepting our recommendations or not. Such circumstances need not automatically be considered either failures or nonanalytic procedures.

Case 5, an Impulsive-Driven Man, an Impulsive Ending: Mr. E

A 6-year analysis had a 10-month termination phase following the analysand's decision to relocate after having achieved a higher level in his profession. A 7-year psychotherapy with another analyst and a year and a half of pre-analytic work had left this man, 34 when the analysis began, still struggling with inner demons. In adolescence, he engaged in dramatically dangerous activities and still had eruptions of risky behavior. The analysis resulted in considerable modulation of drive-eruption and inner turmoil. Mr. E was able to stabilize a shaky marriage, become a father, and advance in his professional career. Financial pressures and opportunities, involving geographic relocation, provided ample external impetus to end-setting. At the time, however, I felt we had entered a termination phase prematurely.

I worked interpretively rather than with confrontation, and the termination phase was unremarkable and quite satisfactory.

External events combining with less-than-complete achievement of analytic goals may give us pause as to the appropriateness of termination. I would now argue that there is always less-than-complete achievement and that there are most often external events which contribute to end-setting. These common conditions should not be considered inappropriate or nonanalytic, but normative. Such a consideration allows for maintenance of an analytic attitude, and a stance that properly accepts analysands as being in charge of their own lives.

Case 6, Learning from Psychotherapy Endings: Ms. F

A 34-year-old divorced mother of a 12-year-old daughter, Ms. F entered analytic psychotherapy on a thrice weekly basis using the couch. After two and a half years, she reduced her session frequency to twice weekly, and after another two and a half years to once a week. Her initial complaints were of promiscuity and inability to trust men, following abandonment by her husband who attempted to kidnap their 5-year-old child. The horror story that came to be revealed included the fact that the marriage was arranged within a therapy cult to which the patient's mother had brought her three children to live after the mother's own divorce when the patient was, herself, twelve.

In this cult, assigned therapists had sex even with early adolescents and directed their lives under the leadership of the guru. Ms. F lived in these circumstances for 14 years, completing college and a master's degree, becoming a wife and mother, and suffering the abandonment before becoming able to extricate herself.

The inability to trust men manifested itself as an important aspect of the transference that resulted in this treatment being a very tense and careful one in which preservation of the patient's sense of autonomy was a principle that most often superseded other treatment principles. This is a woman who would be considered high-strung and temperamental by most people, and would be very easily upset. She had left a treatment with a supportive woman therapist, despite having been helped considerably, when the woman became advising and directive as well as supportive. Ego-boundary issues were of critical importance in the analytic psychotherapy of this borderline woman.

Over time, Ms. F was able to develop a meaningful degree of trust in me. She was able to take a lover who, unlike most she had known, was not exploitative. They married. Much of the latter part of treatment was devoted to her wishes and fears about having a second child while still able to do so. Mothering was the only facet of herself about which she felt mostly good, and her daughter's departure for college left her wanting to reestablish a mothering role.

Ms. F's husband underwent a vasectomy reversal but, in a follow-up consultation over a year after termination, conception had not occurred, and Ms. F was now 43 and obsessively preoccupied with her conflict. During the ending period of treatment and in the consultation, Ms. F begged for my endorsement or dis-endorsement of her wish for a child. Interpretations and clarifications frustrated her but seemed to maintain the effectiveness of the treatment by not stealing her autonomy as she felt her post-cult therapist had done.

This treatment was a psychotherapy that ended in stages by a weaning process directed by the patient. In analysis, appropriate termination is one of several goals; in this therapy, it was a central goal as Ms. F had been in at least a quasi-psychotherapy almost continuously since age 12. The question of termination here had more to do with degrees of improvement rather than idealizations, and with partial solutions that provided degrees of satisfaction rather than resolutions of underlying conflicts.

My point in this example is that we can learn about analytic termination from psychotherapy endings if we recognize that analyses are surely meant to be therapeutic, and that partial solutions, geared to the individual patient's needs, are always the norm.

Case 7, A Forced Termination: Mrs. G

A year of successful twice-weekly exploratory psychotherapy was to come to an end as a result of the therapist's separation from military service. The patient, a married mother in her mid-thirties, had improved considerably. Depressive symptoms, alcohol binges, and promiscuous adultery while her often-abusive husband was on military assignment abroad had been reduced and almost eliminated. On the way to the final session, following some months of dealing with terminating the treatment, which had been her best relationship with a man, Mrs. G had a serious car accident in which the car was totaled, but she sustained only minor injuries. She hypothesized, in the rescheduled final hour, that the accident was unconsciously motivated, and that she needed to pay more attention to such motivations.

This case is offered to emphasize that endings are always to be taken very seriously. Forced terminations do, indeed, occur, and sometimes, as in this example, are unavoidable. Psychoanalysis and exploratory psychotherapies, perhaps any psychotherapies, arouse intense feelings that cannot be resolved quickly or easily. Despite the therapist's focus on the issues of ending, even in this relatively brief treatment, a life-threatening situation occurred.

Discussion

Each of the cases presented includes a termination that may be considered "unorthodox" in one or more of its dimensions. Ms. A's analysis ended with a shared sense of disappointment and with the analytic outcome in serious doubt. Mr. B's termination was externally precipitated, too short, and at reduced frequency. Mr. C's extremely long analysis and its ending were too focused on a symptom, a limb-threatening physical illness. Dr. D's termination involved a weaning process. Mr. E's termination seemed overly determined by external factors, and premature. Ms. F's termination left much work undone. Mrs. G's termination was forced.

These cases seem to me, however, not atypical. Few of our treatments meet the mythological, idealized model of termination that has inadvertently evolved. Even those terminations that seem closer to the ideal may be, like Kris's (1956) apparently good hour, only apparently good when measured against the myth of the endgame.

To replace our idealization, I suggest that terminations are unlikely to be simple matters of following one of a few (never precisely defined) endgame technical sequences that have clear moves. Each ending is, like the analysis of which it has been a part, an idiosyncratic activity that has some orienting principles, but much more ambiguity than clarity. Psychoanalysis is not, like chess, a game; termination is not an endgame.

This assertion defines psychoanalysis as an idiographic enterprise: a study of and a treatment for individuals, from which flexible orienting principles may be derived. Psychoanalytic technique is not rule bound, as Freud's title word "recommendations" (1912) is meant to emphasize.

What might these orienting principles be? I have, in discussing the cases, implied a few. Let me spell out four essential ones. First among these is that analysts try to follow the lead of the analysand. As in the treatment proper, the analysand's concerns need to become ours, and our interventions are designed (following Bibring, 1954) to further the analysis technically by evoking associative material rather than to be more directly curative. This principle does not require that the analysand always raise the matter of termination directly. Loewald (1988) presents several ways that the subject may be broached indirectly by patients. Long analyses with neither direct nor indirect reference to termination may call for the analyst's raising the question by noting its avoidance. Nonetheless, I believe that terminations forced or essentially led by the analyst are not desirable. (For a useful way of looking at the handling of necessarily forced terminations—as in my case of Mrs. G—see Martinez, 1989.)

A second guiding principle would be that terminations follow, in spirit, the technical style of the treatment itself, as it has developed in the individual case (Dewald, 1982). Termination in psychoanalysis is a phase of the therapy with characteristic issues, but except for the common practice of agreeing on a date, there is a general consensus that special techniques are neither required nor appropriate. Lipton (1961) reminded us that this principle applies even in the closing session.

The third principle is that psychoanalysis is always a therapy, and that therapeutic considerations are a central responsibility however else we may characterize the practice of psychoanalysis. Conceptual contrasts between psychotherapy and psychoanalysis are matters of considerable importance in actual practice, but the idea that a therapeutic attitude is not compatible with an analytic one is naive. It exaggerates differences and ignores similarities, an error as substantial as its opposite. Psychoanalysts believe that analytic practice is therapeutic in its effect; it is also often the case that therapeutic considerations that have influenced a particular treatment can be psychoanalytic in their spirit. Among the cases presented here, therapeutic concerns were most pronounced with Ms. F, but were necessarily important in each.

Perhaps the central principle, the fourth, is that endings of treatment need time and thoughtful attention. A psychoanalytic situation is designed to foster powerful transferential affects and fantasies, and therapies that are analytic in orientation do so as well. Ending such a treatment must, therefore, be a careful process in which analyst and analysand pay close attention to the special issues that parting always involves. The forced termination of Mrs. G and her car accident provide a dramatic example of potential consequences of inadequate attention.

These four principles, it turns out, are not unique to the issue of ending treatment. They are, in fact, among the reliable principles of the inherently flexible idiographic practice that characterizes psychoanalysis in general.

Some caution is in order. A flexible idiographic practice, and the variability of endings that I am describing, is hardly a call for an "anything goes" stance. To the contrary, the tenets of our professional training model are designed to foster a self-discipline to protect us and our patients from such a stance. The standard tripartite model of training (study, supervision, and analysis) can be applied, I think, to this issue.

We now have a substantial and growing psychoanalytic literature on termination, the study of which is essential both during coursework and following training. Supervision following graduation is recommended in general, and surely on initial cases entering a termination phase it should be recommended as well. For many psychoanalysts, clinical study groups with a leader or with peers may be considered suitable as an analog, and periodic consultation may also serve. As to the critical third cornerstone of our model, we need to rely, as Renik (1993b), among others, has recently noted, on the analytic superego, which continues to develop as a result both of our continuing analysis or self-analytic work and our careful observation of countertransference manifestations.

Among the reasons for Freud's (1925) consideration that psychoanalysis be included among the impossible professions is that there are no easy answers or guarantees in doing the work. Complexity, conditionality, and individuality make terminations, like psychoanalysis itself, not a game constrained by rules, but an enterprise requiring lifelong instruction, study, and self-exploration. Although we can terminate particular analyses, psychoanalytic training on termination and many other issues, like the self-analyses that we hope will follow a successful treatment, is interminable.

Totem or Taboo? The Ethics of Psychoanalytic Technique

With Special Reference to Influence and Neutrality
Annual Meeting of the American Psychological Association,
August 15, 1998

A 20-ish single woman comes for treatment for multiple problems related to school, work and family. During our third evaluation session, I am considering recommending psychoanalysis. (I am then in training. It is 1970. I might be able to take her on as a control case.) She begins to discuss her recreational drug use and tells me of her plan to experiment with Quaaludes.

A 30-ish mother of two is in psychoanalytic psychotherapy (twice weekly, face-to-face) for depression related to her husband's neglect. He is frequently absent, usually on military assignment. She drinks heavily, has taken to periodic promiscuity, and has herself begun to neglect her two children.

A 35-year-old recently married professional comes to treatment conflicted about his compulsive, anonymous homosexual encounters. His wife is approaching 40 and concerned about her "biological clock." After one miscarriage, she announces her pregnancy. He tacitly betrays his ambivalence about paternity by being less than enthusiastic at her news.

The question, what is good behavior? occupies the philosophical subdiscipline of Ethics. In psychology, this subdiscipline is represented by the Problem of Evil: psychologists ask why do people behave badly (or irrationally)? Clinical psychology and psychiatry are disciplines devoted to answering this age-old question and to providing solutions; psychoanalytic psychology offers one set of answers and a companion set of treatment approaches. Government and Education, (Freud's two other impossible professions), and, of course, Religion are also institutions addressing the Problem of Evil; they offer different answers and methodologies. In a philosophical sense then, evil may be considered the subject matter of psychoanalysis. This view would place ethics at the center of psychoanalytic concerns.

Patients who first sought treatment with Freud had not succeeded in ridding themselves of their Evil symptoms by available social, religious, neurological or psychiatric practices of the day. Our patients, too, present problems they have not been able to resolve with their usual devices. Exhortation and self-exhortation have failed them. In each clinical example here, the focus was on a conflict-laden, unhappy-making activity; even the Quaalude proposal can be seen this way, despite the lack of manifest complaint.

As analysts, we offer help to those who come to us in emotional conflict and distress—or, without awareness, hint at it. Of course, we hope to influence them, and, in cases of ego-dystonic problems, in ways consonant with their own desires. The second patient did not wish to drink to excess, to be promiscuous (her own characterization), nor to neglect her children. The third patient wanted desperately to be unambivalently enthusiastic about his wife's pregnancy, and to be heterosexual and faithful to her, but was not. One can easily infer that the first patient was looking to provoke some controlling external authority in response to what she knew was problematic behavior.

Faced with these problems, Carl Rogers and his non-directive school of therapy (as well as many contemporary cognitive therapies) recommend the technical stance of non-judgmentalism; Freud and psychoanalysis offer neutrality as a technical precept. Rogers offered his construct as a practical necessity to promote his clients' full disclosure in discussing their problems; Freudian neutrality, in reaction to the failure of moralizing and the inadequacy of suggestive techniques, has a similar but more ambitious aim: to allow emergence of unconscious (often shameful and guilty,—read "evil") ideas. Psychoanalytic epistemology, the question of how we come to know, has been a major focus of contention in the past twenty years. We will see that psychoanalytic axiology, the question of values, is no less controversial.

Psychoanalysis may properly be characterized as the rational study of irrationality. It is, likewise, an essentially moral and ethical activity, which, as a matter of technique, avoids moralizing. The rational study of irrationality follows most clearly from Freud's description (some would say discovery) of the ego, and the related clinical dictum, "where there was id, there shall ego be." The moral dimension of psychoanalysis evolves from the very fact that psychoanalysis has a meliorative aim. But Freud's description/discovery of the superego and its development and psychopathology provides its related clinical dicta of nonjudgmental technique and neutrality. Neither of these apparent paradoxes is difficult to understand.

Ego psychological formulations result in the appreciation of irrationality, and the development of adaptive outlets for id derivatives. (Id derivatives, unconscious libidinal and aggressive wishes, may be considered the initial Freudian discovery.) The moral dimension of psychoanalysis, in part stemming from study of the superego, provides context within which ethical matters may be fruitfully discussed. Of course, the essentially meliorative aim of clinical practice requires that a discussion of ethics in psychoanalysis takes up more obvious matters regarding the behavior of the analyst. Confidentiality, fee-setting, and analytic boundaries and their violation have properly received attention in our literature and in those of related clinical fields.

Also worthy of our scrutiny is what we may call the axiology of influence, i.e., the propriety of suggestion, manipulation, and correction (as in "corrective emotional experience") as means of human interaction. This latter topic has even drawn the attention of colleagues in educational psychology (Friedrich and Douglass, "Ethics and the Persuasive Enterprise of Teaching Psychology," *American Psychologist*, May 1998). This matter, of course, was addressed by Freud early on, when he gave up hypnosis and suggestive methods because of their clinical inadequacy.

Classical technique, especially as defined by Glover (1931), went so far as to eschew explicitly suggestive methodologies and to declare such methodologies essentially anti-psychoanalytic. The extremity of Glover's position was recognized well before our current pluralistic discourse. While the idea of "interpretation alone" (Gill, 1954) supported the Glover doctrine, factors other than insight were openly part of analytic discourse (see especially Bibring, 1954, Loewald, 1960, Stone, 1968) presaging more recent relational and social constructivist models. Classical analysis developed at a time when it seemed necessary to argue against accusations that its effects were suggestive, and to promote a standard technique that would be seen as avoiding influencing and manipulation of patients.

While current discussion within psychoanalysis recognizes legitimate influence beyond interpretation (see, e.g., Gedo, 1979), questions of analytic authority, the use and abuse of privilege, and Renik's idea of "irreducible subjectivity" (1998) have brought once again into focus what I am calling the axiology of influence. Whose values shall determine the direction of treatment? Is a conflicted patient the arbiter, or is the analyst, whom we also recognize as a conflicted human being? How is the direction of treatment negotiated in the face of the social and philosophical reduction of analytic authority? Classical technique, cognizant of ubiquitous countertransference, promotes nonetheless a methodology aiming to minimize suggestion as the basis for change in analysis. Let us look back at the clinical cases with which I began.

In the fourth session with the woman planning her Quaalude experiment, which was to conclude the evaluation phase, I recommended psychoanalysis. I also told her that her planned experiment would likely interfere with the treatment and would not be acceptable. She called me a few days later to say she would not be seeing me again.

I was, at the time, young in my psychotherapy career, and still in training to become a psychoanalyst. With hindsight, it is easy to see my mistaken and doctrinaire position. I do not know what happened in this woman's life, but I surely did not provide her with adequate help. Today I would say to myself that this woman may have been offering a challenge which I did not understand well enough. I understood little of her psychology, particularly her defenses. To pose a suggestion, a prohibition, when she could not, at this stage of our relationship, trust me enough to accept such an intervention, was clearly not useful. Especially since I believed psychoanalysis to be the suitable treatment, I should have accepted her challenge as a communication and awaited the opportunity to address it interpretively.

To my second patient, seen in treatment when I had not even begun analytic training, I spoke out, suggestively, about her neglect of her children. This intervention was successful, resulting in increasingly effective parenting. The intervention occurred some months into the work, after a sound and trusting alliance had developed. In that context, it came when I was becoming increasingly concerned and uncomfortable regarding the children's welfare. It was a moral suggestion which enabled me more comfortably to continue the work. It was also an intervention in the context of a time-limited twice weekly face-to-face psychotherapy, determined by my own lack of analytic training and by its setting in a military dependents' clinic at an army base from which clientele would routinely be transferred.

While my suggestion came from a position of morality (or moral outrage), rather than from, as in the first instance, a doctrinaire naivete, I believe, again in hindsight, that my technical handling would have been different in an open-ended treatment, let alone an analysis. I surely would have addressed child neglect, but not with suggestion. I believe, in a more analytic modality, questions and defense interpretations would have produced a similar behavioral result while preserving a non-judgmental technical posture.

My third patient was in the beginning months of treatment, twice weekly, face-to-face, and struggling with my recommendation for psychoanalysis. My ethical and moral position was that he was betraying his wife in several ways. Such betrayal is, in my view, inherently unethical and immoral, but psychodynamically it directly related to his presenting symptomatic behavior. My stance was to address the matter with non-judgmental technique. By this I mean, firstly, that I did indeed address the matter. I did so, though, by helping the patient to note and to reflect upon his ambivalence; he called it his "hedging," his failure to embrace his wife's announcement of pregnancy. There was little doubt that he would discern my moral position; we are not blank screens and what we address or greet with silence reveals more than our technique. The patient felt challenged. I acknowledged that our reflection on his "hedging" (which he himself considered wrong) implied a better way to be. I explicitly added: "if you are able." It was clear to him, in our treatment alliance, that I was as invested in this last phrase as much as I was in joining his moral position. To me, this is an example of "technical" neutrality.

Technical neutrality does not refer to any absence of a position, even a moral position, with regard to an analysand's activities. It is, instead, a recognition that we should not intervene solely on the side of the superego. That we may share a superego position is balanced and made technically neutral by our letting the patient know that we also respect and support the acknowledgement of other factors (unconscious id wishes, for example), and ego-autonomy. I am, in my intervention, trying for Anna Freud's equidistance from (I would also call it respect and acknowledgement of) the several components of psychic life.

Most analysts consider our work to be a moral enterprise. The issue is how to square personal morality with the "Evil" presented by our patients. For some this means working with those who share our most important values. Freud felt that analysis was only to be attempted with persons of good character, whatever that might mean. Robert Waelder is said to have asserted that he couldn't analyze a Republican. For more of us, our own experience on the couch has resulted in great tolerance for differences, and an understanding of the Problem of Evil in psychodynamic terms. We do not say that we have solved the age-old problem but, instead, that psychoanalytic insights have led to a reduction in the zone of evil by successfully explaining and treating a range of its manifestations. The late

Sidney Smith did analytic work in prisons with murderers in order to elucidate the psychology of that manifestation of Evil.

From personal experience on the couch, we are also sensitive to the irrational superego involvement of many moral positions, and from our study of cultural differences we are aware of the great variation in moralities. These sensitivities should allow us to maintain psychoanalytic values in the face of Republicans or others with whom we have moral disagreement. We do not, then, as a rule, when working analytically, assume a moralistic posture with our analysands.

Of course, we may be morally offended at times. The abuse of drugs, the neglect of children, the betrayal of a loved one (both emotionally and by possibly exposing her to HIV infection) were offensive to me. But I am neither a narc, a welfare inspector, a marriage counselor, nor even a close follower of the Tarasoff obligation to warn; I am a psychoanalyst.

I imagine that, even 25 years after completing my training, I might find some individuals too morally repugnant to engage. Nonetheless, as an analyst, I believe that the most effective and ethical contribution I can make is the technical one of analyzing, whenever possible.

I emphasize the word "technical" because the ultimate focus of this paper is on the ethics of technique per se. From early in the century, Freud concerned himself with technique as an ethical matter. His 1905 paper, "On Psychotherapy," addressed the issue of untrained practitioners. His 1910 paper, "Wild Analysis," took up the careless application of psychoanalytic interpretation. His several papers on technique form a compendium of recommendations regarding what behaviors analysts ought to avoid, with several of these recommendations being essentially ethical in nature. These latter would today be considered under the rubric of "boundary violations."

The development of psychoanalytic technique has not proceeded in any clearly articulated form. Freud did not write with specificity on what analysts should do and say, and his own practice, as inferred from the classical case presentations, has engendered multiple interpretations. Glover's (1928) book was the first attempt at a textbook on technique and with Fenichel's (1941) and Greenson's (1967) the list of comprehensive technical treatises is exhausted.

Eissler's (1953) formulation of a standard technique (and its variants) has engendered considerable controversy. Of late, some consider that the very idea of "technique" itself may be inappropriate to describe what occurs in the psychoanalytic situation. Technique may introduce iatrogenic effects by prescribing formulaic responses for what is in essence an idiographic enterprise dealing with human emotion and interaction. Technique may, from this perspective, be thought of as a totem which, in its very nature, contradicts and dehumanizes, and should, therefore, be taboo.

There is little dispute that the notions of classical technique and a "standard model" have often been taken as totemic. This is usual in the case of anxious novices (as I was when faced with the issue of Quaalude use). It was also common in earlier decades of psychoanalytic history when the appearance of professional rectitude was paramount, in the face of the disreputable subject matter and theories of sexuality proposed by Freud. The boundary violations of some psychoanalytic pioneers, recently revealed to a wider audience, led Freud to his technical admonitions, and led the profession to attempt the development of a technique beyond reproach. Such an attempt was premature, at best, and led to the common caricature of the stiff and silent, uninvolved psychoanalyst.

That totemism, not Freud's (nor ever characteristic of sound practice), has been in recent decades (and in the ambience of my own training) debunked. The work of Leo Stone and of Hans Loewald undermined totemic uses of technique by the early sixties. Kohut's focus on analytic empathy to respect narcissistic vulnerabilities, Winnicott's object-relations approach and his delineation of transitional phenomena, and more recent work on relational and intersubjective issues, has served well to undo the analytic caricature and totemic approaches to technique (with the likely exception of anxious novices like my younger self). My own teaching of technique places emphasis on the inherent flexibility within what I consider to be a sound basic model approach.

The accusations of totemism continue, and with them a growing notion that technique should be considered taboo. From what quarters do these accusations arise? In my view they emerge from the misguided approach that leads to overemphasis on any single psychoanalytic discovery to the detriment of important others. It is an approach that Leo Rangell has frequently criticized as *pars pro* totem thinking, in contrast with his own total composite theory of psychoanalysis. The hypertrophied idea in this case is that the psychoanalytic relationship must be authentic and emotional rather than artificial and distant. This leads to an idealization of authenticity, and to the devaluation of technique as being inherently artificial and inauthentic.

It is my thesis, in contrast, that while authenticity is central to the analytic relationship, the use of technique is neither inauthentic nor ethically dispensable. My clinical examples may provide help in clarifying that authenticity and technique are not mutually exclusive. With an authentic feeling that ingesting Quaaludes would serve neither the young woman nor her treatment, I made the error of disregarding my already honed techniques for establishing a treatment alliance. In my authentic concern for the welfare of my patient's children, I considered the technical context of her therapy situation, including the evaluation of our alliance and the situationally defined limits of our psychoanalytic inquiry, in deciding to intervene suggestively. In my authentic concern for my patient's valued marriage, I chose to focus, I would say non-suggestively, on his "hedging" ambivalence. In these examples, authentic moral and ethical feelings have a distinct role in my working life, and my patients can feel my authenticity in my comments as well as in my silent listening. Technical thinking also has a distinct and critical role which conveys my authentic commitment to a way of working, a commitment not lost on patients and analysands.

I would argue that the failure to take technical considerations into account is, itself, unethical, and leads essentially to a mutual catharsis (perhaps even *folie a deux*) rather than a valid treatment process.

What is this technique, then? Like neutrality, it is a widely misunderstood concept. Technique in psychoanalysis and its derivative therapies involves thinking about the various artifices that might be employed to further psychic exploration and to assist the patient or analysand with his or her problems. It has never been formulaic or prescriptive. It is about thoughtfulness in light of the now century-old psychoanalytic therapeutic endeavor. It involves thinking through our interventions and silences as to their likely therapeutic and analytic effects. In practice, and with experience, it usually becomes a preconscious process, serving as backdrop within a session to other aspects of analytic listening. At times it becomes a focally conscious process for the analyst. At other times, thinking about technique occurs in supervision and study groups, or on our own, outside of sessions.

There are broad issues of technique, such as neutrality (the analyst's commitment to help assure that each of the psychic agencies and the external world have voice), and narrower ones, such as whether, when, and how to respond to a direct question. In each instance, the analyst must be committed to the difficult tasks of being engaged with the patient, authentically and with affect, and of thoughtfulness. The analyst must thus be able to sustain what is promoted as well in the analysand, what Sterba (1934) called a therapeutic split of the ego: the ability to oscillate between experience and reflection.

This is not easy, and attempts to simplify it are misguided. To consider technique, as I have discussed it, to be taboo is to consider thoughtfulness and reflection inappropriate. That is an unethical stance.

Speaking with two colleagues at the Division 39 conference in April 1998, the technical matter of the use of the couch in psychoanalysis came up. They expressed some dismay that I would actually use a couch, let alone prefer its use as a technical matter. They elaborated on the authenticity of face-to-face encounters and on the artificiality of my technical preference, and the likelihood that it was dehumanizing. I was equally dismayed at their position—and that they considered themselves to be analysts. We continued to discuss the matter, with obvious attempts at politeness on both sides. In a genial manner, at the conversation's end, they allowed that the use of the couch might work for me because I was so authentically committed to it.

It is quite true that I am authentic in my commitment to my way of practicing analysis and that this is evident to my patients. It is also true that I am authentically committed to many moral and ethical positions about psychoanalysis and about life. I am certain that my patients and analysands come to know many of these commitments as well, despite my technical anonymity.

In closing, I would like to distinguish between morality and ethics, although I have used the terms synonymously. For me, morality is a superego matter, much more prone to regressive enactment and pathological conflict-formation than are ethics. For me, ethics are an ego function, much more prone to engagement with external reality, including the argumentation over ethical constructs which so engages philosophers. Morality, too often, leads to intolerance of differences and authoritarian posturing. I believe that suggestive elements in psychotherapies share this characteristic.

Ethics, as existentialists see it, involves the anguish of freedom and a struggle with the diversity of human values. Moralists have totems and taboos; ethicists have questions and arguments. Psychoanalysts have a generative theory of human psychology and development, and a range of therapeutic approaches which aim both to enhance understanding and relieve suffering. Psychoanalytic technique is central to these approaches, and ethical on its face. Would that our present psychoanalytic pluralism relied more on clarity of thinking, on reflection, and on a respect for the evolution and development of this meliorative movement. We might then have more common ground in place of so much wagging of tongues and pointing of fingers.

The New York Freudian Society: History, Organizational Contributions, Current Program

Psychologist Psychoanalyst (2002)

The 1950s were an especially interesting decade for American psychoanalysis. Psychoanalysts had assumed undisputed leadership in American psychiatry, chairing departments at the most prestigious medical centers. Psychiatric residents assumed psychoanalytic training to be a requirement for pursuing a successful career. The American Psychoanalytic Association (APsaA) had effectively established in the public perception that psychoanalysis was a medical specialty. APsaA had also isolated "wayward" theorists such as Karen Horney and Franz Alexander in its quest to define a "standard" theory and practice. These developments (and their negative consequences) were documented by Eissler (1965) in his book on medical orthodoxy, and later by Richards (1999) in his paper on the politics of exclusion.

Neither psychoanalytic theory nor practice were so easily contained or restricted. Alternate theories, however marginalized, and alternate practices, free from medical orthodoxy, found settings in which to flourish. An especially gifted psychologist, David Rapaport, organized an elaboration of metapsychology to incorporate the contributions of Hartmann and his collaborators. He attracted equally gifted students, many of them not physicians, who went on to make theoretical innovations whose importance was recognized even by the APsaA establishment, despite their explicit rejection of the Hartmann-Rapaport establishment paradigm.

Theodore Reik, the defendant in the earliest dispute over "lay" analysis, created in New York City a psychoanalytic society and institute in which several facets of orthodoxy were eschewed, among them the APsaA requirement that training analysts "report" to training committees about their candidate analysands. By the end of the decade of the '50s, the openness of Reik's group, the National

Psychological Association for Psychoanalysis (NPAP), appeared to some of its own members to make for diminished standards of theory and practice. As has happened all too frequently in the psychoanalytic world, organizational splits ensued.

One new group to emerge was the New York Society of Freudian Psychologists (NYSFP). Founded in 1959 by a strong-willed social worker, European-trained psychoanalyst Gisela Barenbaum, NYSFP attracted a core group of creative individuals committed to building psychoanalysis within the framework of its founder's basic theories, but without the strictures of medical orthodoxy. Like similar groups at their founding, personal ties to the leader were strong; many members and candidates were her supervisees or analysands. By the end of the decade of the '60s, however, NYSFP had added to its ranks several members trained at NPAP or at the newer NYU postdoctoral program. This cadre provided new leadership, expanded the faculty and supervisory ranks, and created a more formal structure for institute training. Society membership included nine graduates by 1969.

In addition to their organizational skills, the new leadership group brought to psychoanalytic training at NYSFP theoretical and practical leanings that were both rigorous and flexible. As the developmental psychology of Mahler and the humanizing approaches of Stone and of Loewald were achieving influence within American psychoanalysis, NYSFP faculty incorporated these approaches with its teaching of modern conflict theory, and added to them the object relations orientation of Winnicott, Balint, Fairbairn and Guntrip. Rangell called this curriculum expansion "total composite theory." (Having been trained at NYSFP during the late '60s and early '70s, I was well aware of being exposed to a curriculum richer than that studied by friends who were in training within APsaA.)

The mid-seventies saw NYSFP change its name to more accurately reflect its diverse membership, becoming the New York Freudian Society (NYFS). Its roots remained both strong and clear. By this time a group of child and adolescent psychoanalysts, many of whom had been trained by Anna Freud at the Hampstead Clinic in England, had been welcomed to membership. This group created for the NYFS institute a strong training program in its subdiscipline, graduating its first candidate in 1980.

The next major expansion of NYFS was the formation, beginning in the mid-1980s, of its Washington, DC training center, the first geographically-distant institute started in the United States outside of APsaA. Before the successful settlement of the Division 39 lawsuit, APsaA arbitrarily rejected a group of candidates, mostly psychologists approved by their local training facilities, for advanced training. The candidates took the initiative in collaborating to be trained by NYFS faculty who would fly to Washington on alternate Saturdays to provide full NYFS training without advanced standing. This initial Washington group has long since graduated and its members have joined the ranks of faculty and supervising analysts. They are frequent contributors at Division 39 programs and have recently taken over administrative direction of the ongoing Washington Division of NYFS.

Following the Division 39 lawsuit, NYFS became one of the first three (now four) groups to become full component societies within the International Psychoanalytical Association (IPA). The NYFS training program had been designed early on to be consistent with IPA standards and philosophy. At the time of its admission, NYFS had graduated 65 psychoanalysts and had become a major training site. Its current graduates number close to 150. NYFS members have made many significant contributions to psychoanalysis. As scholars, they have authored dozens of books and hundreds of articles as well as being regular presenters at national and international professional meetings. Members serve with distinction on editorial boards of several psychoanalytic journals. As organizational leaders, two NYFS members have been president of Division 39, another has been president of APA's Division 42, and seven NYFS members have held the presidency of Section I. NYFS members have also been active on the Boards of Sections III and IV. One member has served on the Executive Council of IPA. Two members are recipients of the coveted Sigourney Award.

In its most recent decade NYFS has continued to grow, both in membership and in its range of activities. The latest IPA roster had NYFS as the fourth largest component society in the world (following APsaA, the Canadian Psychoanalytic Association, and the Argentine Psychoanalytic Association). Its membership ranges geographically beyond the New York tri-state and Washington, DC metropolitan areas to include France, Germany and Mexico, as well as mid-Connecticut, Colorado, Florida, northern Maryland, Massachusetts, Michigan, Missouri, Pennsylvania, and central and southern Virginia. Its newer programs include a parent/infant/toddler training sequence, continuing education for psychologists and social workers at the New York City Board of Education, and divorce and forensics outreach groups. Recently, NYFS has created a clinical services division and it supports the work of a counselor at a private school in Manhattan. NYFS offers the Plumsock Prizes for psychoanalytic writing by candidates and members who are new to publication. A foundation has been established to promote support for its community programs. A psychotherapy training program is scheduled to admit its first class in 2002. NYFS as a society and its members as individuals have also participated generously in the response to the September 11 tragedy in both New York and Washington, and have made a commitment to continue to assist families of the victims. Now in its 43rd year, NYFS looks forward to continuing as a strong member of a renewed and vibrant psychoanalytic movement in the United States and in the international community.

Time and Other Illusions: A Work in Progress

Faculty Psychotherapy Conference at Mount Sinai, September 13, 2016

This date came open just two weeks ago, so I asked for the opportunity to present a work-in-progress, confident that my less-than-polished presentation would be rescued by this group's always-lively and astute commentary. I'm still fascinated by philosophy of science issues that both support and critique our work as psychotherapists. I had hoped naively that my presentations here last year would be definitive, and I published a revised version of last fall's entitled "Psychoanalysis is Science!" in the new on-line edition the APA Division 39 publication. But I've given up my ambition to make a definitive contribution to centuries-old debates. I will offer instead some ideas and leave most of our time for our discussion.

My title word "illusion" is made with my tongue planted firmly in my cheek. I hope to make a case for the proposition that time is real. My focus on "time" was stimulated last semester by our physicist colleague Terry Rogers. He gets to play something of a *bete noire* in this paper but I'm grateful for his prodding. It led to my writing a brief piece for my college class 55th year reunion book, the creative section. I'll begin with that essay, entitled "On Time."

I have a reputation for always being on time. I'm never very early, perhaps five minutes on occasion; and I'm hardly ever late—and always upset and apologetic when I am. Several years ago I decided to address this neurotic symptom by purposely coming late for a committee meeting to be held at my college departmental conference room, a short walk from my private office (my presence was not at all important to the agenda). I was nearly out the door at 10 AM, the meeting time, when my phone rang. The committee chair was calling to see if some terrible accident had occurred—or if I had died! This colleague was not a friend.

479

What is this thing we call time? Much of my musing and writing these days is about philosophy of science issues as they pertain to my field, psychoanalysis. Whether or not this field is a science (or even scientific) is a matter of considerable dispute, with traditional scientists and psychoanalysts on both sides of the argument. The more generous critique is that psychoanalysis is a craft, perhaps an art; more hostile critics call it an obsolete mythology, or charlatanism. Analysts are paid for spending time with people. One naysayer called psychoanalysis "the purchase of friendship."

Surprising as it may be to most non-scientists, Albert Einstein concluded in his later years that past, present, and future all exist simultaneously. In 1952, in his book *Relativity*, Einstein wrote:

Since there exist in this four-dimensional structure [space-time] no longer any sections which represent 'now' objectively, the concepts of happening and becoming are indeed not completely suspended, but yet complicated. It appears therefore more natural to think of physical reality as a four-dimensional existence, instead of, as hitherto, the evolution of a three dimensional existence... Physicists believe the separation between past, present, and future is only an illusion, although a convincing one.

Scientists, Einstein tells us, believe direct experience is an illusion, not merely a lesser reality, like the shadows in Plato's cave. Psychoanalysts focus on personal experience, Freud's "psychological reality."

I recall enjoying the comic strip "Gasoline Alley." I had misremembered it, believing its literary conceit to be condensing time. I thought its characters aged several years each year; in a decade a baby would mature to grandparenthood. When I did some research, I found its format to be real time; the characters aged exactly as we did, with specified birthdays and anniversaries. This error of memory seemed to result from my mental comparison with the usual comic-strip format, timeless, like Einstein's universe—and, I now add, Freud's Unconscious.

And so, fallible memory is the norm, lapses increase with aging; forgetting is no definitive indicator of Alzheimer's Disease. Also common to aging is the strong sense that time is going faster. My sister asked my mother for deathbed words of wisdom; my mother replied, "It goes fast." It's hard to believe my own grandchildren are growing up so quickly. I know that I'm ignorant of entire realms of experience familiar to others. My ignorance, faulty memory, and distorted time sense support the physicists' dismissal of experience. But can psychoanalysis consider dialogue based on that experience to be substantive, or even useful as the basis for treatment? Aristotle contradicted Plato, saying let's not believe only in ideas and ideals. I believe Einstein's confirmed prediction that space is curved; on earth, Newton's Laws apply anyway. Ideas and ideals are important, and I admire the work of physicists, but life is experience.

Psychological reality is not the only reality, but it has its own validity. Life is measured with Dali's distorted clocks. Experience is subject to scientific inquiry; it is not the entire story of the universe, but it counts. Life is time. Life is short, but it's all we have; it's not an illusion. I don't want to waste it. My analytic hour remains fifty minutes, though most therapists now stop at forty-five. I hope to keep being on time for a long time to come. Moments can be momentous.

That was my reunion essay. Now: further thoughts. Human time is real; it is, in fact, our primary, experiential and existential reality. Cosmological time and geologic time are claimed to be objective, but for most non-specialists they are experience-distant concepts, products of refined human thought and methods that are hard to grasp intuitively or emotionally, they are abstractions created by human thought process and supported by human validation methods. It takes effort and focus to appreciate the idea of eons. The translation "appreciation" was my first Freudian teacher's explanation of "cathexis,"—despite his being a native German speaker who knew the literal meaning of bezetzung. Mental effort and focus are psychological matters.

I've been a fan of Laurence Friedman's work since reading his paper on the therapeutic alliance (1969). His first psychoanalytic paper was published in 1953 at age 22. Until his 1988 book, *The Anatomy of Psychotherapy*, I felt he was an underappreciated scholar. In 2012, no longer underappreciated, he was a Sigourney Award honoree. I am in awe of the range of his interests and the clarity of his writing. The most recent issue of JAPA has his essay entitled "Is There a Usable Heidegger for Psychoanalysts?" I thought, before reading the paper: "Why write about this Nazi sympathizer?" I learned a lot, though I lack the skill to provide a summary. What struck me was Friedman's discussion of Heidegger on the issue of time, beginning with the astute observation that tick-tick is the objective sound of a clock, while tick-tock is what we make of it. Heidegger emphasizes the subjective dimension. Time, a la Heidegger, "plausibly is revealed as the central 'matter' of being" (p 609). Friedman's Heidegger is "a defender of mundane experience against philosophers who dismiss common sense as mere shadows of ideal timeless abstractions" (p 618), with time itself "the central philosophical puzzle" (p 620) as it is to "every other serious philosopher." (That's Friedman.)

So we have cosmological time and geologic time, each measured by esoteric and complex methods like spectrography and carbon-dating, though we may choose to accept expert opinion. We also have "real time," measured for millennia with clocks and watches now so precise that periodic adjustments of the calendar by leap-seconds are now made in some years and accepted, while racing results on land or in water are settled by tiny fractions of a second. If time is an illusion, we waste a lot of it in ways that seem exquisitely accurate and useful. And then there is a dimension of time we call "psychological," essentially subjective but with enough commonality so people can appreciate (cathect) the experiences of others. The late Swiss psychoanalyst Danielle Quinodoz wrote about the experience of moments of eternity—awesome experiences, quite brief in real time, but emotionally significant for individuals. That idea resonates for me with "peak experiences," a similar one from my teacher Abraham Maslow. I was sent a paper and video clip last week from the Stanford Medical School newsletter, by a neurosurgeon in anticipation of his own death from cancer at age 37. These documents describe time in the OR residency as "slow days and fast years," and at home recovering from treatment while caring for his infant daughter; each a different experience, though immediately recognizable to most of us (Kalanithi 2015).

These pregnant moments of time refer to present and immediate experience. Time also refers to the past and the future. The past is understood through records—written, artistic, fossil and geological—each method imperfect but each subject to methodological analysis to yield a best-evidence contemporary knowledge base. The individual past is understood through always imperfect memory, to which psychoanalysis has contributed significant understanding. Teleology is eschewed by philosophers and scientists, who assert that a non-existent future can have no effect. I will soon address another so-called illusion: "progress," which, according to Terry Rogers, is not relevant to evolution. But the illusion of a future is no illusion at all; philosopher-psychoanalyst Jonathan Lear has astutely pointed out that goal setting, planning, imagining and fantasizing are part of ordinary thought—and have consequences. Human thinking and experience are the subject matter of our work. Psychological and real time are each central to understanding thought and experience.

I'm not picking on Terry Rogers, but rather appreciating his contribution to our education when I move to the next "illusion," purposelessness. Rogers reminds us that Darwinian evolution is not progressive, having but a singular aim: survival. That reminder seems correct for a biology that precedes human evolution. The emergence of the human mind, however, with its capacity for imagination, creates the means for affecting evolution, not only of other species by agriculture, animal husbandry and environmental protection, but—with the discovery of DNA—also provides tools for modifying the biology of our own genome. The implications are important and scary, as Karen Davis's recent report on CRISPR showed. Science is actively seeking to create an artificial intelligence that might harm, even destroy our own.

Purpose and planning are human capacities that—within historical time—have led to countless changes in the world. The Enlightenment was a progressive period, as were the more recent industrial and scientific revolutions and the technological revolution that is speeding along now. In this, the week of the opening of the Smithsonian National Museum of African American History and Culture, we should also recognize that social progress can be made in human time as a result of human agency. Outcomes like climate change and potential nuclear devastation— as well as major political regressions—warn that human activity is not necessarily progressive, but these are ethical judgments, yet another central dimension of human psychology. Humans value both personal and genetic survival, but these values are not necessarily the top priority of individuals. People sacrifice their lives; many choose not to become parents.

Final judgment on our species is only to be made after extinction—but only if a sentient successor species emerges to treat us like fossils. This idea is at the heart of Sartre's existentialism. A human timeframe includes higher purposes, with intention and action to achieve them. Progress is a value judgment, surely not linear, but humans have aims and values. People without them are said to suffer from anomie, or psychopathy. Darwinian dismissal of purpose in human evolution, like Einstein's dismissal of time, is an unproven idea. Human purpose in real time is validated by nearly universal consensus. Such consensus could change; pragmatism as a philosophical school claims change itself as the essential reality.

Physics envy is unbecoming. Physicists can claim no monopoly on epistemological conclusions. The several dimensions of time should not be dismissed by those whose own major paradigms are incompatible, and whose string theory has yet to find one shred of empirical support. The theory of multiverses, Rogers admits, is an elaborate "workaround" that postulates but does not demonstrate a valid cosmology. It is based on statistics and logical thinking, but a search for evidence is deemed impossible *a priori*. Mathematics and physics use these workarounds so that contradictions and lack of evidence do not hamper theory development and testing. Like us, scientists fantasize. Fantasy and imagination may sometimes lead to demonstrable progress; as did Kekule's dream of the benzene ring.

Human ideas are the stuff of progress, though not all ideas are of value. Psychoanalysis calls many ideas "fantasy." Fantasy or illusion: unproven ideas are the engine of progress. All ideas emerge from the human mind with its inherent subjectivity. Subjectivity exists in the observation of animate objects and other species as well as our selves. Bias is not limited to social and cultural dimensions; fraud occurs in "hard science," for psychological reasons, these reasons also subject to study. Every perception can be erroneous; this does not make all perception illusory. When Renik (1998) speaks of irreducible subjectivity, some take that to mean "not at all reducible," rather than "not reducible to zero." Methods exist in science to reduce both fraud and subjectivity. To believe we are incapable of degrees of objectivity, an apparent tenet of post-modernism, can lead to cynicism; I prefer an attitude of critical hopefulness.

I began early on to reject narrow definitions of science. My freshman biology teacher declared the purpose of life was to pass germ cells; lives as lived were irrelevant. A graduate school instructor asserted that psychology as a discipline aimed for prediction and control. My intuitive response to each claim was: this could not be the whole truth. Different realities lead to different scholarly disciplines. Physicists and mathematicians are people; like most others, prone to overvalue their own subjectivity. Freud's (1914a) paper "On Narcissism" is an introduction to the study of that psychological observation.

Within our discipline of psychotherapy, the mind-brain issue remains unresolved. Descartes' dualism may not satisfy, but alternative answers have yet to achieve consensus. The matter of qualia remains unexplained. Brain science is ascendant these days but a recent *New York Times* opinion piece questions fMRI methodology, likening current brain science to a "new phrenology." Zvi Lothane's on-line response to this report seemed gleeful; others were more circumspect. Scientists take methodological critiques and revisions as routine; an opinion piece is not a scientific paper. Biological approaches to the brain do not all rely on brain localization, for example the work of Rodolfo Llinas. Neuroscientists may have a near-monopoly on mental health research funding but their work has yet to yield helpful results nearly as good as ours.

A more disturbing article appeared in *The Stone* on September 5th. Neurologist Robert Burton wrote "A Life of Meaning: (Reason not required)," in which he challenged the primacy of rational deliberation. This challenge is, of course, a foundational psychoanalytic principle: Freud (1927) wrote of "the voice of the intellect as a soft one." But Burton dismisses both psychology and law, calling the experience of agency a biologically-driven illusion. He asserts that "empirical methods can't help us with abstract, non-measurable, linguistically ambiguous concepts such as purpose and meaning," and he denies altogether the importance of human intellect. "It's no wonder," to Burton, but scary to me "that pre-eminent scientists like Stephen Hawking have gleefully declared, 'Philosophy is dead.'" This arrogant reductionism ignores its own methodological limitations and portends a dystopia in which advances in brain science are sure to resolve Cartesian dualism, and it promotes La Mettrie's "L'homme Machine," a materialistic ideal awaiting only the inevitable development of silicon-based robots to surpass and replace our species. Not so fast, buster!

It may be lazy to repeat the Rashomon story of an elephant being examined by blind people, each describing a part as if it were the whole. Against radical reductionism, many thinkers support the idea of emergence, with emergent phenomena to be studied with methods appropriate for their own subject matter. Scientific disciplines and philosophy can then continue systematic study motivated by what Jaak Panksepp calls the epistemic drive, in the same way that cosmology proceeds with both empirical and conjectural work despite its incompatible master theories. We need serious empirical and rational work, not polemic, to continue to make human progress.

Psychology and psychoanalysis have disciplinary domains, but do not exist in a vacuum. They explore their respective subject matter with focus, but other domains: weather, biology, economics, sociology, even politics impinge; the elephant remains an elephant, with new questions, blind alleys, and failures continuing to excite and motivate exploratory and interdisciplinary activity.

Our chair told us he chose psychiatry because reading novels counts as work. Patients bring a wide variety of beliefs and interest to our consulting rooms. These conferences welcome talks on music and poetry. Keats's Ode on a Grecian Urn is, however, an inspired romantic vision: "Beauty is truth, truth beauty" is neither all we know nor all we need to know.

Psychotherapists must attend to findings in cognate domains like neuroscience, and in hybrid disciplines like neuro-psychoanalysis. Unifying approaches will be attempted and may eventually succeed in providing explanatory power. People create theory and must eschew reification of our mental products. Kurt Lewin said there's nothing as useful as a good theory, but a theory cannot claim truth—it helps us instead to search. I join Allen Fay's condemnation of "schoolism," where theoretical differences lead to hostility rather than respect and possible collaboration. Strong conviction about the truth value of personal subjectivity can lead to a narcissistic disparagement of other subjectivities. Fallible people make these judgments. When these people have power, they can treat their beliefs as proven. Alternatively, my Hungarian mathematician friend's specialty is brain algorithms. He has a low Erdös number, a major honor in the math world. I am in awe of his work, the specifics of which I can hardly grasp. He feels similarly about my work.

We judged from our own value perspectives. The illusion of a future is no illusion: the idea of a future inheres in human thought. The alternatives are learned helplessness, cynicism, or solipsism. I prefer hope, thoughtfulness, planning and meaningfulness as psychological strengths to be supported rather than derogated or dismissed; these are frames of mind, not epiphenomena. Humans make countless mistakes but also demonstrate useful imagination, creativity and occasional genius. Thought changes the world in ways that can be progressive. Projected outcomes are speculative, relying on the same mental processes as fantasy and dreaming. Unpredictability is exciting; it is about differences between and within individuals, rather than the cloning hatchery of Huxley's Brave New World.

In my world there is definable progress over time; there is affect, intellect and agency.

Clinical work and science aim to promote that progress. Some patients get better. We wonder why and think about what worked. Judged retrospectively by historians, the scholars of the human past, progress is erratic. Rumors of an end to history (Francis Fukuyama's claim when the Soviet Empire fell) are premature.

I try to avoid a medical model for thinking about the work I do, but it's hard to avoid medical language. I've called my work non-invasive neurosurgery, but I wasn't happy with that intrusive image. I prefer a description that jumped out of my mouth in casual conversation recently. I now practice "metaphoric cardiology" in real time, and in a real world with real people.

CONCLUDING ESSAYS

How Scientific is Psychoanalysis?

March 15, 2016

This is a follow-up to my philosophy of science paper, "Psychoanalysis is Scientific!" presented in October. Before hearing your comments on it, I naively believed my arguments were definitive and unassailable. This is another attempt to convince you that psychoanalysis—I'll be less categorical—is *scientific*. I will briefly review the points I made last time, insert a disclaimer about my own understanding of the psychoanalytic paradigm, then go on to demonstrate that psychoanalysis is, necessarily, a scientific enterprise. I will conclude by espousing a conceptual inclusiveness to address the ongoing project of understanding the human mind.

Summary of October Paper

1. Science, a la Francis Bacon, is "an attitude toward the universe in which observations are made using the best methods available; logic is employed; and... magical, supernatural, and ad hoc solutions are rejected." Apparent contradictions require further study.
2. Human subjectivity is real, an emergent phenomenon in the evolution of the universe, itself subject to scientific inquiry.
3. All scientific methods and instruments are imperfect; subjectivity (individual perception and interpretation) inheres in every observation. Imperfection is not a basis for ruling out scientific activity—or personal reality-testing.
4. Evolution has enabled the human mind, in Freud's words (1927, p55), to "develop precisely in the attempt to explore the external world." Stanislas Dehaene asserts that "Subjective reports are the key phenomena that neuroscience purports to study." Psychoanalytic approaches prioritize but do not limit themselves to "unconscious subjectivity."

5. Radical reductive science would have it that cosmology is the only basic science; this is an absurd proposition, inadequate for understanding emergent phenomena, be they geological, psychological, or social. Complex phenomena have multiple and often complex determinants.
6. "Best evidence" in any science is always tentative and subject to revision.
7. Scientific advances emerge from scientific ambition, yet scientific claims must be modest.

Disclaimer: "Three Masters"

Psychoanalysis is not only a science; it began and remains a healing artful profession. I agree with Leo Stone and Sinclair Lewis's Martin Arrowsmith that when clinical judgment conflicts with scientific rigor, healing trumps science. I disagree with Freud that the therapy will hurt the science. As a healing art and profession, psychoanalysis must adhere to medical ethics; these include humane relatedness, as well as the use of "best evidence." But a profession with more than aesthetic claims requires ongoing attempts at empirical validation.

Psychoanalysis is also something more than a healing method and scientific discipline; from its beginnings it earned a place in the History of Ideas. Not often credited, psychoanalysis has changed culture; Auden called Freud "a whole climate of opinion." Philosophers partake and contribute to psychoanalytic ideas. In December the Helix Center hosted "A Freudian Perspective on What Ails the World Today," at which humanities and social science professors, psychoanalysts, and cultural and political leaders held roundtable discussions on three themes: identity formation; education and the thirst for knowledge; and knowledge to overcome religious and nationalist extremism. In a talk last month at NYPSI, philosopher-psychoanalyst Jonathan Lear spoke on The Ethics of Psychoanalysis, in which he drew lines between Plato, Aristotle and Freud. A healing practice must concern itself with problems in the world and values: how to have a good life—and how to create a better world. Psychoanalysis addresses ethics and aesthetics. Its developmental psychology complements Piaget's "genetic epistemology" with a "genetic axiology"—the development of values—and a superego psychology to supplement Hartmann's ego psychology.

The psychoanalytic paradigm serves "three masters:" healing, science, and the history of ideas. These are distinct but necessarily interrelated domains, with different, sometimes conflicting, criteria. I am challenged by every patient in every hour to be my best self; I am challenged by the science and the ideas that keep my professional life lively and meaningful.

In preparing this paper, I've collected many ideas before and since October, even as late as yesterday; the literature continues to provide far too many points to organize with the precision I prefer. I will instead present fragments of a paper—a work-in-progress—asking your indulgence while hoping to overwhelm and force you to agree with my thesis (as some here already do). But I expect to be disappointed, so we will continue to debate in the ample time we'll have for discussion. It is also likely that a version of my October paper will be used by an on-line interactive publication to open to debate among its readers.

More Philosophy of Science

September 19, 2017

How do I dare approach this topic again? I've presented about psychoanalysis-as-science for several years, beginning with reviews of major research programs and findings, and I've published one of my more recent efforts. But I come away from these presentations feeling that I've convinced no one who didn't agree with me before. I intended last September's effort, "Time and Other Illusions," to be my last on this theme, but reading new papers and attending recent panels led me to try again. When I decided to reconsider, my next thought was lifted from that magnificent 16th Century psychologist, Will Shakespeare, when his hero in *Henry V* (Act 3, scene 1) declared: "Once more unto the breach, dear friends...." But not so fast....

Just nine days ago I read a paper by Brett Clarke in the current edition of the *Psychoanalytic Quarterly*, just after Ben Roth's new paper on *Schreber*. Clarke is a faculty member at the Cincinnati Psychoanalytic Institute. His paper, "The Epistemology behind the Curtain: Thoughts on the Science of Psychoanalysis" (PsyQ, 86:3, pp. 575-608), made it clear that my own philosophical scholarship was seriously lacking. I restate that I am neither a philosopher nor a research scientist. But rather than chickening out or deferring this talk as I try to master Clarke's arguments, I will instead summarize its essential points. They are more effective than what will follow; his paper provides both a finely nuanced epistemology and a clinical description that is readily recognized as typical. I am delighted that such a paper appears in what used to be the most conservative of psychoanalytic journals.

Clarke describes the respective epistemologies of standard scientific research, and of the special method of psychoanalysis, a distinction too often mistakenly caricatured as either *scientism* (for sound science) or *fuzzy speculation* (for sound psychoanalytic theorizing). Central to the real distinction is a difference in the phenomenology of the two domains. Standard scientific research emphasizes measurement, norms and generalizability. The psychoanalytic associative method attempts to grasp the unique "irreducibly subjective character of psychoanalytic experience" (p 577). I won't repeat the quotation marks to follow, nor the page references, but much of what I'll now say are direct quotes: "Science is more than measurement and calculations of physical forces" (pp 576). "Relativism, or a purely contextual model offers a poor basis for theory and practice; a constrained 'objectivity' is required" (p 577). "Scientific reason is a *subset* of rational inquiry, not the other way around" (p 578). Mental events are "determined by motivations, meanings, [and] will, as surely as mental events are 'real'" (p 579).

"Critical realism," an approach I've spoken of before with reference to Hanly and Hanly (2001), provides for just such a "constrained" objectivity, but an overemphasis on objectivism lends itself to slippage to scientism by creating an implicit hierarchy of knowledge (favoring norms and quantities), in which essential mental activity is considered "prescientific" (p 579). Psychoanalytic "data," and I hesitate to use that word, is about "the particularities of lived experience... .affectively colored, fantasy organized... as played out in the analytic setting and relationship" (p 580). The "quality of excess" (p 581)—or *qualia*—is part of the "fiber of how and what we know psychoanalytically" (p 581). There is a "density" (Clarke's word) or intensity of felt mutual affect in clinical experience that requires a "practical kind of objectivity" (p 587). Its understandings are "partial and ever evolving" (p 589).

All science is a product of the human mind, and subjectivity is not reducible to zero, and may also be distorted by dishonesty, so I believe we must accept psychological reality as real enough, and the psychoanalytic approach to understanding that reality as valid enough.

Not originally planned for publication, this paper is not nearly well enough organized or philosophically sophisticated. Instead it's a compilation of thoughts I haven't stated adequately before, and ideas I've gleaned recently from the papers I've read and panels I've attended. My views supporting the scientific status of psychoanalytic psychology are shared by many, despite ongoing efforts of Freud bashers like Frederick Crews, bashed himself by reviewers of his most recent book, and psychoanalysts who assert their work is essentially artistic.

Everybody is Right

On March 31, the New York Psychoanalytic Society hosted on Oxford-style debate on the proposition that neuro-psychoanalysis makes *no* contribution to "clinical psychoanalytic practice." Mark Solms, a founder and major spokesperson for neuro-psychoanalysis, also the research chair of IPA, began with arguments in opposition to the proposal. Rachel Blass, the Controversies Editor of IJPA, argued the affirmative. Votes were taken in advance of the presentations and following them; very few minds were changed. My own view was that they were each partially right and partially wrong, the apparent paradox of my position was that they were addressing—like the blind men describing an elephant—different aspects of the more comprehensive Freudian corpus and were talking past rather than with each other.

From the perspective of Freud's theory of mind, Solms has the better case. Though Freud never provided a summary, and numerous complexities in his own writing are contradictory, there is little doubt that he would welcome a neurological understanding of his psychological propositions; he did in fact say he expected this eventuality. Freud's theory of treatment also defies summary. From his oft-quoted minimal criteria of "attending to transference and resistance" (1919), to the several metaphors and admonitions in the series of papers on technique written a century ago, Freud seems to argue for a clinical approach based on his practical experience, and the pragmatic goal of helping patients as best one can. This position contrasts, however, with his stated wish not to let the therapy interfere with the science! The much more specific regulations developed in the thirty years following Freud's death were an attempt to define a clinical method that made effective use of the psychoanalytic theory of mind, but—as alternate schools within psychoanalysis made clear—no generally agreed upon standard method has emerged. Instead we have competing positions, often declaring one another "not psychoanalysts." That psychoanalytic theories of mind are related to clinical practice is clear in the competing literatures; theoretical papers most often provide clinical examples. That the relationship is straightforward is far less evident; different schools argue for their own clinical methods, and sound comparative studies are rare. Blass's arguments are correct insofar as any *direct* application of neuro-psychoanalytic findings to technique is unconvincing, and is not even claimed by Dr. Solms.

This debate is yet another example of the story of the rabbi who heard an argument from one congregant, and said "you're right;" then heard an opposing argument, to which he gave the same reply. When a third congregant declared they couldn't both be right, the rabbi said "You're right too." In a June 10, *New York Times* Saturday profile, Isabel Kershner wrote about Micah Goodman, a popular Israeli philosopher: "He gives the Israeli-Palestinian conflict a kind of Talmudic treatment, where everything and its opposite are true." The rabbi and the philosopher might best add to their statements: "Or so it seems with the incomplete state of knowledge today."

Freud created a new paradigm for psychology, matched by his readiness to acknowledge errors, incompleteness, and ignorance. I'm reminded of the CERN scientist saying after the confirmation of the discovery of the Higgs boson, that it would have been more interesting if they had failed. Ignorance motivates scientific enterprise!

We remain far from a complete explanation of mind and/or brain, and we are not alone: Physics has two apparently incompatible theories, and also seeks a Grand Unifying Theory. This lack does not invalidate the pragmatic or theoretical advances of physics any more than it renders our own practices and ideas valueless, though they may be called art when they seem effective, or hogwash when they fail. "Psychoanalytic pluralism," like the Solms/Blass debate, offers exploratory ideas, including theories and tests, about different aspects of our complex domain. We are all experts at different parts of the elephant based on particular experience, and there is empirical support for each conflicting psychoanalytic perspective.

Reductionism: Charles Brenner's Dull Razor

While no psychoanalytic theorist has established a unifying theory, the collaborative and individual efforts of Jacob Arlow and Charles Brenner made that claim. (Arnie Richards has commented that their early Marxist politics made them certain of their assertions, and optimistic about their complete success.) By contrast, what is called psychoanalytic pluralism is the coexistence of several coherent theories, each derived from the Freudian corpus. Arlow, discussing a paper of Madelaine Baranger's from 25 years ago, called it primitive, a pre-structural psychology. Unexcelled in the clarity of his writing, Brenner wielded Occam's razor to cut many basic Freudian concepts out of his "Modern Conflict Theory." The work of Willi and Madeleine Baranger and their colleagues is now flourishing in South American psychoanalysis, with English translations becoming available and influential in North America and Europe. Since Brenner's death, his radical revisionist arguments dismissing Freud's Id-Ego-Superego model have all but dropped out of the discourse, even in Modern Conflict Theory at East 82nd Street. Likewise, the "therapeutic alliance," and "working through"—each idea skewered, sliced, diced, minced and crushed by Brenner—remain popular technical concepts, even for those like me who claim affiliation with Modern Conflict Theory.

Where does pluralism leave those who claim scientific status of psychoanalysis? The best current view is that it underscores the generativity of Freudian thought: the questions and shortcomings of Freud's models have led to more complex understandings of the mind (as F's presentation last week on Andre Green showed), and attempts to fulfill Leo Rangell's goal of a comprehensive unified theory and practice continue.

Determinism, Predetermination and Change: The Copper Sulfate Solution

Without postulating a "ghost" in the machine, there *are* phenomena best described as "emergent," or even "transcendent." Copper sulfate differs from its elements, having properties not like or predictable from its constituents, copper, sulfur and oxygen. Brains produce simple and more complex minds. The relative intelligence of octopuses, dogs, and chimps can be assessed. The human mind produces ideas; ideas rely on brains but (contra Churchland) transcend their materialism. In addition to ideas, people produce art, develop moral and ethical codes, and they love. These are transcendent phenomena, surely with material correlates, but far from adequately understood solely in material terms. Radical reductionism is materialism in spades. It cannot account for or predict evolutionary change. From minds with ideas, creativity emerges—in many forms. Creativity is a non-ghostly transcendence of what was before. Language is a transcendent development; it is real and important, despite—perhaps even because of—reliance on allusion and metaphor. Music relies on sound waves; art on vision, lust on hormones. Collective minds produce values, ethics, organized societies, and politics. Emergent properties create new events that affect our lives, the world, even the universe (note the conclusion last week of the 20 year exploration of Saturn). These developments provide meaning to lives, despite—and perhaps because of—mortality, and our awareness of it. Emergent properties differ from their necessary and even sufficient precursors. The mind is both contained within the body, and relational in its development (recall studies of mirror neurons, and attachment motivation). These phenomena—not just the malfunctions we consider psychopathology—provide the broad subject matter of the humane, individualized and inexact but scientific psychoanalysis.

The "Hard Problem:" Subjectivity as Phenomenal Entity

Subjectivity is seen by some as totally undermining the scientific standing of psychoanalysis. Owen Renik's 1993 influential phrase "irreducible subjectivity" seems to suggest that subjectivity is not at all reducible; I take it instead to mean not reducible to zero. We have degrees of objectivity, never complete no matter whether in physics, chemistry, biology or psychology. Skinner's behaviorism limited scientific psychology to observable behavior, leaving no room for inferred mental operations. His approach lost dominance in North America to Ulric Neisser's "cognitive psychology," wherein subjective responses are a proper focus of research. Freudian psychology is *about* subjectivity, but extended the scope of study beyond consciousness: human subjectivity is more than what we can at any moment report as conscious mentation; much of cognition, affect and conation (will) are not conscious states. Will (will power, intent), is psychological, though not the potent force one may wish, and its variations—omnipotence, stubbornness, inhibition, abulia—are aspects of normal psychological development that might suggest psychopathology.

As Kwame Anthony Appiah, the *New York Times* ethicist and NYU philosophy professor, pointed out in a column last month, science can transcend the subjectivity of scientists by virtue of methodology, or else no science of human beings would be possible. Scientists work at refining methods, recognizing their inevitable limitations. A recent dispute over the very definition of science appeared a few weeks ago on one of the psychoanalytic listservs. Science was defined by Georges Canguilem as "... a contemplative possession of reality through exclusion of all illusion, error and ignorance." This was countered almost immediately by Stephen Soldz with "... an active grappling with our ignorance regarding reality in a manner that systematically takes account of the possibility of error and illusion." The first definition assumes incorrectly that we can know the "the thing in itself," the second leans to a belief that we can hardly know it at all, allowing post-modernists to declare, also incorrectly, that there is no such thing as the thing in itself. They turn a problem of epistemology into a nihilistic ontology.

Subjectivity is a limitation of objectivity; it is also a phenomenon absolutely worthy of scientific scrutiny. Physics Nobel Laureate Murray Gell-Mann, reflecting on Freud the person, considered his self-analysis valid as a contribution to knowledge, since each individual's mind provides instances of general mental functioning.

Another panel at the New York Psychoanalytic Society, sponsored by the interdisciplinary Helix Center on May 20 this year, was entitled, "Complexity and Emergence II: Visions of Cosmic Order, from Particles to People." It was moderated by psychoanalyst Ed Nercessian. (I'd missed the first one.) The five presenters included a social activist/author, an astrobiologist, a philosophy professor, an evolutionary biologist, and an environmental scientist. I'd never heard of any of the speakers but all were highly-credentialed, and I found each to be an effective and creative representative of their respective disciplines. The overall panel defies my ability to summarize. I present instead from among the take-away ideas: "Complexity cannot be scaled;" "Cultural evolution is not random, it is intentional;" "Morality and rationality must count;" "Complexity and beauty are beyond biology." None of these statements was disputed by the three biologists.

T's February 21st presentation outlined his project to describe consciousness in fully biological terms. No one is more of a fan of his than I, and my complete disagreement with the aim of his project is meant respectfully. T has a beautiful mind; I haven't seen his brain. I may be unfair to the project, if so, he'll correct me. My critique is in five points:

1. T equates consciousness with the ability to adapt to changing conditions. This seems a substitution of the word "consciousness" for Darwin's more general word and central idea: "adaptation." It explains nothing more and adds nothing, especially as discussion of fungi and plants are deferred, and Protista are excluded from this ostensibly evolutionary approach.

2. I agree there is good reason and sound evidence to include primates, mammals, octopuses, and perhaps many more creatures as having consciousness. Observables result in inferences that make good sense, though criteria may be in dispute and specifics may be disproven. Similarities can be described. Comparative psychology, though, involves the study of differences as well. To my mind, the differences are at least as important.

3. Differences in consciousness are not limited to those between species; their most significant manifestations are among members of the same species,

most notably our own. Consciousness is, in Freud's still apt metaphor, the tip of an iceberg. Every patient/client/person is unique. Every therapy dyad (similarly each family and every group) is unique. Fixed rules and procedures may work for some individuals, families and groups, but fail for many others; flexibility is necessary for the therapeutic approach I believe to be required for responsible, clinical practice. Our knowledge base cannot provide formulaic procedures for success; scientistic approaches remain the stuff of overambitious fantasy.

4. The basic fallibility of determinism is its pre-determination, i.e., everything cannot be reduced to the Big Bang, a most obvious *reductio ad absurdum*. If we could mentally deconstruct that original first instance Big Bang phenomenon, we would with ultra-reductionism have to postulate that all subsequent phenomena are inherent in the nascent state. The current more probabilistic understanding of the universe may be less satisfying, but as a best tentative theory it seems far more tenable.

5. Perhaps the most important issues for psychological (and social and anthropological) study are values, i.e., ethics and aesthetics: what is good, what is beautiful. Survivability of our planet is not a random consideration; human behavior and misbehavior lend direction to human evolution and survival. These human creations—**values**—highlight differences. Radical post-modernism is the inverse of predetermination, claiming everything comes from what came before; while post-modernism declares there is no essence. In Radical Reductionism, everything is determined; in Radical Postmodernism, nothing is. The scientists on the Helix panel believe in intentionality. Humans influence evolution; with CRISPR we now have the capacity to change the very biology of evolution. A major and appropriate response from scientists is to raise ethical questions, and they are doing just that.

Sir Cyril Burt, FBA (b. 1883) was an English educational psychologist known best for his studies on the heritability of IQ. Shortly after he died in 1971, his studies came into disrepute after evidence emerged indicating he had falsified research data. Some scholars have more recently asserted that Burt did not commit fraud since numerous international studies have since confirmed a high heritability for intelligence. But the honesty of scientific findings must always be checked. On a more fundamental level, experiments by Nazi doctors (described by Robert Lifton) are repudiated on moral grounds, as is the work of psychologists at Guantanamo supporting "advanced interrogation," only recently condemned by the American

Psychological Association as torture. One of those whose ten-year effort led to that change in the APA ethics code is Steven Reisner, who will speak with us in February.

T's project might generate useful ideas. He respects our work as therapists within our experience; how could we work otherwise. We understand the tentative nature of current knowledge. But experiential reality is all we have until more definitive knowledge is experienced, and that too will be experiential. T believes that time is an illusion; there is only space/time; but space/time as a reality seems less relevant psychologically than time itself as it is experienced. I doubt that consciousness, or ideas, ethics or aesthetics will be adequately explained by biology. The valorization of materialism is itself a belief, no longer essential to a scientific attitude—or to defining what is or isn't scientific. Experiential reality is worthy of scientific inquiry. T emphasizes the heuristics of scientific thinking; on this we are in agreement. On the hardest questions, heuristics may be the best we can do. The very idea of "now" is called into question by physics, but "now" is central to experience.

T condemns "flat earth" thinking, but it worked until more useful observations were made. Empiricism confirmed that space is curved, as Einstein theorized, and this fact is essential for accurate astronomy. The curvature of space is small enough though to lack practical import for down-to-earth activities. Einstein's discoveries show the limits of Newton's Laws, which nonetheless work quite well on earth. That molecules and atoms have more space than substance is a fact; that we have a technology of solids is equally true. Biology studies life forms; psychology studies mental events with emergent properties that include consciousness, self-consciousness, reflective consciousness, theory of mind, empathy; and psychoanalysis informs us about unconscious motives. Disciplines have specific methods and methodological limitations. Each is probabilistic, the human sciences more so than physical disciplines.

I support the study of the biological underpinnings of psychology and respect neuro-psychoanalytic research but expect no more from it than correlational findings. I object to the proposition that psychology can be reduced to biology or biology to chemistry: radical reductionism mistakenly treats emergent and transcendent forms with the epithet, *epi*phenomena, but these realities require new disciplines with methods appropriate to their study.

How do we know facts are facts? The political use of "fake news" is disturbing precisely because of the epistemological problem: How do we know anything? Scientific methodology and discourse are subject to ethical and moral judgment.

Social science methods, like all scientific methods, are subject to review, replication, critique and revision. To borrow S's watchwords, this is "the back and forth" of all scientific work. How the balance of empiricism and rationality plays out specifically is beyond the scope of biology.

The ability to distinguish inner (ideational and affective) and outer (perceptual) realities, "reality-testing" is a central ego psychological concept. The ability is imperfect and variable, but its assessment is critical to clinical work. We can distinguish between realistic and delusional or hallucinatory experiences.

I still like Strachey's term "cathexis." An undergrad professor translated this neologism into understandable English, "learning to appreciate." This phrase describes a knowledge laden with affect, personal and interpersonal. Rapaport and his students tried to quantify cathexis; their efforts came to a dead end. I hope Freud's essential "economic point of view" will find more clarity; psychological intensity is real.

Coda

Science is itself a human invention, built on motivations like curiosity. We infer curiosity in infants from their observable exploratory behavior. Its developmental stages can be described normatively: the infant is most interested in "who?" the toddler in "what?" while the preschooler asks "why?" The grade-school pupil discovers "how?" and the teen plaintively asks "when?" Young adults, with freedom to take distance from their parents, ask "where?" Curiosity may not be limited to our species, but it is likely that such refined developmental curiosity is species-specific.

The late Jaak Panksepp's seven drives, correlated with brain locations, include an epistemic urge akin to Freud's perhaps prematurely discarded formulation of Ego instincts. Freud's final dual instinct theory is itself more than "dual;" he writes of life instincts in the plural, and the death instinct, a most controversial idea rejected in much of North American psychoanalysis, with mixed reviews in Europe, yet a central idea for Kleinians, British and South American, and, as we learned last week, for Andre Green. Melanie Klein spoke also of "epistemophilia" as a defense; ego psychologists call it intellectualization. I believe with Panksepp that it is instinctive as well, and with Brenner, that any mental capacity can be used defensively.

Science prides itself on increasingly useful methods. It also considers knowledge always to be tentative, subject to revision and/or rejection. Science makes use of both Platonic rationality and Aristotelian empiricism in an incomplete Kantian synthesis to create methods suited to the phenomena under study. Ideas and observations can be conceptually distinct, but are always joined in the actual work of scientists, and also of those who apply "best evidence" science, like physicians and us psychotherapists.

Thanks for listening.

Defining Science

January 30, 2018

This is the sixth or seventh essay I've written on this topic—the fraught relationship between psychoanalysis and science—in about 12 years. It's increasingly difficult to organize the material, since the sheer quantity of documentation exceeds my ability to condense and summarize, and our time-frame properly values discussion. The scientific status of psychoanalysis is a hot topic, with no sign of cooling but maybe some chance for enlightenment. This essay is aimed at demonstrating the necessity for recognizing psychoanalysis, "the paradigm," as a scientific enterprise, and "the treatment" as but one of several applications of this paradigm. As is true of all health care, psychodynamic therapists try to apply the best available evidence for their work.

My guiding framework is broader than today's specific aim. It is that psychoanalysis the paradigm, like Freud's "Ego" (1923), serves three masters: clinical practice, science, and the history of ideas. These disciplines are not always congruent in their validation criteria.

To return to the aim: why do I persist with philosophy of science? While most appreciate my efforts, and others agree with me, many remain skeptical, or opposed to my position. Still others are primarily interested in directly clinical questions: How does this help with my patients? What's the use of epistemology? My answer will refer to the pragmatic situation of mental health professions, the intellectual ferment within the psychoanalytic discipline, and specific responses to my earlier presentations.

The psychoanalytic paradigm emerged from and continues with clinical practice as its primary source. Its derivative therapies are practical applications. Freud learned by doing, and—still without a Grand Unifying Theory or commonly agreed "best practice"—we all continue to learn from treating individuals or couples or families, groups or organizations (to acknowledge the extended domain of psychoanalytically-informed practice). Mental health careers are predicated on clinical work and/or clinical research. The focus on practice as the major career path is a reason for relative—but only apparent—paucity of research: few practitioners engage in systematic research, and much of this work is conducted by those without much experience-based clinical practice. Freud believed his work was scientific, even fearing that practitioner values would limit scientific discovery. He was dismissive of research data that did not emerge from the consulting room. Andre Green among others shared this view of the proper psychoanalytic "database." Practitioners who don't think much about theory or research literature surely have clinical success, but I believe practice is impoverished if it does not try to understand "therapeutic action," and if it cannot demonstrate the processes that lead to successful and teachable outcomes. I will repeat what I've said before: there are several decades of sound research programs that support psychoanalytic concepts and process and demonstrate successful outcomes. Among these programs are those at Penn, Yale, Columbia, Adelphi and the University of Michigan.

A frankly pragmatic reason exists for establishing that psychoanalytic treatments are scientific. The recently-issued American Psychological Association Treatment Guidelines for PTSD do not include psychodynamic therapies among "evidence-based" treatments, counting Randomized Controlled Trials (RCTs) as essential criteria for this designation. This, the larger APA, lobbies heavily to have psychology itself counted among the STEM fields (Science, Technology, Engineering, and Mathematics), so that research funding will flow. The evidence-based imprimatur, though faulty (Wachtel, 2010), points people to mental health practitioners other than most of us, and directs students to alternate approaches by speaking disparagingly, if at all, of psychoanalysis. Few contemporary clinical psychology programs emphasize psychoanalytically-informed therapies, the dominant modalities when most of my generation trained. Psychodynamic methods occupy a diminishing part of curricula in psychiatry and social work professional training as well. Organizational guidelines, endorsements, and dis-endorsements matter to the survival of this clinical practice. APA says that its Guidelines should not be the basis for insurance or Medicare reimbursement. It is naïve, even absurd, however, to believe that payments will be unaffected by a narrow definition of psychological care that promotes short-term, cheaper therapy.

I also continue my philosophy of science project because I am stimulated by papers that demonstrate the vitality of contemporary psychoanalytic theory. I will quote from several that articulate my argument better than I can.

Science began as "natural philosophy." Knowledge acquisition requires both empiricism and rationality and has proven to have great value when applied. Space is curved, but on Earth the curvature is rarely relevant. Apprenticeship remains central to psychotherapy training, but book learning is also required. Thomas Insel noted when he retired from the National Institute of Mental Health that psychopharmacology hasn't advanced significantly in 60 years despite new drugs, and we know that the economic motivation of Big Pharma makes suspect much of its research. In a paper presented in October 2006, I spoke of the art of clinical work in health care and agreed that talent may be even more important in our field, with its reliance on—and very subject matter—subjectivity. But—I must reiterate: an art whose claims are more than aesthetic needs more than its claims to affirm its value.

This paper's title is "Defining Science" because I believe many of our disagreements are definitional, that is, semantic. Daniel Kahneman's research shows us all wedded to our own opinions, often even more strongly in the face of opposing argumentation or evidence. Language, and its special form of creativity, metaphor, is necessarily subject to disagreement, to *subjectivity*. Robert Stolorow and others indeed define psychoanalysis-the-paradigm as the scientific study of subjectivity.

Science is a human creation, defined in several ways. In earlier presentations, I cited philosopher Francis Bacon (1561-1626), known as the "father of empiricism," whose definition is: "an attitude toward the universe in which observations are made using the best methods available; logic is employed; and contradictions or magical, supernatural, and *ad hoc* solutions are rejected." Charles Brenner (2006) supplemented Bacon, adding that all sciences are inferential and influenced by the observer's psychology, but facts rule. Experimentation may be employed but is not required (e.g., Galileo's astronomy); quantification is a tool of science, not its essence. I add two more principles to the Bacon/Brenner definition: 1) scientific conclusions are always tentative, and 2) though psychological reality is rife with contradiction and paradox (themselves characteristic of human psychology), its methods are rational *and* empirical—therefore, scientific.

In a previous essay I cited two other definitions appearing on one of the psychoanalytic listservs: George Canguilem defined Science as "a contemplative possession of reality through exclusion of all illusion, error and ignorance." This post was countered almost immediately by Stephen Soldz, with "an active grappling with our ignorance regarding reality, in a manner that systematically takes account of the possibility of error and illusion." Canguilem's definition assumes—against the contemporary consensus of philosophers—that we can know the "the thing in itself." Soldz leans to a belief that we can know objective reality hardly at all, allowing post-modernists to declare, also incorrectly in my opinion, that there is *no such thing* as the thing in itself. This turns the problem of epistemology into an ontology of nihilism!

Yet a fourth view appeared in the October 26, 2017 issue of the *New York Review of Books*. According to Lisa Appignanesi, noting Freud's election to the Royal Society "for pioneering work in psychoanalysis" following his flight to England in 1939, "science is not a narrow domain whose residents, like adherents of a strict religion, follow one rigid set of eternal rules, but rather a capacious and diverse mansion where observation of not only the animal but also the human world could count as science, where doubters could live side by side and engage in heated argument." Further, "scientists are not uniformly consistent either in their ideas or in their lives. Nor is it always clear how one shapes the other."

Paul Mosher recommended the first chapter of Joseph Schwartz's 1999 book, *Cassandra's Daughter: A History of Psychoanalysis*, one largely devoted to this subject. Schwartz, a psychoanalyst who also holds a Ph.D. in particle physics (Berkeley), says:

> When psychoanalysis is accused of being unscientific the charge is really that it is subjective, an accusation that raises loud alarms in the Western mind. We learn from an early age, especially if we are men, that we must strive to be objective, that feelings are not to be trusted, that, in some renderings, to be subjective is a peculiar weakness of the female of our species. The fear that psychoanalysis is 'only subjective,' and therefore that it is unreliable or even dangerous, has provoked four distinct responses. The first is to accept as fair the charge that psychoanalysis is unscientific with an ensuing attempt to reconfigure it to produce the controlled studies that have proved so effective in biology. A second response is to accept the characterization of psychoanalysis as unscientific but to insist that scientific criteria are not useful because what is important about psychoanalysis is that it creates meanings in ways that are completely different from the natural sciences. A third is to insist that psychoanalysis is in fact a science, with clinical evidence being a form of evidence valid in its own right. And a fourth reply to the criticism is to argue that the problem lies not with psychoanalysis but with a fallacious concept of science and scientific success. The fourth response is the response we

will explore here because a fallacious concept of science lies at the heart of the critiques of psychoanalysis and the responses to them.

I contend that research programs have made considerable progress and provide lots of evidence. The late Howard Shevrin's program at Michigan finally satisfied the philosopher Adolph Grunbaum, a long-time critic of psychoanalysis. "Scientific" practice should mean making use of available "best evidence." Clinical evidence accumulated for 120 years is considered evidentiary, even by APA. It adds to a knowledge base that can support practice. Practice should not be limited to the results of RCTs. Public respect—and patients and students surely influenced by the *zeitgeist*—are responsive to economic and political considerations. Necessarily imperfect evidence must count as good enough for the moment. "Best practice" must not be an unrealizable ideal.

Measurement is important in science. Psychometrics is a respectable field. It is said anything that exists can be measured. That seems axiomatic until one hears statements like "one knows the cost of everything, but the value of nothing." Statistical significance is not always practically significant. Precision can be useful and is often beautiful, but it may have neither impact nor import. Are values measurable? Psychology produces clever research designs and operational definitions, but psychological research is always limited in its generalizability and application. There are four useful psychometric categories:

1. Nominal scales name and categorize: living/not living; animal/plant; dog/cat; the visible spectrum of colors, not all binaries. Classification (taxonomy) is a primary method of science.

2. Ordinal scales address more and less, the simplest of quantifiers. How hungry? How tired? How intelligent? IQ scores are not precise: 110 IQ does not indicate smarter than 105 despite the 5-point difference. There is a measurable standard error of measurement. Both IQ score and the error of measurement are probable and inexact. Ordinal scales are useful within their limits.

3. Interval scales are exemplified by rulers; cc's of a liquid operationalize temperature. These measures are more specific than more-or-less, but do not mean that 60 degrees F is twice as warm as 30 degrees. For humans in temperate climes, 60 degrees is better described as mild, depending on the season, and 32 degrees F freezes water by the very definition of

the scale; it is also, subjectively, "freezing." These measures are practical and scientific.

4. Ratio scales can properly speak of "twice as much" or "twenty times greater." Kelvin is a ratio-scale measure of heat, its utility limited to chemistry, physics and cosmology.

Scientific methods have degrees of precision and probabilistic results. RCTs may be the ratio scales of science; like Kelvin, however, their utility is limited. The best-controlled experiments in our field yield conclusions that don't apply to patients with co-morbid pathologies, or those with intolerable side effects, or with limited motivation for a difficult treatment. Exposure therapy, for instance, has many dropouts. Non-compliance is rife in all medical fields (my dermatologist says I'm his only patient who follows his advice). Operational definitions are necessary for experimentation, but always compromise generalizability. Patients don't conform well enough to diagnostic criteria, and exclusion criteria for good research (what Alex Charney refers to as "cleaning" data-sets) always limit translation of the cleanest findings into clinical practice.

Our case studies, like field studies in sociology, usually provide better guidance for treating individuals, despite their imprecision. Detailed case material describes situations that, in our field, often preclude focused psychotherapies. The general approach of a psychoanalytic treatment is to understand the complexity of the individual (or couple, family or group), and to work with a modesty appropriate to our ignorance, and with trial-and-error interventions.

Bona fide methods of science include: systematic observation, classification and taxonomy, trial and error, surveys, and correlational studies. They allow scientific work where experiments are inappropriate for practical or ethical reasons. Suicidology is a scientific clinical practice relying on taxonomy and correlation, non-experimental, but scientific nonetheless. When its findings and recommendations are put into practice, suicide is statistically reduced, with no guaranteed prevention for an individual. I wrote this sentence well before the announcement of today's Research Grand Rounds, entitled "The Science of Suicide Prevention: A Path Forward for Clinicians."

Terry Rogers is a *bona fide* scientist, though several of us earned doctorates in the scientist-practitioner training model, the one-time standard for clinical psychology. In an exchange following a presentation, Terry distinguished between scientific findings and psychotherapy practice. He dismissed the findings of psychoanalysis as neither measurable nor reproducible, and its practice as experiential and academic (by which I believe he means rational or philosophical rather than empirical). He counts its findings as reifications of metaphorical structures, violating *his* definition of "scientific." He allows that the brain is beyond all but "around-the-edges" experimentation, and he feels that therapy practice is, like most practical things, a best guess, and therefore—in his judgment—without shame: practice can be good enough without being scientific. Rogers also asserts that quantification is central to science. Dismissing trial-and-error (a practice I promote to students) as unscientific, he accuses psychoanalysis of an absence of rules and lacking in prediction.

As to trial-and-error, I cite H-K Choi, a senior researcher in South Korea. Referring to Kim Jong-un, the North Korean leader, Choi said, "We have never heard of him killing scientists. He is someone who understands that trial-and-error is part of doing science."

As to quantification, the research programs I've cited have measurable outcomes. Jonathan Shedler and Drew Westen developed an assessment instrument (SWAP) with substantial reliability among clinicians judging symptoms, personality characteristics, and changes in each. But numbers can be manipulated.

Psychoanalytic treatments make no claims for prediction, but we are not surprised at frequent reports from supervisees that supervisor speculations about patients we've never met turn out to be what these patients often talk about in the following week's session! It is a far too stringent requirement that we achieve precision to decimal places. Our guesses, which we make every time we say anything to a patient or remain silent, are rarely precise but purposefully unique. They are often effective enough if only, as Fred Busch says, they are "in the ballpark."

In his November 5 presentation, Terry expressed his belief that "psychoanalysis has reached its limit as a model of mind." His reliance for that statement cited only the authority of Eric Kandel who, at a meeting last October 14, claimed "no scientific validation for psychoanalysis in the past 50 years." This statement betrays Kandel's ignorance of the several research programs that remain productive well into a sixth decade.

But Terry's November paper seemed also to respond well to my critique of his February presentation on his work-in-progress. Terry's is no longer a radical reductionist model that limits explanation of psychological matters solely to biological terms. He acknowledged "time" as a psychological reality, despite its loss of ontological standing in contemporary physics. Terry also put "anxiety" at the center of his evolutionary approach, just as it became the center of Freud's clinical theory in 1926. Terry now uses phrases like, "mind is the action of the brain in terms that are relevant to us," and speaks of "feeling states" and "self." These, unlike terms preferred by Churchland, are psychological. "Relevant to us" is a clearly psychological statement.

I applaud Terry's ambitious wish to find common factors throughout the animal kingdom, perhaps among all life, from simple "minds" to the most complex. Despite the great commonality of the human genome with that of our close primate cousins, and with one another, differences among us are central to the psychoanalytic aim of being a comprehensive theory of the human mind and in its products. Like all science, psychoanalysis seeks replicable generalizations. Freud's claims were often overgeneralizations. But one specific difference, language, is a major focus of psychoanalysis; in Lacan's version, the essential one. Other differences are important as well: that humans and our near evolutionary cousins are social creatures. The psychoanalytic paradigm is a bio-psycho-socio-cultural-ecological discipline. I agree with Terry, no paradigm can contradict phenomenal findings from other sciences; and for Freud (1923), "the ego is first and foremost a body ego." A paradigm makes inferences that go beyond the level of observation; not all things are observable. Self-deception is real, as is secrecy. The psychological includes the interpersonal and other phenomenal domains, each of which focus on relevant phenomena. Some prominent analysts (e.g., Green, Irwin Hoffman) limit their focus solely to Freud's *Ucs*. A scientific psychoanalysis aims for a complete theory; human groups small and large are part of the paradigm; thus Freud's anthropological speculations.

For psychoanalysis, the very concept of causality is expanded by multiple function, over-determination, and intentionality. Freud's *Ucs* is the special domain of Psychoanalysis; its method—Free Association—aims to plumb the *Ucs*, but *Cs* and *Pcs* are more than descriptors. Psychodynamic treatments aim to expand consciousness by including the *Ucs*, social values, cultural traditions, economic circumstances and political systems. We'll hear next week from Dr. Steven Reisner on "the political action of psychoanalysis."

Rogers' current model of mind recognizes mental process; perception is, he acknowledges, "in our mind"—but not "all in our mind." It is subjective; subjectivity is real and cannot be ruled out of the scientific endeavor. Science is a human creation; subjectivity underlies human mental activity. Psychoanalysis not only takes this into account, it studies the nature of subjectivity, and individual subjectivities. If Owen Renik's (1993) idea of the mind's "irreducible subjectivity" puts mind beyond science, then science is impoverished by impotence in the face of subjectivity, which is an indisputable fact of nature!

Terry's "unconscious" seems akin to Freud's *Pcs*. We await his comments on a dynamic, conflicted unconscious involving repression and resistance to awareness. But his November model, unlike last February's, is compatible with a scientific psychoanalytic paradigm—even to his inclusion of a "superego" concept.

I am arguing for a psychoanalysis based on sound science. Not all purported science is sound. Ignorance motivates both science and a rush for elusive certainty, because ignorance can trigger anxiety. Ignorance also motivates philosophy.

On October 22, 2017, the *New York Times Magazine* cover story was on Amy Cuddy, a social psychologist specializing in body language. Her TED talk on the dramatic, positive effects on self-confidence of "power poses" had become the second most popular, yet new statistical tools found her findings wanting—and replication failed. Lisa Pryor, MD, in a January 5, 2018 *New York Times* op-ed on countering pseudo-science addressed the dilemma of asserting scientific claims found, while wading through the online world of alternative-health practitioners, wellness bloggers, whole-food chefs and Gwyneth Paltrow. If the psychotherapy most of us practice is similarly categorized because we cannot claim sound evidence, we are doomed to cult status. Pryor goes on:

> Most doctors, especially the good ones, are acutely aware of the limits of their knowledge. I have learned from those much more experienced and qualified than me that humility is something to be cultivated over time, not lost.
>
> Our field is built around trying to prove ourselves wrong. In hospitals we hold morbidity and mortality meetings trying to show where we have failed, what we need to change, how we can do better. Our hospital work is audited to identify where we fell short of our ideals. Through scientific research we try to disprove the effectiveness of treatments. Our failings are exposed from the inside.
>
> The nature of evidence-based health care is that practices change as new evidence emerges.
>
> That is also the case for other health professionals whose practice is based on science, like qualified dieticians, physiotherapists, occupational therapists and psychologists. Guidelines are revised, advice is reversed—

on blood pressure, diet, hormone replacement, opioid prescribing. This can be immensely frustrating for patients, even though it is what we must do to provide the best possible treatment.

Psychological conferences, though not limited to science, are frequently scientific. We argue respectfully with one another, and we learn from our arguments. We accept differences in a field marked by constant internal dispute. Patients rely on our expertise, assuming we are honest practitioners that care about the science underpinning our imprecise clinical methods.

Science is a product of minds in interaction. Definitions vary and can be contradictory. To us, science is a good thing. The educated public concurs, but this concurrence is deceptive. Billions of people place faith above science as guides for living. More people in this country believe angels are real rather than metaphorical, and that there is an afterlife, although theologians themselves question and challenge simple faith-based assertions. A majority of Americans don't believe in evolution, and a significant number reject the assertion of a human contribution to climate change. Few if any of my colleagues subscribe to supernaturalism, but we disagree on what counts as scientific.

Arnold Richards has promoted the ideas of Ludwik Fleck on "thought collectives." Thought collectives operate as silos where differences are treated as better or worse, and inclusion criteria are often stringent. A narrow definition of science can result in isolation and a limit on discovery. We can have instead an anthropology of science to guard against a stifling orthodoxy.

Science is essential for the advancement of knowledge. Treating psychoanalysis as pseudoscience or only an art ignores its knowledge base and undermines its useful practice. Psychoanalytic therapies are evidence-based. Ignoring evidence is just plain bias, confirming the defensiveness Freud attributed to early critics of his formulations. The psychoanalytic paradigm is a scientific work-in-progress, as are its derived therapies. A properly broad definition of science should acknowledge this fact. The contributions of psychoanalysis are far too important to dismiss or relegate to cult status.

Is Psychoanalysis a Science or an Art?

International Journal of Controversial Discussions 1, No. 1, (2020), pp. 668–674

Leo Rangell (2007) pointed out the need for replacing either/or thinking with a both/and formulation to better advance our field. We should apply his recommendation to the science/art binary. Psychoanalysis not only defies such binaries, it goes beyond hybridization. Psychoanalysis is both scientific and artistic, yet it does not fit comfortably with either science or art.

Science makes use of empiricism and rationality to understand reality, and to discover laws of nature. Art makes skillful use of a variety of materials and methods, aiming for originality and an enhanced sense of wonder and beauty. Science also relies on original thinking for solutions to empirical problems. Among the defining elements of psychoanalysis is that much mental functioning is out of awareness and involves non-rational mental operations.

British scientist and novelist C.P. Snow's 1959 Rede Lecture had as its thesis that "the intellectual life of the whole of western society" was split into two cultures: the sciences and the humanities. He claimed that this split was a major hindrance to solving the world's problems. In 2008 the (London) *Times Literary Supplement* included Snow's *The Two Cultures* and *The Scientific Revolution* on its list of 100 books that most influenced Western public discourse since World War II. We might expect that six decades of influence would have made for some reconciliation, but Snow's thesis has been both elaborated and disputed, while science and the humanities (including the arts) are still too often seen as antimonies.

Jaak Panksepp (2012) counted curiosity as not merely a sublimated sexual voyeurism but one of seven inherent human drives. The science or art question addresses psychoanalytic epistemology: how do we slake curiosity and come to know anything? Knowledge acquisition began prehistorically and led to the survival and dominance of our species. Like the Tower of Babel story, a pluralism of epistemologies ensued, with intuition and revelation the first of these, and shamans and priests the earliest non-warrior tribal leaders. The 18th Century Enlightenment and the technology revolution of the last 140 years defined distinct disciplines to expand knowledge and appreciation of the world: theology, philosophy, history, biography, linguistics, mathematics, natural sciences and the arts among them. Advancement and refinement generated subspecialties within each discipline, seeking more nuanced means of increasing human understanding, adaptation and control of natural events. Psychoanalysis emerged from the creative mind of a single genius, claiming as its domain a heretofore little known or dismissed realm of human nature. Freud's ambition went beyond therapeutics; he sought a complete theory of mind and its products. His limitations have provided opportunities for his successors to correct, modify, redirect and expand upon his work.

As Freud wrote of the Ego (1923), psychoanalysis itself serves three masters. It is a treatment method. In fact, the theory informs several related treatment methods usually referred to as "psychodynamic." In the eyes of its founder and of many contemporaries it is a natural science. It is also recognized as a contribution to the history of ideas, that status marked by Freud's inclusion in the *Great Books of the Western World* (1952). These disciplines—therapeutics, science, and intellectual history—differ in their criteria for disciplinary membership; psychoanalysis aspires in each but does not fit easily within them. In a voice recording made in his final year of life, Freud stated that psychoanalysis is "a part of psychology, not medical psychology" (1938b). I will argue that psychoanalysis is unlike other sciences but is and must be scientific. Nor is psychoanalysis art, as that term is commonly and sometimes disparagingly understood, but it includes a central therapeutic enterprise that relies on the creative intuition of clinicians and theorists: its practice is artistic!

Like medical treatment, the practice of psychoanalytic psychotherapies is informed by best evidence. For psychoanalysis, the treatment situation is exquisitely individualized, relying nonetheless on tentative generalizations about the mind's regularities and variations. As a scientific discipline, psychoanalysis rests on a systematic observational methodology that does not lend itself to rigorously controlled experimental design. Its primary database is comprised of 125 years of clinical reportage and attempts at theoretical integration. There is however a vast literature (hundreds of thousands of Google hits) for "psychoanalytic research" that tests hypotheses within and outside the confidential clinical situation. Its scientific aims include validation of therapeutic work while testing and refining psychological propositions and the general theory of mind. The work of the late Sidney Blatt, commemorated in a special issue of Psychoanalytic Psychology (Auerbach, 2019), underscores the essential privacy of the clinical situation, which makes extra-clinical validation essential for scientific acceptance.

Those who dismiss psychoanalysis as unscientific use a narrow definition of science, limited to methodologies that would exclude Darwin and Einstein as well as Freud. I prefer the definition offered by philosopher Francis Bacon (1561-1626), the father of empiricism cited by Brenner (2006). Bacon spoke of science as "an attitude toward the universe in which observations are made using the best methods available; logic is employed; and contradictions or magical, supernatural, and ad hoc solutions are rejected." Brenner added that all sciences are inferential and influenced by the observer's psychology, but "facts must rule." Experimentation may be employed but is not required (e.g., Galileo's astronomy); quantification is a tool of science, not its essence. Two additional principles: scientific conclusions are tentative, and although "psychological reality" is rife with contradiction and paradox, as Freud (1900) showed in his dream book, its methods are rational and empirical. Scientific advances may occur without scientific methods, as with Kekule's dreaming discovery of the benzene ring, and Fleming's incidental observation of the anti-bacterial effects of penicillin.

A clear definition of art is harder to come by. Definitions are verbal; art is not limited to—or by—language. When poets are asked to explain their work, they typically decline, saying the poem speaks for itself. Art history reveals a great variety of forms and subject matter—and striking cultural differences. And art forms evolve: the invention of photography led to obsolescence of still life painting and portraiture. Non-representational art forms emerged early in the 20th Century, with visual aesthetics redefined by Picasso and others. Music also underwent changes in the last century, from tonality to atonality, to jazz and rap among other new genres. Art exceeds its limits through the creative imagination of those who become recognized as artists, often with delay and sometimes posthumously. "Fine" art came to share the word with commercial art and graffiti. Literature evolved to include violation of rigid grammars and "stream of consciousness." Craft is considered essential, but the forms art takes seem limitless. Art is created to express and evoke an experience of beauty. Great artists change the world by expanding collective aesthetic experience.

While the term "applied psychoanalysis" has traditionally been reserved for non-clinical realms, primarily the arts and humanities, therapeutics still comprise the best-known applications of the psychoanalytic paradigm. Scientific applications extend their effectiveness with standardization and generalization, while recognizing the probabilistic and tentative nature of scientific findings.

As with medical applications of science, practice—especially the exquisitely individualized practice of psychoanalytic therapeutics—can only approximate what theory suggests. Jerome Groopman, in a *New Yorker* essay reviewing "Psychiatry's Fraught History" (2019), states, "For a psychiatrist, writing a prescription remains as much an art as a science" (p.68). Thomas Insel, on retiring from his long-term position as NIMH director, stated: "I spent 13 years at NIMH really pushing on neuroscience... I don't think we moved the needle in reducing suicide, reducing hospitalizations, improving recovery for the tens of millions of people who have mental illness. I hold myself accountable for that."

Marvin Goldfried (2019), a prominent psychotherapy researcher, considers the lack of consensus after over a century to indicate that psychotherapy is "pre-paradigmatic" in Kuhnian (1962) terms. Irwin Z. Hoffman (2009), to great applause at a plenary session of the American Psychoanalytic Association, disparaged the entire research enterprise within psychoanalysis. Others demean psychoanalysis as "merely" an art, unacceptable therefore as a clinical treatment.

Yet applications of an evolving body of scientific understanding must be as incomplete and inexact as the state of the science; psychoanalytic practice calls for a talent beyond programmatic skills. Since individual talent is involved, psychoanalysis is artistic. In Insel's judgment, a biological focus reached a dead end: narrow scientism is a premature confidence in current findings, even risking a dystopic and dehumanizing *Brave New World*.

Arlow (1979) discussed the creative phase of interpretive work, which was to be followed by a reflective, thoughtfully focused phase, in order to lead to the fashioning of an intervention. Bion famously described psychoanalytic listening as without memory or desire; the Kleinian psychoanalytic tradition emphasizes countertransference as experience generating thoughts and feelings in the analyst that can help the patient in the moment. Athletes and actors speak of being "in the zone," where focused thinking seems to disappear, but with effective results. Poser (2019), in a recent presentation, played several recordings based on Debussy's Reverie to demonstrate a theme heard differently. He then showed an interview with jazz saxophonist Sonny Rollins, who described his music-making as without focus, but using what he calls his "subconscious experience" of the music to determine what emerges from his instrument. Rollins has surely mastered his craft: melodies, chords, and scales, without which he could not perform, but the performance itself, like the authentic communication of a psychoanalyst in the immediacy of the moment, does not arise solely from focused, evidence-based rationality.

The application of psychoanalysis as paradigm to therapeutics can be described as artful in the same way that mathematical propositions can be considered things of beauty. Freud's Goethe Prize treated his writing as highly artistic literature. The art of Freud's writing is discussed by Blass (2019), commenting on a paper by Joan Riviere (1958). The artful work of clinical psychoanalysis refers to authentic, spontaneous interactions with patients that turn out, though not necessarily immediately, to be helpful.

The curiosity drive (the Kleinian epistemophilic instinct) is renewed with each human birth. We cannot know who will be the next Mozart or Einstein, advancing the range of human experience and knowledge. Curiosity is not to be sated; humans remain novelty-seeking and curious; we become bored with sameness.

A Grand Unifying Theory is likely to remain elusive. If there is a god's-eye view of the universe, we lack the capacity to use it; human limitation must be acknowledged by the godless as well. Ignorance is often motivating and can lead to exploration and discovery. Advancing knowledge requires originality, unbound from contemporary methods. Psychoanalysis is not medicine, nor is it science. Psychoanalysis is a set of ideas, a paradigm, not a fixed entity or restricted domain. The study of the human mind and its products is limitless, and subject to ongoing indeterminacy and generative controversy.

Each new patient presents a challenge to a therapist's knowledge, skill and talent. Stone's (1961) "physicianly attitude" does not require a medical education. Despite all prior experience, therapists are ignorant when meeting a new person. We are also ignorant as to what the next meeting will reveal. We must accept Keats's "negative capability" (rather than philosophical certainty) as essential to achieving understanding that will enhance the adaptation, creativity and joy of the patient. Ulric Neisser, the psychologist who coined the term "cognitive psychology," taught that while the brain has a finite number of synapses, the mind's ability to generate thought is infinite.

Artists may promote art for art's sake; it is its own explanation, ultimately inexplicable but central to the good life. Psychoanalysis is neither science nor art per se, but both scientific and artistic, and its clinical applications are often effective. Yet an art whose claims are more than aesthetic needs more than claims to affirm its value (Golland, 2016). Psychotherapy must be more than art.

Engaging in psychoanalytic practice enhances knowledge and creativity—and can also provide joy for the practitioner. The quest to satisfy curiosity is incomplete but gratifying—and involves debunking false antimonies while providing better resolutions of inner conflict. Irving Steingart (1977) saw the psychoanalytic relationship as "a thing apart," a special case in which the more we learn, the more we recognize the complexity and paradoxical nature of its subject matter. Neither science nor art, but both scientific and artistic, psychoanalysis is itself "a thing apart."

Brandeis Psychology in the Late Fifties:
Further Comment on Feigenbaum

Comparative Civilization Review 86, Spring 2022

Recent articles in this journal (Feigenbaum, 2020, Lester, 2020) spoke about A.H. Maslow and the Brandeis University Psychology Department of the 1960s, the first from a former junior faculty member, the second from a former graduate student. I learned from each of them, and they triggered my own memories as an undergraduate psychology major who went on to earn a PhD in clinical psychology. Maslow taught the introductory course in fall semester; I took it in the spring (1958) with Ricardo Morant, who succeeded Maslow as department chair and held that position for decades. I first met Maslow during my junior year in his course on motivation, already having studied with Walter Toman, Ulric Neisser, Richard Held, James Klee, Richard Jones and David Ricks.

All but Klee were young men who hadn't yet made their mark. Maslow did hire one woman, Eugenia Hanffman, who did not teach, but instead founded the first college counseling service, a facility now universal in American higher education. Friends had told me Maslow's introductory course was excellent; my recollection of his teaching was that it lacked organization and consisted mostly of anecdotes. However, at my graduate admissions interview I was asked to name three psychologists who had most affected my thinking. I cited Freud, Wilhelm Reich, and Maslow.

Later, at the five-year anniversary reunion of my Brandeis class, I saw Dr. Maslow just outside the Brown Building. Eager to tell him I had just completed my doctorate, I thanked him for his leadership of the very special group with whom I had studied (by then several had decamped).

He seemed to this newly-minted clinician to be depressed. He said he was sorry he'd chosen to be a psychologist and regretted much of what he'd written, especially the abnormal psychology text co-authored with Bela Mittelmann. I was shocked, reiterated my appreciation, and backed away. This was a year before his election to the APA presidency. Maslow's "humanistic psychology" could not be considered a specialty; it was instead a general attitude that influenced the entire profession. Ulric Neisser's entry in *A History of Psychology in Autobiography* (Lindzey & Runyan, 2007) spoke of Maslow's Humanistic Psychology as the "third force;" Freud and Skinner were the other two. Known as the father of "cognitive psychology" and coining that term, Neisser ultimately displaced Maslow to become a real third force. Maslow's reputation as an eminent psychologist remained estimable, finding adherents (paradoxically, it seems to me) in Industrial Psychology.

I've often mentioned Maslow as my teacher, and I refer to myself today as a "flexible Freudian," my flexibility related to the humanistic atmosphere conveyed by each of the several members of the Brandeis faculty Maslow assembled. Walter Toman and Richard Jones were the two faculty Freudians. Toman gave a definition of "cathexis"—"learning to appreciate"—that enabled me to resist the word's quantitative implications then in fashion for the neologism, James Strachey's translation of the German *bezetzung*.

Jones's focus on applications of psychoanalysis (which led to his 1968 book, *Fantasy and Feeling in Education*) oriented me to Freudian thinking as a study of the human mind and its products. In several tutorials and a course, Klee exposed students to the multiple manifestations of offbeat ideas. Neisser taught a great statistics course, as well as one on memory, and Held taught the history of Psychology, the best single course I've ever taken. Jones and Ricks jointly led a "personality laboratory," what is now referred to as a process group, not therapy but surely a therapeutic experience. Morant was a steadying influence, a research scientist and humanist who spent his full career at Brandeis.

I like to say that this faculty was—pound for pound—the best psychology department ever established. Like Camelot, that department would not last, but an unusually high number of classmates (plus many students in other classes at the time) became psychiatrists or psychologists, passing on the wisdom of those mostly young men. An important characteristic of contemporary psychoanalysis, which I hope is also true of psychology at large, is respect for multiple perspectives, and Maslow's great accomplishment as founder and chair of that small department at Brandeis was, I believe, to nurture a quality of openness among the undergraduates lucky enough to have been there at the time.

Psychoanalysis vs. Psychotherapy: A 50-Year Retrospective

June 28, 2024

I began formal psychoanalytic training in the late 1960s, when Freud's theory was still dominant in psychology and psychiatry. A proliferation of therapies (e.g., orgone boxes, hallucinogen-aided therapy, sensitivity groups, Rolfing and even nude group therapy), many claiming Freud as basic, were part of what made the sixties the sixties. For much of the preceding decade, the psychoanalytic establishment tried to take distance from such variations; a symposium on differences between psychoanalysis and psychotherapy was published in the second volume of the *Journal of the American Psychoanalytic Association* (1954).

For at least 25 years, my own practice can best be described as psychoanalytic psychotherapy, a less-frequent, usually face-to-face treatment based on the psychoanalytic paradigm. This paper is an attempt to formulate the evolution of my practice over a period of a half century, a timeframe in which psychoanalysis itself devolved from the dominant mental health paradigm and recommended treatment to general disparagement by American establishments in both psychiatry and psychology, and a clinical treatment of last resort.

When I began my psychoanalytic candidacy, a major controversy was whether teaching the intensive, couch-based treatment approach should follow or precede clinical experience with less intensive therapy. The answer seems obvious now: after the first generation of Freud's students, hardly any psychoanalyst would qualify without first having seen patients face-to-face, and less often than daily.

Another major issue at that time was the "medical model." Psychiatrists sought training in psychoanalysis almost routinely, starting "training analyses," while considering themselves people of sound mind. The authenticity of such "treatments" was undermined by the basic compromise of confidentiality, as a matter of policy. As a psychiatrist friend told me: "Why would I say everything to a person who reported to the training committee and could derail my career?" Psychologists more typically began treatment because we were unhappy, hurting inside while successful in our studies, and reasonably well-adjusted socially. We may have had symptoms, but we were not sick; we wanted to be analyzed! Financial limitations had many begin what would evolve into a training analysis from a twice-weekly therapy. In graduate school, psychoanalysis was often discussed as a meta-therapy.

I earned my doctorate in clinical psychology as the Vietnam War was heating up and had to interrupt my treatment to be commissioned as an Army psychologist in lieu of being drafted as a private or fleeing to Canada. Upon discharge I returned to my hometown, New York, at that time the only city in the United States where non-physicians could find formal psychoanalytic training. I had to wait a full year to begin my psychoanalysis, as my analyst—a psychologist—had no immediate availability. I increased my weekly frequency of sessions to four; of course I continued with the couch.

In the Army I did therapy as a Freudian; my graduate school supervisors had even trained in Vienna with Freud! I was not doing psychoanalysis but was applying its theory and methods to evaluate and treat soldiers, their families, and military retirees. Many young colleagues in the large medical center were interested in discussing my work and providing peer supervision. Older career officers, more identified with the military than with their profession, were of little help. I believe I was working psychoanalytically when I saw individuals, couples or families. I started and co-led three therapy groups and initiated a process group for the enlisted men working under my supervision. I understood the psychoanalytic paradigm as an evolving theory of the mind and its products, and I knew that actual practice had always to be adapted to the individual or couple, family or group, and to the situation.

In my formal analytic training, readings were by respected analysts with contradictory positions about both theory and technique. The learning context promoted one's own style of working, and one's own tentative formulations for clinical intervention. Freud's shifts in theory served as a model for flexible thinking and practice, despite his authoritarian organizational leadership.

Articulating clear and substantive differences in analytically informed therapeutics is not easy. I'll telegraph my conclusion: Treatment within the psychoanalytic paradigm is always exquisitely individualized.

One of the rare consensual negative judgments of Freud's theorizing within psychoanalysis is that it was phallocentric. Biographers have noted Freud's idealization of his mother, and his limited attention to the earliest maternal influences on psychic development. Acknowledging his rivalry with his father, he sired a new psychological paradigm as his sublimation. He nonetheless deputized his daughter, welcomed women as full members of the profession, and put mothers at the center of his Oedipus formulation. It is axiomatic for psychoanalysts that people act in complex, conflicted, and contradictory ways; this axiom surely applies to Freud himself.

"Therapy" is a medical term. Freud welcomed non-physicians into his new profession, and wrote a paper, "The Question of Lay Analysis" (1926), in support of his position—and of Theodore Reik. That paper and his Death Instinct concept were Freud's only major positions rejected by the psychoanalytic establishment in the United States during the 20th Century. Internationally, psychotherapists are no longer mostly physicians, and women comprise a majority even among the most recent generations of psychiatrists.

The lawsuit against the American Psychoanalytic Association, the International Psychoanalytical Association, and the New York and Columbia Institutes was settled over three decades ago by the defendants as an unsustainable restraint of trade. I continue to be alert to assertions of medical primacy in psychotherapy. Although psychoanalytically informed therapy would still describe their practice, some among my colleagues consider medicine their primary professional identification. Each of us has a complex set of identifications comprising both personal identity and the way we practice; if we're responsive to change, we change with time. Identifications may also impede effective work. My first course in analytic technique warned against overemphasis on tender-loving-care common to training in social work and nursing, habituated intellectualization central to producing a psychological dissertation, and authoritarianism often fostered in medical training. These styles—or overreactions against them—can undermine our work. Despite the interdisciplinary respect for differences among my colleagues, remnants of prior influences remain.

As to the medical model, some still consider non-physicians to be therapists-manqué, since we cannot prescribe; I reject that view. Until about 30 years ago, the consensual psychoanalytic stance was that medication was incompatible with psychoanalytic work. (Earlier anti-psychotics dramatically changed psychiatry, but were seen as anathema to psychoanalytic treatment.) Selective serotonin reuptake inhibitors (SSRIs) changed that position, and medication became another piece of a common clinical picture. Patients in my practice often begin treatment on medication, too freely dispensed by primary care physicians; analytic work can lead to weaning. Psychiatrists aren't manqué because they lack expertise in statistics or projective testing; I've never felt disadvantaged as a psychoanalyst by not having a prescription pad. While in the Army, I was ordered to use such a pad, signed by my MD colonel, for about three months. Frightened at first that I would poison patients, I became overconfident in prescribing, and got angry when patients did not respond well. It was truly a relief to be relieved of this duty. Thomas Insel, MD, on retiring from the directorship of the National Institute of Mental Health (NIMH), declared no significant progress in biological psychiatry in 50 years: while newer pills have fewer side effects than older ones, he felt no breakthrough had occurred. In light of the contemporary opioid crisis, perhaps reminiscent of *Valley of the Dolls* and "Mama's Little Helper," I find it an advantage rather than a limitation that I am not asked for prescriptions.

Freud has been accused of being too biological in his drive concept, too psychological in his focus on fantasy, and too environmental in his object relations theory. He was, however, an interactionist to the core: psychoanalysis is a bio-psycho-sociocultural paradigm, as it must be; contemporary interactionism extends to political and ecological factors that must also be considered for each patient.

I have argued (2016, 2020) against radical reductionism in the human sciences. The task in these disciplines is to learn more about whatever part of the elephant our blind fingers may touch. Many terms for therapies seem temptations to reductionism: milieu therapy and relational therapy are examples.

Milieu is important. The acute in-patient service at the Army hospital to which I was assigned claimed milieu therapy as the major supplement to medication, straitjackets and ice-baths. That milieu, however, was an intensely hostile one, depicted with humor by the movie and TV series *M*A*S*H* in the fraught relationship between Major "Hotlips" Houlihan, a nurse, and Captain "Hawkeye" Pierce, a surgeon.

Relationship is centrally important in psychotherapy, and always addressed in psychodynamic treatments. But every patient in individual, couple, group or family treatment is in a therapy relationship. To adequately understand the relationship is to define its elements, and how each might be effective. The mid-20th Century clinical psychoanalytic model was Greenson's (1967) tripartite one: real relationship, therapeutic alliance, and transference, with each in subtle interaction with the others. Relationships are complex; psychotherapy should not be "the purchase of friendship," as William Schofield called it (1964). Nor does contemporary psychoanalytic therapy follow Freud's own model—or that of his early colleagues. None of Freud's patients or those of the first generation of analysts had what at mid-20th century or today would be called "traditional" analysis. Anna's analyst was her father; grandson Ernst had his aunt Anna, his surrogate mother, as his analyst.

A mid-20th Century post-war model developed as a strictly defined structure, with variations labeled by Eissler (1953) in the first volume of JAPA as "parameters," to be used only in exceptional circumstances, and then to be undone by analysis. It seemed important at the time that psychoanalysis differentiate itself from the several variations being developed. This period saw the extensive development of group, couple and family therapies. "That is not analysis!" was a phrase used against Franz Alexander, Donald Winnicott and others—while the "mainstream" was engaged in controversy between Kleinians and Anna Freudians as to which group held the keys to the kingdom. The 1954 Symposium (JAPA volume 2) was a schismatic watershed: Alexander's "corrective emotional experience" was out, and the sharp definitions of Rangell (1954) and Gill (1954) became holy writ: resolution of the "transference neurosis by means of interpretation alone" became the official standard. Leo Stone's (1954) "Widening Scope" paper was controversial; Anna Freud's (1954) discussion of that paper recommended analysts keep their focus narrowly on the neuroses. In the context of medical exclusivity, this became a precious ideal; it did not keep alternative psychoanalytically based approaches from flourishing. Kohut (1971) created the next schism from within the establishment, and Greenberg and Mitchell (1983) the next major challenge from "outsider" analysts. The standard was no longer standard; pluralism became the watchword. Psychopharmacology and non-psychoanalytic talk therapies became prominent, each supported with experimental evidence and economic advantage. By 1990, these modalities came to dominate mental healthcare.

The exclusivity claims of the psychoanalytic establishment as a medical specialty also relegated even close variations to an implicitly inferior "psychotherapy." Freud's (1919) "alloy" metaphor seemed disparaging, despite the greater strength and utility of alloys in metallurgy, their home science. But Stone's "widening scope" carried the day even among trained psychoanalysts, leading to isolation and critique of the four-times-weekly, couch-based model. Twenty years after my graduation from the New York Freudian Society's institute, several of my intensive couch-based cases came to termination, their hours to be filled with patients who would attend only once or twice weekly. Though I'd always worked face-to-face and twice-weekly with some patients, until then I'd refused once-a-week treatments, calling them "news of the week in review" and stating they were unlikely to be effective. I had to learn to be useful for weekly patients, since insurance companies had come to control much of the potential patient population, with once-weekly treatment the cultural expectation.

I will try to concretize my understanding of a psychoanalytic psychotherapy. My thinking is chiefly based on my teaching and supervision during the past 15 years, where my students only work face-to-face and non-intensively. They call it "psychodynamic;" I call it "psychoanalytic," since "dynamics" refer—as I tell them—to the sexy and aggressive stuff; the paradigm is far more encompassing than the dynamic meta-psychological point of view.

The axiomatic first principle of both psychoanalysis and psychotherapy—individualization—has been best stated by a colleague: "If you had a recording of my typical workday with eight patients, you'd think the therapist was eight different people." This analyst also defines the work as "conveying wisdom," and his role akin to that of a tailor, trying to fit each patient according to the patient's dimensions. This is not "anything goes," but the down-to-earth descriptions of a well-trained, certified medical psychoanalyst who works within the flexible clinical theory that is today's Freudian paradigm. Nor does every patient get what she or he demands, but rather what clinical judgment calls for.

Common principles of traditional psychoanalysis as treatment, and psychoanalytic psychotherapy, are best summarized by the seven elements described by Shedler (2010): 1) A focus on affect and expression of feelings; 2) exploration of attempts to avoid uncomfortable thoughts and feelings ("resistance"); 3) noting recurrent themes and patterns; 4) discussion of past experiences and the repetition of the past in the present ("transference"); 5) interpersonal relationships; 6) the therapy relationship itself; and 7) exploring wishes and fantasies. Any psychoanalytic treatment will partake of each of these elements to varying degrees.

The implicit goal is to go beyond symptom relief to foster psychological capacities and resources (i.e., resilience or "positive psychology"). Symptoms, as in general medicine, are surface manifestations of disturbance; they exist within a complex and complete personality.

To Shedler's seven characteristics I add what is to my mind an empirical fact: Freud's assertion that much of human psychology is not in conscious awareness. I also find free association foundational as a clinical procedure in both traditional psychoanalysis and its related therapies. In my practice, I begin with this statement of the patient's task: try to say everything. I add that this task is difficult if not impossible, but the attempt is important. I must periodically remind patients of this basic rule.

Additional clinical dicta of which I periodically remind myself: "the patient is doing the best s/he can" and "the patient is always right" (Schlesinger, 2004), and our therapeutic posture is Friedman's (1988) recommendation: "Accept, don't settle." I emphasize in supervision that analysts and therapists have no script; each pairing will develop its own discourse; with the same principles applying to couple, family or group. For the normally anxious beginning student, I add: "You can say anything so long as you mean well and are thoughtful about potential impact." If you are wrong in content (it happens often) or timing (even more frequently), the patient's response will provide a corrective. Patients who bolt at such errors may be more difficult people in general, or more sensitive to the specific comment; they require greater responsiveness and recognition of their discomfort. The analytic stance includes constantly assessing patient responses and reactions to what we say, and to our silences.

I've referred to psychoanalytic psychotherapy in recent years as "open ended therapy." I recently came across the useful phrase, "therapies of insight and relationship," the focus of a new advocacy group, the Psychotherapy Action Network.

The 1954 Symposium included an underappreciated paper by Edward Bibring. In addition to describing a variety of interventions, he categorized them into "psychoanalytic" and "therapeutic" comments; the former aim to promote associations; the latter to calm the patient. I translate this as interventions that might increase anxiety (or other dysphoric affect) versus those that aim at easing ill feelings, "supportive," if you will. Bibring stated that the proportionality of these interventions should define a treatment as psychoanalysis or psychotherapy. For him, psychoanalytic method was inherently flexible, unlike for the Gill of 1954, for whom formal psychoanalysis required a "transference neurosis resolvable by interpretation alone." Gill, until his "relational turn" in the late 1980's, was considered among the most orthodox of Freudians. As to orthodoxy, we could note that Eissler was at pains at several public meetings to express regret for his "parameters" coinage, recognizing it as a far too rigid caricature. His 1965 book was a more general critique of medical orthodoxy in psychoanalysis.

Variations from the Freudian tradition began early and led to frequent schisms, often due to Freud's demands for loyalty. Early variations that Freud welcomed include child treatment—both Anna's and Melanie Klein's, and

Aichhorn's work with adolescents (1925). Martin Bergmann (1993) discussed these in his 1991 plenary address at the American Psychoanalytic Association as extensions, modifications and heresies. Each variation exemplified patient differences, situational factors, and the individuality and creativity of the clinician. Child analysts were ineligible for International Psychoanalytical Association (IPA) membership for many decades unless they also completed adult training. Kernberg's writing on borderline and narcissistic states (1975) was developed primarily in an inpatient setting. His development of "Transference-focused Psychotherapy" is a form of psychoanalytic psychotherapy that has a substantial empirical research base (2008). In the 1950's, Felix Deutsch (1955) developed "Sector Therapy," a time-limited treatment, focused on selected problematic aspects of functioning rather than the open-ended approach of the more traditional method. Leon Hoffman's recent development of Regulation-Focused Psychotherapy for Children is another specific analytic psychotherapy, also with a research base (Hoffman et al, 2016). The late Bertram Karon's career has emphasized the advantage of psychoanalytic treatment with patients diagnosed as psychotic, with or without medication. His research shows good results, often with reduction or full discontinuation of drugs. A book of his collected essays was recently published (Cosgro & Widener, 2019). Group, couple and family therapies originated predominantly outside the auspices of the IPA but have often called themselves psychodynamic therapies.

Too many variations have been considered heretical, leading to different "schools" of analysis hostile to one another, rather than respected alternative contributions. "That's not analysis" accusations fail to recognize the legitimacy of creative extension of the paradigm from the initial—in fact haphazard— development of what is now considered traditional psychoanalytic technique.

The two most obvious differences between psychoanalysis and psychoanalytic therapy are those that describe my own practice in the last 30 years, and those of many colleagues: less than daily frequency and a face-to-face relationship instead of lying on the couch. Freud began working six times weekly, only reducing to five when, having achieved world fame, he was asked by a visiting scholar to add his own treatment to Freud's workday. By mid-century, four-times-weekly was the IPA standard, reduced to three by one of the French schools soon thereafter. That French standard became one of three official IPA training models only in the current century, and it was just three years ago that three became acceptable to the American Psychoanalytic Association, leading to the recent affiliation of the William Alanson White Institute with APsaA. Some still consider this change of the frequency criterion to be slippage. By contrast, for Charles Brenner (1995), psychoanalysis was not defined by frequency or furniture, and even Gill (1954) did not consider these to be intrinsic criteria of the method. I'd also heard some decades ago that Leo Rangell was seeing someone "in analysis" at his weekend country home on Sundays! It is commonplace wisdom that some adept patient/ analyst pairs can develop an "analytic process" at low frequency.

The major force reducing frequency has been economic, both financial and temporal, and has served to make psychotherapies the dominant treatments offered by psychoanalysts. Just two years ago Division 39 of the American Psychological Association changed its name to the Society for Psychoanalysis and Psychoanalytic Psychology.

At times a high frequency of contact may be clinically indicated, and yet be a psychotherapy. I saw a very disturbed woman four times weekly, face-to-face, to deal with her severe symptoms, including suicidality; I would neither suggest nor permit the use of the couch, and my interventions remained primarily supportive through the course of our work—which I considered psychoanalytic in its larger sense, the way in which I understood her and tried to help her understand herself.

Many European analysts make a sharp differentiation between analysis and therapy. Some in this country make no such distinction, defining analysis as "what analysts do." This seems too vague to be useful. Rangell (1954) spoke of differences between night and day, dawn and dusk, black, white, and shades of gray. I've found this a good way to think about the work.

As to the couch, once the very symbol of psychoanalysis, with its absence almost defining a weak alloy, it is no longer sine qua non—especially with the recent development of tele-treatments, and more so since the Covid-19 pandemic moved psychotherapy to remote platforms.

Psychoanalytic psychotherapies are usually conducted once- or twice-weekly, with use of the couch optional. The primary technical issue associated with frequency is the relative activity of the therapist. When seeing a patient almost daily, "expectant" technique urges the patient to take the lead, and to break silences; whatever the analyst wants to say can usually wait until tomorrow. Exceptions are, however, routine. The many jokes about the silent analyst remain a caricature, or an anomaly of a long-gone era of training.

Continuity is usually considered important in any treatment modality and is not easily maintained with low frequency. Freud (1913a) observed a "Monday crust," heightened defensiveness when the one-day Christian Sabbath could interrupt associative flow. Patients often ask where they left off. I may hear a continuity of latent content despite the forgetting of its manifest thoughts. Depending on the patient and my sense of the situation, I often wait, but I am not routinely reluctant to provide the memory. In the Army I initiated a process group for the enlisted men I'd taught to do telephone and intake interviews. Within two sessions, one got ordered to Viet Nam, and his replacement arrived shortly thereafter. This was to be repeated regularly; group continuity was impossible. I defined the group focus as "hello and goodbye," and wrote about it (1971). I nonetheless viewed my approach, before formal training, as psychoanalytic.

Leo Stone's (1954) "widening scope" redefined "indications" for traditional psychoanalysis. Most analysts favor psychodynamic therapy for more disturbed patients. Advances in theory provide technical recommendations: Andre Green (2000) and others (Levine et al, 2018) have addressed patients for whom internal representation is limited, while Charles Brenner's (1979) narrow scope definition would rule out traditional treatment for these patients. How traditional is "traditional" when we are working with pre-oedipal, pre-structural psychology? Much of what are variations in technique get the typical answer to any complex question: "It depends." It depends on the analyst, the patient, the situation.

The heart of the matter is individualization. Contemporary psychoanalytic theory, more complex and pluralistic, guides my understanding. Some will be helped by an approach promoting initiative and autonomy, and a search for meaningful, affective self-understanding. Others will require different approaches consistent with the larger theory. For those in acute crisis, considerable therapist activity is required. Some patients need us to function as auxiliary egos or superegos as our understanding of them and their circumstances indicate. These therapeutic approaches are therapies, acknowledged by Freud, who endorsed simpler and quicker methods, if and when they can be effective (1905). They include educational interventions (McWilliams, 2003). They aim also to bolster functioning toward greater self-awareness. Some patients won't achieve much insight. Some may need indefinite support, or periodic returns to treatment. Any specific intervention might well be included over the course of a more traditional psychoanalysis. Though direct questions are not recommended in "standard technique," Eissler (1958) said, "No analysis has ever been conducted without (them)." Frederic Busch (2019) combines cognitive techniques with psychodynamic ones. The paradigm can include ego-strengthening, and homework may help. Nathan Leites' 1977 paper, "Transference Interpretation Only?" answered "No"—even for the intensive traditional method. Working in the transference is encouraged for psychotherapy, but there is no longer a commitment to attempting blank screen purity for the psychoanalytic therapist. In practice, that posture itself was a caricature, and could be harmful.

A central tenet of all psychoanalytic therapies is what Stone (1961) called a "physicianly attitude," a medical term, but one that does not require a medical education or license. In the clinical situation, the well-being of the patient is the primary concern of any therapist. This caring includes what are known as the "non-specific factors" of therapeutic action: reliability, patience and non-judgmental positive regard. As Fred Pine (1998) reminded us, these factors may be the primary action of treatment for patients whose early life was much more damaging than supportive. Humor is another. To be effective, humor cannot be scripted; it will likely be present in all successful therapies. These are not matters of technique; I doubt they can be taught. It may well be that these non-specific elements have potency for all patients disproportionate to specific interventions of any approach. Some will not benefit from the most accurate interventions. I hesitate to quote Woody Allen, but 80% of success in our work may be just showing up. For many patients treated at hospital out-patient departments, 45 weekly minutes spent with a novice therapist are the sanest and best hours of their often sad lives.

It's been said that free association is only truly approached near the end of treatment. The theoretical aim of traditional psychoanalysis is "structural change" that promotes the mind-stretching that can help keep one aware of unconscious process long after termination. Psychoanalytic treatments all aim to enhance self-awareness; it may also be that whether we have done psychoanalysis or psychotherapy can only be stated with confidence at the conclusion of the work.

I've learned a great deal from colleagues: a few using an entirely different paradigm, some eclectic, others aiming at integration. By any reasonable criteria, all have success with those who seek them out for help. I've become more respectful of differences but will rise to argue with those who insult my approach as false, some—using a severely constricted definition of evidence—even calling it malpractice. We work with the human mind, among the most complex entities of any that might be addressed scientifically or therapeutically. The psychoanalytic paradigm has progressed through the pluralism of recent decades to a more open, yet coherent discipline. I don't believe we can fully understand people, or the next stranger who comes into our office; generalizations won't be adequate for every person. But we can surely hope that ongoing efforts may result in greater understanding and therapeutic effect. That attitude keeps me at work even with my most difficult patients—and hoping to continue to do so.

Afterword

From a very early paper, "A Hello and Goodbye Group," I've been interested in and seen the importance of beginnings and endings. The word "termination" is used for the endings of psychoanalytic treatment. It's an unfortunate word in English, though cognate with the French. Freud's *Endlich* is easier on my ears. I've taken to discussing this phase with my patients, as "satisfactory completion." And, adopting Winnicott's "good enough," as a good enough response to "how are you?" I discuss with my patients that good enough completion is as good as it can be.

The word "psychoanalysis" conjures for most the couch-based therapy invented by Sigmund Freud. The practice has evolved over my lifetime to "exquisitely individual" psychotherapies with clinical extensions to couples, families, and groups small and large. The varieties of therapy approaches are also exquisitely individualized. The word itself is valued by the many varieties that claim it.

The Psychoanalytic Paradigm serves three masters: 1) clinical practice; 2) science; and 3) the history of ideas. The scientist-practitioner model of my doctoral training emphasized the idea that an art that claims more than aesthetic value must be grounded in science. The practice is artful, relying on the skill and talent of the therapist, but an appropriate best-evidence base is required for its legitimacy.

The third "master," the History of Ideas, is for me the guarantor of the eternally valid contribution of psychoanalysis. The "Discovery of the Unconscious" (Ellenberger, 1970) records the ideas of those who preceded and accompanied Freud, but his elaboration, initially in his masterpiece (1900), made solid the knowledge that minds operate mostly without awareness and that these unconscious operations are meaningful.

I saw my first psychotherapy patients as a student, over 60 years ago. Now in the end phase of my career, I am still a student with each patient. They teach me how we can successfully complete our work. There are complex and contradictory feelings on both sides of "the couch" (for me, in recent decades, mostly without the couch). I've enjoyed compiling my written work, especially since I've had the benefit of the editorship and collaboration of my older son. The book is complete. I'm still writing. I hope readers will find some valuable ideas for their own work.

Rereading my papers for this collection, I was able to see more clearly my clinical and theoretical evolution, and to appreciate the evolution of psychoanalysis itself—as both theory and methodology—since my initial exposure to it in 1958 as a college sophomore.

Early in my practice, I thought I knew how to do the work. Now I describe the practice of psychoanalytic psychotherapy as two ignorant individuals trying to understand and help one of them.

Two role models, Martin S. Bergmann and Louis Linn, MD, each worked nearly until death, Martin at 100, Lou in his nineties. Having inherited two patients whose analysts became demented during their "open-ended" treatment, I chose a different course. When I turned 80, I stopped taking new referrals, and I am working with my patients toward "successful completion." My practice is waning but I am satisfied I made the right choice. I already have fewer hours than I had just a few months ago and expect my clinical practice to end in a few short years. Seeing patients has been central to my identity. I will find it challenging to give it up entirely.

References

Abend, S. (2000). "Analytic Technique Today." *Journal of the American Psychoanalytic Association* 48:9–16.

_____ (2001). "Expanding Psychological Possibilities." *Psychological Quarterly* 70:3–14.

Adorno, T., E. Frenkel-Brunswik, D. Levinson, and R. Sanford (1950). *The Authoritarian Personality*. Harpers.

Aichhorn, A. (1925). *Wayward Youth*. London: Imago Publishing Co., 1951.

Ainsworth, M. (1979). "Infant–mother Attachment." *American Psychologist* 34:932–937.

Alexander, F. (1954). "Psychoanalysis and Psychotherapy." *Journal of the American Psychoanalytic Association* 2:722–733.

Allport, G. (1954). *The Nature of Prejudice*. Cambridge, MA: Addison-Wesley.

Arlow, J. (1979). "The Genesis of Interpretation." *Journal of the American Psychoanalytic Association* 27 (Supplement):193–206.

_____ and C. Brenner (1964). *Psychoanalytic Concepts and the Structural Theory*. NY: International Universities Press.

Aron, L. (1996). *A Meeting of Minds*. Hillsdale, NJ: Analytic Press.

Auden, W. (1940). *From Another Time*. NY: Random House.

Auerbach, J. (2019). "Sidney J. Blatt's Contribution to Psychoanalytic Psychology." *Psychoanalytic Psychology* 36:287–290.

Bacon, F. (1993). *Novum Organum*. P. Urbach and J. Gibson (Trans. and Eds.). Chicago, IL: Open Court Publishers (Originally published 1620).

Bekas, V., K. Asfjes-van Doorn, T. Prout, and L. Hoffman (2020). "Stretching the Analytic Frame: Analytic Therapists' Experiences with Remote Therapy During COVID-19." *Journal of the American Psychoanalytic Association* 68:437–446.

Bergmann, M. (1976). "Notes on the History of Psychoanalytic Technique." M. Bergmann and F. Hartmann (Eds.), *Evolution of Psychoanalytic Technique* (pp. 17–40). NY: Basic Books.

_____ (1987). *The Anatomy of Loving.* NY: Columbia University Press.

_____ (1992). *In The Shadow of Moloch: The Effect of the Sacrifice of Children in Western Religions.* NY: Columbia University Press.

_____ (1993). "Reflections on the History of Psychoanalysis." *Journal of the American Psychoanalytic Association* 41:929–955.

_____ and F. Hartman (Eds.) (1976). *The Evolution of Psychoanalytic Technique.* NY: Basic Books.

_____ and M. Jucovy. (1982). *Generations of the Holocaust.* NY: Basic Books.

_____ (1997). "Termination: The Achilles Heel of Psychoanalytic Technique." *Psychoanalytic Psychology* 14:163–174.

Berlin, I. (1980). *Vico and Herder.* London: Chatto & Windus.

Bettelheim, B. (1950). *Love is Not Enough: The Treatment of Emotionally Disturbed Children.* Glencoe, IL: Free Press.

Bibring, E. (1954). "Psychoanalysis and the Dynamic Psychotherapies." *Journal of the American Psychoanalytic Association* 2:745–770.

Biehler, R. (1976). *Child Development: An Introduction*, Boston, Mass.: Houghton Mifflin Company, 1976.

Bion, W. (2001). *Attention and Interpretation: A Scientific Approach to Insight in Psychoanalysis and Groups.* London: Routledge.

Blass, R. (2019). "Freud's Writing as a Living Creative Presence in Our Minds." *International Journal of Psychoanalysis* 100:635–636.

Blatt, S., and G. Shahar (2004). "Psychoanalysis: With whom, for What, and how? Comparisons with Psychotherapy." *Journal of the American Psychoanalytic Association* 52:393–447.

Blum, H. (1989). "The Concept of Termination and the Evolution of Psychoanalytic Thought." *Journal of the American Psychoanalytic Association* 37:275–295.

Bornstein, M. (Ed.) (1982). "Termination." *Psychoanalytic Inquiry* 2:323–499.

Bornstein, R. (1999). "Source Amnesia, Misattribution, and the Power of Unconscious Perceptions and Memories." *Psychoanalytic Psychology* 16:155–178.

_____ (2005). "Reconnecting Psychoanalysis to Mainstream Psychology: Challenges and Opportunities." *Psychoanalytic Psychology* 22:323–340.

_____ (2007). "Nomothetic Psychoanalysis." *Psychoanalytic Psychology* 24:590–602.

Brenman-Gibson, M. (1997). "The Legacy of Erik Homburger Erikson." *Psychoanalytic Review* 84[3], 329–335.

Brenner, C. (1955). *An Elementary Textbook of Psychoanalysis*. NY: International Universities Press.

_____ (1976). *Psychoanalytic Technique and Psychic Conflict*. NY: International Universities Press.

_____ (1979). "The Components of Psychic Conflict and its Consequences in Mental Life." *Psychoanalytic Quarterly* 48:547–567.

_____ (1995). "Some Remarks on Psychoanalytic Technique." *Journal of Clinical Psychoanalysis* 4:413–428.

_____ (2003). "Commentary on Ilany Kogan's 'On Being a Dead, Beloved Child.'" *Psychoanalytic Quarterly* 72:767–776.

_____ (2006). *Psychoanalysis or Mind and Meaning*. NY: The Psychoanalytic Quarterly, Inc.

_____ (2007). "Freud's Great Voyage of Discovery." *Psychoanalytic Quarterly* 76:9–25.

Brenton, M. (1974). "Mainstreaming the Handicapped." *Today's Education*.

Brody, S., and S. Axelrod (1978). *Mothers, Fathers, and Children: Explorations in the Formation of Character in the First Seven Years*, NY: International Universities Press.

Burkeman, O. (2016). "Therapy Wars: The Revenge of Freud." *The Guardian*.

Burston, D. (2007). *Erik Erikson and the American Psyche*. Jason Aronson.

Busch, Fred (1993). "In the Neighborhood: Aspects of a Good Interpretation and a 'Developmental Lag' in Ego Psychology." *Journal of the American Psychoanalytic Association* 41:151–176.

_____ (1994). "Some Ambiguities in the Method of Free Association and their Implications for Technique." *Journal of the American Psychoanalytic Association* 42:363–384

_____ (2015). "Our Vital Profession." *International Journal of Psychoanalysis* 96:553–568.

Busch, Frederick (2019). "Psychodynamic Approaches to Behavioral Change." Paper presented at the Faculty Psychotherapy Conference, Icahn School of Medicine at Mount Sinai, New York, NY.

Campbell, R. (1989). *Psychiatric Dictionary*. NY: Oxford University Press.

Casement, P. (1982). "Some Pressures on the Analyst for Physical Contact during the Reliving of an Early Trauma." *International Review of Psychoanalysis* 9:279–286.

Cavell, M. (2002). "On Reality and Objectivity." *Journal of the American Psychoanalytic Association* 50:319–324.

Charcot, J-M. (1991). "La théorie, c'est bon, mais ça n'empêche pas d'exister." Quoted in D. De Marneffe. "Looking and Listening: The Construction of Clinical Knowledge in Charcot and Freud." *Signs* 17:71–111.

Chein, I. (1972). *The Science of Behavior and the Image of Man.* NY: Basic Books.

Chessick, R. (1989). *The Technique and Practice of Listening in Intensive Psychotherapy.* Northvale, NJ: Jason Aronson.

Churchland, P. (2013). *Touching a Nerve: The Self as Brain.* Norton.

Clark, K. (1971). "The Pathos of Power: A Psychological Perspective." *American Psychologist* 26:1047–1057.

_____ (1980). "Empathy: A Neglected Topic in Psychological Research." *American Psychologist* 35:187–190.

_____, I. Chein, and S. Cook (1952). "The Effects of Segregation and the Consequences of Desegregation Social Science Statement in the Brown v. Board of Education of Topeka Supreme Court Case." *American Psychologist* 59(6):495–501.

Cohen, J. (2018). "Education." In S. Akhtar and S. Twemlow (Eds.). *Textbook of Applied Psychoanalysis.* NY: Routledge.

Collingwood, R. (1969). *An Essay on Metaphysics.* Oxford: Clarendon Press.

Cosgro, M. and A. Widener (Eds.). (2019). *The Widening Scope of Psychoanalysis: Collected Essays of Bertram Karon.* NY: IP Books.

Critchley, S. (2015). "There Is No Theory of Everything." *The New York Times.*

Dehaene, S., and L. Naccache (2001). "Towards a Cognitive Neuroscience of Consciousness: Basic Evidence and a Workspace Framework." *Cognition* 79:1–37.

Deutsch, F., and W. Murphy (1955). *The Clinical Interview, Volume 2: A Method of Teaching Sector Therapy.* NY: International Universities Press.

Dewald, P. (1982). "The Clinical Importance of the Termination Phase." *Psychoanalytic Inquiry* 2:441–461.

Dunn, L. (1973). *Exceptional Children in the Schools*, 2nd ed. Holt, Rinehart and Winston.

Eagle, M. (1997). "Contributions of Erik Erikson." *Psychoanalytic Review* 84[3], 337–347.

_____ (2011). *From Classical to Contemporary Psychoanalysis: A Critique and Integration.* Taylor & Francis.

Eisold, K. (2005). "Psychanalysis and Psychotherapy: A Long and Troubled Relationship." *International Journal of Psychoanalysis* 86:1175–95.

Eissler, K. (1953). "The Effect of the Structure of the Ego on Psychoanalytic Technique." *Journal of the American Psychoanalytic Association* 1:104–143.

_____ (1954). "On the Dream Specimen of Psychoanalysis." *Journal of the American Psychoanalytic Association* 2:5–56.

_____ (1958). "Remarks on Some Variations in Psychoanalytic Technique." *International Journal of Psychoanalysis* 39:222–229.

_____ (1965). *Medical Orthodoxy and the Future of Psychoanalysis*. NY: International Universities Press.

_____ (1974). "On Some Theoretical and Technical Problems Regarding the Payment of Fees for Psychoanalytic Treatment." *International Review of Psychoanalysis* 1:73–101.

Ekstein, R., and R. Motto (1969). *From Learning for Love to Love of Learning: Essays on Psychoanalysis and Education*. NY: Brunner.

Ellenberger, H. (1970). *The Discovery of the Unconscious*. Basic Books.

Erikson, E. (1950, 1962). *Childhood and Society*. NY: Norton.

_____ (1954). "The Dream Specimen of Psychoanalysis." *Journal of the American Psychoanalytic Association* 2:5–50.

Etchegoyan, H. (1991). *The Fundamentals of Psychoanalytic Technique*. London: Karnac.

Fajrajzen, S. (2014). "The Compulsion to Confess and the Compulsion to Judge in the Analytic Situation." *International Journal of Psychoanalysis* 95:977–993.

Feigenbaum, K. (2020). "In the Brandeis University Psychology Department, 1962–65: Recalling A Great American Social Theorist." *Comparative Civilization Review* 82.

Fenichel, O. (1941). *Problems of Psychoanalytic Technique*. Albany: Psychoanalytic Quarterly.

_____ (1945). *The Psychoanalytic Theory of Neurosis*. NY: Norton.

Ferenczi, S. (1950). *Further Contributions to the Theory and Technique of Psychoanalysis*. London: Hogarth Press.

_____ (1955). *Final Contributions to the Problems and Methods of Psychoanalysis*. NY: Brunner/Mazel.

_____ & O. Rank (1925). *The Development of Psychoanalysis*. NY: Nervous and Mental Disease Publishing.

Firestein, S. (1974). "Termination of Psychoanalysis of Adults: A Review of the Literature." *Journal of the American Psychoanalytic Association* 22:873–894.

_____ (1978). *Termination in Psychoanalysis.* NY: International Universities Press.

_____ (1982). "Termination of Psychoanalysis: Theoretical, Clinical, and Pedagogic Considerations." *Psychoanalytic Inquiry* 2:473–497.

Fosshage, J. (1997). "Psychoanalysis and Psychoanalytic Psychotherapy." *Psychoanalytic Psychologist* 14:409–425.

Freud, A. (1954). "The Widening Scope of Indications for Psychoanalysis—Discussion." *Journal of the American Psychoanalytic Association* 2:607–620.

_____ (1966). "The Ego and the Mechanisms of Defense." *The Writings of Anna Freud* (Vol. 2). NY: International Universities Press (Originally published 1936).

Freud, S. (1895). "Project for a Scientific Psychology." J. Strachey (Ed. & Trans.), *The Standard Edition of the Complete Psychological Works of Sigmund Freud.* London: Hogarth Press (hereinafter SE), Vol. 1.

_____ (1900). "The Interpretation of Dreams." SE3, 4, 5.

_____ (1901). "The Psychopathology of Everyday life." SE6.

_____ (1905). "On Psychotherapy." SE7:257–268.

_____ (1909). "Analysis of a Phobia in a Five-Year-Old Boy." SE10:5–147.

_____ (1910). "'Wild' Psychoanalysis." SE11:219–228.

_____ (1912). "Recommendations to Physicians Practicing Psychoanalysis." SE12:109–120.

_____ (1913a). "On Beginning the Treatment." SE12:123–144.

_____ (1913b). "Totem and Taboo." SE13:ix–161.

_____ (1914a). "On Narcissism: An introduction." SE14.

_____ (1914b). "On the History of the Psychoanalytic Movement." SE14:7–66.

_____ (1915). "On Transience." SE14:305–307.

_____ (1917a). "Mourning and Melancholia." SE14:243–258.

_____ (1917b). "Introductory Lectures." SE16.

_____ (1919). "Lines of Advance in Psycho-Analytic Therapy." SE17:159–168.

_____ (1920). "Beyond the Pleasure Principle." SE18:7–64.

_____ (1923). "The Ego and the Id." SE19:3–66.

_____ (1925). "Preface to Aichhorn's Wayward Youth." SE19:273–275.

_____ (1926). "The Question of Lay Analysis." SE20:177–358.

_____ (1927). "The Future of an Illusion." SE21:55.

_____ (1931). "Libidinal Types." SE21:217–220.

_____ (1933). "New Introductory Lectures in Psychoanalysis." SE22:5–182.

_____ (1937). "Analysis Terminable and Interminable." SE23:216–253.

_____ (1938a). "An Outline of Psycho-Analysis." SE23:139–208.

_____ (1938b). "The Voice of Sigmund Freud." Kaplan, D. (Prod.). 33 1/3 LP. National Psychological Association for Psychoanalysis, Inc.

_____ (1939). "Moses and Monotheism." SE23:1–137.

Friedman, L. (1969) "The Therapeutic Alliance." *International Journal of Psychoanalysis* 50:139–153.

_____ (1988). *The Anatomy of Psychotherapy.* Hillsdale, NJ: The Analytic Press.

_____ (2016). "Is There a Usable Heidegger for Psychoanalysts?" *Journal of the American Psychoanalytic Association* 64:587–624.

Friedrich, J., and D. Douglass (1998). "Ethics and the Persuasive Enterprise of Teaching Psychology." *American Psychologist* 53:459–562.

Fromm-Reichman, F. (1950). *Principles of Intensive Psychotherapy.* Chicago: University of Chicago Press.

Frosh, S. (1997). *For and Against Psychoanalysis.* London: Routledge.

Furman, E. (1969). "Techniques of Working with the Mother." In R.A. Furman & A. Karan (Eds.). *The Therapeutic Nursery School.* NY: International Universities Press, pp. 79–84.

Gabbard, G., and D. Westen (2003). "Rethinking Therapeutic Action." *The International Journal of Psychoanalysis* 84:823–841.

Gaines, S., and E. Reed (1995). "Prejudice: From Allport to DuBois." *American Psychologist* 50:96–103.

Gann, E. (2010). Letter to the Editor. *International Journal of Psychoanalysis* 91:199–200.

Gardner, R., P. Holzman, G. Klein, H. Linton, and D. Spence (1959). "Cognitive Control: A Study of Individual Consistencies in Cognitive Behavior." *Psychological Issues* 1[4]:1–185.

Gedo, J. (1979). *Beyond Interpretation: Toward a Revised Theory for Psychoanalysis.* International Universities Press.

Gill, M. (1951). "Ego Psychology and Psychotherapy." *Psychoanalytic Quarterly* 20:62–71.

_____ (1954). "Psychoanalysis and Exploratory Psychotherapy." *Journal of the American Psychoanalytic Association* 2:771–797.

_____ (1984). "Psychoanalysis and Psychotherapy: A Revision." *International Review of Psychoanalysis* 11:161–179.

Gillman, R. (1982). "The Termination Phase in Psychoanalytic Practice: A Survey of 48 Completed Cases." *Psychoanalytic Inquiry* 2:463–472.

Glover, E. (1928/1955). *The Technique of Psychoanalysis.* International Universities Press.

_____ (1931). "The Therapeutic Effect of Inexact Interpretation: A Contribution to the Theory of Suggestion." *International Journal of Psychoanalysis* 12:397–411.

Goldberg, A. (2008). Review of "Psychoanalytic Disagreements in Context." *International Journal of Psychoanalysis* 89:1294–1289.

Goldfried, M. (2019). "Obtaining Consensus in Psychotherapy: What Holds Us Back?" *American Psychologist* 74:484–496.

Golland, D. (2011). *Constructing Affirmative Action: The Struggle for Equal Employment Opportunity.* University Press of Kentucky.

_____ (2019). *A Terrible Thing to Waste: Arthur Fletcher and the Conundrum of the Black Republican.* University Press of Kansas.

Golland, J. (1971). "A 'Hello' and 'Goodbye' Group." *International Journal of Group Psychotherapy* 22:258–261.

_____ (1975). "Mainstreaming and Teacher Preparation." in L. Golubchick and B. Persky. *Innovations in Education.* Kendall/Hunt.

_____ (1991). "The Politics of Psychoanalytic Training." *Psychologist Psychoanalyst* 11, No.1:10–12.

_____ (1995). "Compare and Contrast." *The Round Robin* 11:2–3.

_____ (1997). "Not an Endgame: Terminations in Psychoanalysis." *Psychoanalytic Psychology* 14:259–270.

_____ (1999). "If it's All the Same to you...: The Politics of Leveling." *Psychoanalytic Psychologist* 16:103–9.

_____ (2002). "What do Teachers Want (from Psychoanalysts)?" *Journal of Applied Psychoanalytic Studies* 4:275–281.

_____ (2005). Review of Rangell, "My Life in Theory." *Psychologist Psychoanalyst* 25[2]:42–43.

_____ (2007). Review of Brenner, "Psychoanalysis or Mind and Meaning." *PsycCRITIQUES* 52, Rel. 33, Art. 164.

_____ (2016). "Psychoanalysis is Scientific!" *Division/Review Forum.*

_____ (2020). "Is Psychoanalysis a Science or Art?" *International Journal of Controversial Discussions* 1:68–74.

_____, M. Brenman-Gibson, M. Eagle, and I. Steingart (1997). "Erik Erikson's Clinical Contributions: A Symposium in Memorial Tribute." *The Psychoanalytic Review* 84:325–364.

Goodale, J. (2018). "Putting Profits Over People." *The New York Times.*

Green, A. (2000). "The Central Phobic Position: A New Formulation of the Free Association Method." *International Journal of Psychoanalysis* 81:429–451.

Greenacre, P. (1941). "The Predisposition to Anxiety." *Psychoanalytic Quarterly* 10:66–94.

Greenberg, J., and S. Mitchell (1983). *Object Relations in Psychoanalytic Therapy*. Cambridge, MA: Harvard University Press.

Greenson, R. (1967). *The Technique and Practice of Psychoanalysis*. NY: International Universities Press.

Groopman, J. (2019). "Medicine in Mind: Psychiatry's Fraught History." *The New Yorker*.

Hammerstein, O. (1943). *Oklahoma*.

Hanly, C. (2014). "Skeptical Reflection on Subjectivist Epistemologies." *Psychoanalytic Quarterly* 83:949–968.

_____, and M. Hanly (2001). "Critical Realism: Distinguishing the Psychological Subjectivity of the Analyst from Epistemological Subjectivism." *Journal of the American Psychoanalytic Association* 49:515–532.

Hartmann, H. (1944/1964). *Essays on Ego Psychology*. NY: International Universities Press.

Heffernan, M. (1974). "Special Education for Everyone." *Changing Education* 6:28–30.

Hetherington, E. (1979). "Divorce: A Child's Perspective." *American Psychologist* 34(10), 851–858.

Hofer, P. (2005). "Reflections on Cathexis." *Psychoanalytic Quarterly* 74[4]:1127–1135.

Hoffman, I. (2009). "Doublethinking Our Way to 'Scientific' Legitimacy: The Desiccation of Human Experience." *Journal of the American Psychoanalytic Association* 57:1043–1069.

Hoffman, L., (1979). "Maternal Employment: 1979." *American Psychologist* 34:859–865.

_____, T. Rice, and T. Prout (2016). *Manual of Regulation-Focused Psychotherapy for Children (RFP-C) with Externalizing Behaviors: A Psychodynamic Approach*. NY: Routledge.

Holt, R. (1973). "On Reading Freud." Rothgeb, C. (Ed.). *Abstracts of The Standard Edition of the Complete Psychological Works of Sigmund Freud*. NY: Jason Aronson.

Hutchens, R., and M. Adler, Eds. (1952). *Great Books of the Western World* 54. Chicago: University of Chicago Press.

Jones, R. (1968). *Fantasy and Feeling in Education*. NY: New York University Press.

Kahneman, D., and A. Tversky (1979). "Prospect Theory: An Analysis of Decision under Risk." *Econometrica* 47:263–292.

Kaiser, H. (1955). "The Problem of Responsibility in Psychotherapy." *Psychiatry* 18:205–211.

Kalanithi, P. (2015). "Before I Go: Time Warps for a Young Surgeon with Metastatic Lung Cancer." *Stanford Medicine Magazine*.

Kaplan, D. (1995). "The Future of Classical Psychoanalysis." *Clinical and Social Realities*. Northvale, NJ: Jason Aronson.

Kernberg, O. (1975). *Borderline Conditions and Pathological Narcissism*. NY: Jason Aronson.

_____, F. Yeomans, J. Clarkin, and K. Levy (2008). "Transference Focused Psychotherapy: Overview and Update." *International Journal of Psychoanalysis* 89:601–620.

Klein, G. (1973). "Two Theories or One?" *Bulletin of the Menninger Clinic* 37:102–132.

Kogan, I. (2003). "On Being a Dead, Beloved Child." *Psychoanalytic Quarterly* 72:727–766.

Kohut, H. (1971). *The Analysis of the Self*. NY: International Universities Press.

_____ (1977). *The Restoration of the Self*. NY: International Universities Press.

Kris, E. (1949). "Roots of Hostility and Prejudice." *Family in a Democratic Society: Anniversary Papers of the C. C. S. of New York*.

_____ (1956). "On Some Vicissitudes of Insight in Psycho-Analysis." *International Journal of Psycho-Analysis* 37:445–455.

_____ (1975). "The Nature of Psychoanalytic Propositions and their Validation." Kernberg, O. *Selected Papers of Ernst Kris*. New Haven: Yale University Press (Originally published 1947).

Kuhn, T. (1962). *The Structure of Scientific Revolutions*. University of Chicago Press.

Langer, S. (1942). *Philosophy in a New Key: A Study of the Symbolism of Reason, Rite and Art*. New American Library.

Lasch, C. (1978). *The Culture of Narcissism*. NY: Norton.

Lear, J. (2017). *Wisdom Won from Illness*. Harvard University Press.

Leites, N. (1977). "Transference Interpretations Only?" *International Journal of Psychoanalysis* 58:275–287.

Lester, D. (2020). "The Psychology Department, Brandeis University in the 1960s: A Comment on Feigenbaum's Memoir." *Comparative Civilization Review* 83.

Levine, H. (2016). "Psychoanalysis and the Problem of Truth." *Psychoanalytic Quarterly* 85:391–409.

_____, G. Reed, and D. Scarfone (2018). *Unrepresented States and the Construction of Meaning*. NY: Routledge.

Limentani, A. (1982). "On the 'Unexpected' Termination of Psychoanalytic Therapy." *Psychoanalytic Inquiry* 2:419–440.

Lindzey, G., and W. Runyan (2007). *A History of Psychology in Autobiography* 9[8]:269–301. American Psychological Association.

Lipsitt, L. (1979). "Critical Conditions in Infancy: A Psychological Perspective." *American Psychologist* 34:973–980.

Lipton, S. (1961). "The Last Hour." *Journal of the American Psychoanalytic Association* 9:325–330.

Loewald, H. (1960). "On the Therapeutic Action of Psychoanalysis." *International Journal of Psychoanalysis* 41:16–33.

_____ (1988). "Termination Analyzable and Unanalyzable." *Psychoanalytic Study of the Child* 43:155–166.

"Lucy Daniels Center for Early Childhood Serving on the Front Lines of Its Community" (2005). *The American Psychoanalyst* 39[2].

Martinez, D. (1989). "Pains and Gains: A Study of Forced Terminations." *Journal of the American Psychoanalytic Association* 37:89–115.

Maslow, A., and B. Mittelmann (1951). *Principles of Abnormal Psychology*. Harper.

McWilliams, N. (2003). "The Educative Aspects of Psychoanalysis." *Psychoanalytic Psychology* 20:245–260.

Meehl, P. (1954). *Clinical Versus Statistical Prediction: A Theoretical Analysis and a Review of the Evidence*. University of Minnesota Press.

Miermont-Schilton, D., and F. Richard (2020). "The Current Sociosanitary Coronavirus Crisis: Remote Psychoanalysis by Skype or Telephone." *The International Journal of Psychoanalysis* 101:572–579.

Moore, B., and B. Fine (1990). *Psychoanalytic Terms and Concepts*. New Haven, CT: Yale University Press.

Moraitis, G. (1995). "The Relevance of the Couch in Contemporary Psychoanalysis." *Psychoanalytic Inquiry* 15[3]:406–412.

Myrdal, G. (1944). *An American Dilemma: The Negro Problem and Modern Democracy*. New York: Harper.

Nagel, J. (2010). "Psychoanalytic and Musical Ambiguity: The Tritone in 'Gee, Officer Krupke.'" *Journal of the American Psychoanalytic Association* 58:9–25.

Nicoli, L., and S. Tugnoli (2020). "'Bringing the Plague:' Groundwork for a Transformative Outreach of Psychoanalysis." *The International Journal of Psychoanalysis* 101:549–571.

Novick, J. (1982). "Termination: Themes and Issues." *Psychoanalytic Inquiry* 2:329–365.

_____ (1997) "Termination Conceivable and Inconceivable." *Psychoanalytic Psychology* 14:145–162.

_____ and K. Novick (2002). "Reclaiming the Land." *Psychoanalytic Psychology* 19:348–377.

Olinick, S. (1954). "Some Considerations of the Use of Questioning as a Psychoanalytic Technique." *Journal of the American Psychoanalytic Association* 2:57–66.

_____ (1957). "Questioning and Pain, Truth and Negation." *Journal of the American Psychoanalytic Association* 5:302–324.

Oremland, J., K. Blacker, and H. Norman (1975). "Incompleteness in 'Successful' Psychoanalyses: A Follow-Up Study." *Journal of the American Psychoanalytic Association* 23:819–844.

Paniagua, C. (1995). "Common Ground, Uncommon Methods." *International Journal of Psychoanalysis* 76:357–371.

Panksepp, J., and L. Biven (2012). *The Archaeology of Mind: Neuroevolutionary Origins of Human Emotion.* NY: W. W. Norton.

Pine, F. (1990). *Drive, Ego, Object and Self: A Synthesis for Clinical Work.* NY: Basic Books.

_____ (1998). *Diversity and Direction in Psychoanalytic Technique.* New Haven, CT: Yale University Press.

_____ (2006). "The Psychoanalytic Dictionary: A Position Paper on Diversity and its Unifiers." *Journal of the American Psychoanalytic Association* 54:463-491.

Poser, S. (2019). "Debussy Comes to Harlem." Presented to the Group and Family Therapy Conference, Mount Sinai School of Medicine.

Racker, H. (1968). *Transference and Countertransference.* Routledge.

Rangell, L. (1954). "Similarities and Differences Between Psychoanalysis and Dynamic Psychotherapy." *Journal of the American Psychoanalytic Association* 2:734–744.

_____ (1980). *The Mind of Watergate.* New York: Norton.

_____ (1981). "Psychoanalysis and Dynamic Psychotherapy—Similarities and Differences Twenty-Five Years Later." *Psychoanalytic Quarterly* 50:665–693.

_____ (1982). "Some Thoughts on Termination." *Psychoanalytic Inquiry* 2:367–392.

_____ (1988). "The Future of Psychoanalysis: The Scientific Crossroads." *Psychoanalytic Quarterly* 57:313–340.

_____ (1990). *The Human Core: The Intrapsychic Base of Behavior*. Madison, CT: International Universities Press.

_____ (2004). *My Life in Theory*. NY: Other Press.

_____ (2005). "The Psychology of Public Opinion: The Public as Jury." *Psychoanalytic Psychology* 22:3–20.

_____ (2007). *The Road to Unity in Psychoanalytic Theory*. NY: Jason Aronson.

Redl, F., and D. Wineman (1957). *The Aggressive Child*. Free Press.

Reed, G., and F. Baudry (1997). "Susan Isaacs and Anna Freud on Fantasy." *Journal of the American Psychoanalytic Association* 45:465–490.

Reich, A. (1973). "On the Termination of Analysis." *Psychoanalytic Contributions*. NY: International Universities Press. (Originally published 1950).

Reich, W. (1972). *Character Analysis*, Third Enlarged Edition (V. Carfagn, Trans.). Farrar, Strauss and Geroux. (Originally published 1933).

Reik, T. (1948). *Listening with the Third Ear*. NY: Farrar, Straus.

Renik, O. (1993a). "Analytic Interaction: Conceptualizing Technique in Light of the Analyst's Irreducible Subjectivity." *Psychoanalytic Quarterly* 62:553–571.

_____ (1993b). "Countertransference Enactment and the Psychoanalytic Process." M. Horowitz, O. Kernberg, and E. Weinshel. *Psychic Structure and Psychic Change*. NY: International Universities Press.

_____ (1998). "The Analyst's Subjectivity and the Analyst's Objectivity." *International Journal of Psychoanalysis* 79:487–497.

Richards, A. (1997). "The Relevance of Frequency of Sessions to the Creation of an Analytic Experience." *Journal of the American Psychoanalytic Association* 47:1241–1251.

_____ (1999). "A. A. Brill and The Politics of Exclusion." *Journal of the American Psychoanalytic Association* 47:9–28.

Riviere, J. (1958/2019). "A Character Trait of Freud's." *International Journal of Psychoanalysis* 100[4]:637–639.

Roazen, P. (1975). *Freud and His Followers*. NY: Knopf.

Rogers, T. (2014). "Consciousness and the Brain: Deciphering How the Brain Codes Our Thoughts." *Neuropsychoanalysis: An Interdisciplinary Journal for Psychoanalysis and the Neurosciences*.

Sandler, J., H. Kennedy, and R. Tyson (1980). *The Technique of Child Analysis: Discussions with Anna Freud*. Cambridge, Massachusetts: Harvard University Press.

Scarfone, D., (2013). "A Brief Introduction to the Work of Jean Laplanche." *International Journal of Psychoanalysis* 94:545–566.

Scarr, S. (1979). "Psychology and Children: Current Research and Practice." *American Psychologist* 34:809–1039.

Schafer, R. (1976). *A New Language for Psychoanalysis.* New Haven: Yale University Press.

_____ (1985). "Wild Analysis." *Journal of the American Psychoanalytic Association* 33:275–299.

_____ (1995). *The Contemporary Kleinians of London.* NY: International Universities Press.

Schlesinger, H. (2004). *The Texture of Treatment: On the Matter of Psychoanalytic Technique.* Hillsdale, NJ: The Analytic Press.

_____ (2005). *Ending and Beginning: On the Technique of Terminating Psychotherapy and Psychoanalysis.* Hillsdale, NJ: The Analytic Press.

Schofield, W. (1964). *Psychotherapy: The Purchase of Friendship.* Saddle River, NJ: Prentice-Hall.

"The Schoolyard Bully Meets the Peaceful Schools Project" (2005). *The American Psychoanalyst* 39[1].

Schwaber, E. (1985). *The Transference in Psychotherapy: Clinical Management.* NY: International Universities Press.

Seligman, S. (1998). "Child Psychoanalysis, Adult Psychoanalysis, and Developmental Psychology: Introduction to Symposium on Child Analysis, Part II." *Psychoanalytic Dialogues* 8:79–86.

Shane, M., and E. Shane (1984). "The End Phase of Analysis: Indicators, Functions, and Tasks of Termination." *Journal of the American Psychoanalytic Association* 32:739–772.

Shapiro, D. (1965). *Neurotic Styles.* NY: Basic Books.

Shapiro, E. (1990). "The Future of Psychoanalytic Education." In M. Meisels and E. Shapiro. *Tradition and Innovation in Psychoanalytic Education.* Hillsdale, NJ: Erlbaum.

Shedler, J. (2010). "The Efficacy of Psychodynamic Psychotherapy. *American Psychologist* 65:98–109.

_____ (2015). "Where is the Evidence for 'Evidence-Based' Therapy?' *The Journal of Psychological Therapies in Primary Care* 4:47–59.

Shevrin, H. (2012). "A Contribution Toward a Science of Psychoanalysis." *Psychoanalytic Review* 99:491–509.

Siegel, B. (1982). "Some Thoughts on 'Some Thoughts on Termination' by Leo Rangell." *Psychoanalytic Inquiry* 2:393–398.

Silverman, D. (1986). "A Multi-Model Approach: Looking at Clinical Data from Three Theoretical Perspectives." *Psychoanalytic Psychology* 3:121–132.

Silverman, M. (2013). Review of Günter, M. (Ed.), "Technique in Child and Adolescent Analysis." *Psychoanalytic Quarterly* 82:528-535.

Sklarew, B., J. Krupnick, D. Ward-Wimmer, and C. Napoli (2002). "The School-based Mourning Project: A Preventive Intervention in the Cycle of Inner-city Violence." *Journal of Applied Psychoanalytic Studies* 4[3]: 317-330.

Sklarew, B., S. Twemlow, and S. Wilkinson (2004). *Analysts in the Trenches: Streets, Schools, War Zones.* NY: Routledge.

Smith, H. (2007). "In Search of a Theory of Therapeutic Action." *Psychoanalytic Quarterly* 76:1735–1761.

Snow, C. (1959). *The Two Cultures and the Scientific Revolution.* NY: Oxford University Press.

Spock, B. (1946). *The Common Sense Book of Baby and Child Care.* NY: Duell, Sloane and Pearce.

Steingart, I. (1977/1995). *A Thing Apart: Love and Reality in the Therapeutic Relationship.* NY: Jason Aronson.

_____ (1997). "Erik Erikson's Work: Clinical Implications and Applications." *Psychoanalytic Review* 84[3], 349-362.

Sterba, R. (1934). "The Fate of the Ego in Analytic Therapy." *International Journal of Psychoanalysis* 15:117–126.

Stone, L. (1954). "The Widening Scope of Indications for Psychoanalysis." *Journal of the American Psychoanalytic Association* 2:567–594.

_____ (1961). *The Psychoanalytic Situation.* NY: International Universities Press.

_____ (1968) "The Psychoanalytic Situation." *Journal of the American Psycho-analytic Association* 43[1]:197–205.

_____ (1982). "The Influence of the Practice and Theory of Psychotherapy on Education in Psychoanalysis." In E. Joseph and R. Wallerstein. *Psychotherapy: Impact on Psychoanalytic Training.* NY: International Universities Press.

Strachey, J. (1934). "The Nature of the Therapeutic Action of Psycho-Analysis." *International Journal of Psychoanalysis* 15:127–159.

Strenger, C. (2004). "Nobrow: Identity Formation in a Fatherless Generation." *Psychoanalytic Psychology* 21:499–515.

Summers, F. (2011). "Psychoanalysis: Romantic, Not Wild." *Psychoanalytic Psychology* 28:13–32.

Tauber, A. (2010). Freud, The Reluctant Philosopher. Princeton University Press.

Ticho, E. (1972). "Termination of Psychoanalysis: Treatment Goals, Life Goals." *Psychoanalytic Quarterly* 41:315–333.

Viorst, J. (1982). "Experiences of Loss at the End of Analysis: The Analyst's Response to Termination." *Psychoanalytic Inquiry* 2:399–418.

Wachtel, P. (2010). "Beyond 'ESTs': Problematic Assumptions in the Pursuit of Evidence-Based Practice." *Psychoanalytic Psychology* 27:251-272.

Waelder, R. (1936). "The Principle of Multiple Function: Observations on Overdetermination." *Psychoanalytic Quarterly* 5:1, 45-62.

_____ (1962). "Psychoanalysis, Scientific Method, and Philosophy." *Journal of the American Psychoanalytic Association* 10:617–637.

Wallerstein, R. (1986). *Forty-Two Lives in Treatment: A Study of Psychoanalysis and Psychotherapy*. NY: Guilford Press.

_____ (1988). "One Psychoanalysis or Many?" *International Journal of Psycho-Analysis* 69:5-21.

_____ (1990). "Psychoanalysis: The Common Ground." *International Journal of Psychoanalysis* 71:3–20.

_____ (1995). "Obituary: Erik Erikson (1902–1994)." *International Journal of Psychoanalysis* 76:173–175.

White, R. (1963). *The Study of Lives: Essays on Personality in Honor of Henry A. Murray*. NY: Atherton Press.

White, S. (1979). "Children in Perspective: Introduction to the Section." *American Psychologist* 34:812–814.

Wolberg, L. (1954). *The Technique of Psychotherapy*. NY: Grune & Stratton.

Young-Bruehl, E. (1996). *The Anatomy of Prejudices*. Cambridge, MA: Harvard University Press.

Zamanian, K. (2011). "Attachment Theory as Defense: What Happened to Infantile Sexuality?" *Psychoanalytic Psychology* 28:33–47.

Author's Acknowledgments

There are far too many people to thank for a nearly six-decade career, much of it as a full-time academic with a part-time practice. As a young man, I thought the acknowledgment of patients was simply routine. I now understand its authenticity. Likewise the acknowledgment of teachers and supervisors. I am surprised to be grateful for my time in the United States Army, despite feeling compelled to enlist as a psychologist/captain rather than leave the country or be drafted into a war that was ill-conceived, poorly conducted, far too long, and a total failure. Professionally, however, I could not have had a better post-doctoral experience. It preceded my entry to a psychoanalytic institute free from the medical model, with its courses taught by superb educators.

I was brought into organizational leadership by Moss L. Rawn, PhD, and William M. Greenstadt, PhD, and encouraged in my scholarship by Donald M. Kaplan, PhD, supervisor, mentor, colleague and friend.

I met Don Kaplan at the start of my psychoanalytic training. A charismatic teacher with his notes propped on a music stand, he riffed on assignments in a Freud early papers course. I chose him to supervise my first training case. He encouraged me to apply for graduation before I felt ready ("Nobody should feel ready," he chided) and then to present my first public paper, a discussion of the work of a senior analyst. We became colleagues, then friends, until his untimely death in 1994 at age 67.

Kaplan seemed confident in what he taught. I was surprised when a friend I'd referred to him as a patient reported on his conversational clinical manner. The last page of his 1966 paper, "The Future of Classical Psychoanalysis," shows this apparent paradox. In criticizing what he called "the liberal point of view" toward psychoanalysis, he finds it "bereft of criteria for determining when in the course of unraveling a sock he has finally lost the garment and is in possession instead of a tangle of wool." Yet he concludes this paper with "psychoanalysis is after all a limited thing. But there too, though it is bound to perish, it will also survive." As Freud taught, contradictory ideas coexist in the unconscious. The work is to become more conscious of the contradictions within us.

Psychoanalytic psychologists did not find a welcome in psychology departments when I first looked for a job. Being a full-time teacher education faculty member at the City University of New York provided 35 years of economic stability to enable a part-time practice in my preferred profession while enlightening me as to the central relevance of the psychoanalytic paradigm beyond the consulting room. "Retirement" was nominal, as I left CUNY for Mount Sinai's Psychiatry Department, where I was welcomed by the late Hillel Swiller, MD, who became a good friend—and a foil for refining my ideas and my practice.

The actual list of names here is short and does not include that of my personal analyst (for the better part of two decades), still working well into his nineties, but I am most grateful for his tough love and flexible model of psychoanalytic practice. I am also grateful for the long-term support of my close and extended family, now four generations, and in this project, for my older son and editor, David Hamilton Golland, PhD.

About the Author and the Editor

Dr. Jeffrey Harris Golland is Clinical Professor in the Department of Psychiatry at Mount Sinai School of Medicine, and a member of the editorial board of the *Journal of the American Psychoanalytic Association.* He holds a PhD and an MA from New York University and a BA from Brandeis University. Prior to his appointment at Mount Sinai, he was for 35 years a teacher education professor at the City University of New York, serving two terms as Chair of Education at Baruch College.

Dr. David Hamilton Golland is Dean of the Wayne D. McMurray School of Humanities and Social Sciences, and Professor of History, at Monmouth University. The author of three books, he holds a PhD from the City University of New York and an MA from the University of Virginia. Prior to his appointment at Monmouth, he was Professor of History at Governors State University, where he led the social sciences and humanities faculty for eight years and served four years as President of the University Faculty Senate.

Editor's Acknowledgments

The easiest part of editing this work was ensuring that my voice did not occlude that of the author, my father; I will not break that pattern with these acknowledgments. Let me simply thank Arnold D. Richards, Editor-in-Chief of International Psychoanalytic Books and Noel S. Morado, typesetter extraordinaire; join Dad in thanking the late Hillel Swiller; express gratitude to my academic home, Monmouth University; and of course, thank Dad for the decades of work he put into this book, which has, after all, needed only a light dusting.